INSURANCE RISK MODELS

Harry H. Panjer, FSA, FCIA
Gordon E. Willmot, FSA, FCIA

published by the
SOCIETY OF ACTUARIES

funded by the
ACTUARIAL EDUCATION AND RESEARCH FUND

475 NORTH MARTINGALE ROAD, SUITE 800 • SCHAUMBURG, IL 60173-2226

Library of Congress Cataloging-in-Publication Data

Panjer, Harry H.
     Insurance risk models / H.H. Panjer, G.E. Willmot.
     442 p. cm.
     "Course notes for Actuarial science 431/831."
     Includes bibliographical references (p.) and index.
     ISBN 0-938959-25-5
     1. Insurance--Mathematics--Mathematical models. 2. Risk
(Insurance)--Mathematical models. I. Willmot, G.E. (Gordon E.),
1957- . II. Title.
HG8781.P26 1992
368' .01--dc20
                                                       92-16373
                                                       CIP

ISBN 0-938959-25-5

TABLE OF CONTENTS

PART V: RUIN THEORY

11. Ruin Probability Calculations

Preface

This book was originally conceived in 1984 following the publication of the book *Loss Distributions*, by Robert V. Hogg and Stuart A. Klugman published by John Wiley and Sons, Inc. That book deals with statistical modelling of the sizes of insurance losses from real data. It includes a large amount of distribution theory in addition to statistical estimation procedures for data that is in the form often available from insurance companies. At the same time we were active in a new area of research which examined insurance claim frequency distributions from the point of view of carrying out efficient numerical procedures for the calculation of the distribution of total losses of an insurance portfolio.

This book is devoted to this end. However, it has taken a long time to be finally published. In fact many, if not most, of the theoretical results have been developed since 1984 during the writing of the book! Consequently, there have been many drafts of this book over the years. These drafts have been tested on hundreds of senior undergraduate and graduate students at the University of Waterloo.

The basic theme of the book is that the distribution of aggregate claims for an insurer can be computed by simple recursive algorithms for a very wide range of claim number models with any loss distribution. Related quantities, such as stop-loss premiums, and expected losses for layers of reinsurance can then be computed easily. The theory was developed at the same time that computer costs plummeted with the development of micro- and mini-computers. The theory allows the user to harness the power of computing to provide exact solutions to problems for which the development of approximations had always been the focus. The subject matter falls within the field that has been traditionally called risk theory. We devote much less attention to ruin theory which had been the primary area of research in the broader field of risk theory. However, we have not abandoned ruin theory. In fact, the last chapter is devoted entirely to theoretical and computational aspects of ruin theory.

Chapters 1-4 provide the basic mathematical and statistical tools that are used in the remaining chapters. These chapters can be read first, or can be used as a reference for readers who begin with chapter 5. Chapter 1 develops the Laplace transform which is the basic mathematical tool used throughout the book to develop the theory. For the reader interested only in the results of the theory this can be skipped. However, it should be noted that readers familiar with moment (and other) generating functions, this chapter should not be too painful. The Laplace transform is used rather than the moment generating function because of the non-existence of the moment generating function for many models presented in the book. Chapter 2 provides the basic probabilistic background necessary for the book. Readers who have studied probability and statistics can skim this material. Likewise for chapter 3 which deals with basic stochastic processes. Chapter 4 provides the plethora of continuous and discrete distributions used in the subsequent chapters. This provides a good reference for the reader as a lot of information is provided for each distribution. Chapter 5 deals with what has been traditionally called the "individual risk" model with its background in life insurance. The computational results presented were all developed in the 1980's and are related to those in chapter 6. Chapters 6-9 deal with the "collective" risk with its background in primarily non-life branches of insurance such as health, property, casualty, liability and catastrophe insurance. Chapter 6 focuses on the Poisson, negative binomial, binomial and related distributions for claim counts. Generalizations of these models through the mechanism of compounding are given in chapter 7. Similar generalizations using mixing or "parameter uncertainty" are the subject of chapter 8. In chapter 9, the problems of selection , fitting and validation of the distributions is addressed. This parallels the corresponding material in Hogg and Klugman's book which deals with continuous distributions only. Chapter 10 is different in the sense that simple analytic formulas for the extreme right hand tail of the distribution of aggregate claims are developed. This provides insight into the effect of the selection of any of the claim count of size-of-loss distributions and useful approximations when computations become prohibitive or when a quick estimate is required. Chapter 11 is devoted to traditional ruin theory. The emphasis is on approximate and exact calculation of ruin probabilities used the mathematical tools in previous chapters.

The book is intended for a broad audience. The theory is developed from the perspective of application to real insurance data. Many examples and numerical illustrations in a wide range of insurance applications are provided. The book can be used as a text for university courses at the undergraduate and graduate level. Exercises are provided to emphasize the techniques developed in the chapters and to provide additional results that can be derived from the theory. The researcher can used the book as a modern reference to the literature on numerical techniques for solving this class of problems. Although not all related papers published are included in the reference list, the energetic and thorough researcher can find many other sources by scouring the references listed within each these references!

The authors would like to acknowledge the support provided by the Actuarial Education Research Fund, Schaumburg IL, and the Institute of Insurance and Pension Research at the University of Waterloo. We would like to acknowledge especially Lynda Clarke for her unflagging energy in typesetting the various drafts over the many years of this project. However, any errors or omissions remain entirely the responsibility of the authors.

Harry H. Panjer
Gordon E. Willmot
May, 1992

About the Authors

Harry H. Panjer

Harry Panjer, a native of the Netherlands, emigrated to Canada at the age of five with his family. He grew up in the small town of Blenheim, Ontario in the extreme southwestern part of Ontario close to the US border.

He received Bachelor's, Master's and PhD degrees in actuarial science and statistics, all from the University of Western Ontario. He is a Fellow of the Society of Actuaries and of the Canadian Institute of Actuaries. He has devoted most of his career to teaching and research in actuarial science at the University of Western Ontario, The University of Texas at Austin and the University of Waterloo where he is Professor in the Department of Statistics and Actuarial Science. He has served as the Director of the Institute of Insurance and Pension Research at the University of Waterloo.

His research interests span the subject of this book as well as other aspects of modelling in actuarial science. He is an associate editor of several actuarial journals. His papers have appeared in most actuarial and insurance journals. His research has been awarded best paper prizes by several journals. He has lectured in many other countries. In addition he has worked in actuarial positions in both the US and Canada. He has served on many professional actuarial committees in Canada, the US and internationally and is currently Vice-President of the Society of Actuaries.

He is an avid pilot, preferring to spend his time flying his airplane rather than writing books like this one. This explains, in part, why it took so long to complete the book.

About the Authors

Gordon E. Willmot

Gordon Willmot was born and raised in St. Catharines, Ontario, Canada. He received Bachelor's, Master's, and PhD degrees in actuarial science and statistics from the University of Waterloo. He is a Fellow of both the Society of Actuaries and the Canadian Institute of Actuaries. He has worked in group insurance where he specialized in analysis and modelling of life, health, and disability claims. He is currently an Associate Professor in the Department of Statistics and Actuarial Science at the University of Waterloo where he has been on faculty since receiving his doctorate in 1986.

He has done extensive research in the areas of risk theory, as well as in other mathematically related areas such as statistics and queueing theory. He has authored or co-authored papers which have appeared in most actuarial journals as well as in various other statistical and applied probability journals. He was the winner of the International Actuarial Association's 1987 ASTIN competition for young researchers which was held in Scheveningen, the Netherlands. He has served on various committees of the Society of Actuaries and of the Canadian Institute of Actuaries.

He would have preferred to spend more time on the completion of this book; but unfortunately, he found that minor irritations such as writing actuarial exams and a doctoral thesis as well as playing squash took priority. In any event, it is his contention that any errors or omissions remaining in the book are not a result of these other activities but rather are the result of the first named author having spent too much time flying.

CHAPTER 1

INTRODUCTION AND MATHEMATICAL BACKGROUND

1.1 INTRODUCTION TO THE BOOK

Risk is the essence of insurance. Insurance is a mechanism for transferring risk from one party to another party that is better able to manage it. Through laws of probabilities, insurance companies are able to diversify risks so that losses associated with unexpected events have a relatively smaller impact.

The actuary is directly involved in assessing the quality or the quantity of risk to be covered by the insurer. For any type of risk, the actuary must attempt to understand the nature of both the frequency of such unexpected events and nature of the financial impact on the parties involved of each of the events. From the point of view of the insurer, the relevant unexpected events are the claims that are made to it by insured parties who experience losses covered by an insurance contract. The nature of the financial impact is the size of the claims made to the insurance company. Consequently, the actuary is interested in both the **frequency** and the **size** or **severity** of claims. When these are combined for some accounting period such as one year, the relevant quantity is the total of all claims for the period, often called the **total claims** or **aggregate claims.** Furthermore, the insurance company actuary is interested in assessing the total claims not only for individual insured parties but also for collections or **portfolios** of risks covered by the insurer in order to make business decisions for the company. The insured parties could be individual risks such as human lives covered for the event of death, buildings covered for fire or automobiles covered for damages resulting from accidents. The insured parties could also be collections of such individual risks such as a fleet of automobiles or an employee group insured against the death of individuals in the group. These collections are themselves the risks covered by the insurer. Actuaries are interested in making decisions about risks such as setting premium levels, developing reinsurance strategies and making judgements about the surplus needs of the insurer. Probability and statistics are basic tools used by the actuary to develop models that describe the nature of both claim frequency and claim severity. By developing a mathematical model of the physical phenomenon which generates the insurance claims, the actuary is able to study the model and to study the impact of various possible decisions.

Models for claims severity have been studied extensively by Hogg and Klugman (1984). They discuss fitting probability distribution models describing the size of claims associated with single occurrences of unexpected events. In this book, we study models of the frequency of occurrence of claims and models of total claims or aggregate claims that result when models of frequency and severity are combined. In other words, we are primarily interested in the monetary effect of total claims in some fixed time period. This requires modeling claim frequencies and severities separately and developing numerical procedures for combining them.

In the past, approximations were heavily relied upon in making probability statements about total claims. This was a direct consequence of the enormous number of calculations required to obtain exact results numerically. These approximate methods date back to the early part of the twentieth century when all numerical results were obtained by hand or mechanical calculation. With the introduction of digital computers to insurance companies in the 1950's and 1960's, the emphasis changed somewhat. The development of computer simulation techniques provided the actuary with a powerful tool for risk analysis. The primary disadvantage of these techniques was the amount and cost of computer time required to carry out large scale simulations. Furthermore, the results were necessarily approximations. These approximations could be improved, but often at great expense of computer time. Numerically exact results for large scale problems were often obtainable only at prohibitive costs.

In the 1970's, computer costs and operating times decreased dramatically. Minicomputers and microcomputers were introduced in the late 1970's and improved dramatically in the early 1980's to the point where small inexpensive desk-top microcomputers have the capability of the large mainframe computers of the early 1970's.

Concurrent with this dramatic reduction in the cost of computing were a number of theoretical developments that provided new procedures for obtaining numerically exact solutions to the class of actuarial problems that are the subject of this book. The numerical procedures reduced the volume of computations required to obtain numerical results to a more manageable size. As a consequence of these two advances, numerically exact solutions are now obtainable at a tiny fraction of the previous costs as measured in terms of computer time and cost. It is this combination of events that provide the central theme of this book.

Chapters 1 to 4 provide the basic tools of mathematics, probability and statistics that are used in later chapters. Chapters 5 and 6 provide the basic tools of the simplest models while chapters 7 and 8 deal with more complex models. Chapter 9 deals with the ancillary problem of fitting distributions to data. Chapter 10 provides approximations that have been developed to provide "quick" results. Chapter 11 examines the related question of when an insurance enterprise is "ruined" as a result of excessive claims. It gives numerical procedures related to those in previous chapters. Although the reader may be somewhat overwhelmed by the "theoretical" nature of this book, the theory presented is motivated by real insurance problems. The methods developed in this book are intended to provide the actuary the technical tools to address a wide range of problems of the real world.

1.2 ORDINARY GENERATING FUNCTIONS

In this section the basic properties of a very powerful mathematical tool will be summarized. The ordinary generating function is a most useful tool in insurance modeling and will be used extensively throughout this book for various purposes.

Consider a sequence $\{a_n; \ n = 0,1,2,...\}$ of real numbers. The **ordinary generating function** of this sequence is defined to be the sum

$$A(z) = \sum_{n=0}^{\infty} a_n z^n \qquad (1.2.1)$$

for values of z for which the sum is convergent. While it is not necessary, it is sufficient for our purposes to assume that z is a real number. It is easily shown that, if the sequence is bounded, i.e. $|a_n| \leq M$, $n = 0,1,2,...$, then the sum $A(z)$ is convergent for $|z| < 1$ (at least).

Example 1.2.1.

Suppose $a_n = 1$, $n = 0,1,2,....$ Then

$$A(z) = \sum_{n=0}^{\infty} z^n$$

$$= (1-z)^{-1}, \quad |z| < 1.$$

Example 1.2.2.

Suppose $a_n = \dfrac{1}{n!}$, $n = 0,1,2,....$ Then

$$A(z) = \sum_{n=0}^{\infty} \frac{z^n}{n!}$$

$$= e^z, \quad |z| < \infty.$$

It can be shown that **there is a one-to-one correspondence between a sequence** $\{a_n; \ n = 0,1,2,...\}$ **and its ordinary generating function** $A(z)$. In other words, a sequence has only one ordinary generating function (at most), and conversely, the sequence corresponding to a particular generating function is unique. It is this property which is of paramount importance for our purposes. We will often have situations where we first obtain the ordinary generating function and then attempt to obtain the coefficient of z^n in (1.2.1) which is a_n and is unique. In fact,

$$a_n = \frac{1}{n!} \frac{d^n}{dz^n} A(z)|_{z=0}. \tag{1.2.2}$$

In most situations z^n in (1.2.1) is viewed as a "marker", which "keeps track" of the coefficient a_n. For many of our purposes, it will be clear that the sum is convergent but this must, of course, be checked in any particular situation.

Some elementary properties of ordinary generating functions are now given. Suppose $A(z) = \sum_{n=0}^{\infty} a_n z^n$, $B(z) = \sum_{n=0}^{\infty} b_n z^n$, and $C(z) = \sum_{n=0}^{\infty} c_n z^n$. Then

$$\text{I. } c_n = \alpha a_n + \beta b_n, \quad n = 0,1,... \tag{1.2.3}$$

if and only if

$$C(z) = \alpha A(z) + \beta B(z).$$

Also,

$$\text{II. } c_n = \sum_{k=0}^{n} a_k b_{n-k}, \quad n = 0,1,... \tag{1.2.4}$$

if and only if

$$C(z) = A(z)B(z).$$

It can be shown that if $A(z)$ is convergent for all $|z|<R$, then the derivative $A'(z)$ is convergent for all $|z|<R$ as well, and furthermore that

$$\text{III. } zA'(z) = \sum_{n=0}^{\infty} n a_n z^n. \tag{1.2.5}$$

To illustrate some of the uses of this tool, we give a famous example where the sequence $\{a_n; \; n = 0,1,2,...\}$ is not known explicitly, but certain information about it is known.

Example 1.2.3. The Fibonacci Numbers

The sequence $\{a_n; \; n = 0,1,2,...\}$ is defined by $a_0 = 0$, $a_1 = 1$, and

$$a_n = a_{n-1} + a_{n-2}, \quad n \geq 2.$$

We wish to use ordinary generating functions to obtain an explicit expression for $a_n; \; n \geq 2$. Since

$$a_n = a_{n-1} + a_{n-2}$$

for $n \geq 2$, we may multiply this relationship by z^n to obtain

$$a_n z^n = a_{n-1} z^n + a_{n-2} z^n.$$

Since this latter expression is true for all $n \geq 2$, we may substitute successively $n = 2, 3, 4, \ldots$, etc. and sum all the equations, obtaining,

$$\sum_{n=2}^{\infty} a_n z^n = \sum_{n=2}^{\infty} a_{n-1} z^n + \sum_{n=2}^{\infty} a_{n-2} z^n.$$

In other words, using (1.2.1), we have

$$A(z) - a_0 - a_1 z = z[A(z) - a_0] + z^2 A(z)$$

or

$$A(z)[1 - z - z^2] = z.$$

Thus the ordinary generating function is

$$A(z) = \frac{z}{1 - z - z^2}.$$

It now remains to extract the coefficient of z^n. By the method of partial fractions we may write

$$A(z) = \frac{1}{\sqrt{5}} \left[\frac{1}{1 - \{(1+\sqrt{5})/2\}z} - \frac{1}{1 - \{(1-\sqrt{5})/2\}z} \right]$$

$$= \frac{1}{\sqrt{5}} \left[\sum_{n=0}^{\infty} \left\{ \frac{1+\sqrt{5}}{2} \right\}^n z^n - \sum_{n=0}^{\infty} \left\{ \frac{1-\sqrt{5}}{2} \right\}^n z^n \right]$$

$$= \frac{1}{\sqrt{5}} \sum_{n=0}^{\infty} \left[\left\{ \frac{1+\sqrt{5}}{2} \right\}^n - \left\{ \frac{1-\sqrt{5}}{2} \right\}^n \right] z^n.$$

Hence, by the uniqueness of the coefficient of z^n, it follows that

$$a_n = \frac{1}{\sqrt{5}} \left[\left\{ \frac{1+\sqrt{5}}{2} \right\}^n - \left\{ \frac{1-\sqrt{5}}{2} \right\}^n \right]; \quad n = 0,1,2,\dots \; .$$

Ordinary generating functions are of great use in solving simple difference equations (as in the above example) and in many other situations. In particular, with the advent of computers, it is not always necessary to obtain an explicit expression for a_n. The following example illustrates this.

Example 1.2.4.

Suppose $a_0 \neq 0$, and $A(z) = \sum_{n=0}^{\infty} a_n z^n$. Let $B(z) = [A(z)]^\alpha$ where α is not necessarily an integer. It is of interest to obtain the sequence $\{b_n; \; n = 0,1,2,\dots\}$ such that $B(z) = \sum_{n=0}^{\infty} b_n z^n$. In some situations one can recognize b_n explicitly (for example, if $A(z) = e^z$). Otherwise, if α is a postive integer, one could use (1.2.4) and obtain b_n using a finite number of "convolutions", but this would have to be done numerically. A much more effective approach is as follows. Since

$$B(z) = [A(z)]^\alpha,$$

it follows that

$$B'(z) = \alpha [A(z)]^{\alpha-1} A'(z)$$

which may be rewritten as

$$A(z)[zB'(z)] = \alpha B(z)[zA'(z)].$$

By the uniqueness property, the coefficients of z^n on both sides of this equation must be equal. The coefficient of z^n on the left side is, by (1.2.5) and (1.2.4),

$$\sum_{k=0}^{n} (n-k)b_{n-k}a_k$$

and similarly, the coefficient on the right side is

$$\alpha \sum_{k=0}^{n} kb_{n-k}a_k.$$

Thus, for all n,

$$\sum_{k=0}^{n} (n-k)b_{n-k}a_k = \alpha \sum_{k=0}^{n} kb_{n-k}a_k.$$

Solving this latter expression for b_n yields

$$b_n = \frac{1}{na_0} \sum_{k=1}^{n} [(\alpha+1)k-n]b_{n-k}a_k, \quad n>0$$

which, together with

$$b_0 = a_0^{\alpha},$$

yields a recursive formula for b_n in terms of the sequence $\{a_n;\ n = 0,1,2,...\}$ and $b_0, b_1, \ldots, b_{n-1}$.

The previous example demonstrates how ordinary generating functions may be used to derive computationally useful formulas for the coefficients even though they cannot easily be obtained analytically. This important application of ordinary generating functions will be used throughout this book.

In conclusion, it is often easier to work with ordinary generating functions than it is with the original sequence, and in many instances valuable information about the sequence may be extracted from the generating function. The treatment of ordinary generating functions in this section is extremely brief, and more details (including proofs) concerning their properties may be obtained by consulting references given at the end of this chapter.

1.3 LAPLACE TRANSFORMS

The ordinary generating function considered in the previous section is very useful when working with sequences (or discrete countable functions). In this section a similar tool is considered for use with continuous (or piecewise continuous) functions.

Let $h(x)$ be a function defined for $x>0$. The Laplace transform of $h(x)$ is defined to be

$$\bar{h}(z) = \int_0^\infty e^{-zx} h(x)\,dx. \tag{1.3.1}$$

For our purposes it will be sufficient to assume that z is a positive real number (more advanced theory allows for z to be a complex number with the real part assumed to be positive). It can be shown that the integral (1.3.1) exists if $h(x)$ is (piecewise) continuous and there exist $\alpha_1, \beta > 0$ and α_2 such that $|h(x)| < \alpha_1 e^{\alpha_2 x}$ for all $x > \beta$.

Example 1.3.1.

If $h(x) = e^{\mu x}$, $x > 0$, then

$$\bar{h}(z) = \int_0^\infty e^{-zx} e^{\mu x}\,dx$$

$$= \int_0^\infty e^{-(z-\mu)x} dx$$

$$= \frac{1}{z-\mu}, \quad z > \mu.$$

It can be shown that **there is a one-to-one correspondence between a function and its Laplace transform** so that it makes sense to talk about "the" Laplace transform corresponding to a function and "the" inverse function corresponding to a given Laplace transform. The general formula for the inverse of a Laplace transform is quite complicated and will not be given here. Rather, we will attempt to "recognize" the required function through tables of well known transform pairs (found in most mathematical handbooks), or we will perform some operation with the transform rather than invert it directly.

We now summarize some of the basic properties of Laplace transforms without proof. If (1.3.1) holds, then the following results also hold:

$$\text{I. } \bar{h}(z-a) = \int_0^\infty e^{-zx}[e^{ax}h(x)]dx \tag{1.3.2}$$

$$\text{II. } e^{-az}\bar{h}(z) = \int_0^\infty e^{-zx}k(x)dx \tag{1.3.3}$$

where

$$k(x) = \begin{cases} h(x-a), & x \ge a \\ 0, & x < a. \end{cases}$$

$$\text{III. } \frac{1}{a}\bar{h}(\frac{z}{a}) = \int_0^\infty e^{-zx}h(ax)dx \tag{1.3.4}$$

$$\text{IV. } z\bar{h}(z) - h(0) = \int_0^\infty e^{-zx} h'(x)dx \tag{1.3.5}$$

$$\text{V. } \frac{\bar{h}(z)}{z} = \int_0^\infty e^{-zx} \left[\int_0^x h(y)dy\right] dx \tag{1.3.6}$$

$$\text{VI. } \bar{h}'(z) = \int_0^\infty e^{-zx} [-xh(x)]dx \tag{1.3.7}$$

$$\text{VII. } \bar{h}^{(n)}(z) = \int_0^\infty e^{-zx} [(-1)^n x^n h(x)]dx \tag{1.3.8}$$

$$\text{VIII. } \int_z^\infty \bar{h}(s)ds = \int_0^\infty e^{-zx} [\frac{h(x)}{x}]dx \tag{1.3.9}$$

IX. If

$$\bar{h}_i(z) = \int_0^\infty e^{-zx} h_i(x)dx; \quad i = 1,2,$$

then

$$\alpha\bar{h}_1(z) + \beta\bar{h}_2(z) = \int_0^\infty e^{-zx} [\alpha h_1(x) + \beta h_2(x)]dx \tag{1.3.10}$$

and

$$\bar{h}_1(z)\bar{h}_2(z) = \int_0^\infty e^{-zx} \left[\int_0^x h_1(y)h_2(x-y)dy\right] dx. \tag{1.3.11}$$

The properties of Laplace transforms listed above are useful when operations are performed on the functions involved. In general, it is difficult to invert Laplace transform exactly, but there are exceptions (found in tables of transform pairs). The following examples illustrate this.

Example 1.3.2. Polynomials

If $h(x) = x^n$, $n \varepsilon \{0,1,2,...\}$, then

$$\bar{h}(z) = \int_0^\infty e^{-zx} x^n dx$$

$$= \frac{n!}{z^{n+1}}$$

Repeated integration by parts can be used to obtain this result.

Example 1.3.3. Rational Functions

In some instances the Laplace transform of a function is known to be the ratio of polynomials in z. Partial fraction expansion may then be carried out and then the inverse transform may be obtained. For example, if

$$\bar{h}(z) = \frac{z^2+2z+3}{z^3-12z-16}$$

$$= \frac{z^2+2z+3}{(z-4)(z+2)^2} .$$

The partial fraction expansion is

$$\bar{h}(z) = \frac{3}{4} \left[\frac{1}{z-4} \right] + \frac{1}{4} \left[\frac{1}{z+2} \right] - \frac{1}{2} \left[\frac{1}{z+2} \right]^2 .$$

Hence, by examples 1.3.1 and 1.3.2 as well as equation (1.3.2) or (1.3.7) and equation (1.3.10), it follows that

$$h(x) = \frac{3}{4} e^{4x} + \frac{1}{4} e^{-2x} - \frac{1}{2} x e^{-2x} .$$

The above example illustrates one of the most common techniques for inverting Laplace transforms. The many uses of these transforms include solving differential equations, integral equations, and integro-differential equations. The following example illustrates this.

Example 1.3.4. A Volterra Integral Equation

Suppose we know that the function $h(x)$ satisfies the integral equation

$$h(x) = J(x) + \int_0^x K(x,y)h(y)dy, \quad x>0, \tag{1.3.12}$$

where $J(x)$ and $K(x,y)$ are known functions. The above equation is called a **Volterra integral equation of the second kind with kernel** K and will be encountered repeatedly throughout this book. Laplace transforms can often be used to solve this type of equation. For example, suppose

$$h(x) = \frac{\theta\lambda e^{-\lambda x}}{-\log(1-\theta)} + \theta\int_0^x (1-\frac{y}{x})h(x-y)\lambda e^{-\lambda y}dy.$$

We are now in a position to take Laplace transforms. We wish to take the Laplace transform of each side of this equation. But first, it is expedient to rewrite it as

$$xh(x) = -\frac{\theta\lambda}{\log(1-\theta)}\left[xe^{-\lambda x}\right] + \theta\lambda\int_0^x (x-y)h(x-y)e^{-\lambda y}dy.$$

From (1.3.7), the Laplace transform of $xh(x)$ is $-\bar{h}'(z)$. The Laplace transform of the first term on the right hand side is $-\frac{\theta\lambda}{\log(1-\theta)}\frac{1}{(z+\lambda)^2}$ as can be seen from example 1.3.1 and equation (1.3.7). The second term on the right hand side is $\theta\lambda$ times the convolution of $xh(x)$ with $e^{-\lambda x}$. Hence, by example 1.3.1 and equations (1.3.7) and (1.3.11), it has Laplace transform $-\frac{\theta\lambda\bar{h}'(z)}{z+\lambda}$. Hence, taking Laplace transforms of the whole equation yields,

$$-\tilde{h}'(z) = -\frac{\theta\lambda}{\log(1-\theta)}\frac{1}{(z+\lambda)^2} - \frac{\theta\lambda\tilde{h}'(z)}{z+\lambda}.$$

Thus,

$$\tilde{h}'(z) = \frac{\theta\lambda}{\log(1-\theta)}\frac{\dfrac{1}{(z+\lambda)^2}}{1-\dfrac{\theta\lambda}{z+\lambda}}$$

$$= \frac{\theta\lambda}{\log(1-\theta)}\frac{1}{[z+\lambda][z+\lambda(1-\theta)]}.$$

It would be easy to obtain $\tilde{h}(z)$ but it is not necessary to do so to obtain $h(x)$. We have, by partial fractions,

$$\tilde{h}'(z) = \frac{1}{\log(1-\theta)}\left[\frac{1}{z+\lambda(1-\theta)} - \frac{1}{z+\lambda}\right].$$

Written in this form, the equation may be inverted using (1.3.7) and (1.3.10) as well as example 1.3.1 to obtain

$$-xh(x) = \frac{e^{-\lambda(1-\theta)x} - e^{-\lambda x}}{\log(1-\theta)}$$

and thus

$$h(x) = \frac{e^{-\lambda(1-\theta)x} - e^{-\lambda x}}{-x\,\log(1-\theta)}.$$

Laplace transforms are of use in solving integral equations if the integral is expressible as a convolution. In many situations in this book, it will not be possible to obtain an explicit formula for the solution (unlike this example); but techniques for the numerical solution of Volterra integral equations can be used with the help of a computer.

The uses of Laplace transforms are quite varied. For example, some functions are more easily differentiable using Laplace transforms than the standard calculus. We illustrate this idea in the following example.

Example 1.3.5. Derivative of a Convolution

Suppose one wishes to evaluate the following expression:

$$\frac{d}{dx}\int_0^x f(y)g(x-y)dy.$$

It is easy using Laplace transforms. Let

$$h(x) = \int_0^x f(y)g(x-y)dy.$$

Then, in an obvious notation, $\bar{h}(z) = \bar{f}(z)\bar{g}(z)$ and so by (1.3.5) $h'(x)$ has Laplace transform $z\bar{f}(z)\bar{g}(z)$ since $h(0) = 0$. To obtain an explicit formula for $h'(x)$ we write

$$z\bar{f}(z)\bar{g}(z) = [z\bar{f}(z) - f(0)]\bar{g}(z) + f(0)\bar{g}(z).$$

The first term on the right hand side is the Laplace transform of the convolution of $f'(x)$ and $g(x)$ by (1.3.5) and (1.3.10), and the second term is the Laplace transform of $f(0)g(x)$. Hence,

$$h'(x) = \int_0^x f'(y)g(x-y)dy + f(0)g(x).$$

(Note that f and g may be interchanged.)

There are many situations where it is of use to extend these concepts to functions of more than one variable. For example, if we have a function $h(x,y)$ of two variables, the **bivariate Laplace transform** of $h(x,y)$ is defined to be

$$\bar{h}(z_1,z_2) = \int_0^\infty\int_0^\infty e^{-z_1 x - z_2 y} h(x,y)\,dx\,dy. \qquad (1.3.13)$$

Most of the results for single-variable functions (including uniqueness of the Laplace transform) extend to the bivariate case in an obvious manner.

The Laplace transform is, like the ordinary generating function, a most useful tool in working with continuous functions and will be extensively used throughout this book. These two transforms are often used in conjunction with each other; for example, it is sometimes expedient to work with the Laplace transform of an ordinary generating function. However they are used, they are most useful in insurance modeling to obtain otherwise complicated results.

1.4 BIBLIOGRAPHIC NOTES

A good reference on ordinary generating functions is contained in Riordan (1958). More elementary discussions are given in many textbooks on combinatorial theory. Example (1.2.4) is taken from Knuth (1981).

The Laplace transform is discussed in many textbooks such as Widder (1946) and Feller (1971). Extensive tables of Laplace transform pairs are also given in many different sources, including Oberhettinger and Badii (1973).

EXERCISES

1. **Binomial Series**
   Show, using formula (1.2.2) that if $-\infty < \alpha < \infty$, then

$$(1+z)^\alpha = \sum_{n=0}^\infty \binom{\alpha}{n} z^n, \quad |z| < 1$$

where $\displaystyle \binom{\alpha}{n} = \frac{\alpha(\alpha-1)\cdots(\alpha-n+1)}{n!}$.

What happens if α is a positive integer? What if $\alpha = -1$?

2. Logarithmic Series

(a) Show that $-\log(1-z) = \sum_{n=1}^{\infty} \dfrac{z^n}{n}$, $|z|<1$.

(b) How would you compute the coefficient of z^n in $C(z) = [-\log(1-z)]^\alpha$?
Hint: let $A(z) = -z^{-1}\log(1-z)$ and use example 1.2.4.

3.

(a) Suppose that $A(z) = \sum_{n=0}^{\infty} a_n z^n$.

Deduce that $A(kz) = \sum_{n=0}^{\infty} (a_n k^n) z^n$.

(b) Show, using example 1.2.2 that $e^{\alpha z} = \sum_{n=0}^{\infty} \dfrac{\alpha^n}{n!} z^n$, $|z|<\infty$.

(c) Show, using exercise 2 that

$$-\log(1-qz) = \sum_{n=1}^{\infty} \dfrac{q^n}{n} z^n, \quad |qz|<1.$$

4. Suppose that $a_0 = 1-p$, $a_1 = p(1-p)$, and

$$a_n = (1+p)a_{n-1} - pa_{n-2}, \quad n \geq 2.$$

Use the method of example 1.2.3 to show that

$$a_n = (1-p)p^n, \quad n \geq 0.$$

5. Suppose that $a_0 = 2$, $a_1 = 5$, and $a_n = 5a_{n-1} - 6a_{n-2}$, $n \geq 2$.

Use the method of example 1.2.3 to show that $a_n = 2^n + 3^n$, $n \geq 0$.

6. Suppose that $a_0 = 1$, $a_1 = 2$, and $a_n = 2a_{n-1} - a_{n-2}$, $n \geq 2$.

    Use the method of example 1.2.3 to show that $a_n = n+1$, $n \geq 0$.

7. (a) Using the definition given in exercise 1, show that

    $$(-1)^n \begin{pmatrix} -\alpha \\ n \end{pmatrix} = \begin{pmatrix} \alpha+n-1 \\ n \end{pmatrix}$$

    (b) Suppose that $b>0$, $\alpha>0$, and that

    $$na_n = [b(n-1)+\alpha]a_{n-1}, \quad n \geq 1.$$

    Use generating functions to show that

    $$a_n = a_0 \begin{pmatrix} \dfrac{\alpha}{b}+n-1 \\ n \end{pmatrix} b^n, \quad n \geq 0.$$

8. (a) Prove that

    $$\begin{pmatrix} -.5 \\ n \end{pmatrix} = \begin{pmatrix} 2n \\ n \end{pmatrix} \left(-\frac{1}{4} \right)^n$$

    (b) Let $a_{2n} = \begin{pmatrix} 2n \\ n \end{pmatrix} p^n(1-p)^n$, $n \geq 0$, and $a_{2n+1} = 0$, $n \geq 0$.

    Show that $A(z) = [1-4p(1-p)z^2]^{-\frac{1}{2}}$.

    Hence show that if $0<p<1$, $p \neq \frac{1}{2}$, then $\sum_{n=0}^{\infty} a_n = (|1-2p|)^{-1}$.

9. Suppose $a_n = \dfrac{1}{n(n+1)}$, $n = 1,2,3,...$ and $a_0 = 0$.

(a) Show that $A(z) = 1 + \dfrac{(1-z)}{z}\log(1-z)$ and that $A'(z) = -\dfrac{1}{z} - \dfrac{\log(1-z)}{z^2}$.

(b) Hence conclude that $\sum\limits_{n=1}^{\infty} a_n = 1$ but $\sum\limits_{n=1}^{\infty} na_n = \infty$. This shows that if $A(z)$ is convergent for all $|z| \leq R$, then $A'(z)$ is not necessarily convergent at $z = R$ (see (1.2.5) and exercise 2).

10. Let $A(z) = \sum\limits_{n=0}^{\infty} a_n z^n$, $B(z) = \sum\limits_{n=0}^{\infty} b_n z^n$ and m be a positive integer.

(a) Suppose $b_n = a_{n+m}$. Show that $B(z) = z^{-m}[A(z) - \sum\limits_{n=0}^{m-1} a_n z^n]$

(b) Suppose $b_n = a_{n-m}$, $n \geq m$ and $b_n = 0$ otherwise. Show that $B(z) = z^m A(z)$.

(c) Suppose $b_{mn} = a_n$, $n = 0,1,2,3,\ldots$, and $b_n = 0$ otherwise. Show that $B(z) = A(z^m)$.

11. Let $A(z) = \sum\limits_{n=0}^{\infty} a_n z^n$, $B(z) = \sum\limits_{n=0}^{\infty} b_n z^n$ and $C(z) = \sum\limits_{n=0}^{\infty} c_n z^n$.

(a) Suppose $b_n = \sum\limits_{m=n+1}^{\infty} a_m$, $n = 0,1,2,...$. Show that

$$B(z) = \frac{A(1)-A(z)}{1-z}.$$

(b) Suppose $c_n = \sum\limits_{m=n}^{\infty} (m-n)a_m$, $n = 0,1,2,...$. Show that, if $A'(1) < \infty$,

$$C(z) = \frac{A'(1)-z[\frac{A(1)-A(z)}{1-z}]}{1-z}.$$

(c) Suppose $a_n = p^n$, $n = 0,1,2,...$, $0<p<1$. Show that $B(z) = \frac{p}{1-p}A(z)$ and that $C(z) = \frac{p}{(1-p)^2}A(z)$.

12. Let $A(z) = \sum_{n=0}^{\infty}a_n z^n$, $B(z) = \sum_{n=0}^{\infty}b_n z^n$ and $B(z) = [A(z)]^{\alpha}$.

   (a) Suppose $a_n = 0$ for $n \geq m$. Show that the quantities b_n, $n = 0,1,2,...$ can be written recursively using at most m terms.

   (b) If $a_0 = .990$, $a_1 = .009$, $a_2 = .001$ and $\alpha = 100$, give the recursive formula for b_n and calculate b_n, $n = 0,1,2, \ldots, 10$.

13. Verify each of the properties of Laplace transforms given by equations (1.3.2) - (1.3.11).

14. Suppose that $\tilde{f}(z) = \int_0^{\infty}e^{-zx}f(x)dx.$

   (a) Let $g(x) = \int_x^{\infty}f(y)dy.$ Show that $\tilde{g}(z) = \int_0^{\infty}e^{-zx}g(x)dx$ is given by $\tilde{g}(z) = \frac{\tilde{f}(0)-\tilde{f}(z)}{z}.$

   (b) Let $h(x) = \int_x^{\infty}(y-x)f(y)dy.$ If $\tilde{f}'(0)<\infty$, show that $\tilde{h}(z) = \int_0^{\infty}e^{-zx}h(x)dx$ is given by $\tilde{h}(z) = \frac{-\tilde{f}'(0)-[\tilde{f}(0)-\tilde{f}(z)]/z}{z}.$

   (c) If $f(x) = e^{-\lambda x}$, $x>0$, show that $\tilde{g}(z) = \lambda^{-1}\tilde{f}(z)$ and that $\tilde{h}(z) = \lambda^{-2}\tilde{f}(z).$

15. Consider the function $h(x)$ with Laplace transform

$$\bar{h}(z) = \frac{z+\lambda}{\lambda} \; \frac{\log(1-\frac{\theta\lambda}{\lambda+z})}{\log(1-\theta)} + \frac{\theta}{\log(1-\theta)}, \quad 0<\theta<1, \; \lambda>0.$$

(a) Show that $h(x)$ satisfies the Volterra integral equation

$$h(x) = \frac{\theta[e^{-\lambda(1-\theta)x}-e^{-\lambda x}]}{-x \, \log(1-\theta)} - \frac{1}{x}\int_0^x e^{-\lambda y} h(x-y)dy, \quad x>0.$$

(b) Show that

$$h(x) = \frac{e^{-\lambda(1-\theta)x}-e^{-\lambda x}}{\lambda x^2 \log(1-\theta)} - \frac{\theta e^{-\lambda(1-\theta)x}}{x \, \log(1-\theta)}, \quad x>0.$$

16. Let $A(z) = \sum_{n=0}^{\infty} a_n z^n$, $|z|<R$ and $\bar{h}(z) = \int_0^{\infty} e^{-zx} h(x)dx$. Suppose $a_0 = 0$, $a_n = \theta^n$,

$n = 1,2,3,...$ and $h(x) = h(x;\lambda) = e^{-\lambda x}$, $x>0$. Let $\bar{g}(z) = A(\bar{h}(z)) = \int_0^{\infty} e^{-zx} g(x)dx$.

Show that $g(x) = \theta h(x;\lambda-\theta)$.

CHAPTER 2

PROBABILITY
AND RANDOM VARIABLES

2.1 INTRODUCTION

This chapter provides a review of the basic tools of probability and statistics which will be used in the remaining chapters of this book. This review is carried out without reference to the models or applications being considered in later chapters. The reader who has a strong background in the topics covered in this chapter can skip forward to later chapters directly. Other readers may wish to read this chapter thoroughly as background to the technical material in later chapters.

A number of features of this chapter should be noted by the reader. The contents of sections 2.2 to 2.6 are standard topics in most basic books on probability and statistics although Laplace transforms are not usually used. Sections 2.7 to 2.12 deal with topics that will be used in various places in this book. Laplace transforms of random variables are introduced in section 2.4. Along with probability generating functions, they will be used in deriving most results in later chapters.

2.2 RANDOM VARIABLES

Let X denote a **random variable** taking on values on a subset of the real line. For any subset A of the real line, we denote the probability that X takes on a value contained in A by $Pr\{X \varepsilon A\}$.

The **distribution function** (df) of the random variable X is defined for any real number x by

$$F_X(x) = Pr\{X \le x\} = Pr\{X \varepsilon \, (-\infty, x]\,\}. \qquad (2.2.1)$$

The subscript X indicates the random variable under consideration. When there is no ambiguity created by dropping the subscript, we shall do so for the sake of notational convenience.

Note that the distribution function $F_X(x)$ has the following properties:

(a) $F_X(-\infty) = \lim\limits_{x \to -\infty} F_X(x) = 0.$ $\qquad (2.2.2)$

(b) $F_X(\infty) = \lim\limits_{x \to +\infty} F_X(x) = 1.$ $\qquad (2.2.3)$

(c) $F_X(x)$ is non-decreasing, i.e. for $x < y$,

$$F_X(x) \le F_X(y). \qquad (2.2.4)$$

(d) $F_X(x)$ is right continuous, i.e. for any x,

$$F_X(x+0) = F_X(x). \qquad (2.2.5)$$

We now classify random variables into three types on the basis of the properties of their distribution functions.

A random variable X is said to be "of the **discrete** type" if its distribution function is a step function with a countable number of discontinuities or "jump points". For discrete random variables, the distribution function (2.2.1) can be written as

$$F_X(x) = \sum_{y \le x} Pr\{X=y\} \qquad (2.2.6)$$

where the sum is taken over all jump points of the distribution function $F_X(x)$. A discrete random variable X is said to be **arithmetic with span h** if the set of possible values of X consists of integral multiples of h; that is, the set of possible values of X is contained in the set $\{x=ih; \; i=0,\pm1,\pm2,...\}$. We shall often use the term **arithmetic** for distributions with span $h = 1$. We can do so without loss of generality since, measuring X in units of size h is equivalent to measuring $Y = X/h$ in units of size 1. An arithmetic distribution taking on only non-negative integral values is sometimes called a **counting**

distribution since it is often used to count events.

For a discrete random variable X, the function

$$f_X(x) = Pr\{X=x\} = F(x) - F(x-0) \qquad (2.2.7)$$

is called the **probability function** (pf) of X.

A random variable X is said to be "of the **continuous** type" if $F_X(x)$ is a continuous function. A continuous random variable is said to be **absolutely continuous** if $F_X(x)$ is differentiable everywhere on the real line. For a continuous random variable X, the function $f_X(x)$ defined by

$$f_X(x) = \frac{d}{dx} F_X(x) \qquad (2.2.8)$$

at the points where the derivative exists is called the **probability density function** (pdf) of X.

A random variable X is said to be "of the **mixed** type" if it is neither continuous nor discrete. Much of this book is concerned with random variables of the mixed type. If x is a jump point of $F_X(x)$, then we say that X has probability mass $Pr\{X=x\}$ at the point x or equivalently that X has a probability atom of size $Pr\{X=x\}$ at the point x. At points of absolute continuity of $F_X(x)$ we refer to the pdf of $F_X(x)$ as in the case of continuous distributions.

The **support** of a distribution is the set of points x for which $f(x)>0$.

We now consider the joint distribution of a pair of random variables X,Y. Let X,Y be a pair of random variables taking on values on a subset of the Cartesian plane. The **distribution function** of the random variables X and Y is defined by

$$F_{X,Y}(x,y) = Pr\{X \le x \text{ and } Y \le y\} = Pr\{X \le x, Y \le y\} \qquad (2.2.9)$$

for any real pair (x,y). The **marginal distribution functions of** the random variables X and Y are defined by

$$F_X(x) = F_{X,Y}(x,\infty) = \lim_{y \to \infty} F_{X,Y}(x,y) \tag{2.2.10}$$

and

$$F_Y(y) = F_{X,Y}(\infty,y) = \lim_{x \to \infty} F_{X,Y}(x,y). \tag{2.2.11}$$

The random variables X and Y are said to be **independent** if

$$F_{X,Y}(x,y) = F_X(x)F_Y(y). \tag{2.2.12}$$

We now consider the joint distribution of a set of real-valued variables $X_1, X_2, \ldots, X_n$. The **joint distribution function** is defined as

$$F_{X_1,X_2,\ldots,X_n}(x_1,x_2,\ldots,x_n) = Pr\{X_1 \le x_1, X_2 \le x_2, \ldots, X_n \le x_n\}$$

$$= Pr\{X_1 \varepsilon(-\infty,x_1] \text{ and } X_2 \varepsilon(-\infty,x_2] \text{ and } \cdots \text{ and } X_n \varepsilon(-\infty,x_n]\}. \tag{2.2.13}$$

The **marginal distribution function** of the random variable X_i is

$$F_{X_j}(x_j) = F_{X_1,X_2,\ldots,X_n}(\infty, \ldots, \infty, x_j, \infty, \ldots, \infty) \tag{2.2.14}$$

$$= Pr\{X_j \le x_j\}.$$

The random variables $X_1, X_2, \ldots, X_n$ are said to be **(mutually) independent** if

$$F_{X_1,X_2,\ldots,X_n}(x_1,x_2,\ldots,x_n) = \prod_{j=1}^{n} F_{X_j}(x_j). \tag{2.2.15}$$

In the case in which the random variables $X_1, X_2, \ldots, X_n$ are continuous, their **joint probability density function** is defined as

$$f_{X_1,X_2,\ldots,X_n}(x_1,x_2,\ldots,x_n) = \frac{\partial^n F_{X_1,X_2,\ldots,X_n}(x_1,x_2,\ldots,x_n)}{\partial x_1 \partial x_2 \cdots \partial x_n}$$

(2.2.16)

Now suppose $Y_1,Y_2,\ldots,Y_n$ is a one-to-one function of $X_1,X_2,\ldots,X_n$. If the joint pdf of $X_1,X_2,\ldots X_n$ is given, and we wish to perform a **change of variables** to $Y_1,Y_2,\ldots,Y_n$, we obtain their joint density as

$$f_{Y_1,Y_2,\ldots,Y_n}(y_1,y_2,\ldots,y_n) = f_{X_1,X_2,\ldots,X_n}(x_1,x_2,\ldots,x_n) \left| \frac{\partial(x_1,x_2,\ldots,x_n)}{\partial(y_1,y_2,\ldots,y_n)} \right|$$

(2.2.17)

where the right hand side of (2.2.17) is evaluated at $(y_1,y_2,\ldots,y_n)$ and

$$\left| \frac{\partial(x_1,x_2,\ldots,x_n)}{\partial(y_1,y_2,\ldots,y_n)} \right|$$

is the absolute value of the determinant of the matrix with (i,j)th entry $\frac{\partial x_i}{\partial y_j}$. This matrix is called the **Jacobian.** In the special case of (2.2.17) when $n=1$, we obtain

$$f_Y(y) = f_X(x) \left| \frac{dx}{dy} \right|$$

(2.2.18)

2.3 EXPECTED VALUES OF RANDOM VARIABLES

The **expectation** or **expected value** of a random variable X, denoted by $E[X]$, is defined by the Stieltjes integral

$$E[X] = \int x \, dF(x)$$

(2.3.1)

where the integral is taken over the set of all possible values of X. When X is of the discrete type, this reduces to

$$E[X] = \sum y \, f_X(y) \qquad (2.3.2)$$

where the summation is taken over all jump points of the distribution function $F_X(x)$. When X is of the continuous type, equation (2.3.1) can be rewritten as

$$E[X] = \int x \, f_X(x) dx. \qquad (2.3.3)$$

When X is of the mixed type, equation (2.3.1) can be rewritten as

$$E[X] = \int x \, f_X(x) dx + \sum x \, f_X(x)$$

where the integral is taken over all points of absolute continuity of $F_X(x)$ and the summation is over all jump points of $F_X(x)$.

Because we will be dealing with all three types of distributions, it will be notationally convenient to use the Stieltjes integral form (2.3.1) throughout the book.

Equation (2.3.1) yields the following generalization for the expectation of any function $g(X)$ of the random variable

$$E[g(X)] = \int g(x) dF_X(x). \qquad (2.3.4)$$

The **raw moments** or **moments about the origin** , denoted by μ_k', of the random variable X are obtained by setting

$$g(x) = x^k, \quad k = 1,2,3,... \qquad (2.3.5)$$

so that

$$\mu_k' = E[X^k], \quad k = 1,2,\dots \; . \tag{2.3.6}$$

The **factorial moments** , denoted by $\mu_{(k)}$, of the random variable X are obtained by setting

$$g(x) = x(x-1) \cdots (x-k+1) = x^{(k),} \; k = 1,2,3,\dots \tag{2.3.7}$$

so that

$$\mu_{(k)} = E[X^{(k)}]. \tag{2.3.8}$$

The first four factorial moments in terms of the raw moments are

$$\mu_{(1)} = \mu_1' \tag{2.3.9}$$

$$\mu_{(2)} = \mu_2' - \mu_1' \tag{2.3.10}$$

$$\mu_{(3)} = \mu_3' - 3\mu_2' + 2\mu_1' \tag{2.3.11}$$

$$\mu_{(4)} = \mu_4' - 6\mu_3' + 11\mu_2' - 6\mu_1'. \tag{2.3.12}$$

The first four raw moments in terms of the factorial moments are

$$\mu_1' = \mu_{(1)} \tag{2.3.13}$$

$$\mu_2' = \mu_{(2)} + \mu_{(1)} \tag{2.3.14}$$

$$\mu_3' = \mu_{(3)} + 3\mu_{(2)} + \mu_{(1)} \tag{2.3.15}$$

$$\mu_4' = \mu_{(4)} + 6\mu_{(3)} + 7\mu_{(2)} + \mu_{(1)}. \tag{2.3.16}$$

The **central moments** or **moments about the mean,** denoted by μ_k, of the random variable X are obtained by setting

$$g(x) = (x - \mu_1')^k, \quad k = 2, 3, \ldots \tag{2.3.17}$$

so that

$$\mu_k = E[(X - \mu_1')^k]. \tag{2.3.18}$$

The **variance** of the random variable X is the special case of (2.3.18) when $k = 2$

$$Var(X) = E[(X - \mu_1')^2]. \tag{2.3.19}$$

Two useful indices of the shape of a distribution are the **index of skewness,** $\mu_3\{\mu_2\}^{-\frac{3}{2}}$, and the **index of kurtosis,** $\mu_4\{\mu_2\}^{-2}$. The index of skewness is a measure of asymmetry of a distribution. The index of kurtosis is a measure of the thickness of the tails of a distribution. The normal distribution has skewness 0 since it is symmetric and kurtosis 3.

The first four central moments in terms of the raw moments are

$$\mu_1 = 0 \tag{2.3.20}$$

$$\mu_2 = \mu_2' - \mu_1'^2 \tag{2.3.21}$$

$$\mu_3 = \mu_3' - 3\mu_2'\mu_1' + 2\mu_1'^3 \tag{2.3.22}$$

$$\mu_4 = \mu_4' - 4\mu_3'\mu_1' + 6\mu_2'\mu_1'^2 - 3\mu_1'^4. \tag{2.3.23}$$

The first four raw moments in terms of the central moments and the mean are

$$\mu_1' = \mu_1' \tag{2.3.24}$$

$$\mu_2' = \mu_2 + \mu_1'^2 \tag{2.3.25}$$

$$\mu_3' = \mu_3 + 3\mu_1'\mu_2 + \mu_1'^3 \tag{2.3.26}$$

$$\mu_4' = \mu_4 + 4\mu_1'\mu_3 + 6\mu_1'^2\mu_2 + \mu_1'^4. \tag{2.3.27}$$

The expectation of the sum of two random variables X and Y is

$$E[X+Y] = E[X] + E[Y]. \tag{2.3.28}$$

The **covariance** of two random variables is defined to be

$$Cov(X,Y) = E\{(X-E[X])(Y-E[Y])\}$$
$$= E[XY] - E[X]E[Y] \tag{2.3.29}$$

where

$$E[XY] = \iint xy \, dF_{X,Y}(x,y). \tag{2.3.30}$$

If X and Y are independent random variables, then

$$E[XY] = E[X]E[Y]$$

and so

$$Cov(X,Y) = 0. \tag{2.3.31}$$

Extensions to the multivariate case of a set of n random variables is immediate using the generalization of (2.3.4)

$$E[g(X_1,X_2,\ldots,X_n)] = \iint \cdots \int g(x_1,x_2,\ldots,x_n)dF(x_1,x_2,\ldots,x_n) \tag{2.3.32}$$

where $F(x_1,x_2,\ldots,x_n)$ is given by (2.2.13). If $X_1,X_2,\ldots,X_n$ are mutually independent random variables, then

$$E[\prod_{j=1}^{n} X_j] = \prod_{j=1}^{n} E[X_j]. \tag{2.3.33}$$

2.4 GENERATING FUNCTIONS AND TRANSFORMS

Consider the univariate case (2.3.4) with the following functions:

(a) $g(x) = e^{zx}$

(b) $g(x) = z^x$

(c) $g(x) = e^{izx}$

(d) $g(x) = e^{-zx}$.

In each case, evaluation of (2.3.4) leads to a function of z as x is removed through the integration process. This function is called a **transform.**

The **moment generating function** (mgf) of X, denoted by $M_X(z)$, is defined by

$$M_X(z) = E[e^{zX}] = \int e^{zx} dF_X(x). \tag{2.4.1}$$

This integral does not always converge. When it does not the moment generating function is said to not exist. Note that we can write the mgf as

$$M_X(z) = \int \{1 + zx + \frac{(zx)^2}{2!} + \cdots \} dF_X(x)$$

$$= 1 + \mu_1' z + \mu_2' \frac{z^2}{2!} + \mu_3' \frac{z^3}{3!} + \cdots . \tag{2.4.2}$$

Raw moments are obtained by differentiating the mgf and setting $z = 0$,

$$\mu_k' = E[X^k] = \frac{d^k}{dz^k} M_X(z)|_{z=0} = M_X^k(0), \quad k = 1,2,3,\dots \quad . \tag{2.4.3}$$

The **probability generating function** (pgf) of X, denoted by $P_X(z)$, is defined as

$$P_X(z) = E[z^X] = \int z^x dF_X(x). \tag{2.4.4}$$

It is most frequently used for discrete random variables defined on the non-negative integers. In this case

$$P_X(z) = \sum_{k=0}^{\infty} z^k f_X(k). \tag{2.4.5}$$

The probabilities $f_X(k)$ are obtained by differentiating the pgf k times, setting $z = 0$ and dividing by $k!$,

$$f_X(k) = \frac{1}{k!} \frac{d^k}{dz^k} P_X(z)|_{z=0} = P_X^k(0). \tag{2.4.6}$$

Factorial moments can be obtained by differentiating the pgf k times and setting $z = 1$,

$$\mu_{(k)} = \frac{d^k}{dz^k} P_X(z)|_{z=1} = P_X^k(1). \tag{2.4.7}$$

The **characteristic function** (cf) of X, denoted by $\phi_X(z)$, is defined as

$$\phi_X(z) = E[e^{izX}] = \int e^{izx} dF_X(x). \tag{2.4.8}$$

In contrast to the moment generating function, the characteristic function always exists. Moments can be obtained from the cf in a manner similar to that for the mgf.

The **Laplace transform** (*LT*) of X or its distribution, denoted by $L_X(z)$, is defined as

$$L_X(z) = E[e^{-zX}] = \int e^{-zx} dF_X(x).$$ (2.4.9)

It is usually used only with random variables that do not take on negative values. For non-negative random variables, the LT always exists for complex values of z with a positive real part. For our purposes, it is usually sufficient to assume that z is a real variable.

The Laplace transform (2.4.9) of X is, in fact, the Laplace-Stieltjes transform of the df $F(x)$. Since it will be clear in any particular situation that we are dealing with the Laplace transform of a random variable as opposed to the Laplace transform of a function (in the sense of section 1.3), we shall henceforth use the same terminology in dealing with both. Note that if X is a continuous random variable with pdf $f_X(x)$, then the Laplace transform of X is the same as the Laplace transform of $f_X(x)$ defined in section 1.3. When X is a random variable of the mixed type, it will suffice to treat its probability density function as the sum of a (piecewise) continuous function and a discrete function and to use the results of section 1.3 on the (piecewise) continuous portion.

Each of the above transforms uniquely determine the corresponding distribution. It will be more convenient to obtain many results contained in this book in terms of transforms rather than in terms of the distribution function. Note that the various transforms may be obtained from each other by simple substitutions. For example, the transforms in terms of the mgf are given by:

$$P_X(z) = M_X(\ln z)$$ (2.4.10)

$$\phi_X(z) = M_X(iz)$$ (2.4.11)

$$L_X(z) = M_X(-z)$$ (2.4.12)

If X and Y are independent random variables, then each of the above transforms of the sum $X+Y$ can be written as the product of the corresponding transforms of X and Y. For example, in the case of Laplace transforms

$$L_{X+Y}(z) = L_X(z)L_Y(z). \tag{2.4.13}$$

For each of the transforms, we can define the multivariate analogue in the case of a set of n random variables $X_1, X_2, \ldots, X_n$. In this case we define

$$M_{X_1,X_2,\ldots,X_n}(z_1,z_2,\ldots,z_n) = E\left[\exp\left\{\sum_{j=1}^{n} z_j X_j\right\}\right], \tag{2.4.14}$$

$$P_{X_1,X_2,\ldots,X_n}(z_1,z_2,\ldots,z_n) = E\left[\prod_{j=1}^{n} z_j^{X_j}\right], \tag{2.4.15}$$

$$\phi_{X_1,X_2,\ldots,X_n}(z_1,z_2,\ldots,z_n) = E\left[\exp\left\{i\sum_{j=1}^{n} z_j X_j\right\}\right], \tag{2.4.16}$$

and

$$L_{X_1,X_2,\ldots,X_n}(z_1,z_2,\ldots,z_n) = E\left[\exp\left\{-\sum_{j=1}^{n} z_j X_j\right\}\right]. \tag{2.4.17}$$

If $X_1, X_2, \ldots, X_n$ are independent random variables, the transform of the sum can be written as the product of the corresponding transforms of the random variables $X_1, X_2, \ldots, X_n$. Hence,

$$L_{X_1+X_2+\cdots+X_n}(z) = \prod_{j=1}^{n} L_{X_j}(z). \tag{2.4.18}$$

Another transform of interest is the logarithm of the moment generating function, often called the **cumulant generating function** (cgf). It is defined as

$$C_X(z) = \log M_X(z). \qquad (2.4.19)$$

The cgf may easily be related to other transforms (for example by (2.4.11)). If (2.4.19) is expanded in a power series in z, we obtain

$$C_X(z) = \kappa_1 z + \kappa_2 \frac{z^2}{2!} + \kappa_3 \frac{z^3}{3!} + \cdots . \qquad (2.4.20)$$

The quantities $(\kappa_r, \; r = 1,2,3,...)$ are called the **cumulants** or the **semi-invariants** of the distribution. From (2.4.20), we see that

$$\kappa_r = \frac{d^r}{dz^r} C_X(z)|_{z=0}. \qquad (2.4.21)$$

The cumulants can be related to other moments (see section 2.3) and the r-th cumulant exists if all moments of order r exist. For example, the first four cumulants in terms of the central moments and the mean are

$$\kappa_1 = \frac{d}{dz} \log M_X(z)|_{z=0}$$

$$= \frac{M_X'(z)}{M_X(z)}|_{z=0}$$

$$= \mu_1' \qquad (2.4.22)$$

$$\kappa_2 = \mu_2 \qquad (2.4.23)$$

$$\kappa_3 = \mu_3 \qquad (2.4.24)$$

$$\kappa_4 = \mu_4 - 3(\mu_2)^2. \qquad (2.4.25)$$

Note that the first two cumulants are the mean and variance.

If X and Y are independent random variables, we have

$$C_{X+Y}(z) = \log\{M_X(z)M_Y(z)\}$$

$$= \log M_X(z) + \log M_Y(z)$$

$$= C_X(z) + C_Y(z) \tag{2.4.26}$$

and so the r-th cumulant of $X+Y$ is the sum of the r-th cumulant of X and the r-th cumulant of Y. Hence, the cumulants of independent random variables are additive.

2.5 CONDITIONAL DISTRIBUTIONS

If X and Y are any two random variables, the **conditional distribution function** of X, given $Y=y$, is

$$F(x|y) = F_{X|Y}(x|y) = Pr\{X \leq x | Y=y\} \tag{2.5.1}$$

The conditional distribution function is related to the distribution function by the "law of total probability", namely

$$F_X(x) = \int F_{X|Y}(x|y)dF_Y(y). \tag{2.5.2}$$

If both X and Y are continuous random variables, the law of total probability can be expressed in terms of probability density function as

$$f_X(x) = \int f_{X|Y}(x|y)f_Y(y)dy. \tag{2.5.3}$$

In the discrete case, the analogous expression is

$$f_X(x) = \sum_y f_{X|Y}(x|y)f_Y(y).$$
(2.5.4)

If X and Y are independent random variables, then from (2.2.12) it follows that

$$F_{X,Y}(x|y) = F_X(x).$$
(2.5.5)

The **conditional expectation** or **conditional mean** of X, given $Y=y$, is

$$E[X|Y=y] = \int x \, dF_{X|Y}(x|y).$$
(2.5.6)

If X and Y are independent random variables, then from (2.5.5) it follows that

$$E[X|Y=y] = E[X].$$
(2.5.7)

For any function $h(x)$, the conditional expectation of $h(X)$, given $Y=y$, is

$$E[h(X)|Y=y] = \int h(x) dF_{X|Y}(x|y).$$
(2.5.8)

It is easy to show that (when the expectations exist),

$$E[h(X)] = E_Y E_X[h(X)|Y]$$
(2.5.9)

where the inner expectation is first taken over X, for Y fixed, and the outer expectation is then taken over Y.

In equations similar to (2.5.9) in which the order of operations is obvious, we will often drop the subscripts for notational convenience. A particularly useful formula for the variance of a random variable in terms of conditional variances is given by the equation

$$Var(X) = E[Var(X|Y)] + Var[E(X|Y)]. \qquad (2.5.10)$$

Generalization of conditional probability concepts to multivariate situations follows directly along the same lines.

2.6 SUMS OF RANDOM VARIABLES

Suppose that X and Y are independent random variables. The distribution of the sum $S = X+Y$ is denoted by

$$F_S(s) = F_X * F_Y(s)$$

and called the **convolution** of F_X and F_Y. The df of S is evaluated as

$$\begin{aligned}
F_S(s) &= Pr\{S \le s\} \\
&= \int Pr\{S \le s | Y = y\} dF_Y(y) \\
&= \int Pr\{X \le s - y | Y = y\} dF_Y(y) \\
&= \int F_{X|Y}(s - y | y) dF_Y(y) \\
&= \int F_X(s - y) dF_Y(y)
\end{aligned}$$

by (2.5.5). Hence, the df of the sum of two random variables is evaluated as

$$F_S(s) = F_X * F_Y(s) = \int F_X(s - y) dF_Y(y). \qquad (2.6.1)$$

The corresponding pdf or pf of S is similarly denoted as

$$f_S(s) = f_X * f_Y(s) = \int f_X(s - y) dF_Y(y). \qquad (2.6.2)$$

If both X and Y are continuous random variables, the pdf of S is obtained by differentiating (2.6.1) with respect to s, yielding

$$f_S(s) = f_X * f_Y(s) = \int f_X(s-y) f_Y(y) dy. \tag{2.6.3}$$

If both X and Y are discrete random variables, the pf of S is likewise

$$f_S(s) = f_X * f_Y(s) = \sum_y f_X(s-y) f_Y(y). \tag{2.6.4}$$

Equations (2.6.1) to (2.6.4) show how the convolution of two df's, pdf's or pf's can be evaluated.

Since X and Y are independent by assumption, the distribution of $S = X+Y$ can be studied by examining any of the transforms in section 2.4 by using equations such as (2.4.13). Since the convolution operator $*$ must have the same properties as the addition operator $+$, it is both associative and commutative. Hence, we write symbolically

$$f_X * f_Y = f_Y * f_X \tag{2.6.5}$$

and

$$f_X * (f_Y * f_Z) = (f_X * f_Y) * f_Z. \tag{2.6.6}$$

This tells us that the results do not depend on the sequence in which the convolutions are carried out.

For the multivariate case of n independent random variables, the sum $S = X_1 + X_2 + \cdots + X_n$ can be obtained by convoluting successively over the random variables in any order. Hence, we could first obtain in sequence the partial sums recursively. By starting with, for example $S_1 = X_1$, we then obtain successively the distributions of the partial sums

$$S_j = S_{j-1} + X_j, \quad j = 2,3,\ldots,n \tag{2.6.7}$$

to finally yield the distribution of $S = S_n$. Equivalently, we could use a transform to obtain the distribution of S. For example, the LT of S is

$$L_S(z) = \prod_{j=1}^{n} L_{X_j}(z). \tag{2.6.8}$$

In this case, the resulting df and pdf (or pf) are denoted by

$$F_S(x) = F_{X_1} * F_{X_2} * \cdots * F_{X_n}(x) \tag{2.6.9}$$

and

$$f_S(x) = f_{X_1} * f_{X_2} * \cdots * f_{X_n}(x) \tag{2.6.10}$$

If $X_1, X_2, \ldots, X_n$ are identically distributed with df $F_X(x)$ and pdf (or pf) $f_X(x)$ as well as being independent, we denote the df and pdf (or pf) of S as

$$F_S(x) = F_X^{*n}(x) \tag{2.6.11}$$

and

$$f_S(x) = f_X^{*n}(x) \tag{2.6.12}$$

where the superscript $*n$ denotes to the "n-fold convolution of X". In this case, from (2.6.8), $S = X_1 + X_2 + \cdots + X_n$ has a transform that is the nth power of the transform of X. For example, for the pgf

$$P_S(z) = \{P_X(z)\}^n. \tag{2.6.13}$$

2.7 INFINITE DIVISIBILITY

The concept of infinite divisibility of a random variable or distribution will be used in later chapters as a basis for classifying distributions.

A real valued random variable X or its distribution is said to be **infinitely divisible** if for all values of $n = 1, 2, 3, \ldots$, its characteristic function $\phi(z)$ can be written as

$$\phi(z) = \{\phi_n(z)\}^n \tag{2.7.1}$$

where $\phi_n(z)$ is the characteristic function of some distribution.

From this equation it can be seen that any random variable X can be written as

$$X = X_1 + X_2 + \cdots + X_n \tag{2.7.2}$$

for all values of $n = 1,2,3,...$ where for each n, the random variables, $X_1, X_2, \ldots, X_n$ are identically distributed.

We now consider a further restriction on infinitely divisible distributions. Let X denote a random variable with support on some subset A of the set of real numbers R. Then X is said to be **infinitely divisible on A** if X is infinitely divisible and the support of the distributions with cf $\phi_n(z)$ is contained in A for all values of $n = 1,2,3,...$. From this definition it is clear that "infinite divisibility on R" implies "infinite divisibility".

From section 2.4, it is clear that if equation (2.7.1) holds for any of the transforms, it also holds for the cf and vice versa providing that the transform exists.

Example 2.7.1. Normal Distribution

The normal distribution with mean μ and variance σ^2 and pdf

$$f(x) = \frac{1}{\sqrt{2\pi}\,\sigma} \exp\{-\frac{1}{2}(\frac{x-\mu}{\sigma})^2\}, \quad -\infty < x < \infty$$

and cf

$$\phi(z) = \exp\{i\mu z - \frac{1}{2}\sigma^2 z^2\}$$

is infinitely divisible (on R) since for any value of $n = 1,2,...$, we can write $\phi_n(z)$ as

$$\phi_n(z) = \exp\{i\frac{\mu}{n}z - \frac{1}{2}\frac{\sigma^2}{n}z^2\}$$

which is the cf of a normal random variable with mean μ/n and variance σ^2/n.

Example 2.7.2. Gamma Distribution

The gamma distribution with parameters α and β and pdf

$$f(x) = \frac{\beta^\alpha}{\Gamma(\alpha)}x^{\alpha-1}e^{-\beta x}, \quad x>0$$

and cf

$$\phi(z) = \left(\frac{\beta}{\beta-iz}\right)^\alpha$$

is infinitely divisible (on $R_+ = [0,\infty)$) since for any value of $n = 1,2,3,\ldots$, we can write $\phi_n(z)$ as

$$\phi_n(z) = \left(\frac{\beta}{\beta-iz}\right)^{\frac{\alpha}{n}}$$

which is the characteristic of a gamma distribution with parameters α/n and β.

Example 2.7.3. Poisson Distribution

The Poisson distribution with mean λ and pf

$$f(x) = \frac{\lambda^x}{x!}e^{-x}, \quad x = 0,1,2,\ldots$$

and cf

$$\phi(z) = \exp\{\lambda(e^{iz}-1)\}$$

is infinitely divisible (on $N_+ = \{0,1,2,...\}$) since for any value of $n = 1,2,\ldots$, we can write $\phi_n(z)$ as

$$\phi_n(z) = \exp\{\frac{\lambda}{n}(e^{iz}-1)\}$$

which is the characteristic function of a Poisson random variable with mean λ/n.

Example 2.7.4. Negative Binomial Distribution

The negative binomial distribution with parameters r and q and pf

$$f(x) = \frac{\Gamma(r+x)}{\Gamma(r)x!}p^r q^x, \quad x = 0,1,2,3...,$$

when $p = 1-q$, and cf

$$\phi(z) = \left(\frac{p}{1-qe^{iz}}\right)^r$$

is infinitely divisible (on N_+) since for any value of $n = 0,1,2,\ldots$, we can write $\phi_n(z)$ as

$$\phi_n(z) = \left(\frac{p}{1-qe^{iz}}\right)^{\frac{r}{n}}$$

which is the characteristic function of a negative binomial distribution with parameters r/n and q. We often use parameterization $p = (1+\beta)^{-1}$ and so the cf can be written as

$$\phi(z) = \{1-\beta(e^{iz}-1)\}^{-r}.$$

Example 2.7.5. Binomial Distribution

The binomial distribution with parameters m and q and pf

$$f(x) = \binom{m}{x} q^x p^{m-x}, \quad x = 0,1,2,\ldots,m$$

where $p = 1-q$ and cf

$$\phi(z) = \{1+q(e^{iz}-1)\}^m$$

is not infinitely divisible since

$$\phi_n(z) = \{1+q(e^{iz}-1)\}^{m/n}$$

is only a cf when m/n is an integer.

Example 2.7.6. One Point Distribution

The degenerate distribution with point mass 1 at $x = 1$ and cf

$$\phi(z) = e^{iz}$$

is infinitely divisible since

$$\phi_n(z) = e^{i\frac{z}{n}}$$

is the cf of a degenerate distribution with point mass 1 at $x = 1/n$, but is not infinitely divisible on N_+ since the support of the distribution with cf $\phi_n(z)$ is not contained in N_+.

The notion of infinite divisibility can be extended to multivariate distributions. A multivariate distribution (or its associated characteristic function) is said to be infinitely divisible if its characteristic function $\phi(z_1,z_2,\ldots,z_n)$ can be written as

$$\phi(z_1, z_2, \dots, z_n) = \{\phi_n(z_1, z_2, \dots, z_n)\}^n$$

for $n = 1, 2, 3, \dots$ and $\phi_n(z_1, z_2, \dots, z_n)$ is a characteristic function.

Example 2.7.7. Multivariate Normal Distribution

If $X_1, X_2, \dots, X_n$ has joint pdf

$$f(x_1, \dots, x_n) = (2\pi)^{-\frac{n}{2}} (|\textstyle\sum|)^{-\frac{1}{2}} \exp\{-\frac{1}{2}(\mathbf{x} - \boldsymbol{\mu})' \textstyle\sum^{-1}(\mathbf{x} - \boldsymbol{\mu})\},$$

where $\mathbf{x}' = (x_1, x_2, \dots, x_n)$, $\boldsymbol{\mu}' = (\mu_1, \mu_2, \dots, \mu_n)$, and $\sum = [\sigma_{ij}]_{n \times n}$, then $(X_1, X_2, \dots, X_n)$ is said to have a multivariate normal distribution. The characteristic function is

$$\phi(\mathbf{z}') = \exp\{i\mathbf{z}'\boldsymbol{\mu} - \frac{1}{2}\mathbf{z}'\textstyle\sum\mathbf{z}\}$$

where $\mathbf{z}' = (z_1, z_2, \dots, z_n)$. Clearly,

$$\phi_n(\mathbf{z}') = \exp\{\frac{i}{n}\mathbf{z}'\boldsymbol{\mu} - \frac{1}{2n}\mathbf{z}'\textstyle\sum\mathbf{z}\}$$

is again a multivariate normal cf and so the distribution is infinitely divisible. $\sum$ must be a positive definite symmetric matrix in this expression. It is easily shown that X_i has a normal distribution with mean μ_i and variance σ_{ii} and that $Cov(X_i, X_j) = \sigma_{ij} = \sigma_{ji}$. Furthermore, any linear combination of the X_i's has again a normal distribution.

Example 2.7.8. Multinomial Distribution

If $X_1, X_2, \dots, X_n$ has joint probability function

$$f(x_1,x_2,\ldots,x_n) = \begin{pmatrix} m \\ x_1,x_2,\ldots,x_{n-1} \end{pmatrix} q_1^{x_1} q_2^{x_2} \cdots q_n^{x_n}$$

where $x_1 + x_2 + \cdots + x_n = m$ and $q_1 + q_2 + \cdots + q_n = 1$, then $(X_1, X_2, \ldots, X_n)$ is said to have a $(n-1)$-variate multinomial distribution. The characteristic function is

$$\phi(z_1, z_2, \ldots, z_n) = (q_1 e^{iz_1} + q_2 e^{iz_2} + \cdots + q_n e^{iz_n})^m.$$

As for the binomial distribution,

$$\phi_n(z_1, z_2, \ldots, z_n) = [\phi(z_1, z_2, \ldots, z_n)]^{\frac{1}{n}}$$

is only a characteristic function if m/n is a positive integer and so the distribution is not infinitely divisible. It is easily shown that X_i has a binomial distribution with parameters m and q_i and that $Cov(X_i, X_j) = -mq_i q_j$.

2.8 MIXTURES OF DISTRIBUTIONS

Suppose X is a random variable with df $F_X(x;\theta)$ and pf $f_X(x;\theta)$ indexed by some parameter θ. The parameter θ is normally considered a fixed but unknown quantity. In this section, θ is considered to be the outcome of some "random parameter" θ. In a typical situation, the quantity θ is unknown and can only be estimated from the observed data using some procedure from the field of statistical inference. We will often use the notation $F_X(x|\theta)$ to emphasize when θ is fixed or given.

Further suppose that θ is distributed over its range of possible values according to a df $U(\theta)$ and pf or pdf $u(\theta)$.

Then we define the df of the **mixture of distributions** of the form $F_X(x|\theta)$ to be

$$F_X(x) = \int_\theta F_X(x|\theta)dU(\theta) = E_\theta F_X(x|\theta). \tag{2.8.1}$$

Equation (2.8.1) defines the unconditional distribution of X in terms of the conditional distribution of X given $\theta = \theta$. Consequently, the results for conditional random variables and expectations of section 2.5 hold. The unconditional pf of X is then

$$f_X(x) = \int_\theta f_X(x|\theta)dU(\theta) = E_\theta f_X(x|\theta); \tag{2.8.2}$$

the unconditional raw moments are

$$E[X^k] = \int_\theta E[X^k|\theta]dU(\theta) = E_\theta E[X^k|\theta], \quad k = 1,2,...; \tag{2.8.3}$$

and the unconditional transforms are obtained by taking the expected value over the set of possible parameter values in accordance with the distribution of θ. Hence we write

$$M_X(z) = E_\theta M_X(z|\theta) \tag{2.8.4}$$

$$P_X(z) = E_\theta P_X(z|\theta) \tag{2.8.5}$$

$$\phi_X(z) = E_\theta \phi(z|\theta) \tag{2.8.6}$$

$$L_X(z) = E_\theta L_X(z|\theta) \tag{2.8.7}$$

Example 2.8.1. Poisson Mixtures

Suppose X has a Poisson distribution with pf

$$f_X(x|\theta) = e^{-\theta}\frac{\theta^x}{x!}, \quad x = 0,1,2,...$$

and mgf

$$M_X(z|\theta) = \exp\{\theta(e^z-1)\}.$$

Then for any distribution $U(\theta)$, the unconditional mgf of X is given by

$$M_X(z) = E_\theta M_X(z|\theta)$$

$$= E_\theta[\exp\{\theta(e^z-1)\}]$$

$$= M_\theta(e^z-1)$$

which is the mgf of θ evaluated at e^z-1.

A (possibly) different form of mixture of distributions can be constructed as follows. Let $p_1, p_2, p_3,...$ denote a series of non-negative weights satisfying $\sum p_j = 1$. Let $F_1(x), F_2(x), F_3(x),...$ denote an arbitrary sequence of distribution functions. Then, the df

$$F_X(x) = \sum p_j F_j(x) \tag{2.8.8}$$

is called a mixture. This is more general than (2.8.1) in the sense that the weights are not necessarily related to any parameter. For example, one can construct a mixture of a degenerate distribution

$$F_1(x) = \begin{cases} 0, & x<0 \\ 1, & x\geq 0 \end{cases}$$

and an exponential distribution

$$F_2(x) = 1 - e^{-\lambda x}, \quad x > 0$$

with weights p_1 and $1-p_1$ as

$$F_X(x) = p_1 1 + (1-p_1)(1-e^{-\lambda x})$$

$$= 1 - (1-p_1)e^{-\lambda x}, \quad x > 0. \tag{2.8.9}$$

In this example the LT of X is

$$L_X(z) = p_1 L_1(z) + (1-p_1)L_2(z)$$

$$= p_1 + (1-p_1)\frac{\lambda}{\lambda + z}. \tag{2.8.10}$$

Equation (2.8.8) could be considered different from equation (2.8.1) for a discrete variable θ since the distributions $F_j(x)$ in (2.8.8) are not necessarily from the same parametric family. Using the technique of mixing, one can construct a wide range of distributions. This technique will be considered in later chapters.

2.9 DISTRIBUTION OF RANDOM SUMS

Suppose $X_1, X_2, X_3, ...$ is a sequence of independent and identically distributed (iid) random variables with common df $F_X(x)$, cf $\phi_X(z)$, mean μ_X and variance σ_X^2. Then the sum $X_1 + X_2 + \cdots + X_n$ has df $F_X^{*n}(x)$, cf $\{\phi_X(z)\}^n$, mean $n\mu_X$ and variance $n\sigma_X^2$ for $n = 1,2,3,... $.

Now consider the random sum

$$S = X_1 + X_2 + \cdots + X_N \tag{2.9.1}$$

where N has a counting distribution and $S = 0$ when $N = 0$. Then, the df of X can be obtained as

$$F_S(x) = Pr\{S \le x\}$$

$$= \sum_{n=0}^{\infty} Pr\{N=n\} Pr\{S \le x | N=n\}$$

$$= \sum_{n=0}^{\infty} Pr\{N=n\} F_X^{*n}(x) \tag{2.9.2}$$

where

$$F_X^{*0}(x) = \begin{cases} 0, & x<0 \\ 1, & x \ge 0 \end{cases}.$$

This distribution of the random sum (2.9.1) is called a **compound distribution.** The cf of the compound distribution is given by

$$\phi_S(z) = E[\exp\{izS\}]$$

$$= \sum_{n=0}^{\infty} E[\exp\{iz(X_1+X_2+\cdots+X_n)\} | N=n] Pr\{N=n\}$$

$$= \sum_{n=0}^{\infty} Pr\{N=n\} [\phi_X(z)]^n. \tag{2.9.3}$$

This can be rewritten as

$$\phi_S(z) = P_N(\phi_X(z)). \tag{2.9.4}$$

For the other transforms, equations (2.9.3) and (2.9.4) hold with ϕ replaced by the appropriate symbol. Hence, for the compound distribution,

$$M_S(z) = P_N(M_X(z)) \tag{2.9.5}$$

$$P_S(z) = P_N(P_X(z)) \tag{2.9.6}$$

and

$$L_S(z) = P_N(L_X(z)). \qquad (2.9.7)$$

If the distribution of N is Poisson, then the distribution of (2.9.1) is called the compound Poisson distribution. Similarly, for the compound binomial distribution, the compound negative binomial distribution and so forth. It can be shown that the only infinitely divisible distributions on $\{0,1,2,...\}$ are compound Poisson distributions (cf. Feller, 1968).

Example 2.9.1. Compound Geometric-Exponential

Suppose $X_1, X_2, X_3,...$ are iid with common exponential distribution with mean $1/\theta$, pdf

$$f_X(x) = \theta e^{-\theta x}, \quad x>0,$$

and LT

$$L_X(z) = \frac{\theta}{\theta+z}.$$

According to (2.9.3) the LT of S is

$$L_S(z) = \sum_{n=0}^{\infty} Pr\{N=n\} \left(\frac{\theta}{\theta+z}\right)^n.$$

Further, suppose that N is a geometric random variable with pf

$$Pr\{N=n\} = pq^n, \quad n = 0,1,2,...$$

and pgf

$$P_N(z) = \frac{p}{1-qz}.$$

Then, from (2.9.7), the LT of S becomes

$$L_S(z) = p \left[1 - \frac{q\theta}{\theta + z} \right]^{-1}$$

$$= p \left[\frac{\theta + z}{p\theta + z} \right]$$

$$= p + q\frac{p\theta}{p\theta + z}$$

$$= pL_1(z) + qL_2(z)$$

where $L_1(z) = 1$ is the LT of the degenerate distribution with probability 1 at $x = 0$, and $L_2(z)$ is the LT of the exponential distribution with mean $(p\theta)^{-1}$. This is of the form (2.8.10) with $p_1 = p$ and $\lambda = p\theta$. Hence, by the uniqueness of the LT, the random sum S has a distribution which has density

$$f_S(x) = \begin{cases} p, & x=0 \\ pq\theta e^{-p\theta x}, & x>0 \end{cases}$$

and df

$$F_S(x) = 1 - qe^{-p\theta x}, \quad x \geq 0.$$

Note that the distribution of S may be thought of as a mixture of two other distributions.

The moments of random sums can be evaluated by differentiating equation (2.9.5) and setting $z = 0$ or directly using conditional probability arguments. Differentiating equation (2.9.5) once yields

$$M_S'(z) = P_N'(M_X(z))M_X'(z). \tag{2.9.8}$$

Setting $z = 0$ and using equations (2.4.3) and (2.4.7) yields

$$M_S'(0) = P_N'(1)M_X'(0)$$

and so

$$E[S] = E[N]E[X]. \tag{2.9.9}$$

Differentiating equation (2.9.8) again yields

$$M_S''(z) = P_N''(M_X(z))[M_X'(z)]^2 + P_N'(M_X(z))M_X''(z). \tag{2.9.10}$$

Setting $z = 0$ yields

$$M_S''(0) = P_N''(1)\{M_X'(0)\}^2 + P_N'(1)M_X''(0) \tag{2.9.11}$$

and so

$$E[S^2] = E[N(N-1)]\{E[X]\}^2 + E[N]E[X]. \tag{2.9.12}$$

Subtracting the square of equation (2.9.9) and reorganizing yields the variance of S

$$Var(S) = Var(N)\{E[X]\}^2 + E[N]Var(X). \tag{2.9.13}$$

To obtain third moments, differentiating (2.9.10) and setting $z = 0$ yields

$$M_S'''(0) = P_N'''(1)\{M_X'(0)\}^3 + 3P_N''(1)M_X'(0)M_X''(0) + P_N'(1)M_X'''(0) \tag{2.9.14}$$

and so

$$E[S^3] = E[N(N-1)(N-2)]\{E[X]\}^3 + 3E[N(N-1)]E[X]E[X^2] + E[N]E[X^3].$$

$$\tag{2.9.15}$$

This general procedure can be used to obtain higher moments of S in terms of moments of N and X.

2.10 ORDER STATISTICS

Suppose that $X_1, X_2, \ldots, X_n$ are n identically distributed random variables with common df $F(x)$. If they are rearranged in ascending order of magnitude and then written as

$$X_{(1)} \leq X_{(2)} \leq \cdots \leq X_{(n)},$$

we call $X_{(r)}$ the r-th **order statistic** $(r = 1, 2, \ldots, n)$. The unordered variables may be independent or dependent. In any case, the ordered variables are dependent.

Let $F_r(x)$ $(r = 1, 2, \ldots, n)$ denote the df of $X_{(r)}$. Then the distribution function of the maximum $X_{(n)}$ is

$$F_n(x) = Pr\{X_{(n)} \leq x\}$$

$$= Pr\{\text{all } X_i \leq x\}$$

$$= [F(x)]^n. \tag{2.10.1}$$

Similarly, the distribution of the minimum is

$$F_1(x) = Pr\{X_{(1)} \leq x\}$$

$$= 1 - Pr\{X_{(1)} > x\}$$

$$= 1 - Pr\{\text{all } X_i > x\}$$

$$= 1 - [1 - F(x)]^n. \tag{2.10.2}$$

When one considers the distribution of $X_{(r)}$, the above arguments can be generalized to

$$F_r(x) = Pr\{X_{(r)} \leq x\}$$

$$= Pr\{\text{at least } r \text{ of the } X_i \text{ are less than or equal to } x\}$$

$$= \sum_{j=r}^{n} \binom{n}{j} [F(x)]^j [1-F(x)]^{n-j}. \tag{2.10.3}$$

In order to obtain the df of $X_{(r)}$ when the X_i are continuous random variables, we consider the probability $Pr\{X_r \varepsilon(x,x+h]\}$ for small positive values of h. For this event to occur for sufficiently small values of h, $r-1$ values of the X_i must be less than or equal to x and $n-r$ of them must be greater than $x+h$. For sufficiently small values of h, only one of the X_i can be in the interval of length h from x to $x+h$. Hence we can write

$$Pr\{X_r \varepsilon(x,x+h]\} = \binom{n}{r-1,1} [F(x)]^{r-1} [F(x+h)-F(x)][1-F(x)]^{n-r} \tag{2.10.4}$$

$$+ \text{ terms involving higher powers of } F(x+h)-F(x)$$

where

$$\binom{n}{r-1,1} = \frac{n!}{(r-1)!\,1!\,(n-r)!} \tag{2.10.5}$$

represents the number of combinations of the X_i. For small values of h, this becomes approximately

$$Pr\{X_r \varepsilon(x,x+h]\} = \binom{n}{r-1,1} [F(x)]^{r-1} f(x)h[1-F(x)]^{n-r} + o(h^2) \tag{2.10.6}$$

when $o(h^2)$ means of order h^2. A function $k(x)$ is $o(h^2)$ if

$$\lim_{h \to 0} \frac{k(h^2)}{h^2} = 0.$$

Dividing by h and letting h approach zero, yields

$$f_r(x) = \binom{n}{r-1,1} [F(x)]^{r-1} f(x)[1-F(x)]^{n-r}. \tag{2.10.7}$$

For the joint distribution of k ($1 \leq k \leq n$) order statistics $X_{(n_1)}, X_{(n_2)}, \ldots, X_{(n_k)}$ where $1 \leq n_1 \leq n_2 \leq \cdots \leq n_k \leq n$, similar arguments result in

$$f_{n_1 n_2 \cdots n_k}(x_1, x_2, \ldots, x_k) = \frac{n!}{(n_1-1)!(n_2-n_1-1)! \cdots (n-n_k)!}$$

$$\times [F(x_1)]^{n_1-1} f(x_1)[F(x_2)-F(x_1)]^{n_2-n_1-1}$$

$$\times f(x_2) \cdots f(x_k)[1-F(x_k)]^{n-n_k} \tag{2.10.8}$$

where $x_1 \leq x_2 \leq \cdots \leq x_k$.

From (2.10.8), the joint pdf of all n order statistics is

$$f_{1,2\ldots n}(x_1, x_2, \ldots, x_n) = n! f(x_1)f(x_2) \cdots f(x_n) \tag{2.10.9}$$

where $x_1 \leq x_2 \leq \cdots \leq x_n$. This result reflects the fact that there are $n!$ ways of ordering the X_i.

Example 2.10.1. Order statistics from the Uniform Distribution

Suppose that the X_i are from a uniform distribution on $(0,t]$

$$f(x) = 1/t, \quad 0 < x \leq t.$$

Then the joint pdf of n order statistics is

$$f_{1,2\ldots n}(x_1, x_2, \ldots, x_n) = n!/t^n, \quad 0 < x_1 \leq x_2 \cdots \leq x_n \leq t.$$

This fact will be used in the next chapter.

2.11 CENTRAL LIMIT THEOREM

Suppose we have a sequence of iid random variables $X_1, X_2,...$ each with finite mean μ and variance σ^2. Then, consider the sequence $S_1, S_2,...$ where

$$S_n = \frac{(\sum_{i=1}^{n} X_i) - n\mu}{\sigma\sqrt{n}}, \quad n = 1,2,3,... \tag{2.11.1}$$

For large n, the distribution of S_n is now shown to be approximately normal (see example 2.7.1).

Theorem 2.11.1. The sequence of random variables defined by (2.11.1) converges (as $n \to \infty$) to a normal distribution with mean 0 and variance 1.

Proof

Let the characteristic function of $Y_i = X_i - \mu$ be $\phi_Y(z)$. Then the characteristic function of S_n is

$$\phi_{S_n}(z) = E[e^{izS_n}]$$

$$= \{\phi_Y(\frac{z}{\sigma\sqrt{n}})\}^n. \tag{2.11.2}$$

The mean of Y_i is 0 and the variance is σ^2. Hence we may expand $\phi_Y(t)$ in a Taylor series about $z = 0$, i.e.

$$\phi_Y(z) = 1 - \frac{1}{2}\sigma^2 z^2 + o(z^2)$$

and thus

$$\phi_{S_n}(z) = \{1 - \frac{1}{2}\frac{z^2}{n} + o(\frac{z^2}{n})\}^n.$$

(2.11.3)

Hence, since $\lim_{n \to \infty} \{1 + \frac{A}{n} + o(\frac{1}{n})\}^n = e^A$, we obtain,

$$\lim_{n \to \infty} \phi_{S_n}(z) = e^{-\frac{z^2}{2}}.$$

(2.11.4)

By example 2.7.1, this is the cf of a normal variate with mean 0 and unit variance.

This theorem states the distribution of the sum $\sum_{i=1}^{n} X_i$ is approximately normal with mean $n\mu$ and variance $n\sigma^2$ if n if sufficiently large. The rate of convergence to normality is slower as the distribution of the X_i's becomes more skewed.

This theorem gives an approximate distribution for any variate expressible as a sum of independent and identically distributed (iid) variates. It is useful when, as is often the case, the exact distribution is difficult to obtain.

2.12 BIBLIOGRAPHIC NOTES

A good introduction to many of the statistical concepts is given by Hogg and Craig (1978), Fisz (1963), Feller (1968), or Kendall and Stuart (1977).

The use of generating functions and transforms in statistics is covered by Giffin (1975) and Feller (1971). Infinite divisibility is discussed by Feller (1968) in connection with distributions of random sums. Bühlmann (1970) discusses infinite divisibility and its uses in an insurance situation. Laha and Rohatgi (1979) discuss it from a more mathematical viewpoint as does Feller (1971). Mixtures of distributions in connection with claim size distributions are considered by Hogg and Klugman (1984), and Kupper (1960, 1962). Ord (1972), and Bühlmann (1970) also discuss mixtures of distributions. An introduction to random sums can be found in Feller (1968). Order statistics are discussed by Hogg and Craig (1978), Kendall and Stuart (1977), and more extensively by David (1981).

CHAPTER 3

STOCHASTIC PROCESSES

3.1 INTRODUCTION

The body of actuarial literature known as "risk theory" with origins that date back to the first decade of this century was based on modeling a **random process** or **stochastic process** which generates claims over time. The concept of "ruin", which has been explored extensively by many authors over the years, is based directly upon the model of the stochastic claim process.

In this book we place relatively less emphasis on the concept of ruin and hence the underlying stochastic process than have previous authors. Nevertheless, there are references to stochastic processes in various chapters. The brief summary of some stochastic process concepts in this chapter is intended to provide the reader with the necessary background. The reader who has a strong background in stochastic processes should feel free to skip forward to the next chapter.

3.2 STOCHASTIC PROCESSES

Let $X(t)$ denote a random variable indexed by a real-valued parameter t. The set of all possible values T of the parameter t is called the **index set.** The collection of random variables $\underline{X} = \{X(t); t \varepsilon T\}$ is called a **stochastic process.**

The parameter t usually refers to time measured by real time or some transformation of real time. For the purpose of this book we shall henceforth refer to t as the "time parameter". If the index set T is a continuous set of points, the process $\underline{X}$ is called a **continuous-time stochastic process.**

If the index set T is a set of countable points, the process $\underline{X}$ is called a **discrete-time stochastic process.**

The set of possible values of outcomes of the random variable $X(t)$ for fixed t is called the **sample space** of $X(t)$. A realization or outcome of the process $\underline{X} = \{X(t); t\varepsilon T\}$ is called a **sample space.** The set of possible values of outcomes of the process $\underline{X} = \{X(t); t\varepsilon T\}$ is called the **state space** of $\underline{X}$.

Example 3.2.1. Claim Counter

Let $T = (0,\infty)$ denote the set of time points (measured in months) beginning at January 1, 1980. Let $N(t)$ denote the number of third party liability claims settled since January 1, 1980 resulting from automobile accidents occurring in the calendar 1980. Then $\underline{N} = \{N(t); t\varepsilon T\}$ takes on values $0,1,2,\ldots$, successively. It is a continuous-time stochastic process with discrete state space.

Example 3.2.2. Total Loss Costs

Let $\underline{X} = \{X(t); t\geq 0\}$ be a stochastic process that is identical to $\underline{N}$ in the previous example except that $X(t)$ denotes the total amounts paid in $(0,t]$ for third party liability claims resulting from automobile accidents occurring in 1980. Then $\underline{X}$ is a continuous-time stochastic process with a continuous state space.

A number of properties of stochastic processes are important in characterizing certain classes of continuous-time processes. A continuous-time process has **independent increments** if for all possible choices of $t_0 < t_1 < t_2 \cdots < t_n$, the random variables

$$X(t_1) - X(t_0), \; X(t_2) - X(t_1), \ldots, \; X(t_n) - X(t_{n-1})$$

are mutually independent. A process has independent increments if the changes in the value of the process in non-overlapping time intervals are independent.

A continuous-time stochastic process has **stationary increments** if $X(t+h) - X(t)$ has the same distribution for all values of t. A process has stationary increments if the change in the value of the process over a time interval depends only on the length of the interval and not on its location.

A stochastic process $\underline{X} = \{X(t); t\varepsilon T\}$ is said to be a **Markov process** if, for any $n = 1,2,3,\ldots$, and arbitrary $t_m\varepsilon T$, $(m = 0,1,2,\ldots,n)$ where $t_0<t_1<t_2<\cdots<t_n$, and for any real x and y, the equality

$$Pr\{X(t_n){\le}y\,|X(t_{n-1}) = x, \; X(t_{n-2}) = x_{n-2},\ldots, \; X(t_0) = x_0\}$$

$$= Pr\{X(t_n){\le}y\,|X(t_{n-1}) = x\}$$

holds for every real $x_0,x_1,x_2,\ldots,x_{n-2}$. This definition states that the future values of the process given its (partial) history depends only on the value of the process at the most recent point in its history. In other words, once a particular position is attained, the future behaviour of the process does not depend upon how that position was attained.

A very important class of stochastic processes is now defined. A **counting process** $\underline{N} = \{N(t); t{\ge}0\}$ is a process that represents the total number of events that have occurred up to time t. A counting process satisfies the following properties:

(a) $N(t){\ge}0$.

(b) $N(t)$ is integer valued.

(c) $N(t)$ is non-decreasing, i.e. for $s<t$, $N(s){\le}N(t)$.

(d) for $s<t$, the quantity $N(t) - N(s)$ represents the number of events

that have occurred in the interval $(s,t]$.

We shall use a counting process to model the number of claims occurring over time.

3.3 THE POISSON PROCESS

The Poisson process is a special counting process in which the number of events in any time period has a Poisson distribution. It can be formally defined as follows.

A counting process $\underline{N} = \{N(t);\ t \geq 0\}$ is said to be a **Poisson process** with rate λ, $\lambda > 0$, if it satisfies the following conditions:

(a) $N(0) = 0$.

(b) The process $\underline{N}$ has stationary and independent increments

(c) $Pr\{N(t+h)-N(t)=1\} = \lambda h + o(h)$ for all $t \geq 0$.

(d) $Pr\{N(t+h)-N(t)>1\} = o(h)$ for all $t \geq 0$.

The term $o(h)$ means of order h. A function $f(x)$ is $o(h)$ if

$$\lim_{h \to 0} \frac{f(h)}{h} = 0.$$

Intuitively, conditions (c) and (d) state that in sufficiently short intervals, no more than one event can occur. This eliminates the possibility of multiple events at a single point in time and the possibility of an infinite number of events in a finite interval.

Theorem 3.3.1. For any counting process $\{N(t);\ t \geq 0\}$ satisfying conditions (a)-(d) above, the number of events in any interval of length t is Poisson distributed with mean λt. That is, for all $s, t \geq 0$

$$Pr\{N(t+s)-N(s)=n\} = \frac{e^{-\lambda t}(\lambda t)^n}{n!}, \quad n = 0,1,2,\dots \ . \tag{3.3.1}$$

Proof

Let $p_n(t) = Pr\{N(t)=n\}$ denote the probability that exactly n events occurr before time t. Then we can write the probability of no claims up to time $t+h$ as

$$p_0(t+h) = Pr\{N(t+h)=0\}$$

$$= Pr\{N(t)=0,\ N(t+h)-N(t)=0\}$$

$$= Pr\{N(t)=0\}\, Pr\{N(t+h)-N(t)=0\}$$

from condition (b). Hence

$$p_0(t+h) = p_0(t)[1-\lambda h + o(h)]$$

from conditions (c) and (d) since $Pr\{N(t+h)-N(t)=0\} = 1-\lambda h + o(h)$. Subtracting $p_0(t)$ from both sides and dividing by h yields

$$\frac{p_0(t+h)-p_0(t)}{h} = -\lambda p_0(t) + \frac{o(h)}{h}.$$

Letting $h \rightarrow 0$ yields the differential equation

$$p_0'(t) = -\lambda p_0(t) \qquad\qquad\text{(A)}$$

Similarly, for $n \geq 1$

$$p_n(t+h) = Pr\{N(t+h)=n\}$$

$$= \sum_{j=0}^{n} Pr\{N(t)=n-j,\ N(t+h)-N(t)=j\}$$

$$= \sum_{j=0}^{n} Pr\{N(t)=n-j\}Pr\{N(t+h)-N(t)=j\}$$

Using conditions (b), (c) and (d), we obtain

$$p_n(t+h) = (1-\lambda h)p_n(t) + \lambda h p_{n-1}(t) + o(h).$$

Subtracting $p_n(t)$ from both sides, dividing by h, and letting $h \rightarrow 0$ yields

$$p_n'(t) = -\lambda p_n(t) + \lambda p_{n-1}(t) \tag{B}$$

Let

$$P(z,t) = \sum_{n=0}^{\infty} p_n(t)z^n$$

denote the probability generating function of the random variable $N(t)$. Then

$$\frac{\partial}{\partial t}P(z,t) = \sum_{n=0}^{\infty} p_n'(t)z^n.$$

Substituting (A) and (B) into the above equation yields

$$\frac{\partial}{\partial t}P(z,t) = -\lambda \sum_{n=0}^{\infty} p_n(t)z^n + \lambda \sum_{n=1}^{\infty} p_{n-1}(t)z^n$$

$$= -\lambda P(z,t) + \lambda z P(z,t)$$

$$= \lambda(z-1)P(z,t).$$

Hence,

$$\ln P(z,t) = \lambda t(z-1) + c(z).$$

Since $p_0(0) = 1$ and $p_n(0) = 0$, $n>0$, we have $P(z,0) = 1$, and so $c(z) = 0$.

Consequently,

$$P(z,t) = e^{\lambda t(z-1)}$$

which is the probability generating function of a Poisson random variable with mean λt. Hence,

$$p_n(t) = \frac{e^{-\lambda t}(\lambda t)^n}{n!}, \quad n = 0,1,2,\dots .$$

Since by condition (b), the increments of the process are stationary,

$$p_n(t) = Pr\{N(t+s)-N(s)=n\}$$

and so the theorem is proved.

The Poisson process will be seen to play a very important role in this book where the 'events' correspond to the claims of an insurance portfolio. We now study the distribution of the time between events.

Let $0<T_1<T_2<T_3<\cdots$ denote the times of occurrence of the events of a Poisson process. Let $W_1 = T_1$ and $W_j = T_j - T_{j-1}$, $j = 2,3,\dots$ denote the interoccurrence times of the Poisson process. The distribution of the interoccurrence times are now shown to be exponential.

Theorem 3.3.2. The interoccurrence times of the Poisson process with mean rate λ are independent and identically distributed random variables with a common exponential distribution with mean $1/\lambda$.

Proof

Consider the time, $W_1 = T_1$, of the first event. The probability that it exceeds t is given by

$$Pr\{W_1>t\} = Pr\{N(t)=0\} = e^{-\lambda t}.$$

Hence, the df of W_1 is given by

$$Pr\{W_1 \leq t\} = 1 - e^{-\lambda t}$$

which is the df of an exponential distribution with mean $1/\lambda$. Furthermore,

$$Pr\{W_2>t\,|\,W_1=s\} = Pr\{T_2>s+t\,|\,T_1=s\}$$

$$= Pr\{N(s+t)=1\,|\,N(s)=1\}$$

$$= Pr\{N(s+t)-N(s)=0\,|\,N(s)=1\}$$

$$= Pr\{N(s+t)-N(s)=0\}$$

since increments are independent. Hence,

$$Pr\{W_2>t\,|\,W_1=s\} = Pr\{N(t)-N(0)=0\}$$

since increments are stationary. Consequently,

$$Pr\{W_2>t\,|\,W_1=s\} = e^{-\lambda t}.$$

Hence W_2 is independent of W_1 and has the same distribution as W_1, i.e. exponential with mean $1/\lambda$. Repeating the arguments for $W_3, W_4, \dots$ shows that the interoccurrence times of a Poisson process with mean rate λ are independent and identically distributed random variables with an exponential distribution with mean $1/\lambda$.

A related result for the conditional distribution of the occurrence times $T_1, T_2, \dots, T_n$, given that $N(t) = n$ is now given.

Theorem 3.3.3. Given that $N(t) = n$, the n occurrence times $T_1, T_2, \dots, T_n$ have the same distributions as the order statistics corresponding to n independent random variables uniformly distributed on the interval $(0, t]$.

Proof

Consider the times $0 < t_1 < t_2 < \cdots < t_{n+1} = t$. Let h_i be smaller than the minimum difference $t_{i+1} - t_i$, $i = 1, \dots, n$. Then the joint distribution of the times $T_1, T_2, \dots, T_n$, conditional on $N(t) = n$, can be obtained from

$$Pr\{t_i \le T_i \le t_i + h_i, \ i = 1, 2, \dots, n\,|\,N(t)=n\}$$

$$= \frac{Pr\{\text{one event in } [t_i, t_i + h_i), \ i = 1,2,3,\dots,n \text{ and no other events in}(0,t)\}}{Pr\{N(t){=}n\}}$$

$$= \frac{\prod\limits_{j=1}^{n} (\lambda h_j) e^{-\lambda h_j} \ e^{-\lambda(t - h_1 - h_2 - \cdots - h_n)}}{(\lambda t)^n \ e^{-\lambda t}/n!}$$

$$= \frac{n!}{t^n} \prod\limits_{j=1}^{n} h_j.$$

Dividing by h_j and letting $h_j \to 0$, $j = 1,2,\dots,n$, the conditional distributional distribution of the occurrence times is given by

$$f(t_1, t_2, \dots, t_n) = \frac{n!}{t^n} \qquad 0 < t_1 < t_2 \cdots < t_n$$

as in example 2.10.1.

This result shows that if the number of events in a time interval are known, their times are uniformly distributed over that interval.

3.4 THE NONHOMOGENEOUS POISSON PROCESS

The Poisson process is now generalized to allow the rate of the process to vary with time. The rate λ in the previous function is replaced by $\lambda(t)$, a function of time t.

A counting process $\{N(t); \ t{\geq}0\}$ is said to be a **nonhomogeneous Poisson process** with rate $\lambda(t)$, where $\lambda(t){\geq}0$, for $t{\geq}0$, if it satisfies the following conditions:

(a) $N(0) = 0$.

(b) The process $\underline{N}$ has independent increments.

(c) $Pr\{N(t+h)-N(t)=1\} = \lambda(t)h + o(h)$ for all $t \geq 0$.

(d) $Pr\{N(t+h)-N(t)>1\} = o(h)$ for all $t \geq 0$.

The only difference between the nonhomogeneous Poisson process and the (homogeneous) Poisson process is that the rate may vary with time resulting in the loss of the stationary increment property.

Theorem 3.4.1. For any counting process $\{N(t); t \geq 0\}$ satisfying conditions (a)-(d) above, the number of events in the interval $(t, t+s]$ is Poisson distributed with mean $m(t,s) = \int_{t}^{t+s} \lambda(u)du$. That is, for all $s,t \geq 0$

$$Pr\{N(t+s)-N(t)=n\} = \frac{e^{-m(t,s)}[m(t,s)]^n}{n!} \tag{3.4.1}$$

Proof

Let $p_n(t,s) = Pr\{N(t+s)-N(t)=n\}$ denote the probability that n events occur between times t and $t+s$. Then, in a similar manner to the proof of theorem 3.3.1, we can write the probability of no claims between t and $t+s+h$ as

$$p_0(t,s+h) = Pr\{N(t+s+h)-N(t)=0\}$$

$$= Pr\{N(t+s)-N(t)=0, N(t+s+h)-N(t+s)=0\}$$

$$= Pr\{N(t+s)-N(t)=0\}Pr\{N(t+s+h)-N(t+s)=0\}$$

from condition (b). Thus

$$p_0(t,s+h) = p_0(t,s)[1-\lambda(t+s)h+o(h)]$$

from conditions (c) and (d). Subtracting $p_0(t,s)$ from both sides, dividing by h and letting $h \to 0$ yields

$$\frac{\partial}{\partial s} p_0(t,s) = -\lambda(t+s)p_0(t,s).$$
(A)

For $n \geq 1$

$$p_n(t,s+h) = Pr\{N(t+s+h)-N(t)=n\}$$

$$= \sum_{j=0}^{n} Pr\{N(t+s)-N(t)=n-j, N(t+s+h)-N(t+s)=j\}$$

$$= \sum_{j=0}^{n} Pr\{N(t+s)-N(t)=n-j\}Pr\{N(t+s+h)-N(t+s)=j\}$$

from condition (b). Thus, from conditions (c) and (d),

$$p_n(t,s+h) = [1-\lambda(t+s)h]p_n(t,s)+\lambda(t+s)hp_{n-1}(t,s)+o(h).$$

Subtracting $p_n(t,s)$ from both sides, dividing by h, and letting $h \to 0$ yields

$$\frac{\partial}{\partial s} p_n(t,s) = -\lambda(t+s)p_n(t,s)+\lambda(t+s)p_{n-1}(t,s).$$
(B)

To solve, the system of equations defined by (A) and (B), let

$$P(z,t,s) = \sum_{n=0}^{\infty} p_n(t,s)z^n$$

be the probability generating function of $N(t+s)-N(t)$. Multiplying (B) by z^n and summing from $n=1$ to ∞ yields

$$\frac{\partial}{\partial s} P(z,t,s)-\frac{\partial}{\partial s} p_0(t,s) = -\lambda(t+s)\{P(z,t,s)-p_0(t,s)\}+\lambda(t+s)zP(z,t,s).$$

Using equation (A) and rearranging yields

$$\frac{\partial}{\partial s} \ln P(z,t,s) = \lambda(t+s)[z-1]. \tag{C}$$

Since

$$\lambda(t+s) = \frac{\partial}{\partial s} m(t,s),$$

substitution into (C) yields

$$\frac{\partial}{\partial s} \ln P(z,t,s) = \{\frac{\partial}{\partial s} m(t,s)\}[z-1].$$

Thus

$$\ln P(z,t,s) = m(t,s)[z-1] + c(z,t).$$

Clearly, $p_0(t,0) = 1$ and so $P(z,t,0) = 1$. Since $m(t,0) = 0$, this implies that $c(z,t) = 0$.

Finally,

$$P(z,t,s) = e^{m(t,s)[z-1]}$$

and so $N(t+s)-N(t)$ is a Poisson variate with mean $m(t,s)$.

3.5 THE MIXED POISSON PROCESS

The concept of mixtures of distributions of section 2.8 is now generalized to stochastic processes, specifically the Poisson process. Let $\{N(t;\lambda); t \geq 0\}$ denote a Poisson process indexed by parameter or rate λ. As in section 2.8, λ is considered to be the outcome of a "random parameter" Λ. Consequently, we will use the notation $\{N(t|\lambda); t \geq 0\}$ to emphasize that Λ is fixed or given.

Further suppose that Λ is distributed over its range of possible values according to a df $U(\lambda)$. The unconditional process $\{N(t); t \geq 0\}$ satisfying

(a) $N(0) = 0$,

(b) $Pr\{N(t+s)-N(s)=n\} = \int_0^\infty Pr\{N(t+s)-N(s)=n \mid \Lambda=\lambda\} dU(\lambda)$

$$= \int_0^\infty e^{-\lambda t} \frac{(\lambda t)^n}{n!} dU(\lambda) \tag{3.5.1}$$

is called a **mixture of Poisson processes** or a **mixed Poisson process.** It is sometimes termed a **conditional Poisson process** since, conditional on the event that $\Lambda=\lambda$, it is a Poisson process with rate λ.

It should be noted that a mixture of Poisson processes is itself not a Poisson process. From (3.5.1), it is clear that the unconditional process $\{N(t);\ t\geq 0\}$ has stationary increments. However, the increments are not independent. This can be seen from the fact that, for $t_0 < t_1 < t_2$

$$Pr\{N(t_1)-N(t_0)=n_1, N(t_2)-N(t_1)=n_2\}$$

$$= \int Pr\{N(t_1)-N(t_0)=n_1, N(t_2)-N(t_1)=n_2 \mid \lambda\} dU(\lambda)$$

$$= \int Pr\{N(t_1)-N(t_0)=n_1 \mid \lambda\} Pr\{N(t_2)-N(t_1)=n_2 \mid \lambda\} dU(\lambda)$$

$$\neq \int Pr\{N(t_1)-N(t_0)=n_1 \mid \lambda\} dU(\lambda)$$

$$\times \int Pr\{N(t_2)-N(t_1)=n_2 \mid \lambda\} dU(\lambda)$$

$$= Pr\{N(t_1)-N(t_0)=n_1\} \times Pr\{N(t_2)-N(t_1)=n_2\}.$$

The mixed Poisson process is very convenient for insurance modeling. It should be noted that theorem 3.3.3 holds for the mixed Poisson process as well.

3.6 BIRTH PROCESSES

We now consider a generalization of both the nonhomogeneous Poisson process and the mixed Poisson process. The rate of the process now varies with time and the state of the process.

A counting process $\{N(t);\ t \geq 0\}$ is said to be a **birth process** with transition probabilities

$$p_{m,n}(t,s) = Pr\{N(t+s)-N(t)=n \mid N(t)=m\} \qquad (3.6.1)$$

if it satisfies the following conditions

(a) $N(0) = 0$.

(b) The process $\{N(t);\ t \geq 0\}$ is a Markov process.

(c) $p_{m,1}(t,h) = \lambda_m(t)h + o(h),\ m = 0,1,2,...$

(d) $p_{m,n}(t,h) = o(h),\ n > 1,\ m = 0,1,2,...$

where $\lambda_n(t) \geq 0$.

The relationship between the transition probabilities (3.6.1) is given in the following lemma.

Lemma 3.6.1. For any birth process satisfying conditions (a) - (d) above, the transition probabilities satisfy the differential difference equations

$$\frac{\partial}{\partial s}p_{m,0}(t,s) = -\lambda_m(t+s)p_{m,0}(t,s) \qquad (3.6.2)$$

and

$$\frac{\partial}{\partial s}p_{m,n}(t,s) = -\lambda_{m+n}(t+s)p_{m,n}(t,s) + \lambda_{m+n-1}(t+s)p_{m,n-1}(t,s),\ n \geq 1.$$

$$(3.6.3)$$

Proof

To prove (3.6.2), note that

$$p_{m,0}(t,s+h) = Pr\{N(t+s+h)-N(t)=0 \,|\, N(t)=m\}$$

$$= Pr\{N(t+s+h)=m \,|\, N(t)=m\}$$

$$= Pr\{N(t+s+h)=m \,|\, N(t+s)=m, N(t)=m\}$$

$$\times Pr\{N(t+s)=m \,|\, N(t)=m\}$$

$$= Pr\{N(t+s+h)=m \,|\, N(t+s)=m\}$$

$$\times Pr\{N(t+s)=m \,|\, N(t)=m\}$$

from condition (b). Thus,

$$p_{m,0}(t,s+h) = p_{m,0}(t,s)[1-\lambda_m(t+s)h+o(h)]$$

from conditions (c) and (d). If we subtract $p_{m,0}(t,s)$ from both sides, divide by h and let $h \to 0$, we obtain (3.6.2).

The proof of (3.6.3) is similar. We have

$$p_{m,n}(t,s+h) = Pr\{N(t+s+h)=m+n \,|\, N(t)=m\}$$

$$= \sum_{j=0}^{n} \left[Pr\{N(t+s+h)=m+n \,|\, N(t+s)=m+j, N(t)=m\} \right.$$

$$\left. \times Pr\{N(t+s)=m+j \,|\, N(t)=m\} \right]$$

$$= \sum_{j=0}^{n} \left[Pr\{N(t+s+h)=m+n \,|\, N(t+s)=m+j\} \right.$$

$$\left. \times Pr\{N(t+s)=m+j \,|\, N(t)=m\} \right]$$

from condition (b). Thus,

$$p_{m,n}(t,s+h) = \lambda_{m+n-1}(t+s)h p_{m,n-1}(t,s)$$

$$+ \left[1-\lambda_{m+n}(t+s)h\right]p_{m,n}(t,s) + o(h)$$

from conditions (c) and (d). Subtraction of $p_{m,n}(t,s)$ from both sides, division by h, and letting $h \to 0$ yields (3.6.3).

It is easily seen that the transition probabilities (3.6.1) may be obtained recursively from (3.6.2) and (3.6.3). In fact, the general solution is

$$p_{m,0}(t,s) = \exp\{-\int_t^{t+s} \lambda_m(u)du\} \tag{3.6.4}$$

$$p_{m,n}(t,s) = \int_t^{t+s} p_{m,n-1}(t,u-t)\lambda_{m+n-1}(u)p_{m+n,0}(u,t+s-u)du. \tag{3.6.5}$$

Some special choices for $\lambda_n(t)$ are of interest. If $\lambda_n(t) = \lambda_n$, independently of t, the process is called a **homogeneous birth process**. If $\lambda_n(t)$ depends on t, it is called a **nonhomogeneous birth process**. In addition, if $\lambda_n(t) = \lambda(t)$, independently of n, then the resulting process is a **nonhomogeneous Poisson process**. To see this, note that the system of equations (3.6.2) and (3.6.3) becomes the same system as that defined by equations (A) and (B) of section (3.4), but with $p_{m,n}(t,s)$ replacing $p_n(t,s)$. Thus, $p_{m,n}(t,s)$ has probabilities given by (3.4.1) and are independent of m. Using this fact, it is easy to show that in this case the process has independent increments and therefore that all the conditions for $\{N(t); t \geq 0\}$ to be a nonhomogeneous Poisson process are satisfied. In general, however, the birth process does not have independent increments, but instead has the Markov property.

An important special case of the birth process is that for which

$$\lambda_n(t) = \lambda(t)\{\alpha+\beta n\}, \quad n = 0,1,2,\ldots,N \tag{3.6.6}$$

where $\lambda(t) \geq 0$, $\alpha > 0$, $-\infty < \beta < \infty$, and $N \leq \infty$. Explicit solutions for the transition probabilities are obtainable in this case. Let

$$P_m(z,t,s) = \sum_{n=0}^{\infty} p_{m,n}(t,s)z^n. \tag{3.6.7}$$

We have the following lemma.

Lemma 3.6.2. For the birth process with rates given by (3.6.6) with $\beta \neq 0$, the pgf defined by (3.6.7) has the solution

$$P_m(z,t,s) = \left[\frac{e^{-\beta\gamma(t,s)}}{1-z\{1-e^{-\beta\gamma(t,s)}\}} \right]^{\frac{\alpha}{\beta}+m} \tag{3.6.8}$$

where $\gamma(t,s) = \int_t^{t+s} \lambda(v)dv$.

Proof

Multiplication of (3.6.3) by z^n and summing over $n \geq 1$ yields

$$\frac{\partial}{\partial s}P_m(z,t,s) = \frac{\partial}{\partial s}p_{m,0}(t,s) + \lambda(t+s)$$

$$\times \left[-(\alpha+\beta m)\{P_m(z,t,s)-p_{m,0}(t,s)\} - \beta z\frac{\partial}{\partial z}P_m(z,t,s) \right.$$

$$\left. + (\alpha+\beta m)zP_m(z,t,s) + \beta z^2\frac{\partial}{\partial z}P_m(z,t,s) \right].$$

Using (3.6.2), and rearranging yields

$$\frac{\partial}{\partial s}P_m(z,t,s) = \lambda(t+s)\left[(\alpha+\beta m)(z-1)P_m(z,t,s) + \beta z(z-1)\frac{\partial}{\partial z}P_m(z,t,s) \right].$$

To solve this partial differential equation for $P_m(z,t,s)$, we use the method of Lagrange and write

$$\frac{ds}{1} = \frac{dz}{\beta z(1-z)\lambda(t+s)} = \frac{dP_m}{(\alpha+\beta m)(z-1)\lambda(t+s)P_m}.$$

Since $\lambda(t+s) = \dfrac{\partial}{\partial s}\gamma(t,s)$, we may solve the first two to obtain

$$\beta\gamma(t,s) = \ln\left[\frac{z}{1-z}\right]+k$$

which may be written as

$$\left[\frac{z}{1-z}\right]e^{-\beta\gamma(t,s)} = c_1.$$

Similarly, from the last two equations, we obtain

$$-\left[\frac{\alpha+\beta m}{\beta}\right]\frac{dz}{z} = \frac{dP_m}{P_m}$$

and so

$$P_m z^{\frac{\alpha}{\beta}+m} = c_2.$$

The general solution is

$$P_m(z,t,s) = z^{-\frac{\alpha}{\beta}-m}\phi\left[\frac{z}{1-z}e^{-\beta\gamma(t,s)}\right].$$

Clearly, $P_m(z,t,0) = 1$ and so

$$\phi\left(\frac{z}{1-z}\right) = z^{\frac{\alpha}{\beta}+m}$$

or

$$\phi(w) = \left(\frac{w}{1+w}\right)^{\frac{\alpha}{\beta}+m}.$$

Hence,

$$P_m(z,t,s) = z^{-\frac{\alpha}{\beta}-m} \left[\frac{ze^{-\beta\gamma(t,s)}}{1-z+ze^{-\beta\gamma(t,s)}}\right]^{\frac{\alpha}{\beta}+m}$$

$$= \left[\frac{e^{-\beta\gamma(t,s)}}{1-z\{1-e^{-\beta\gamma(t,s)}\}}\right]^{\frac{\alpha}{\beta}+m}$$

as required.

The solution to the transition probabilities depends upon whether β is negative or positive.

Theorem 3.6.1. For the birth process with rates given by (3.6.6) and $\beta>0$, the transition probabilities have a **negative binomial** distribution with probabilities

$$p_{m,n}(t,s) = \frac{\Gamma\left(\frac{\alpha}{\beta}+m+n\right)}{\Gamma\left(\frac{\alpha}{\beta}+m\right)n!}\left[e^{-\beta\gamma(t,s)}\right]^{\frac{\alpha}{\beta}+m}\left[1-e^{-\beta\gamma(t,s)}\right]^n, \quad n = 0,1,2,...$$

$$(3.6.9)$$

where $\gamma(t,s) = \int_t^{t+s}\lambda(u)du.$

Proof

The pgf (3.6.8) is simply that of a negative binomial distribution (see example 2.7.4) and thus the transition probabilities are obtained on expansion.

An important special case of (3.6.9) is now considered.

Example 3.6.1. The Polya process

Consider the process with intensity function

$$\lambda_n(t) = \frac{\alpha+n}{\beta+t}, \quad n = 0,1,2,\dots .$$

From (3.6.9), the transition probabilities are

$$p_{m,n}(t,s) = \binom{\alpha+m+n-1}{n} \left(\frac{\beta+t}{\beta+t+s}\right)^{\alpha+m} \left(\frac{s}{\beta+t+s}\right)^n, \quad n = 0,1,2,\dots .$$

Since $N(0) = 0$, the unconditional state probabilities are

$$p_m(t) = Pr\{N(t)=m\}$$

$$= p_{0,m}(0,t)$$

$$= \binom{\alpha+m-1}{m} \left(\frac{\beta}{\beta+t}\right)^\alpha \left(\frac{t}{\beta+t}\right)^m, \quad m = 0,1,2,\dots .$$

It is clear that the Polya process does not have independent increments. It does, however, possess stationary increments. To see this, we write

$$Pr\{N(t+s)-N(t)=n\}$$
$$= \sum_{m=0}^{\infty} Pr\{N(t+s)-N(t)=n \mid N(t)=m\}Pr\{N(t)=m\}$$
$$= \sum_{m=0}^{\infty} p_m(t)p_{m,n}(t,s)$$

$$= \sum_{m=0}^{\infty} \binom{\alpha+m-1}{m} \left(\frac{\beta}{\beta+t}\right)^{\alpha} \left(\frac{t}{\beta+t}\right)^{m} \binom{\alpha+m+n-1}{n} \left(\frac{\beta+t}{\beta+t+s}\right)^{\alpha+m} \left(\frac{s}{\beta+t+s}\right)^{n}$$

$$= \sum_{m=0}^{\infty} \frac{(\alpha+m+n-1)!}{(\alpha-1)!m!n!} \frac{\beta^{\alpha}t^{m}s^{n}}{(\beta+t+s)^{\alpha+m+n}}$$

$$= \frac{(\alpha+n-1)!}{(\alpha-1)!n!} \frac{\beta^{\alpha}s^{n}}{(\beta+s)^{\alpha+n}} \sum_{m=0}^{\infty} \binom{\alpha+n+m-1}{m} \left(\frac{t}{\beta+t+s}\right)^{m} \left(\frac{\beta+s}{\beta+t+s}\right)^{\alpha+n}$$

$$= \binom{\alpha+n-1}{n} \left(\frac{\beta}{\beta+s}\right)^{\alpha} \left(\frac{s}{\beta+s}\right)^{n}$$

$$= p_n(s)$$

$$= Pr\{N(s)=n\}.$$

The final summation in the above argument is equal to unity since it is simply the sum of negative binomial probabilities.

The special case of (3.6.6) when $\beta<0$ is now considered.

Theorem 3.6.2. For the birth process with rates given by (3.6.6) and $\beta<0$ where $-\frac{\alpha}{\beta}$ is a positive integer r, the transition probabilities have a **binomial** distribution with probabilities

$$p_{m,n}(t,s) = \binom{r-m}{n} \left[1-e^{\beta\gamma(t,s)}\right]^{n} \left[e^{\beta\gamma(t,s)}\right]^{r-m-n}, \quad n = 0,1,2,... \tag{3.6.10}$$

where $\gamma(t,s) = \int_{t}^{t+s} \lambda(u)du.$

Proof

From (3.6.8),

$$P_m(z,t,s) = \left[e^{\beta\gamma(t,s)} + z\{1 - e^{\beta\gamma(t,s)}\} \right]^{r-m}$$

and the result follows. (See example 2.7.5).

Hence the negative binomial probabilities may arise when the occurrence of an event increases the likelihood of another, and the binomial probabilities when the likelihood of a further event is decreased. These models thus allow for a dependency of sorts between the events in a process.

It can be shown that the **mixed Poisson process** with probabilities given by (3.5.1) is a birth process with stationary increments. If we define

$$L(t) = \int_0^\infty e^{-\lambda t} dU(\lambda) \tag{3.6.11}$$

then the intensity function of the process is given by

$$\lambda_n(t) = -\frac{\dfrac{d^{n+1}}{dt^{n+1}} L(t)}{\dfrac{d^n}{dt^n} L(t)}, \quad n = 0,1,2,\dots \; . \tag{3.6.12}$$

The Polya process is, in fact, a mixed Poisson process. The mixing function is the gamma density (see example 2.7.2).

3.7 COMPOUND STOCHASTIC PROCESSES

Let $\{N(t); t \geq 0\}$ denote a counting process and let $X_1, X_2, X_3, \dots\}$ be a sequence of independent and identically distributed random variables with common df $F_X(x)$. Furthermore, assume that the process $\{N(t); t \geq 0\}$ and the sequence $\{X_1, X_2, X_3, \dots\}$ are independent. Then the process defined, for $t \geq 0$, by

$$S(t) = X_1 + X_2 + \cdots + X_{N(t)}, \tag{3.7.1}$$

with $S(t) = 0$ when $N(t) = 0$, is called a **compound stochastic process.**

The various transforms of the random variable $S(t)$, for some fixed t, can be evaluated by considering equation (3.7.1) as a random sum as in equation (2.9.1). For example, equation (2.9.7) yields

$$L_{S(t)}(z) = P_{N(t)}(L_X(z)). \tag{3.7.2}$$

An important compound stochastic process is that for which $\{N(t); t \geq 0\}$ is a Poisson process with rate λ. The resulting process, called a **compound Poisson process** has Laplace transform

$$L_{S(t)}(z) = e^{\lambda t [L_X(z) - 1]}. \tag{3.7.3}$$

Since $\{N(t); t \geq 0\}$ has stationary and independent increments and the sequence $\{X_1, X_2, X_3, \dots\}$ is independent of the process $\{N(t); t \geq 0\}$, it is clear that the process $\{S(t); t \geq 0\}$ also has stationary and independent increments.

3.8 BIBLIOGRAPHIC NOTES

The stochastic processes discussed in this chapter and others which may be of use in insurance modeling (eg. renewal processes, semi-Markov processes, birth-death processes, point processes, Brownian motion and diffusion processes, and martingales) are discussed in more detail in a number of textbooks. Ross (1985) provides a good introduction. Other references include Feller (1968, 1971), Cox and Miller (1965), Karlin and Taylor (1975, 1981), Parzen (1962), and Ross (1983).

Mixtures of Poisson processes are discussed in detail by Lundberg (1940), and Haight (1967). The relationship between birth processes and mixed Poisson processes is discussed by McFadden (1965) and Lundberg (1940). Birth processes are discussed by Feller (1968) and Parzen (1962). Karlin and Taylor (1981) discuss many of the properties of the compound Poisson process.

Buhlmann (1970), gives a brief survey of many of these processes and their applications to insurance.

CHAPTER 4

PROBABILITY DISTRIBUTIONS

4.1 INTRODUCTION

In this chapter some of the more important parametric discrete and continuous probability distributions used in insurance modeling are discussed. Many of the continuous random variables may be used to model the costs of claims payable by an insurer. The discrete distributions may serve either to describe the number of claims or the claims costs payable by an insurer over a specified period of time.

Many distributions other than the ones described in this chapter may also be used. Some other distributions will be discussed in later chapters.

4.2 THE POISSON DISTRIBUTION

This distribution is one of the most important in insurance modeling. The **pf** of the Poisson distribution with mean λ is

$$f(x) = \frac{\lambda^x e^{-\lambda}}{x!}, \quad x = 0,1,2,... \tag{4.2.1}$$

where $\lambda > 0$. The **pgf** of a variate X with pf (4.2.1) is

$$P(z) = \sum_{x=0}^{\infty} \frac{z^x \lambda^x e^{-\lambda}}{x!}$$

$$= e^{\lambda(z-1)}. \tag{4.2.2}$$

The factorial moments of this distribution are easily obtainable from (4.2.2). The k-th derivative is

$$\frac{d^k}{dz^k}P(z) = \lambda^k e^{\lambda(z-1)}$$

and so, according to (2.4.7), the **k-th factorial moment** is

$$\mu_{(k)} = \lambda^k. \tag{4.2.3}$$

The **mean** of the Poisson distribution is

$$\kappa_1 = \mu_{(1)}$$

$$= \lambda. \tag{4.2.4}$$

The **variance** is

$$\kappa_2 = \mu_{(2)} + \mu_{(1)} - \{\mu_{(1)}\}^2$$

$$= \lambda. \tag{4.2.5}$$

Thus the variance of the Poisson distribution is equal to the mean.

Suppose X_1 and X_2 have Poisson distributions with means λ_1 and λ_2 respectively and that X_1 and X_2 are independent. Then, the pgf of $S = X_1 + X_2$ is

$$P_S(z) = P_{X_1}(z)P_{X_2}(z)$$

$$= e^{(\lambda_1+\lambda_2)(z-1)}.$$

Hence, by the uniqueness of the pgf, S is again a Poisson variate with mean $\lambda_1+\lambda_2$. By induction, it is easily seen that the sum of a finite number of Poisson variates is again a Poisson variate. Therefore, by the central limit theorem, a Poisson variate with mean λ is close to a normal variate if λ is large.

The Poisson distribution is infinitely divisible by example 2.7.3, a fact that is of central importance in the study of stochastic processes (see chapter 3). For this and other reasons (including its many desirable mathematical properties), it is often used to model the number of claims of an insurer. In this connection, one major drawback of the Poisson is the fact that the variance is restricted to being equal to the mean, a situation which may not be consistent with observation.

As will be seen later, this distribution tends to arise in many different situations and is closely related to many other distributions.

4.3 THE BINOMIAL DISTRIBUTION

Another distribution which arises in a great many practical situations is the **binomial** with **pf**

$$f(x) = \binom{m}{x} q^x (1-q)^{m-x}, \quad x = 0,1,2, \ldots , m \tag{4.3.1}$$

where $0 < q < 1$ and m is a non-negative integer. The **pgf** is

$$P(z) = \sum_{x=0}^{m} z^x \binom{m}{x} q^x (1-q)^{m-x}$$

$$= \{1 + q(z-1)\}^m. \tag{4.3.2}$$

The **k-th factorial moment** is easily obtained from (4.3.2). It is

$$\mu_{(k)} = \frac{d^k}{dz^k} P(z)|_{z=1}$$

$$= m(m-1) \cdots (m-k+1) q^k. \tag{4.3.3}$$

In particular, the **mean** and **variance** are

$$\kappa_1 = \mu_{(1)}$$

$$= mq \qquad\qquad (4.3.4)$$

$$\kappa_2 = \mu_{(2)} + \mu_{(1)} - \{\mu_{(1)}\}^2$$

$$= mq(1-q) \qquad\qquad (4.3.5)$$

Thus, since $0<q<1$, the binomial has variance less than the mean.

It is easily seen by considering the pgf that if a sequence of independent random variables $\{X_i; \ i = 1, 2, \ldots, n\}$ are such that X_i is a binomial variate with parameters m_i and q, then $X_1 + \cdots + X_n$ is a binomial variate with parameters $m_1 + m_2 + \cdots + m_n$ and q. This means that for large m, the binomial is approximately normal by the central limit theorem.

The binomial also has another limiting form. Consider a binomial variate with parameters m and q. Let $m \to \infty$, $q \to 0$ such that $\lambda = mq$ remains constant. In terms of the pgf, we have

$$P(z) = \{1 + q(z-1)\}^m$$

$$= \{1 + \lambda \frac{(z-1)}{m}\}^m.$$

As $m \to \infty$, $P(z) \to e^{\lambda(z-1)}$. In other words, the Poisson distribution is the limiting form and thus, for large m and small q, the binomial distribution may be approximated by the Poisson. Unlike the Poisson, however, the binomial is not infinitely divisible (see example 2.7.5).

In the special case of (4.3.1) when $m = 1$, the resulting two-point random variable is called a **Bernoulli** or indicator variable.

The binomial may arise naturally in some insurance situations. For example, suppose a portfolio of m risks is such that each risk has probability q of having one claim and $1-q$ of having no claims. Then the number of claims is a binomial variate with parameters m and q.

The binomial, like the Poisson, often arises in connection with other distributions, as will be seen in subsequent sections.

4.4 THE GEOMETRIC DISTRIBUTION

Consider the discrete random variable with **pf**

$$f(x) = \frac{1}{1+\beta} \left(\frac{\beta}{1+\beta} \right)^x, \quad x = 0,1,2,... \tag{4.4.1}$$

where $\beta > 0$. This distribution is termed a **geometric** distribution. It has df

$$F(x) = \sum_{y=0}^{x} f(y)$$

$$= \frac{1}{1+\beta} \sum_{y=0}^{x} \left(\frac{\beta}{1+\beta} \right)^y$$

$$= 1 - \left(\frac{\beta}{1+\beta} \right)^{x+1}, \quad x = 0,1,2,... \ . \tag{4.4.2}$$

The **pgf** is

$$P(z) = \sum_{x=0}^{\infty} \frac{1}{1+\beta} \left(\frac{\beta}{1+\beta} \right)^x z^x$$

$$= [1 - \beta(z-1)]^{-1}, \quad |z| < \frac{1+\beta}{\beta}. \tag{4.4.3}$$

The **k-th factorial moment** is easily obtainable from (4.4.3) by differentiation. We have

$$\mu_{(k)} = \frac{d^k}{dz^k} P(z)|_{z=1}$$

$$= \beta^k k!. \tag{4.4.4}$$

The **mean** and **variance** are thus

$$\kappa_1 = \beta \qquad\qquad\qquad (4.4.5)$$

$$\kappa_2 = \mu_{(2)} + \mu_{(1)} - \{\mu_{(1)}\}^2$$

$$= \beta(1+\beta). \qquad\qquad\qquad (4.4.6)$$

The geometric distribution also arises as a Poisson mixture (see example 2.8.1). Suppose that X has a (conditional) Poisson distribution with mean λ, but λ itself has an exponential distribution (see example 2.9.1). Then, the pgf of the resulting distribution is (from (2.8.5))

$$P(z) = \int_0^\infty e^{\lambda(z-1)}\theta e^{-\theta\lambda}d\lambda$$

$$= \{1-\frac{1}{\theta}(z-1)\}^{-1}$$

which is of the form (4.4.3).

The geometric distribution is a special case of the negative binomial distribution (see example 2.7.4) and, as such, further properties will be discussed in the next section. Like the Poisson and binomial distributions, the geometric arises in a variety of situations.

4.5 THE NEGATIVE BINOMIAL DISTRIBUTION

Also known as the **Polya** distribution, the **negative binomial** distribution has **pf**

$$f(x) = \frac{\Gamma(r+x)}{\Gamma(r)x!}\left[\frac{1}{1+\beta}\right]^r\left[\frac{\beta}{1+\beta}\right]^x, \quad x = 0,1,2,... \qquad (4.5.1)$$

where $r,\beta > 0$.

The **pgf** is

$$P(z) = \sum_{x=0}^{\infty} \frac{\Gamma(r+x)}{\Gamma(r)x!} \left[\frac{1}{1+\beta} \right]^r \left[\frac{\beta z}{1+\beta} \right]^x$$

$$= \sum_{x=0}^{\infty} \binom{-r}{x} \left[\frac{1}{1+\beta} \right]^r \left[\frac{-\beta z}{1+\beta} \right]^x$$

$$= \{1-\beta(z-1)\}^{-r}, \quad |z| < \frac{1+\beta}{\beta}. \tag{4.5.2}$$

The **k-th factorial moment,** easily obtained from (4.5.2), is

$$\mu_{(k)} = (r)(r+1) \cdots (r+k-1)\beta^k. \tag{4.5.3}$$

The **mean** and **variance** are

$$\kappa_1 = r\beta \tag{4.5.4}$$

$$\kappa_2 = r\beta(1+\beta). \tag{4.5.5}$$

Thus the variance exceeds the mean. This is one reason why the negative binomial is often used to model claim numbers in situations where the Poisson is inadequate.

If a sequence of independent negative binomial variates $\{X_i; i = 1,2,\ldots,n\}$ are such that X_i has parameters r_i and β, then $X_1+X_2+\cdots+X_n$ is again negative binomial with parameters $r_1+r_2+\cdots+r_n$ and β. Thus, for large r, the negative binomial is approximately normal by the central limit theorem. Alternatively, the negative binomial, like the binomial, has a Poisson limiting form. If $r\to\infty$, $\beta\to0$ such that $r\beta=\lambda$ remains constant, the limiting distribution is Poisson with mean λ. Thus, the Poisson is a good approximation if r is large and β is small.

When $r = 1$ the **geometric** distribution is obtained. When r is an integer the **Pascal** distribution is obtained. The Pascal distribution can be shown to be a compound binomial random variable (see section 2.9). Using (4.5.2), we obtain

$$P(z) = \{1-\beta(z-1)\}^{-r}$$

$$= \left\{1+\frac{\beta}{1+\beta}[Q(z)-1]\right\}^{r} \qquad (4.5.6)$$

where $Q(z) = z[1-\beta(z-1)]^{-1}$ is the pgf of $1+X$ and X is a geometric variate. Clearly, $P(z)$ in (4.5.6) is of the form (2.9.6) where N is a binomial variate with parameters r and $\beta(1+\beta)^{-1}$.

The negative binomial distribution also arises as a mixed Poisson variate (see example 2.8.1). If X is (conditionally) Poisson with mean λ where λ itself has a gamma distribution (see example 2.7.2), then the unconditional distribution of X is negative binomial.

The negative binomial (including the geometric) is infinitely divisible (see example 2.7.4). As will be demonstrated in section 4.6, it is a compound Poisson (see section 2.9) random variable.

Closely related to many other distributions, it is also important in its own right in modeling claim numbers.

4.6 THE LOGARITHMIC DISTRIBUTION

The random variable X has a **logarithmic** or **logarithmic series** distribution if its **pf** is

$$f(x) = \frac{q^x}{-x\,\log(1-q)} = \frac{1}{x\,\log(1+\beta)}(\frac{\beta}{1+\beta})^x, \quad x = 1,2,3,\ldots \qquad (4.6.1)$$

where $0 < q = \dfrac{\beta}{1+\beta} < 1$. The **pgf** is

$$P(z) = \sum_{k=1}^{\infty} \frac{(qz)^k}{-k\,\log(1-q)}$$

$$= \frac{\log(1-qz)}{\log(1-q)}, \qquad (4.6.2)$$

$$= \frac{\log[1-\beta(z-1)]-\log(1+\beta)}{-\log(1+\beta)}, \quad |z| < \frac{1}{q}.$$

The k-th factorial moment is

$$\mu_{(k)} = \frac{d^k}{dz^k}P(z)|_{z=1}$$

$$= \frac{q^k(k-1)!}{[-\log(1-q)](1-q)^k} = \frac{\beta^k(k-1)!}{\log(1+\beta)}. \tag{4.6.3}$$

The **mean** and **variance** are

$$\kappa_1 = \frac{q}{-(1-q)\log(1-q)} = \frac{\beta}{\log(1+\beta)} \tag{4.6.4}$$

$$\kappa_2 = \frac{-q[q+\log(1-q)]}{(1-q)^2[\log(1-q)]^2} = \frac{\beta(1+\beta)\log(1+\beta)-\beta^2}{[\log(1+\beta)]^2}. \tag{4.6.5}$$

Unlike all the distributions discussed previously, the logarithmic distribution has no probability mass at $x=0$. Another disadvantage of this distribution from the point of view of modeling is that $f(x)$ is strictly decreasing in x. This distribution will arise in chapters 6, 7, and 8 in the modeling of claim frequencies.

The logarithmic distribution is closely related to the negative binomial and Poisson distributions. It is a limiting form of a truncated negative binomial distribution. Consider the distribution of $Y = X|X>0$ where X has the negative binomial distribution (4.5.1). The pf of Y is

$$g(y) = \frac{Pr\{X=y\}}{1-Pr\{X=0\}}, \quad y = 1,2,3,...$$

$$= \frac{\dfrac{\Gamma(r+y)}{\Gamma(r)y!} \left[\dfrac{\beta}{1+\beta}\right]^y}{\left[1+\beta\right]^r - 1}.$$

This may be rewritten as

$$g(y) = \frac{\Gamma(r+y)}{\Gamma(r+1)y!} \frac{r}{(1+\beta)^r - 1} \left[\frac{\beta}{1+\beta}\right]^y.$$

Letting $r \to 0$, we obtain

$$\lim_{r\to 0} g(y) = \frac{1}{y} \left[\frac{\beta}{1+\beta}\right]^y \lim_{r\to 0} \frac{r}{\left[1+\beta\right]^r - 1}$$

$$= \frac{1}{y} \left[\frac{\beta}{1+\beta}\right]^y \frac{1}{\log(1+\beta)}$$

$$= \frac{\left(\dfrac{\beta}{1+\beta}\right)^y}{-y \log \left[1 - \dfrac{\beta}{1+\beta}\right]} = \frac{q^y}{-y \log(1-q)}$$

where $q = \beta/(1+\beta)$. Thus, the logarithmic distribution is a limiting form of the truncated negative binomial distribution.

Also, one may rewrite the negative binomial pgf (4.5.2). We have

$$P(z) = [1-\beta(z-1)]^{-r} = e^{\lambda[Q(z)-1]} \tag{4.6.6}$$

where

$$\lambda = r \log(1+\beta) \tag{4.6.7}$$

and

$$Q(z) = \frac{\log\left(1 - \frac{\beta z}{1+\beta}\right)}{\log\left(1 - \frac{\beta}{1+\beta}\right)}. \tag{4.6.8}$$

Thus $Q(z)$ is a logarithmic pgf and on comparison of (4.6.6) with (4.3.2) and (2.9.6) it is clear that the negative binomial (and geometric) is a compound Poisson-logarithmic variate.

The logarithmic distribution, while not as common as the distributions discussed earlier, does tend to arise in some situations.

4.7 MIXED AND COMPOUND DISCRETE DISTRIBUTIONS

A technique for generating new probability distributions is that of mixing distributions, as discussed in section 2.8. In this section a few discrete mixtures are discussed. Of central importance in this class is the **mixed Poisson** distribution, a few of whose properties are given in example 2.8.1. It will be discussed in more detail in chapter 8. Other examples include the following.

Example 4.7.1. Polya-Eggenberger Distribution

Suppose we have the binomial distribution (4.3.1) where q has a **beta** distribution with pdf

$$f(x) = \frac{\Gamma(a+b)}{\Gamma(a)\Gamma(b)} x^{a-1}(1-x)^{b-1}, \quad 0 < x < 1 \tag{4.7.1}$$

where $a, b > 0$. The resulting pf is

$$f(x) = \int_0^1 \binom{m}{x} q^x (1-q)^{m-x} \frac{\Gamma(a+b)}{\Gamma(a)\Gamma(b)} q^{a-1}(1-q)^{b-1} dq$$

$$= \frac{\Gamma(a+b)\Gamma(m+1)}{\Gamma(a)\Gamma(b)\Gamma(x+1)\Gamma(m-x+1)} \int_0^1 q^{a+x-1}(1-q)^{b+m-x-1} dq$$

$$= \frac{\Gamma(a+b)\Gamma(m+1)\Gamma(a+x)\Gamma(b+m-x)}{\Gamma(a)\Gamma(b)\Gamma(x+1)\Gamma(m-x+1)\Gamma(a+b+m)}$$

$$= \frac{\binom{-a}{x}\binom{-b}{m-x}}{\binom{-a-b}{m}}, \quad x = 0,1,2,\ldots,m$$

This distribution is also termed **binomial-beta,** or **negative hypergeometric.**

Example 4.7.2. Generalized Waring Distribution

Consider the negative binomial distribution (4.5.1) where the parameter $p = (1+\beta)^{-1}$ is treated as having a beta distribution (4.7.1). The resulting pf is

$$f(x) = \frac{\Gamma(r+x)}{\Gamma(r)x!} \frac{\Gamma(a+b)}{\Gamma(a)\Gamma(b)} \int_0^1 p^{a+r-1}(1-p)^{b+x-1} dp$$

$$= \frac{\Gamma(r+x)}{\Gamma(r)x!} \frac{\Gamma(a+b)}{\Gamma(a)\Gamma(b)} \frac{\Gamma(a+r)\Gamma(b+x)}{\Gamma(a+r+b+x)}, \quad x = 0,1,2,\ldots$$

The special case where $b = 1$ is the **Waring** distribution and if both $r = 1$ and $b = 1$ it is termed a **Yule** distribution.

A second technique for generating discrete distributions is that of compounding, considered in section 2.9. A random sum of discrete variates is again a discrete variate. These **compound** (or **contagious** or **stopped** or **generalized**) distributions are very useful in insurance modeling and are discussed in chapter 7. The connection between mixed and compound Poisson distributions is discussed in chapter 8. In general, the pf of these contagious distributions is only expressible as an infinite sum using equation 2.9.2 but, as we shall see, that is of little consequence in dealing with these distributions. They are more easily characterized by the pgf which is given for the following examples.

Example 4.7.3. Neyman Type A Distribution

The pgf of this distribution, which is a Poisson sum of Poisson variates, is given by

$$P(z) = e^{\lambda_1[e^{\lambda_2(z-1)}-1]}.$$

Example 4.7.4. Poisson-Inverse Gaussian Distribution

The pgf of this variate is

$$P(z) = e^{-\frac{\mu}{\beta}\{[1+2\beta(1-z)]^{\frac{1}{2}}-1\}}.$$

Example 4.7.5. Generalized Poisson-Pascal Distribution

This distribution has pgf

$$P(z) = e^{\lambda[Q(z)-1]}$$

where

$$Q(z) = \frac{[1-\beta(z-1)]^{-r}-(1+\beta)^{-r}}{1-(1+\beta)^{-r}} \qquad (4.7.2)$$

and $\lambda>0$, $\beta>0$, $r>-1$. This distribution has many special cases including the **Poisson-Pascal** $(r>0)$, the **Poisson-Inverse Gaussian** $(r=-.5)$ and the **Polya-Aeppli** $(r=1)$. It is easy to show that the **negative binomial** distribution obtained in the limit as $r\to 0$ and using (4.6.6) and (4.6.8). To see that the negative binomial is a special case, note that (4.7.2) is a logarithmic series pgf when $r=0$ by the results of section (4.6). The **Neyman Type A** is also a limiting form, obtained by letting $r\to\infty$, $\beta\to 0$ such that $r\beta=\lambda_1$ remains constant.

The three previous examples are all both mixed and compound Poisson distributions. They are extremely useful in modeling claim frequencies, and are discussed in more detail in chapters 7 and 8.

Other mixed and contagious distributions may be used, and more involved discussion of their many and varied uses in insurance modeling are given in chapters 7 and 8.

4.8 OTHER DISCRETE DISTRIBUTIONS

Other discrete distributions can be used in insurance modeling. There are other techniques which may be used to generate new discrete variates from known ones for use in insurance modeling. One such technique involves the use of shifting distributions. Hence we take a random variable N with probabilities $f(x)$ and define a new variate $N^* = N+m$ where m is an integer. Then the new variate N^* has probabilities $f^*(x) = f(x-m)$. An example is now given.

Example 4.8.1. Shifted Logarithmic Distribution

Consider the logarithmic distribution (4.6.1). From this distribution, define a new pf defined by

$$f(x) = \frac{q^{x+1}}{-(x+1)\log(1-q)}, \quad x = 0,1,2,\dots \ .$$

The support of this distribution now includes 0. The pf, moments, and other characteristics can be deduced from the fact that the associated random variable can be expressed as $X-1$ where X has the logarithmic distribution (4.6.1). For example, the pgf is, (using (4.6.2)),

$$P(z) = E(z^{X-1})$$
$$= \frac{\log(1-qz)}{z \log(1-q)}.$$

Another technique involves the use of modifying distributions. Certain probabilities are changed arbitrarily, and others multiplied by a constant so that the sum is unity. Two examples are now given.

Example 4.8.2. Log-Zero Distribution

Consider the logarithmic distribution (4.6.1) and define a zero probability by $f(0) = \alpha$. Then multiply the remaining probabilities by a constant so that the sum is unity. We thus have the pf

$$f(0) = \alpha$$

$$f(x) = \frac{(1-\alpha)q^x}{-x \, \log(1-q)}, \quad x = 1,2,3,\dots \quad .$$

The associated pgf is

$$P(z) = \alpha + (1-\alpha)\frac{\log(1-qz)}{\log(1-q)}.$$

From (4.3.2), (4.6.2), and (2.9.6) it is clear that the distribution is a compound Bernoulli-logarithmic distribution or a mixture of a degenerate and logarithmic distribution.

Example 4.8.3. Truncated Poisson Distribution

If the Poisson distribution has the probability mass at zero omitted and the remaining probabilities standardized, the resulting pf is

$$f(x) = \frac{\lambda^x}{(e^\lambda - 1)x!}, \quad x = 1,2,\dots \quad .$$

This distribution has pgf

$$P(z) = \frac{e^{\lambda z} - 1}{e^\lambda - 1}.$$

Combinations of shifting and modifying distributions are also used.

Many other discrete distributions may be used in insurance modeling and will be discussed in subsequent chapters. Only the most common parametric forms have been described here. We now proceed to the examination of some continuous distributions which are used to model the size of insurance claims.

4.9 THE EXPONENTIAL DISTRIBUTION

Consider the random variable with **pdf**

$$f(x) = \lambda e^{-\lambda x}, \quad x > 0 \tag{4.9.1}$$

where $\lambda > 0$. The **df** is

$$F(x) = 1 - e^{-\lambda x}, \quad x > 0. \tag{4.9.2}$$

This distribution is termed an **exponential** distribution. In many situations, the pdf defined by

$$f_1(x) = f(x-c) = \lambda e^{-\lambda(x-c)}, \quad x > c \tag{4.9.3}$$

is used. This distribution is often called the **two-parameter exponential** distribution. The Laplace transform of (4.9.1) is

$$L(z) = \frac{\lambda}{\lambda + z}, \quad z > -\lambda. \tag{4.9.4}$$

From (4.9.4) we may derive the **k-th moment about the origin** of an exponential variate. We have

$$\mu_k' = (-1)^k d^k \frac{L(z)}{dz^k}\Big|_{z=0}$$

$$= \frac{k!}{\lambda^k}. \tag{4.9.5}$$

The **mean** and **variance** are thus

$$\kappa_1 = \lambda^{-1} \tag{4.9.6}$$

$$\kappa_2 = \mu_2' - (\mu_1')^2$$

$$= \lambda^{-2}. \tag{4.9.7}$$

If X has pdf (4.9.1), then the scale family of variates $Y = aX$, $a > 0$ has Laplace transform

$$E(e^{-zY}) = E(e^{-azX})$$

$$= L(az)$$

$$= \frac{\lambda a^{-1}}{\lambda a^{-1} + z}$$

and thus Y is exponential with mean $a\lambda^{-1}$.

The exponential distribution, like the geometric, has the **memoryless** property and is sometimes referred to as the continuous analogue of the geometric. We have, for a variate X with pdf (4.9.1),

$$P\{X - y > x \mid X > y\} = P\{X > x + y \mid X > y\}$$

$$= \frac{1 - F(x+y)}{1 - F(y)}$$

$$= e^{-\lambda x}$$

$$= P(X > x), \quad x > 0. \tag{4.9.8}$$

The distribution of the conditional random variable $X - y \mid X > y$ is thus the same as that of X.

The exponential distribution is closely related to many distributions. For example, it arises as the interoccurrence times of the events in a **Poisson process** (see section 3.3).

The n-th root of (4.9.4) is $(\frac{\lambda}{\lambda+z})^{\frac{1}{n}}$ which is the Laplace transform of a gamma variate (see example 2.7.2) and thus the exponential distribution is infinitely divisible. More generally, it can be shown (Steutel, 1970) that a mixed df of the form

$$F(x) = \int_0^\infty [1 - e^{-\lambda x}] dU(\lambda)$$

$$= 1 - L(x) \qquad\qquad (4.9.9)$$

where $U(\lambda)$ is a df and $L(z)$ its associated Laplace transform, is infinitely divisible.

The **order statistics** (see section 2.11) in a sample of size n from the pdf (4.9.1) are of a particularly simple form.

Theorem 4.9.1. Suppose $X_1, X_2, \ldots, X_n$ is a sample of size n from the exponential (4.9.1). Let $X_{(1)}, X_{(2)}, \ldots, X_{(n)}$ be the order statistics of this sample. Define $X_{(0)} = 0$ and

$$W_i = (n-i+1)(X_{(i)} - X_{(i-1)}), \quad i = 1, 2, \ldots, n. \qquad (4.9.10)$$

Then the variates $W_1, W_2, \ldots, W_n$ are independent exponential variates, each with pdf (4.9.1).

Proof

From (2.10.9), the joint pdf of the order statistics is

$$f(x_{(1)}, x_{(2)}, \ldots, x_{(n)}) = n! \lambda^n e^{-\lambda \left(\sum_{i=1}^{n} x_{(i)} \right)}. \tag{4.9.11}$$

The joint pdf of $W_1, W_2, \ldots, W_n$ is

$$g(w_1, w_2, \ldots, w_n) = f(x_{(1)}, x_{(2)}, \ldots, x_{(n)}) \left| \frac{\partial(x_{(1)}, x_{(2)}, \ldots, x_{(n)})}{\partial(w_1, w_2, \ldots, w_n)} \right| \tag{4.9.12}$$

We first note that

$$X_{(i)} = \sum_{j=1}^{i} (X_{(j)} - X_{(j-1)})$$

$$= \sum_{j=1}^{i} (n-j+1)^{-1} W_j \tag{4.9.13}$$

from (4.9.10). Hence

$$\frac{\partial x_{(i)}}{\partial w_j} = \begin{cases} 0, & i < j \\ (n-j+1)^{-1}, & i \geq j \end{cases} \tag{4.9.14}$$

and so the Jacobian in (4.9.12) is lower triangular, and its determinant is the product of the diagonal entries (i.e., the special case of (4.9.14) when $j = i$). Thus, the determinant is

$$\left| \frac{\partial(x_{(1)}, x_{(2)}, \ldots, x_{(n)})}{\partial(w_1, w_2, \ldots, w_n)} \right| = \frac{1}{n!}. \tag{4.9.15}$$

Also, from (4.9.10),

$$\sum_{i=1}^{n} W_i = \sum_{i=1}^{n} (n-i+1)(X_{(i)} - X_{(i-1)})$$

$$= \sum_{i=1}^{n}(n-i+1)X_{(i)} - \sum_{i=0}^{n-1}(n-i)X_{(i)}$$

$$= X_{(n)} + \sum_{i=1}^{n-1}(n-i+1-n+i)X_{(i)}$$

$$= \sum_{i=1}^{n}X_{(i)}. \tag{4.9.16}$$

Finally, substituting (4.9.15), (4.9.16), and (4.9.11) into (4.9.12) yields

$$g(w_1,w_2,\ldots,w_n) = \lambda^n e^{-\lambda\sum_{i=1}^{n}w_i}, \quad w_i>0. \tag{4.9.17}$$

Since the joint pdf (4.9.17) factors, the result follows.

It easily follows from (4.9.13) that

$$E(X_{(i)}) = \lambda^{-1}\sum_{j=1}^{i}(n-j+1)^{-1}. \tag{4.9.18}$$

The exponential distribution is often used in developing models of insurance risks. This usefulness stems in large part from its many and varied tractable mathematical properties, a few of which have been demonstrated in this section. However, a disadvantage of the exponential distribution is that its density is monotone decreasing, a situation which may not be appropriate in some practical situations.

4.10 THE PARETO DISTRIBUTION

Suppose that a variate X has (conditional on θ) an exponential distribution with mean θ^{-1}. Further suppose that θ itself has a gamma pdf (see example 2.7.2). The unconditional distribution of X is a mixture (see section 2.8 and equation 4.9.9) and is called the **Pareto** distribution. The Laplace transform of the gamma variate is

$$L_\theta(z) = \left[\frac{\lambda}{\lambda+z}\right]^\alpha.$$

Hence, the Pareto **df** is given by

$$F(x) = \int_0^\infty [1-e^{-\theta x}]\frac{\lambda(\lambda\theta)^{\alpha-1}e^{-\lambda\theta}}{\Gamma(\alpha)}d\theta$$

$$= 1-L_\theta(x)$$

$$= 1-(\frac{\lambda}{\lambda+x})^\alpha, \quad x>0. \tag{4.10.1}$$

Clearly, λ and α are both non-negative. The **pdf** is thus

$$f(x) = \frac{\alpha\lambda^\alpha}{(\lambda+x)^{\alpha+1}}, \quad x>0. \tag{4.10.2}$$

As with the exponential distribution, the pdf defined by

$$f_1(x) = f(x-\lambda) = \frac{\alpha\lambda^\alpha}{x^{\alpha+1}}, \quad x>\lambda \tag{4.10.3}$$

is often used. To derive the **k-th moment about the origin** of $f(x)$, we write

$$\mu_k' = \int_0^\infty \alpha\lambda^\alpha(\lambda+x)^{-\alpha-1}x^k dx$$

$$= \int_0^\infty \frac{\alpha x^k}{\lambda}(\frac{\lambda}{\lambda+x})^{\alpha+1}dx.$$

Then making the change of variable $y = \lambda(\lambda+x)^{-1}$, we obtain

$$\mu_k' = \int_0^1 \frac{\alpha}{\lambda} \left\{ \frac{\lambda(1-y)}{y} \right\}^k y^{\alpha+1} \lambda y^{-2} dy$$

$$= \alpha \lambda^k \int_0^1 y^{\alpha-k-1} (1-y)^k dy.$$

This integral is a beta function (see appendix B) and thus

$$\mu_k' = \frac{\alpha \lambda^k \Gamma(\alpha-k) \Gamma(k+1)}{\Gamma(\alpha+1)}$$

$$= \lambda^k k! \frac{\Gamma(\alpha-k)}{\Gamma(\alpha)}, \quad \alpha > k. \qquad (4.10.4)$$

The **mean** and **variance** are thus

$$\kappa_1 = \frac{\lambda}{\alpha-1}, \quad \alpha > 1 \qquad (4.10.5)$$

$$\kappa_2 = \frac{\alpha \lambda^2}{(\alpha-1)^2(\alpha-2)}, \quad \alpha > 2. \qquad (4.10.6)$$

It is clear that only a finite number of moments exist, and even the mean and variance may not exist. Thus, the Pareto distribution has very thick tails.

If X has the Pareto pdf (4.10.2), then the scaled variate $Y = aX, a > 0$, has df

$$P(Y < y) = P(X < \frac{y}{a})$$

$$= 1 - (\frac{\lambda a}{\lambda a + y})^\alpha, \quad y > 0$$

which is again Pareto with parameters λa and α. Thus, the Pareto distribution is closed under scale transformations.

It can be shown that if X is an exponential random variable and Y is a gamma random variable, then XY^{-1} is a Pareto random variable.

If X has the Pareto pdf (4.10.2), then it is easily seen that

$$Pr\{\log(1+\frac{X}{\lambda})\leq y\} = 1 - e^{-\alpha y}, \quad y>0 \tag{4.10.7}$$

and so $\log(1 + \frac{X}{\lambda})$ is exponential with mean α^{-1}.

This result may be used to obtain the distribution of the **order statistics** from the Pareto distribution.

Theorem 4.10.1. Suppose $X_{(1)}, X_{(2)}, \ldots, X_{(n)}$ are the order statistics from a sample of size n from the Pareto pdf (4.10.2). Then

$$X_{(i)} = \lambda \left[\prod_{j=1}^{i}(1+V_j)-1 \right] \tag{4.10.8}$$

where the V_j are independent Pareto variates with df

$$Pr(V_j<v) = 1-(1+v)^{-\alpha(n-j+1)}. \tag{4.10.9}$$

Proof

From (4.10.7), we may write

$$X_i = \lambda(e^{Y_i}-1) \tag{4.10.10}$$

where X_i is from the original sample and Y_i is exponential with mean α^{-1}. Since (4.10.10) defines a monotone increasing function of Y_i, the corresponding order statistics satisfy

$$X_{(i)} = \lambda(e^{Y_{(i)}} - 1). \tag{4.10.11}$$

But, from (4.9.13)

$$Y_{(i)} = \sum_{j=1}^{i} (n-j+1)^{-1} W_j$$

where the W_j are independent exponentials with mean α^{-1}. Then $Z_j = (n-j+1)^{-1} W_j$ is exponential with mean $[\alpha(n-j+1)]^{-1}$. We thus have

$$V_j = e^{Z_j} - 1 \tag{4.10.12}$$

and on comparison with (4.10.7), the V_j are independent Pareto random variables with df (4.10.9). Thus, from (4.10.11) and (4.10.12),

$$X_{(i)} = \lambda(e^{Y_{(i)}} - 1)$$

$$= \lambda(e^{\sum_{j=1}^{i} Z_j} - 1)$$

$$= \lambda\{\prod_{j=1}^{i} e^{Z_j} - 1\}$$

$$= \lambda\{\prod_{j=1}^{i} (1+V_j) - 1\}$$

as required.

Moments for the order statistics are easily obtainable from (4.10.8) and (4.10.4). For example,

$$E(X_{(i)}) = \lambda\{\prod_{j=1}^{i} E(1+V_j) - 1\}$$

$$= \lambda\{\prod_{j=1}^{i} (1+[\alpha(n-j+1)-1]^{-1}) - 1\}, \quad \alpha > (n-i+1)^{-1}. \tag{4.10.13}$$

The Pareto distribution is a mixed exponential variate and hence infinitely divisible by (4.9.9). This distribution is very useful in modeling claim costs in insurance, due in large part to its extremely thick tail. Its main drawback lies in its lack of mathematical tractability in some situations. For example, the Laplace transform does not exist in closed form.

4.11 THE LOGNORMAL DISTRIBUTION

Consider a random variable X which has the normal distribution (see example 2.7.1) with pdf

$$f_X(x) = \frac{1}{\sqrt{2\pi}\sigma} e^{-\frac{1}{2}\left(\frac{x-\mu}{\sigma}\right)^2}, \quad -\infty < x < \infty.$$

Let $Y = \exp X$ so that $X = \log Y$. The **pdf** of Y is

$$f_Y(y) = f_X(\log y) \frac{1}{y}$$

$$= \frac{1}{\sqrt{2\pi}\sigma y} e^{-\frac{1}{2}\left(\frac{\log y - \mu}{\sigma}\right)^2}, \quad y > 0 \qquad (4.11.1)$$

where $\sigma > 0$, $-\infty < \mu < \infty$. The distribution of Y is termed a **lognormal** distribution. The **df** is given by

$$F(y) = \Phi(\frac{\log y - \mu}{\sigma}), \quad y > 0 \qquad (4.11.2)$$

where $\Phi(.)$ is the standard normal (with mean 0 and variance 1) df.

The **k-th moment about the origin** of the lognormal can be easily derived using results from normal theory. We have

$$\mu'_k = E(Y^k)$$

$$= E(e^{kX})$$

$$= M_X(k)$$

where $M_X(z)$ is the mgf of the normal distribution. Hence,

$$\mu'_k = \exp(\mu k + \frac{\sigma^2 k^2}{2}). \qquad (4.11.3)$$

In particular, the **mean** and **variance** are

$$\kappa_1 = \exp(\mu + \frac{\sigma^2}{2}) \qquad \qquad (4.11.4)$$

$$\kappa_2 = \exp(2\mu + \sigma^2)[\exp(\sigma^2) - 1]. \qquad (4.11.5)$$

Consider the tranformed variate $Z = aY^b$ where $a,b > 0$. We may write $Z = ae^{Xb} = e^{bX + \log a}$. But $bX + \log a$ is a normal variate with mean $\mu b + \log a$ and variance $b^2 \sigma^2$. Thus, Z is again a lognormal variate. Thus, the lognormal family is closed under both scale and power transformations.

If $\{X_1, X_2, ...\}$ is a sequence of independent and identically distributed positive random variables such that $\log X_i$ has finite mean and variance, then by the central limit theorem (section 2.11) $\sum_{i=1}^{n} \log X_i$ converges to a normal variate. Thus, whatever the distribution of the $X_i's$, $T_n = \prod_{i=1}^{n} X_i$ has an approximate lognormal distribution for large n. By the same reasoning, if the distribution of the $X_i's$ is in fact lognormal, then so is that of T_n (if the $X_i's$ are independent, though not necessarily identically distributed).

The lognormal distribution is very useful in modeling of claims costs. It has a thick right tail and fits many situations well. For small σ it resembles a normal distribution, although this is not always desirable. The fact that the class of lognormal distributions is closed under scale and power transformations is a useful feature. It suffers from some drawbacks mathematically, most notably that the Laplace transform does not have a closed form representation and it has no moment generating function. It is, however, infinitely divisible.

4.12 THE GAMMA DISTRIBUTION

The distribution with **pdf**

$$f(x) = \lambda(\lambda x)^{\alpha-1} \frac{e^{-\lambda x}}{\Gamma(\alpha)}, \quad x>0 \tag{4.12.1}$$

where $\lambda, \alpha > 0$ is termed a **gamma** distribution. It is also known as a **Pearson's Type III** distribution. If $\alpha = 1$ the **exponential** distribution results. If α is a positive integer it is termed an **Erlang** distribution. If $\lambda = \frac{1}{2}$ and $\alpha = \frac{1}{2}\nu$ then it is termed a **chi-squared distribution with ν degrees of freedom.**

The **df** corresponding to (4.12.1) is

$$F(x) = \int_0^x \lambda(\lambda y)^{\alpha-1} e^{-\lambda y} \frac{dy}{\Gamma(\alpha)} = I(\alpha, \lambda x) \tag{4.12.2}$$

where $I(\alpha, z)$ is the incomplete gamma function (see appendix A). Thus, for the Erlangian case when α is a positive integer,

$$F(x) = 1 - \sum_{j=0}^{\alpha-1} \frac{(\lambda x)^j e^{-\lambda x}}{j!}. \tag{4.12.3}$$

In other words, the left tail of the Erlang distribution is equal to the right tail of the Poisson distribution (see section 4.2).

The Laplace transform of the distribution is

$$L(z) = \int_0^\infty \frac{e^{-zx}\lambda(\lambda x)^{\alpha-1}e^{-\lambda x}}{\Gamma(\alpha)}dx$$

$$= \frac{\lambda^\alpha}{\Gamma(\alpha)}\int_0^\infty x^{\alpha-1}e^{-(\lambda+z)x}dx$$

$$= (\frac{\lambda}{\lambda+z})^\alpha, \quad z > -\lambda \qquad (4.12.4)$$

where the last step follows on making the substitution $y = (\lambda+z)x$.

The **k-th moment about the origin** is easily derived from (4.12.4). We have,

$$\mu_k' = (-1)^k \frac{d^k L(z)}{dz^k}\big|_{z=0}$$

$$= \frac{\alpha(\alpha+1)\cdots(\alpha+k-1)}{\lambda^k}$$

$$= \frac{\Gamma(\alpha+k)}{\Gamma(\alpha)\lambda^k}. \qquad (4.12.5)$$

The **mean** and **variance** are

$$\kappa_1 = \frac{\alpha}{\lambda} \qquad (4.12.6)$$

and

$$\kappa_2 = \frac{\alpha}{\lambda^2}. \qquad (4.12.7)$$

If X has pdf (4.12.1), then aX, $a>0$ has Laplace transform

$$(\frac{\lambda a^{-1}}{\lambda a^{-1}+z})^\alpha$$

and so aX has a gamma distribution with parameters λa^{-1} and α. Thus the gamma family is closed under scale changes.

Suppose we have a sequence of independent variates $\{X_1, X_2,...\}$ such that X_i has a gamma distribution with parameters λ and α_i. Then, from (4.12.4) the sum $\sum_{i=1}^{n} X_i$ has a gamma distribution with parameters λ and $\sum_{i=1}^{n} \alpha_i$. If $\alpha_i = 1$ for all i, we see that the sum of exponential variates has a gamma (in fact an Erlang) distribution.

It was shown in example 2.7.2 that the gamma distribution is infinitely divisible.

The gamma distribution is closely related to many distributions. For example, as was shown earlier, the tails of the Erlang and Poisson distributions are closely related. In addition, the time until the occurrence of the rth event in a Poisson process (see section 3.3) has an Erlang distribution since the event interoccurrence times are exponentially distributed. A mixed Poisson distribution (see section 2.8) with gamma mixing distribution is negative binomial (see section 4.5). Also, the sum of squares of n independent normal random variables with zero mean and unit variance has a chi-squared distribution with n degrees of freedom.

Many other relationships exist between the gamma and other variates. The Pareto distribution (section 4.10) was derived by mixing an exponential parameter λ over a gamma distribution.

Suppose X_1 and X_2 are independent gamma random variables with parameters λ and α_1 and λ and α_2 respectively. It can be shown that $Y_2 = X_1 + X_2$ has a gamma distribution with parameters λ and $\alpha_1 + \alpha_2$, and that $Y_1 = X_1(X_1 + X_2)^{-1}$ has a beta distribution (4.7.1). Furthermore, Y_1 and Y_2 are independent.

It is clear from the central limit theorem (section 2.11) that, for large α, the gamma approaches a normal distribution.

The gamma distribution is sometimes a reasonable model for insurance claim costs. It is, however, one of the most important distributions for modeling both because it has very tractable mathematical properties and because it is related to so many other important distributions. The number of these relationships is large, and only a few of them are listed here. It is very useful in creating other distributions for modeling insurance costs.

4.13 THE INVERSE GAUSSIAN DISTRIBUTION

If X has a **pdf**

$$f(x) = \mu(2\pi\beta x^3)^{-\frac{1}{2}} \exp\{-\frac{(x-\mu)^2}{2\beta x}\}, \quad x>0 \tag{4.13.1}$$

where $\beta, \mu > 0$, then X is said to have an **inverse Gaussian** distribution. Also known as an **inverse normal** or **Hadwiger** distribution, the special case of (4.13.1) when $\mu = 1$ is often called a **Wald** distribution. The **df** of the inverse Gaussian distribution is

$$F(x) = \Phi[(\beta x)^{-\frac{1}{2}}(x-\mu)] + e^{2\mu\beta^{-1}}\Phi[-(\beta x)^{-\frac{1}{2}}(x+\mu)], \quad x>0 \tag{4.13.2}$$

where $\Phi(.)$ is the standard normal df.

The Laplace transform of the distribution is obtained as

$$L(z) = \int_0^\infty e^{-zx}\mu(2\pi\beta x^3)^{-\frac{1}{2}} e^{-\frac{(x-\mu)^2}{2\beta x}} dx$$

$$= e^{\frac{\mu}{\beta}[1-(1+2\beta z)^{\frac{1}{2}}]}, \quad z \geq -\frac{1}{2\beta} \tag{4.13.3}$$

This can be seen by rewriting the integral in terms of an inverse Gaussian pdf with $\beta_1 = \beta(1+2\beta z)^{-1}$, and $\mu_1 = \mu(1+2\beta z)^{-\frac{1}{2}}$. The cumulants are quite simple to obtain. We have

$$\log L(z) = \frac{\mu}{\beta}[1-(1+2\beta z)^{\frac{1}{2}}].$$

Thus, the **k-th cumulant** $(k \geq 2)$ is

$$\kappa_k = (-1)^k \frac{d^k \log L(z)}{dz^k}|_{z=0}$$

$$= \mu \beta^{k-1}(1)(3)(5)\cdots(2k-3), \quad k \geq 2. \tag{4.13.4}$$

The **mean** and **variance** are

$$\kappa_1 = \mu \tag{4.13.5}$$

$$\kappa_2 = \mu \beta. \tag{4.13.6}$$

If X has pdf (4.13.1), then the Laplace transform of aX, $a>0$ is

$$L(z) = e^{\frac{a\mu}{a\beta}\{1-[1+2(a\beta)z]^{\frac{1}{2}}\}}$$

and hence aX is inverse Gaussian with parameters $a\beta$ and $a\mu$. Thus the inverse Gaussian family is closed under scale transformations.

If we consider the n-th root of (4.13.3), we obtain

$$\{L(z)\}^{\frac{1}{n}} = e^{\frac{\mu}{n\beta}[1-(1+2\beta z)^{\frac{1}{2}}]}$$

which is the Laplace transform of an inverse Gaussian variate with parameters β and $\frac{\mu}{n}$. Thus the inverse Gaussian distribution is infinitely divisible.

The inverse Gaussian distribution has a property which is similar to that of the gamma distribution. If we have a sequence of independent inverse Gaussian variates $\{X_1, X_2, \ldots\}$ such that X_i has parameters β and μ_i, then $\sum_{i=1}^{n} X_i$

is again inverse Gaussian with parameters β and $\sum_{i=1}^{n}\mu_i$. Thus, by the central limit theorem (see section 2.11), the inverse Gaussian approaches a normal distribution for large μ.

There are some other interesting relationships between the gamma and inverse Gaussian variates. First, consider the random variable $Y=(X-\mu)^2X^{-1}$ where X has the pdf (4.13.1). The Laplace transform of Y is

$$L_Y(z) = E[e^{-zY}]$$

$$= \int_0^\infty e^{-z\frac{(x-\mu)^2}{x}} \mu(2\pi\beta x^3)^{-\frac{1}{2}} e^{-\frac{(x-\mu)^2}{2\beta x}} dx$$

$$= \int_0^\infty \mu(2\pi\beta x^3)^{-\frac{1}{2}} e^{-\frac{1+2\beta z}{2\beta x}(x-\mu)^2} dx$$

$$= (1+2\beta z)^{-\frac{1}{2}} \int_0^\infty \mu(2\pi\beta_1 x^3)^{-\frac{1}{2}} e^{-\frac{(x-\mu)^2}{2\beta_1 x}} dx$$

$$= (1+2\beta z)^{-\frac{1}{2}}, \quad z \geq -\frac{1}{2\beta}$$

where $\beta_1 = \beta(1+2\beta z)^{-1}$ on the second last line. The integral in the second last line is that of an inverse Gaussian pdf with parameters β_1 and μ and hence equals 1. The variate Y is thus a gamma variate with parameters $\lambda = \frac{1}{2\beta}$ and $\alpha = \frac{1}{2}$ (see (4.12.4)).

Now consider the variate $Y = X^{-1}$ where X has pdf (4.13.1). The pdf of Y is

$$g(y) = f(x) \left| \frac{dx}{dy} \right|$$

$$= \mu \left(\frac{y^3}{2\beta\pi} \right)^{\frac{1}{2}} e^{-\frac{y}{2\beta}(\frac{1}{y}-\mu)^2} \frac{1}{y^2}$$

$$= \mu (2\pi\beta y)^{-\frac{1}{2}} e^{-\frac{(1-\mu y)^2}{2\beta y}}, \quad y>0. \tag{4.13.7}$$

Y is said to be a **reciprocal inverse Gaussian** variate. The Laplace transform of Y can be shown to be

$$L(z) = \left(\frac{\mu^2}{\mu^2 + 2\beta z} \right)^{\frac{1}{2}} e^{\frac{\mu}{\beta}[1-(1+\frac{2\beta z}{\mu^2})^{\frac{1}{2}}]}, \quad z \geq -\frac{\mu^2}{2\beta}. \tag{4.13.8}$$

From (4.13.8), the reciprocal of an inverse Gaussian variate with pdf (4.13.1) is equal to a gamma variate with parameters $\lambda = \frac{\mu^2}{2\beta}$ and $\alpha = \frac{1}{2}$ plus an independent inverse Gaussian variate with parameters $\frac{\beta}{\mu^2}$ and $\frac{1}{\mu}$. It is easily shown that, if Y is a reciprocal inverse Gaussian variate, so is aY, $a>0$.

The inverse Gaussian distribution has only recently been utilized in modeling claims costs to any great degree. It has thick tails and is very similar to the lognormal distribution in shape. It is a reasonable candidate for modeling in many insurance situations, therefore, and has the distinct advantage over the lognormal distribution of having many desirable mathematical properties, most notably a closed form expression for the Laplace transform. As well as being a good candidate for claims costs, the inverse Gaussian can be used to generate other useful distributions through mixing and other statistical techniques.

4.14 OTHER CONTINUOUS DISTRIBUTIONS

Many distributions which are of use in modeling can be obtained by transforming to a new variate and using this new distribution. If X has a known distribution, then the distribution of $h(X)$ is often useful. For all the continuous distributions considered so far, the distribution of scalar multiples is of the same family, so no new distributions are created.

One usual transform is the **exponential transform** $Y = e^X$. In terms of the df, this means that

$$F_Y(y) = F_X(\log y), \quad y > 0. \tag{4.14.1}$$

In terms of the pdf, we thus obtain

$$f_Y(y) = f_X(\log y)\frac{1}{y}, \quad y > 0. \tag{4.14.2}$$

One common example of this type of distribution is the lognormal (section 4.11). Another distribution of this form is given in the following example. Further examples are given in the exercises.

Example 4.14.1. The Log-logistic Distribution

The **log-logistic** distribution has pdf

$$f(y) = \frac{c\lambda y^{c-1}}{(\lambda + y^c)^2}, \quad y > 0$$

where $c > 0$, $\lambda > 0$. The df is

$$F(y) = 1 - (\frac{\lambda}{\lambda + y^c}), \quad y > 0.$$

The k-th moment about the origin is

$$\mu_k' = \lambda^{\frac{k}{c}}\Gamma(1 - \frac{k}{c})\Gamma(1 + \frac{k}{c}), \quad k < c.$$

The distribution of $X = \log Y$ is known as the **logistic** distribution, which looks very much like the normal except the tails are much thicker. As a result, the log-logistic looks very much like the lognormal, except in the extreme tails.

Another useful transform is the class of **power transformations** $Y = X^{1/c}$ where $c > 0$. In terms of the df, we have

$$F_Y(y) = F_X(y^c), \quad y > 0. \tag{4.14.3}$$

The relation in terms of the pdf is

$$f_Y(y) = f_X(y^c)cy^{c-1}, \quad y > 0. \tag{4.14.4}$$

It is easy to see that if X has distribution which is a member of a family that is closed under scale changes, then so does Y. This is because $aY = (a^c X)^{1/c}$ and $a^c X$ is a member of the same family as X so $(a^c X)^{1/c}$ is a member of the same family as $X^{1/c}$.

Some examples are now given.

Example 4.14.2. The Weibull Distribution

Suppose X has the exponential distribution (4.9.1). The distribution of $Y = X^{1/c}$ is called the **Weibull** distribution. Then, from (4.14.3), the df of Y is

$$F_Y(y) = 1 - e^{-\lambda y^c}, \quad y > 0.$$

The pdf is thus

$$f_Y(y) = c\lambda y^{c-1} e^{-\lambda y^c}, \quad y > 0.$$

The k-th moment about the origin can be shown to be

$$\mu_k' = \frac{\Gamma(1+\frac{k}{c})}{\lambda^{\frac{k}{c}}}.$$

The **exponential** distribution $(c=1)$ is a special case.

Example 4.14.3. The Burr Distribution

If X has the Pareto distribution (4.10.2), the distribution of $Y = X^{1/c}$ is known as the **Burr** distribution. Thus the df of Y is

$$F_Y(y) = 1 - (\frac{\lambda}{\lambda+y^c})^\alpha, \quad y>0.$$

The pdf is

$$f_Y(y) = \frac{c\alpha\lambda^\alpha y^{c-1}}{(\lambda+y^c)^{\alpha+1}}, \quad y>0.$$

The k-th moment about the origin is

$$\mu_k' = \frac{\lambda^{\frac{k}{c}}\Gamma(\alpha-\frac{k}{c})\Gamma(1+\frac{k}{c})}{\Gamma(\alpha)}, \quad k<c\alpha.$$

The **Pareto** $(c=1)$ and the **log-logistic** $(\alpha=1)$ are special cases.

Example 4.14.4. The Generalized Gamma Distribution

Also referred to as the **transformed gamma,** this distribution is derived by letting $Y = X^{1/c}$ where X has the gamma pdf (4.12.1). Thus, the df is, from (4.12.2) and (4.14.3),

$$F_Y(y) = I(\alpha, \lambda y^c), \quad y>0$$

where $I(\alpha, z)$ is the incomplete gamma function (see appendix A). The pdf is

$$f_Y(y) = \frac{c\lambda^\alpha y^{c\alpha-1}e^{-\lambda y^c}}{\Gamma(\alpha)}, \quad y>0.$$

The k-th moment about the origin of Y is

$$\mu_k' = \frac{\Gamma(\alpha+\frac{k}{c})}{\lambda^{\frac{k}{c}}\Gamma(\alpha)}.$$

This class of distribution includes the **exponential** ($c=1, \alpha=1$), **Weibull** ($\alpha=1$) and **gamma** ($c=1$) distributions as special cases.

Another useful way of deriving distributions is by taking ratios of known distributions. In other words, the variate of interest is $Y = X_1/X_2$ where X_1 and X_2 are known independent distributions. Change of variable techniques yield the required pdf as (in an obvious notation)

$$f_Y(y) = \int_0^\infty x_2 f_{X_1}(x_2 y) f_{X_2}(x_2) dx_2, \quad y>0. \tag{4.14.5}$$

Some examples are now given.

Example 4.14.5. The Generalized Pareto Distribution

Suppose X_1 is a gamma variate with parameters $\lambda = 1$, $\alpha = \beta$ in the notation of section 4.12. Furthermore, suppose X_2 is also a gamma variate with parameters λ, α, independent of X. The pdf of Y is, from (4.14.5)

$$f_Y(y) = \int_0^\infty x_2 \frac{(x_2 y)^{\beta-1} e^{-x_2 y}}{\Gamma(\beta)} \frac{\lambda(\lambda x_2)^{\alpha-1} e^{-\lambda x_2}}{\Gamma(\alpha)} dx_2$$

$$= \frac{\lambda^\alpha y^{\beta-1}}{\Gamma(\alpha)\Gamma(\beta)} \int_0^\infty x_2^{\alpha+\beta-1} e^{-(\lambda+y)x_2} dx_2$$

$$= \frac{\Gamma(\alpha+\beta)}{\Gamma(\alpha)\Gamma(\beta)} \frac{\lambda^\alpha y^{\beta-1}}{(\lambda+y)^{\alpha+\beta}}, \quad y>0.$$

This distribution is known as a **generalized Pareto** distribution. The last line follows on making the substitution $z = (\lambda+y)x_2$ and recognizing the integral as being that of a gamma function (see appendix A). The df can be shown to be

$$F_Y(y) = B(\beta,\alpha,\frac{y}{\lambda+y}), \quad y>0$$

where $B(a,b,x)$ is the incomplete beta function (see appendix B). The k-th moment about the origin is

$$\mu'_k = \frac{\lambda^k \Gamma(\beta+k)\Gamma(\alpha-k)}{\Gamma(\beta)\Gamma(\alpha)}, \quad k<\alpha.$$

This distribution has several special cases including the **Pareto** ($\beta = 1$), and the **F** ($\beta = \frac{m}{2}, \alpha = \frac{n}{2}, \lambda = \frac{n}{m}$) with m and n degrees of freedom.

Example 4.14.6. The Transformed Beta Distribution

If X_1 is a generalized gamma variate (example 4.14.4) with parameters $\lambda = 1$, $\alpha = \beta$, and c, and X_2 is also a generalized gamma variate, independent of X_1, with parameters λ, α, and c, the pdf of Y is easily shown to be (from 4.14.5)

$$f_Y(y) = \frac{\Gamma(\alpha+\beta)c\lambda^\alpha y^{c\beta-1}}{\Gamma(\alpha)\Gamma(\beta)(\lambda+y^c)^{\alpha+\beta}}, \quad y>0.$$

This four parameter family of distributions, known as the **transformed Beta** distribution is very flexible and has many distributions as special cases including the **generalized Pareto** ($c=1$), the **Pareto** ($c=1, \beta=1$), the **Burr** ($\beta=1$), and the **log-logistic** ($\beta=1, \alpha=1$). This density can also be derived by mixing one of the parameters of a generalized gamma variate by another generalized gamma variate. The k-th moment about the origin is

$$\mu_k' = \lambda^{\frac{k}{c}} \frac{\Gamma(\alpha-\frac{k}{c})\Gamma(\beta+\frac{k}{c})}{\Gamma(\alpha)\Gamma(\beta)}, \quad k<c\alpha.$$

The df is

$$F_Y(y) = B(\beta,\alpha,\frac{y^c}{\lambda+y^c}), \quad y>0$$

where $B(a,b,x)$ is the incomplete beta function (see appendix B). The transformed beta has several limiting forms. If $\alpha \to \infty$ the generalized gamma distribution is obtained (example 4.15.3) along with its special cases. If $\alpha \to \infty$, $\beta \to \infty$ the lognormal distribution is obtained. The family of distributions obtained by letting $\alpha \le \infty$, $\beta \le \infty$ has been termed the **generalized F** distribution. Since we will have occasion to distinguish between the case where $\alpha < \infty$, $\beta < \infty$ and the case where $\alpha \le \infty$, $\beta \le \infty$, we shall refer to the family obtained by insisting that $\alpha < \infty$, $\beta < \infty$ as the "transformed beta" distribution. The use of the distribution may be primarily in distinguishing between distributions which are special cases of it. Model fitting can cause difficulties due to the large number of parameters and it has been suggested by Prentice (1975) that the reparameterization

$$\mu = (\frac{1}{\beta} - \frac{1}{\alpha})(\frac{1}{\beta} + \frac{1}{\alpha})^{\frac{1}{2}}, \quad \sigma = \frac{2}{\alpha+\beta}$$

may be useful in this regard.

Another important technique used for generating random variables is mixing (section 2.8). In many instances, several different techniques yield the same distribution. For example, if X is a generalized Pareto variate, then $Y = X^{1/c}$ is a transformed beta variate. These and other relationships will be explored in the exercises. Other transforms, may also be used (e.g. $\log(1+X)$ could also be used to generate non-negative variates).

Other distributions can often be used in insurance modeling which may not arise by taking simple functions $h(X)$ of known variates X. An example is now given.

Example 4.14.7. The Generalized Inverse Gaussian Distribution

The generalized inverse Gaussian distribution has pdf

$$f(x) = \frac{\mu^{-\lambda} x^{\lambda-1} e^{-\frac{(x^2+\mu^2)}{2\beta x}}}{2K_\lambda(\mu\beta^{-1})}, \quad x>0$$

where $\mu>0$, $\beta>0$, $-\infty<\lambda<\infty$, and $K_\lambda(x)$ is the modified Bessel function of the third kind with index λ (see appendix C). This distribution includes the **inverse Gaussian** ($\lambda=-.5$) and the **reciprocal inverse Gaussian** ($\lambda=.5$) as special cases. The Laplace transform of the distribution is

$$L(z) = (1+2\beta z)^{-\frac{\lambda}{2}} \frac{K_\lambda\{\mu\beta^{-1}(1+2\beta z)^{\frac{1}{2}}\}}{K_\lambda(\mu\beta^{-1})}, \quad z \geq -\frac{1}{2\beta}.$$

The k-th moment about the origin is

$$\mu_k' = \mu^k \frac{K_{\lambda+k}(\mu\beta^{-1})}{K_\lambda(\mu\beta^{-1})}.$$

It is easily shown that every distribution in this section is closed under scale transformations.

Many other distributions can be used in modeling insurance costs. Some of these include the **Gompertz, Makeham,** and **Rayleigh** distributions.

It will be seen that in many instances, it is not important that a parametric distribution always be specified, and in these instances the reader should not feel restricted to use a parametric form when a non-parametric or empirical distribution will suffice.

4.15 BIBLIOGRAPHIC NOTES

The properties of many of the probability distributions discussed in this chapter are outlined by Johnson and Kotz (1969, 1970a, 1970b). Patil and Joshi (1968) survey a wide variety of discrete distributions. Other useful references on distributions include Ord (1972), Patel, Kapadia, and Owen (1976), and Haight (1967) who discusses the Poisson distribution and its applications.

The generalized Waring distribution is discussed by Seal (1978) in an insurance context and more generally by Irwin (1975).

The contagious distributions are discussed by Douglas (1980). Holla (1966) discusses the Poisson-Inverse Gaussian distribution.

Proof of the infinite divisibility of exponential mixtures is given by Steutel (1970). The distribution of the order statistics from the Pareto distribution was given by Huang (1975). Thorin (1977) proved that the lognormal distribution is infinitely divisible. Folks and Chhikara (1978) survey some of the basic properties of the inverse Gaussian distribution. Many of the distributions discussed in section 4.14 (Weibull, Burr, generalized gamma, generalized Pareto) are discussed in an insurance context by Hogg and Klugman (1984). Venter (1983) discusses the transformed beta and generalized gamma distributions. Kalbfleisch and Prentice (1980) discuss the log-logistic and transformed beta (generalized F). The generalized inverse Gaussian distribution is discussed by Jorgensen (1982).

CHAPTER 5

INDIVIDUAL RISK MODELS

5.1 INTRODUCTION

In this chapter, we begin to introduce insurance problems. Specifically, we will be concerned with modeling the total losses associated with a portfolio of heterogeneous insurance risks. We use the term **insurance risks** loosely to describe an insured entity such as a person insured against financial losses associated with death, a building insured to cover fire damage or a professional person insured for malpractice. The term **portfolio** is used to describe a collection or aggregation of insurance risks. The class of models discussed in this chapter may be viewed as a special case of models which will be discussed in later chapters. However, we believe that the **individual risk model** deserves special attention due to the facts that it is widely used in certain applications, especially in life and health insurance, and that it is more difficult to deal with mathematically in spite of the simplicity of the model.

5.2 THE MODEL

Consider a portfolio of n insurance risks. We assume that the risks are statistically independent so that the claim costs or losses of one risk have no influence on any other risk in the portfolio. This assumption may seem appropriate in some types of insurance (for example, life insurance sold on an individual basis) but will be inappropriate for other types of insurance.

The individual risk model is characterized by the assumption that each risk in the portfolio can experience at most one claim. A somewhat general formulation is that either a claim will or will not occur for each risk and that all claim costs arising from a particular risk are amalgamated and treated as a single claim. The first characterization is appropriate for life insurance covering a closed group of lives since no more than one claim per risk can occur. The second interpretation may be desirable in some types of insurance. For example, in dental insurance, an insured individual may visit a dentist several times during a one-year insurance period. Another individual may make only one or two visits to a dentist and have the same services provided. It is desirable to treat these individuals identically for several reasons. First, the way in which the risk is modeled should not depend upon the way in which a particular dentist handles his or her patients. A dentist who does more work per visit and does the same amount of work over the one-year period of observation is no different (at least from the insurer's point of view) from the dentist who does less work per visit. The critical factor is whether the insured risk did or did not make a claim during the year. All claim costs should be amalgamated and treated as a single claim. Secondly, some types of insurance have a deductible associated with the period of insurance, typically one year. This occurs in some types of medical or drug expense insurance plans in which the insured individual is required to pay the first, say one hundred dollars or five hundred dollars, of expenses incurred in a particular year. In this case, all the expenses in a particular year must be amalgamated and treated as a single claim for the year. To avoid repetition of the above arguments, we will subsequently treat the risks as having at most one claim.

The total loss associated with a portfolio of n independent heterogeneous risks is the sum of the losses from each risk. Hence, we write

$$S = X_1 + X_2 + \cdots + X_n \qquad (5.2.1)$$

to represent the total losses where X_i represents the loss associated with the i-th risk. Thus, taking expectations and using the independence of the X_j's, we have

$$E(S) = E(X_1) + E(X_2) + \cdots + E(X_n), \qquad (5.2.1)$$

$$Var(S) = Var(X_1) + Var(X_2) + \cdots + Var(X_n). \qquad (5.2.2)$$

In general, the distribution of S is quite complicated, but in certain instances simplification is possible. The use of transforms is a substantial convenience in these situations. The Laplace transform of S is

$$L_S(z) = E(e^{-zS})$$

$$= E\{e^{-z(X_1+X_2+\cdots+X_n)}\}$$

$$= E\{e^{-zX_1}e^{-zX_2}\cdots e^{-zX_n}\}$$

$$= E(e^{-zX_1})E(e^{-zX_2})\cdots E(e^{-zX_n})$$

$$= \prod_{i=1}^{n} L_{X_i}(z). \tag{5.2.3}$$

Since the Laplace transform uniquely defines the distribution, it may be possible to identify (5.2.3) as the Laplace transform of some distribution, which is therefore that of S. The following example illustrates this idea.

Example 5.2.1. Sum of Gamma Random Variables

Suppose that X_j has a gamma distribution (section 4.12) with pdf

$$f_{X_j}(x) = \frac{\lambda(\lambda x)^{\alpha_j-1}e^{-\lambda x}}{\Gamma(\alpha_j)}, \quad x>0 \tag{5.2.4}$$

and Laplace transform

$$L_{X_j}(z) = \left(\frac{\lambda}{\lambda+z}\right)^{\alpha_j}. \tag{5.2.5}$$

From (5.2.3), it follows that

$$L_S(z) = \left(\frac{\lambda}{\lambda+z}\right)^{\alpha_1+\alpha_2+\cdots+\alpha_n}. \tag{5.2.6}$$

We recognize (5.2.6) as the Laplace transform of a gamma random variable with parameters λ and $\alpha_1+\alpha_2+\cdots+\alpha_n$. Thus S is also a gamma random variable, with pdf

$$f_S(x) = \frac{\lambda(\lambda x)^{\alpha_1+\alpha_2+\cdots+\alpha_n-1}e^{-\lambda x}}{\Gamma(\alpha_1+\alpha_2+\cdots\alpha_n)}, \quad x>0. \tag{5.2.7}$$

In most practical applications, it is not possible to recognize (5.2.3) as the Laplace transform of a particular distribution. For large n, however, one may use the central limit theorem to approximate the distribution of S by a normal distribution with mean and variance given by (5.2.1) and (5.2.2) respectively.

Example 5.2.2.

A study of a group insured for drug claims reveals the following claim patterns, on an annual basis.

Coverage	Number insured	Expected cost per insured	Standard Deviation per insured
Single	786	76	42
Family	592	187	77

From (5.2.1) and (5.2.2), we obtain

$$E(S) = 786(76) + 592(187) = 170{,}440$$

$$Var(S) = 786(42)^2 + 592(77)^2 = (2{,}212.8)^2.$$

Thus

$$F_S(x) \approx \Phi(\frac{x-170{,}440}{2{,}212.8})$$

where $\Phi(x)$ is the standard normal cdf. For example, the probability of observing claims in excess of 175,000 dollars is

$$1 - F_S(175{,}000) \approx 1 - \Phi(2.06) = .0197.$$

More accurate methods for the approximation of the distribution of S are described in later chapters. For small n one can calculate the distribution of S recursively in some instances by using the following procedure.

Let $S_k = X_1 + X_2 + \cdots + X_k$, $k=1,2,\ldots,n$, denote the sum of the first k random variables. We shall assume for simplicity that the distribution of the X_k's is discrete, defined on the non-negative integers. Then, for $k=1,2,\ldots,n$, the pf of the partial sum S_k is

$$f_{S_k}(x) = Pr\{X_1 + X_2 + \cdots + X_k = x\}; \quad x = 0,1,2,\ldots \quad . \tag{5.2.8}$$

Now, $f_{S_1}(x) = Pr\{X_1 = x\} = f_{X_1}(x)$, and for $k>1$,

$$f_{S_k}(x) = \sum_{y=0}^{x} f_{S_{k-1}}(x-y) f_{X_k}(y); \quad x = 0,1,2,\ldots \quad . \tag{5.2.9}$$

Thus one can compute $f_{S_2}(x)$ from (5.2.9), and then $f_{S_3}(x)$, $f_{S_4}(x)$,... until one obtains $f_{S_n}(x) = f_S(x)$. This "brute force" method is not recommended if there is a special structure inherent in the distribution of the X_k's, as is the case in life insurance and when the X_k are identically distributed, as well as independent. Furthermore, if the X_k's have a continuous distribution, the sum in (5.2.9) are replaced by integrals, which are normally less convenient computationally.

Example 5.2.3.

Three independent risks have the following claim size distributions $f_{X_j}(x) = Pr(X_j = x)$:

$$Pr\{X_j = x\}$$

j	$x=0$	$x=1$	$x=2$	$x=3$
1	.3	.2	.4	.1
2	.6	.1	.3	0
3	.4	.2	0	.4

We first compute the distribution $f_{S_2}(x)$ of X_1+X_2 from (5.2.9) with $f_{S_1}(x) = f_{X_1}(x)$. Substitution of $x = 0$ into (5.2.9) yields, for example

$$f_{S_2}(0) = f_{X_1}(0)f_{X_2}(0) = (.3)(.6) = .18$$

$$f_{S_2}(1) = f_{X_1}(0)f_{X_2}(1) + f_{X_1}(1)f_{X_2}(0) = (.3)(.1) + (.2)(.6) = .15$$

Continuing in this manner, we find the following values for $f_{S_2}(x)$:

x	0	1	2	3	4	5
$f_{S_2}(x)$	.18	.15	.35	.16	.13	.03

Next we use these values in a second application of (5.2.9) with $k = 3$. Thus, for example,

$$f_{S_3}(0) = f_{S_2}(0)f_{X_3}(0) = .072$$

$$f_{S_3}(1) = f_{S_2}(0)f_{X_3}(1) + f_{S_2}(1)f_{X_3}(0) = .096.$$

Again we continue, and obtain the following values for $f_{S_3}(x)$:

x	0	1	2	3	4	5	6	7	8
$f_{S_3}(x)$	.072	.096	.170	.206	.144	.178	.070	.052	.012

This procedure is normally continued until we compute $f_{S_n}(x) = f_S(x)$. In this particular case, $n = 3$, and so the procedure is complete.

In many cases, there is a non-zero probability that a no claim occurs for the j-th risk. Thus, let

$$q_j = Pr(X_j > 0) \qquad (5.2.10)$$

and so $1 - q_j = Pr(X_j = 0)$. Then

$$Pr(X_j \leq x) = 1 - q_j + q_j Pr(X_j \leq x \mid X_j > 0).$$

If we let $Y_j = X_j \mid X_j > 0$ represent the claim costs when a positive claim occurs, then the df of X_j can be written in terms of the df of Y_j as

$$F_{X_j}(x) = 1 - q_j + q_j F_{Y_j}(x), \quad x \geq 0, \tag{5.2.11}$$

where $F_{Y_j}(0) = 0$ by definition. F_{Y_j} is called the claim size distribution or the severity distribution for the j-th risk. From (5.2.11),

$$\int_0^\infty e^{-zx} dF_{X_j}(x) = 1 - q_j + q_j \int_0^\infty e^{-zx} dF_{Y_j}(x),$$

or

$$L_{X_j}(z) = 1 - q_j + q_j L_{Y_j}(z). \tag{5.2.12}$$

Thus, the Laplace transform of the total claims (5.2.3) becomes

$$L_S(z) = \prod_{i=1}^n \{1 - q_j + q_j L_{Y_j}(z)\}. \tag{5.2.13}$$

Various methods for the evaluation of the distribution of S for special cases of (5.2.13) will be discussed in following sections.

Numerical Illustration 5.2.1.

Three independent risks have claim probabilities, claim size distributions and moments as follows:

j	q_j	$Pr\{Y_j=y\}$ $y=1$	$y=2$	$y=3$	$y=4$	$E[Y_j]$	$E[Y_j^2]$	$E[Y_j^3]$
1	.10	.10	.20	.30	.40	3.0	10.0	35.4
2	.20	.20	.30	.50	0	2.3	5.9	16.1
3	.30	0	0	.50	.50	3.5	12.5	45.5

The unconditional distributions of claim costs for the three risks are as follows:

j	$Pr\{X_j=x\}$ $x=0$	$x=1$	$x=2$	$x=3$	$x=4$
1	.90	.01	.02	.03	.04
2	.80	.04	.06	.10	0
3	.70	0	0	.15	.15

The distribution of $S = X_1 + X_2 + X_3$ is computed in the following table by first obtaining the distribution of $X_1 + X_2$; i.e.

$$f_{X_1+X_2}(x) = f_{X_1}*f_{X_2}(x) = \sum_{y=0}^{x} f_{X_1}(y)f_{X_2}(x-y)$$

and then computing

$$f_{X_1+X_2+X_3}(x) = f_{X_1+X_2}*f_{X_3}(x).$$

x	$f_{X_1}(x)$	$f_{X_2}(x)$	$f_{X_3}(x)$	$f_{X_1}*f_{X_2}(x)$	$f_{X_1}*f_{X_2}*f_{X_3}(x)$
(1)	(2)	(3)	(4)	(5)=(2)*(3)	(6)=(5)*(4)
0	.90	.80	.70	.7200	.50400
1	.01	.04	-	.0440	.03080
2	.02	.06	-	.0704	.04928
3	.03	.10	.15	.1154	.18878
4	.04	-	.15	.0354	.13938
5	-	-	-	.0054	.02094
6	-	-	-	.0054	.03165
7	-	-	-	.0040	.02542
8	-	-	-	-	.00612
9	-	-	-	-	.00162
10	-	-	-	-	.00141
11	-	-	-	-	.00060
Total	1.00	1.00	1.00	1.0000	1.00000

The moments of S are calculated by differentiating (5.2.13) as

$$\mu_1' = \sum_{j=1}^{3} q_j E[Y_j] = .10(3.0) + .20(2.3) + .30(3.5) = 1.81,$$

$$\mu_2 = \sum_{j=1}^{3} q_j E[Y_j^2] - \sum_{j=1}^{3} q_j^2 \{E[Y_j]\}^2 = 4.5259,$$

$$\mu_3 = \sum_{j=1}^{3} q_j E[Y_j^3] - 3\sum_{j=1}^{3} q_j^2 E[Y_j]E[Y_j^2] + 2\sum_{j=1}^{3} q_j^3 \{E[Y_j]\}^3 = 8.63302201.$$

Alternatively, the moments can be calculated directly from the distribution of $f_{X_1}*f_{X_2}*f_{X_3}(x)$ as given above.

Numerical Illustration 5.2.2. Group Life Insurance

A small manufacturing business in Canada has a group life insurance contract on its 14 permanent employees. The actuary for the insurer has selected the 1969-75 Canadian Institute of Actuaries Mortality Table (ultimate rates) to represent the mortality of the group.

Each employee is insured for the amount of his or her salary rounded up to the next 1,000 dollars. The group's data are given below:

Employee j	Age	Sex	Benefit b_j	Mortality Rate q_j
1	20	M	15,000	.00149
2	23	M	16,000	.00142
3	27	M	20,000	.00128
4	30	M	28,000	.00122
5	31	M	31,000	.00123
6	46	M	18,000	.00353
7	47	M	26,000	.00394
8	49	M	24,000	.00484
9	64	M	60,000	.02182
10	17	F	14,000	.00050
11	22	F	17,000	.00050
12	26	F	19,000	.00054
13	37	F	30,000	.00103
14	55	F	55,000	.00479
Total			373,000	

As in numerical illustration 5.2.1, the first three moments are calculated as:

$$\mu_1' = \sum_{j=1}^{14} q_j b_j = 2,054.41,$$

$$\mu_2 = \sum_{j=1}^{14} q_j b_j^2 - \sum_{j=1}^{14} q_j^2 b_j^2 = \sum_{j=1}^{14} q_j (1-q_j) b_j^2 = 1.025335632 \times 10^8$$

and

$$\mu_3 = \sum_{j=1}^{14} q_j b_j^3 - 3\sum_{j=1}^{14} q_j^2 b_j^3 + 2\sum_{j=1}^{14} q_j^3 b_j^3 = \sum_{j=1}^{14} q_j (1-q_j)(1-2q_j) b_j^3 = 5.4687849 \times 10^{12}.$$

The **index of skewness** is calculated as

$$\mu_3\{\mu_2\}^{-\frac{3}{2}} = 5.26734515.$$

5.3 EVALUATION OF THE DISTRIBUTION OF TOTAL CLAIMS

The distribution of S based on equations (5.2.8) and (5.2.9) is not easily evaluated in general when the number of risks is large because the required computer time grows rapidly as n increases. Some simplification is possible when the severities are of some convenient form or when all the claim probabilities or severities are equal, as the following examples demonstrate.

Example 5.3.1. Distributions closed under convolution

Suppose that the claim severities, which are assumed to be strictly positive, are of the same form with one parameter varying from risk to risk. Further suppose that the distribution of the sum of two severities is of the same form but with the parameter replaced by the sum of the parameters of the two severity distributions; i.e., if

$$F_{Y_j}(x) = F(x;\theta_j) \text{ for } j = 1,2,\ldots,n \tag{5.3.1}$$

then

$$F_{Y_i+Y_j}(x) = F_{Y_i}*F_{Y_j}(x) = F(x;\theta_i+\theta_j). \tag{5.3.2}$$

Then from (5.2.3), the LT of the total loss S becomes

$$
\begin{aligned}
L_S(z) &= \prod_{j=1}^{n}\{p_j+q_jL_{Y_j}(z)\} \\
&= \{\prod_{j=1}^{n}p_j\}\{\prod_{j=1}^{n}[1+\frac{q_j}{p_j}L(z;\theta_j)]\} \\
&= \{\prod_{j=1}^{n}p_j\}\{1+\sum_{j=1}^{n}\frac{q_j}{p_j}L(z;\theta_j)+\sum_{j=1}^{n}\sum_{k=1}^{n}\frac{q_jq_k}{p_jp_k}L(z;\theta_j+\theta_k)+\cdots\}
\end{aligned}
\tag{5.3.3}
$$

where $L(z;\theta)$ is the LT associated with $F(x;\theta)$. The right-hand side of equation (5.3.3) can be seen to be a linear combination of transforms of the same type. If n is not too large, one can evaluate (5.3.3) quite easily. For $n = 3$, it becomes after inversion

$$F_S(x) = p_1p_2p_3 + q_1p_2p_3F(x;\theta_1) + p_1q_2p_3F(x;\theta_2) + p_1p_2q_3F(x;\theta_3)$$

$$+ q_1q_2p_3F(x;\theta_1+\theta_2) + q_1p_2q_3F(x;\theta_1+\theta_3) + p_1q_2q_3F(x;\theta_2+\theta_3)$$

$$+ q_1q_2q_3F(x;\theta_1+\theta_2+\theta_3).$$

If the q_j's are small, one can obtain an approximate distribution by taking a few terms in the final expression of (5.3.3).

Severity distributions satisfying (5.3.2) include the gamma (4.12.1) with $\alpha = \theta$ and the inverse Gaussian (4.13.2) with $\mu = \theta$.

Example 5.3.2. Identical Risks

If all risks are identical, equation (5.2.13) becomes the LT for the compound binomial distribution

$$L_S(z) = \{p+qL_Y(z)\}^n$$

$$= \{1+q[L_Y(z)-1]\}^n \qquad\qquad (5.3.4)$$

which is the Laplace transform of a compound binomial distribution (see (2.9.7) and (4.3.2)).

Evaluation of this function will be discussed in chapter 6.

These examples demonstrate how the computations are simplified in some situations. In general, one may be forced to convolute recursively over the partial sums $S_j = X_j + S_{j-1}$ for $j = 2,3,\ldots,n$ beginning with $S_1 = X_1$. In the discrete case this yields

$$f_{S_j}(x) = f_{S_{j-1}} * f_{X_j}(x) \qquad\qquad (5.3.5)$$

and, in the continuous case, the density of S_j satisfies

$$f_{S_j}(x) = \{\prod_{i=1}^{j-1} p_i\} q_j f_{Y_j}(x) + p_j f_{S_{j-1}}(x) + q_j \int_0^x f_{S_{j-1}}(x-y) f_{Y_j}(y) dy \qquad (5.3.6)$$

in terms of the distribution of Y_j in (5.2.11). Clearly, the number of computations using (5.3.5) quickly becomes large for large values of n, and an approximate method may be desirable. Similarly in (5.3.6), numerical integration procedures are usually required. Use of these procedures at each stage of the calculations can easily become unwieldy. In the next two sections we examine how the computations can be carried out efficiently in the case of a typical life insurance portfolio.

5.4 LIFE INSURANCE

In some insurance situations, the size of the claim or the severity is fixed in advance. A typical situation is a life insurance with a fixed benefit of say 10,000 dollars or 100,000 dollars. Although it may not be apparent, the situation of fixed severity also arises in disability insurance if at the time of disability a disabled life reserve is set up and the subsequent period of disability is treated separately with an annuity on a disabled life.

We shall assume that the amounts of insurance are all multiples of some convenient unit such as 1,000 dollars or 10,000 dollars. In the case where the lowest common divisor of the amounts of insurance is too small (e.g. one dollar), for the purpose of the subsequent calculations, one might simply round each amount to some more convenient unit. This will generally give sufficiently accurate results as long as the unit used is not too large.

We now use the selected unit of measurement so that all policies are of integral amounts. We will consider two methods of calculation of the distribution of total claims.

Method 1: Direct Calculation

Suppose that the portfolio consists of n risks with claim probabilities q_j; $j = 1, 2, \ldots, n$ and insured amount b_j; $j = 1, 2, \ldots, n$. Then the pf of total claims is given by

$$f_S(x) = f_{X_1} * f_{X_2} * \cdots * f_{X_n}(x) \tag{5.4.1}$$

where

$$f_{X_j}(x) = \begin{cases} p_j, & x{=}0; \\ q_j, & x{=}b_j. \end{cases} \tag{5.4.2}$$

The distribution (5.4.1) can be calculated recursively over the partial sums $S_j = S_{j-1} + X_j$ for $j = 2, 3, \ldots, n$ beginning with $S_1 = X_1$. In this case, formula (5.3.5) reduces to

$$f_{S_j}(x) = \begin{cases} f_{S_{j-1}}(x) f_{X_j}(0), & x < b_j; \\ f_{S_{j-1}}(x) f_{X_j}(0) + f_{S_{j-1}}(x - b_j) f_{X_j}(b_j), & x \geq b_j \end{cases}$$

$$= \begin{cases} p_j f_{S_{j-1}}(x), & x < b_j; \\ p_j f_{S_{j-1}}(x) + q_j f_{S_{j-1}}(x - b_j), & x \geq b_j. \end{cases} \tag{5.4.3}$$

If one wishes to calculate the distribution of total claims up to some value r, the computer time involved, as measured by the number of multiplications, can be seen to be of order nr. If both r and n are large, e.g. $r = 10{,}000$ and $n = 10{,}000$, the number of computations can be prohibitive. However, it can be seen that this method can be computationally much more efficient than using equation (5.3.5) directly since (5.3.5) requires a number of multiplications that is of order nr^2. The method of this section simply eliminates $x-1$ multiplications of zero in (5.3.5).

Numerical Illustration 5.4.1.

Consider the group life insurance portfolio of 14 lives considered in numerical illustration 5.2.2. To begin calculations, we let $f_{S_1}(x) = f_{X_1}(x)$ and proceed to use equation (5.4.3) successively for $j = 2, 3, \ldots, 14$. The first few calculations are as follows (using units of 1,000 dollars):

$$f_{S_1}(0) = .99851,$$

$$f_{S_1}(15) = .00149,$$

$$f_{S_2}(0) = p_2 f_{S_1}(0) = .99709212,$$

$$f_{S_2}(15) = p_2 f_{S_1}(15) = .00148788,$$

$$f_{S_2}(16) = p_2 f_{S_1}(16) + q_2 f_{S_1}(0) = .00141788,$$

$$f_{S_2}(31) = p_2 f_{S_1}(31) + q_2 f_{S_1}(15) = .0000021158.$$

The final values of the df $F_S(x)$ are given below for $x = 0, \ldots, 79$ are given below:

x	$F_S(x)$	x	$F_S(x)$	x	$F_S(x)$	x	$F_S(x)$
0	0.95273905	20	0.96157969	40	0.97335098	60	0.99933062
1	0.95273905	21	0.96157969	41	0.97335892	61	0.99933187
2	0.95273905	22	0.96157969	42	0.97338128	62	0.99933191
3	0.95273905	23	0.96157969	43	0.97338740	63	0.99933193
4	0.95273905	24	0.96621337	44	0.97340884	64	0.99933198
5	0.95273905	25	0.96621337	45	0.97341351	65	0.99933202
6	0.95273905	26	0.96998201	46	0.97342561	66	0.99933206
7	0.95273905	27	0.96998201	47	0.97342840	67	0.99944309
8	0.95273905	28	0.97114577	48	0.97343397	68	0.99933217
9	0.95273905	29	0.97114648	49	0.97343866	69	0.99933450
10	0.95273905	30	0.97212950	50	0.97345889	70	0.99934141
11	0.95273905	31	0.97330507	51	0.97346040	71	0.99934796
12	0.95273905	32	0.97330747	52	0.97346606	72	0.99935031
13	0.95273905	33	0.97331344	53	0.97346608	73	0.99936659
14	0.95321566	34	0.97331962	54	0.97347547	74	0.99937973
15	0.95463736	35	0.97332386	55	0.97806678	75	0.99941735
16	0.95599217	36	0.97332585	56	0.97807068	76	0.99944759
17	0.95646878	37	0.97332829	57	0.97807536	77	0.99945823
18	0.95984386	38	0.97333493	58	0.97807660	78	0.99953355
19	0.96035862	39	0.97334251	59	0.97807808	79	0.99956734

This approach is reasonable when n is not too large, but for larger groups an alternative method is needed. The following approach allows for the distribution to be calculated recursively.

Method 2: Recursive Calculation

We first subdivide the portfolio into subportfolios according to policy size and claim probability. Let n_{ij} be the number of policies of size i (where $i = 1,2,\ldots,r$) and claim probability q_j (where $j = 1,2,\ldots,m$). Then the pgf of total claims may be written as

$$P_S(z) = \prod_{i=1}^{r} \prod_{j=1}^{m} (1-q_j+q_j z^i)^{n_{ij}}. \tag{5.4.4}$$

The logarithm of the pgf is

$$\log P_S(z) = \sum_{i=1}^{r} \sum_{j=1}^{m} n_{ij} \log(1-q_j+q_j z^i). \tag{5.4.5}$$

We now differentiate (5.4.5) to obtain

$$P_S'(z) = \{\sum_{i=1}^{r} \sum_{j=1}^{m} i q_j n_{ij} z^{i-1}(1-q_j+q_j z^i)^{-1}\} P_S(z). \tag{5.4.6}$$

Setting $z = 1$ in (5.4.6) yields the mean of the total claims distribution, namely

$$E(S) = P_S'(1) = \sum_{i=1}^{r} \sum_{j=1}^{m} i q_j n_{ij}. \tag{5.4.7}$$

Now, (5.4.6) may be rewritten as

$$zP_S'(z) = \{\sum_{i=1}^{r} \sum_{j=1}^{m} i n_{ij} (\frac{q_j}{1-q_j} z^i)(1 + \frac{q_j}{1-q_j} z^i)^{-1}\} P_S(z)$$

$$= \{\sum_{i=1}^{r} \sum_{j=1}^{m} i n_{ij} \sum_{k=1}^{\infty} (-1)^{k-1} (\frac{q_j}{1-q_j})^k z^{ik}\} P_S(z) \tag{5.4.8}$$

for $|z| < \min_{i,j}\{q_j^{-1}(1-q_j)\}^{\frac{1}{i}}$. The first term on the right hand side of (5.4.8) may be rewritten as

$$\sum_{i=1}^{r} \sum_{k=1}^{\infty} h(i,k) z^{ik}$$

where

$$h(i,k) = i(-1)^{k-1} \sum_{j=1}^{m} n_{ij} (\frac{q_j}{1-q_j})^k. \tag{5.4.9}$$

Thus, (5.4.8) may be written as

$$zP'_S(z) = \{\sum_{i=1}^{r} \sum_{k=1}^{\infty} h(i,k) z^{ik}\} P_S(z). \tag{5.4.10}$$

The coefficient of z^x on the left hand side of (5.4.10) is $x f_S(x)$ where $f_S(x)$ is the coefficient of z^x in $P_S(z)$. The right hand side of (5.4.10) is a convolution, and the coefficient of z^x is thus given by

$$\sum_{ik \leq x} h(i,k) f_S(x-ik). \tag{5.4.11}$$

A simpler way of writing (5.4.11) is

$$\sum_{i=1}^{x} \sum_{k=1}^{[\frac{x}{i}]} h(i,k) f_S(x-ik) \tag{5.4.12}$$

where $[x]$ denotes the greatest integer in x. Finally, since $h(i,k) = 0$ if $i > x$, one may equate coefficients of z^x on both sides of (5.4.10) and divide by x to obtain

$$f_S(x) = \frac{1}{x} \sum_{i=1}^{\min(x,r)} \sum_{k=1}^{[\frac{x}{i}]} h(i,k) f_S(x-ik); \quad n \geq 1. \tag{5.4.13}$$

Now,

$$f_S(0) = P_S(0) = \prod_{i=1}^{r} \prod_{j=1}^{m} (1-q_j)^{n_{ij}}, \tag{5.4.14}$$

and from (5.4.13),

$$f_S(1) = h(1,1) f_S(0), \tag{5.4.15}$$

$$f_S(2) = \frac{1}{2} \{h(1,1) f_S(1) + [h(1,2) + h(2,1)] f_S(0)\}, \ldots \tag{5.4.16}$$

The probabilities $\{f_S(x); x = 1,2,\ldots,\}$ may be calculated recursively using (5.4.13), beginning with (5.4.14).

It can be seen from (5.4.9) that $h(i,k)$ is a weighted sum of the k-th power of $\frac{q_j}{1-q_j}$, $j = 1,2,\ldots,m$. When q_j is close to zero, $(\frac{q_j}{1-q_j})^k$ is small. Consequently, the magnitude of $h(i,k)$ decreases rapidly as k increases. This suggests that the inner summation in (5.4.13) can be limited to a small number of terms without significant loss of accuracy in computations while speeding up the computations considerably.

If we limit k to a maximum of K terms, let

$$f_S^{(K)}(x) = \frac{1}{x} \sum_{i=1}^{\min(x,r)} \sum_{k=1}^{\min(K,[\frac{x}{i}])} h(i,k) f_S^{(K)}(x-ik) \qquad (5.4.17)$$

denote the approximation using at most K terms in (5.4.13). De Pril (1988) shows that if $q_j < 1/2$, $j = 1, 2, \ldots, m$, then

$$\sum_{x=0}^{M} |f_S(x) - f_S^{(K)}(x)| < e^{\delta(K)} - 1 \qquad (5.4.18)$$

where

$$\delta(K) = \frac{1}{K+1} \sum_{i=1}^{r} \sum_{j=1}^{m} n_{ij} \frac{1-q_j}{1-2q_j} \left(\frac{q_j}{1-q_j}\right)^{K+1} \qquad (5.4.19)$$

and $M = \sum_{i=1}^{r} \sum_{j=1}^{m} i n_{ij}$ is the maximum possible aggregate claim amount.

The value of $\delta(K)$ is easily calculated for any value of K. Equation (5.4.18) provides an upper bound on the sum of the absolute errors over the entire distribution of aggregate claims and can be used to guarantee accuracy of results when a limited number of terms is used in (5.4.17).

Numerical Illustration 5.4.2.

The group life insurance portfolio considered in the previous numerical illustrations is reconsidered here to demonstrate the application of the recursive method. The value of q_j and the non-zero rows of the matrix of $n_{i,j}$ values are as follows:

j	$1000q_j$	$i=14$	15	16	17	18	19	20	24	26	28	30	31	55	60
1	.50	1	0	0	1	0	0	0	0	0	0	0	0	0	0
2	.54	0	0	0	0	0	1	0	0	0	0	0	0	0	0
3	1.03	0	0	0	0	0	0	0	0	0	0	1	0	0	0
4	1.22	0	0	0	0	0	0	0	0	0	1	0	0	0	0
5	1.23	0	0	0	0	0	0	0	0	0	0	0	1	0	0
6	1.28	0	0	0	0	0	0	1	0	0	0	0	0	0	0
7	1.42	0	0	1	0	0	0	0	0	0	0	0	0	0	0
8	1.49	0	1	0	0	0	0	0	0	0	0	0	0	0	0
9	3.53	0	0	0	0	1	0	0	0	0	0	0	0	0	0
10	3.94	0	0	0	0	0	0	0	0	1	0	0	0	0	0
11	4.79	0	0	0	0	0	0	0	0	0	0	0	0	1	0
12	4.84	0	0	0	0	0	0	0	1	0	0	0	0	0	0
13	21.82	0	0	0	0	0	0	0	0	0	0	0	0	0	1

Using (5.4.19), we find that $\delta(1) = 5.947 \times 10^{-4}$, $\delta(2) = 1.170 \times 10^{-5}$, $\delta(3) = 2.548 \times 10^{-7}$ and $\delta(4) = 5.656 \times 10^{-9}$. Hence, equation (5.4.17) with $K = 4$ will give us about 8 decimal place accuracy. The (non-zero) values of $h(i,k)$ computed using (5.4.9) are as follows:

i	$k=1$	$k=2$	$k=3$	$k=4$
14	7.0035018E-03	-3.5035025E-06	1.7526276E-09	-8.7675218E-13
15	2.2383351E-02	-3.3400962E-05	4.9841694E-08	-7.4374944E-11
16	2.2752309E-02	-3.2354221E-05	4.6008325E-08	-6.5424723E-11
17	8.5042522E-03	-4.2542531E-06	2.1281907E-09	-1.0646277E-12
18	6.3765090E-02	-2.2588816E-04	8.0020991E-07	-2.8347477E-09
19	1.0265543E-02	-5.5463884E-06	2.9966680E-09	-1.6190750E-12
20	2.5632810E-02	-3.2852048E-05	4.2104515E-08	-5.3962851E-11
24	1.1672495E-01	-5.6769638E-04	2.7610139E-06	-1.3428300E-08
26	1.0284521E-01	-4.0681297E-04	1.6091833E-06	-6.3652612E-09
28	3.4201726E-02	-4.1777074E-05	5.1030287E-08	-6.2332996E-11
30	3.0931860E-02	-3.1892665E-05	3.2883315E-08	-3.3904736E-11
31	3.8176959E-02	-4.7015487E-05	5.7900266E-08	-7.1305033E-11
55	2.6471800E-01	-1.2741022E-03	6.1323232E-06	-2.9515207E-08
60	1.3384040E-00	-2.9855420E-02	6.6597689E-04	-1.4855768E-05

The values of $f_S(x)$ and the associated cdf $F_S(x)$ calculated using (5.4.17) with $K = 4$ and (5.4.14) are as follows:

x	$f_S(x)$	$F_S(x)$	x	$f_S(x)$	$F_S(x)$
0	9.5273905E-01	0.95273905	38	6.6436439E-06	0.97333493
14	4.7660783E-04	0.95321566	39	7.5742253E-06	0.97334251
15	1.4216995E-03	0.95463736	40	8.4744508E-06	0.97335098
16	1.3548133E-03	0.95599217	41	7.9416543E-06	0.97335892
17	4.7660783E-04	0.95646878	42	2.2356100E-05	0.97338128
18	3.3750829E-03	0.95984386	43	6.1253961E-06	0.97338740
19	5.1475706E-04	0.96035862	44	2.1435448E-05	0.97340884
20	1.2210690E-03	0.96157969	45	4.6721584E-06	0.97341351
24	4.6336840E-03	0.96621337	46	1.2100769E-05	0.97342561
26	3.7686403E-03	0.96998201	47	2.7915140E-06	0.97342840
28	1.1637614E-03	0.97114577	48	5.5621896E-05	0.97343397
29	7.1120536E-07	0.97114649	49	4.6964950E-06	0.97343866
30	9.8301077E-04	0.97212950	50	2.0226469E-05	0.97345889
31	1.1755723E-03	0.97330507	51	1.5103585E-06	0.97346040
32	2.3995910E-06	0.97330747	52	5.6661624E-06	0.97346607
33	5.9716305E-06	0.97331344	53	1.3705553E-08	0.97346608
34	6.1784053E-06	0.97331962	54	9.3923168E-06	0.97347547
35	4.2424878E-06	0.97332386	55	4.5913084E-03	0.97806678
36	1.9938909E-06	0.97332585	56	3.9003832E-06	0.97807068
37	2.4343694E-06	0.97332829	57	4.6823253E-06	0.97807536

It can be seen that the values in the last column of this table are identical to the corresponding values from numerical illustration 5.4.1 based on the first method.

Numerical Illustration 5.4.3.

For the purpose of illustrating the effect of the size of the portfolio, consider a portfolio consisting of 1400 independent lives, with exactly 100 lives like each life in the group life portfolio of the previous numerical illustrations. From numerical illustration 5.2.2, it is seen that the mean and variance of the distribution of total claims are 205,441 and $1.025335632 \times 10^{10}$ respectively. The values of $n_{i,j}$ are now either 100 or 0. From (5.4.9), it can be seen that each $h(i,k)$ is now 100 times larger than that of the previous example. The distribution of total claims can be computed as in the previous example. The following table gives some values of the distribution function of total claims (as before x is measured in units of 1000 dollars).

x	$F_S(x)$	x	$F_S(x)$	x	$F_S(x)$	x	$F_S(x)$
0	.00789581	200	.51793382	400	.96031865	600	.99927281
8	.00789581	208	.55208736	408	.96528977	608	.99939248
16	.01059183	216	.57594360	416	.96999808	616	.99950270
24	.01906263	224	.60583632	424	.97360199	624	.99958630
32	.02561396	232	.63412023	432	.97694855	632	.99965590
40	.02979597	240	.66687534	440	.98031827	640	.99971784
48	.03774849	248	.68632432	448	.98297484	648	.99976679
56	.04770335	256	.71292641	456	.98515668	656	.99980876
64	.06976756	264	.73984823	464	.98728185	664	.99984205
72	.07610528	272	.76061061	472	.98914069	672	.99987063
80	.10013432	280	.78007667	480	.99068429	680	.99989481
88	.12399672	288	.80016248	488	.99194854	688	.99991371
96	.13839960	296	.82073766	496	.99321771	696	.99992950
104	.15945674	304	.83672920	504	.99421982	704	.99994275
112	.18004988	312	.85121374	512	.99504627	712	.99995364
120	.22162539	320	.86849112	520	.99580992	720	.99996222
128	.23569706	328	.88253629	528	.99644624	728	.99996932
136	.26335063	336	.89343529	536	.99701494	736	.99997545
144	.30172723	344	.90530546	544	.99745896	744	.99998004
152	.33041683	352	.91610001	552	.99785787	752	.99998383
160	.35497038	360	.92599796	560	.99821941	760	.99998707
168	.38635038	368	.93340851	568	.99850204	768	.99998955
176	.42177800	376	.94180939	576	.99873887	776	.99999162
184	.45476409	384	.94903173	584	.99895067	784	.99999326
192	.47881084	392	.95482932	592	.99912971	792	.99999461

From numerical illustration 5.2.2, the mean and variance of total claims for this portfolio of 1400 lives are $\mu_1 = 205{,}441$ dollars and $\mu_2 = 1.025335632 \times 10^{10}$. The coefficient of skewness is calculated as $\mu_3\{\mu_2\}^{-3/2} = .5267345$ which is exactly one-tenth of the value of 5.26734515 for the corresponding group of 14 lives. This indicates that the distribution is much more symmetric.

5.5 APPROXIMATIONS TO THE DISTRIBUTION OF TOTAL CLAIMS

For large portfolios, it may be useful to consider approximating the distribution of total claims. This can be done in a variety of ways, most of which are sufficiently general in nature to be applied not only to the models in this chapter but also to the models considered in later chapters. Consequently, we consider here only the normal approximation based on the **central limit theorem** for non-identical random variables which is now stated without proof.

Theorem 5.5.1. Let $X_1, X_2, \ldots$ be a sequence of independent random variables with df's $F_1(x), F_2(x), \ldots$, means $\mu_1, \mu_2, \ldots$ and variances $\sigma_1^2, \sigma_2^2, \ldots$. Let $S = X_1 + X_2 + \cdots + X_n$, $\mu = \mu_1 + \mu_2 + \cdots + \mu_n$ and $\sigma^2 = \sigma_1^2 + \sigma_2^2 + \cdots + \sigma_n^2$. Then a necessary and sufficient condition for

$$\lim_{n \to \infty} Pr\{\frac{S-\mu}{\sigma} \leq x\} = \Phi(x) \tag{5.5.1}$$

where Φ is the standard normal df, is that for arbitrary $t > 0$,

$$\lim_{n \to \infty} \frac{1}{\sigma^2} \sum_{j=1}^{n} \int_{|y| > t\sigma} (y - \mu_j)^2 dF_j(y) = 0. \tag{5.5.2}$$

The regularity condition (5.5.2), known as the Lindeberg condition, (cf. Feller, 1971), is meant to ensure that the individual variances σ_j^2 are small as compared to their sum σ^2 in the sense that for given $\varepsilon > 0$ and all n sufficiently large

$$\frac{\sigma_j}{\sigma} < \varepsilon, \quad j = 1, 2, \ldots, n. \tag{5.5.3}$$

In most actuarial applications, the Lindeberg condition is satisfied and can be ignored. However, the reader should be aware of the regularity conditions, since they are not always satisfied. Feller (1971) constructs some examples where the condition is not satisfied. Approximate probability values for total claims can be obtained using (5.5.1), so that the sum S can be thought of as having a normal distribution with mean μ and variance σ^2.

In the special case where the true distribution of S is discrete on $\{0,1,2,...\}$, an improvement can be obtained by using a continuity correction to reflect the fact that a discrete distribution is being approximated by a continuous one. In this case, we adjust the value of S by a one-half interval so that

$$Pr\left\{\frac{S+\frac{1}{2}-\mu}{\sigma} \le x\right\} \approx \Phi(x). \tag{5.5.4}$$

The continuity correction will make very little difference when S is large; it is useful only for small values of S.

Numerical Illustration 5.5.1.

Consider the group life portfolio of numerical illustrations 5.2.2, 5.4.1 and 5.4.2. From numerical illustration 5.2.2, we have $\mu = 2,054.41$ dollars and $\sigma = 10,125.88574$ dollars. The probability that total claims will exceed 40,000 dollars is calculated using equation (5.5.4) as

$$Pr\{S>40\} = 1 - Pr\{S\le40\}$$

$$= 1 - Pr\left\{\frac{S+\frac{1}{2}-2.05441}{10.1258984} \le \frac{40.5-2.05441}{10.1258894}\right\}$$

$$\approx 1 - \Phi(3.79676) = 1-.9999 = .0001.$$

From numerical illustration 5.4.1, it can be seen that the true value is .02664902 which is significantly larger than the value based on the normal approximation. This is largely due to the fact that the distribution is not shaped like a normal distribution as exhibited by an index of skewness 5.27 (see numerical illustration 5.2.2) rather than zero. Since the normal approximation is based on large n, it is inappropriate to use this approximation for such a small portfolio.

Numerical Illustration 5.5.2.

We now reconsider the group life portfolio of 1400 lives of numerical illustration 5.4.3. For this group, we have $\mu = 205{,}441$ dollars and $\sigma = 101{,}258.8474$ dollars. The probability that total claims will exceed $1000n$ dollars is approximated as

$$Pr\{S>n\} = 1-Pr\{S\leq n\}$$

$$= 1-Pr\left\{ \frac{S+\frac{1}{2}-205.441}{101.258984} \leq \frac{n+.5-205.441}{101.258984} \right\}$$

$$\approx 1-\Phi\left(\frac{n-204.941}{101.258985} \right).$$

The true and approximate values are given below for a few values of n:

n	True	Approximate	Percentage Error
320	.1315	.1278	-2.8%
360	.0740	.0628	-15%
400	.0397	.0270	-32%
440	.0197	.0101	-49%
480	.0093	.0033	-65%
520	.0042	.0009	-79%
560	.0018	.0002	-89%
600	.0007	.0000	-100%

From the above values it can be seen that the approximate values underestimate the true probabilities with right-hand tail of the distribution. This results from the fact that some skewness remains in the portfolio as is exhibited by a coefficient of skewness of .5259.

Numerical Illustration 5.5.3.

We now increase the size of the group by a factor of 10 so that 14,000 lives are included. For this group, $\mu = 2{,}054{,}410$ dollars and $\sigma = 320{,}208.62$ dollars. The coefficient of skewness is .1666 indicating that some skewness still exists. Repeating the exercise of the previous numerical illustration for this group gives the following probabilities:

n	True	Approximate	Percentage Error
2400	.1409	.1402	-.5%
2450	.1106	.1083	-2%
2500	.0855	.0821	-4%
2550	.0650	.0690	-6%
2600	.0487	.0442	-9%
2650	.0359	.0314	-13%
2700	.0260	.0219	-16%
2750	.0186	.0149	-20%
2800	.0131	.0099	-24%
2850	.0091	.0065	-29%
2900	.0062	.0041	-34%
2950	.0042	.0026	-38%
3000	.0028	.0016	-43%
3050	.0018	.0009	-50%

It can be seen that even for such a large group, the normal approximations still underestimates the right-hand tail as a result of the remaining skewness.

5.6 REINSURANCE

The insurer's risk can be reduced by the use of reinsurance, in which another insurer (the reinsurer) acts as an insurer of the insurance company (the ceding company) originally covering the risk.

The reinsurance can take on several forms. If the reinsurer pays individual losses in excess of some limit, it is often called excess-of-loss (XL) reinsurance. The limit, which can be viewed as a deductible, has different names in different branches of insurance. In life insurance it is called the ceding company's retention level, because the company "retains" insurance up to that level. In other branches of insurance where the size of loss is unknown in advance, as in life insurance, the limit is variously called a deductible, a limit, a pooling point or an attachment point depending on the application.

The reinsurer may not insure all of the risk but rather assume a layer of reinsurance either directly or by itself obtaining reinsurance from another reinsurer.

Coinsurance is a mechanism where the insurance losses are split in some proportion between the reinsurer and the insurance company. Other reinsurance arrangements involving a combination of a deductible and coinsurance are common.

In most branches of insurance, reinsurance arrangements covering the aggregate of all risks in some pool also exist. For example, an insurer may obtain reinsurance coverage for losses in excess of some limit for all losses in its professional liability line. This type of reinsurance is useful in protecting the company against insolvency due to excessive claims on this coverage. Reinsurance covering a pool of risks in aggregate is called aggregate loss reinsurance or stop-loss reinsurance.

In group life and health insurance, frequently discussed in this chapter, the insurance programs are often "self-insured" up to some level by the sponsor of the group life or health insurance plan. In this case the plan sponsor, usually the employer or the employer's union acts as the insurer and an insurance company acts as reinsurer. This concept of self-insurance extends to individuals who cover losses up to some deductible.

Consider the individual risk model (5.2.1) in which the reinsurer pays losses in excess of some limit d for each of the n risks in the portfolio.

In this case, the maximum insurer's cost for an individual risk's loss is d. Consequently the insurer's claim size distribution can be described by

$$f_X^I(x) = \begin{cases} f_X(x), & x<d \\ 1-F_X(d-0), & x=d \\ 0, & x>d \end{cases} \tag{5.6.1}$$

where $f_X(x)$ is the probability density of the individual loss. The reinsurer will only suffer a loss when an individual loss exceeds d and the reinsurer's loss will be that portion in excess of d. Hence, the probability that the reinsurer will not suffer a loss for an individual risk is

$$p_j^* = p_j + q_j Pr\{X \le d\} = p_j + q_j F_X(d). \tag{5.6.2}$$

The distribution of the reinsurer's loss for the j-th risk is then,

$$f_X^R(x) = \begin{cases} p_j^*, & x=0 \\ f_X(x+d), & x>0. \end{cases} \qquad (5.6.3)$$

In the case of aggregate or stop-loss reinsurance, the reinsurer pays the excess of the sum of all claims combined for the risk over a deductible or limit, called the stop-loss or attachment point. If the distribution of aggregate losses is given by $f_S(x)$, $x \geq 0$, then the insurer's distribution of losses, $S_d^I = \min(S, d)$, is

$$f_{S_d^I}(x) = \begin{cases} f_S(x), & x<d \\ 1-F_S(x-0), & x=d \\ 0, & x>d \end{cases} \qquad (5.6.4)$$

and the distribution of the reinsurer's losses, $S_d^R = \max\{(S-d),0\} = (S-d)_+$, is

$$f_{S_d^R}(x) = \begin{cases} F_S(d), & x=0 \\ f_S(x+d), & x>d. \end{cases} \qquad (5.6.5)$$

The expected value of the reinsurer's losses is called the net stop-loss premium and is evaluated as

$$E[S_d^R] = E[(S-d)_+]$$

$$= \int_0^\infty (x-d)dF_S(x) - \int_0^d (x-d)dF_S(x) \qquad (5.6.6)$$

$$= E[S] - d + \int_0^d (x-d)\, d(1-F_S(x))$$

$$= E[S] - \int_0^d 1-F_S(x)dx \qquad (5.6.7)$$

upon integration by parts.

Since the reinsurer's expected losses and the insurer's expected losses must in total equal the total expected losses, we have

$$E[S_d^I] = E[S] - E[S_d^R]$$

$$= \int_0^d 1 - F_S(x)dx. \tag{5.6.8}$$

When the stop-loss limit d increases without limit, the insurer's cost is then

$$E[S] = \lim_{d \to \infty} E[S_d^I] = \int_0^\infty 1 - F_S(x)dx \tag{5.6.9}$$

and so the reinsurer's expected losses (5.6.7) can be rewritten as

$$E[S_d^R] = \int_d^\infty 1 - F_S(x)dx. \tag{5.6.10}$$

Example 5.6.1. Normal Distribution

Suppose that the distribution of S can be approximated by a Normal distribution with mean μ and variance σ^2. Then the net stop-loss premium is

$$E[S_d^R] = \int_d^\infty (x-d)dF_S(x)$$

$$= \int_d^\infty (x-d)f_S(x)dx$$

$$= \int_d^\infty (x-d) \frac{1}{\sqrt{2\pi}\sigma} e^{-\frac{1}{2}(\frac{x-\mu}{\sigma})^2} dx$$

$$= \int_d^\infty (x-\mu) \frac{1}{\sqrt{2\pi}\sigma} e^{-\frac{1}{2}(\frac{x-\mu}{\sigma})^2} dx - (d-\mu)[1-\Phi(\frac{d-\mu}{\sigma})]$$

$$= \frac{\sigma}{\sqrt{2\pi}} e^{-\frac{1}{2}(\frac{d-\mu}{\sigma})^2} - (d-\mu)[1-\Phi(\frac{d-\mu}{\sigma})].$$

Example 5.6.2. Exponential Tails

Suppose that the right-hand tail of the total claims distribution has an approximately exponential shape, i.e.

$$f_S(x) \approx c\alpha e^{-\alpha x}$$

for x sufficiently large. If d is also large, then the net stop-loss premium can be approximated as

$$E[S_d^R] = \int_d^\infty 1 - F_S(x)dx$$

$$= \int_d^\infty ce^{-\alpha x} dx$$

$$= \frac{c}{\alpha} e^{-\alpha d}, \quad d>0.$$

In this chapter (as well as in subsequent ones), we focus on arithmetic loss distributions; i.e. ones defined on the positive integers where the unit of measurement is some convenient one, such as 1,000 dollars. If $f_S(x)$ is defined only on the non-negative integers, then (5.6.6), (5.6.7) and (5.6.8) become

$$E[S_d^R] = \sum_{x=d+1}^{\infty} (x-d)f_S(x) \tag{5.6.11}$$

$$= E[S] - \sum_{x=0}^{d-1}\{1-F_S(x)\} \tag{5.6.12}$$

$$= \sum_{x=d}^{\infty}\{1-F_S(x)\}. \tag{5.6.13}$$

From (5.6.13), it can be seen that the net stop-loss premiums can be computed recursively as

$$E[S_{d+1}^R] = E[S_d^R] - \{1-F_S(d)\} \tag{5.6.14}$$

beginning with $E[S_0^R] = E[S]$. This recursive formula is very convenient since the starting point $E[S]$ can be calculated directly.

Similarly, it can be shown that the second raw moment can be calculated recursively as

$$E[(S_{d+1}^R)^2] = E[(S_d^R)^2] - 2E[S_d^R] + \{1-F_S(d)\}. \tag{5.6.15}$$

Subtracting the square of (5.6.14) from (5.6.15) yields

$$Var(S_{d+1}^R) = Var(S_d^R) - F_S(d)\{2E[S_d^R] - 1 + F_S(d)\}. \tag{5.6.16}$$

The recursion (5.6.16) begins with $Var(S_0^R) = Var(S)$ which can be calculated separately.

Numerical Illustration 5.6.1.

Consider the group life case considered in numerical illustration 5.2.2 and 5.4.1. The expected claim cost is 2,054.41 dollars. Using (5.6.14) and (5.6.16) gives the following table of net stop loss premiums and the standard deviation of stop-loss claims for various stop-loss levels.

d	$F_S(d)$	$E[S_d^R]$	$\sigma(S_d^R)$
0	0.95273905	2.05441	51.26678
1	0.95273905	2.00715	48.80718
2	0.95273905	1.95989	46.41511
3	0.95273905	1.91263	44.09059
4	0.95273905	1.86537	41.83361
5	0.95273905	1.81811	39.64416
6	0.95273905	1.77084	37.52226
7	0.95273905	1.72358	35.46791
8	0.95273905	1.67632	33.48109
9	0.95273905	1.62906	31.56181
10	0.95273905	1.58180	29.71007
11	0.95273905	1.53454	27.92588
12	0.95273905	1.48728	26.20922
13	0.95273905	1.44002	24.56011
14	0.95321566	1.39276	22.97854
15	0.95463736	1.34597	21.46375
16	0.95599217	1.30061	20.01370
17	0.95646878	1.25660	18.62663
18	0.95984386	1.21307	17.30202
19	0.96035862	1.17291	16.03540
20	0.96157969	1.13327	14.82595

When the distribution of total claims is arithmetic, the net stop-loss premium for values of d which are not integers can be obtained by linear interpolation between the adjacent integer values of d. This can be shown as follows:

$$E[S_d^R] = \sum_{x>d} (x-d)f_S(x)$$

$$= \sum_{x>d} \{x-[d]\}f_S(x) - \sum_{x>d} \{d-[d]\}f_S(x)$$

$$= E[S_{[d]}^R] - \{d-[d]\}\{1-F_S(d)\}$$

$$= E[S_{[d]}^R] - \{d-[d]\} \{E[S_{[d]}^R] - E[S_{[d]+1}^R]\}$$

$$= \{1-(d-[d])\}E[S_{[d]}^R] + \{d-[d]\}E[S_{[d]+1}^R]. \tag{5.6.17}$$

5.7 BIBLIOGRAPHIC NOTES

The distribution of total claims for individual risk models has traditionally been calculated using computer simulation methods (cf. Collins, 1962). Rosenthal (1947) discusses approximations in connection with applications in life insurance.

The recursive approach is based on De Pril (1986). It improves a method of Kornya (1983) and extends the method of Panjer (1981) which is discussed in the next chapter. Error bounds are discussed by Hipp (1986). Practical comparisons are done by Kuon, Reich, and Reimers (1987) and Vandebroek and De Pril (1988).

Various approximations to the distribution of total claims are discussed by Beard, Pesonen and Pentikäinen (1984). Some of these methods are also discussed in chapter 10 in connection with compound risk models. Feller (1971) discusses the regularity conditions for the central limit theorem.

EXERCISES

1. A portfolio of six independent insurance risks has the following benefit amounts and claim probabilities:

Risk	Claim Probability	Benefit
A	.01	10,000
B	.04	30,000
C	.07	60,000
D	.02	20,000
E	.06	40,000
F	.08	10,000

At most one claim can occur for each risk.

a) Calculate the expected total claim costs.

b) Calculate the standard deviation of total claim costs.

c) Calculate the index of skewness of total claim costs.

d) Calculate directly the probability that total claims costs will be exactly 60,000 dollars.

e) Calculate the distribution function of total claim costs up to 60,000 dollars.

f) If total claim costs are 60,000 dollars and it is known that risk C does not have a claim, calculate the probability that risk A has a claim.

g) Using the normal approximation, calculate the probability that total claims do not exceed 60,000 dollars.

2. A portfolio consists of 6 independent risks. If a claim occurs, it will be of size 10,000, 20,000, 30,000 or 40,000 dollars. At most one claim can occur per risk. The claim probabilities and claim size distributions are:

	Claim	$Pr\{Y=y\}$			
Risk	Probability	$y=10{,}000$	20,000	30,000	40,000
A	.01	.10	.20	.30	.40
B	.02	.25	.25	.25	.25
C	.03	.40	.30	.20	.10
D	.04	.0	0	.50	.50
E	.05	.50	.50	0	0
F	.06	.50	0	0	.50

Repeat parts a) to f) of question 1 above for this portfolio.

3. Two independent risks have claim probabilities .01 and .02 respectively. At most one claim can occur for each risk. If a claim occurs for the first risk, its size has a probability density function that decreases linearly from its value at 0 dollars to its value of 0 at 200,000 dollars. For the second risk the corresponding pdf increases linearly from zero at 20,000 dollars to 100,000 dollars. Obtain the probability distribution function of the total claim costs from the two risks.

4. Three independent risks have claim probabilities 0.01, 0.02 and 0.03 respectively. At most one claim occurs per risk. Each risk has an inverse Gaussian distribution of claim sizes with means 2,000, 3,000 and 4,000 dollars respectively. For each distribution the variance is twice the mean. Use the method of example 5.3.1 and to evaluate the probability that total claim costs will not exceed 500 dollars.

5. A risk has claim probability .01 and an exponential claim size distribution with mean 20,000. If a claim occurs, the insurer pays 80% of the excess of claim over 2,000 dollars with a maximum payment of 40,000 dollars. Obtain the exact form of the distribution of the costs to the insurer for this risk.

6. Consider the individual risk model where each of the X_i's has the inverse Gaussian pdf

$$f_{X_i}(x) = \frac{\mu_i}{2}(\frac{\beta}{\pi x^3})^{1/2}e^{-\frac{(2x-\mu_i\beta)^2}{4\beta x}}, \quad x>0,$$

where $\mu_i>0$, $\beta>0$.

a) Show that the Laplace transform of the pdf of X_i is

$$L_{X_i}(s) = e^{-\mu_i\{(1+\beta s)^{1/2}-1\}}, \quad s\geq-1/\beta.$$

b) Find the mean and variance of X_i.

c) Consider the distribution of the total claims $X_1+X_2+\cdots+X_n$ where the X_i's are independent. Write down the associated pdf, and give the mean and variance.

d) It can be shown that the cdf of X_i is

$$Pr\{X_i\leq x\} = \Phi\{\frac{2x-\mu_i\beta}{\sqrt{2\beta x}}\} + e^{2\mu_i}\Phi\{-\frac{2x+\mu_i\beta}{\sqrt{2\beta x}}\}$$

where $\Phi(\cdot)$ is the $N(0,1)$ cdf. If the expected total claims was 1.7044 and the standard deviation .022128 (in hundreds of thousands), find the probability that the total claims exceed 1.72 assuming the pdf obtained in c) for the total claims (with the mean and variance as given), and then assuming a normal distribution. Compare your answers.

7. Consider the following four independent risks, with probability distributions as follows:

		$f_{X_j}(x)$				
		0	1	2	3	4
	1	0	.1	.2	.3	.4
j	2	0	.2	.3	.5	0
	3	0	0	0	.5	.5
	4	.1	0	.4	.2	.3

a) Find the pgf of the total claims and use this to find the mean and standard deviation.

b) Find the probability function of the total claims.

8. Suppose that X_i has probability function

$$f_{X_i}(x) = \frac{\Gamma(r_i+x)}{\Gamma(r_i)x!}\left(\frac{1}{1+\beta_i}\right)^{r_i}\left(\frac{\beta_i}{1+\beta_i}\right)^x; \quad x = 0,1,2,...,$$

and pgf

$$P_{X_i}(z) = \{1-\beta_i(z-1)\}^{-r_i}.$$

a) Write down the pgf $P_S(z)$ for the sum $S = X_1+X_2+\cdots+X_n$ and identify the distribution of S when $\beta_i = \beta$ for all i. Show more generally that

$$P'_S(z) = P_S(z)\{\sum_{i=1}^{n} r_i\beta_i[1-\beta_i(z-1)]^{-1}\}.$$

b) Use (a) to show that

$$f_S(0) = \prod_{i=1}^{n}(1+\beta_i)^{-r_i},$$

and for $x>0$

$$f_S(x+1) = \frac{1}{x+1}\sum_{y=0}^{x} f_S(x-y)\{\sum_{i=1}^{n}(\frac{r_i\beta_i}{1+\beta_i})(\frac{\beta_i}{1+\beta_i})^y\}.$$

c) Use the recursion developed in (b) to calculate the distribution of S when $n = 5$, $r_i = i/2$ and $\beta_i = 2/i$.

9. Consider the following life insurance portfolio, where the table entries are n_{ij}.

q_j	i 1	2	3	4	5
.00094	12	1	-	19	6
.00191	23	-	3	32	14
.00501	2	6	13	24	1
.01320	14	7	31	5	36
.03407	20	-	-	31	22

a) Find the mean and standard deviation of the total claims.

b) Set up the $h(i, k)$ matrix and calculate the total claims distribution up to 50 recursively so that the approximating cdf is accurate to 5 decimal places. What was the largest value of k needed in evaluation of $h(i, k)$?

c) Calculate the exact distribution up to 50 recursively using the direct method. Compare the results to those in b). Comment on the difference in computing time as compared to b).

d) Obtain the net stop-loss reinsurance premiums and the standard deviations to reinsurance claims with deductibles $d = 0, 1, 2,..., 50$.

e) Recompute a) to c) for the insurer that retains only that portion of any claim up to 20.

f) Recompute a) to c) for the reinsurer in e).

10. Prove (5.6.12), (5.6.13) and (5.6.15).

11. a) Show that the cdf of the reinsurer's losses satisfies

$$F_{S_d^I}(x) = \begin{cases} 0, & x<0 \\ F_S(x+d), & x\geq 0. \end{cases}$$

b) For any non-negative random variable X,

$$E(X) = \int_0^\infty Pr\{X>x\}dx.$$

Use this fact and a) to prove (5.6.10).

12. a) Prove that the reinsurer's losses, S_d^R, and the direct insurer's losses, S_d^I, are positively correlated.

b) Using a), show that the variance of total losses, S, is larger than the sum of the variance of the reinsurer's losses, S_d^R, and the variance of the direct insurer's losses, S_d^I. Hence, two insurers can mutually reduce risk by acting as each other's reinsurer when the risks insured are independent.

CHAPTER 6

BASIC COMPOUND RISK MODELS

6.1 INTRODUCTION

In this chapter, we consider a basic class of risk models in which all risks in a portfolio are treated implicitly as being identical. This requirement is not always needed explicitly. We will show that, in some cases, a portfolio of heterogeneous risks can be treated mathematically as a portfolio of homogeneous risks. This will allow us to greatly simplify the computational aspects associated with calculating the distribution of total claims over a fixed period such as one year.

We consider only the class of compound Poisson, compound negative binomial and compound binomial distributions in this chapter since they are the most well known, the easiest to work with, and the most frequently used distributions. Besides, they fall into a natural class of distributions as will be seen in later sections.

In some cases, the number of risks in the portfolio is reflected in the parameters of the distribution although knowledge of the parameters will not necessarily yield the number of risks in the portfolio. Consequently, we will often speak of a single compound risk as referring to a portfolio of risks each of which may themselves be compound risks. For example, a fire insurance policy on a building may be treated mathematically in an equivalent manner to a group life insurance plan for a group of employees. The random variable of interest is the total cost of all claims arising from the risk under consideration, not the costs of a particular claim, be it the result of a fire or the death of an employee. Consequently, it is not necessary to restrict consideration to collections of insured entities such as fleets of automobiles, or groups of persons insured against loss of income due to disability resulting from sickness or accident. We can equivalently consider a single automobile insurance policy or a disability policy.

The most popular distribution, the compound Poisson will be considered first, followed by the compound negative binomial and the compound binomial distributions.

Compound distributions arise from consideration of random sums of the form

$$S = X_1 + X_2 + \cdots + X_N \tag{6.1.1}$$

where $X_1, X_2, \ldots$ represent the amounts of the successive claims and N represents the number of claims occurring in a fixed time period, typically one year.

We now make two important assumptions. For fixed $N = n$, it is assumed that $X_1, X_2, \ldots, X_n$ are mutually independent and identical random variables. Furthermore, it is assumed that the distributions of $X_1, X_2, \ldots$ are independent of N, the number of claims that have occurred.

In this case, we write the pdf (or pf) of total claims as

$$f_S(x) = \sum_{k=0}^{\infty} f_S(x | N=k) Pr\{N=k\} = \sum_{k=0}^{\infty} p_k f_{X_1 + X_2 + \cdots + X_k}(x)$$

$$= \sum_{k=0}^{\infty} p_k f_X^{*k}(x). \tag{6.1.2}$$

In equation (6.1.2), it should be noted that $f_X^{*0}(0) = 1$ and that $f_X^{*0}(x) = 0$ when $x \neq 0$. Also $f_{X_1 + X_2 + \cdots + X_k}(x) = f_X^{*k}(x)$ since the X_j's are assumed to be independent for fixed N. Furthermore in (6.1.2), $p_k = Pr\{N=k\}$ represents the probability of k claims in the fixed time period. The Laplace transform of S is

$$L_S(z) = E[e^{-zS}] = \sum_{k=0}^{\infty} p_k E[e^{-zS} | N=k]$$

$$= \sum_{k=0}^{\infty} p_k \{L_X(z)\}^k = P_N(L_X(z)). \tag{6.1.3}$$

where $P_N(z)$ is the pgf of the number of claims. From (6.1.3), (2.4.10) and

(2.4.12), the corresponding cgf can be written conveniently as

$$C_S(z) = C_N(C_X(z)).\tag{6.1.4}$$

The cumulants of S can be written in terms of the cumulants of N and X. They are (using an obvious notation) obtained by differentiating (6.1.4) and setting $z = 0$. The results for the first four cumulants are:

$$\kappa_{S1} = \kappa_{N1}\kappa_{X1},\tag{6.1.5}$$

$$\kappa_{S2} = \kappa_{N2}\kappa_{X1}^2 + \kappa_{N1}\kappa_{X2},\tag{6.1.6}$$

$$\kappa_{S3} = \kappa_{N3}\kappa_{X1}^3 + 3\kappa_{N2}\kappa_{X1}\kappa_{X2} + \kappa_{N1}\kappa_{X3},\tag{6.1.7}$$

and

$$\kappa_{S4} = \kappa_{N4}\kappa_{X1}^4 + 6\kappa_{N3}\kappa_{X1}^2\kappa_{X2} + 3\kappa_{N2}\kappa_{X2}^2 \tag{6.1.8}$$

$$+ 4\kappa_{N2}\kappa_{X1}\kappa_{X3} + \kappa_{N1}\kappa_{X4}$$

where the first subscript indicates the random variable under consideration.

Because the pgf (2.9.6) of S is of the same form as (6.1.4), formulas for the factorial moments are the same as (6.1.5) to (6.1.8) with the cumulants replaced by factorial moments. The raw moments or central moments can be obtained by appropriate substitution of equations (2.4.22) to (2.4.25) into equations (6.1.5) to (6.1.8). We will do this when we consider the three distributions separately. We choose to use cumulants at this stage because of the relationships (2.4.22) to (2.4.25) between cumulants and central moments.

Numerical Illustration 6.1.1. Group Dental Insurance

Under a group dental insurance plan covering employees and their families, the premium for each married employee is the same regardless of the number of family members. The insurance company has compiled statistics showing that the annual cost (adjusted to current dollars) of dental care per person for the benefits provided by the plan has the following distribution (given in units of 25 dollars):

x	1	2	3	4	5	6	7	8	9	10
$f_X(x)$	.150	.200	.250	.125	.075	.050	.050	.050	.025	.025

Furthermore, the distribution of the number of persons per insurance certificate (i.e. per employee) receiving dental care in any year has the distribution:

n	0	1	2	3	4	5	6	7	8
p_n	.05	.10	.15	.20	.25	.15	.06	.03	.01

The insurer is now in a position to calculate the distribution of the cost per year per married employee in the group. The cost per married employee is

$$f_S(x) = \sum_{n=0}^{8} p_n f_X^{*n}(x).$$

The distribution up to amounts up to 525 dollars is given in the following table. To obtain $f_S(x)$, each row of the matrix of convolutions of $f_X(x)$ is multiplied by the probabilities from the row below the table and the products are summed.

The reader may wish to verify using equations (6.1.5) to (6.1.8) that the first four moments of the distribution $f_S(x)$ are

$$\mu'_{S1} = \kappa_1 = 12.58,$$

$$\mu_{S2} = \kappa_2 = 58.7464,$$

$$\mu_{S3} = \kappa_3 = 235.02314,$$

$$\mu_{S4} = \kappa_4 + 3\kappa_2^2 = 10868.0166.$$

Hence the annual cost of the dental plan has mean $12.58 \times 25 = 314.50$ dollars and standard deviation 191.6155 dollars.

x	$f_X^{*0}(x)$	$f_X^{*1}(x)$	$f_X^{*2}(x)$	$f_X^{*3}(x)$	$f_X^{*4}(x)$	$f_X^{*5}(x)$	$f_X^{*6}(x)$	$f_X^{*7}(x)$	$f_X^{*8}(x)$	$f_S(x)$
0	1	0	0	0	0	0	0	0	0	.05000
1	0	.150	0	0	0	0	0	0	0	.01500
2	0	.200	.02250	0	0	0	0	0	0	.02338
3	0	.250	.06000	.00338	0	0	0	0	0	.03468
4	0	.125	.11500	.01350	.00051	0	0	0	0	.03258
5	0	.075	.13750	.03488	.00270	.00008	0	0	0	.03579
6	0	.050	.13500	.06144	.00878	.00051	.00001	0	0	.03981
7	0	.050	.10750	.08569	.01999	.00198	.00009	.00000	0	.04356
8	0	.050	.08813	.09750	.03580	.00549	.00042	.00002	.00000	.04752
9	0	.025	.07875	.09841	.05266	.01194	.00136	.00008	.00000	.04903
10	0	.025	.07063	.09338	.06682	.02138	.00345	.00031	.00002	.05190
11	0	0	.06250	.08813	.07597	.03282	.00726	.00091	.00007	.05138
12	0	0	.04500	.08370	.08068	.04450	.01305	.00218	.00022	.05119
13	0	0	.03125	.07673	.08266	.05486	.02062	.00448	.00060	.05030
14	0	0	.01750	.06689	.08278	.06314	.02930	.00808	.00138	.04818
15	0	0	.01125	.05377	.08081	.06934	.03826	.01304	.00279	.04576
16	0	0	.00750	.04125	.07584	.07361	.04677	.01919	.00505	.04281
17	0	0	.00500	.03052	.06811	.07578	.05438	.02616	.00829	.03938
18	0	0	.00313	.02267	.05854	.07552	.06080	.03352	.01254	.03575
19	0	0	.00125	.01673	.04878	.07263	.06573	.04084	.01768	.03197
20	0	0	.00063	.01186	.03977	.06747	.06882	.04775	.02351	.02832
21	0	0	0	.00800	.03187	.06079	.06982	.05389	.02978	.02479
$P_n=$	.05	.10	.15	.20	.25	.15	.06	.03	.01	

6.2 THE COMPOUND POISSON DISTRIBUTION

Consider the fixed time period $(0,t]$ over which claims can arise for some risk (or collection of risks). Let $X_1, X_2,...$ denote the sizes (or severity) of the corresponding claims with common distribution given by pdf (or pf) $f_X(x)$. Furthermore, let $N(t)$ denote the number of claims occurring in $(0,t]$ and let

$$S(t) = X_1 + X_2 + \cdots + X_{N(t)} \qquad (6.2.1)$$

denote the total (or aggregate) claims occurring in $(0,t]$.

Suppose that we make the following assumptions about the claim number process $\underline{N} = \{N(t); t{\geq}0\}$:

(a) $N(0) = 0$. The number of claims at time zero is zero.

(b) The process $\underline{N}$ has independent increments. The number of claims in any interval is independent of the number of claims in any other (non-overlapping) interval.

(c) $Pr\{N(t+h)-N(t)=1\} = \lambda h + o(h)$ for all $t{\geq}0$.

(d) $Pr\{N(t+h)-N(t)>1\} = o(h)$ for all $t{\geq}0$. For sufficiently small time intervals, at most one claim can occur. The function λ is the rate (or intensity) function of the process.

From section 3.3, it can be seen that $\underline{N}$ is a homogeneous Poisson process. According to theorem 3.3.1, the distribution of $N(t)$ is Poisson with parameter λt and according to equation (3.7.3), the distribution of $S = S(1)$, the aggregate claims for a single time period, is compound Poisson with Poisson parameter λ and claim size (or severity) distribution $f_X(x)$.

The compound Poisson distribution has df

$$F_S(x) = \sum_{k=0}^{\infty} e^{-\lambda} \frac{\lambda^k}{k!} F_X^{*k}(x) \qquad (6.2.2)$$

and LT

$$L_S(z) = \exp\{\lambda[L_X(z)-1]\}. \qquad (6.2.3)$$

The first four moments of the Poisson distribution can be obtained from (4.2.3). They are

$$\mu'_{N1} = \lambda \qquad (6.2.4)$$

$$\mu_{N2} = \lambda \qquad (6.2.5)$$

$$\mu_{N3} = \lambda \tag{6.2.6}$$

$$\mu_{N4} = \lambda + 3\lambda^2 \tag{6.2.7}$$

The first four moments of the compound Poisson are

$$\mu'_{S1} = \lambda \mu'_{X1} \tag{6.2.8}$$

$$\mu_{S2} = \lambda \mu'_{X2} \tag{6.2.9}$$

$$\mu_{S3} = \lambda \mu'_{X3} \tag{6.2.10}$$

$$\mu_{S4} = \lambda \mu'_{X4} + 3\lambda^2 (\mu'_{X2})^2. \tag{6.2.11}$$

The above results can be obtained from equations (6.1.5) to (6.1.8). In fact, these are special cases of the formula

$$\kappa_{Sj} = \lambda \mu'_{Xj}, \quad j = 1, 2, \dots \tag{6.2.12}$$

where κ_{Sj} is the j-th cumulant of S and μ'_{Xj} is the j-th moment about the origin of X.

The following theorem gives a very powerful computing tool that significantly reduces the number of computations required to evaluate $f_S(x)$ when the claim size distribution is defined on the positive integers.

Theorem 6.2.1. The compound Poisson distribution defined by (6.2.2) with the claim size distribution defined on the positive integers with probability function $f_X(x)$, $x = 1,2,3,\dots$ satisfies

$$f_S(x) = \frac{\lambda}{x} \sum_{y=1}^{x} y f_X(y) f_S(x-y), \quad x = 1,2,3,\dots \tag{6.2.13}$$

with $f_S(0) = e^{-\lambda}$.

Proof

For the Poisson distribution

$$np_n = \lambda\, p_{n-1}, \quad n = 1,2,3,\ldots$$

Multiplying each side by $\{L_X(z)\}^{n-1}L_X'(z)$ and summing over n yields

$$\sum_{n=1}^{\infty} np_n\{L_X(z)\}^{n-1}L_X'(z) = \lambda\sum_{n=1}^{\infty} p_{n-1}\{L_X(z)\}^{n-1}L_X'(z).$$

Since $L_S(z) = \sum_{n=0}^{\infty} p_n\{L_X(z)\}^n$, the previous equation can be recognized as

$$L_S'(z) = \lambda\, L_X'(z)L_S(z).$$

Inversion of this, when X is defined only on positive integers yields

$$xf_S(x) = \lambda\sum_{y=1}^{x} yf_X(y)f_S(x-y).$$

The recursive formula (6.2.13) allows one to avoid the calculation of the convolutions of the claim size distribution and the "convolution table" (as in numerical illustration 6.1.1) by making use of the properties of the Poisson distribution. This can reduce computational time dramatically when a large number of claims are expected to occur. The following example illustrates the recursive evaluation of the distribution $f_S(x)$.

Numerical Illustration 6.2.1.

An insurer expects 0.2 claims per year from a compound Poisson risk. For any claim, there is an 80% chance that the insurer's loss is 10,000 dollars and a 20% chance that the loss is 20,000 dollars. The probabilities of possible total losses from the risk are calculated using the recursive formula (6.2.13) (in units of 10,000 dollars):

$$f_S(0) = e^{-\lambda} = 0.818731$$

$$f_S(1) = \lambda f_X(1) f_S(0) = (.2)(.8)(.818731) = 0.130997$$

$$f_S(2) = \frac{\lambda}{2} \{f_X(1) f_S(1) + 2f_X(2) f_S(0)\} = 0.043229$$

$$f_S(3) = \frac{\lambda}{3} \{f_X(1) f_S(2) + 2f_X(2) f_S(1)\} = 0.005799$$

$$f_S(4) = \frac{\lambda}{4} \{f_X(1) f_S(3) + 2f_X(2) f_S(2)\} = 0.001097$$

Note that there are only two terms and no convolutions required in calculating each point of the distribution. The pf and cdf of the total claims up to 60,000 dollars (in units of 10,000) are:

x	$f_S(x)$	$F_S(x)$
0	.818731	.818731
1	.130997	.949728
2	.043229	.992957
3	.005799	.998755
4	.001097	.999852
5	.000128	.999980
6	.000018	.999998

Since $\mu'_{X1} = 1.2$, $\mu'_{X2} = 1.6$, $\mu'_{X3} = 2.4$ and $\mu'_{X4} = 4.0$, the first four moments of the compound Poisson distribution are $\mu'_{S1} = .24$, $\mu'_{S2} = .32$, $\mu'_{S3} = .48$ and $\mu'_{S4} = 1.1072$.

The following example shows how a nonhomogeneous Poisson process arises naturally in connection with group life insurance. The corresponding compound Poisson distribution will be developed in a later example.

Example 6.2.1. Group Life Insurance

Consider a group life insurance contract covering a group of n employees for a one year period. Using the standard actuarial notation, the 'force of mortality' at time t for an individual aged x at the beginning of the year, is μ_{x+t}. For convenience, we let $\mu_j(t) = \mu_{x+t}$ for the j-th individual aged x at the beginning of the year. The probability that the j-th individual will survive the year is $1 - q_j = \exp\{-\int_0^1 \mu_j(t)\}$. Assuming independence between the survival of persons in the group, the probability of all persons surviving the year is $\prod_{j=1}^{n}(1-q_j) = \exp\{-\sum_{j=1}^{n}\mu_j(t)dt\}$. In the individual risk model of chapter 5, the expected number of deaths during the year is $\sum_{j=1}^{n}q_j$. Let us now assume that upon death, each member is immediately replaced by a new member with identical mortality characteristics. In group life insurance, this is a reasonable assumption for many groups. For example, if the insured group is a group of hourly paid workers, the death of a worker will immediately precipitate the hiring a replacement worker. Often this worker will be approximately the same age as the deceased worker because of the nature of the job. Even if this is not the case, the fact that very few deaths are expected to occur, due to very small probabilities of death, the error introduced by the "replacement" assumption will be negligible.

The number of deaths arising from the j-th member of the group (including replacements) in the time interval $(0,t]$ can be viewed as a nonhomogeneous Poisson process $\{N_j(t); t\geq0\}$ with mean $E[N_j(t)] = \int_0^t \mu_j(s)ds$. Hence the number of deaths over the full year has a Poisson distribution with mean

$$\lambda_j = \int_0^1 \mu_j(s)ds = -\log(1-q_j). \tag{6.2.14}$$

Assuming independence of the survival of persons in the group, the number of deaths from the group forms a nonhomogeneous Poisson process $\{N(t); t\geq0\}$ with $N(t) = \sum_{j=1}^{n}N_j(t)$. The number of deaths in the year is then Poisson distributed with mean $\lambda = \sum_{j=1}^{n}\lambda_j$. Note that for the individual risk model and the Poisson model in this example have identical "'probabilities of no deaths" for each person as well as for the entire group.

For other types of insurance, this "replacement" assumption is equivalent to the assumption that the insured risk is re-exposed immediately following each claim. This is appropriate (at least approximately) for automobile insurance in which a driver can be driving again immediately following an accident or a car is immediately re-exposed following repairs or replacement. The same is, of course, true for most types of insurance, e.g., medical costs, fire, liability of various types, and theft.

6.3 COMBINING COMPOUND POISSON RISKS

It is not necessary that all risks in a portfolio have exactly the same claim size (or severity) distribution. Indeed, any collection of independent compound Poisson risks can be treated as a single compound risk. This is now proved in the following theorem.

Theorem 6.3.1. Let $S_1, S_2, \ldots, S_n$ denote independent compound Poisson random variables with Poisson parameters $\lambda_1, \lambda_2, \ldots, \lambda_n$ and claim size (severity) distribution functions $F_1(x), F_2(x), \ldots, F_n(x)$. Then

$$S = S_1 + S_2 + \cdots + S_n \tag{6.3.1}$$

is a compound Poisson random variable with Poisson parameter

$$\lambda = \lambda_1 + \lambda_2 + \cdots + \lambda_n \tag{6.3.2}$$

and claim size (severity) distribution function

$$F_X(x) = \sum_{j=1}^{n} \frac{\lambda_j}{\lambda} F_j(x). \tag{6.3.3}$$

Proof

The LT of S_j is

$$L_{S_j}(z) = \exp\{\lambda_j[L_j(z)-1]\}$$

where $L_{S_j}(z)$ is the LT corresponding to $F_j(x)$. Since $S_1, S_2, \ldots, S_n$ are independent, the LT of S is

$$L_S(z) = \prod_{j=1}^{n} L_j(z) = \exp\{\sum_{j=1}^{n} \lambda_j [L_j(z)-1]\}$$

$$= \exp\{\sum_{j=1}^{n} \lambda_j L_j(z)-\lambda\} = \exp\{\lambda [\sum_{j=1}^{n} \frac{\lambda_j}{\lambda} L_j(z)-1]\}$$

$$= \exp\{\lambda [L_X(z)-1]\}.$$

Since the LT is unique, the result follows.

This result is very useful in all types of insurance applications and is one of the reasons that the compound Poisson model has great appeal for the practitioner. It allows one to combine various Poisson risks and treat the aggregation as a single risk of the same type.

Numerical Illustration 6.3.1.

An insurer has two independent insurance coverages on a risk. The first is compound Poisson with $\lambda_1 = .2$ and $f_1(1) = .8$, $f_1(2) = .2$ as in numerical illustration 6.2.1. The second coverage is compound Poisson with $\lambda_2 = .3$ and $f_2(2) = .5$, $f_2(4) = .5$. Then from (6.3.3), we have $\lambda = \lambda_1 + \lambda_2 = .5$ and

$$f_X(x) = \frac{\lambda_1}{\lambda_1+\lambda_2} f_1(x) + \frac{\lambda_2}{\lambda_1+\lambda_2} f_2(x) = .4f_1(x) + .6f_2(x)$$

$$= \begin{cases} .32, & x = 1 \\ .38, & x = 2 \\ .30, & x = 4. \end{cases}$$

Hence, providing insurance covering both compound Poisson risks is equivalent to covering a single risk with $.5$ expected claims and claim size distribution $f_X(x)$ as given above.

In the situation of life insurance with a fixed benefit of b_j for the j-th risk, one can view the individuals in the portfolio as independent Poisson risks, assuming, of course, that replacement occurs at the moment of death by an identical risk with the same insurance benefit. In this case, from (6.2.13)

$$\lambda_j = -\log(1-q_j) \tag{6.3.4}$$

and

$$f_j(x) = \begin{cases} 1, & x=b_j \\ 0, & x \neq b_j. \end{cases} \tag{6.3.5}$$

Combining all risks yields, according to Theorem 6.3.1,

$$\lambda = \lambda_1 + \lambda_2 + \cdots + \lambda_n \tag{6.3.6}$$

and

$$f_X(x) = \sum_{j=1}^{n} \frac{\lambda_j}{\lambda} f_j(x) = \sum_{b_j=x} \frac{\lambda_j}{\lambda}, \quad x > 0. \tag{6.3.7}$$

The summation in equation (6.3.7) is taken over all risks with benefit amount x.

In other types of insurance, various independent coverages can be easily combined. For example, comprehensive and liability coverages in automobile insurance can be combined if one is interested in examining total claims in conjunction with a single risk or a collection of risks. Similarly, life and health coverages can be combined, as long as it is assumed that these benefits are independent.

The distribution given by $F_X(x)$ is interpreted as the distribution of the severity of a claim arising from the portfolio as a whole without reference to the type of claim.

Numerical Illustration 6.3.2. Group Life Insurance

Consider the group life insurance portfolio of 14 lives considered in numerical illustrations 5.2.2, 5.4.1, 5.4.2 and 5.5.1. Since there is no more than one policy at any given benefit amount, the summation in formula (6.3.7) will have at most one term for any given value of x. The group's data, including the values of $\lambda_j = -\log(1-q_j)$, $j = 1, 2, \ldots, 14$ are given below (see example 6.2.1 for notation):

j	Age	Sex	Benefit	Mortality Rate	λ_j
1	20	M	15,000	.00149	.0014911
2	23	M	16,000	.00142	.0014210
3	27	M	20,000	.00128	.0012808
4	30	M	28,000	.00122	.0012207
5	31	M	31,000	.00123	.0012308
6	46	M	18,000	.00353	.0035362
7	47	M	26,000	.00394	.0039478
8	49	M	24,000	.00484	.0048518
9	64	M	60,000	.02182	.0220616
10	17	F	14,000	.00050	.0005001
11	22	F	17,000	.00050	.0005001
12	26	F	19,000	.00054	.0005401
13	37	F	30,000	.00103	.0010305
14	55	F	55,000	.00479	.0048015
			373,000		.0484142

Using (6.3.7), the following distribution of claim sizes is obtained (using units of 1000 dollars):

x	$f_X(x)$	$F_X(x)$	x	$f_X(x)$	$F_X(x)$
14	.0103296	.0103301	24	.1002133	.2916773
15	.0307990	.0411291	26	.0815418	.3732191
16	.0293511	.0704802	28	.0252146	.3984336
17	.0103301	.0808103	30	.0212857	.4197193
18	.0730414	.1538518	31	.0254214	.4451407
19	.0111568	.1650085	55	.0991756	.5443163
20	.0264554	.1914640	60	.4556837	1

The distribution of total claims for the group is compound Poisson with .0484142 expected claims and claim size distribution given by $f_X(x)$ above. When the distribution is used together with $\lambda = .0484142$ as in numerical illustration 6.3.1, the resulting distribution function of total claims is given below:

x	$F_S(x)$	x	$F_S(x)$	x	$F_S(x)$	x	$F_S(x)$
0	0.9527391	20	0.9615705	40	0.9733303	60	0.9990849
1	0.9527391	21	0.9615705	41	0.9733382	61	0.9990861
2	0.9527391	22	0.9615705	42	0.9733604	62	0.9990869
3	0.9527391	23	0.9615705	43	0.9733666	63	0.9990870
4	0.9527391	24	0.9661930	44	0.9733879	64	0.9990870
5	0.9527391	25	0.9661930	45	0.9733926	65	0.9990871
6	0.9527391	26	0.9699542	46	0.9734047	66	0.9990872
7	0.9527391	27	0.9699542	47	0.9734075	67	0.9990872
8	0.9527391	28	0.9711174	48	0.9734242	68	0.9990873
9	0.9527391	29	0.9711181	49	0.9734289	69	0.9990897
10	0.9527391	30	0.9721016	50	0.9734491	70	0.9990966
11	0.9527391	31	0.9732765	51	0.9734506	71	0.9991031
12	0.9527391	32	0.9732799	52	0.9734637	72	0.9991055
13	0.9527391	33	0.9732858	53	0.9734637	73	0.9991217
14	0.9532155	34	0.9732921	54	0.9734731	74	0.9991348
15	0.9546362	35	0.9732963	55	0.9780534	75	0.9991720
16	0.9559900	36	0.9733043	56	0.9780580	76	0.9992019
17	0.9564665	37	0.9733067	57	0.9780627	77	0.9992125
18	0.9598356	38	0.9733135	58	0.9780639	78	0.9992868
19	0.9603503	39	0.9733210	59	0.9780654	79	0.9993204

It should be noted that the values of $F_S(x)$ are very similar to (but not larger than) those of numerical illustration 5.4.2. They are necessarily equal at $x = 0$.

When the portfolio (i.e. the expected number of claims) becomes larger, the difference between the individual risk model and the compound Poisson model becomes larger due to the effect of the "replacements".

6.4 DECOMPOSING COMPOUND POISSON RISKS

For a variety of purposes associated with calculating the distribution of total claims, it is useful to consider the distribution of total claims for various subsets of the claims. The subsets will be based on the size of the individual claims. It will be shown that the totals of claims for the subsets of sizes are mutually independent compound Poisson random variables.

First, suppose that the support of the claim sizes is partitioned into m disjoint non-empty sets $A_1, A_2, \ldots, A_m$ such that the union of the A_i's is the complete support of the claim sizes.

Let p_i denote the probability that any given claim will fall into claim size class A_i, i.e.

$$p_i = Pr\{X_k \in A_i\} \quad i = 1, 2, 3, \ldots, m \tag{6.4.1}$$

where X_k is the size of the k-th claim from the portfolio as a whole.

Let N_i denote the number of claims for claim size class A_i. Hence

$$N = N_1 + N_2 + \cdots + N_m \tag{6.4.2}$$

where N is the number of claims for the portfolio as a whole.

It is apparent that for fixed $N=n$, the joint distribution of $(N_1, N_2, \ldots, N_{m-1}, N_m)$ is multinomial with parameters $(n, p_1, p_2, \ldots, p_m)$ and that for fixed $N=n$, the marginal distribution of N_j is binomial with parameters (n, p_j). We now use these facts to show that $N_1, N_2, \ldots, N_m$ are mutually independent Poisson random variables.

Theorem 6.4.1. Suppose that the number of claims N is a Poisson random variable with mean λ. Then the number of claims $N_1, N_2, \ldots, N_m$ corresponding to claim size categories $A_1, A_2, \ldots, A_m$ respectively are mutually independent Poisson random variables with means $\lambda p_1, \lambda p_2, \ldots, \lambda p_m$ respectively.

Proof

The joint pf of $(N_1, N_2, \ldots, N_m)$ is given by

$$Pr\{N_1=n_1, \ldots, N_m=n_m\} = Pr\{N_1=n_1, \ldots, N_n=n_m \mid N=n\}Pr\{N=n\}$$

$$= \binom{n}{n_1, \ldots, n_{m-1}} p_1^{n_1} \cdots p_m^{n_m} \frac{e^{-\lambda} \lambda^n}{n!}$$

$$= \prod_{i=1}^{m} e^{-\lambda p_i} \frac{(\lambda p_i)^{n_i}}{n_i!}.$$

where $n = n_1 + n_2 + \cdots + n_m$. Similarly, the marginal pf of N_i is given by

$$Pr\{N_i = n_i\} = \sum_{n=n_i}^{\infty} Pr\{N_i = n_i | N = n\} Pr\{N = n\}$$

$$= \sum_{n=n_i}^{\infty} \binom{n}{n_i} p_i^{n_i} (1-p_i)^{n-n_i} \frac{e^{-\lambda} \lambda^n}{n!}$$

$$= e^{-\lambda} \frac{(\lambda p_i)^{n_i}}{n_i!} \sum_{n=n_i}^{\infty} \frac{[\lambda(1-p_i)]^{n-n_i}}{(n-n_i)!}$$

$$= e^{-\lambda} \frac{(\lambda p_i)^{n_i}}{n_i!} e^{\lambda(1-p_i)}$$

$$= e^{-\lambda p_i} \frac{(\lambda p_i)^{n_i}}{n_i!}.$$

Hence the joint pf is the product of the marginal pf's, establishing mutual independence.

We now generalize the result to compound Poisson distributions. Let $X_{i,j}$ denote the j-th claim arising from size class A_i and let

$$S_i = X_{i,1} + X_{i,2} + \cdots + X_{i,N_i} \qquad (6.4.3)$$

denote the total claims associated with size class A_i. Hence

$$S = S_1 + S_2 + \cdots + S_m. \qquad (6.4.4)$$

The distribution of claim size distribution for the size class A_i is then

$$f_i(x) = \begin{cases} f_X(x)/p_i, & x \varepsilon A_i, \\ 0, & \text{otherwise.} \end{cases} \tag{6.4.5}$$

Note that the supports of $f_i(x)$, $i = 1,2,\ldots,m$ are non-overlapping and that the severity for the portfolio has pdf (or pf)

$$f_X(x) = \sum_{i=1}^{m} p_i f_i(x) \tag{6.4.6}$$

and Laplace transform

$$L_X(z) = \sum_{i=1}^{m} p_i L_i(z). \tag{6.4.7}$$

Since $X_{i,1}, X_{i,2},\ldots$ are mutually independent for a fixed class size A_i and since N_i is a Poisson variate with mean λp_i, it follows that S_i is a compound Poisson variate with Poisson parameter λp_i and severity distribution $f_i(x)$. We now show that the S_i's are independent random variables.

Theorem 6.4.2. Suppose that the total claims S is a compound Poisson random variable with Poisson parameter λ and severity distribution $f_X(x)$. Then the total claims $S_1, S_2, \ldots, S_m$ associated with claim size classes $A_1, A_2, \ldots, A_m$ are mutually independent compound Poisson random variables with Poisson parameters $\lambda p_1, \lambda p_2, \ldots, \lambda p_m$ and severity distributions $f_1(x), f_2(x), \ldots, f_m(x)$ respectively.

Proof

The joint pdf of $(N_1, N_2, \ldots, N_m, S_1, S_2, \ldots, S_m)$ is obtained by conditioning successively as

$$\frac{e^{-\lambda}\lambda^n}{n!}\binom{n}{n_1,\ldots,n_{m-1}}p_1^{n_1}\cdots p_m^{n_m}f_1^{*n_1}(s_1)\cdots f_m^{*n_m}(s_m)$$

$$= \prod_{i=1}^{m}e^{-\lambda p_i}\frac{(\lambda p_i)^{n_i}}{n_i!}f_i^{*n_i}(s_i).$$

Summing over all possible values of $N_1, N_2, \ldots, N_m$ turns the left-hand side into the joint pdf of $(S_1, S_2, \ldots, S_m)$ and the right-hand side into

$$\prod_{i=1}^{m}\sum_{n_i=0}^{\infty}e^{-\lambda p_i}\frac{(\lambda p_i)^{n_i}}{n_i!}f_i^{*n_i}(s_i)$$

which is the product of the marginal pdf's of $S_1, S_2, \ldots, S_m$. Hence, the result follows.

This theorem is very useful in a variety of situations in which one wishes to classify claims by size. Some examples are now given.

Example 6.4.1. Group Life Insurance

A group of employees are joint participants in a group life insurance plan. The benefits under the plan are multiples of 10,000 dollars up to 100,000 dollars. Let the sets $A_1, A_2, \ldots, A_m$ correspond to the amounts 10,000 dollars, 20,000 dollars, ..., 100,000 dollars respectively. Thus $m = 10$. According to the theorem the number of claims at the various amounts are independently Poisson distributed. Furthermore we can write

$$S = \sum_{i=1}^{10}iN_i = \sum_{i=1}^{10}S_i$$

where S is measured in units of 10,000 dollars and N_i has a Poisson distribution

$$Pr\{N_i=n_i\} = e^{-\lambda p_i}\frac{(\lambda p_i)^{n_i}}{n_i!}$$

and so the distribution of $S_i = iN_i$ is given by

$$Pr\{S_i{=}in_i\} = Pr\{N_i{=}n_i\}$$

$$= e^{-\lambda p_i} \frac{(\lambda p_i)^{n_i}}{n_i!}$$

and 0 elsewhere. The resulting distributions can then be convoluted to obtain the final distribution of total claims

$$f_S(x) = f_{S_1} {}^* f_{S_2} {}^* \cdots {}^* f_{S_m}(x).$$

This is a useful computational tool when m is relatively small since only $m{-}1$ convolutions are involved.

Numerical Illustration 6.4.1.

Consider the compound Poisson risk of numerical illustration 6.2.1 with $\lambda = .2$ and $f_X(1) = .8$ and $f_X(2) = .2$. Then, N_1, the number of claims of size 1 (in units of 10,000 dollars), and N_2, the numbers of claims of size 2, are independent Poisson variables with means $\lambda f_X(1) = .16$ and $\lambda f_X(2) = .04$ respectively. Letting $S_i = iN_i$, $i = 1,2$, we see that $S = S_1 + S_2$ and $f_S(x) = f_{S_1} {}^* f_{S_2}(x)$. The distribution of S is as follows:

x	$f_{S_1}(x)$	$f_{S_2}(x)$	$f_S(x)$
0	.8521438	.9607894	.818731
1	.1363430	0	.130997
2	.0109074	.0384316	.043229
3	.0005817	0	.005799
4	.0000233	.0007686	.001097
5	.0000007	0	.000128
6	.0000000	.0000102	.000018

This is an alternative to the calculations in numerical illustration 6.2.1.

Example 6.4.2. Continuous Severity with a Maximum

In many types of insurance, the insurer is exposed to a maximum amount of risk either because a maximum is specified in the insurance contract or because the insurer is covered for excess losses on each risk through a reinsurance agreement. If the severity without the maximum is a (piecewise) continuous positive random variable, then when a maximum is used, a spike or atom at the maximum is created. In this situation it is usually worth separating the spikes from the continuous portion of the severity. If the original severity with no maximum is of the form $f_X(x)$ and a maximum of m is imposed, then the revised severity for $Y = \min(X,m)$ is

$$f_Y(x) = \begin{cases} f_X(x), & 0<x<m, \\ 1-F_X(m-0), & x=m. \end{cases}$$

In the notation of this section, we let

$$p_1 = F_X(m-0),$$

$$p_2 = 1-F_X(m-0),$$

$$f_1(x) = f_X(x)/p_1, \quad 0<x<m,$$

$$f_2(x) = \begin{cases} 1, & x=m, \\ 0, & x\neq m. \end{cases}$$

Hence the distribution of total claims is $S = S_1 + S_2$ where S_1 represents the total of non-maximal claims and has compound Poisson distribution

$$f_{S_1}(x) = \sum_{n=0}^{\infty} e^{-\lambda p_1} \frac{(\lambda p_1)^n}{n!} f_1^{*n}(x)$$

which is continuous on the positive axis with a spike of size $\exp(-\lambda p_1)$ at the origin. The random variable S_2, representing the total of all "maximal" claims, is independent of S_1, is arithmetic with span m and has probabilities

$$f_{S_2}(x) = e^{-\lambda p_2}\frac{(\lambda p_2)^n}{n!}, \quad x = 0, m, 2m, \ldots,$$

where $n = x/m$.

The distribution of the total claims $S = S_1 + S_2$ has spikes at $x = 0, m, 2m, \ldots$ with the spikes being of mass

$$f_S(x) = f_{S_1}(0)f_{S_2}(x) = e^{-\lambda}\frac{(\lambda p_2)^n}{n!}$$

where $n = x/m$.

Between these spikes, it is piecewise continuous. Consider some point $rm+x$ where r is a non-negative integer and $x<m$. Then at most r maximum claims could have occurred. Consequently, the pdf at points of continuity is

$$f_S(rm+x) = \sum_{n_2=0}^{r} e^{-\lambda p_2}\frac{(\lambda p_2)^{n_2}}{n_2!}f_{S_1}(rm+x-n_2 m).$$

Example 6.4.3. Positive or Negative Severity

In some situations, a "claim" may result in a gain or loss for the insurer. This could be described through a severity distribution that takes on negative values as well as positive ones. The positive and negative parts of the severity can be separated and dealt with separately. The distribution totals of all gains and of all losses can be calculated as independent compound Poisson random variables if desired. In a later section dealing with the computation of the distribution of total claims, it will be seen that this splitting of positive and negative claims is useful.

Example 6.4.4. Insurance with Deductibles

Suppose that when a loss occurs, a deductible of d applies so that the claims to the insurer is given by

$$Y = \begin{cases} X-d, & X>d, \\ 0, & X\leq d. \end{cases}$$

If the number of losses in a fixed time period is a Poisson variate with mean λ, then the number of claims is a Poisson variate with mean λp where

$$p = Pr\{X>d\} = Pr\{Y>0\}$$

and the severity for (positive) claims is

$$f_Y(x) = f_X(x+d)/p, \quad x>0$$

so that the total claim cost is a compound Poisson random variable with Poisson parameter λp and claim severity distribution given by $f_Y(x)$.

Numerical Illustration 6.4.2. Major Medical Insurance

Under a major medical insurance plan it is assumed that claims occur randomly through any year in accordance with a Poisson process with intensity function $\lambda = .120$. The claim sizes are assumed to be independent with distribution given (in units of 50 dollars) below:

x	$f_X(x)$	$F_X(x)$	x	$f_X(x)$	$F_X(x)$	x	$f_X(x)$	$F_X(x)$	x	$f_X(x)$	$F_X(x)$
1	.02	.02	6	.04	.15	11	.09	.50	16	.06	.89
2	.02	.04	7	.05	.20	12	.09	.59	17	.04	.93
3	.02	.06	8	.06	.26	13	.09	.68	18	.03	.96
4	.02	.08	9	.07	.33	14	.08	.76	19	.02	.98
5	.03	.11	10	.08	.41	15	.07	.83	20	.02	1.00

The insured is required to pay the first 150 dollars on any claim. The insurer pays the remaining cost subject to a maximum payment of 750 dollars on any claim. The probability that a given claim exceeds 150 dollars is $1-F_X(3) = .94$. The distribution of the insurer's cost for any claim exceeding 150 dollars is

$$f_1(x) = \begin{cases} f_X(x+3)/.94, & x = 1,2,\ldots,14, \\ [1-F_X(17)]/.94, & x = 15. \end{cases}$$

Hence, the distribution of the insurer's total cost of a one year policy is compound Poisson with Poisson parameter $.12\times.94 = .1128$ and claim cost distribution $f_1(x)$ given below:

x	$f_1(x)$	$F_1(x)$	x	$f_1(x)$	$F_1(x)$	x	$f_1(x)$	$F_1(x)$
1	.0212766	.0212766	6	.0744681	.2872340	11	.0851064	.7446809
2	.0319149	.0531915	7	.0851064	.3723404	12	.0744681	.8191489
3	.0425532	.0957447	8	.0957447	.4680851	13	.0638298	.8829787
4	.0531915	.1489362	9	.0957447	.5638298	14	.0425532	.9255319
5	.0638298	.2127660	10	.0957447	.6595745	15	.0744681	1

6.5 APPROXIMATING THE INDIVIDUAL RISK MODEL BY THE COMPOUND POISSON MODEL

Because of the computational complexity of calculating the distribution of total claims for a portfolio of n risks using the individual risk model described in chapter 5, it has been popular to attempt to approximate the distribution by using the compound Poisson distribution. As was seen in section 6.2, use of the compound Poisson allows calculation of the total claims distribution using a very simple recursive procedure. In the notation of chapter 5, the distribution of total claims has Laplace transform

$$L_S(z) = \prod_{j=1}^{n}\{p_j+q_jL_{Y_j}(z)\}$$

$$= \prod_{j=1}^{n}\{1+q_j[L_{Y_j}(z)-1]\}. \tag{6.5.1}$$

For any value of z for which $L_{Y_j}(z)$ exists, the logarithm of the LT is

$$\log L_S(z) = \sum_{j=1}^{n} \log\{1+q_j[L_{Y_j}(z)-1]\} \tag{6.5.2}$$

$$= \sum_{j=1}^{n} \sum_{k=1}^{\infty} \frac{(-1)^{k+1}}{k} \{q_j[L_{Y_j}(z)-1]\}^k \tag{6.5.3}$$

using the series expansion for the logarithm function.

Retaining only first order terms in the claim probabilities (i.e. $k=1$ only) yields the approximation

$$\log L_S(z) \sum_{j=1}^{n} q_j[L_{Y_j}(z)-1] = \left(\sum_{j=1}^{n} q_j\right)\left(\frac{\sum_{j=1}^{n} q_j L_{Y_j}(z)}{\sum_{j=1}^{n} q_j} - 1\right)$$

$$= \lambda[L_X(z)-1] \tag{6.5.4}$$

where

$$\lambda = \sum_{j=1}^{n} q_j \tag{6.5.5}$$

and

$$L_X(z) = \frac{\sum_{j=1}^{n} q_j L_{Y_j}(z)}{\sum_{j=1}^{n} q_j}. \tag{6.5.6}$$

Note that (6.5.4) is the logarithm of the LT of a compound Poisson distribution. Consequently, we can approximate the individual risk model by a compound Poisson model with the same expected number of claims (6.5.5) and the claim severity distribution

$$F_X(x) = \frac{\sum_{j=1}^{n} q_j F_{Y_j}(x)}{\sum_{j=1}^{n} q_j}. \tag{6.5.7}$$

The severity distribution is the weighted average of the n individual claim size distributions $F_{Y_j}(x)$, $j = 1,2,\ldots,n$ where the weights are the expected number of claims q_j, $j = 1,2,\ldots,n$. Note that this construction is essentially the same as in Theorem 6.3.1 in which independent compound Poisson risks were combined using expected number of claims as weights. This should be expected because in the approximation (6.5.4), the logarithm of the LT for each individual risk was approximated by the quantity $q_j[L_{Y_j}(z)-1]$, the corresponding quantity for a compound Poisson distribution with q_j expected claims. From (6.5.4)- (6.5.6), it can be seen that the mean and variance of the approximating compound Poisson distribution are

$$E[S] = \sum_{j=1}^{n} q_j E[Y_j] \tag{6.5.8}$$

and

$$Var[S] = \sum_{j=1}^{n} q_j E[Y_j^2]. \tag{6.5.9}$$

On comparison with Numerical Illustration 5.2.1, one sees that (6.5.9) "overestimates" the variance by the quantity $\sum_{j=1}^{n} q_j^2 \{E[Y_j]\}^2$. Consequently, the approximation using the compound Poisson distribution is considered to be "conservative" in the sense that it assumes greater "spread" of the distribution of total claims than is the actual case.

It is also possible to measure the "distance" of the approximating distribution (the compound Poisson) from the true distribution based on the individual risk model. A useful measure of distance between distributions F and G is that of Le Cam (1960). It is defined as

$$d(F,G) = \sup_A\{|P_G(A)-P_F(A)|\} \tag{6.5.10}$$

where $P_F(A)$ is the probability that $X \in A$ based on distribution F where A is any subset of the support of F. Hence, the distance $d(F,G)$ can be viewed as the maximum possible "error" in any probability statement about total claims when F and G are two distributions of total claims. Gerber (1984) considers the distance (6.5.10) in assessing the compound Poisson approximation. He shows that the distance between the distribution for the individual risk model and the approximating compound Poisson distribution satisfies

$$d(F_S^{ind}, F_S^{cp}) \le \sum_{j=1}^{n} q_i^2 \tag{6.5.11}$$

The sum on the right-hand side of (6.5.11) is an upper bound on the maximum possible error. If the q_i's are small (as in the case of life insurance) and n is not too large, the bound is small.

Numerical Illustration 6.5.1.

Consider the three risks used in numerical illustration 5.2.1. The data for the three risks are as follows:

j	q_j	$f_{Y_1}(1)$	$f_{Y_2}(2)$	$f_{Y_3}(3)$	$f_{Y_4}(4)$
1	.10	.10	.20	.30	.40
2	.20	.20	.30	.50	0
3	.30	0	0	.50	.50
Combined	.60	.083333	.133333	.466667	.316667

The approximate distribution of total claims using the method described within this section is given in the following table together with the exact results from numerical illustration 5.2.1:

	Exact		Approximate		
x	$f_S(x)$	$F_S(x)$	$f_S(x)$	$F_S(x)$	Difference
0	.50400	.50400	.5488116	.5488116	.0448116
1	.03080	.53480	.0274406	.5762522	.0414522
2	.04928	.58408	.0445909	.6208432	.0367632
3	.18878	.77286	.1558739	.7767171	.0038571
4	.13938	.91224	.1137688	.8904859	-.0217541
5	.02094	.93318	.0177879	.9082738	-.0249062
6	.03165	.96483	.0306526	.9389264	-.0259036
7	.02542	.99205	.0312012	.9701276	-.0201224
8	.00612	.99637	.0134838	.9836115	-.0127585
9	.00162	.99799	.0049926	.9886041	-.0093859
10	.00141	.99940	.0051912	.9937953	-.0056047
11	.00060	1	.0032816	.9970769	-.0029231
12	0	1	.0012863	.9983632	-.0016368

The maximum error occurs at $x = 0$ and is .0448116. The error bound (6.5.11) yields $(.1)^2 + (.2)^2 + (.3)^2 = .14$ significantly greater than the actual error.

Numerical Illustration 6.5.2. Group Life Insurance

Consider the group life case of numerical illustration 5.2.2. Using the compound Poisson approximation of this section with Poisson parameter $\sum q_j = .04813$, the following distribution function is obtained:

x	$F_S(x)$	x	$F_S(x)$	x	$F_S(x)$	x	$F_S(x)$
0	.9530099	20	.9618348	40	.9735771	60	.9990974
1	.9530099	21	.9618348	41	.9735850	61	.9990986
2	.9530099	22	.9618348	42	.9736072	62	.9990994
3	.9530099	23	.9618348	43	.9736133	63	.9990995
4	.9530099	24	.9664473	44	.9736346	64	.9990995
5	.9530099	25	.9664473	45	.9736393	65	.9990996
6	.9530099	26	.9702022	46	.9736513	66	.9990997
7	.9530099	27	.9702022	47	.9736541	67	.9990997
8	.9530099	28	.9713650	48	.9736708	68	.9990998
9	.9530099	29	.9713657	49	.9736755	69	.9991022
10	.9530099	30	.9723490	50	.9736956	70	.9991091
11	.9530099	31	.9735235	51	.9736971	71	.9991156
12	.9530099	32	.9735268	52	.9737101	72	.9991179
13	.9530099	33	.9735328	53	.9737102	73	.9991341
14	.9534864	34	.9735391	54	.9737195	74	.9991470
15	.9549064	35	.9735433	55	.9782901	75	.9991839
16	.9562597	36	.9735512	56	.9782947	76	.9992135
17	.9567362	37	.9735536	57	.9782994	77	.9992239
18	.9601003	38	.9735604	58	.9783006	78	.9992973
19	.9606149	39	.9735679	59	.9783021	79	.9993307

When these values are compared to those of numerical illustration 5.4.1, it can be seen that the maximum error of .0002708 occurs at $x = 0$. The upper bound on the error given by formula (6.5.11) is $\sum q_j^2 = .0005612$.

6.6 COMPUTATION FOR ARITHMETIC SEVERITIES

We now consider compound distributions of the form

$$f_S(x) = \sum_{n=0}^{\infty} p_n f_X^{*n}(x), \quad x \geq 0 \tag{6.6.1}$$

where p_n is the probability function of the Poisson, negative binomial (including geometric) or binomial distributions and generalize the recursive formula (6.2.13). In this section we will restrict (unless otherwise stated) the claim sizes to be positive. In this case, the probability that total claims are zero is just the probability that no claims occur and so we write

$$F_S(0) = p_0 \qquad (6.6.2)$$

with equation (6.6.1) holding for values of $x > 0$.

Evaluation of (6.6.1) may be difficult to carry out, even on a high-speed computer. If $F_X(x)$ is a continuous function, its convolutions need to be obtained analytically or numerically. If $F_X(x)$ is discrete on the positive integers, such convolutions can be carried out on a computer but may become very time consuming if a large number of points on the total claims distribution are required and if a large number of terms in the infinite sum are required before the terms become negligible. If $F_X(x)$ is a mixed distribution, analytic results are usually not possible and numerical evaluation would be required.

A simplified procedure for the evaluation of the distribution of total claims was introduced into the actuarial literature by Panjer (1980, 1981). The procedure is based on a simple recurrence relation when the claim sizes are discrete on the positive integers (or equivalently on some multiple thereof) and on a recurrence relation in the form of a Volterra integral equation when the claim sizes are from a continuous distribution. If claim sizes are from a distribution of the mixed type, or from a discrete distribution with an irregular span, discretization procedures can be used to obtain upper and lower bounds and approximations to the distribution of total claims. The results are now developed.

Consider the class of claim frequency distribution for which the recurrence relation

$$\frac{p_n}{p_{n-1}} = a + \frac{b}{n}, \quad n = 1,2,3,\dots \qquad (6.6.3)$$

holds. Members of this class and the corresponding parameter values are given in table 6.6.1.

We now show that the distributions given in table 6.6.1 are the only members of the class satisfying (6.6.3).

TABLE 6.6.1

Distribution	Formula	Value of a	Value of b
Poisson	4.2.1	0	λ
Binomial	4.3.1	$-\dfrac{q}{1-q}$	$(m+1)\dfrac{q}{1-q}$
Geometric	4.4.1	$\dfrac{\beta}{1+\beta}$	0
Negative Binomial	4.5.1	$\dfrac{\beta}{1+\beta}$	$(r-1)\dfrac{\beta}{1+\beta}$

FIGURE 6.6.1

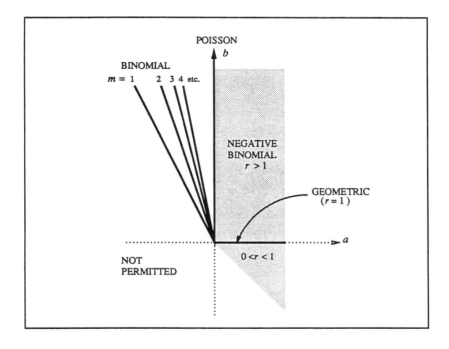

Lemma 6.6.1. The only members of the class of discrete distributions on the non-negative integers satisfying (6.6.3) are the Poisson, binomial, negative binomial and geometric distributions.

Proof

In figure 6.6.1, the lines of the form $b = -(m+1)a$ for $m = 1,2,3,...$ and $a<0$ corresponds to the binomial distribution. The positive vertical axis corresponds to the Poisson distribution. The region with $b>-a$ and $0<a<1$ corresponds to the negative binomial distribution. Consider the region for which $b<-a$. In this region $b+a<0$ so that $(a+b)p_0<0$. Consequently (6.6.3) cannot hold for $n = 1$. Now consider the region for which $a<0$ and $b\geq-a$. The line $b = -a$ for $a<0$ corresponds to the degenerate distribution at the origin since $p_1 = (a+b)p_0 = 0$. For any point in the region, excluding the lines $b = -(m+1)a$, $m = 1,2,3,...$, application of the recurrence relation (6.6.3) will ultimately result in negative values for p_n. Finally, for the region for which $a\geq1$ and $b>-a$, it is clear that $a+b/n\geq a(1-1/n)\geq(n-1)/n$. For this region, successive application of (6.6.3) results in $p_2>p_1/2$, $p_3>p_1/3$, ..., $p_n>p_1/n$,.... . Summing the p_j's yield

$$\sum_{n=1}^{\infty} p_n > p_1 \left[1 + \frac{1}{2} + \frac{1}{3} + \cdots \right]$$

which diverges. Hence, the distribution satisfying (6.6.3) cannot exist in this region. Consequently, the Poisson, binomial, negative binomial and geometric distributions are the only distributions satisfying (6.6.3).

The following theorem gives the basic result in terms of Laplace transforms and applies for any severity distribution. The corollary give the result for discrete claim severity distributions.

Theorem 6.6.1. For the class of distributions defined by (6.6.3), the following relationship holds:

$$L_S'(z) = aL_X(z)L_S'(z) + (a+b)L_X'(z)L_S(z). \tag{6.6.4}$$

Proof

The recursion (6.6.3) can be rewritten as

$$np_n = a(n-1)p_{n-1} + (a+b)p_{n-1}.$$

Multiplying this equation by $\{L_X(z)\}^{n-1}L_X'(z)$ and summing over n yields

$$\sum_{n=1}^{\infty} np_n\{L_X(z)\}^{n-1}L_X'(z) = a\sum_{n=1}^{\infty}(n-1)p_{n-1}\{L_X(z)\}^{n-1}L_X'(z)$$

$$+ (a+b)\sum_{n=1}^{\infty}p_{n-1}\{L_X(z)\}^{n-1}L_X'(z).$$

Since

$$L_S(z) = \sum_{n=0}^{\infty}p_n\{L_X(z)\}^n,$$

the previous equation can be recognized as

$$L_S'(z) = aL_X(z)L_S'(z) + (a+b)L_X'(z)L_S(z).$$

Corollary 6.6.1. For the class of distributions defined by (6.6.3) with claim sizes defined on the positive integers, the following recursive formula for the distribution of total claims holds:

$$f_S(x) = \sum_{y=1}^{x}(a+b\frac{y}{x})f_X(y)f_S(x-y), \quad x = 1,2,3,\dots \ . \qquad (6.6.5)$$

Proof

Inversion of (6.6.4) when X is defined only on positive integers yields

$$x\,f_S(x) = a\sum_{y=1}^{x}(x-y)f_X(y)f_S(x-y) + (a+b)\sum_{y=1}^{x}yf_X(y)f_S(x-y).$$

Rearrangement yields (6.6.5).

For the situation in which the claim sizes are defined on the positive integers, equation (6.6.1) reduces to

$$f_S(x) = \sum_{n=1}^{x}p_n f_X^{*n}(x), \quad x = 1,2,3,\dots \tag{6.6.7}$$

since a maximum of x claims (each of size 1) can occur when total claims are exactly x units. In order to compare the computational efficiency of (6.6.5) over (6.6.7), we count only the number of multiplications required to carry out the calculations for $f_S(x)$, $x = 1,2,\dots,m$ where m is the maximum value for which values of the distribution of total claims is required.

The number of computations required to calculate $f_X^{*n}(x)$ can be obtained by examining

$$f_X^{*n}(x) = \sum_{y=1}^{x}f_X(y)f_X^{*(n-1)}(x-y) \tag{6.6.8}$$

the recurrence relationship for convolutions. Here exactly x multiplications are required. Consequently, the calculation of all values of $f_X^{*n}(x)$ for n fixed and $x = 1,2,3,\dots,m$ requires $1+2+3+\cdots+m = m(m+1)/2$ multiplications. This must be done for $n = 1,2,3,\dots,m$. Consequently, the total number of multiplications is of order m^3.

The number of computations to evaluate (6.6.5) is of order x for each value of $f_S(x)$. Hence, summing over $x = 1,2,\dots,m$ yields a total which is of order m^2.

In many practical applications carried out by the authors, the value of m was often of size 1000 or larger. Use of (6.6.5) instead of (6.6.8) reduces the computer time for these calculations by a factor of about 1000 when $m = 1000$. At this rate, what can be done in 1 minute of computer time using (6.6.5) requires approximately 16 2/3 hours of computer time using (6.6.7) at a cost that would typically be prohibitive. Since computer speeds have increased by many orders of magnitude in the past decade, the use of equation (6.6.5) allows one to carry out exact calculations that would be virtually (or practically) impossible previously using equation (6.6.7). The one minute time mentioned above on an older computer is now more realistically only a fraction of a second on a high-speed computer. Microcomputers with high speed microprocessors can easily be used to evaluate (6.6.5) even for large values of m.

In addition, from a computational point of view, equation (6.6.5) has the advantage that it requires much less storage than (6.6.7) since only the values of $f_X(x)$, $x = 1,2,\ldots,m$ and the previously computed $f_S(x)$ need be maintained in computer memory.

In the above analysis we have assumed that the severity distribution $f_X(x)$ is positive for large values of x. If the support of $f_X(x)$ is restricted to $x = 1,2,\ldots,r$, then equation (6.6.5) reduces to

$$f_S(x) = \sum_{y=1}^{s}(a+b\frac{y}{x})f_X(y)f_S(x-y), \quad x = 1,2,3,\ldots \qquad (6.6.9)$$

where $s = \min\{x,r\}$. Thus, equation (6.6.9) contains at most r terms, speeding up the calculations even further. A finite value of r occurs in all situations in which the liability is restricted by a maximum value as a result of excess-of-loss (XL) reinsurance, as a result of contractual provisions in the insuring contract or as a consequence of the nature of the insurance. For example, reinsurance sold in "layers" to various reinsurers has a defined maximum. Similarly, the life insurance portfolio has a maximum severity that is the size of the largest policy.

The recursive formula (6.6.5) uses as an initial value $f_S(0) = p_0$. When carrying out these calculations on a computer, one may encounter difficulty if p_0 is sufficiently small to be represented on the computer hardware as zero indicating "underflow". In this case, (6.6.5) will generate a vector of zeros and fail to compute the probabilities as desired. For the Poisson frequency distribution, this occurs when λ is too large; for the negative binomial, when $r \log(1+\beta)$ is too large; and for the binomial, when $-m \log q$ is too large. There are several ways to overcome this difficulty, the simplest of which is now described.

Let e^{-k} denote the smallest number that can be represented on the computer (this varies by computer type and by computer language). Then underflow occurs when $\lambda > k$ for the Poisson distribution, when $r \log(1+\beta) > k$ for the negative binomial, and when $-m \log q > k$ for the binomial. The Laplace transform of the distribution of total claims can be written as

$$L_S(z) = \{L(z)\}^\alpha$$

for each of these distributions where $\alpha = \lambda$ for the Poisson, $\alpha = r$ for the negative binomial and $\alpha = m$ for the binomial.

For the Poisson, let $\lambda^* = \lambda/2^n$ where n is the smallest integer so that $\lambda^* < k$. Then one computes (using (6.6.5)) the distribution with Laplace transform $L_1(z) = \{L(z)\}^{\lambda^*}$ (from the definition of n, underflow cannot occur). This distribution can be convoluted with itself to produce the distribution with Laplace transform $L_2(z) = \{L_1(z)\}^2 = \{L(z)\}^{2\lambda^*}$. The resulting distribution is convoluted with itself to produce the distribution with Laplace transform $L_3(z) = \{L_2(z)\}^2 = \{L_1(z)\}^4 = \{L(z)\}^{4\lambda^*}$. This process is repeated until the distribution with Laplace transform $L_S(z) = \{L(z)\}^{2^n \lambda^*}$ is produced. Since the number of computations in evaluating the distribution using (6.6.5) is roughly the same as in doing one convolution, this procedure will require about $(n+1)$ times the computational time as a single application of (6.6.5).

For the negative binomial, let $r^* = r/2^n$ where n is the smallest integer so that $r^* \log(1+\beta) < k$. Initially the distribution with Laplace transform $L_1(z) = \{L(z)\}^{r^*}$ is calculated using (6.6.5) and an analogous procedure is carried out.

For the binomial, it should be noted that m must be integral so that a modification is required. Let $m^* = [m/2^n]$ where [.] indicates the "greatest integer less than " function. Similar calculations are carried out until the distribution with Laplace transform $G(z) = \{L(z)\}^{2^n m^*}$ is produced. Then the distribution with Laplace transform $H(z) = \{L(z)\}^{m - 2^n m^*}$ is calculated separately. The final distribution is calculated by convoluting these two distributions since

$L_S(z) = G(z)H(z)$. Consequently, the number of calculations are about $(n+3)$ times the number using (6.6.5) alone.

This simple method produces a fool proof way of avoiding underflow. However it is at the expense of additional computing time. If n is judged to be too large, the expected number of claims is large and approximations discussed in chapter 10 may also be useful. Other methods are discussed by Panjer and Willmot (1986).

6.7 COMPOUND NEGATIVE BINOMIAL AS A MIXTURE

In this and the subsequent three sections, we give some theoretical justification for the use of the negative binomial distribution as a model of claims frequency.

The compound negative binomial distribution is of the form (6.1.2) with claim frequency probabilities given by

$$p_k = \frac{\Gamma(r+k)}{\Gamma(r)k!} \left[\frac{1}{1+\beta}\right]^r \left[\frac{\beta}{1+\beta}\right]^k, \quad k = 0,1,2,... \tag{6.7.1}$$

and pgf (from equation (4.5.2)

$$P_N(z) = \{1-\beta(z-1)\}^{-r}, \quad |z|<(1+\beta)/\beta. \tag{6.7.2}$$

Again here p_k is to be interpreted as the number of claims in a fixed period of time such as one year.

Derivation of (6.7.2) by mixing a Poisson distribution can be done by using pgf's and the results of section 2.8. Suppose for known or fixed θ, the distribution of $N(t)$, the number of claims occurring in time interval $(0,t]$, has a Poisson distribution with mean θt, and pgf given by

$$P_{N(t)}(z \mid \theta) = e^{\theta t(z-1)}. \tag{6.7.3}$$

The unconditional distribution of $N(t)$ (for unknown θ) has a pgf of the form

$$P_{N(t)}(z) = E_\theta P_{N(t)}(z \mid \theta = \theta) = E_\theta[e^{\theta t(z-1)}] = L_\theta[t(1-z)]. \qquad (6.7.4)$$

Further suppose that θ has a gamma distribution of the form (4.12.1) with LT

$$L_\theta(z) = \left(\frac{\lambda}{\lambda + z}\right)^\alpha. \qquad (6.7.5)$$

Then, substituting this result into (6.7.4) yields

$$P_{N(t)}(z) = L_\theta(t(1-z)) = \left[\frac{\lambda}{\lambda + t(1-z)}\right]^\alpha = \left\{1 - \frac{t}{\lambda}(z-1)\right\}^{-\alpha} \qquad (6.7.6)$$

which is of the form (6.7.2) with $\beta = t/\lambda$ and $r = \alpha$. Hence, the unconditional distribution of $N(t)$ is negative binomial.

The mixing of the claim frequency distribution can be justified in an insurance context as follows. Suppose that the claim frequency for any risk follows a compound Poisson distribution if its risk parameter θ is known. Further suppose that the population of risks is heterogeneous with respect to the risk parameter θ and that the values of θ in the population are distributed in accordance with the gamma distribution. The insurer of the risk is unable to determine the risk parameter θ for any particular risk in the population. Consequently, the risk is taken as a risk from the population as a whole.

This situation is natural in most insurance contexts. Insurance classification systems recognize only some characteristics of the risks. For example, in fire insurance, a variety of buildings with different susceptibility to fire will occur within any particular class. Similarly, for life insurance, a simple age and sex classification system will not recognize such factors as variations in build, family history and personal habits which might affect an individual's risk.

The negative binomial has appeal because its variance exceeds its mean unlike the Poisson for which the mean and variance are equal. However, all mixtures of Poisson distributions has this property. From example 2.8.1, it is easy to show that the ratio of the variance to the mean is of the form

$$Var[N(t)]/E[N(t)] = 1 + t \ Var(\theta)/E(\theta) \qquad (6.7.7)$$

which exceeds 1 for all non-degenerate mixing distributions. Other choices of mixing functions will be considered in chapter 7 which deals with more advanced models.

In terms of the mean μ_1' and the variance μ_2, the skewness of the negative binomial distribution may be written as

$$\mu_2^{-\frac{3}{2}}\{3\mu_2 - 2\mu_1' + 2(\mu_2 - \mu_1')^2/\mu_1'\}. \qquad (6.7.8)$$

This will be compared with alternative distributions in chapter 7.

Numerical Illustration 6.7.1. Automobile Insurance.

The following two data sets record the number of accidents over a fixed time period by drivers in the state of California. The first data set is taken from Weber (1970) and presents the number of accidents over a two year period (1961-2) for 148,006 drivers. The second set is based on the period November 1959 to February 1968 for 7,482 drivers and is taken from Seal (1982). Using the maximum likelihood method (see chapter 9), a negative binomial distribution is fitted to each data set. The expected number of persons in each category and the parameter estimators are given in the following table:

| Number of | Weber (1970) | | Seal (1982) | |
Accidents	Actual	Theoretical	Actual	Theoretical
0	129,524	129,527.10	5,147	5,147.94
1	16,267	16,261.21	1,859	1,859.84
2	1,966	1,955.21	595	586.33
3	211	231.63	167	175.85
4	31	27.24	54	51.39
5	5	3.19	14	14.78
6	1	.37	5	4.21
7	1	.04	0	1.19
8	-	.00	0	.33
9	-	.00	0	.09
10	-	.00	0	.03
11	-	.00	1	.01
Total	148,006	148,006.00	7,842	7,842.00
$\hat{r}$		1.0923183		1.3418374
$\hat{\beta}$		.12985739		.36844195

Comparing (6.7.6) and (6.7.2), the maximum likelihood estimates of the parameters λ and α of the gamma distribution (6.6.5) are $\hat{\lambda} = t/\hat{\beta}$ and $\hat{\alpha} = \hat{r}$. For the first data set, $t = 2$, and so $\hat{\lambda} = 2/.12985739 = 15.401511$ and $\hat{\alpha} = 1.0923183$. For the second data set $t = 8.25$ so that $\hat{\lambda} = 8.25/.36844195 = 22.391587$ and $\hat{\alpha} = 1.3418374$. Using the model of this section, the results can be interpreted as follows. Each driver experiences accidents in accordance with a homogeneous Poisson process. In the population of drivers, the Poisson risk parameter for the drivers is distributed in accordance with a gamma distribution with mean α/λ and variance α/λ^2. For the two data sets, the gamma distributions have means .07092280 and .05992596 and standard deviations .06785960 and .05173269 respectively. In order to model the distribution of claim costs of a one-year insurance plan, the actuary may wish to use such a model. Since the mixed Poisson process does not possess independent increments, it is assumed that the portfolio being modeled starts again at $N(0) = 0$ at the issue of the insurance policy. In this case, we can model $N(1)$, the number of claims in a single year, as a negative binomial distribution with parameters $r = \hat{\alpha}$ and $\beta = 1/\hat{\lambda}$.

It should be noted that we have mixed only the claims frequency distribution. If it is assumed that the severity distribution does not depend upon the risk parameter, the resulting mixed distribution of total claims will have the same severity distribution as the conditional distribution of total claims. We now consider the situation where the compound Poisson random variable is itself a sum of compound Poisson random variables, a situation for which the severity does depend upon the various Poisson parameters.

In section 6.3, we considered sums of compound Poisson variables and showed that such a sum was itself a compound Poisson variable with claim severity distribution of the form (6.3.3) with pf (or pdf) given by

$$f_X(x) = \sum_{j=1}^{n} \frac{\lambda_j}{\lambda} f_j(x). \tag{6.7.9}$$

In order for one to carry out the mixing as was done in this section, it will be necessary for the severity of the combined model, $F_X(x)$, to be independent of λ. This is true if the proportions, λ_j/λ, do not vary as λ varies, i.e., if

$$\lambda_j = \lambda \pi_j, \quad j = 1, 2, \ldots, n. \tag{6.7.10}$$

This has a very useful and simple interpretation in the life insurance situation described in section 6.3 with associated formulas (6.3.4) to (6.3.7). In this situation, the severity is of the form (from 6.3.7)

$$f_X(x) = \sum_{b_j=x} \pi_j \tag{6.7.11}$$

where the summation is taken over all risks with benefit amount x. It is clear that this severity does not depend upon λ. Varying λ causes λ_i to vary at the same rate (from 6.7.10). Since λ_j is interpreted as the integrated force of mortality at amount b_j, changes in λ and λ_j can be interpreted as a result of a constant multiplicative change in the basic force of mortality at all ages. Consequently, a mixed model could be interpreted as reflecting the uncertainty in the overall level of the mortality table. The mixing distribution reflects the uncertainty about the level of the overall level of mortality. The relative levels of mortality (as measured by the integrated forces of mortality) remain constant.

It should be noticed that the corresponding mixture of Poisson processes is referred to as a Polya process. The transition probabilities will be of compound negative binomial form when the mixing distribution is a gamma distribution. This can be seen from section 3.5 and formula (3.5.1).

Numerical Illustration 6.7.2. Group Life Insurance

Consider the group life insurance portfolio of 14 lives of numerical illustration 6.3.2 where the compound Poisson model is used to represent the distribution of total claims. The mean number of claims is .04841423259 based on the 1969-75 Canadian Institute of Actuaries Mortality Table. The actuary is uncertain about the appropriateness of this table for the group of 14 lives and it is impractical to obtain additional underwriting information on the group. The actuary is willing to express his or her uncertainty about the expected number of claims as a gamma distribution with mean .0484142 and standard deviation .01. The actuary makes this assessment on the basis of his professional experience in group insurance. The parameters of the gamma distribution are obtained by solving

$$\frac{\alpha}{\lambda} = .04841423259$$

and

$$\frac{\alpha}{\lambda^2} = (.01)^2.$$

This yields $\alpha = 23.43937917$ and $\lambda = 484.1423259$. The actuary now replaces the Poisson distribution by the negative binomial distribution with parameters $r = 23.43937917$ and $\beta = 1/\lambda = .002065508316$. The unconditional distribution of total claims can now be calculated as a compound negative binomial distribution. The individual claim size distribution is that used in numerical illustration 6.3.2. The distribution of total claims is most easily calculated using the recursive formula (6.6.9) described in section 6.6. The calculations are carried out in the next numerical illustration.

Numerical Illustration 6.7.3. Group Life Insurance

Consider the group life portfolio of 14 lives in numerical illustration 6.7.2 where the negative binomial distribution with parameters $r = 23.43937917$ and $\beta = .002065508316$ was developed as the claim frequency distribution. For the negative binomial, $a = \beta/(1+\beta)$ and $b = (r-1)\beta/(1+\beta)$ and the recursive formula (6.6.9) reduces to

$$f_S(x) = \frac{1}{x}\frac{\beta}{1+\beta}\sum_{y=1}^{s}\{x+(r-1)y\}f_X(y)f_S(x-y), \quad x = 1,2,3,\dots \; .$$

Using this formula and the claim size distribution developed in numerical illustration 6.3.2, the distribution of total claims can easily be calculated. The resulting distribution up to $x = 77$ is given in the following table:

x	$F_S(x)$	x	$F_S(x)$	x	$F_S(x)$	x	$F_S(x)$
0	0.9527866	30	0.9721104	46	0.9734161	62	0.9990503
13	0.9527866	31	0.9732830	47	0.9734189	63	0.9990503
14	0.9532622	32	0.9732864	48	0.9734364	64	0.9990504
15	0.9546799	33	0.9732926	49	0.9734412	65	0.9990505
16	0.9560311	34	0.9732991	50	0.9734622	66	0.9990506
17	0.9565066	35	0.9733035	51	0.9734637	67	0.9990506
18	0.9598689	36	0.9733118	52	0.9734773	68	0.9990507
19	0.9603825	37	0.9733143	53	0.9734773	69	0.9990532
20	0.9616004	38	0.9733214	54	0.9734871	70	0.9990604
23	0.9616004	39	0.9733292	55	0.9780584	71	0.9990671
24	0.9662135	40	0.9733388	56	0.9780632	72	0.9990696
25	0.9662135	41	0.9733470	57	0.9780681	73	0.9990865
26	0.9699671	42	0.9733701	58	0.9780694	74	0.9991000
27	0.9699671	43	0.9733765	59	0.9780709	75	0.9991387
28	0.9711280	44	0.9733987	60	0.9990481	76	0.9991698
29	0.9711287	45	0.9734035	61	0.9990494	77	0.9991807

Note that for large values of x $(x \geq 60)$, the distribution function of the compound negative binomial distribution is less than that of the corresponding compound Poisson distribution (see numerical example 6.3.3). This means that the mixing function has introduced additional risk for the insurer. The amount of additional risk is very small since the portfolio is very small. The situation for larger portfolios is illustrated in the next numerical illustration.

Numerical Illustration 6.7.4. Group Life Insurance

Suppose that the group of 14 lives in the previous numerical illustration is increased by a factor of 100 so that the group now consists of 1400 lives and the mean number of claims is 4.841423259. If, as in numerical illustration 6.7.2, the actuary expresses his or her uncertainty about the true mortality rates as a gamma distribution with mean 4.841423259 and standard deviation 1. Then, as in numerical illustration 6.7.2, one obtains $\alpha = 23.43937917$ and $\lambda = 4.841423259$ so that the negative binomial parameters are $r = 23.43937917$ and $\beta = 1/\lambda = .2065508316$. When the distribution of total claims is calculated and compared with the corresponding compound Poisson distribution, the following results are obtained (only values for multiples of 40,000 dollars are given):

	Distribution Function		Tail Probabilities		
x	Poisson $F_S(x)$	Neg. Bin. $F_S(x)$	Poisson $1-F_S(x)$	Neg. Bin. $1-F_S(x)$	Increase
0	.0078958	.0122637			
40	.0297674	.0395700			
80	.0996608	.1194133			
120	.2199202	.2444101			
160	.3517526	.3712274			
200	.5130186	.5221847			
240	.6609470	.6584125			
280	.7739436	.7630714	.2260564	.2369286	4.8%
320	.8630801	.8477731	.1369199	.1522269	11%
360	.9217728	.9062252	.0782272	.0937748	20%
400	.9572480	.9440844	.0427520	.0559156	31%
440	.9783364	.9683916	.0216636	.0316084	46%
480	.9894971	.9826694	.0105029	.0173306	65%
520	.9951368	.9908064	.0048632	.0091936	89%
560	.9978685	.9952880	.0021315	.0047120	121%
600	.9990985	.9976449	.0009015	.0023551	161%

The right-hand tail probabilities indicate that the introduction of uncertainty can have a significant effect on the right-hand tail probabilities.

6.8 COMPOUND NEGATIVE BINOMIAL AS A COMPOUND POISSON WITH MULTIPLE CLAIMS

The homogeneous and nonhomogeneous Poisson processes, as described in sections 3.3 and 3.4, satisfy the condition that for sufficiently small time intervals no more than one event can occur. For the purpose of this section, we shall refer to these events as "claim-causing events" or accidents. Consequently, no more than one accident can occur in a sufficiently small time interval. We now consider the possibility of multiple claims arising from a single accident. This is natural in most types of insurance, e.g. automobile, group life, fire or workmen's compensation. We are interested in the number of claims over a fixed time period.

Let $N(t)$ be the stochastic process representing the number of accidents up to time t. Let $M_1, M_2, \ldots, M_{N(t)}$ denote the number of claims for the successive accidents. Then

$$R(t) = M_1 + M_2 + \cdots + M_{N(t)} \tag{6.8.1}$$

is a stochastic process representing the total number of claims.

We assume that the number of claims per accident are independent and identically distributed random variables and that they are independent of the number of accidents. Consequently from (2.9.6), $R(t)$ is a compound random variable with pgf

$$P_{R(t)}(z) = P_{N(t)}(P_M(z)). \tag{6.8.2}$$

For convenience, we now drop the time variable t since we are concerned with the distribution of total claims for some fixed time period. When N is a Poisson variate with mean λ, (6.8.2) becomes

$$P_R(z) = e^{\lambda\{P_M(z)-1\}}. \tag{6.8.3}$$

We now make the assumption that the number of claims per accident has a logarithmic distribution with pf given by (4.6.1) and pgf

$$P_M(z) = \frac{\log(1-qz)}{\log(1-q)}. \tag{6.8.4}$$

Then the pgf of R becomes

$$P_R(z) = \left[\frac{1-qz}{1-q}\right]^{\lambda/\log(1-q)} = \{1-\beta(z-1)\}^{-r} \tag{6.8.5}$$

which is the pgf of the negative binomial distribution where

$$\beta = q/(1-q) \tag{6.8.6}$$

and

$$r = -\lambda/\log(1-q). \tag{6.8.7}$$

Hence, if the number of claims per accident is a logarithmic random variable, and the number of accidents over the time interval of interest is a Poisson random variable, the total number of claims for the time interval can be modeled by the negative binomial distributions. If the usual assumptions of independence of the claim severities is made, the distribution of total claims over the time interval can be modeled using a compound negative binomial distribution.

Numerical Illustration 6.8.1. Automobile Insurance

In a study of claims on automobile insurance, Lemaire (1985) (see also Gossiaux and Lemaire, 1981) reports the following results for a sample of 4000 policies:

Number of Claims	Actual	Theoretical	
		Poisson	Negative Binomial
0	3719	3668.54	3719.22
1	232	317.33	229.90
2	38	13.72	39.91
3	7	.40	8.42
4	3	.01	1.93
5	1	.00	0.46
Total	4000	4000	3999.85
$\hat{\lambda}$		.0865	
$\hat{r}$			.216600
$\hat{\beta}$			.399354

Using the method of maximum likelihood (see chapter 9), the Poisson and negative binomial distributions are fitted to the observed data. From the above table it is clear that the Poisson distribution fits badly and that the negative binomial distribution fits very well. Under both models the expected number of claims is .0865. The variance of the actual data is .1225 which exceeds the mean significantly, demonstrating the inadequacy of the Poisson model. If the negative binomial model is viewed as being based on a compound Poisson distribution of the number of accidents and a logarithmic distribution of the number of claims per accident, the parameter estimates are $\hat{\lambda} = \hat{r} \log(1+\hat{\beta}) = .0727799$ for the expected number of accidents and $\hat{q} = \hat{\beta}/(1+\hat{\beta}) = .285231$ for the logarithmic distribution parameter. The logarithmic probabilities are:

n	1	2	3	4	5
p_n	.84942	.12114	.02304	.00493	.00112

Under this model, 84.942% of all accidents giving rise to claims will result in only one claim, 12.114% will result in two claims, and so forth. In practice, this distribution will vary from insurance company to insurance company since it depends heavily upon the companies market share. For a small company, the probability that more than one claim will arise from an accident is much smaller than that of a large company which could have more than one of its insureds involved in an accident with greater likelihood.

6.9 COMPOUND NEGATIVE BINOMIAL AS A CONTAGION MODEL

In this section we derive the negative binomial from a physical phenomenon that is apparently different from the one considered in the last section. Suppose that the number of claims process $N(t)$, which describes the number of claims occurring up to time t, is a birth process (see section 3.6) and has the property that its intensity function or rate depends on both the time parameter t and the history of the process up to time t. We then write the intensity as $\lambda_n(t)$.

In particular we consider the special case of "positive contagion" (cf. Bühlmann, 1970) for which

$$\lambda_n(t) = \lambda(t)\{\alpha + \beta n\}, \quad \alpha, \beta > 0. \tag{6.9.1}$$

The form of the intensity function indicates that for fixed t, the intensity of the $(n+1)$-st claim increases linearly as a function of n. This effect may be interpreted as increased accident proneness or increased contagion. If it is believed that the risk of contracting a particular illness or disease is increased as the number in the population who are already ill or diseased increases, this model may be useful in modeling the total number of claims related to such illness or disease in the population.

Results of section 3.6 are now used to generate the compound negative binomial distribution. The intensity given by equation (6.9.1) is that of equation (3.6.6) and so according to theorem 3.6.1, the number of claims occurring between time t and time $t+s$ has a negative binomial distribution that depends upon the values of both t and s. Consequently the process is nonstationary.

The Polya process, as described in example 3.6.1 does possess stationary increments (see example 3.6.1) and is consequently more appealing. The process is a special case of (6.9.1) and is of the form

$$\lambda_n(t) = \frac{\alpha + n}{\beta + t}. \tag{6.9.2}$$

Lundberg (1940) shows that the processes described by (6.9.2) and the mixed

Poisson process of section 6.7 are identical. Consequently, the formulations of the process are equivalent descriptions of the same process.

6.10 COMPOUND BINOMIAL AS A CLOSED GROUP MODEL

The compound binomial distribution is a natural extension of the individual risk model when all risks are identical. The Laplace transform of total claims is given by

$$L_S(z) = \{1 + q[L_X(z) - 1]\}^r.$$

(6.10.1)

It occurs naturally in situations where at most one claim per risk can occur in the relevant time period. In equation (6.10.1), q represents the probability of claim for a single risk and r represents the number of risks. The restriction of at most one claim occurs in life insurance as well as other forms such as in dental insurance in which the variable of interest for each risk is the cost of all dental visits in a year or in some forms medical expense insurance in which all costs for a time period are claimed once per year because of a deductible that applies to the one year time period.

It is not necessary for r to refer to individual risks in the usual sense. It could refer for example to the number of weeks and the severity would refer to the claim costs per week given that a claim occurred. This could be used to model costs associated with workmen's compensation insurance, although in practice, the situation is more complicated because of dependence between time periods.

6.11 COMPOUND BINOMIAL AS A CONTAGION MODEL

It is not necessary to restrict the parameter β in equation (6.9.1) representing the number of claims to positive values. A more general phenomenon giving rise to the compound binomial distribution is given in this section.

Consider a general nonhomogeneous birth process that gives rise to claims with intensity function given by

$$\lambda_n(t) = \lambda(t)\{\alpha + \beta n\}, \quad n = 0, 1, 2, \ldots, r \qquad (6.11.1)$$

where

$$\alpha + \beta r = 0 \qquad (6.11.2)$$

and $\beta < 0$. It will be further assumed that $\lambda_n(t) = 0$ for $n > r$. According to theorem 3.6.2, the distribution of the number of claims in a fixed time interval has a binomial distribution. This model is sometimes called a "negative linear contagion" model.

The intensity function (6.11.1) with negative β indicates that the likelihood of the next claim decreases as the number of past claims increase. This suggests a decreasing propensity of death, accident or illness as the number of claims increase.

It is a natural model for a group of life insurance risks in which the lives are not "replaced" after death as was the case in section 6.2. In this case the total remaining force of mortality is the sum of the forces of mortality of those also remain alive. Consequently the intensity for a group of identical lives at time t is

$$\lambda_n(t) = \mu_{x+t}\{r - n\} \qquad (6.11.3)$$

where μ_{x+t} is the force of mortality of an individual life at time t who was age x at the beginning of the time interval, r is the number of lives at the beginning of the time interval, and n is the number of deaths that have already occurred.

6.12 ANALYTIC RESULTS FOR CERTAIN CLAIM SIZE DISTRIBUTIONS

When the claim severity distribution is the exponential (4.9.1), the incomplete gamma function can be used to obtain analytic results for the distribution of total claims. The exponential distribution with mean $1/\theta$ has LT (from 4.9.4) given by

$$L_X(z) = \frac{\theta}{\theta+z}, \quad z > -\theta. \tag{6.12.1}$$

Then, the sum of n independent and identically distributed random variables with common distribution defined by (6.12.1) has a gamma distribution (4.12.1) with LT (from 4.12.4) given by

$$L_{X_1+X_2+\cdots+X_n}(z) = \left[\frac{\theta}{\theta+z}\right]^n. \tag{6.12.2}$$

Then the df of $X_1 + X_2 + \cdots + X_n$ can be written as an incomplete gamma function

$$F_X^{*n}(x) = I(n, \theta x) \tag{6.12.3}$$

where

$$I(k,x) = \int_0^x s^{k-1} e^{-s}/\Gamma(k)\,ds, \quad k > 0.$$

For integral values of k we can write (see appendix A)

$$I(k,x) = 1 - \sum_{j=0}^{k-1} \frac{x^j e^{-x}}{j!}, \quad k = 1,2,3,\dots \quad . \tag{6.12.4}$$

Substituting (6.12.4) into (6.12.3) and evaluating the df of total claims yields

$$F_S(x) = p_0 + \sum_{n=1}^{\infty} p_n \left\{ 1 - \sum_{j=0}^{n-1} \frac{(\theta x)^j e^{-\theta x}}{j!} \right\}$$

$$= 1 - \sum_{n=1}^{\infty} p_n \sum_{j=0}^{n-1} \frac{(\theta x)^j e^{-\theta x}}{j!}, \quad x \geq 0. \tag{6.12.5}$$

When the number of claims has a Poisson distribution with mean λ, equation (6.12.5) becomes

$$F_S(x) = 1 - \sum_{n=1}^{\infty} \frac{e^{-\lambda}\lambda^n}{n!} \sum_{j=0}^{n-1} \frac{(\theta x)^j e^{-\theta x}}{j!}$$

$$= 1 - e^{-(\lambda+\theta x)} \sum_{n=1}^{\infty} \frac{\lambda^n}{n!} \sum_{j=0}^{n-1} \frac{(\theta x)^j}{j!}, \quad x \geq 0. \tag{6.12.6}$$

Consequently, numerical values of the df can be obtained (at any point x) by taking a sufficient number of terms in (6.12.6).

When the number of claims has a binomial distribution with parameters m and q, equation (6.12.5) becomes

$$F_S(x) = 1 - \sum_{n=1}^{m} \binom{m}{n} q^n (1-q)^{m-n} \sum_{j=0}^{n-1} \frac{(\theta x)^j e^{-\theta x}}{j!}, \quad x \geq 0. \tag{6.12.7}$$

Consequently, numerical values of the df can be obtained exactly since only a finite number of terms are required in (6.12.7).

When the number of claims has a negative binomial distribution, the summation over n in equation (6.12.5) remains infinite. However, Panjer and Willmot (1981) showed that if the parameter r of the negative binomial distribution (4.5.1) is an integer, then a finite sum can be obtained. To show this, consider first the LT of the total claims S when the claim frequency is negative binomial,

$$L_S(z) = \left\{ 1 - \beta \left[\frac{\theta}{\theta+z} - 1 \right] \right\}^{-r}$$

$$= \left\{ 1 + \frac{\beta}{1+\beta} \left[\frac{\frac{\theta}{1+\beta}}{\frac{\theta}{1+\beta}+z} - 1 \right] \right\}^{r}. \tag{6.12.8}$$

Note that for positive integral values of r, (6.12.8) is the LT of the compound binomial distribution with exponential claim sizes with mean $(1+\beta)/\theta$ where the binomial parameters are $m = r$ and $q = \frac{\beta}{1+\beta}$. Consequently, we can obtain the df for the compound negative binomial distribution by substituting into (6.12.7):

$$F_S(x) = 1 - \sum_{n=1}^{r} \binom{r}{n} \left(\frac{\beta}{1+\beta}\right)^n \left(\frac{1}{1+\beta}\right)^{r-n} \sum_{j=0}^{n-1} \frac{(\frac{\theta x}{1+\beta})^j \exp\{-\frac{\theta x}{1+\beta}\}}{j!}. \tag{6.12.9}$$

In the special case of the geometric claim number distribution with exponential claim sizes, we let $r = 1$ in (6.12.9), yielding

$$F_S(x) = 1 - \frac{\beta}{1+\beta} \exp\left\{-\frac{\theta x}{1+\beta}\right\}$$

$$= \frac{1}{1+\beta} 1 + \frac{\beta}{1+\beta} \left[1 - \exp\left\{-\frac{\theta x}{1+\beta}\right\}\right] \tag{6.12.10}$$

which is the mixture of two distribution functions with weights $1/(1+\beta)$ and $\beta/(1+\beta)$. The respective distributions are the degenerate distribution with probability mass 1 at $x = 0$ and the exponential distribution with mean $(1+\beta)/\theta$. Hence, the probability density of total claims has mass $1/(1+\beta)$ at $x = 0$ and a continuous exponential portion on the positive axis.

For severities with distributions which are closed under convolution, formula (6.1.2) is useful in determining the pdf of the total claims.

Example 6.12.1. Gamma Severity Distribution

If the claim severities have the gamma pdf (4.12.1), then pdf of total claims is easily seen to be

$$f_S(x) = \sum_{n=1}^{\infty} p_n f^{*n}(x) = \sum_{n=1}^{\infty} p_n \frac{\lambda(\lambda x)^{n\alpha-1} e^{-\lambda x}}{\Gamma(n\alpha)}, \quad x > 0.$$

This formula may be useful in determining the density of total claims directly by taking a finite number of terms. In addition, if α is an integer, then $n\alpha$ is an integer as well and the df becomes

$$F_S(x) = 1 - \sum_{n=1}^{\infty} p_n \sum_{j=0}^{n\alpha-1} \frac{(\lambda x)^j e^{-\lambda x}}{j!}, \quad x \geq 0$$

which is a generalization of (6.12.5).

Example 6.12.2. Inverse Gaussian Severity Distribution

If the claim severities have the inverse Gaussian pdf (4.13.1), the pdf of total claims is

$$f_S(x) = \sum_{n=1}^{\infty} p_n f^{*n}(x) = \sum_{n=1}^{\infty} p_n \mu n (2\pi\beta x^3)^{-\frac{1}{2}} e^{-\frac{(x-n\mu)^2}{2\beta x}}, \quad x > 0.$$

This formula is also useful in obtaining the density of total claims directly.

6.13 REMOVAL OF ZERO CLAIMS

Up to this point in this chapter, it was assumed that all claims were positive valued. Although it may seem somewhat surprising at first glance, claims of size zero arise in some insurance contexts. If a company records all claims as they are presented to the company, and some claims are resisted, refused or a complete recovery of losses is made from another insurer, the net cost of the claim is zero. A similar situation arises in the context of reinsurance. A reinsurer with an excess-of-loss portfolio may use, as a claim frequency distribution, the basic claim frequency distribution of the primary insurer. This makes sense in the situation of life (with replacement), disability or medical cost reinsurance. A further similar situation arises in the case of deductibles for which the insurer pays only that portion of a claim in excess of the prescribed deductible. When no claim is paid because of the imposition of the deductible, a zero claim arises.

In this section, we show that these situations present no difficulties in the calculation of the distribution of total claim costs to the insurer or reinsurer. This is done by adjusting the claim frequency and the severity distributions slightly.

Suppose that the claim severity has a spike or atom of size f_0 at $X = 0$. Then the Laplace transform of X can be written as

$$L_X(z) = f_0 + (1-f_0)L_{X_+}(z) \qquad (6.13.1)$$

where $L_{X_+}(z)$ is the severity distribution of the conditional random variable

$$X_+ = X|X > 0. \qquad (6.13.2)$$

We obtain results for the Poisson, binomial and negative binomial (including geometric) claim frequency distributions by considering them as a part of a much larger class defined by

$$P_N(z;\theta) = B[\theta(z-1)] \qquad (6.13.3)$$

where θ is some parameter and $B(z)$ is some function which does not depend on θ. From (4.2.2), (4.5.2) and (4.3.2) it can be seen that for the Poisson $B(x) = e^x$ and $\theta = \lambda$; for the negative binomial $B(x) = (1-x)^{-r}$ and $\theta = \beta$; and for the binomial $B(x) = (1+x)^m$ and $\theta = q$.

The distribution of total claims has Laplace transform

$$L_S(z) = P_N[L_X(z);\theta]. \qquad (6.13.4)$$

The following theorem due to Panjer and Willmot (1984a) summarizes the results for the distributions under consideration.

Theorem 6.13.1. For any claim frequency distribution satisfying (6.13.3) and any claim severity distribution satisfying (6.13.1), the Laplace transform of S can be rewritten as

$$L_S(z) = P_N[L_{X_+}(z); (1-f_0)\theta].$$

(6.13.5)

Proof

Substitution of (6.13.1) and (6.13.3) into (6.13.4) yields

$$L_S(z) = P_N[f_0+(1-f_0)L_{X_+}(z);\theta]$$

$$= B[\theta\{f_0+(1-f_0)L_{X_+}(z)-1\}]$$

$$= B[(1-f_0)\theta\{L_{X_+}(z)-1\}]$$

$$= P_N[L_{X_+}(z);(1-f_0)\theta]$$

as required.

Theorem 6.13.1 states that we can consider only positive claims by using the conditional claim severity distribution. Furthermore, the number of positive claims has a distribution that is of the same form as the original distribution but with the parameter θ replaced by $(1-f_0)\theta$ reflecting the fact that the expected proportion of positive claims.

This means that the spike at zero can be easily removed. When this is done, the model is reduced to one of positive claims only, so that all results derived in previous sections in this chapter can be used. It is also possible to reflect the spike at zero in the recursive or integral equation formulas for the distribution of total claims. We choose to consider only positive claims since it is easily done and because the notation would become somewhat clumsy by continually allowing for a spike at zero.

The results of this section will be used in chapter 7 which deals with more advanced models.

Numerical Illustration 6.13.1. Excess-of-Loss Reinsurance

Under an automobile liability reinsurance treaty, the reinsurer pays the excess of any claim over $d = 100,000$ dollars. The direct insurer has a portfolio of risks with a negative binomial number of claims distribution with mean 400 and variance 600, i.e.

$r = 800$ and $\beta = .5$. The distribution of the size of any given claim has a Pareto distribution (4.10.2) with mean 15,000 dollars and standard deviation 60,000 dollars, i.e. $\lambda = 17,000$ and $\alpha = 32/15$. From (4.10.1), the probability that a given claim does not exceed 100,000 dollars is $(17/117)^{32/15} = .983676$. Then, the distribution of the reinsurer's total claim costs is compound negative binomial with parameters $r = 800$ and $\beta = .5$ and single claims cost distribution

$$f_X(x) = \begin{cases} .983676, & x = 0, \\ \dfrac{\alpha\lambda^\alpha}{(\lambda+d+x)^{\alpha+1}}, & x > 0. \end{cases}$$

Using theorem 6.13.1, the reinsurer's distribution of total claim costs can be rewritten as negative binomial with parameters $r = 800$ and $\beta = (1 - .983676).5 = .008162$ and single claim cost distribution

$$f_X(x) = \frac{\alpha(\lambda+d)^\alpha}{(\lambda+d+x)^{\alpha+1}}, \quad x > 0,$$

which is again of Pareto form with parameters $\lambda+d$ and α. This form is rather more convenient since it ignores all claims for which a claim is payable by the direct insurer but not by the reinsurer.

6.14 COMPUTATION FOR CONTINUOUS SEVERITIES

When the claim severity distribution is of the continuous type with support on the positive real line, the distribution of total claims has a spike or atom at zero and is of the continuous type on the positive real line. A recurrence type relationship exists for the density of total claims in the form of an integral equation.

Theorem 6.14.1. For the class of distributions defined by (6.6.3) with a claim size distribution of the continuous type with support on the positive real line, the following integral equation holds:

$$f_S(x) = p_1 f_X(x) + \int_0^x (a+b\frac{y}{x}) f_X(y) f_S(x-y) dy, \quad x > 0. \qquad (6.14.1)$$

Proof

Let $\tilde{g}(z) = L_S(z) - p_0$ denote the Laplace transform of the continuous portion of the distribution of S. Substituting into (6.6.4) yields

$$\tilde{g}'(z) = a L_X(z)\tilde{g}'(z) + (a+b)L_X'(z)\tilde{g}(z) + (a+b)p_0 L_X'(z).$$

Since $p_1 = (a+b)p_0$, inversion of the previous equation yields

$$x f_S(x) = a\int_0^x (x-y)f_X(y)f_S(x-y)dy + (a+b)\int_0^x y f_X(y)f_S(x-y)dy$$

$$+ p_1 x f_X(x).$$

Rearrangement of this equation yields (6.14.1).

Equation (6.14.1) is of the form

$$h(x) = J(x) + \int_0^x K(x,y)h(y)dy \qquad (6.14.2)$$

which is a Volterra integral equation of the second kind. Solutions to this type of equation have been developed in the field of numerical analysis. This type of equation arises frequently throughout this book. Consequently, the solution of equations of the form (6.14.2) is left for a later chapter. The reader interested in these procedures should proceed directly to appendix D.

6.15 COMPUTATIONAL TECHNIQUES FOR NON-ARITHMETIC SEVERITIES

In sections 6.6 and 6.14, the claim severity distributions were discrete on the positive integers or were of the continuous type on the positive real line. In section 6.12, the results were specialized to the case of exponential claim size distributions. In this section, we deal with all other distributions of positive severity. These distributions are of two basic types:

a) Discrete Severities with an Irregular Span.

These severity distributions arise in at least two contexts. When an empirical distribution is constructed, based on previous actual claim costs (possibly normalized for inflation), the resulting distribution will consist of spikes or atoms at amounts that may be expressed in dollars or some other monetary unit. They also arise in connection with life insurance severities, which are constructed based on mortality tables and actual amounts insured (net of policy reserves, usually). Such severities were constructed in section 6.3. Although distributions such as this can be considered arithmetic with span of size one dollar, it is impractical to use recursive calculation techniques for each single dollar of claims. It is usually sufficient to evaluate the distribution of total claims using a convenient span such as 1,000 dollars, 10,000 dollars or 100,000 dollars depending on the size of the portfolio and the sizes of the individual claims under consideration. The methods described in this chapter can be used to replace the original distribution by an arithmetic distribution with a span of any size.

b) Severities of the Mixed Type.

These severities contain both continuous portions and point masses (or "spikes") at specific claim sizes. These severities can arise in the case of a maximum claim cost due to reinsurance or can arise when risks with continuous severities and risks with discrete severities are included in a single portfolio. This might arise when the distribution of total group insurance claims is required and the benefits consist of life insurance (at some fixed level for each member of the group) and of other insurance coverages which have continuous or mixed severities.

In this situation, if the claim frequency distribution is Poisson, it is advisable to separate the continuous and discrete portions and decompose the portfolio according to the methods of section 6.14. After the distribution of total claims is calculated for each portion, they can be recombined. In any case, for any frequency distribution, the methods given in this chapter can be used to replace the severity distribution by an arithmetic distribution with a span of any size.

Various methods of "arithmetizing" distributions will be considered and their properties discussed. Each method attempts to replace the original severity distribution by an arithmetic distribution while preserving the essential characteristics of the original distribution. Generally, the more sophisticated the technique used for arithmetization, the larger the span of the arithmetic distribution can be to maintain a prescribed degree of accuracy.

In this section, the arithmetized severity distribution will be denoted by

$$k_j = Pr\{X=jh\}, \quad j = 0,1,2,... \tag{6.15.1}$$

where X denotes the "arithmetized" claim size and h is the span of the arithmetic distribution. The corresponding df will be denoted by $K(x)$.

Methods of arithmetization were introduced by Gerber and Jones (1976) and Gerber (1982) and studied extensively by Panjer and Lutek (1983) in connection with the calculation of stop-loss premiums. Only the method of rounding (sometimes called mass dispersion) and the method of moments matching will be discussed here since the method of rounding is simplest to apply and provides upper and lower bounds and the method of moment matching is more general and yields highly accurate results.

Method of Rounding

We consider three cases:

A. Rounding to lower unit

$$k_0^A = F_X(h-0),$$

$$k_j^A = F_X(jh+h-0) - F_X(jh-0), \quad j = 1,2,... \tag{6.15.2}$$

B. Rounding to nearest unit

$$k_0^B = F_X(\frac{h}{2}-0)$$

$$k_j^B = F_X(jh+\frac{h}{2}-0) - F_X(jh-\frac{h}{2}-0), \quad j = 1,2,...$$ (6.15.3)

C. Rounding to upper unit

$$k_0^C = 0$$

$$k_j^C = F_X(jh+0) - F_X(jh-h+0), \quad j = 1,2,...$$ (6.15.4)

The superscripts A, B, and C will be used only when comparing methods and will become subscripts in the corresponding distribution function, e.g.

$$K_A(x) = \sum_{j=0}^{[x]} k_j^A, \quad x \geq 0.$$ (6.15.5)

From the above definitions, it is obvious that

$$K_A(x) \geq F_X(xh) \geq K_C(x), \quad x \geq 0,$$ (6.15.6)

and that

$$K_A(x) \geq K_B(x) \geq K_C(x), \quad x \geq 0.$$ (6.15.7)

Consequently, for the compound distributions, we have the same ordering of their convolutions, which results in a corresponding ordering of the compound distributions

$$\sum_{n=0}^{\infty} p_n K_A^{*n}(x) \geq \sum_{n=0}^{\infty} p_n F_X^{*n}(xh) \geq \sum_{n=0}^{\infty} p_n K_C^{*n}(x), \quad x \geq 0,$$ (6.15.8)

and

$$\sum_{n=0}^{\infty} p_n K_A^{*n}(x) \geq \sum_{n=0}^{\infty} p_n K_B^{*n}(x) \geq \sum_{n=0}^{\infty} p_n K_C^{*n}(x), \quad x \geq 0. \tag{6.15.9}$$

Hence, upper and lower bounds of the true compound distribution are easily obtained by the discrete recursive method described in section 6.6. From equations (6.15.8) and (6.15.9) it can be seen that the method based on rounding to the nearest unit can be viewed as yielding an approximation to the true distribution. In practice, it would be wisest to use the lower and upper bounds as well as the approximation in order to evaluate the error introduced by rounding.

It should be noticed that the mean of the approximating distribution is not necessarily equal to the mean of the true distribution. The same can be said of higher moments. The method of moment matching will be used to ensure that the approximate distribution and the true distribution have an arbitrary number of raw moments matched both globally and locally in some sense.

Method of Local Moment Matching

In order that the approximating distribution and the original severity distribution be similar, we impose the restriction that a specified number, say p, of moments of the original distribution be preserved by the approximating distribution. We impose this requirement for successive portions of length ph of the original severity distribution so that the number of constraints equals the number of unknown points.

Consider an arbitrary interval of length ph, denoted by $(x_k, x_k+ph]$. We aim to determine $p+1$ point masses $m_0^k, m_1^k, \ldots, m_p^k$ to be located at $x_k, x_k+h, \ldots, x_k+ph$ so that the first p moments are preserved. The system of equations reflecting these conditions are

$$\sum_{j=0}^{p} (x_k+jh)^r m_j^k = \int_{x_k}^{x_k+ph} x^r dF_X(x) \quad r = 0,1,2,\ldots,p. \tag{6.15.10}$$

The condition with $r = 0$ preserves the total probability mass over the interval. The following theorem gives the solution of this system of $p+1$ equations.

Theorem 6.15.1. The solutions of (6.15.10) is

$$m_j^k = \int_{x_k}^{x_k+ph} \prod_{i \neq j} \frac{x-x_k-ih}{(j-i)h} dF_X(x), \quad j = 0,1,\ldots,p \tag{6.15.11}$$

where the product is taken over $i = 0,1,\ldots,j-1,j+1,\ldots,p$.

Proof

The Lagrange formula for collocation of a polynomial $f(y)$ at points $y_0, y_1, \ldots, y_n$ is

$$f(y) = \sum_{j=0}^{n} f(y_j) \prod_{i \neq j} \left(\frac{y-y_i}{y_j-y_i} \right).$$

Applying this formula to the polynomial $f(y) = y^r$ over the points $x_k, x_k+h, \ldots, x_k+ph$ respectively yields

$$x^r = \sum_{j=0}^{p} (x_k+jh)^r \prod_{i \neq j} \frac{(x-x_k-ih)}{(j-i)h}, \quad r = 0,1,\ldots,p.$$

Integrating over the interval $(x_k, x_k+ph]$ with respect to the probability measure defined by the severity distribution results in

$$\int_{x_k}^{x_k+ph} x^r dF_X(x) = \sum_{j=0}^{p} (x_k+jh)^r m_j^k$$

where m_j^k is given by (6.15.11). Hence the solution (6.15.11) preserves the first p moments as required.

The procedure described above is carried out for intervals $(0,ph]$, $(ph,2ph]$, $(2ph,3ph]$, corresponding to $k = 0,1,2,\ldots$.

The final probabilities are the point masses (6.15.11) in each interval except that the two point masses coinciding at the end points of each interval of length ph are summed. It is clear that the total probability and the moments of the original distribution are preserved by this preservation of the local raw moments.

This moment matching method was studied by Panjer and Lutek (1983) for a variety of empirical and analytic severity distributions. In assessing the error in the stop-loss premiums, they found that two moments were usually sufficient and that adding a third moment added only marginally to the accuracy. Furthermore, the second moment method always performed better than the method of rounding while the rounding and first moment methods have roughly the same degree of accuracy. This suggests using $p = 2$ will give good numerical results.

In applying (6.15.11), it is necessary to be able to evaluate the integral. When the claim severity is discrete (but not necessarily arithmetic with the desired span), the integral reduces to a summation and presents no problem. When the severity over the interval is of exponential or gamma form, the integral may be easy to evaluate. However, for more complicated severities, no analytic expression may be possible. In this case, it is recommended that the rounding method given in this section or the methods of appendix D be used.

To conclude this section we note that any severity distribution can be easily arithmetized so that recursive calculations of total claims can be carried out. It is worth noting that the numerical solutions to the Volterra integral equations that arise in connection with continuous severities involve a discretization (or arithmetization) and weighted recursive formula for total claims. This formula is similar to the discrete recursions discussed in this chapter but includes weights with each term. This procedure is studied in a more general context in appendix D.

Numerical Illustration 6.15.1.

To illustrate the methods of this section, consider the group life case of 1400 lives of 6.6.3. The claim size distribution, $f_X(x)$, is given below:

x	$f_X(x)$	$F_X(x)$
14	.0103301	.0103301
15	.0307990	.0411291
16	.0293511	.0704802
17	.0103301	.0808103
18	.0730414	.1538518
19	.0111568	.1650088
20	.0264554	.1914640
24	.1002133	.2916773
26	.0815418	.3732191
28	.0252146	.3984336
30	.0212857	.4197183
31	.0254214	.4451407
55	.0991756	.5443163
60	.4556837	1

We wish to replace this distribution by one that has support on multiples of 20,000 dollars only. Using the method of rounding yields the following distributions:

j	k_j^A	k_j^B	k_j^C	$K_A(j)$	$K_B(j)$	$K_C(j)$
0	.1650085	0	0	.1650085	0	0
1	.2801322	.3984336	.1914640	.4451407	.3984336	.1914640
2	.0991756	.0467071	.2536767	.5443163	.4451407	.4451407
3	.4556837	.5548593	.5548593	1	1	1

These distributions are used with a Poisson claim frequency distribution with mean 4.841423259. The results are given below and compared with the exact values from numerical illustration 6.6.3.

x	Exact	A Upper	B Approx.	C Lower
0	.0079	.0176	.0079	.0079
40	.0298	.0659	.0396	.0283
80	.0997	.1881	.1227	.0896
120	.2199	.3368	.2363	.1923
160	.3518	.4992	.3851	.3173
200	.5130	.6603	.5431	.4643
240	.6609	.7828	.6789	.6086
280	.7739	.8708	.7919	.7293
320	.8631	.9296	.8739	.8250
360	.9218	.9635	.9273	.8939
400	.9573	.9821	.9609	.9388
440	.9783	.9918	.9800	.9666
480	.9895	.9964	.9902	.9827
520	.9951	.9985	.9955	.9915
560	.9979	.9994	.9980	.9960
600	.9991	.9998	.9991	.9982

The approximation B is surprisingly accurate in spite of the fact that the claim size distribution is very crude. This suggests that for very large portfolios, a significant amount of discretization will not affect the results materially.

6.16 MODIFICATION OF THE CLAIM NUMBER DISTRIBUTION

In this section we generalize the class of frequency distributions to allow for the recurrence relation (6.6.3) to hold only for values of n larger than some value m. These distributions have the essential shape of the Poisson binomial or negative binomial (including geometric) distributions to the right of the point m. The basic distributions are modified to the left of the point m. In this region they could have zero values, a situation which arises in catastrophe reinsurance when claims are only paid if at least m claims occur. Alternately, they could occur as modifications to the original distributions. Examples 4.8.2, 4.8.3 and 4.8.4 illustrate how these distributions could arise. The logarithmic distribution (4.6.1) satisfies the recurrence relation (6.6.3) only for values of $n \geq 2$. It satisfies

$$\frac{p_n}{p_{n-1}} = q(1 - \frac{1}{n}) \tag{6.16.1}$$

so that $a = q$ and $b = -q$.

Let the class of distributions under consideration satisfy

$$\frac{p_n}{p_{n-1}} = a + \frac{b}{n}, \quad n = m+1, m+2, \dots \ . \tag{6.16.2}$$

The following theorem gives the result analogous to Theorem 6.6.1.

Theorem 6.16.1. For the class of counting distributions defined by (6.16.2), the following relationship holds:

$$L_S'(z) = aL_X(z)L_S'(z) + (a+b)L_X'(z)L_S(z) \tag{6.16.3}$$

$$+ \sum_{n=1}^{m} \{p_n - (a + \frac{b}{n})p_{n-1}\} \frac{d}{dz} \{L_X(z)\}^n.$$

Proof

The recursion (6.16.2) can be rewritten as

$$np_n = a(n-1)p_{n-1} + (a+b)p_{n-1}, \quad n = m+1, m+2, \dots \ .$$

Multiplying this equation by $\{L_X(z)\}^{n-1}L_X'(z)$ and summing over n yields

$$\sum_{n=m+1}^{\infty} np_n\{L_X(z)\}^{n-1}L_X'(z) = a \sum_{n=m+1}^{\infty} (n-1)p_{n-1}\{L_X(z)\}^{n-1}L_X'(z)$$

$$+ (a+b) \sum_{n=m+1}^{\infty} p_{n-1}\{L_X(z)\}^{n-1}L_X'(z).$$

Adding terms of the form of the left hand side for $n = 1, 2, \dots, m$ to both sides of the above equation and rearrangement of the right hand side results in, after a bit of algebra,

$$L'_S(z) = aL_X(z)L'_S(z) + (a+b)L'_X(z)L_S(z)$$

$$+ \sum_{n=1}^{m}\{np_n - (an+b)p_{n-1}\}\{L_X(z)\}^{n-1}L'_X(z).$$

Since

$$\frac{d}{dz}\{L_X(z)\}^n = n\{L_X(z)\}^{n-1}L'_X(z),$$

the result follows.

Corollary 6.16.1. For the class of counting distributions defined by (6.16.2) with claim sizes defined on the positive integers, the following recursive formula for the distribution of total claims holds:

$$f_S(x) = \sum_{y=1}^{x}(a+b\frac{y}{x})f_X(y)f_S(x-y) + \sum_{n=1}^{m}\{p_n-(a+\frac{b}{n})p_{n-1}\}f_X^{*n}(x). \tag{6.16.4}$$

Proof

Inversion of (6.16.3) when X is defined only on positive integers yields

$$x\,f_S(x) = a\sum_{y=1}^{x}(x-y)f_X(y)f_S(x-y) + (a+b)\sum_{y=1}^{x}yf_X(y)f_S(x-y)$$

$$+ \sum_{n=1}^{m}\{p_n-(a+\frac{b}{n})p_{n-1}\}xf_X^{*n}(x).$$

Division by x and rearrangement yields (6.16.4).

Corollary 6.16.2. For the class of counting distributions defined by (6.16.2) with a claim size distribution of the continuous type with support on the positive real line, the following equation holds:

$$f_S(x) = p_1 f_X(x) + \sum_{n=2}^{m} \{p_n - (a + \frac{b}{n})p_{n-1}\} f_X^{*n}(x)$$

$$+ \int_0^x (a + b\frac{y}{x}) f_X(y) f_S(x-y) dy, \quad x > 0. \tag{6.16.5}$$

where the summation is 0 if $m < n$.

Proof

Let $\tilde{g}(z) = L_S(z) - p_0$ denote the Laplace transform of the continuous portion of the distribution of S. Substituting into (6.16.3) yields

$$\tilde{g}(z) = aL_x(z)\tilde{g}'(z) + (a+b)L_X'(z)\{\tilde{g}(z) + p_0\}$$

$$+ \sum_{n=1}^{m} \{p_n - (a + \frac{b}{n})p_{n-1}\} \frac{d}{dz} \{L_X(z)\}^n.$$

Inversion of this equation yields

$$x f_S(x) = a\int_0^x (x-y) f_X(y) f_S(x-y) dy + (a+b)\int_0^x y f_X(y) f_S(x-y) dy$$

$$+ (a+b)p_0 x f_X(x) + \sum_{n=1}^{m} \{p_n - (a + \frac{b}{n})p_{n-1}\} x f_X^{*n}(x)$$

$$= \int_0^x (ax+by) f_X(x) f_S(x-y) dy + p_1 x f_X(x)$$

$$+ \sum_{n=2}^{m} \{p_n - (a + \frac{b}{n})p_{n-1}\} x f^{*n}(x).$$

Division by x yields the result.

When the value of m is small the "adjustment term" in each of (6.16.4) and (6.16.5) can be evaluated without difficulty. Equation (6.16.4) is a recursive formula and can be easily evaluated while equation (6.16.5) is a Volterra integral equation of the second kind (6.14.2). It can be solved numerically using the methods of section 6.15. Alternatively, the methods used for evaluating this type of equation are considered in appendix D.

Example 6.16.1. Logarithmic Distribution

Suppose the claim frequencies satisfy the logarithmic distribution with pf (4.6.1). Then, by (6.16.1), it is clear that if we put $m = 1$, $a = q$, $b = -q$, and $p_0 = 0$ into (6.16.4) we obtain, for discrete severities,

$$f_S(x) = p_1 f_X(x) + q \sum_{y=1}^{x} (1 - \frac{y}{x}) f_X(y) f_S(x-y)$$

and for continuous severities, from (6.16.5),

$$f_S(x) = p_1 f_X(x) + q \int_0^x (1 - \frac{y}{x}) f_X(y) f_S(x-y) dy.$$

Note that there is no spike at 0 if claim sizes are strictly positive.

It is easy to see that example 6.16.1 can be generalized to the log-zero distribution by adding a spike at zero.

6.17 REINSURANCE

Basic reinsurance concepts were introduced in section 5.6 in connection with individual risk models. There both reinsurance based on individual losses and reinsurance based on aggregate (or total) losses were introduced. It should be noted that formulas (5.6.1) to (5.6.17) relate to any aggregate loss (or claims) distribution and do not depend upon the form of the aggregate losses, although examples 5.6.1 and 5.6.2 give results for special cases. Consequently, the results of section 5.6 apply equally to the models in this chapter and to those in subsequent ones.

In this chapter, the focus has been on specific choices of the frequency model (Poisson, negative binomial, binomial, etc.) with general severity distributions and the construction of the aggregate claims distribution. Once the distribution is constructed, the results given in section 5.6 apply directly. Hence, the results will not be repeated here.

In this section, we discuss the effect on both the insurer's and the reinsurer's frequency distribution, severity distribution and total claims distribution when reinsurance is based on the size of individual losses.

Consider first excess-of-loss (XL) reinsurance in which the reinsurer pays that part of each claim in excess of a reinsurance limit, m. Then the maximum loss to be paid by the direct insurer is m. This situation, in connection with a Poisson claims frequency distribution, is illustrated in example 6.4.2. The example shows that total "maximal" claims and total "non-maximal" claims are each compound Poisson and that they are independent. The distribution of aggregate claims of the direct insurer are given in example 6.4.2.

In the above situation, the distribution of the reinsurer is simply that of an insurer where a deductible of m is applied to each loss. Example 6.4.4 shows that the reinsurer's losses are compound Poisson with a modified Poisson parameter (the expected number of reinsurance claims) and a truncated distribution of the size of any reinsurance claim. This allows the use of the methods described in this chapter in the evaluation of the reinsurer's aggregate claims distribution.

More generally, in the case of excess-of-loss reinsurance, similar results hold for the binomial and negative binomial distributions. Section 6.13 shows that the reinsurer's aggregate claims can be viewed as a compound distribution with a modified parameter for the frequency distribution and a truncated distribution of the size of any reinsurance claim, as in the Poisson case.

However, it should be noted that for the direct insurer, the "maximal" and "non-maximal" claims are not independent for binomial and negative binomial frequencies as in the Poisson case. In fact, only in the Poisson case are they independent. Hence, one cannot take advantage of this property in evaluating the distribution of the direct insurer's aggregate claims as in example 6.4.2. It is still not difficult to evaluate the distribution. One simply needs to note that a "spike" of probability exists at the maximal level. When using a discretization method as in section 6.14, to produce a discretized severity, the maximal level can be the highest mass point. The discretized distribution is "exact" with respect to the maximal loss. The distribution of the direct insurer's claims can be calculated using the recursive method (6.6.5).

6.18 BIBLIOGRAPHICAL NOTES

The formula (6.2.13) was given by Panjer (1980) based on Adelson (1966) and extended by Panjer (1981) and Sundt and Jewell (1981). Other contributions to this chapter are from Panjer and Willmot (1981, 1982, 1984a, 1986) and Panjer and Lutek (1983). In general, these papers deal with recursive evaluation of the aggregate claims distribution and the corresponding stop-loss premiums. Numerical stability of the recursive methods is studied by Panjer and Wang (1992).

Some other authors have examined other methods of evaluation of the aggregate claims distribution. Ströter (1985) examines numerical integration of the integral equation (6.14.1) using methods described in appendix D. Bertram (1981) uses direct inversion of the Fourier transform of the distribution using the fast Fourier transform. This method is compared to the recursive method by Bühlmann (1984). Heckman and Meyers (1983) invert the Fourier transform directly by making the severity distribution function piecewise linear. This property of the severity distribution can be used to dramatically speed up the calculation of the aggregate claims distribution.

The exercises dealing with reinsurance are based on Panjer and Willmot (1984a) and the references therein.

EXERCISES

1. The "geometric with zeros" distribution has probabilities of the form

$$p_0 = \pi_0$$

$$p_n = (1-\pi_0)pq^{n-1}, \quad n = 1,2,3,\dots .$$

   Describe how you could use the results of section 6.16 to calculate the distribution of total claims for an arbitrary arithmetic claim size distribution.

2. Consider the compound distribution with logarithmic frequency distribution (4.6.1) and exponential severity distribution (4.9.1).

   (a) Show that the density may be expressed as

$$f_S(x) = \sum_{n=1}^{\infty} \frac{q^n}{-n \, \log(1-q)} \frac{\lambda(\lambda x)^{n-1}e^{-\lambda x}}{(n-1)!}.$$

   (b) Show that this can be simplified to

$$f_S(x) = \frac{e^{-\lambda(1-q)x}-e^{-\lambda x}}{-x \, \log(1-q)}.$$

3. **Excess-of-Loss Reinsurance with Coinsurance**

   Consider a compound Poisson model (6.2.2) of losses for which the reinsurer pays $100k\%$ of the excess of any claim over a deductible d. Let $Y = k \max\{(X-d),0\}$ denote the reinsurer's cost for a loss of X.

   a) Verify that the distribution of the reinsurer's total cost is a compound Poisson distribution with Poisson parameter λ and severity distribution given by

$$f_Y(x) = \begin{cases} F_X(d), & x=0 \\ f_X(\frac{x}{k}+d), & x>0. \end{cases}$$

b) By comparing Laplace transforms, show that the distribution in a) can be equivalently written as a compound Poisson distribution with Poisson parameter $\lambda(1-F_X(d))$ and severity distribution

$$f_{Y_+}(x) = \frac{f_X(\frac{x}{k}+d)}{1-F_X(d)}, \quad x>0.$$

c) Show that a corresponding result holds when the Poisson model is replaced by any claim frequency model satisfying (6.13.3).

d) If the claim sizes are exponentially distributed with mean μ, show that the reinsurer's distribution in c), is identical to the distribution of aggregate losses, except that μ is replaced by $k\mu$.

4. Catastrophic Reinsurance

Suppose that the losses arise from a number of claim-causing events (accidents), each of which contributes a number of losses, each of which has a common distribution of size. Let $N(t) = \sum_{i=1}^{M(t)} N_i$ denote the total number of losses in time interval $(0,t]$, where $M(t)$ is the number of accidents in $(0,t]$ and $N_1, N_2, ...$ are the number of losses in the successive accidents.

The catastrophic reinsurance agreement pays $100k\%$ of all losses in excess of some amount d on each accident.

a) Show that the reinsurer's total losses in $(0,t]$ is

$$R(t) = \sum_{i=1}^{M(t)} k \max\{(S_i - d), 0\} \quad \text{where} \quad S_i = \sum_{j=1}^{N_i} X_{i,j}.$$

b) Assuming independence between amounts of losses and between amounts of losses, numbers of losses and numbers of accidents, with the number of accidents having a distribution satisfying (6.13.3) for a fixed time interval, show that the distribution of the reinsurer's total losses is identical to that in the case of excess-of-loss reinsurance in exercise 3 above.

5. Cumulative Loss Reinsurance

This agreement is identical to that of catastrophe reinsurance except that the excess for an accident is not paid unless at least m losses arise from the accident.

a) Show that the reinsurer's total losses in $(0, t]$ is the same as in exercise 4a) above with S_i replaced by

$$S_i = \begin{cases} 0, & N_i < m \\ \sum_{j=1}^{N_i} X_{i,j}, & N_i \geq m. \end{cases}$$

b) Let $p_k = Pr\{N_i = k\}$.

If the number of losses from an accident is binomial, Poisson or negative binomial, show that the common distribution of S_i is given by

$$f(0) = \sum_{k=0}^{m-1} p_k$$

and

$$f(x) = p_m f^{*m}(x) + \int_0^x (a+b\frac{y}{x}) f_X(y) f(x-y) dy, \quad x>0$$

for appropriate choices of a and b when $f_X(x)$ is the pdf of the size of any loss arising from any accident if X is of the continuous type; or,

$$f(x) = \begin{cases} 0 & x = 1, 2, \ldots, m-1 \\ p_m f^{*m}(x) - (a+b)f(0)f_X(x) + \sum_{y=1}^{x}(a+b\frac{y}{x})f_X(y)f(x-y), & x = m, m+1, m+2 \end{cases}$$

if X is defined on positive integers.

6. Consider the recursive formula (6.6.5) when the claim numbers are binomially distributed (4.3.1). Suppose that individual claim sizes are defined on positive integers with a maximum size of r per claim.

a) Show that

$$f_S(x) = \frac{1}{g(x)}[f_S(x+m) - \sum_{y=1}^{m-1}(a+b\frac{m-y}{x+m})f_X(m-y)f_S(x+y)], \quad x = 1, 2, 3,\ldots$$

where

$$g(x) = f_X(m)\left\{a + \frac{bm}{x+m}\right\}.$$

b) How can the recursive formula in a) be used to compute the right-hand tail of the total claims distribution? What are the initial values required to begin the recursive calculation in a)?

7. Consider the portfolio of six risks in exercise 2 of chapter 5. Use the compound Poisson approximation of section 6.5 to redo the exercise. Compare your results with those obtain in chapter 5 using the individual risk model.

8. Consider the life insurance portfolio of exercise 9 of chapter 5. Use the compound Poisson approximation of section 6.5 to redo that exercise. Compare the results.

9. Repeat exercise 8 above using the compound Poisson model of example 6.2.1 in which each life is "replaced" by an identical one upon death. Compare the results with those of exercise 8.

CHAPTER 7

COMPOUND CLAIM FREQUENCY MODELS

7.1 INTRODUCTION

The purpose of this and the subsequent chapter is to generalize the claim frequency models which were considered in chapter 6; namely, the Poisson, binomial, negative binomial and geometric distributions. When this class of distributions is judged to inadequately describe a given set of claim frequency data or a physical phenomenon, alternative distributions should be available to the actuary. Judging the adequacy of a model and estimating model parameters will be considered in chapter 9.

In this chapter we investigate the class of models for which the claims frequency distribution is itself a compound distribution. These distributions are sometimes called **contagious** or **generalized** distributions (cf. Johnson and Kotz, 1969) or **stopped** distributions (cf. Douglas, 1980). A **compound claim frequency distribution** has probability generating function of the form

$$P_N(z) = P_1(P_2(z)) \tag{7.1.1}$$

where $P_1(z)$ and $P_2(z)$ are themselves pgf's. The distributions associated with $P_1(z)$ and $P_2(z)$ will be referred to as the **primary** and **secondary** distributions respectively. This concept can be extended to the case of multiple compounding; that is, to distributions with pgf's of the form

$$P(z) = P_1(P_2(P_3 \cdots (P_m(z)))). \tag{7.1.2}$$

The number of parameters in the distribution with pgf given by (7.1.2) is the sum of the number of parameters in each of the m consituent distributions. Because of the nature of the data normally available to the actuary, we will consider models with no more than three parameters. Consequently, the value of m in (7.1.2) will take on values 1, 2 or occasionally 3. Extensions to higher parameter models can be made using the techniques of this chapter in a routine way. It is the experience of the authors that three parameters are adequate to describe most practical situations.

In section 6.8, an example of a compound claim frequency distribution was described. In that example, the primary distribution describing the **number of accidents in a fixed time period** was assumed to be Poisson and the secondary distribution describing the **number of claims per accident** was assumed to be logarithmic. The resulting distribution of the **number of claims in the fixed time period** was shown to be negative binomial. The models in this chapter are natural extensions of this example. We allow a greater choice of primary and secondary distributions and also allow for more levels of modeling by considering models with three (or possibly more) constituent distributions.

When the various constituent distributions; i.e. the number of accidents and the number of claims per accident, can be modeled and estimated separately, compound claim frequency distributions arise naturally. However, they are also useful alternatives when the actuary has difficulty in fitting one of the distributions of chapter 6 to claims frequency data.

As in chapter 6, the Laplace transform of total claims can be written as

$$L_S(z) = P_N(L_X(z)) \qquad (7.1.3)$$

where $P_N(z)$ is the pgf of the number of claims distribution and $L_X(z)$ is the LT of the claim size (severity) distribution. Upon substitution of (7.1.2), (7.1.3) becomes

$$L_S(z) = P_1(P_2 \cdots (P_m(L_X(z))). \qquad (7.1.4)$$

The distribution of S can be evaluated by first evaluating the compound distribution with LT

$$L_m(z) = P_m(L_X(z)).$$ (7.1.5)

The resulting distribution is then used as a "severity" distribution in evaluating the compound distribution with LT

$$L_{m-1}(z) = P_{m-1}(L_m(z)).$$ (7.1.6)

This recursive process is repeated until the distribution of s with LT

$$L_S(z) = P_1(L_2(z))$$ (7.1.7)

is obtained. If compound distributions with transforms of the form (7.1.3) are easily evaluated for all of the frequency distributions with LT's $P_1(z)$, $P_2(z), \ldots, P_m(z)$, then the distributions with LT given by (7.1.4) can be also easily evaluated using the procedure described by equations (7.1.5) to (7.1.7) since each stage involves the calculation of a distribution of the form (7.1.3). It is for this reason that we will restrict the frequency distributions with LT's $P_1(z)$, $P_2(z), \ldots, P_m(z)$ to be members of a class of distributions which is a slight generalization of the class of distributions (6.6.3) used in developing recursive algorithms in chapter 6. For these distributions, one can use the recursive techniques described in section 6.6 and 6.14 at each stage of the calculations in (7.1.5) to (7.1.7).

Consider the class of counting distributions (with support on the non-negative integers) for which the recurrence relation

$$\frac{p_n}{p_{n-1}} = a + \frac{b}{n}, \quad n = 2,3,\ldots \ .$$ (7.1.8)

Here, the recursive relation starts at $n = 1$ rather than at $n = 0$ as in (6.6.3). It is in fact a special case of (6.16.2) with $m = 1$. Consequently, from theorem 6.16.1, the Laplace transform relationship for a distribution of the form (7.1.3) is

$$L_S'(z) = aL_X(z)L_S'(z) + (a+b)L_X'(z)L_S(z) + \{p_1-(a+b)p_0\}L_X'(z). \tag{7.1.9}$$

If the original severity is defined on the non-negative integers, then so is the distribution at each stage of the calculations. In this case, inversion of (7.1.9) yields (exercise 7.1) for $x = 1,2,...,$ the recursion

$$f_S(x) = \left[\sum_{y=1}^{x}(a+b\frac{y}{x})f_X(y)f_S(x-y) + \{p_1-(a+b)p_0\}f_X(x)\right]/\{1-af_X(0)\}.$$

$$\tag{7.1.10}$$

If the original severity is of the continuous type on the positive axis with a possible spike or atom of $f_X(0)$ at 0, then so is the distribution at each stage of the calculations. In this case, inversion of (7.1.9) yields (exercise 7.2) for $x>0$, the Volterra type integral equation

$$f_S(x) = \left[\int_0^x(a+b\frac{y}{x})f_X(y)f_S(x-y)dy + \{p_1+(a+b)[f_S(0)-p_0]\}f_X(x)\right]/\{1-af_X(0)\}.$$

$$\tag{7.1.11}$$

In either case, the probability mass at zero is

$$f_S(0) = P_N(f_X(0)). \tag{7.1.12}$$

These formulas can be used at each stage to obtain the distribution of S with LT (7.1.4). The methods of discretization, which are described in section 6.15, can be used for continuous or more complicated severities. Alternatively, the integral equation methods described in appendix D can be used.

The moments of compound claim frequency distributions can be evaluated in terms of the moments of the constituent distributions by differentiating the cgf

$$C_N(z) = C_1(C_2(z))$$ (7.1.13)

and setting $z = 0$. From the analogous exercise in section 6.1, the results for the first four cumulants are:

$$\kappa_1 = \kappa_{1,1}\kappa_{2,1}$$ (7.1.14)

$$\kappa_2 = \kappa_{1,2}\kappa_{2,1}^2 + \kappa_{1,1}\kappa_{2,2}$$ (7.1.15)

$$\kappa_3 = \kappa_{1,3}\kappa_{2,1}^3 + 3\kappa_{1,2}\kappa_{2,1}\kappa_{2,2} + \kappa_{1,1}\kappa_{2,3}$$ (7.1.16)

and

$$\kappa_4 = \kappa_{1,4}\kappa_{2,1}^4 + 6\kappa_{1,3}\kappa_{2,1}^2\kappa_{2,2} + 3\kappa_{1,2}\kappa_{2,2}^2 + 4\kappa_{1,2}\kappa_{2,1}\kappa_{2,3} + \kappa_{1,1}\kappa_{2,4}$$

(7.1.17)

where $\kappa_{i,j}$ is the j-th cumulant for the distribution with cgf $C_i(z)$.

7.2 THE (a,b) CLASS OF DISTRIBUTIONS

We shall call the class of distributions (7.1.8) the **(a,b) class** of distributions. The subclass (6.6.3) will be called the **(a,b,0) subclass** and the subclass satisfying (7.1.8) with the additional restriction that $p_0 = 0$ will be called the **(a,b,1) subclass.** The third argument in the triplet describing the class gives the point at which the support of the distribution begins.

It is easy to see that the $(a,b,0)$ and the $(a,b,1)$ subclasses do not constitute the entire (a,b) class of distributions. Any distribution satisfying (7.1.8) with an arbitrary probability at the origin is also a member. It is easy to show (see exercise 7.3) that all such distributions have probabilities of the form

$$q_0 = (1-\pi) + \pi p_0$$

$$q_n = \pi p_n, \quad n = 1,2,3,...$$ (7.2.1)

where p_n is a member of the $(a,b,0)$ or the $(a,b,1)$ subclass. Distributions of this type are sometimes called **modified** or the term "with zeros" is used as in "Poisson with zeros" (cf. Johnson and Kotz, 1969). No other members of the (a,b) class are possible.

In section 6 of chapter 6, it was seen that the only members of the $(a,b,0)$ subclass are the Poisson, binomial and negative binomial (including geometric) distributions. We now examine the membership of the $(a,b,1)$ subclass.

FIGURE 7.2.1

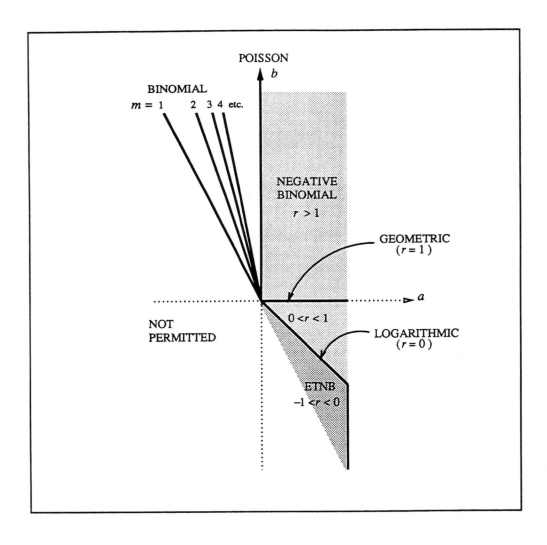

Figure 7.2.1 is identical to figure 6.6.1 except that a region has been added; namely, the region for which $0<a\leq1$ and $-2a<b\leq-a$. We first consider the region $0<a\leq1$ and $-2a<b<-a$. In this region, it is clear that $a+b/n>0$ for $n>2$. Consequently, we have

$$p_n = p_1(a+\frac{b}{2})(a+\frac{b}{3})\cdots(a+\frac{b}{n}) >0, \quad n = 2,3,\ldots \quad . \tag{7.2.2}$$

Letting $f_{n+1}=p_n$ and $A=-b/a>1$, we have

$$\frac{f_{n+1}}{f_n} \leq 1 - \frac{A}{n}, \quad n = 2,3,\ldots \quad .$$

By Raabe's test (c.f. Marsden, 1974, p. 60), $\sum_{n=2}^{\infty}f_n = \sum_{n=1}^{\infty}p_n < \infty$. Hence, imposing the conditional that $p_1 + p_2 + p_3 + \cdots = 1$ results in valid probabilities $p_1, p_2, p_3,\ldots$ with (from 7.2.2)

$$p_n = p_1\frac{\Gamma(n+1+b/a)}{n!\Gamma(2+b/a)}a^{n-1}, \quad n = 1,2,3,\ldots \quad . \tag{7.2.3}$$

When $a<1$, letting $a = \beta/(1+\beta)$ and $b = (r-1)\beta/(1+\beta)$, it follows that

$$p_n = \frac{p_1}{r}\binom{r+n-1}{n}\left(\frac{\beta}{1+\beta}\right)^{n-1}, \quad n = 1,2,3,\ldots$$

where $\beta>0$ and $-1<r<0$. These probabilities differ in form from the negative binomial probabilities (4.5.1) only by a constant. Since $p_0 = 0$, they must have a pgf of the form

$$P(z) = \frac{[1-\beta(z-1)]^{-r}-(1+\beta)^{-r}}{1-(1+\beta)^{-r}} \tag{7.2.4}$$

which is of the same form as the truncated (at zero) negative binomial distribution except that $r = 1+b/a$ takes on values in the range $1 < r \leq 0$.

When $a = 1$ and $-2 < b < -1$, let $b = -(\alpha+1)$ so that $0 < \alpha < 1$. Hence (7.2.3) becomes

$$p_n = \frac{p_1}{n!} \frac{\Gamma(n-\alpha)}{\Gamma(1-\alpha)}$$

and the pgf is

$$P(z) = \sum_{n=1}^{\infty} \frac{p_1}{n!} \frac{\Gamma(n-\alpha)}{\Gamma(1-\alpha)} = \sum_{n=1}^{\infty} \frac{p_1}{-\alpha} \begin{pmatrix} -\alpha+n-1 \\ n \end{pmatrix} z^n$$

$$= \frac{p_1}{-\alpha} \sum_{n=1}^{\infty} \begin{pmatrix} \alpha \\ n \end{pmatrix} (-z)^n = \frac{p_1}{-\alpha} [(1-z)^{\alpha}-1].$$

Since $P(1) = 1$, $p_1 = \alpha$ and the pgf can be rewritten as

$$P(z) = 1 - (1-z)^{\alpha}, \quad 0 < \alpha < 1. \tag{7.2.5}$$

This distribution corresponds to the line $a = 1$ over the range $-2 < b < -1$. Note that for $a = 1$ and $b \geq -1$, no distribution is possible. The distribution with pgf (7.2.5) can be seen to have an infinite mean and, in fact, infinite moments of all orders. Since this distribution is not of much interest in insurance contexts (due to uninsurability of risks with infinite expected claims!), we will not consider it further and ignore it as a member of the $(a,b,1)$ subclass.

From (4.6.1), it can be seen that, for the logarithmic distribution, $p_0 = 0$ and

$$\frac{p_n}{p_{n-1}} = q - \frac{q}{n}, \quad n = 2,3,\dots . \tag{7.2.6}$$

Hence, the logarithmic distribution is a member of the $(a,b,1)$ subclass with $b = -a$ and $0 < a < 1$.

The distribution in the $(a,b,1)$ class corresponding to the region satisfying $0<a<1$ and $-2a<b<-a$ will be called the **extended truncated negative binomial** distribution because of its relation to the negative binomial distribution. Like the logarithmic distribution and the negative binomial distribution with $r<1$, it has decreasing probabilities. This is because the quantity $a+b/n<1$ for $n=2,3,...$. The **extended truncated negative binomial** distribution can be parametrized consistently with the negative binomial and logarithmic distributions by letting $a=q=\beta/(1+\beta)$ and $b=(r-1)q$ where $0<q<1$ and $-1<r<0$. The logarithmic distribution is obtained by letting $r=0$. The negative binomial parametrization in chapter 6 has $q=\beta/(1+\beta)$.

The other members of the $(a,b,1)$ subclass are the truncated versions of the Poisson, binomial, geometric and negative binomial distributions. The truncation is carried out by removing the probability mass at 0 and normalizing the remaining probabilities so that they sum to one. The region in figure 7.2.1 for which $b<-2a$ is an "impossible" region since $p_1(a+b/2)<0$. The line $b=-2a$ corresponds to the degenerate distribution with $p_1=1$ and $p_n=0$ for $n>1$. The relevant members of the $(a,b,1)$ subclass are listed in table 7.2.1.

The properties of the distributions on the $(a,b,1)$ subclass can be obtained directly for each of the truncated distributions by appealing to the properties of the corresponding (untruncated) distributions as described in chapter 4. For example, the factorial moments can be obtained using the formula

$$E[X_{(k)}] = \frac{E[X^*_{(k)}]}{1-f_{X^*}(0)} \tag{7.2.7}$$

where X^* is the untruncated random variable.

Because the extended truncated negative binomial distribution can be parametrized as a truncated negative binomial distribution with $q=\beta/(1+\beta)$, formulas for the extended truncated negative binomial distribution will be identical to those of the truncated negative binomial distribution except that r can take on negative values. For example, from (4.5.2) the pgf of the extended truncated negative binomial distribution is

TABLE 7.2.1

Distribution	Value of a	Value of b
Truncated Poisson	0	λ
Truncated Binomial	$-\dfrac{q}{1-q}$	$(m+1)\dfrac{q}{1-q}$
Truncated Geometric	$\dfrac{\beta}{1+\beta}$	0
Truncated Negative Binomial	$\dfrac{\beta}{1+\beta}$	$(r-1)\dfrac{\beta}{1+\beta},\ r>0$
Logarithmic	$q=\dfrac{\beta}{1+\beta}$	$-q$
Extended Truncated Negative Binomial	$q=\dfrac{\beta}{1+\beta}$	$(r-1)q,\ -1<r<0$

$$P(z) = \frac{[1-\beta(z-1)]^{-r}-(1+\beta)^{-r}}{1-(1+\beta)^{-r}}$$

$$= \frac{(1-qz)^{-r}-1}{(1-q)^{-r}-1}, \qquad 0<q<1, \qquad -1<r<0. \tag{7.2.8}$$

The pgf (4.6.2) of the logarithmic distribution can be obtained from (7.2.8) by taking the limit as $r \to 0$. It should be noted that we interpret $\Gamma(r+x)/\Gamma(r)$ in (4.5.2) as

$$\frac{\Gamma(r+x)}{\Gamma(r)} = (r+x-1)(r+x-2) \cdots (r+1)r. \tag{7.2.9}$$

Consequently the pf becomes

$$p_n = \frac{-r\Gamma(n+r)}{n!\Gamma(1+r)[1-(1+\beta)^r]}\left(\frac{\beta}{1+\beta}\right)^n, \quad n = 1,2,\dots \quad . \tag{7.2.10}$$

The moments are easily obtained from (7.2.8). We have

$$P'(z) = \frac{r\beta}{1-(1+\beta)^{-r}}[1-\beta(z-1)]^{-(1+r)}$$

and so the mean is

$$\mu_{(1)} = \frac{r\beta}{1-(1+\beta)^{-r}}. \tag{7.2.11}$$

The last term on the right hand side of the expression for $P'(z)$ is of the form (4.5.2) and hence the k-th factorial moment is, from (4.5.3),

$$\mu_{(k)} = \frac{r(r+1)\cdots(r+k-1)\beta^k}{1-(1+\beta)^{-r}}. \tag{7.2.12}$$

It is convenient to defer until section 7.7 specific consideration of modified distributions such as the "Poisson with zeros" since these are distributions with an additional parameter, namely, π. Furthermore, these adjustments of the zero probability are often of no consequence. For example, consider the model (7.1.1). If the secondary distribution is modified "with zeros" and the primary distribution is from the $(a,b,0)$ subclass (binomial, Poisson, geometric or negative binomial), then the resulting compound distribution is equivalent to a compound distribution whose constituent distributions are of the same form as before but with the zero of the secondary distribution eliminated. The proof of this statement is given by theorem 6.14.1 for which the secondary distribution is the severity distribution. Furthermore, as a consequence of this fact, it is immediately seen that if the primary distribution is of the $(a,b,0)$ subclass, then it makes no difference whether the secondary distribution is in its untruncated or its truncated form. The parameter values of the primary distribution are adjusted accordingly.

Example 7.2.1. Geometric-Poisson Distribution

Consider the model for which

$$P_N(z) = \{1-\beta[e^{\lambda(z-1)}-1]\}^{-1}.$$

Here, the primary distribution is geometric with pgf

$$P_1(z) = \{1-\beta(z-1)\}^{-1}$$

and the secondary distribution is Poisson with pgf

$$P_2(z) = e^{\lambda(z-1)}.$$

Now consider a model for which

$$P_1(z) = \{1-\beta(1-e^{-\lambda})(z-1)\}^{-1}$$

and

$$P_2(z) = \frac{e^{\lambda(z-1)}-e^{-\lambda}}{1-e^{-\lambda}}.$$

Here, the primary distribution is geometric with parameter $\beta(1-e^{-\lambda})$ and the secondary distribution is truncated Poisson. When these two distributions are combined the resulting pgf can be seen to be of the same form as before.

When members of the (a,b) family are used to construct claim frequency distributions, there are a large number of compound distributions possible. In the next few sections, we examine a few of the more important combinations.

7.3 COMPOUND POISSON CLAIM FREQUENCY MODELS

If one takes the primary distribution in (7.1.1) to be Poisson, the resulting distribution has pgf

$$P(z) = e^{\lambda[P_2(z)-1]} \tag{7.3.1}$$

where $P_2(z)$ is the pgf of the secondary distribution. Since the pgf of the Poisson exists for all real z, the pgf (7.3.1) is valid for all values of z for which $P_2(z)$ exists. Moments for this distribution are easily obtainable from formula (7.1.13) to (7.1.16). Alternatively, the cumulants are easily obtainable from (6.2.13). The probabilities corresponding to the distribution can be computed from formula (7.1.10) with $a = 0$ and $b = \lambda$. This yields

$$p_n = \frac{\lambda}{n} \sum_{j=1}^{n} j q_j p_{n-j}, \quad n = 1,2,3,... \tag{7.3.2}$$

beginning with

$$p_0 = e^{-\lambda(1-q_0)} \tag{7.3.3}$$

where the q_j's are the probabilities with pgf $P_2(z)$ and the p_n's have pgf $P(z)$. Sometimes simpler computational formulae are available; for example, if $P_2(z)$ is a logarithmic pgf it follows from section (6.7) that $P(z)$ is a negative binomial pgf and the probabilities are easily obtainable.

The compound Poisson frequency distribution is very convenient for several reasons. First, if N_i has pgf (7.3.1) with $\lambda = \lambda_i$, then $\sum N_i$ has pgf (7.3.1) with $\lambda = \sum \lambda_i$, as long as $P_2(z)$ is the same for all i and the N_i are independent. Hence the distribution is closed under convolution. In particular, the sum of n independent variates, each with pgf (7.3.1), has pgf (7.3.1) with parameter $n\lambda$. This is useful when applying this distribution to groups or portfolios of business. Secondly, one can easily define a compound Poisson process (section 3.7) for the number of claims. The distribution of the number of claims in an interval of length t could be obtained by letting $\lambda = \lambda t$. Thirdly, in fitting probability models, it is desirable to try to fit a model with relatively few parameters. Clearly, in fitting compound frequency models, it is then desirable to select as primary and or secondary distributions those with relatively few parameters. As we shall see in chapter 9, a Poisson primary distribution will usually give a good fit if the secondary distribution is appropriately chosen.

In light of the results of sections 7.1 and 7.2, it is of interest to consider distributions from the (a,b) class as secondary distributions. It should be clear from the comments following (7.2.10) that the only distributions which need be considered are those from the $(a,b,1)$ subclass, since q_0 can be ''absorbed'' into the parameter λ. More generally, we leave it to the reader to verify that the possible choices of secondary distributions are the Poisson, binomial, negative binomial, geometric, logarithmic, and extended truncated negative binomial.

When the secondary distribution is logarithmic, the resulting distribution is negative binomial, a distribution which requires no further analysis. When the secondary distribution is Poisson, the resulting distribution is a Neyman Type A distribution, which is discussed in section (7.4). When the secondary distribution is geometric, negative binomial, or extended truncated negative binomial, (7.3.1) may be parameterized in a uniform way. These three are discussed jointly in section (7.5). If the secondary distribution is binomial, the resulting distribution is considered in the next example.

Example 7.3.1. The Poisson-Binomial Distribution

The pgf for this distribution is

$$P(z) = e^{\lambda\{[1+q(z-1)]^m - 1\}}.$$

The probabilities are easily obtainable from (7.3.2) and (7.3.3). If $m = 1$, the distribution is simply Poisson with parameters λq. If $m = 2$, the resulting distribution is called the **Hermite** distribution. The mean and variance are

$$\mu_1' = m\lambda q,$$

$$\mu_2 = \mu_1'[1+(m-1)q].$$

The skewness in terms of the mean and variance is

$$\mu_2^{-\frac{3}{2}}\{3\mu_2 - 2\mu_1' + \frac{m-2}{m-1}\frac{(\mu_2 - \mu_1')^2}{\mu_1'}\}.$$

Since $0 < (m-2)(m-1)^{-1} < 1$ for $m = 2,3,4, \ldots$, it is clear that, for fixed mean and variance, there is a narrow range of possible values that the skewness may assume.

As will be discussed in chapter 8, there is a close connection between mixed Poisson and compound Poisson variates. It will be shown that many of the distributions considered here are both mixed Poisson and compound Poisson.

7.4 NEYMAN TYPE A DISTRIBUTION

This two-parameter distribution, which was discussed in example 4.8.6, has the Poisson for both primary and secondary distributions. The pgf of the Neyman Type A distribution is

$$P(z) = \exp\{\lambda_1[e^{\lambda_2(z-1)} - 1]\}. \tag{7.4.1}$$

From (7.1.10), it follows that the probabilities of this distribution can be written recursively as

$$p_n = \frac{\lambda_1}{n}\sum_{j=1}^{n} jq_j p_{n-j}, \quad n = 1,2,\ldots \tag{7.4.2}$$

where

$$p_0 = e^{-\lambda_1(1-q_0)} \tag{7.4.3}$$

and $\{q_n; n = 0,1,\ldots\}$ are Poisson probabilities (with mean λ_2) which can be calculated recursively as

$$q_n = \frac{\lambda_2}{n} q_{n-1} \tag{7.4.4}$$

beginning with

$$q_0 = e^{-\lambda_2}. \tag{7.4.5}$$

The secondary distribution is given recursively since it is the most convenient way to generate it on a computer.

Using the pgf, it is easy to show that the Neyman Type A distribution has mean

$$\mu_1' = \lambda_1 \lambda_2, \tag{7.4.6}$$

variance

$$\mu_2 = \lambda_1 \lambda_2 (1 + \lambda_2), \tag{7.4.7}$$

skewness

$$\frac{1 + 3\lambda_2 + \lambda_2^2}{(\lambda_1 \lambda_2)^{\frac{1}{2}} (1 + \lambda_2)^{\frac{3}{2}}} \tag{7.4.8}$$

and kurtosis

$$3 + \frac{1 + 7\lambda_2 + 6\lambda_2^2 + \lambda_2^3}{\lambda_1 \lambda_2 (1 + \lambda_2)^2}. \tag{7.4.9}$$

The variance always exceeds the mean. In terms of the mean and variance, the skewness can be written as

$$\mu_2^{-\frac{3}{2}} \{ 3\mu_2 - 2\mu_1' + (\mu_2 - \mu_1')^2 / \mu_1' \}. \tag{7.4.10}$$

On comparison with (6.7.8), it is seen that the skewness (7.4.10) is less than that of the negative binomial for given mean and variance.

It will be seen in chapter 8 that the Neyman Type A is also a mixed Poisson.

It is interesting to note that this distribution can have one or more modes depending on the relationship between λ_1 and λ_2. When λ_1 is small, the distribution is approximately a "Poisson with zeros" with pgf

$$P(z) = \lambda_1 + (1-\lambda_1)e^{\lambda_2(z-1)}. \qquad (7.4.11)$$

When λ_2 is small, the distribution is approximately a Poisson with mean $\lambda_1\lambda_2$.

Although we do not give a specific analysis, this distribution can be generalized to a three-parameter model by introducing a tertiary distribution that is also Poisson. Three applications of the Poisson will yield total claims since the LT of total claims is $P_S(x) = P_1(P_2(P_3(L_X(z))))$.

In section 6.4, it was shown that severities with deductibles, maxima, or positive and negative components could be handled easily for a Poisson claims frequency distribution. Since the Neyman Type A claims frequency distribution involves two applications of the Poisson distribution in calculating total claims, the same comments apply here. At each stage the "severity" is split into the appropriate components. The compound Poisson recursion is used to evaluate each part and these parts are combined to give the result for the next stage. The ease with which one can handle more complicated severities is one of the most useful aspects of this distribution.

7.5 GENERALIZED POISSON-PASCAL DISTRIBUTION

This three-parameter distribution has a Poisson primary distribution and a secondary distribution that is truncated negative binomial or extended truncated negative binomial. Consequently, its pgf is (from 7.2.8)

$$P(z) = \exp\left[\lambda\left\{\frac{[1-\beta(z-1)]^{-r}-(1+\beta)^{-r}}{1-(1+\beta)^{-r}}-1\right\}\right], \quad r>-1, \ \lambda, \beta>0. \qquad (7.5.1)$$

In the case when $r>0$, this pgf is that of the **Poisson-Pascal** distribution with a Poisson primary distribution with mean $\lambda[1-(1+\beta)^{-r}]^{-1}$ and a negative binomial secondary distribution. When $r=1$ this distribution is known as the **Polya-**

Aeppli. When $r = -.5$ the distribution is known as the **Poisson-Inverse Gaussian** distribution (see chapter 8 for details).

The Poisson-Pascal distribution is generalized by extending the range of r to -1. In this case, it is necessary to consider the primary distribution to be Poisson with mean λ and the secondary distribution to be truncated at zero.

The probabilities of the generalized Poisson-Pascal distribution can be calculated recursively as

$$p_n = \frac{\lambda}{n} \sum_{j=1}^{n} j q_j p_{n-j}, \quad n = 1, 2, \ldots, \tag{7.5.2}$$

where

$$p_0 = e^{-\lambda} \tag{7.5.3}$$

and $\{q_n; \; n = 1, 2, \ldots\}$ are probabilities from the (extended) truncated negative binomial distribution which can be calculated recursively as

$$q_n = \frac{n+r-1}{n} \frac{\beta}{1+\beta} q_{n-1}, \quad n = 2, 3, \ldots \tag{7.5.4}$$

beginning with

$$q_1 = \frac{r}{(1+\beta)^r - 1} \frac{\beta}{1+\beta}. \tag{7.5.5}$$

From (7.2.7) and (4.5.3), the factorial moments of the extended truncated negative binomial distribution are

$$\mu_{(k)} = \frac{(r+k-1)^{(k)} \beta^k}{1 - (1+\beta)^{-r}}. \tag{7.5.6}$$

Consequently the first four factorial moments of the generalized Poisson-Pascal distribution are

$$\mu_{(1)} = \lambda^* r\beta = \lambda[1-(1+\beta)^{-r}]^{-1}r\beta, \tag{7.5.7}$$

$$\mu_{(2)} = \mu_{(1)}\{(r+1)\beta+\mu_{(1)}\}, \tag{7.5.8}$$

$$\mu_{(3)} = \mu_{(1)}\{(r+2)(r+1)\beta^2+3(r+1)\beta\mu_{(1)}+\mu_{(1)}^2\}, \tag{7.5.9}$$

$$\mu_{(4)} = \mu_{(1)}\{(r+2)(r+2)(r+1)\beta^3+(7r+11)(r+1)\beta^2\mu_{(1)} + 6(r+1)\beta\mu_{(1)}^2+\mu_{(1)}^3\} \tag{7.5.10}$$

which can be seen to be the corresponding formulas for the Poisson-Pascal model with Poisson parameter $\lambda^* = \lambda[1-(1+\beta)^{-r}]^{-1}$ and an (untruncated) negative binomial secondary distribution with parameters r and β.

The variance of the generalized Poisson-Pascal can be shown to be

$$\mu_2 = \mu_1'[1+(r+1)\beta] \tag{7.5.11}$$

for which we can see that the variance can exceed the mean by any quantity. Furthermore, it can be shown that the skewness in terms of the mean, variance and r is

$$\mu_2^{-\frac{3}{2}}\left\{3\mu_2-2\mu_1'+\frac{r+2}{r+1}\frac{(\mu_2-\mu_1')^2}{\mu_1'}\right\}. \tag{7.5.12}$$

Since $(r+2)/(r+1)$ is a decreasing function of r, for $r>-1$, the skewness increases without bound as $r\to-1$ from the right and decreases to one as $r\to\infty$. Consequently, this distribution can handle heavily skewed distributions very easily.

The Poisson-Pascal distributions, for which r must be positive, has a skewness that is bounded above by (7.5.12) for $r=0$. This is the skewness for the negative binomial distribution (i.e., Poisson-logarithmic). Extending the values of r to -1 by truncating the secondary distribution without loss of generality gives a very flexible three-parameter model by allowing the skewness to be unbounded. Consequently, we focus much attention on this distribution.

It should be noted that, by letting $\beta\to 0$, $r\to\infty$ with $r\beta=\lambda>0$, the Neyman Type A distribution results. This follows directly from the fact that the truncated negative binomial has the truncated Poisson as its limit. Furthermore, from section 6.14, a compound claim frequency distribution with a Poisson primary distribution and a truncated negative binomial secondary distribution is equivalent to a model with a Poisson primary and a negative binomial secondary distribution.

Since the geometric distribution is a special case of the negative binomial distribution with $r = 1$, the Polya-Aeppli distribution, i.e. Poisson primary and geometric secondary distributions, is a special case of the Poisson-Pascal and the generalized Poisson-Pascal.

Since the logarithmic distribution is the limit, as $r \to 0$, of both the truncated negative binomial and the extended truncated negative binomial, the negative binomial distribution is a limiting case with $r = 0$.

The Poisson distribution can also be considered a limit of the generalized Poisson-Pascal distribution. If one lets $r \to -1$ or $\beta \to \infty$ a limiting Poisson form is obtained.

This distribution (and its two-parameter special cases) provides a very powerful alternative in situations in which the data indicates that the variance exceeds the mean and the skewness does not correspond to that of any of the two parameter models discussed in previous sections.

It will be seen in chapter 8 that the generalized Poisson-Pascal is a mixed Poisson distribution (as are its special cases).

7.6 ONE PARAMETER PRIMARY AND MODIFIED DISTRIBUTIONS

In sections 7.4 and 7.5, we considered three new two-parameter models, namely the Neyman Type A, the Polya-Aeppli and the Poisson-Inverse Gaussian distributions, and one three-parameter distribution, the generalized Poisson-Pascal.

Each of these distributions had a Poisson as a primary distribution. It is possible to combine many other pairs of one or two-parameter models to produce two, three or four-parameter models. The choice of the Poisson distribution as a primary distribution has great appeal since it can be viewed as the distribution of the number of "accidents" which occur randomly through time, i.e. according to a Poisson process. The secondary distribution (truncated or untruncated) can be viewed as the number of claims per accident. Furthermore, the Poisson distribution has a positive probability at zero. In practical applications in which we have data based on the number of accidents per risk, the largest frequency often occurs at zero. Consequently, when the primary distribution is interpreted as the number of accidents, it is desirable to choose a primary distribution that has a positive probability at zero.

As will be seen in chapter 8, many of the claims frequency distributions with a Poisson primary distribution and a secondary distribution from the (a,b) class can also be interpreted as a mixed Poisson model. This is another appealing argument for use of the Poisson distribution as a primary distribution.

The reader should not feel restricted to these models since it is not imperative to interpret the models as was done in the previous two paragraphs. It is possible to use geometric or logarithmic primary distributions. The logarithmic distribution should only be used with a secondary distribution possessing a positive probability at zero since it does not possess one itself.

Example 7.6.1 Geometric-Geometric

Consider a claim frequency model in which both primary and secondary distributions are geometric. This distribution has pgf

$$P(z) = P_1(P_2(z))$$

$$= \{1 - \beta_1 [\frac{1}{1 - \beta_2(z-1)} - 1]\}^{-1}.$$

It can be shown (see exercise 7.6) that this distribution has a greater skewness than the Polya-Aeppli (Poisson-Geometric) with the same first two moments. Furthermore, it can be shown (see exercise 7.7) that the pgf can be rewritten as

$$P(z) = 1 + \frac{\beta_1}{1 + \beta_1} [\frac{1}{1 - \beta_2(1+\beta_1)(z-1)} - 1]$$

which is the pgf of a compound distribution with a Bernoulli (with mean $q = \beta_1(1+\beta_1)^{-1}$) primary distribution and a geometric (with mean $\beta_2(1+\beta_1)$) secondary distribution. When the pgf is rewritten as

$$P(z) = 1 - \frac{\beta_1}{1+\beta_1} + \frac{\beta}{1+\beta_1}[1-\beta_2(1+\beta_1)(z-1)]^{-1}$$

$$= 1 - \pi + \pi[1-\beta(z-1)]^{-1}$$

it can be seen that the Geometric-Geometric distribution is simply a modified geometric or "geometric with zeros" distribution. Since this distribution is a member of the (a,b) class, only one recursion of the form (7.1.10) or (7.1.11) is necessary to compute total claims rather than two which is suggested by treating the distribution as a compound geometric with a geometric secondary distribution.

It can further be seen (see exercise 7.8) that for distributions with equal first two moments, the skewness of a Geometric-Logarithmic distribution exceeds that of a Geometric-Geometric.

In chapter 6, it was shown that a Binomial-Exponential distribution and a Negative Binomial-Exponential (for integer values of r, i.e. Pascal) distribution are equivalent. The discrete analogue is also true. Using example 7.6.1, one can show that the Binomial-Geometric and the Negative Binomial-Geometric distributions are equivalent (see exercise 7.9).

When it appears that a claims frequency distribution does not adequately fit a set of sample data due to a difference at the probability at the point zero (i.e., the no claims probability), the distribution can be modified by adding (or subtracting) some quantity at the zero point and normalizing the remaining probabilities. Such **modified distributions** were considered in section 7.2 in connection with the membership of the (a,b) class of distributions. In that section, it was shown that making such an adjustment in a secondary distribution, when the primary distribution was Poisson, binomial, geometric or negative binomial, was of no consequence.

We now consider adjustments to the primary distribution so that the modified probabilities are

$$q_0 = 1-\pi+\pi p_0$$

$$q_n = \pi p_n, \quad n = 2,3,... \tag{7.6.1}$$

where p_n is a member of the (a,b) class. From section 7.2, the modified distribution is also a member of the (a,b) class. Consequently, equations (7.1.10) and (7.1.11) can be used for these distributions to calculate total claims.

It can be noticed that the modified distribution has pgf

$$Q(z) = 1-\pi+\pi P(z)$$

$$= 1+\pi\{P(z)-1\}$$

$$= P_1(P(z)) \tag{7.6.2}$$

where $P_1(z)$ is the pgf of a Bernoulli (with mean π) distribution. Hence modified distributions are **compound Bernoulli** variates. From (7.6.2) it is immediately obvious that the k-th factorial moments of the modified distribution can be rewritten as π times the k-th factorial moment of the original distribution. The central moments are affected in a more complicated way.

A simple interpretation of a modified claim frequency distribution is possible. From (7.6.2), the distribution can also be seen as a weighted average of a degenerate distribution (with all probability at zero) and the original distribution. This suggests that the population of risk are of two types: a proportion π whose claim frequency distribution has pgf $P(z)$ and a proportion $1-\pi$ who will never make a claim. This kind of situation is possible in group health insurance or group dental insurance where an employee may never make a claim because the benefits are covered under another (say spouse's group) insurance plan. It is easy to imagine other situations which give rise to the same situation (e.g. lack of knowledge of coverage).

Example 7.6.2. Poisson with zeros

Perhaps the most well known modified distribution, the pgf is $P(z) = 1-\pi+\pi e^{\lambda(z-1)}$.

Another two-parameter distribution of this type is the **log-zero** distribution discussed in example 4.8.2. This distribution simply includes an arbitrary probability at zero for the logarithmic distribution. For fixed mean and variance, the log-zero distribution has greater skewness than the Poisson with zeros distribution (see exercise 7.10).

7.7 OTHER COMPOUND DISTRIBUTIONS

Many other frequency distributions with pgf's of the form (7.1.1) or (7.1.2) can have been used. The authors have selected several distributions which they feel are reasonably suited for modeling in insurance. Some others will be introduced in chapter 8. Other distributions may be appropriate in certain situations, however. Two examples are now given.

Example 7.7.1. Log-Zero-Poisson Distribution

This three parameter model has been used previously and is flexible in fitting a wide variety of distributions. It has a log-zero primary distribution and a Poisson secondary distribution. The pgf is thus

$$P(z) = 1-\pi+\pi\frac{\log[1-qe^{\lambda(z-1)}]}{\log(1-q)}.$$

Example 7.7.2. The Pascal-Pascal Distribution

A four parameter model can be easily constructed by choosing a negative binomial primary and secondary distribution. The resulting pgf is thus

$$P(z) = \{1-\beta_1[(1-\beta_2[z-1])^{-r_2}-1]\}^{-r_1}.$$

It can be extended by truncating the secondary distribution at zero and extending the range of r_2 to -1.

Clearly, many other choices are possible by choosing primary and secondary distributions from the (a,b) class. Some secondary distributions have also been used which are not members of the (a,b) class with a Poisson primary. These include the **Thomas** and **Neyman-type** distributions. See Johnson and Kotz (1969) for descriptions of these distributions.

7.8 REMOVAL OF ZERO CLAIMS

In section 6.13 the claims of size zero are easily "removed" for the $(a,b,0)$ subclass in the calculation of the distribution of total claims with LT

$$L_S(z) = P_N(L_X(z);\theta) \qquad (7.8.1)$$

by adjusting both the frequency and severity distribution to reflect the elimination of claims of size zero. We now extend these results to the $(a,b,1)$ subclass. As in section 6.13, we consider the members of the $(a,b,1)$ subclass to be members of the larger class defined by

$$P_N(z;\theta) = \frac{B[\theta(z-1)] - B(-\theta)}{B(0) - B(-\theta)} \qquad (7.8.2)$$

where θ is some parameter and $B(z)$ is some function which does not depend on θ. It can be seen that $B(x) = e^x$ and $\theta = \lambda$ yields the truncated Poisson distribution; $B(x) = (1+x)^m$ and $\theta = q$ yields the truncated negative binomial and $B(x) = (1-x)^{-r}$ and $\theta = \beta$ yields the truncated negative binomial distributions; and $B(x) = \log(1-x)$ and $\theta = \beta = q/(1-q)$ yields the logarithmic distribution. Note that $B(x)$ is not uniquely defined for any distribution since replacing it by $a+bB(x)$ yields the same distribution.

We again consider the claim severity distribution, with an atom at zero, with LT

$$L_X(z) = f_0 + (1-f_0)L_{X_+}(z). \qquad (7.8.3)$$

Theorem 7.8.1. For any claim frequency distribution satisfying (7.8.2) and any severity distribution satisfying (7.8.3), the Laplace transform $L_S(z)$ can be rewritten as

$$L_S(z) = P_N(f_0) + \{1 - P_N(f_0)\}P_N\{L_{X_+}(z);(1-f_0)\theta\}. \qquad (7.8.4)$$

Proof

Substitution of (7.8.2) and (7.8.3) into (7.8.1) yields

$$L_S(z) = P_N[f_0 + (1-f_0)L_{X_+}(z); \theta]$$

$$= \frac{B[\theta\{f_0 + (1-f_0)L_{X_+}(z) - 1\}] - B(-\theta)}{B(0) - B(-\theta)}$$

$$= \frac{B[(1-f_0)\theta\{L_{X_+}(z) - 1\}] - B[-(1-f_0)\theta] + B[-(1-f_0)\theta] - B(-\theta)}{B(0) - B(-\theta)}$$

$$= \pi_0 + (1-\pi_0)P_N[L_{X_+}(z); (1-f_0)\theta]$$

where

$$\pi_0 = \frac{B[-(1-f_0)\theta] - B(-\theta)}{B(0) - B(-\theta)} = P_N(f_0) = Pr\{S=0\}.$$

It can be seen that (7.8.4) can be written

$$L_S(z) = P(P_N\{L_{X_+}(z); (1-f_0)\theta\})$$

where $P(.)$ is a compound Beroulli pgf. Hence, we could consider (7.8.4) as a distribution of the "with zeros" type.

This result is particularly useful for any compound distribution when the logarithmic distribution or the ETNB distribution is used as a component of the claims frequency distribution by allowing one to ignore the probability at zero and then adjusting the result by an addition of zero.

7.9 BIBLIOGRAPHIC NOTES

Douglas (1980) gives a detailed discussion of many of the distributions discussed in this chapter. Johnson and Kotz (1969), Haight (1967), and Patil and Joshi (1968) also discuss many of them.

Sundt and Jewell (1981) discuss the (a,b) class of distributions. The extended truncated negative binomial distribution was introduced by Engen (1974). The generalized Poisson-Pascal distribution was used to fit claim frequency data by Thyrion (1961). Hofmann (1955) discusses many of its properties.

EXERCISES

1. If X is defined on the non-negative integers, show that the inversion of (7.1.9) yields (7.1.10).

2. If X is of the continuous type on the positive axis and has a point mass of $f_X(0)$ at zero, show that inversion of (7.1.9) yields (7.1.11).

3. Show that all distributions of the form (7.2.1) are members of the (a,b) class. Furthermore show that they, together with the $(a,b,0)$ and $(a,b,1)$ subclasses, constitute the entire (a,b) class.

4. Use the cumulant generating function and equations (6.1.4) - (6.1.8) to verify (7.4.6) - (7.4.10).

5. Use the cumulant generating function and equations (6.1.4) - (6.1.8) to obtain the first four cumulants of the generalized Poisson-Pascal distribution. Use the results to verify (7.5.11) and (7.5.12).

6. Show that the Geometric-Geometric distribution (see example 7.6.1) has greater skewness than the Polya-Aeppli distribution when the means and the variances of the two distributions are equated.

7. Show that the Geometric-Geometric distribution (see example 7.6.1) can be viewed as a compound distribution with a Bernoulli primary distribution and a geometric secondary distribution or equivalently a geometric with zeros distribution.

8. Show that the Geometric-Logarithmic distribution has greater skewness than the Geometric-Geometric distribution when the means and the variances of the two distributions are equated.

9. Prove that the compound claim frequency distribution with a negative binomial primary distribution with pgf

$$P_1(z) = [1 - \beta_1(z-1)]^{-r}$$

(where r is a positive integer) and a geometric secondary distribution with pgf

$$P_2(z) = [1 - \beta_2(z-1)]^{-1}$$

can be written as a compound distribution with a binomial primary distribution with pgf

$$Q_1(z) = [1 + \frac{\beta_1}{1+\beta_1}(z-1)]^r$$

and a geometric secondary distribution with pgf

$$Q_2(z) = [1 - \beta_2(1+\beta_1)(z-1)]^{-1}.$$

10. Show that the log-zero distribution (see example 4.8.2) has greater skewness than the Poisson with zeros distribution (see example 7.6.2) when the means and variances of the two distributions are equated.

11. Use example 2.9.1 to show that the Polya-Aeppli distribution (section 7.5) with exponential claim amounts may be written as a Poisson-exponential distribution.

CHAPTER 8

MIXED CLAIM FREQUENCY MODELS

8.1 INTRODUCTION

In section 2.8, we introduced the concept of a "random parameter" in order to model uncertainty about the value of the parameter. This concept was applied to the distribution of the number of claims in section 6.7. There it was assumed that for a "fixed" or "known" parameter, the claim frequencies for some insurance risks were distributed in accordance with a Poisson distribution. Furthermore, the parameters themselves were assumed to be distributed over the population of risks under consideration (often termed the **collective**) in accordance with a gamma distribution. The resulting "unconditional" distribution was shown to be a negative binomial distribution. This unconditional distribution was interpreted to be the distribution that would apply to a risk selected randomly from the population.

These uncertainty models stress that risks in a particular insurance class do not have identical risk characteristics. Classification schemes in insurance are designed so that risks within a single class (and with the same premium rate) are as homogeneous as is reasonable from a practical point of view. For example, in automobile insurance it is reasonable to expect that the mileage driven per year relates directly to the level of risk of accident. However, it is considered impractical to attempt to determine the level of exposure on the basis of mileage from each insured driver. Consequently, any class of automobile insurance risks will be heterogeneous with respect to the level of risk exposure measured by mileage driven.

The level of risk may be quantified by one or more parameters. However, we will usually consider uncertainty for a single parameter only. In this chapter, we consider only uncertainty for claim frequencies and not uncertainty for claim severities. Hogg and Klugman (1984) devote significant attention to claim severity models with parameter uncertainty.

Let N be a random variable denoting the number of claims over a fixed time period for some risk. From equation (2.5.10), the variance of the number of claims for a risk selected randomly from the collective can be decomposed into two parts as

$$Var(N) = E_\theta[Var_N(N|\theta)] + Var_\theta[E_N(N|\theta)]. \qquad (8.1.1)$$

The first term is the expected value of the conditional variance whereas the second term is the variance of the conditional mean. The first term reflects the variation in claim numbers due to the randomness of N and the second term reflects the randomness (or uncertainty) of the parameter θ. Of course, when the parameter θ is fixed so that $\theta = \theta$, then the second term becomes zero since there is no variation associated with θ. Consequently, the second term reflects the increase in the total variance due to the heterogeneity of the risk characteristics within the population of risks under consideration.

The two components in (8.1.1) play an important part in **credibility theory** which deals with determining a premium for future claims based on a history of prior claims. The first term is called the **expected value of the process variance** and the second term is called the **variance of the hypothetical means.**

More generally, other characteristics, such as higher moments, generating functions and transforms for the collective can be obtained using formula (2.5.9) by first conditioning on the risk parameter and then taking an appropriate expectation.

The variance of the distribution of total claims, $S = X_1 + X_2 + \cdots + X_N$, can be decomposed in similar fashion to (8.1.1),

$$Var(S) = E_\theta\{Var_X(X|\theta)\} + Var_\theta\{E_X(S|\theta)\}. \qquad (8.1.1)$$

Now substituting

$$E_X(S|\theta) = E_N E_X(S|\theta) \qquad (8.1.2)$$

and

$$Var_X(S|\theta) = E_N Var_X(S|\theta,N) + Var_N E_X(S|\theta,N) \tag{8.1.3}$$

yields

$$Var(S) = E_\theta\{E_N[Var_X(S|\theta,N)]\} + E_\theta\{Var_N[E_X(S|\theta)]\}$$

$$+ Var_\theta\{E_N[E_X(S|\theta,N)]\}. \tag{8.1.4}$$

Equation (8.1.4) gives the contributions of the variances of the claim sizes, the claim frequency an the parameter uncertainty. Since the serverities do not depend upon θ, (8.1.4) reduces to

$$Var(S) = E_\theta[E_N(N|\theta)]Var(X) + E_\theta[Var_N(N|\theta)]E(X)^2$$

$$+ Var_\theta[E_N(N|\theta)]E(X)^2. \tag{8.1.5}$$

8.2 MIXED POISSON DISTRIBUTIONS

As discussed in the previous section, a natural method of incorporating the assumption of heterogeneity in the portfolio is to assume that the risk parameter θ varies within the portfolio. To quantify this assumption, suppose that any particular risk in the portfolio has a Poisson distribution of claim frequencies with mean $\lambda\theta$ where θ is itself a random variable with distribution representing the expected risks inherent in the given portfolio. The distribution function of θ is given by $U(\theta)$ and the (unconditional) distribution of claim frequencies of an individual risk drawn from the portfolio is mixed Poisson (see example 2.8.1).

The Poisson assumption is made as a matter of convenience and in the absence of any evidence to the contrary, since there is in general no method of checking the distributional assumption with respect to a particular individual risk. Other mixtures are, however, discussed in section 8.5.

Before considering the choice of any particular mixing function $U(\theta)$, some general results for Poisson mixtures are now given.

The pgf of the number of claims N is easily seen to be (by conditioning on θ),

$$P_N(z) = \int_0^\infty e^{\lambda\theta(z-1)} dU(\theta). \tag{8.2.1}$$

If the Laplace transform of the mixing variate θ is given by

$$L_\theta(z) = \int_0^\infty e^{-z\theta} dU(\theta), \tag{8.2.2}$$

then

$$P_N(z) = L_\theta[\lambda(1-z)]. \tag{8.2.3}$$

The first result concerning mixed Poisson random variables is obtained by noticing that (8.2.3) is of the same form as (6.13.3). Consequently, claim severities of size 0 may be removed (see section 6.13).

Moments of N are easily obtained from (8.2.1). Clearly,

$$\frac{d^k}{dz^k} P_N(z) = \int_0^\infty (\lambda\theta)^k e^{\lambda\theta(z-1)} dU(\theta)$$

and so the k-th factorial moment of N is given by

$$\mu_{(k)} = \lambda^k E(\theta^k), \quad k = 1,2,3,... \tag{8.2.4}$$

Thus mean and variance of the mixed Poisson distribution are

$$E(N) = \lambda E(\theta) \tag{8.2.5}$$

and

$$Var(N) = \lambda^2 Var(\theta) + \lambda E(\theta). \tag{8.2.6}$$

On comparison of the second term of (8.2.6) with (8.2.5), it is clear that mixed Poisson variates have variance exceeding the mean (unlike the Poisson). This condition, which is usually the case in practical situations, is normally desirable from the insurer's standpoint in that the mixed distribution can be thought of as being "safer" than the original Poisson.

From (8.1.5), the variance of total claims for the compound mixed Poisson distribution is

$$Var(S) = \lambda E(\theta)E(X^2) + \lambda^2 Var(\theta)E(X)^2.$$

Douglas (1980) proves that Poisson mixtures are identifiable. This means that

$$\int_0^\infty e^{\lambda\theta(z-1)}dU_1(\theta) = \int_0^\infty e^{\lambda\theta(z-1)}dU_2(\theta)$$

implies that $U_1(\theta) = U_2(\theta)$. Thus, in discussing Poisson mixtures, one can discuss the unique mixing function.

The convolution of two mixed Poisson variates is again a mixed Poisson variate. If $P_1(z) = L_1[\lambda(1-z)]$ and $P_2(z) = L_2[\lambda(1-z)]$ are two mixed Poisson pgf's and $P(z)$ is the pgf of their convolution then

$$P(z) = P_1(z)P_2(z) = L_1[\lambda(1-z)]L_2[\lambda(1-z)] = L[\lambda(1-z)]$$

where $L(z) = L_1(z)L_2(z)$ which is the LT of the convolution of the two mixing distributions. Hence mixed Poisson distributions are closed under convolution. In particular, if the mixing distribution is from a family of distributions which is closed under convolution, i.e. if $[L_\theta(z)]^\alpha$ differs from $L_\theta(z)$ by a change in parameter only (see example 5.3.1), then the same is true for the resulting mixed Poisson, since $[P(z)]^\alpha$ then differs from $P(z)$ by a parameter change only (see 8.2.3).

There is a very close relationship between mixed and compound Poisson variates (section 7.3) which is given in the following theorem.

Theorem 8.2.1. Suppose $P(z)$ is a mixed Poisson pgf with infinitely divisible mixing function $U(\theta)$. Then $P(z)$ is also a compound Poisson pgf and may be expressed as

$$P(z) = e^{\lambda[Q(z)-1]}$$

where $\lambda > 0$ is a parameter and $Q(z)$ a pgf. Furthermore, if one adopts the convention that $Q(0) = 0$, then λ and $Q(z)$ are unique.

Proof

From (8.2.3),

$$P(z) = L_\theta[\lambda(1-z)].$$

Thus

$$[P(z)]^{\frac{1}{n}} = \{L_\theta[\lambda(1-z)]\}^{\frac{1}{n}}$$

and, since $L_\theta(z)$ is infinitely divisible,

$$L_n(z) = [L_\theta(z)]^{\frac{1}{n}}$$

is again a Laplace transform. Thus

$$[P(z)]^{\frac{1}{n}} = L_n[\lambda(1-z)]$$

is again a pgf (in fact, a mixed Poisson pgf). Hence $P(z)$ is an infinitely divisible pgf. But Feller (1968, p. 290) shows that any infinitely divisible pgf is a compound Poisson variate. If $Q(0) = 0$, then $\lambda = -\log p_0$ and $Q(z) = 1 + \lambda^{-1}\log P(z)$.

It was shown in sections 6.7 and 6.8 that the negative binomial was both a mixed and compound Poisson variate. By the above theorem and the fact that the gamma distribution (section 4.12) is infinitely divisible, this is not a coincidence. It will be shown subsequently that many of the compound distributions discussed in chapter 7 are also mixed Poisson variates.

The fact that a particular distribution arises both as a mixture and as a compound model may be unsettling to the actuary as it may be difficult to determine the underlying process. However, if one remembers that there is no "correct" model to describe a particular situation in any event, it seems clear that this gives more scope to the actuary in modeling.

It should be noted that a mixed Poisson process does not have independent increments (see section 3.5). This may be considered a desirable characteristic in situations where it is felt that the independence assumption is too strong.

To this point, no assumption as to the support of the df $U(\theta)$ has been made. In a practical situation, a nonparametric discrete distribution may be chosen, corresponding roughly to a risk classification system in the collective. This would normally give rise to a **finite mixture** of the form

$$P(z) = \sum_{i=1}^{k} p_i e^{\lambda \theta_i (z-1)}. \tag{8.2.7}$$

Strictly speaking, if k is large and the p_i's were all unknown, model fitting would be a formidable task. The more tractable case where $k = 2$ may be referred to as a **two-point mixture,** perhaps corresponding to a "standard" and a "substandard" risk classification system. In this case (8.2.7) may be rewritten as

$$P(z) = p e^{\lambda_1 (z-1)} + (1-p) e^{\lambda_2 (z-1)}. \tag{8.2.8}$$

Even in this simple case, three parameters $(p, \lambda_1, \lambda_2)$ would normally have to be estimated. Tröbliger (1961) used a model of this form for claim frequencies. Everitt and Hand (1981) discuss model fitting for finite Poisson mixtures of the form (8.2.7), paying special attention to the special case (8.2.8).

Due to the fact that a large number of parameters may have to be estimated in (8.2.7), it may be expedient to use parametric discrete mixing distributions in many practical situations. If one considers $U(\theta)$ to correspond to a **discrete** distribution with pgf $P_\theta(z)$, then (8.2.1) may be rewritten as

$$P(z) = P_\theta[e^{\lambda(z-1)}] \tag{8.2.9}$$

which is seen to be a compound distribution with Poisson secondary distribution on comparison with (7.1.1). Hence we are again in a situation where mixing has generated a compound distribution! Conversely, any compound pgf of the form (7.1.1) with Poisson secondary distribution is also a mixture. If one chose as primary distribution a member of the (a,b) class of sections 7.1 and 7.2, then computation of the total claims density is straightforward using the results of these sections. This is the case in the following example.

Example 8.1.1. Neyman Type A Distribution

If, in (8.2.9), we choose

$$P_\theta(z) = e^{\mu(z-1)},$$

we obtain

$$P(z) = e^{\mu[e^{\lambda(z-1)}-1]}$$

and so this distribution is both a compound Poisson distribution and a mixed Poisson distribution with a Poisson mixing function.

As was mentioned in section 7.4, the Neyman Type A distribution may have more than one mode. This may be an undesirable feature of the distribution, particularly if one chooses a unimodal mixing function. This property is often a feature of discrete mixtures. An additional drawback to parametric discrete mixing functions is that the support of the expected frequencies is normally $\{0,\lambda,2\lambda,...\}$ which is an arithmetic set. This assumption seems to be rather difficult to justify in practice since one would have little reason to believe that the set of possible values of the expected frequencies would form an arithmetic sequence.

For these and other reasons, parametric mixing functions are normally taken to be continuous, although distributions with mixed support could be used. Holgate (1970) has shown that if the mixing function is absolutely continuous and unimodal, then so is the mixed Poisson which results. Hence multimodality cannot occur in this case.

Suppose that one chooses as mixing function a distribution which is closed under scale changes, as are virtually all continuous distributions discussed in chapter 4. This means that if $L_\theta(z;\lambda)$ is the LT of θ, then the LT of

$a\theta$ is $L_\theta(z;\lambda a^{-1})$. Then the the pgf (8.2.3) can arise by assuming a (conditional) Poisson distribution with mean θ, where θ has distribution with Laplace transform $\tilde{u}(\lambda z)$ and is thus distributed as λ times the original variate with Laplace transform $\tilde{u}(z)$. If the original mixing distribution is closed under scale changes, then $\tilde{u}(\lambda z)$ is simply another member of the same family, but with different parameters. Hence, if the mixing distribution chosen is closed under scale changes then we assume without loss of generality that $\lambda = 1$ in (8.2.1) and subsequent formulae.

The most common and convenient choice of mixing function is the gamma distribution, and the resulting mixed Poisson distribution is then the negative binomial. This model is discussed in detail in section 6.7. Consequently, no further discussion of this model will be given here. In subsequent sections, other mixing distributions will be discussed. As will be seen in chapter 9, situations often arise when the negative binomial does not provide an adequate fit to the data, and in these situations alternatives may be considered. A good alternative to the gamma mixing distribution is the inverse Gaussian distribution, for which the resulting mixed Poisson has a thicker right tail and is thus more suitable in many insurance applications, since the negative binomial often understates the tail. In addition, this model provides an alternative if the actuary desires an additional degree of conservatism, and is no more difficult to fit to the data than the negative binomial (and often easier).

8.3 THE POISSON-INVERSE GAUSSIAN DISTRIBUTION

An important distribution in insurance modeling is obtained by choosing as mixing distribution the inverse Gaussian distribution for the parameter θ in section 8.2. Since many of its elementary properties may be derived by considering it as a special case of the distribution obtained by mixing over the generalized inverse Gaussian distribution (example 4.14.7), we begin by considering this more general Poisson mixture, known as **Sichel's** distribution.

Since the generalized inverse Gaussian distribution is closed under scale transformations, we set $\lambda = 1$ in (8.2.3) and note that, by example 4.14.7, the pgf of Sichel's distribution is

$$P(z) = \frac{K_\lambda\{\mu\beta^{-1}[1-2\beta(z-1)]^{\frac{1}{2}}\}}{K_\lambda(\mu\beta^{-1})}[1-2\beta(z-1)]^{-\frac{\lambda}{2}}. \tag{8.3.1}$$

where $K_\lambda(x)$ is the modified Bessel function of the third kind wth index λ (see appendix C).

The probabilities $\{p_n; \ n = 0,1,2,...\}$ can be obtained from (8.3.1) as the coefficient of z^n, or more simply from a direct argument. By conditioning on θ, we note that

$$p_n = \int_0^\infty \frac{\theta^n e^{-\theta}}{n!} \mu^{-\lambda}\theta^{\lambda-1} \frac{e^{-\frac{(\theta-\mu)^2}{2\beta\theta}}}{2K_\lambda(\mu\beta^{-1})} d\theta$$

from example 4.14.7. This expression may be rewritten as

$$p_n = \frac{\mu^n(1+2\beta)^{-\frac{n+\lambda}{2}}}{2n!K_\lambda(\mu\beta^{-1})} \int_0^\infty (\mu_1)^{-(n+\lambda)}\theta^{n+\lambda-1}e^{-\frac{1+2\beta}{2\beta\theta}(\theta-\mu)^2} d\theta$$

where $\mu_1 = \mu(1+2\beta)^{-\frac{1}{2}}$. This is of the same form as the numerator of the generalized inverse Gaussian pdf and thus

$$p_n = \frac{\mu^n}{n!} \frac{K_{\lambda+n}[\mu\beta^{-1}(1+2\beta)^{\frac{1}{2}}]}{K_\lambda(\mu\beta^{-1})} (1+2\beta)^{-\frac{\lambda+n}{2}}, \quad n = 0,1,2,... \tag{8.3.2}$$

Using the result (C3) from the appendix, it follows easily that

$$(1+2\beta)n(n-1)p_n = 2\beta(n-1)(\lambda+n-1)p_{n-1}+\mu^2p_{n-2}, \quad n = 2,3,4,... \tag{8.3.3}$$

which may be used to calculate the probabilities recursively, once p_0 and p_1 have been obtained.

If one denotes the Laplace transform of the generalized inverse Gaussian by $L(z;\lambda)$, it can be shown using the results in the appendix that

$$\frac{\partial}{\partial x}K_\lambda(x) = \frac{\lambda}{x}K_\lambda(x) - K_{\lambda+1}(x)$$

and hence

$$\frac{\partial}{\partial z}L(z;\lambda) = -\mu\frac{K_{\lambda+1}(\mu\beta^{-1})}{K_\lambda(\mu\beta^{-1})}L(z;\lambda+1).$$

Thus

$$\frac{\partial^k}{\partial z^k}L(z;\lambda) = (-1)^k\mu^k\frac{K_{\lambda+k}(\mu\beta^{-1})}{K_\lambda(\mu\beta^{-1})}L(z;\lambda+k) \qquad (8.3.4)$$

and so, using (8.2.4) and (8.3.4), the **k-th factorial moment** of Sichel's distribution is

$$\mu_{(k)} = \mu^k\frac{K_{\lambda+k}(\mu\beta^{-1})}{K_\lambda(\mu\beta^{-1})}. \qquad (8.3.5)$$

As was mentioned in example 4.14.7, the inverse Gaussian distribution is the special case of the generalized inverse Gaussian distribution obtained by setting $\lambda = -.5$ in the above formulas. The Poisson mixed over the inverse Gaussian distribution is thus obtained as the same special case. The pgf is

$$P(z) = e^{-\frac{\mu}{\beta}\{[1+2\beta(1-z)]^{\frac{1}{2}}-1\}}. \qquad (8.3.6)$$

From (8.3.2), the probabilities of the Poisson-Inverse Gaussian distribution are given by

$$p_0 = e^{-\frac{\mu}{\beta}[(1+2\beta)^{\frac{1}{2}}-1]} \tag{8.3.7}$$

and

$$p_n = p_0 \frac{\mu^n}{n!} \left[\sum_{m=0}^{n-1} \frac{(n-1+m)!}{(n-1-m)!m!} (\frac{\beta}{2\mu})^m (1+2\beta)^{-\frac{n+m}{2}} \right], \quad n = 1,2,3,... \tag{8.3.8}$$

The probabilities are more easily calculated from the recursive formula

$$p_n = \frac{\beta}{1+2\beta}(2-\frac{3}{n})p_{n-1} + \frac{\mu^2}{1+2\beta}\frac{1}{n(n-1)}p_{n-2}, \quad n = 2,3,4,... \tag{8.3.9}$$

beginning with (8.3.7) and

$$p_1 = \mu(1+2\beta)^{-\frac{1}{2}} p_0. \tag{8.3.10}$$

From (8.3.5), the k-th factorial moment of the distribution is

$$\mu_{(k)} = \mu^k \sum_{m=0}^{k-1} \frac{(k-1+m)!}{(k-1-m)!m!} (\frac{\beta}{2\mu})^m. \tag{8.3.11}$$

The mean and variance are

$$\kappa_1 = \mu \tag{8.3.12}$$

and

$$\kappa_2 = \mu(1+\beta). \tag{8.3.13}$$

Like the negative binomial distribution, the Poisson-Inverse Gaussian distribution has two parameters. It is easily shown that if each of these two distributions has mean μ and variance σ^2, the skewness of the Poisson-Inverse

Gaussian exceeds that of the negative binomial by $(\mu\sigma^3)^{-1}(\sigma^2-\mu)^2$. Thus the Poisson-Inverse Gaussian has a thicker tail, which, as we shall see in the next chapter, makes it more suitable for modeling claim frequencies in some situations.

Also like the negative binomial, it is closed under convolutions. If N_i has pgf (8.3.6) with parameters β and μ_i and $N_1, N_2, \ldots, N_k$ are independent, then $N_1 + N_2 + \cdots + N_k$ has pgf (8.3.6) with parameters β and $\mu_1 + \mu_2 + \cdots + \mu_k$.

If one notes the identity

$$x = [(1+x)^{\frac{1}{2}}-1][(1+x)^{\frac{1}{2}}+1], \quad x>0, \tag{8.3.14}$$

and chooses $x = 2\beta(1-z)$, then (8.3.6) may be rewritten as

$$P(z) = e^{2\mu(z-1)/\{1+[1-2\beta(z-1)]^{\frac{1}{2}}\}^{-1}}$$

When written in this form, it is easy to see that

$$\lim_{\beta \to 0} P(z) = e^{\mu(z-1)}$$

and so the Poisson-Inverse Gaussian has a limiting Poisson form, obtained when $\beta \to 0$.

This model may be used quite naturally in the context of a mixed Poisson process (section 3.5). It also may be used in the context of a compound Poisson process, because the Poisson-Inverse Gaussian is a compound Poisson distribution. Since the inverse Gaussian is infinitely divisible, it follows from Theorem 8.2.1 that this is in fact the case and so we may express (8.3.6) in the form

$$e^{\lambda[Q(z)-1]}. \tag{8.3.15}$$

Imposing the condition that $Q(0) = 0$, it is clear that

$$\lambda = \frac{\mu}{\beta}[(1+2\beta)^{\frac{1}{2}}-1] \tag{8.3.16}$$

and

$$Q(z) = \frac{[1+2\beta(1-z)]^{\frac{1}{2}}-(1+2\beta)^{\frac{1}{2}}}{1-(1+2\beta)^{\frac{1}{2}}}. \tag{8.3.17}$$

On comparison of (8.3.17) with (7.2.8), we see that $Q(z)$ is the pgf of an extended truncated negative binomial distribution with parameter $r = -.5$. Thus, from (7.2.10), it follows that the probabilities $\{q_n; n = 1,2,3,...\}$ with pgf (8.3.17) are given by

$$q_n = \frac{\frac{1}{2}\Gamma(n-\frac{1}{2})(1+2\beta)^{\frac{1}{2}}(\frac{2\beta}{1+2\beta})^n}{n!\Gamma(\frac{1}{2})[(1+2\beta)^{\frac{1}{2}}-1]}, \quad n = 1,2,3,... \tag{8.3.18}$$

The moments of the distribution with pgf (8.3.17) are given by (7.2.11) and (7.2.12) with $r = -.5$ and β replaced by 2β. Using (8.3.14) one may express the mean as

$$\kappa_1 = \frac{1}{2}[(1+2\beta)^{\frac{1}{2}}+1]. \tag{8.3.19}$$

We see that the Poisson-Inverse Gaussian is a special case of the generalized Poisson-Pascal and so one can compute the aggregate claims density using the recursions developed in sections 7.1 and 7.2. Hence one could define a compound Poisson process with this distribution, as well as a mixed Poisson process.

Two other attributes of this distribution are its relative ease in model fitting (as will be seen in chapter 9) and the resulting fit, which is often superior to that obtained by the distributions discussed in chapter 6.

Although this model provides a good alternative to the negative binomial in many situations, other Poisson mixtures may be desirable in some situations. A few of these are discussed in the following section.

8.4 OTHER MIXED MODELS

Other choices for the mixing distribution may be used in some situations. **Sichel's** distribution, discussed in the previous section, tends to be more difficult to work with if λ is unknown. Atkinson and Yeh (1982) have discussed estimation procedures for λ. Willmot (1986) and Willmot and Panjer (1986) have derived recursive formulas for the total claims distribution for this model.

Another generalization of the Poisson-Inverse Gaussian is the **generalized Poisson-Pascal** (section 7.5). This distribution is also a mixed Poisson variate as is now demonstrated. If $r = 0$ in (7.5.1) the distribution is known to be a mixed Poisson since it is negative binomial. If $r > 0$, then (7.5.1) satisfies (8.2.3) with

$$L_\theta(z) = e^{\lambda_1[(1+\beta_1 z)^{-r} - 1]} \tag{8.4.1}$$

and $\lambda_1 > 0$, $\beta_1 > 0$ appropriately chosen parameters. The Laplace transform (8.4.1) is easily seen to be a compound Poisson variate with gamma (section 4.12) severity distribution. If $-1 < r < 0$, (7.5.1) may be reparameterized as

$$P(z) = e^{-\lambda\{[1-\mu(z-1)]^\alpha - 1\}} \tag{8.4.2}$$

where $\lambda > 0$, $\mu > 0$, and $0 < \alpha < 1$.

If one sets $\lambda = 1$ in (8.2.3), then (8.4.2) satisfies (8.2.3) with

$$L_\theta(z) = e^{-\lambda[(1+\mu z)^\alpha - 1]}. \tag{8.4.3}$$

To show that (8.4.3) is the Laplace transform of an absolutely continuous pdf, consider the transform

$$L_\alpha(z) = e^{-z^\alpha}. \tag{8.4.4}$$

Feller (1971, p. 448, 581) shows that for $0<\alpha<1$, (8.4.4) satisfies

$$L_\alpha(z) = \int_0^\infty e^{-zx} f_\alpha(x) dx$$

where

$$f_\alpha(x) = \frac{1}{\pi} \sum_{k=1}^\infty \frac{\Gamma(k\alpha+1)}{k!} (-1)^{k-1} x^{-(k\alpha+1)} \sin(\alpha k\pi), \quad x>0 \tag{8.4.5}$$

is the pdf of a random variable, known as a **stable** variate. We leave it as an exercise to show that (8.4.3) is the Laplace transform of

$$u(x) = \frac{e^\lambda}{\mu\lambda^{1/\alpha}} e^{-\frac{x}{\mu}} f_\alpha\left(\frac{x}{\mu\lambda^{1/\alpha}}\right), \quad x>0. \tag{8.4.6}$$

The function $u(x)$ in (8.4.6) is a pdf since $u(x)\geq 0$ for all $x>0$ and $L_\theta(0) = 1$ in (8.4.3). It is the mixing density for the mixed Poisson variate with pgf (8.4.2).

In conclusion, the generalized Poisson-Pascal is a mixed Poisson, although the mixing distribution is complicated and varies with r. In light of the complexity of the mixing function, it may seem a bit artificial to treat it as a mixed Poisson. However it will be seen in chapter 9 that the generalized Poisson-Pascal does fit frequency data and may be justified as a mixed model.

Other mixed Poisson variates may be used. Albrecht (1984) discusses some other mixing functions. In addition, (more complicated) recursions for the total claims density have been derived by Willmot and Panjer (1986) and Willmot (1986) for some Poisson mixtures.

Mixtures of other variates such as binomials and negative binomials have also been used. The Polya-Eggenberger (example 4.7.1) and the generalized Waring (example 4.7.2) are two such examples. The generalized Waring is also a mixed Poisson variate. The mixing variate θ is distributed as XY

where X is a gamma variate independent of Y which is a generalized Pareto (example 4.14.5). See Panjer and Willmot (1983) for details.

8.5 OTHER FREQUENCY MODELS

It is possible to combine the concepts of chapters 7 and 8 to reflect both mixing and compounding in a single model. Suppose that the number of "accidents" in a fixed time period has a mixed distribution with pgf of the form $P_1(P_2(z))$ and that the number of "claims per accident" has pgf $P_3(z)$, then the distribution of the number of claims has pgf $P_1(P_2(P_3(z)))$. If all three of these distributions are from the (a,b) class, the distribution of total claim costs has Laplace Transform $P_1(P_2(P_3(L_X(z))))$ and can be calculated using three applications of the recursive formulas (7.1.10) and (7.1.11).

In addition to the distributions considered as models in the last three chapters, other discrete distributions certainly may be used. The authors have attempted to choose models which they feel are appropriate in most insurance situations. Other models may be used, however, and the interested reader may wish to consult Johnson and Kotz (1969) or Patil and Joshi (1968) for other choices.

8.6 BIBLIOGRAPHIC NOTES

More detailed discussions of mixed Poisson variates may be found in Lundberg (1940), McFadden (1965), Ord (1972), Douglas (1980), Haight (1967), and Johnson and Kotz (1969).

The Poisson-Inverse Gaussian distribution was introduced by Holla (1966) and subsequently studied by Sankaran (1968) and Sichel (1971). Sichel's distribution was introduced by Sichel (1971) and was subsequently studied by Atkinson and Yeh (1982). Hofmann (1955) discusses the generalized Poisson-Pascal as a mixed Poisson. Albrecht (1984) and Willmot and Panjer (1986) discuss other Poisson mixtures.

EXERCISES

1. Using result (C3) from the appendix, prove that equations (8.3.3), (8.3.7) and (8.3.8) hold for Sichel's distribution.

2. Using (8.3.6) show that, if the negative binomial distribution and the Poisson Inverse Gaussian distribution have mean μ and variance σ^2, the skewness of the Poisson-Inverse Gaussian exceeds that of the negative binomial by $(\mu\sigma^3)^{-1}(\sigma^2-\mu)^2$.

3. Using (8.3.14) show that (8.3.6) can be rewritten as

$$P(z) = e^{2\mu(z-1)\{1+[1+2\beta(z-1)]^{\frac{1}{2}}\}^{-1}}.$$

4. Show that (8.4.3) is the Laplace transform of (8.4.6).

5. Show that, if the Poisson distribution is mixed over the **reciprocal inverse Gaussian** distribution (section 4.13), then the resulting distribution is a compound Poisson distribution, and the secondary distribution is a weighted average of a logarithmic distribution and an extended truncated negative binomial distribution.

6. A **non-central chi-squared** random variable with m degrees of freedom and non-centrality parameter λ has Laplace transform

$$L(z) = (1+2z)^{-\frac{m}{2}} \exp\{\frac{\lambda}{2}[(1+2z)^{-1}-1]\}.$$

Show that, if the Poisson distribution is mixed over this distribution, then the resulting distribution is a compound Poisson distribution with secondary distribution a weighted average of a logarithmic distribution and a geometric distribution.

7. Suppose that the Poisson distribution is mixed over the negative binomial distribution. Show that the resulting distribution is a compound negative binomial with Poisson secondary, which may be viewed as a compound Poisson distribution with secondary distribution itself a compound logarithmic distribution (with Poisson secondary distribution).

8. Suppose that the number of accidents in a year are modeled by a mixed Poisson distribution with an exponential mixing function. If the number of claims per accident is modeled as a truncated (at zero) geometric distribution, prove that the total number of claims has a geometric distribution.

9. The Poisson-Lindley distribution (Sankaran, 1970) has probabilities of the form

$$p_n = \frac{\theta^2(\theta+2+n)}{(\theta+1)^{n+3}}, \quad n = 0,1,2,...$$

(a) Show that it is a mixed Poisson distribution

$$p_n = \int_0^\infty e^{-\lambda} \frac{\lambda^n}{n!} u(\lambda) d\lambda$$

with mixing density

$$u(\lambda) = \frac{\theta^2}{\theta+1}(\lambda+1)e^{-\lambda\theta}, \quad \lambda > 0.$$

(b) Show that the mixing distribution is itself a mixture of a gamma and an exponential distribution.

(c) Prove that the Poisson-Lindley distribution is also a mixture of two negative binomial distributions.

(d) Hence show how recursive techniques of chapter 7 can be used to calculate the distribution of total claims for an arithmetic severity distribution.

10. Suppose that the Poisson distribution is mixed over a shifted gamma distribution, that is, the Poisson mean is itself distributed as $\Lambda+\mu$ where Λ is gamma distributed and $\mu > 0$ is constant.

a) Show that the unconditional distribution (called Delaporte's distribution) is the convolution of a Poisson and a negative binomial distribution.

b) If Λ has an arbitrary distribution, show that the unconditional distribution is the convolution of a Poisson and a Poisson mixed by the distribution of Λ.

11. If $U(\lambda)$ is a distribution function and

$$p_n = \int_0^\infty \frac{\lambda^n e^{-\lambda}}{n!} dU(\lambda); \quad n = 0,1,2,...,$$

show that

$$\sum_{k=n+1}^\infty p_k = \int_0^\infty \frac{\lambda^n e^{-\lambda}}{n!} \{1 - U(\lambda)\} d\lambda, \quad n = 0,1,2,... \ .$$

CHAPTER 9

FITTING RISK MODELS

9.1 INTRODUCTION

Up to this point in the book, little discussion has been given to the important problem of model selection and fitting. Briefly, model fitting involves using the available information to select one or more parameter values for use in a given model. One such situation was described in section 6.5 with Poisson claim frequencies. In this chapter we will concentrate on the selection and fitting of claim frequency models. Hogg and Klugman (1984) give a detailed discussion of fitting claim severity distributions. The few exercises dealing with fitting continuous distributions given at the end of the chapter are intended primarily to augment their results.

One major difficulty in a general discussion of claim frequency model fitting is the definition of a "standard" set of data with which to work. The available information is often quite varied in scope and format. For example, the actuary may not know how many claims a particular risk has incurred, but merely whether claims have been incurred or not. Or it may be of interest to fit a model when one only has information on claims which did occur, and no information on risks with no claims. In some situations one may only be able to obtain a few "pieces" of information, such as the mean claim frequency and perhaps the degree of one's uncertainty about this mean. If one knows only the mean, a one parameter model is the only type which may be fitted satisfactorily, since any other parameters would be arbitrary. More generally, if one knows k "pieces" of information, a k parameter model may be fitted, and it is partly for this reason that the authors have frequently classified models by the number of parameters.

The type of information available, therefore, heavily influences the choice of model and the model fitting technique. While some of the particular situations mentioned previously will be discussed, it is the purpose of this chapter to discuss some general considerations, but the analysis in any particular situation rests primarily with the actuary and his or her judgement.

We now turn our attention to the problem of choosing an appropriate model.

9.2 MODEL SELECTION

In choosing a model, one must consider the extent and format of the data, as mentioned above. In general, the more extensive the data, the more complicated the model one can fit. However, this is not necessarily desirable. Even with extensive data, a simpler model which gives an adequate fit is to be preferred to a more complicated model due to ease of interpretation of the results and ease of model fitting. In addition, a model which gives a good fit to the data is not necessarily a good predictor of future events. Hence, in order to be parsimonious, we would like to find a simple model which gives an adequate fit. A good discussion of these ideas may be found in Linhart and Zucchini (1986).

It is often desirable to fit more than one model in a given situation. It is possible that more than one model adequately describes the data and one would hope for good agreement between these models. There is no such thing as a ''correct'' model, and a model's primary purpose is to capture the essential features of any real situation.

It should be clear to the reader at this point that there are great advantages in having a fitted parametric claim frequency distribution rather than an empirical one based on the ''unsmoothed'' data above. Fitted parametric models usually allow many useful questions about the total claim and claim frequency processes to be answered.

To formulate the problem, we define several different quantities, some or all of which may be available in a given situation. Let $X_1, X_2, \ldots, X_n$ be the n observed values of a random quantity, which are assumed to be independent and identically distributed. The **sample moments** are defined by

$$M_r = \frac{1}{n} \sum_{i=1}^{n} X_i^r; \quad r = 1,2,3,\ldots \tag{9.2.1}$$

From these, we may determine the **sample mean**, the **sample variance**, and the **sample third central moment,** defined by

$$\bar{X} = M_1,\tag{9.2.2}$$

$$S^2 = M_2 - M_1^2,\tag{9.2.3}$$

$$K = M_3 - 3M_2M_1 + 2M_1^3.\tag{9.2.4}$$

(The reader may wish to compare (9.2.4) to (2.3.22) in order to get an idea of the motivation for the sample third central moment.) In many situations the **sample moments** may be available, but not the original X_i's.

When working with claim frequency data, there are only a countable set of possible values for the X_i's, and so repeated values often occur. Hence, it is often convenient to assume that the data are given in terms of the **observed frequencies**

$$N_k = \{\text{number of } X_i\text{'s for which } X_i = k\}, \quad k = 0,1,2,...\tag{9.2.5}$$

Then (9.2.1) becomes

$$M_r = \frac{1}{n}\sum_{k=1}^{\infty} k^r N_k, \quad r = 1,2,3,...\tag{9.2.6}$$

where the upper limit of the summation is actually finite for any finite sample.

The **empirical distribution function** is defined to be

$$G_n(x) = \{\text{number of } X_i\text{'s for which } X_i \le x\}; \quad x \ge 0.\tag{9.2.7}$$

Another set of quantities which are useful (particularly in working with data where the zero frequency class N_0 is missing) are the **frequency ratios**

$$T_k = (k+1)\frac{N_{k+1}}{N_k}, \quad k = 0,1,2,\dots \tag{9.2.8}$$

Before selecting a model, it is often desirable to compute the first few sample moments (e.g. $\bar{X}, S^2$, and K) and the frequency ratios.

As an initial step, one may wish to determine if the $(a,b,0)$ class of frequency distributions (Poisson, binomial, or negative binomial) may be appropriate. For this class, (6.6.3) holds, and since we might expect N_k/n to be close to p_k, it follows that

$$T_k \approx (a+b)+ak, \quad k = 0,1,2,\dots \tag{9.2.9}$$

and so a plot of T_k vs. k should resemble a straight line. If this is the case, then a comparison of $\bar{X}$ to S^2 could be used to choose between members of the $(a,b,0)$ class since for the Poisson $\bar{X}$ and S^2 should be close and T_k has slope 0, but for the binomial $\bar{X}>S^2$ and T_k is decreasing and for the negative binomial $\bar{X}<S^2$ and T_k is increasing. Typically in insurance situations $\bar{X}\leq S^2$, indicating that a Poisson or negative binomial may be appropriate.

Cox and Lewis (1966) describe some other tests which are appropriate to determine if a Poisson distribution is appropriate, often in the context of a stochastic process (see chapter 3).

If the curve defined by (9.2.9) increases more quickly than linearity (as is often the case) then a choice of distributions with thicker right tail (and hence higher skewness) may be appropriate. More generally, since the skewness of the negative binomial is given by (6.7.8) a comparison of K with

$$3S^2 - 2\bar{X} + 2\frac{(S^2-\bar{X})^2}{\bar{X}} \tag{9.2.10}$$

is informative. If K is roughly equal to (9.2.10), then the negative binomial may be appropriate. If K is less than (9.2.10), then one may wish to try to use the generalized Poisson-Pascal (or its special case, the Poisson-Inverse Gaussian, in order to choose a simpler model). If K exceeds (9.2.10), then the Neyman Type A, Polya-Aeppli, or Poisson-Pascal may be appropriate (or even the Poisson-binomial). Chapters 7 and 8 discuss these distributions.

In the interests of being conservative, one would like the right tail of the fitted model to be at least as large as the data would suggest. From the insurer's point of view, this represents conservatism. In other words, one might be content with the Poisson if $\bar{X} > S^2$, or the negative binomial if K exceeded (9.2.10). In practice, however, the opposite is often true, and the generalized Poisson-Pascal or Poisson-Inverse Gaussian distributions are good alternatives.

The above discussion is meant to be a rough guideline only, and for a clear choice of model there must be a great discrepancy between the above quantities. Thus the above considerations should be used with great caution and one may wish to proceed with a particular model choice despite some apparent evidence to the contrary. However, the fitted model should then be checked very carefully for adequacy of fit.

9.3 METHODS OF ESTIMATION

Once a model has been selected, one must then obtain parameter estimates. Any estimation method used should satisfy certain criteria. If a one is trying to estimate a parameter, say θ, from a model which has been selected, one would generally select an estimator $\hat{\theta}$ which is a function of the data and thus a random variable. It would be desirable if $E(\hat{\theta}) = \theta$, and any estimator satisfying this criterion is said to be **unbiased.**

For example, suppose that $E(X_i) = \mu$ and $Var(X_i) = \sigma^2$. Then $\bar{X}$ is unbiased for μ since $E(\bar{X}) = E(\frac{1}{n}\sum_{i=1}^{n}X_i) = \frac{1}{n}\sum_{i=1}^{n}E(X_i) = \frac{1}{n}\sum_{i=1}^{n}\mu = \mu$. It is natural to ask whether S^2 is unbiased for σ^2. We first write S^2 as

$$S^2 = \frac{1}{n}\sum_{i=1}^{n}X_i^2 - \bar{X}^2$$

$$= \frac{1}{n}\sum_{i=1}^{n}X_i^2 - \frac{1}{n}(2n\bar{X}^2 - n\bar{X}^2)$$

$$= \frac{1}{n}\{\sum_{i=1}^{n}X_i^2 - 2n\bar{X}^2 + n\bar{X}^2\}$$

$$= \frac{1}{n} \{\sum_{i=1}^{n} X_i^2 - 2\bar{X} \sum_{i=1}^{n} X_i + \sum_{i=1}^{n} \bar{X}^2\}$$

$$= \frac{1}{n} \sum_{i=1}^{n} \{X_i^2 - 2\bar{X}X_i + \bar{X}^2\}$$

$$= \frac{1}{n} \sum_{i=1}^{n} (X_i - \bar{X})^2. \tag{9.3.1}$$

To find the expected value of S^2, we note that

$$\sum_{i=1}^{n} (X_i - \mu)^2 = \sum_{i=1}^{n} (X_i - \bar{X} + \bar{X} - \mu)^2$$

$$= \sum_{i=1}^{n} (X_i - \bar{X})^2 + \sum_{i=1}^{n} 2(X_i - \bar{X})(\bar{X} - \mu) + \sum_{i=1}^{n} (\bar{X} - \mu)^2$$

$$= nS^2 + 2(\bar{X} - \mu) \sum_{i=1}^{n} (X_i - \bar{X}) + n(\bar{X} - \mu)^2$$

$$= nS^2 + n(\bar{X} - \mu)^2$$

since $\sum_{i=1}^{n}(X_i - \bar{X}) = 0$. In other words

$$S^2 = \frac{1}{n} \sum_{i=1}^{n} (X_i - \mu)^2 - (\bar{X} - \mu)^2. \tag{9.3.2}$$

Thus,

$$E(S^2) = \frac{1}{n} \sum_{i=1}^{n} E\{(X_i - \mu)^2\} - E\{(\bar{X} - \mu)^2\}$$

$$= \frac{1}{n} \sum_{i=1}^{n} Var(X_i) - Var(\bar{X})$$

$$= \frac{1}{n} \sum_{i=1}^{n} \sigma^2 - \frac{1}{n} \sigma^2$$

$$= (\frac{n-1}{n}) \sigma^2.$$

Clearly $E(S^2) \neq \sigma^2$, but

$$\frac{n}{n-1}S^2 = \frac{\sum\limits_{i=1}^{n}(X_i-\bar{X})^2}{n-1} \tag{9.3.3}$$

is unbiased for σ^2. It is worth noting that $\bar{X}$ and (9.3.3) are unbiased for μ and σ^2 even if the X_i's are independent but not necessarily identically distributed.

It turns out that many good estimators are biased, and consequently a better criterion for estimators in most situations is the notion of **consistency**, which states that an estimator $\hat{\theta}$ is consistent if $\hat{\theta} \rightarrow \theta$ in probability. Consistent estimators are asymptotically unbiased, i.e. $E(\hat{\theta}) \rightarrow \theta$ as $n \rightarrow \infty$. Another criterion for judging estimators is based on the precision with which one may estimate the parameter, since an estimator whose distribution is tightly centred around the parameter is to be preferred to one whose distribution is more spread out. We may quantify this by stating that $\hat{\theta}_1$ is to be preferred to $\hat{\theta}_2$ (all else equal) if $Var(\hat{\theta}_1) < Var(\hat{\theta}_2)$. In this case $\hat{\theta}_1$ is said to be more **efficient** than $\hat{\theta}_2$. There are many other criteria with which one may judge the quality of an estimator. The above, however, appear to be sufficient in most situations. See Barnett (1982), for further details.

It is often of interest to determine whether a particular value, eg. θ_0, is consistent with the data. This is often done by constructing a **confidence interval** for the parameter θ and determining if the value θ_0 is contained in the interval. The confidence interval is often based on the asymptotic distribution of the estimator, and is the set of values deemed "acceptable" in light of the data. The mean and variance of $\hat{\theta}$ are often of use in determining this asymptotic distribution. More generally, confidence intervals are often based on the distribution of a pivotal quantity, i.e. a random variable which is a function of θ but whose distribution does not depend on θ. See Hogg and Craig (1978) for a more detailed discussion.

Many estimation procedures have been used and studied in statistics, and it is impossible to outline all of them in a brief discussion. We shall consider a few of the more important techniques for use with claim frequency data, namely **moment estimation, maximum likelihood estimation,** and some "ad hoc" techniques for use in particular situations. Some other techniques which may be suited for use with claim frequency data include **least squares,**

minimum chi-squared, and **Bayesian** estimation. The interested reader should consult Hogg and Klugman (1984) for an introduction to the latter three methods, as well as some other techniques. For a thorough discussion of estimation, the interested reader should consult Hogg and Craig (1978), or Cox and Hinkley (1974) for a more advanced discussion.

As was previously mentioned, the form of the information may dictate the estimation technique used. For example, if one knows only the mean claim frequency, then the only possibility is to equate this to the theoretical mean of a selected model and determine the parameter of interest in this manner. Of course, little can be said about the quality of such an estimation technique since there is so little information to go on.

9.4 TESTING THE FIT OF THE MODEL

Once a model has been chosen and fitted based on available information, it remains to test whether the fit is adequate. This may be based on a comparison of the fitted model with that of the actual data. Again, if one has little data, adequacy of fit may be difficult to check and a subjective method based on judgement may be required.

A very natural statistic for use with claim frequency data is the **goodness-of-fit** statistic obtained as follows. For the random sample $X_1, X_2, \ldots, X_n$, divide the real line into k intervals $[a_0, a_1), [a_1, a_2), \ldots, [a_{k-1}, \infty)$. Let O_i be the number of the X_i which are observed to fall into the $i+1$-st interval. Let p_i be the probability under the fitted model that an observation falls into the $i+1$-st interval. Then the statistic

$$D = \sum_{i=0}^{k-1} \frac{(O_i - np_i)^2}{np_i} \tag{9.4.1}$$

may be used to judge the fit of the model. In general, the intervals should be chosen such that np_i is no smaller than 4 or 5 for almost all of the intervals. Under these circumstances, if we have used the data to estimate r parameters, then, for large n, D has an approximate chi-squared distribution with $(k-r-1)$ degrees of freedom (section 4.12). In general, the better the fit, the smaller D is, and so we say that the fit is acceptable if $D > D_0$ where D_0 is a selected percentile of the distribution, i.e.

$$Pr\{\chi^2_{(k-r-1)} \le D_0\} = 1-\alpha. \tag{9.4.2}$$

Normally α is chosen to be .05 or .10. The value of D_0 can be obtained from tables, or from the series expansion for the incomplete gamma function (see appendix A). The significance level or p-value

$$p = Pr\{\chi^2_{(k-r-1)} > D\} \tag{9.4.3}$$

can be computed similarly.

In general, the selection of the intervals is fairly arbitrary, but considerably less so with claim frequency data. If one chooses the "intervals" to be the integers, one obtains

$$D = \sum_{i=0}^{k-1} \frac{(N_i - np_i)^2}{np_i} \tag{9.4.4}$$

where N_i is the number of risks observed to have i claims. Of course, one may wish to group the value of i for which np_i is small with other values of i so that all classes have sufficiently large expected frequencies.

This test becomes more discriminating as the sample size becomes larger. This may be interpreted as reflecting the more detailed information about the parameters. In any event, it is sensitive to deviations in the tails (which are of considerable interest to actuaries, since the "high risks" are reflected in the right-hand tail), and provides a good relative yardstick to compare models with the same number of parameters.

A second measure of fit which is useful when working with grouped and discrete data is the **likelihood ratio statistic**

$$2\sum_{i=0}^{k-1} O_i \log(\frac{O_i}{np_i}) \tag{9.4.5}$$

in the notation of (9.4.11). Like the goodness of fit statistic, (9.4.5) has an approximate chi-squared distribution with $(k-r-1)$ degrees of freedom if r parameters have been estimated.

Other methods of testing the adequacy of fit of the model include an examination of the empirical distribution function (9.2.7) and a comparison with that of the fitted model. Specifically, one can use the Kolmogorov-Smirnov statistic to measure the adequacy of fit. See Hogg and Klugman (1984) for details. A thorough discussion of goodness of fit is given by Lawless (1982).

It should be noted that when a fitted model based on a particular estimation technique may give an inadequate fit, it does not necessarily mean that the model is inadequate. Another estimation technique may give an adequate fit. In particular, moment estimation techniques are fairly simple to apply but often do not give as good a fit as other more sophisticated techniques, such as maximum likelihood estimation, which are often more difficult computationally.

9.5 SAMPLE DATA SETS

The methods discussed in this chapter will be illustrated with the data sets given in table 9.1, taken from the insurance literature. The numbers are the observed frequencies N_k. Data set A gives the number of accidents per policy on a class of ''business and tourism'' automobile insurance taken from Thyrion (1961). Data set B also gives the number of claims in a year on automobile insurance and was given by Tröbliger (1961). Beard et al. (1984, p. 45) gives the number of claims on comprehensive motor policies, listed in column C. The number of claims on Swiss automobile liability policies was given by Bühlmann (1970, p. 107), and are listed in column D. The data in column E on motor vehicle policies was given by Hossack et al. (1983, p. 121). The data in column F refer to the number of injuries in traffic accidents involving bodily injury and is taken from Kupper (1965). The data in column G are taken from Simon (1961). While many of these data are related to automobile insurance, the methods clearly apply to other types of insurance as well.

For the above data sets, we will fit distributions to the individual risks. The pgf of the number of claims for n risks is then the n-fold convolution of the pgf of one risk. It is for this reason that frequency distributions which are closed under convolution (such as compound Poisson model, see chapter 7) are useful, since normally only a parameter change in the distribution is required.

TABLE 9.1

TYPICAL CLAIM FREQUENCY DATA

k	A	B	C	D	E	F	G
0	7,840	20,592	370,412	103,704	565,664	0	99
1	1,317	2,651	46,545	14,075	68,714	4,121	65
2	239	297	3,935	1,766	5,177	430	57
3	42	41	317	255	365	71	35
4	14	7	28	45	24	19	20
5	4	0	3	6	6	6	10
6	4	1	0	2	0	4	4
7	1	0	0	0	0	0	0
8	0	0	0	0	0	0	3
9	0	0	0	0	0	0	4
10	0	0	0	0	0	0	0
11	0	0	0	0	0	1	1
Total	9,461	23,589	421,240	119,853	639,950	4,652	298

9.6 MOMENT ESTIMATION

An estimation technique which is very common and of considerable importance for claim frequency data is moment estimation.

To employ this technique in fitting a model with k parameters, one computes (or estimates) the first k moments defined by (9.2.1). These are then equated to the first k moments of the model, and the resulting equations solved for the parameters.

The technique is most useful if the chosen model has relatively simple expressions for the moments. In addition, it is sometimes inapplicable. For example, any mixed Poisson distribution has variance exceeding the mean (section 8.2), so the method is inapplicable if $S^2 < \bar{X}$ (as defined in 9.2.2 and 9.2.3), since this will lead to invalid parameter estimates.

The method may be employed in some situations in a different form. Suppose one knows the mean aggregate claim amount and the mean claim severity amount only. An estimate of the mean claim frequency is simply the former divided by the latter, and a parameter estimate is obtainable from this (e.g. Poisson parameter λ). As a second example, one may have an estimate of the mean claim frequency plus an estimate of one's uncertainty in the form of a variance of the estimate of the mean. One could decide that the mean claim frequency is roughly .5, but is reasonably sure that it is between .4 and .6. To estimate, the variance, one could assume that (.4,.6) is a 95% confidence interval for the mean and use the normal approximation. The variance is roughly given by $.6-.4 = 2(1.96)\sigma$, or $\sigma^2 = .0026$. Then one could choose a mixing distribution with mean .5 and variance .0026. From the formulae for the moments of a mixed Poisson in section (8.2), it follows that an estimate of the mean is .5 and the variance $.5+.0026 = .5026$. These quantities could replace $\bar{X}$ and S^2 in moment estimation techniques. If one chooses as mixing distribution a gamma, one would then fit a negative binomial (see section 6.7) or if one chooses an inverse Gaussian distribution, a Poisson-Inverse Gaussian distribution would result (see section 8.3). The skewness of the latter is greater, and consequently it is a "safer" choice, reflecting a higher degree of uncertainty about large values of the mean.

In the general situation, it is assumed that one has data of the form $X_1, X_2, \ldots, X_n$, or, equivalently $N_0, N_1,\ldots$. The quantities $M_r, \ r = 1,2,3,\ldots,k$ can then be computed. For example, if one wishes to fit a negative binomial distribution (4.5.1) to some claim frequency data, then equating (4.5.4) to $\bar{X}$ and (4.5.5) to S^2 yields the estimates

$$\hat{\beta} = \frac{S^2}{\bar{X}} - 1, \tag{9.6.1}$$

$$\hat{r} = \frac{\bar{X}^2}{S^2 - \bar{X}}. \tag{9.6.2}$$

As an example, we use the method of moments to fit the negative binomial distribution to data set B. Using formula (9.2.6) we obtain $M_1 = .1442$ and $M_2 = .1847$. Thus, from (9.2.3), $S^2 = .1639$ which exceeds M_1. Hence, one may use the method of moments. From (9.6.1) and (9.6.2), we obtain $\hat{\beta} = .1362$ and $\hat{r} = 1.0589$. We compute the negative binomial probabilities (4.5.1) with these as our parameter values, and multiply them by 23,489 to obtain the expected frequencies 20,605.80, 2,615.52, 322.76, 39.45, 4.80, 0.58, 0.07. Since the last two expected frequencies are much less than 4 or 5, we group all classes from 4 up. The chi-squared statistic is

$$D = \frac{(20,605.80-20,592)^2}{20,605.80} + \frac{(2,615.52-2,651)^2}{2,615.52}$$
$$+ \frac{(322.76-297)^2}{322.76} + \frac{(39.45-41)^2}{39.45} + \frac{(5.47-8)^2}{5.47} = 3.78.$$

Since we have used 5 classes and estimated 2 parameters, the number of degrees of freedom is $5-1-2=2$. Thus, $p = Pr\{\chi^2_{(2)}>3.78\} = .15$. Since we expect a chi-squared value at least as large as 3.79 roughly 15% of the time, we accept the fit as adequate.

Moment estimators, while often convenient due to their simplicity, tend to have poor statistical properties. By this is meant that the variance of the estimators can be quite large. We omit a discussion of these statistical properties (the interested reader should consult Douglas, 1980) since it is felt by the authors that the main advantage of this technique is the simplicity, and a reader interested enough to examine the statistical properties of the estimators should probably use a more sophisticated technique with better statistical properties, such as maximum likelihood estimation.

Nevertheless, moment estimation is a useful technique for obtaining "quick" parameter estimates which may be used in their own right or as initial parameter estimates for iterative numerical procedures for more sophisticated techniques.

9.7 AD HOC ESTIMATION

In the previous section it was suggested that moment estimation often leads to simple estimates for parameters. There are situations, however, where moment estimation does not lead to simple estimates, and since the quality of the estimates is poor anyway one might wish to consider alternative simple procedures.

Consider, for example, the logarithmic distribution (section 4.6). Since there is one parameter q, moment estimation involves equating the sample mean $\bar{X}$ to the theoretical mean (4.6.4). This means that the moment estimate

$\hat{q}$ satisfies $\bar{X} = \hat{q}/\{-(1-\hat{q})\log(1-\hat{q})\}$. This cannot be solved explicitly for $\hat{q}$ so an alternative may be sought.

The idea of ad hoc estimation is to equate sample statistics to corresponding theoretical quantities, such that the corresponding parameter estimates are simple to obtain (there is no unique way to do this, even in a given situation). Thus moment estimation is a special case of this approach.

In the logarithmic case, one can show from (4.6.1) and (4.6.4) that

$$q = 1 - \frac{p_1}{\mu_1'} \qquad (9.7.1)$$

so that one could replace p_1 and μ_1' by their corresponding sample values, yielding the estimate

$$\hat{q} = 1 - \frac{N_1}{n\bar{X}}. \qquad (9.7.2)$$

For most of the models considered here, the use of the mean μ_1' is reasonable. In the logarithmic case, the use of p_1 is also reasonable since p_1 is the mode of the distribution (the most likely value) and thus most of the observations should be in this part of the distribution. Hence (9.7.2) should be a reasonable estimate in many situations.

As an example, for date set F of table 9.1, we obtain $\hat{q} = .2276$. The fitted frequencies are thus 4099.96, 466.48, 70.76, 12.08, 2.20, .42, .08, .02. The chi-squared test for goodness-of-fit yields $D = 18.57$ on 2 degrees of freedom for a p-value of .00, implying a poor fit.

For most models there may be several ways to estimate the parameters, and "better" estimates (i.e. with smaller variance) are often obtained by equating sample characteristics where "most of the probability" is, to corresponding model characteristics. For example, for each of the first five data sets, there is a high proportion of zeros. Hence, one might expect to obtain fairly efficient estimates by equating the proportion of zeros to p_0 from the chosen model. For example, if one chose to equate $n^{-1}N_0$ to p_0 and $\bar{X}$ to μ_1' for a two parameter model, we might expect to get better estimates (for these data) than those based on straight moment estimation. Unfortunately, for the negative binomial distribution, this leads to equations which must be solved numerically. For the Poisson-Inverse Gaussian distribution, however, we have from (8.3.7)

$$p_0 = e^{-\frac{\mu}{\beta}[(1+2\beta)^{\frac{1}{2}}-1]}$$

and so replacing p_0 by $n^{-1}N_0$, using (4.13.5) and (8.3.14), we obtain the estimates

$$\hat{\mu} = \bar{X}, \tag{9.7.3}$$

$$\hat{\beta} = \frac{2\bar{X}[\bar{X}+\log(N_0/n)]}{[\log(N_0/n)]^2}. \tag{9.7.4}$$

In an example, Lundberg (1940) gives the average number of claims over a six-year interval as 3.0956 and the proportion of policies with no claims as .1563. The 6-year parameter estimates are $\hat{\mu} = 3.0956$ and $\hat{\beta} = 2.2280$. The corresponding one year estimate of μ is .5159 and $\hat{\beta}$ remains the same.

While some ad hoc techniques give rise to reasonably accurate estimators, others do not, and may only be appropriate as initial estimates for a more sophisticated estimation technique, such as maximum likelihood estimation, which is now discussed.

9.8 MAXIMUM LIKELIHOOD ESTIMATION

One of the most important methods of obtaining good estimates of parameters is through a technique known as maximum likelihood estimation. One of the reasons for its importance is due to the fact that it usually gives accurate, sensible estimates.

Suppose one wishes to use maximum likelihood estimation to estimate a parameter θ from a set of independent and identically distributed data $\{X_1, X_2, \ldots, X_k\}$ with probability function $p_n(\theta)$ (or pdf $f(x;\theta)$, if the X_i's have absolutely continuous distribution). The **likelihood function** is

$$L(\theta) = \prod_{i=1}^{n} p_{n_i}(\theta). \tag{9.8.1}$$

The **log-likelihood** is defined to be

$$l(\theta) = \log L(\theta) = \sum_{i=1}^{n} \log p_{n_i}(\theta). \tag{9.8.2}$$

For discrete data, it is often more convenient to work with the observed frequencies (9.2.5), and in this case (9.8.1) and (9.8.2) become

$$L(\theta) = \prod_{k=0}^{\infty} [p_k(\theta)]^{N_k} \tag{9.8.3}$$

and

$$l(\theta) = \sum_{k=0}^{\infty} N_k \log p_k(\theta). \tag{9.8.4}$$

The **maximum likelihood estimator** is the random variable $\hat{\theta}$ for which the likelihood function (or, equivalently, the log likelihood) is a maximum. This seems reasonable, since it is the value of θ for which the probability of observing what did occur is a maximum. In many situations it can be determined by differentiation.

For example, consider the Poisson distribution with pf given by

$$p_k(\lambda) = \frac{\lambda^k e^{-\lambda}}{k!}, \quad k = 0,1,2,... \tag{9.8.5}$$

Hence, from (9.8.4), we obtain the log-likelihood,

$$l(\theta) = \sum_{k=0}^{\infty} N_k [k \log \lambda - \lambda - \log (k!)]. \tag{9.8.6}$$

To obtain the maximum likelihood estimate of λ we differentiate (9.8.6) and set the derivative equal to 0. We thus have

$$l'(\theta) = \sum_{k=0}^{\infty} N_k [\frac{k}{\lambda} - 1].$$

Setting this expression equal to 0 yields the equation which the maximum likelihood estimate must satisfy. Noting that

$$n\overline{X} = \sum_{k=0}^{\infty} kN_k, \qquad (9.8.7)$$

and

$$n = \sum_{k=0}^{\infty} N_k, \qquad (9.8.8)$$

we obtain

$$0 = \frac{n\overline{X}}{\hat{\lambda}} - n. \qquad (9.8.9)$$

We may now easily solve for $\hat{\lambda}$, obtaining the maximum likelihood estimator (MLE), namely

$$\hat{\lambda} = \overline{X}. \qquad (9.8.10)$$

At this point we wish to make several comments. First, the maximum likelihood estimate of λ is also the estimate obtained by using the method of moments. Second, we consider the expected value of $\hat{\lambda}$. It is clear that

$$E[\hat{\lambda}] = \lambda \qquad (9.8.11)$$

and that

$$Var(\hat{\lambda}) = \lambda/n. \qquad (9.8.12)$$

Thus, $\hat{\lambda}$ is unbiased.

In general, MLE's are consistent, and hence asymptotically unbiased. The exact distribution of $\hat{\lambda}$ is easy in this case, but we use the following theory to approximate the distribution of the MLE in a more general situation.

If the log-likelihood is differentiable three times with respect to θ (which is in the interior of the parameter space) and the third derivative is bounded, it can be shown (Cox and Hinkley, 1974) that the maximum likelihood estimator $\hat{\theta}$ is asymptotically normal with mean θ and variance given by

$$Var(\hat{\theta}) \approx \left\{ -nE[\frac{\partial^2}{\partial\theta^2}\log p_X(\theta)] \right\}^{-1}$$

(9.8.13)

$$= \left\{ nE\left[\{\frac{\partial}{\partial\theta}\log p_X(\theta)\}^2 \right] \right\}^{-1}.$$

The reader should be aware of the above regularity conditions but in most practical situations they are satisfied and may be ignored. It can be shown that any unbiased estimator of θ has variance at least as large as (9.8.13). This result, known as the Rao-Cramer inequality, is given in Hogg and Craig (1978). Since $\hat{\theta}$ is asymptotically unbiased, this says that the MLE is asymptotically the "best" estimator of θ in the sense of unbiasedness and minimum variance. While this is an asymptotic result, MLE's tend to be good estimates and have relatively small variance even in finite samples.

For the above example of the Poisson distribution, we have

$$-\frac{\partial^2}{\partial\lambda^2}\log p_X(\lambda) = \frac{X}{\lambda^2}.$$

Since X is random in this expression, we have

$$E\left[-\frac{\partial^2}{\partial\lambda^2}\log p_X(\lambda)\right] = E[\frac{X}{\lambda^2}] = \frac{1}{\lambda}.$$

Thus, from (9.8.13), we have

$$Var(\hat{\lambda}) \approx \frac{\lambda}{n} \qquad (9.8.14)$$

which is exact in this case.

For example, using data set A, we obtain $\hat{\lambda} = .21435$, and the fitted values 7,635.62, 1,636.72, 175.42, 12.53, 0.67, 0.03. The resulting fit is poor. Using (9.8.14), the estimated standard error is .00476. A 95% confidence interval for λ is thus given by $\hat{\lambda} \pm 1.96(.00476) = (.2050, .2237)$.

A desirable property of MLE's is their invariance under parameter transformations. In other words, if one reparameterizes so that $\beta = g(\theta)$, then the MLE of β is $\hat{\beta} = g(\hat{\theta})$. (This is easily seen by considering the derivative of the log-likelihood). For example if we let $\beta = \lambda^2$, then $\hat{\beta} = \hat{\lambda}^2$. As a result, we often use the most convenient parameterization and obtain the parameter of interest later. It should be noted that the accuracy of the normal approximation to the distribution of the MLE depends heavily on both the parameterization chosen and on the sample size n.

In most situations the distribution of the estimator is difficult to obtain, but in some situations it may be obtained exactly as above.

A similar approach is often possible with more than one parameter. If one considers maximum likelihood estimation for the negative binomial distribution (4.5.1), then from (9.8.4), we have

$$l(r,\beta) = \sum_{k=0}^{\infty} N_k[k\log\beta - (r+k)\log(1+\beta)] + \sum_{k=1}^{\infty} N_k[\sum_{m=0}^{k-1}\log(r+m)] - \sum_{k=0}^{\infty} N_k(\log k!).$$

$$(9.8.15)$$

The MLE's of r and β may be obtained by taking partial derivatives of (9.8.15) with respect to r and β, yielding

$$\frac{\partial}{\partial \beta} l(r,\beta) = \sum_{k=0}^{\infty} N_k [\frac{k}{\beta} - \frac{r+k}{1+\beta}], \tag{9.8.16}$$

$$\frac{\partial}{\partial r} l(r,\beta) = -\sum_{k=0}^{\infty} N_k [\log(1+\beta)] + \sum_{k=1}^{\infty} N_k \left[\sum_{m=0}^{k-1} \frac{1}{r+1} \right]. \tag{9.8.17}$$

Setting each of these equations equal to 0 and using (9.8.7) and (9.8.8) yields, respectively,

$$\hat{r}\hat{\beta} = \overline{X}, \tag{9.8.18}$$

$$n \log(1+\hat{\beta}) = \sum_{k=1}^{\infty} N_k \left[\sum_{m=0}^{k-1} \frac{1}{\hat{r}+m} \right]. \tag{9.8.19}$$

As before, we see from (9.8.18) that the MLE of the mean is the sample mean. Replacing β by $\overline{X}/\hat{r}$ in (9.8.19) yields the equation

$$H(\hat{r}) = n \log(1+\frac{\overline{X}}{\hat{r}}) - \sum_{k=1}^{\infty} N_k [\sum_{m=0}^{k-1} \frac{1}{\hat{r}+m}] = 0. \tag{9.8.20}$$

Clearly, we cannot obtain an expression for $\hat{r}$ explicitly from (9.8.20). It can be shown (Johnson and Kotz, 1969), that if $n(n-1)^{-1}S^2 > \overline{X}$, there is a unique positive solution to (9.8.20). If not, then $\hat{r} = \infty$ and a negative binomial may not be appropriate.

The equation (9.8.20) may normally be solved numerically for $\hat{r}$ using a Newton-Raphson approach. Since

$$H'(r) = \sum_{k=1}^{\infty} N_k [\sum_{m=0}^{k-1} \frac{1}{(r+m)^2}] - \frac{n\overline{X}}{r^2+r\overline{X}}, \tag{9.8.21}$$

We may calculate the MLE at the k-th iteration as

$$r_k = r_{k-1} - \frac{H(r_{k-1})}{H'(r_{k-1})} \tag{9.8.22}$$

beginning with the moment estimate (9.6.2) for r_0. Normally, one would use (9.8.22) repeatedly until r_k is sufficiently close to r_{k-1}. If convergence does not occur (which normally will not happen), then an alternate choice of r_0 may be used.

For example, from data set D, the moment estimate of r is 0.9956. Successive iterations using (9.8.22) produced the values 1.0297, 1.0326, and 1.0327. From (9.8.18) the estimate of β is 0.1502. The fitted values 103,723.61, 13,989.95, 1857.08, 245.19, 32.29, 4.24, and 0.56 produced a goodness-of-fit statistic of 12.37 on 3 degrees of freedom, which is a poor fit.

Variance estimates for the MLE's are also easily obtainable. If one has parameters $\theta = (\theta_1, \theta_2, \dots, \theta_p)$, then the asymptotic distribution of the MLE $\hat{\theta} = (\hat{\theta}_1, \hat{\theta}_2, \dots, \hat{\theta}_p)$ is multivariate normal (example 2.7.7) with mean θ and covariance matrix $[A(\theta)]^{-1}$ where the entry in the i-th row and j-th column of $A(\theta)$ is

$$a_{ij} = -nE\left[\frac{\partial^2}{\partial\theta_i\partial\theta_j}\log p_X(\theta)\right]$$

$$\tag{9.8.23}$$

$$= E\left[\left\{\frac{\partial}{\partial\theta_i}\log p_X(\theta)\right\}\left\{\frac{\partial}{\partial\theta_j}\log p_X(\theta)\right\}\right]$$

Often when working with discrete distributions $A(\theta)$ is estimated by $A(\hat{\theta})$.

For the negative binomial case with $\theta_1 = \beta$ and $\theta_2 = r$, we find that

$$\frac{\partial^2}{\partial\beta^2}\log p_X = -\frac{X}{\beta^2} + \frac{(r+X)}{(1+\beta)^2} \tag{9.8.24}$$

and, since X, the random quantity in (9.8.23), has a negative binomial distribution, we have

$$a_{11} = \frac{nr}{\beta(1+\beta)}. \tag{9.8.25}$$

Similarly,

$$\frac{\partial^2}{\partial\beta\partial r}\log p_X = -\frac{1}{1+\beta}, \tag{9.8.26}$$

so that

$$a_{12} = a_{21} = \frac{n}{1+\beta}. \tag{9.8.27}$$

Finally,

$$\frac{\partial^2}{\partial r^2}\log p_X = -\sum_{m=0}^{X-1}\frac{1}{(r+m)^2}, \quad X = 1,2,3,... \tag{9.8.28}$$

and so

$$a_{22} = n\sum_{k=1}^{\infty}p_k\sum_{m=0}^{k-1}\frac{1}{(r+m)^2}. \tag{9.8.29}$$

Hence

$$A^{-1} = \frac{1}{(a_{11}a_{22}-a_{12}^2)}\begin{bmatrix} a_{22} & -a_{12} \\ -a_{12} & a_{11} \end{bmatrix}. \tag{9.8.30}$$

One would normally replace β and r by the MLE's $\hat{\beta}$ and $\hat{r}$ in computing (9.8.30). Note that a_{22} in (9.8.29) may be computed numerically by first computing p_k with $r=\hat{r}$ and $\beta=\hat{\beta}$ and then obtaining the sum numerically. A sufficient number of terms should be taken such that $p_k\sum_{m=0}^{k-1}\frac{1}{(r+m)^2}$ is close to 0.

It turns out that $\hat{r}$ and $\hat{\beta}$ are highly correlated so that it is difficult to interpret the variance of one estimate without considering the other parameter. As in the univariate case, maximum likelihood estimates are preserved under parameter transformations (i.e. the maximum likelihood estimate of $\phi(\theta_1, \theta_2, \ldots, \theta_p)$ is $\phi(\hat{\theta}_1, \hat{\theta}_2, \ldots, \hat{\theta}_p)$) and it is useful if we can find parameterizations which are uncorrelated ($a_{ij} = 0$ if $i \neq j$).

If we have a set of parameters $\theta_1, \theta_2, \ldots, \theta_p$ and we are interested in $\phi_i = \phi_i(\theta_1, \theta_2, \ldots, \theta_p)$ for $i = 1, 2, \ldots, k$, then the maximum likelihood estimates of $\phi_1, \phi_2, \ldots, \phi_k$ are asymptotically multivariate normal with variance matrix $DA^{-1}D^T$ where A is given by (9.8.23). In this case D is a $k \times p$ matrix with ij-th entry $\partial \phi_i / \partial \theta_j$. See Serfling (1980, p. 122) for a proof of this result. This result allows one to quickly obtain the asymptotic variance matrix of $\phi_1, \phi_2, \ldots, \phi_k$.

In the negative binomial example we may identify $\theta_1 = \beta$ and $\theta_2 = r$. If we reparameterize by replacing β by the mean $\mu = r\beta$, we may choose $\phi_1 = \mu = r\beta = \theta_1 \theta_2$ and $\phi_2 = r = \theta_2$. Then D is a 2×2 matrix given by

$$D = \begin{bmatrix} \theta_2 & \theta_1 \\ 0 & 1 \end{bmatrix} = \begin{bmatrix} r & \beta \\ 0 & 1 \end{bmatrix}. \tag{9.8.31}$$

The asymptotic variance matrix of (μ, r) is thus $DA^{-1}D^T$ where A is given by (9.8.30). After some algebra, one finds that

$$DA^{-1}D^T = \begin{bmatrix} \dfrac{\mu(\mu+r)}{nr} & 0 \\ 0 & \{a_{22} - \dfrac{n\mu}{r(\mu+r)}\}^{-1} \end{bmatrix}. \tag{9.8.32}$$

From (9.8.32), one finds that $\hat{r}$ and $\hat{\mu}$ are asymptotically uncorrelated. Also, $\mu(\mu+r)/(nr)$ is the exact variance of $\hat{\mu} = \hat{r}\hat{\beta} = \bar{X}$.

Hence it is convenient for negative binomial maximum likelihood estimation to parameterize in terms of r and the mean since they are asymptotically normal and uncorrelated (and thus independent). For data set D, we obtain $\hat{\mu} = \hat{r}\hat{\beta} = 0.1551$ and the estimated standard error of $\hat{\mu}$ is (replacing μ and r by their estimates in (9.8.32)) thus .00118. Hence, a 95% confidence interval for μ is given by $.1551 \pm 1.96(.00118) = (.1527, .1575)$. Similarly, computing a_{22} from (9.8.29) using the MLE's, and then the approximate variance of $\hat{r}$ from

(9.8.33), we obtain a 95% confidence interval for r as $1.0327 \pm 1.96\sqrt{Var(\hat{r})} = (.9465, 1.1189)$.

Maximum likelihood estimation for some other frequency distributions are considered in the next two sections.

9.9 MLE FOR POWER SERIES DISTRIBUTIONS

In the previous section it was found that the maximum likelihood estimate of the mean was the sample mean $\bar{X}$ for both distributions considered. As shall be seen in this and the following section, this is a common phenomenon. We shall show that this is the case for many of the distributions discussed earlier.

Suppose that the pgf of the frequency distribution may be written as

$$P(z) = \frac{A(\theta z)}{A(\theta)} \tag{9.9.1}$$

for some function $A(.)$ and parameter θ (a reparameterization may be necessary, but this does not affect any of the results since the MLE is invariant under parameter transformations; see section 9.8). Such distributions are said to be power series distributions. For example, if one chooses $A(x) = e^x$, then the Poisson distribution results. Other power series distributions include the binomial, geometric, negative binomial, logarithmic, and shifted logarithmic (example 4.8.1).

We now show that the maximum likelihood estimate of the mean is the sample mean by deriving the likelihood equation corresponding to θ.

From (9.9.1),

$$\frac{\partial}{\partial z}P(z) = \frac{\theta A'(\theta z)}{A(\theta)} \tag{9.9.2}$$

and so the mean is obtained by setting $z = 1$, i.e.

$$\mu_1' = \frac{\theta A'(\theta)}{A(\theta)}. \tag{9.9.3}$$

Taking the partial derivative of (9.9.1) with respect to θ yields

$$\frac{\partial}{\partial\theta}P(z) = \frac{zA'(\theta z)}{A(\theta)} - \frac{A(\theta z)}{[A(\theta)]^2}A'(\theta)$$

$$= \frac{z}{\theta}\frac{\partial}{\partial z}P(z) - \frac{A'(\theta)}{A(\theta)}P(z). \tag{9.9.4}$$

Now, the coefficient of z^k of the left hand side is the partial derivative of p_k with respect to θ. Thus, using (9.9.4) and (1.2.5), we see that equating coefficients of z^k yields

$$\frac{\partial}{\partial\theta}p_k = \frac{kp_k}{\theta} - \frac{A'(\theta)}{A(\theta)}p_k. \tag{9.9.5}$$

From the log-likelihood (9.8.4) we thus obtain

$$\frac{\partial}{\partial\theta}l(\theta) = \sum_{k=0}^{\infty}N_k\frac{\partial}{\partial\theta}\log p_k = \sum_{k=0}^{\infty}\frac{N_k}{p_k}\frac{\partial}{\partial\theta}p_k$$

$$= \sum_{k=0}^{\infty}N_k[\frac{k}{\theta} - \frac{A'(\theta)}{A(\theta)}].$$

Using (9.8.7) and (9.8.8) and setting the left side to 0, yields the equation satisfied by the maximum likelihood estimates, namely,

$$\bar{X} = \frac{\hat{\theta}A'(\hat{\theta})}{A(\hat{\theta})}. \tag{9.9.6}$$

Hence, for all one parameter distribution satisfying (9.9.1), the method of moments estimates are the maximum likelihood estimates. This includes the Poisson, geometric, logarithmic, and binomial distributions, among others. For the geometric with mean β, it is clear that maximum likelihood estimation is easy. We have $\hat{\beta} = \bar{X}$, and so

$$Var(\hat{\beta}) = \frac{\beta(1+\beta)}{n}. \tag{9.9.7}$$

However, for the logarithmic, it is clear from (4.6.4) that one will have to solve for the MLE of q numerically.

For estimation with truncated distributions, one notes that if the zero probabilities are missing, then the truncated distribution has pgf

$$P_1(z) = \frac{P(z)-p_0}{1-p_0}. \tag{9.9.8}$$

If $P(z)$ satisfies (9.9.1), then

$$P_1(z) = \frac{A(\theta z)-A(0)}{A(\theta)-A(0)} \tag{9.9.9}$$

and so $P_1(z)$ also satisfies (9.9.1) with $A(x)$ replaced by $A(x)-A(0)$. Hence, the truncated distribution is a power series distribution if the original distribution is.

As a further example, consider the secondary distribution for the Poisson-Inverse Gaussian distribution which was shown in section 8.3 to be an extended truncated negative binomial distribution with parameter $r = -.5$. While it is not a truncated distribution, it is easily seen that an approach such as that leading to (9.9.9) may be used. The pgf is (from section 8.3)

$$P(z) = \frac{[1+2\beta(1-z)]^{.5} - (1+2\beta)^{.5}}{1-(1+2\beta)^{.5}}. \tag{9.9.10}$$

If we set $\theta = 2\beta(1+2\beta)^{-1}$ and $A(x) = 1-(1-x)^{.5}$, we see that (9.9.10) satisfies (9.9.1) and so the MLE of the mean is the sample mean. Thus, from (8.3.19), we have

$$\bar{X} = \frac{1}{2}[(1+2\hat{\beta})^{.5}+1] \tag{9.9.11}$$

and so the MLE of $\hat{\beta}$ is

$$\hat{\beta} = 2\bar{X}(\bar{X}-1). \tag{9.9.12}$$

Using the fact that the variance of the distribution with pgf (9.9.10) is given by

$$\kappa_2 = \frac{\beta}{2}(1+2\beta)^{.5}, \tag{9.9.13}$$

it is easily seen that

$$E(\hat{\beta}) = \beta + \frac{\beta(1+2\beta)^{.5}}{n}. \tag{9.9.14}$$

The asymptotic variance of $\hat{\beta}$ may be shown to be

$$Var(\hat{\beta}) \approx \frac{2\beta(1+2\beta)^{1.5}}{n} \tag{9.9.15}$$

using the approach given in section 9.8.

Fitting this distribution to data set F, we obtain $\hat{\beta} = .33675$, and the fitted values 4,124.03, 414.93, 83.49, 21.00, 5.92, 1.79, 0.56, 0.18, 0.06, 0.02, 0.01 using (7.5.4) and (7.5.5) with a reparameterization. The chi-squared goodness of fit statistic is 3.31 on 3 degrees of freedom. The resulting significance level is .35 which is an adequate fit. The distribution has a long tail, as can be seen from the fitted values, which often makes it a good one-parameter alternative to the logarithmic for data with no zeroes. Hence the Poisson-Inverse Gaussian distribution is a good candidate as a compound distribution (as well as a mixture) in some situations.

9.10 MLE FOR SOME OTHER FREQUENCY MODELS

In this section we will demonstrate how to obtain maximum likelihood estimates for a wide variety of frequency models including the Poisson-Inverse Gaussian, the Polya-Aeppli, the Neyman Type A, the Hermite, and other distributions. The same algorithm may be used in each case.

We assume that the model depends on two parameters μ and θ where μ is the mean, and that there exists a function $A(x)$ not depending on μ and θ such that the pgf may be expressed as

$$P(z) = e^{A\{\theta + \frac{\mu}{A'(\theta)}(z-1)\} - A(\theta)}. \tag{9.10.1}$$

The family defined by (9.10.1) is quite large and includes (among others) the distributions listed in table 9.10.1.

TABLE 9.10.1

Distribution	Pgf	$A(x)$	μ	θ
Poisson-Inverse Gaussian	(8.3.6)	$-x^{1/2}$	μ	$\mu^2\beta^{-2}$
Polya-Aeppli	$e^{\lambda\{[1-\beta(z-1)]^{-1}-1\}}$	x^{-1}	$\lambda\beta$	λ^{-1}
Neyman Type A	(7.4.1)	e^x	$\lambda_1\lambda_2$	$\log\lambda_1$
Hermite	$e^{\lambda\{[1+q(z-1)]^2-1\}}$	x^2	$2q\lambda$	$\lambda^{1/2}$
Poisson-Binomial (m fixed)	ex. (7.3.1)	x^m	$mq\lambda$	$\lambda^{1/m}$
Generalized Poisson-Pascal (r fixed)	$e^{\lambda\{[1-\beta(z-1)]^{-r}-1\}}$	x^{-r}	$\lambda\beta r$	$\lambda^{-1/r}, r>0$
		$-x^{-r}$	$\lambda\beta r$	$(-\lambda)^{-1/r}, -1<r<0$

To begin the analysis, note that

$$P'(z) = \frac{\mu}{A'(\theta)}A'\{\theta + \frac{\mu}{A'(\theta)}(z-1)\}P(z) \tag{9.10.2}$$

from which it follows on setting $z=1$ that μ is the mean. Also,

$$\frac{\partial}{\partial\mu}P(z) = \frac{A'\{\theta + \frac{\mu}{A'(\theta)}(z-1)\}(z-1)}{A'(\theta)}P(z) = \frac{z-1}{\mu}P'(z).$$ (9.10.3)

Since the coefficient of z^k of the left hand side is the partial of p_k with respect to μ, we may use (1.2.5) and equate coefficients of z^k on both sides of (9.10.3) to obtain

$$\frac{\partial}{\partial\mu}p_k = \frac{kp_k - (k+1)p_k}{\mu},$$

and division by p_k gives

$$\frac{\partial}{\partial\mu}\log p_k = \frac{k-t_k}{\mu}$$ (9.10.4)

where

$$t_k = \frac{(k+1)p_{k+1}}{p_k}.$$ (9.10.5)

From (9.10.1), one finds that the variance of the distribution is

$$\sigma^2 = \mu + \mu^2\frac{A''(\theta)}{\{A'(\theta)\}^2}.$$ (9.10.6)

Then, one obtains the identity

$$\frac{\partial}{\partial\theta}P(z) = \frac{A'(\theta)}{\mu}\{zP'(z) - \mu P(z) - \sigma^2\frac{\partial}{\partial\mu}P(z)\}.$$ (9.10.7)

Extraction of the coefficient of z^k from (9.10.7) and division by p_k yields

$$\frac{\partial}{\partial\theta}\log p_k = \frac{A'(\theta)}{\mu}\{(k-\mu)-\sigma^2(\frac{\partial}{\partial\mu}\log p_k)\}. \qquad (9.10.8)$$

Thus, the partial of the log-likelihood (9.8.4) with respect to μ is, from (9.10.4),

$$\frac{\partial l}{\partial\mu} = \sum_{k=0}^{\infty}N_k(\frac{\partial}{\partial\mu}\log p_k) = \sum_{k=0}^{\infty}N_k\{\frac{k-t_k}{\mu}\}$$

$$= \frac{1}{\mu}\{n\bar{X}-\sum_{k=0}^{\infty}N_k t_k\}.$$

Setting this equation equal to 0 yields the maximum likelihood equation corresponding to μ, namely

$$n\bar{X} = \sum_{k=0}^{\infty}N_k\hat{t}_k \qquad (9.10.9)$$

where $\hat{t}_k$ is the maximum likelihood estimate of t_k. Similarly from (9.8.4) and (9.10.8), one finds that

$$\frac{\partial l}{\partial\theta} = \sum_{k=0}^{\infty}N_k(\frac{\partial}{\partial\theta}\log p_k) = \frac{A'(\theta)}{\mu}\{\sum_{k=0}^{\infty}N_k(k-\mu)-\sigma^2\frac{\partial l}{\partial\mu}\}$$

$$= \frac{A'(\theta)}{\mu}\{n\bar{X}-n\mu-\sigma^2\frac{\partial l}{\partial\mu}\}.$$

Setting this equation equal to 0 yields the maximum likelihood estimate of μ, namely

$$\hat{\mu} = \bar{X}. \qquad (9.10.10)$$

Since (9.10.10) holds, it follows from (9.10.9) that the maximum likelihood estimate $\hat{\theta}$ of θ satisfies

$$H(\theta) = \sum_{k=0}^{\infty} N_k \iota_k^*(\theta) - n\bar{X} = 0. \tag{9.10.11}$$

In (9.10.11), $\iota_k^*(\theta)$ is ι_k as a function of θ only, obtained by replacing μ by $\bar{X}$. The solution $\hat{\theta}$ to (9.10.11) may normally be obtained numerically using a Newton-Raphson approach, i.e. the value of $\hat{\theta}$ at the $(i+1)$-st iteration is given by

$$\hat{\theta}_{i+1} = \hat{\theta}_i - \frac{H(\hat{\theta}_i)}{H'(\hat{\theta}_i)}. \tag{9.10.12}$$

To obtain $H'(\theta)$, one finds from (9.10.11) that

$$
\begin{aligned}
H'(\theta) &= \sum_{k=0}^{\infty} N_k \{\frac{d}{d\theta} \iota_k^*(\theta)\} \\
&= \sum_{k=0}^{\infty} N_k \iota_k^*(\theta) \{\frac{d}{d\theta} \log \iota_k^*(\theta)\} \\
&= \sum_{k=0}^{\infty} N_k \iota_k^*(\theta) \{\frac{d}{d\theta} \log p_{k+1}^*(\theta) - \frac{d}{d\theta} \log p_k^*(\theta)\}.
\end{aligned}
$$

Using (9.10.8), one finds after some algebra that

$$H'(\theta) = \{\frac{A'(\theta)}{\bar{X}} + \frac{A''(\theta)}{A'(\theta)}\} \sum_{k=0}^{\infty} N_k \iota_k^*(\theta)[\iota_{k+1}^*(\theta) - \iota_k^*(\theta)] \tag{9.10.13}$$

$$- \frac{A''(\theta)}{A'(\theta)} \sum_{k=0}^{\infty} N_k \iota_k^*(\theta).$$

Normally, an initial value of $\hat{\theta}_0$ may be obtained using moment estimation or some other ad hoc technique. At each stage of the iteration, $\hat{\theta}_{i+1}$ is obtained from (9.10.12). The function $A(\theta)$ depends on the distribution and may normally be found in table 9.10.1. Using $\mu = \bar{X}$ and the current value $\hat{\theta}_i$ of θ, one computes $p_k^*(\hat{\theta}_i)$, usually using one of the recursive formulae of the previous chapters. Then $\iota_k^*(\hat{\theta}_i)$ is obtainable from (9.10.5), and $H(\hat{\theta}_i)$ and $H'(\hat{\theta}_i)$ are obtainable from (9.10.11) and (9.10.13) respectively.

While it may appear complicated, the approach is quite straightforward on a computer. Convergence to several significant digits is typically obtained after four to six iterations from the moment estimates.

As an example, the Poisson-Inverse Gaussian was fitted to data set D. One finds that $\hat{\mu} = \bar{X} = .15514$, and the moment estimate of β is $.15582$. Thus, the moment estimate of θ is $\hat{\theta}_0 = (.15514/.15582)^2 = .99563$ from table 9.10.1. The distribution $p_k(\hat{\theta}_0)$ is computed using these values and (8.3.7), (8.3.10), and (8.3.9). The function $\iota_k^*(\theta)$ is then computed using (9.10.5), and then $H(\theta)$ and $H'(\theta)$ from (9.10.11) and (9.10.13) with $A(\theta) = -\theta^{1/2}$. From (9.10.12), the value of θ at the first iteration is $\hat{\theta}_1 = .99829$. Hence $\hat{\beta}_1 = \hat{\mu}/\hat{\theta}_1^{1/2} = .15595$ and the process is repeated with the new parameter values. Two more iterations give $\hat{\theta} = .99835$ accurate to seven decimal places. Hence $\hat{\beta} = .15527$. The fitted distribution is then obtained from (8.3.7), (8.3.10), and (8.3.9). Multiplication by 119,853 yields the fitted values 103,710.03, 14,054.65, 1,784.91, 254.49, 40.42, 6.94, and 1.26. The fit is very good as is verified by the goodness-of-fit statistic of .78 on 3 degrees of freedom for a p-value of .85.

In order to assess the accuracy of the estimates, we derive the (inverse of) the asymptotic variance matrix of $\hat{\mu}$ and $\hat{\theta}$. Since

$$\sum_{k=0}^{\infty} p_k \iota_k = \mu$$

and

$$\sum_{k=0}^{\infty} k p_k \iota_k = \sigma^2 + \mu^2 - \mu,$$

it follows from (9.10.4) that

$$a_{11} = n \sum_{k=0}^{\infty} p_k \left(\frac{\partial}{\partial \mu} \log p_k \right)^2 = \frac{n}{\mu^2} \{ 2\mu - (\sigma^2 + \mu^2) + \phi \} \qquad (9.10.14)$$

where

$$\phi = \sum_{k=0}^{\infty} p_k t_k^2.$$ (9.10.15)

Using the fact that

$$\sum_{k=0}^{\infty} p_k (k-\mu)(\frac{\partial}{\partial \mu} \log p_k) = 1,$$

one finds that

$$a_{21} = a_{12} = n\sum_{k=0}^{\infty} p_k (\frac{\partial}{\partial \mu} \log p_k)(\frac{\partial}{\partial \theta} \log p_k) = \frac{A'(\theta)}{\mu}(n - \sigma^2 a_{11}).$$ (9.10.16)

Also, since

$$\sigma^2 = \sum_{k=0}^{\infty} p_k (k-\mu)^2,$$

one finds that

$$a_{22} = n\sum_{k=0}^{\infty} p_k (\frac{\partial}{\partial \theta} \log p_k)^2 = \frac{-\sigma^2 A'(\theta) a_{12}}{\mu}.$$ (9.10.17)

The asymptotic variance matrix of $\hat{\mu}$ and $\hat{\theta}$ is A^{-1} where $A = \{a_{ij}\}_{2\times 2}$, and is normally estimated using the values $\hat{\mu}$ and $\hat{\theta}$. Care must be taken to use a sufficient number of terms in (9.10.15) to ensure accuracy. The variance matrix for a different parameterization may normally be obtained from this.

For the Poisson-Inverse Gaussian, one finds that $\hat{\mu} = .15514$ has an estimated standard error of .00122 and that of $\hat{\theta} = .99835$ is .08988, and the estimated correlation between $\hat{\mu}$ and $\hat{\theta}$ is $-.02354$. If one were interested in μ and $\beta = \mu/\theta^{1/2}$, then the asymptotic variance matrix of μ and β is $DA^{-1}D^T$, where

$$D = \begin{bmatrix} 1 & 0 \\ 1/\theta^{1/2} & -\frac{1}{2}\mu/\theta^{3/2} \end{bmatrix}$$

as follows from the discussion in section 9.8 on reparameterization. One finds for this data set that $\hat{\beta} = .15527$ has an estimated standard error of .00712, and the estimated correlation between $\hat{\mu}$ and $\hat{\beta}$ is .195.

9.11 ESTIMATION FOR THE GENERALIZED POISSON PASCAL

The generalized Poisson-Pascal distribution, with pgf

$$P(z) = e^{\mu\{[1-\beta(z-1)]^{-r}-1\}} \tag{9.11.1}$$

is useful both for fitting distributions which are not fit easily by other distributions and also since the Polya-Aeppli $(r = 1)$, the Poisson-Inverse Gaussian $(r = -.5)$, and the negative binomial $(r = 0$, reparameterized, see section 7.5), are special cases and this distribution gives a good method of discriminating between them. The possible parameter values are $\beta > 0$, $r > -1$, and $r\mu > 0$. The limiting case as $r \to \infty$ is the Neyman Type A distribution.

To use moment estimation for this distribution, we need the first three moments, since there are three parameters. Equivalently, we may use $\bar{X}, S^2$, and K as defined by (9.2.2) through (9.2.4). When written in this form, we see that the mean, variance, and third central moment of the distribution are given by

$$\kappa_1 = \mu\beta r, \tag{9.11.2}$$

$$\kappa_2 = \mu\beta r[1+\beta(r+1)], \tag{9.11.3}$$

$$\kappa_3 = \mu\beta r[1+3\beta(r+1)+\beta^2(r+1)(r+2)]. \tag{9.11.4}$$

Hence, equating these quantities to (9.2.2) through (9.2.4) yields

$$\hat{r} = -\frac{\bar{X}(K-3S^2+2\bar{X})-2(S^2-\bar{X})^2}{\bar{X}(K-3S^2+2\bar{X})-(S^2-\bar{X})^2},$$

(9.11.5)

$$\hat{\beta} = \frac{S^2-\bar{X}}{\bar{X}(1+\hat{r})},$$

(9.11.6)

$$\hat{\mu} = \frac{\bar{X}}{\hat{\beta}\hat{r}}.$$

(9.11.7)

If one fits the negative binomial distribution by the method of moments, the third central moment of the fitted distribution is, from (6.7.8), given by

$$K(NB) = 3S^2-2\bar{X}+2\frac{(S^2-\bar{X})^2}{\bar{X}}.$$

(9.11.8)

Similarly, if the Neyman Type A distribution is fitted by the method of moments from (7.10), the third central moment is given by

$$K(NTA) = 3S^2-2\bar{X}+\frac{(S^2-\bar{X})^2}{\bar{X}}.$$

(9.11.9)

Thus (9.11.5) may be rewritten as

$$\hat{r} = -\frac{K-K(NB)}{K-K(NTA)}.$$

(9.11.10)

Since $K(NTA)<K(NB)$, we see that if the sample third central moment K exceeds that predicted by the negative binomial, i.e. $K(NB)$, then $-1<\hat{r}<0$. If $K(NTA)<K<K(NB)$ then $\hat{r}>0$ but if $K<K(NTA)$, then $\hat{r}<-1$ which is inadmissible.

Thus we conclude that we may use the method of moments for this distribution as long as $S^2>\bar{X}$ and $K<K(NTA)$. In these circumstances we have seen that $\hat{r}>-1$ and thus by (9.11.6), $\hat{\beta}>0$. Similarly, from (9.11.7) $\hat{\mu}\hat{r}>0$ and so all parameter estimates will be valid. If $K<K(NB)$ it is clear that we are actually fitting the Poisson-Pascal distribution since $\hat{\mu}$, $\hat{\beta}$, $\hat{r}$ are all non-negative.

For example, using data set E, we find $\hat{r} = -.8472$, $\hat{\beta} = .2346$, and $\hat{\mu} = -.6312$. The fitted values are obtainable using (7.5.2) through (7.5.5) with $\lambda = \mu[1-(1+\beta)^{-r}]$ and are given by 565,662.44, 68,719.30, 5,172.04, 363.13, 29.68, and 2.99. The fit is good, as confirmed by $\chi^2_{(1)} = .30$.

One difficulty involved in the use of moment estimation is the high sampling variability involved in the third sample central moment K, which can often cause a loss of efficiency. An alternative ad hoc procedure which has very high efficiency when the proportion of sample zeroes and ones is high involves the use of equations (9.11.6) and (9.11.7), but (9.11.5) is replaced by

$$\hat{r} = \frac{S^2\hat{p}_1 - \bar{X}^2\hat{p}_0}{(S^2 - \bar{X}^2)\hat{p}_0\log\hat{p}_0 + \bar{X}(\bar{X}\hat{p}_0 - \hat{p}_1)} \tag{9.11.11}$$

where $\hat{p}_k = N_k/n$ is the sample proportion of k's. We leave it to the reader to verify that (9.11.11) holds in the theoretical population. For most of the data sets in this chapter, this estimation procedure has much higher efficiency than moment estimation, yet is equally simple to use.

Estimation of the parameters using maximum likelihood estimation is generally straightforward numerically, but can occasionally cause problems. The likelihood equations corresponding to μ and β are easily seen from the last section to be

$$n\bar{X} = \sum_{k=0}^{\infty} N_k \hat{t}_k \tag{9.11.12}$$

and (9.11.7).

The likelihood equation for r can be derived in an analogous manner. One of the parameters can be eliminated by (9.11.7) leading to two equations in two unknowns which may be solved numerically. This approach has been suggested by Douglas (1980).

An alternative approach is to use a common statistical technique called the **method of scoring** to obtain the MLE's. This approach may be used in general with discrete distributions and so is discussed in more detail here.

If one has p parameters $\boldsymbol{\theta} = (\theta_1, \theta_2, \ldots, \theta_p)$ and log-likelihood $l(\boldsymbol{\theta})$ given, for example, by (9.8.4), then the **score function** is defined to be the $p \times 1$ matrix $S(\boldsymbol{\theta})$ with j-th element

$$S_j(\boldsymbol{\theta}) = \frac{\partial}{\partial \theta_j} l(\boldsymbol{\theta}), \quad j = 1, 2, \ldots, p. \tag{9.11.13}$$

Clearly, the maximum likelihood estimate $\hat{\boldsymbol{\theta}} = (\hat{\theta}_1, \hat{\theta}_2, \ldots, \hat{\theta}_p)$ satisfies $S(\hat{\boldsymbol{\theta}}) = 0$.

A standard p-dimensional Newton-Raphson technique would give $\hat{\boldsymbol{\theta}}$ iteratively at the $m+1$-st iteration using the iterative formula

$$\boldsymbol{\theta}_{m+1} = \boldsymbol{\theta}_m + [I(\boldsymbol{\theta}_m)]^{-1} S(\boldsymbol{\theta}_m) \tag{9.11.14}$$

where $I(\boldsymbol{\theta})$ is the $p \times p$ matrix with (ij)-th entry

$$I_{ij}(\boldsymbol{\theta}) = -\frac{\partial^2 l(\boldsymbol{\theta})}{\partial \theta_i \partial \theta_j}. \tag{9.11.15}$$

This matrix is called the **observed information matrix** and the inverse of the final iterated value $[I(\hat{\boldsymbol{\theta}})]^{-1}$ is an estimate of the covariance matrix of $\hat{\boldsymbol{\theta}}$.

Another approach is to replace $I(\boldsymbol{\theta})$ in (9.11.14) by an estimate of the **Fisher information matrix** with (ij)-th entry given by (9.8.23). This approach, known as the **method of scoring,** is useful for discrete distributions such as the models considered here, because we only need first derivatives (whereas (9.11.15) requires two), and the expectation may be obtained numerically. In other words, we compute the matrix $A(\boldsymbol{\theta})$ with (ij)-th entry

$$a_{ij}(\boldsymbol{\theta}) = n \sum_{k=0}^{\infty} p_k [\frac{\partial}{\partial \theta_i} \log p_k][\frac{\partial}{\partial \theta_j} \log p_k] \tag{9.11.16}$$

using the current parameter values. The iterated value of $\hat{\boldsymbol{\theta}}$ at the $(m+1)$-st iteration is then given by

$$\hat{\boldsymbol{\theta}}_{m+1} = \hat{\boldsymbol{\theta}}_m + [A(\hat{\boldsymbol{\theta}}_m)]^{-1} S(\hat{\boldsymbol{\theta}}_m) \tag{9.11.17}$$

and the final iterated value $[A(\hat{\boldsymbol{\theta}})]^{-1}$ serves as an estimate of the covariance matrix of $\hat{\boldsymbol{\theta}}$.

For the generalized Poisson-Pascal with pgf (9.11.1), we have easily from the results of the previous section that

$$\frac{\partial}{\partial \mu} \log p_k = \frac{1+\beta}{\mu r \beta} t_k - \frac{k}{\mu r} - 1, \tag{9.11.18}$$

$$\frac{\partial}{\partial \beta} \log p_k = \frac{k - t_k}{\beta}. \tag{9.11.19}$$

The derivative with respect to r is slightly more difficult. We have

$$\frac{\partial}{\partial z} P(z) = \mu r \beta [1 - \beta(z-1)]^{-r-1} P(z) \tag{9.11.20}$$

and so

$$\frac{\partial}{\partial r} P(z) = -\mu \log[1-\beta(z-1)][1-\beta(z-1)]^{-r} P(z)$$

$$= \frac{[1-\beta(z-1)]}{r\beta} \frac{\partial}{\partial z} P(z) \left\{ -\log(1+\beta) - \log\left(1 - \frac{\beta}{1+\beta} z\right) \right\}$$

$$= \log(1+\beta) \left\{ \frac{1}{r} z \frac{\partial}{\partial z} P(z) - \frac{1+\beta}{r\beta} \frac{\partial}{\partial z} P(z) \right\}$$

$$+ \left\{ -\log\left(1 - \frac{\beta}{1+\beta} z\right) \right\} \left\{ \frac{1+\beta}{r\beta} \frac{\partial}{\partial z} P(z) - \frac{1}{r} z \frac{\partial}{\partial z} P(z) \right\}.$$

The first term is easily inverted using (1.2.5). The first factor in the second term is simply a logarithmic type generating function and the second term a convolution. Thus, inverting this expression and dividing by p_k yields

$$\frac{\partial}{\partial r} \log p_0 = -\frac{(1+\beta)\log(1+\beta)}{r\beta} t_0,$$

$$\frac{\partial}{\partial r} \log p_k = \frac{\log(1+\beta)}{r} \left[k - \frac{(1+\beta)}{\beta} t_k \right]$$

$$(9.11.21)$$

$$+ \frac{1}{r p_k} \sum_{m=0}^{k-1} \frac{p_m}{k-m} \left(\frac{1+\beta}{\beta} t_m - m \right) \left(\frac{\beta}{1+\beta} \right)^{k-m}.$$

The score function is thus the (3×1) matrix obtained by multiplying (9.11.18), (9.11.19), and (9.11.21) in turn by the frequency N_k and summing over k. For example, if we designate $\theta_1 = r$, $\theta_2 = \beta$, and $\theta_3 = \mu$, the second element of the score vector is

$$S_2 = \sum_{k=0}^{\infty} N_k \frac{\partial}{\partial \beta} \log p_k = \sum_{k=0}^{\infty} N_k (\frac{k-t_k}{\beta}).$$

Similarly, the matrix A is obtained by taking the product of two of (9.11.18), (9.11.19), and (9.11.21), and multiplying them by p_k, summing over k and multiplying by the number of observations n. For example, the entry in the second row, third column (also third row, second column) is

$$a_{23} = a_{32} = n \sum_{k=0}^{\infty} p_k (\frac{k-t_k}{\beta}) (\frac{1+\beta}{\mu r \beta} t_k - \frac{k}{\mu r} - 1).$$

At each stage of the iteration, the score function and A matrix are calculated using the current parameter values. The probabilities p_k would normally be computed using formulae such as (7.5.4) and (7.5.5) followed by (7.5.2) using the appropriate parameter values. The values of t_k are obtained from (9.10.5) and then the score function and the matrix A as described above. The new estimated parameter values are then obtained using (9.11.17). This procedure would be repeated until (hopefully) convergence occurs.

Initial parameter values could be taken as the moment estimates (9.11.5), (9.11.6), and (9.11.7) or the ad hoc estimates (9.11.6), (9.11.7), and (9.11.11). For example, using data set E, after 2 iterations from the moment estimates, the MLE's are obtained as $\hat{r} = -.8469$, $\hat{\beta} = .2339$, and $\hat{\mu} = -.6335$. These are quite close to the moment estimates in this case.

Occasionally this does not lead to convergence. For example, using data set G, the moment estimates are $\hat{r} = .0009$, $\hat{\beta} = 1.1340$, and $\hat{\mu} = 1,602.59$. Often the conditions $\mu r > 0$ leads to numerical difficulties when one iterated value is positive while the other is negative. This only occurs, however, when r is very close to 0 (as in this case), or when μ is close to 0 (i.e. where r is close to -1). Difficulties were only obtained when r was within .01 of 0 or within .02 of -1 for these data sets. When r is close to -1 is rarely of concern, however. If the initial value of r is close to 0, one can choose a different initial estimate, and if the final value of r is close to 0, the negative binomial is probably appropriate anyway. For data set G convergence did not occur from the moment estimates. However, the Polya-Aeppli $(r = 1)$ had a higher maximum log likelihood than either the negative binomial $(r = 0)$ or the Poisson-Inverse Gaussian $(r = -.5)$. Hence, we chose as initial values for the iteration $r = 1$, $\beta = .5450$, $\mu = 3.1338$ (the latter two are the MLE's of β and μ for the Polya-Aeppli). This led to convergence to the MLE's $\hat{r} = 1.173$, $\hat{\beta} = .4984$, and $\hat{\mu} = 2.9212$ after about eight iterations (convergence is slower for flat likelihoods and a reparameterization may help).

If use of the simple estimates or one of the three special cases does not lead to convergence, one may wish to see if the maximum log-likelihood for the Neyman Type A exceeds that of the above three distributions. If this is the case, then the MLE of r could well be ∞ and convergence will not occur. Otherwise, one could choose a grid of r values and maximize β and μ for given r using the techniques of the previous section, then choose as initial estimates those values which give the highest log-likelihood.

For many data sets, a wide variety of parameter values will fit the frequencies quite closely (such as data set G) and often moment, ad hoc, or other estimates are just as satisfactory as MLE's.

The final value of A obtained from the iterative procedure is an estimate of the covariance matrix of $\hat{r}$, $\hat{\beta}$, and $\hat{\mu}$. However the assumption that the MLE's are approximately normal appears to be inappropriate, even for large samples (such as data set E).

To demonstrate this, we used the following approach. If one takes the maximum value of the log likelihood, say $l(\hat{r},\hat{\beta},\hat{\mu})$, and then chooses a particular value of r, say r_0, then one can maximize the log likelihood for that value of r by finding the MLE's $\hat{\beta}(r_0)$ and $\hat{\mu}(r_0)$, and then compute the statistic

$$m(r_0) = -2\{l[r_0,\hat{\beta}(r_0),\hat{\mu}(r_0)] - l(\hat{r},\hat{\beta},\hat{\mu})\}. \tag{9.11.22}$$

This **likelihood ratio statistic,** under the hypothesis that $r = r_0$, has approximately a $\chi^2_{(1)}$ distribution, and this approximation is better in general than that obtained from the asymptotic distribution of the MLE's. (For more details the interested reader should see Cox and Hinkley, 1974). Hence a better 95% confidence interval for r is given by the set of r values for which $m(r) < \chi^2_{(1)}(.95) = 3.84$. This interval can be obtained by using the results of the previous section to maximize the other two parameters for given r, and then computing (9.8.22). For data set E, this procedure resulted in a confidence interval for r of $(-.90,-.72)$ whereas that based on the normal distribution of $\hat{r}$ was $(-.92,-.77)$, which is rather different in light of the large number of observations. The results are even more striking for data set G, however. This procedure resulted in an interval of $(-.55,\infty)$ since we could not reject any positive value of r. The interval based on the MLE is $(-3.28,5.63)$ which is nonsensical since $r > -1$.

This approach can also be used to test the **goodness of fit** for any distribution which is a special case of the generalized Poisson Pascal. For example, $r = -.5$, 0, or 1 are values of interest, corresponding to the Poisson-Inverse Gaussian, negative binomial, or Polya-Aeppli, respectively. For data set D, we have $l(\hat{r},\hat{\beta},\hat{\mu}) = -54,609.59$ from the generalized Poisson Pascal. For the Poisson-Inverse Gaussian, the maximum log-likelihood is $-54,609.76$. Thus $m(.5) = .34$ and $SL = Pr\{\chi^2_{(1)} > .34\} = .56$. The corresponding figures for the negative binomial case are $m(0) = 11.44$ and significance level .00, consistent with our earlier findings.

The problem is further compounded by the fact that the estimates are very highly correlated (i.e. correlation of r and μ is $-.98$), making the problem of parameter inference more difficult. In conclusion, the asymptotic theory of the distribution of the estimates should be treated with extreme caution.

9.12 OTHER FITTING PROBLEMS

The techniques described in the previous section (i.e. Newton-Raphson and method of scoring) can be used in general to find MLE's numerically. For example, if one had chosen other distributions to fit these techniques could be used, or if the data were truncated in some manner. If the zero class is missing, the analysis would proceed using $p_n^* = p_n(1-p_0)$, $n = 1,2,...$ in place of p_n in deriving the formulas. Similarly, if the data were grouped from k on, (i.e. only observations greater than or equal to k were recorded, and not the exact number) one would replace p_n by

$$
p_n^* = \begin{cases} p_n, & n < k \\ \sum_{m=k}^{\infty} p_m, & n = k \\ 0, & \text{otherwise.} \end{cases}
$$

Another situation which may arise is when certain covariate information on the risks is available (i.e. age, type of car, etc. on automobile insurance). In this case regression type models can be used to model the claim frequencies to account for this. A common type of model for this situation is the **log-linear Poisson regression model,** discussed at length by McCullagh and Nelder (1983), and Bishop, Feinberg, and Holland (1975). The same approach can be used for claim severities, and two particular severity models which may be of use in this regard are gamma and inverse Gaussian regression models, discussed in some detail by McCullagh and Nelder (1983).

9.13 BIBLIOGRAPHIC NOTES

A thorough and practical discussion of estimation for these compound models is given by Douglas (1980). Hogg and Klugman (1984) discuss many of the estimation techniques for severity data. Hogg and Craig (1978) give a good discussion of estimation techniques. More advanced discussions, including asymptotic theory are given by Cox and Hinkley (1974), Lehmann (1983), or Silvey (1975).

Willmot (1988) discussed maximum likelihood estimation for frequency distributions with pgf's of the form (9.10.1). Anscombe (1950) and Simon (1961) discuss maximum likelihood estimation for the negative binomial model.

EXERCISES

1. Suppose that one wishes to estimate the parameters of the **log-logistic** distribution (example 4.14.1) by percentile estimation.

   Show that, if

   $$G_n(x_i) = 1 - \hat{\lambda}(\hat{\lambda} + x_i^{\hat{c}})^{-1}, \quad i = 1,2,$$

   then

   $$\hat{c} = \frac{\log G_n(x_2) + \log[1 - G_n(x_1)] - \log G_n(x_1) - \log[1 - G_n(x_2)]}{\log x_2 - \log x_1},$$

   $$\hat{\lambda} = \left[\frac{G_n(x_1)}{1 - G_n(x_1)}\right]^{\log x_2 [\log(\frac{x_1}{x_2})]^{-1}} \left[\frac{G_n(x_2)}{1 - G_n(x_2)}\right]^{\log x_1 [\log(\frac{x_2}{x_1})]^{-1}}.$$

2. Suppose that one wishes to estimate the parameters of the **Poisson-Inverse Gaussian** (section 8.3) distribution by equating $\hat{p}_0 = F_0/n$ to p_0 and $\hat{p}_1 = F_1/n$ to p_1.

   Show that

$$\hat{\beta} = \frac{1}{2}\left[\left(\frac{\hat{p}_0\log\hat{p}_0}{2\hat{p}_1+\hat{p}_0\log\hat{p}_0}\right)^2 - 1\right],$$

and

$$\hat{\mu} = \frac{-\hat{p}_1\log\hat{p}_0}{2\hat{p}_1+\hat{p}_0\log\hat{p}_0}.$$

3. Consider the **inverse Gaussian** distribution with density given by (4.13.1). Reparameterize the model by letting $\beta = \theta\mu^2$.

a) Show that

$$\sum_{i=1}^{n}\frac{(x_i-\mu)^2}{x_i} = \mu^2\sum_{i=1}^{n}(\frac{1}{x_i} - \frac{1}{\bar{x}}) + \frac{n}{\bar{x}}(\bar{x}-\mu)^2.$$

b) For a sample of size n (i.e. $X_1, X_2, \ldots, X_n$), show that the maximum likelihood estimates of θ and μ are

$$\hat{\mu} = \bar{X}$$

and

$$\hat{\theta} = \frac{1}{n}\sum_{i=1}^{n}(\frac{1}{X_i} - \frac{1}{\bar{X}}).$$

c) Show that $\hat{\mu}$ has an inverse Gaussian distribution with parameter θ replaced by θn^{-1} and μ remaining the same.

d) Show that the joint density of $\bar{X}, X_2, X_3, \ldots, X_n$ is

$$g(\bar{x}, x_2, \ldots, x_n) = n(2\pi\theta)^{-\frac{n}{2}}(n\bar{x}-\sum_{i=2}^{n}x_i)^{-\frac{3}{2}}(\prod_{i=2}^{n}x_i^{-\frac{3}{2}})\exp\{-\frac{n\hat{\theta}}{2\theta} - \frac{n(\bar{x}-\mu)^2}{2\theta\mu^2\bar{x}}\}.$$

Hint: Let $Z_1 = \bar{X}$, $Z_i = X_i$ for $i = 2, 3, \ldots, n$. Then change variables to the Z_i's from the X_i's, noting that the Jacobian of the transformation equals n. Then show that

$$\hat{\theta} = \frac{1}{n}\{[(nz_1 - \sum_{i=2}^{n} z_i)^{-1} - z_1^{-1}] + \sum_{i=2}^{n} (z_i^{-1} - z_1^{-1})\}.$$

e)   Show that the conditional density of $X_2, X_3, \ldots, X_n$ given $\bar{X}$ is

$$h(x_2, x_3, \ldots, x_n | \bar{x}) = n^{\frac{1}{2}} (2\pi\theta)^{-(\frac{n-1}{2})} [n - \sum_{i=2}^{n} x_i \bar{x}^{-1}][\prod_{i=2}^{n} x_i^{-\frac{3}{2}}] \exp\{\frac{-n\hat{\theta}}{2\theta}\}.$$

f)   By noting that the integral over $x_2, x_3, \ldots, x_n$ (from 0 to ∞ for each) of the pdf in (e) must equal 1 for any $\theta > 0$, show that the conditional Laplace transform of $\hat{\theta}$ given $\bar{x}$ is

$$L_{\hat{\theta}}(z | \bar{x}) = (\frac{n}{n + 2\theta z})^{\frac{n-1}{2}}.$$

Hint: Note that

$$L_{\hat{\theta}}(z | \bar{x}) = E(e^{-z\hat{\theta}} | \bar{x})$$

$$= \iint \cdots \int_{x_2 x_3 \quad x_n} h(x_2, x_3, \ldots, x_n | \bar{x}) e^{-\hat{\theta} z} dx_2, dx_3, \ldots, dx_n$$

and that the integrand is a constant times $h(x_2, x_3, \ldots, x_n | \bar{x})$, but with θ replaced by $\theta^* = \theta n (n + 2\theta z)^{-1}$.

g)   Hence conclude that the exact distribution of $\hat{\theta}$ is that of a gamma distribution (4.12.1) with $\lambda = n(2\theta)^{-1}$ and $\alpha = (n-1)2^{-1}$, and that $\hat{\mu}$ is independent of $\hat{\theta}$.

4. The Truncated Negative Binomial Distribution

a) For a sample of size n from the distribution with pf (7.2.10), show
    that the maximum likelihood estimates $\hat{\beta}$ and $\hat{r}$ satisfy

$$\text{i) } \bar{X} = \frac{\hat{r}\hat{\beta}}{1-(1+\hat{\beta})^{-\hat{r}}}$$

$$\text{ii) } \frac{n\bar{X}}{\hat{\beta}}\log(1+\hat{\beta}) = \sum_{k=1}^{\infty} N_k \{ \sum_{m=0}^{k-1} (1 - \frac{m}{\hat{r}+m}) \}.$$

b) Treating β in equation i) implicitly as a function of r fixed, show
    that it may be obtained iteratively from the formula

$$\beta_{i+1} = \beta_i - \frac{h(\beta_i)}{h'(\beta_i)}$$

where

$$h(\beta) = \frac{r\beta}{1-(1+\beta)^{-r}} - \bar{X}$$

and

$$h'(\beta) = \frac{r}{1-(1+\beta)^{-r}} - \frac{r^2\beta(1+\beta)^{-r-1}}{[1-(1+\beta)^{-r}]^2}.$$

c) Using (7.2.12), show that

$$\beta = \frac{\mu_{(2)}}{\mu_{(1)}(1+r)}$$

and thus describe how to obtain an initial estimate for the iterative
routine in (b).

d) Equation (ii) in (a) may be considered as a function of r alone with β implicitly defined by (i). In other words, let

$$g(r) = \sum_{k=1}^{\infty} N_k \{ \sum_{m=0}^{k-1} (1 - \frac{m}{r+m}) \} - \frac{n\overline{X}}{\beta} \log(1+\beta)$$

where β is defined as a function of r by (i). To obtain the root $\hat{r}$ satisfying $g(\hat{r}) = 0$ numerically, show that

$$g'(r) = \sum_{k=1}^{\infty} N_k \{ \sum_{m=0}^{k-1} \frac{m}{(r+m)^2} \} - \frac{n\overline{X}}{\beta} \{ \frac{1}{1+\beta} - \frac{\log(1+\beta)}{\beta} \} \frac{d\beta}{dr}.$$

Differentiate (i) implicitly as a function of r to show that

$$\frac{d\beta}{dr} = \frac{\overline{X}(1+\beta)^{-r} \log(1+\beta) - \beta}{r - r\overline{X}(1+\beta)^{-r-1}}.$$

e) Show that the maximum likelihood estimate of r may be obtained numerically using the formula

$$\hat{r}_{i+1} = \hat{r}_i - \frac{g(\hat{r}_i)}{g'(\hat{r}_i)}$$

where g and g' are defined in (d). Note that, at each stage of the iteration, the value of β to be used with r in computing g and g' may be obtained numerically using the algorithm in (b).

f) Using (7.2.12), show that a starting value for r may be obtained by noting that

$$r = \left[\frac{\mu_{(3)} \mu_{(1)}}{\mu_{(2)}^2} - 1 \right]^{-1} - 1$$

The above algorithm may be used whether r and β are positive, or if $-1 < r < 0$. It can happen that the initial estimate of r has a different sign than the MLE. In this case a better starting value may be obtained by calculating, for fixed r, the MLE $\hat{\beta}(r)$ which satisfies equation (i) in (a). This may be obtained numerically from the algorithm in (b). Normally, one would calculate the maximum log likelihood for a series of r values, and choose as starting value that value of r for which the maximum likelihood is the highest.

CHAPTER 10

TAIL BEHAVIOUR OF THE AGGREGATE CLAIMS DISTRIBUTION

10.1 INTRODUCTION

Up to this point in the book, methods for computing the distribution of aggregate claims using recursive approaches have been described. There are other approximations which have been suggested and used due to the relative complexity of the calculations involved in the recursive approach.

One of these techniques involve approximations for the right tail of the compound distribution. This is a convenient approach in conjunction with the recursive approach, since the latter is more cumbersome to apply in the right tail. Thus, the recursive approach could be used until the point in the right tail when the approximate formula becomes sufficiently accurate. See Willmot (1989) for further discussion on this point.

10.2 TAIL BEHAVIOR FOR CERTAIN CLAIM NUMBER MODELS

Asymptotic formulas (i.e. for the right tail) can be obtained for the aggregate claims distribution for certain frequency models and a wide variety of severity distributions.

We assume that the aggregate claims distribution has cdf $F_S(x)$ and Laplace transform $L_S(z) = P[L_X(z)]$ where

$$P(z) = \sum_{n=0}^{\infty} p_n z^n \qquad (10.2.1)$$

is the pgf of a counting distribution and $L_X(z)$ is the Laplace transform of a non-arithmetic distribution (any distribution which has a continuous portion is non-arithmetic). Discrete distributions are usually, however, arithmetic.

We shall use the notation $A(x) \sim B(x)$ as $x \to \infty$ to denote that

$$\lim_{x \to \infty} \frac{A(x)}{B(x)} = 1.$$

A function $C(x)$ is said to be **slowly varying at infinity** if $C(tx) \sim C(x)$ as $x \to \infty$ for all $t > 0$. For example, $\log x$ is slowly varying at ∞ since

$$\lim_{x \to \infty} \frac{\log(tx)}{\log x} = \lim_{x \to \infty} \frac{\log x + \log t}{\log x} = \lim_{x \to \infty} \left\{ 1 + \frac{\log t}{\log x} \right\} = 1$$

for all $t > 0$. Any constant function is trivially slowly varying at infinity. The function e^x is not, however.

The following theorem is now stated without proof. The interested reader is referred to Embrechts, Maejima, and Teugels (1985) for details.

Theorem 10.2.1. Suppose that p_n as defined by (10.2.1) satisfies

$$p_n \sim \theta^n n^\gamma C(n), \quad n \to \infty \tag{10.2.2}$$

for $0 < \theta < 1$, $\gamma \varepsilon R$ and $C(x)$ slowly varying at ∞. If, in addition, there exists a number $\kappa > 0$ satisfying

$$\theta^{-1} = L_X(-\kappa) \tag{10.2.3}$$

for X non-arithmetic and if $-L_X'(-\kappa) < \infty$, then

$$1 - F_S(x) \sim \frac{x^\gamma e^{-\kappa x} C(x)}{\kappa[-\theta L_X'(-\kappa)]^{\gamma+1}}, \quad x \to \infty. \tag{10.2.4}$$

Before proving that some of the frequency models discussed earlier satisfy (10.2.2), we consider (10.2.3). Clearly, for such a $\kappa > 0$ to exist the variate X must have a moment generating function (excluding many of the severity distributions of chapter 4).

Consider for example, the inverse Gaussian distribution with Laplace transform (4.13.3). It is easily seen that the maximum value of $L_X(z)$ is $e^{\mu\beta^{-1}}$. Hence a κ will exist if $e^{\mu\beta^{-1}} \geq \theta^{-1}$. In this case, we have, from (10.2.3) and (4.13.3),

$$\kappa = -\frac{\log\theta}{\mu}\left[1 + \frac{\beta}{2\mu}\log\theta\right].$$

We now demonstrate that many of the more common frequency distributions discussed earlier satisfy (10.2.2).

Example 10.2.1. Negative Binomial Distribution

For the negative binomial distribution with pf

$$p_n = \frac{\Gamma(r+n)}{\Gamma(r)n!}\left(\frac{1}{1+\beta}\right)^r\left(\frac{\beta}{1+\beta}\right)^n, \tag{10.2.5}$$

we have, using the asymptotic formulas for the gamma functions in the appendix,

$$\lim_{n\to\infty} n^{1-r}\left(\frac{1+\beta}{\beta}\right)^n p_n = \lim_{n\to\infty} n^{1-r}\frac{\Gamma(r+n)}{\Gamma(r)n!}(1+\beta)^{-r}$$

$$= \frac{(1+\beta)^{-r}}{\Gamma(r)}\lim_{n\to\infty} n^{1-r}\frac{\sqrt{2\pi}e^{-r-n}(r+n)^{r+n-\frac{1}{2}}}{\sqrt{2\pi}e^{-n}n^{n+\frac{1}{2}}}$$

$$= \frac{(1+\beta)^{-r}e^{-r}}{\Gamma(r)} \lim_{n\to\infty} (1+\frac{r}{n})^{n+r-\frac{1}{2}} = \frac{(1+\beta)^{-r}}{\Gamma(r)}.$$

Thus

$$p_n \sim \frac{n^{r-1}}{\Gamma(r)} (\frac{1}{1+\beta})^r (\frac{\beta}{1+\beta})^n, \quad n\to\infty \qquad (10.2.6)$$

and so (10.2.2) is satisfied with $\theta = \beta(1+\beta)^{-1}$, $\gamma = r-1$ and $C(n) = (1+\beta)^{-r}[\Gamma(r)]^{-1}$. Thus, (10.2.4) becomes

$$1-F_S(x) \sim \frac{x^{r-1}e^{-\kappa x}}{\kappa\Gamma(r)[-\beta L_X'(-\kappa)]^r}, \quad x\to\infty. \qquad (10.2.7)$$

Corresponding results for the **geometric** distribution are obtained by setting $r = 1$. In this case we see that (10.2.6) is an exact result and (10.2.7) becomes

$$1-F_S(x) \sim \frac{e^{-\kappa x}}{-\beta\kappa L_X'(-\kappa)}, \quad x\to\infty. \qquad (10.2.8)$$

Example 10.2.2. The Generalized Poisson Pascal Distribution

For the generalized Poisson Pascal distribution with pgf

$$P(z) = e^{\mu\{[1-\beta(z-1)]^{-r}-1\}} \qquad (10.2.9)$$

it can be shown (Teugels and Willmot, 1987) that if $-1 < r < 0$,

$$p_n \sim \frac{r\mu(1+\beta)^{-r}e^{-\mu}}{\Gamma(1+r)} (\frac{\beta}{1+\beta})^n n^{r-1}, \quad n\to\infty \qquad (10.2.10)$$

and so (10.2.2) is satisfied with $\theta = \beta(1+\beta)^{-1}$, $\gamma = r-1$, and $C(n) = r\mu(1+\beta)^{-r}e^{-\mu}[\Gamma(1+r)]^{-1}$. Thus (10.2.4) becomes

$$1 - F_s(x) \sim \frac{r \mu e^{-\mu}}{\kappa \Gamma(1+r)[-\beta L_X'(-\kappa)]^r} x^{r-1} e^{-\kappa x}, \quad x \to \infty. \tag{10.2.11}$$

The corresponding formulas for the **Poisson-Inverse Gaussian** distribution with pgf (8.3.6) may be obtained by replacing μ by $-\mu \beta^{-1}$, β by 2β and r by $-\frac{1}{2}$ in (10.2.10) and (10.2.11). Thus, we obtain from (10.2.10),

$$p_n \sim \frac{\mu e^{\mu \beta^{-1}}}{\sqrt{2 \pi \beta}} \left(\frac{2\beta}{1+2\beta}\right)^{n - \frac{1}{2}} n^{-\frac{3}{2}}, \quad n \to \infty \tag{10.2.12}$$

and from (10.2.11),

$$1 - F_S(x) \sim \frac{\mu e^{\mu \beta^{-1}}}{\kappa} \left[-\frac{L_X'(-\kappa)}{2 \pi \beta}\right]^{\frac{1}{2}} x^{-\frac{3}{2}} e^{-\kappa x}, \quad x \to \infty. \tag{10.2.13}$$

Example 10.2.3 Mixed Poisson Distributions

For the mixed Poisson distribution with pgf

$$P(z) = \int_0^\infty e^{\lambda \theta(z-1)} dU(\theta) \tag{10.2.14}$$

where $U(\theta)$ is the cdf of the mixing distribution with (discrete or continuous) density $u(\theta)$ which satisfies

$$u(\theta) \sim C(\theta) \theta^\alpha e^{-\beta \theta}, \quad \theta \to \infty. \tag{10.2.15}$$

In (10.2.15), $C(\theta)$ varies slowly at infinity, and is locally bounded on $(0, \infty)$, i.e. is bounded on compact subsets of $(0, \infty)$. Also, $\alpha \in (-\infty, \infty)$ and $\beta \geq 0$. Then the mixed Poisson probabilities with pgf (10.2.14) satisfy (cf. Willmot, 1990)

$$p_n \sim \frac{C(n)}{(\lambda+\beta)^{\alpha+1}} \left[\frac{\lambda}{\lambda+\beta}\right]^n n^\alpha, \quad n \to \infty. \tag{10.2.16}$$

Evidently, (10.2.16) is of the form (10.2.2). Furthermore, the previous two examples are special cases of this result.

Example 10.2.4 Discrete Compound Distributions

Consider the compound distribution with pgf

$$P(z) = K\{F(x)\} \tag{10.2.17}$$

where $K(z) = \sum_{n=0}^{\infty} k_n z^n$ and $F(z) = \sum_{n=0}^{\infty} F_n z^n$ are themselves pgf's. Then if $k_n \sim Cn^\alpha \theta^n$, $n \to \infty$ where $C>0$, $\alpha \in (-\infty,\infty)$,{and $\theta \in (0,1)$, and if there exists $\tau>1$ satisfying $F(\tau) = \theta^{-1}$, then

$$p_n \sim \frac{Cn^\alpha \tau^{-n}}{\{\theta\tau F'(\tau)\}^{\alpha+1}}, \quad n \to \infty. \tag{10.2.18}$$

Note that (10.2.18) is of the form (10.2.2) and that this example is basically a discrete version of (10.2.1).

On the other hand, suppose (10.2.17) holds with $f_n \sim Cn^\phi \tau^{-n}$, $n \to \infty$ with $C>0$, $\phi<-1$, and $\tau>1$. Suppose also that $K(z)$ has radius of convergence exceeding $F(\tau)$. Then

$$p_n \sim CK'\{F(\tau)\}n^\phi \tau^{-n}, \quad n \to \infty, \tag{10.2.19}$$

again of the form (10.2.2). See Willmot (1989), for details.

Useful formulas for the right tail of the compound distribution are thus obtainable in many situations. These approximate formulas may be used in conjunction with the recursions, since one could stop computing the distribution when the above approximations become sufficiently close.

In addition, these formulas are very useful in obtaining quick approximations for the stop loss premiums. For a random variable X, we define the **stop-loss premium** to be

$$R_X(x) = E[\max(X-x,0)] = \int_x^\infty [1-F_X(y)]dy. \tag{10.2.20}$$

For the examples in this section, simple approximate formulas for the stop-loss premiums associated with the compound distributions are easily obtainable. Since all the examples have $C(n)$ independent of n, we may write (10.2.4) in the form

$$1-F_S(x) \sim Cx^\gamma e^{-\kappa x}, \quad x \to \infty \tag{10.2.21}$$

for some constant C. We thus have, by L'Hopital's rule,

$$\lim_{x\to\infty} \frac{x^\gamma e^{-\kappa x}}{R_S(x)} = \lim_{x\to\infty} \frac{\gamma x^{\gamma-1}e^{-\kappa x}-\kappa x^\gamma e^{-\kappa x}}{-[1-F_S(x)]} = \lim_{x\to\infty} \frac{x^\gamma e^{-\kappa x}}{1-F_S(x)}[\kappa - \frac{\gamma}{x}] = \kappa C^{-1}.$$

In other words, the stop-loss premium satisfies

$$R_S(x) \sim \frac{C}{\kappa} x^\gamma e^{-\kappa x}, \quad x \to \infty. \tag{10.2.22}$$

The constants C and γ are obtained from the formula corresponding to (10.2.21) from each example. In some situations it may be more convenient to estimate the stop-loss premium using (10.2.22) rather than obtaining the df $F_S(x)$ recursively and then using (10.2.20).

10.3 TAIL BEHAVIOR FOR CERTAIN SEVERITY MODELS

For a large number of severity distributions, the results of the previous section do not apply since (10.2.3) is not satisfied. However, in many instances asymptotic formulas for the right tail of the cdf are obtainable using different arguments.

A wide class of severity distributions for which (10.2.3) does not hold but asymptotic formulas are obtainable is the class of **subexponential** distributions with df satisfying

$$\lim_{x \to \infty} \frac{1-F_X^{*2}(x)}{1-F_X(x)} = 2. \tag{10.3.1}$$

It can be shown that

$$\lim_{x \to \infty} \frac{1-F_X^{*n}(x)}{1-F_X(x)} = n, \quad n = 1,2,3,\dots \quad . \tag{10.3.2}$$

This class of distributions is quite broad and includes many of the common severity distributions of chapter 4. Embrechts and Veraverbeke (1982) give a good summary of the properties of this class. It can be shown (Embrechts, Goldie, Veraverbeke, 1979) that if the claim frequency distribution has a moment generating function for some $z > 0$ and has mean $E(N)$, and subexponential severity distribution, then

$$\lim_{x \to \infty} \frac{1-F_S(x)}{1-F_X(x)} = E(N). \tag{10.3.3}$$

Virtually all of the claim frequency models considered in chapters 6, 7, and 8 satisfy this criterion. Some members of the subexponential class include distributions with df satisfying

$$1-F_X(x) \sim x^{-\gamma}C(x) \tag{10.3.4}$$

where $C(x)$ is slowly varying at infinity (see previous section) and $|\gamma| < \infty$. Several distributions from chapter 4 satisfy (10.3.4) as the following examples suggest.

Example 10.3.1. The Transformed Beta Distributions

The transformed beta distribution (example 4.14.6) with pdf

$$f_X(x) = \frac{\Gamma(\alpha+\beta)}{\Gamma(\alpha)\Gamma(\beta)} \frac{c\lambda^\alpha x^{c\beta-1}}{(\lambda+x^c)^{\alpha+\beta}} \tag{10.3.5}$$

satisfies (10.3.4). We have, by L'Hopital's rule,

$$\lim_{x\to\infty} \frac{1-F_X(x)}{x^{-c\alpha}} = \lim_{x\to\infty} \frac{-f_X(x)}{-c\alpha x^{-c\alpha-1}} = \frac{\Gamma(\alpha+\beta)\lambda^\alpha}{\Gamma(\alpha+1)\Gamma(\beta)} \lim_{x\to\infty} (\frac{x^c}{\lambda+x^c})^{\alpha+\beta}.$$

In other words,

$$1-F_X(x) \sim \frac{\lambda^\alpha\Gamma(\alpha+\beta)}{\Gamma(\alpha+1)\Gamma(\beta)} x^{-c\alpha}, \quad x\to\infty. \tag{10.3.6}$$

Thus (10.3.4) is satisfied with $\gamma = c\alpha$ and $C(x) = \lambda^\alpha\Gamma(\alpha+\beta)[\Gamma(\beta)\Gamma(\alpha+1)]^{-1}$. The df of the aggregate distribution satisfies (using (10.3.3)),

$$1-F_S(x) \sim \frac{E(N)\lambda^\alpha\Gamma(\alpha+\beta)}{\Gamma(\alpha+1)\Gamma(\beta)} x^{-c\alpha}, \quad x\to\infty. \tag{10.3.7}$$

Similarly, the stop-loss premium (10.2.14) satisfies

$$R_S(x) \sim \frac{E(N)\lambda^\alpha\Gamma(\alpha+\beta)}{(c\alpha-1)\Gamma(\alpha+1)\Gamma(\beta)} x^{-c\alpha+1}, \quad x\to\infty \tag{10.3.8}$$

if the mean exists, i.e. if $c\alpha>1$. The corresponding formula for the **Pareto** $(c = 1, \beta = 1)$, the **Burr** $(\beta = 1)$, the **generalized Pareto** $(c = 1)$, and the **log-logistic** $(\beta = 1, \alpha = 1)$ are the respective special cases of the above formulas.

Example 10.3.2. The Lognormal Distribution

Embrechts, Goldie, and Veraverbeke (1979) have shown that the lognormal distribution with pf

$$f_X(x) = \frac{e^{-\frac{1}{2}(\frac{\log x - \mu}{\sigma})^2}}{\sqrt{2\pi}\sigma x} \tag{10.3.9}$$

is subexponential. The df satisfies

$$1 - F_X(x) \sim (2\pi)^{-\frac{1}{2}} \left(\frac{\sigma}{\log x - \mu}\right) e^{-\frac{1}{2}(\frac{\log x - \mu}{\sigma})^2}, \quad x \to \infty \tag{10.3.10}$$

and so the df of the compound distribution satisfies

$$1 - F_S(x) \sim E(N)(2\pi)^{-\frac{1}{2}} \left(\frac{\sigma}{\log x - \mu}\right) e^{-\frac{1}{2}(\frac{\log x - \mu}{\sigma})^2}, \quad x \to \infty. \tag{10.3.11}$$

Similarly, the stop-loss premium (10.2.14) satisfies

$$R_S(x) \sim E(N)\sigma^3 (2\pi)^{-\frac{1}{2}} \frac{x}{(\log x - \mu)^2} e^{-\frac{1}{2}(\frac{\log x - \mu}{\sigma})^2}, \quad x \to \infty. \tag{10.3.12}$$

An intermediate class of distributions has been discussed by Embrechts and Goldie (1982). This class of medium tailed distributions may or may not determine the tail. A distribution is defined to be medium tailed if there exists $\gamma > 0$ with

$$\text{i) } \lim_{x \to \infty} \frac{1 - F_X^{*2}(x)}{1 - F_X(x)} = 2L_X(-\gamma) < \infty$$

$$\tag{10.3.13}$$

$$\text{ii) } \lim_{x \to \infty} \frac{1 - F_X(x - y)}{1 - F_X(x)} = e^{\gamma y} \text{ for } y \varepsilon \mathbf{R}.$$

It can be shown that the Laplace transform $L_X(z)$ exists for all $z \geq -\gamma$ and $L_X(-\gamma) < \infty$. If $\gamma = 0$ the subexponential class results. For the medium tailed class, (10.3.3) generalizes to (Teugels, 1985)

$$\lim_{x \to \infty} \frac{1-F_S(x)}{1-F_X(x)} = P'[L_X(-\gamma)] \tag{10.3.14}$$

if $P'[L_X(-\gamma)] < \infty$.

An example of a medium tailed distribution is now given.

Example 10.3.3. The Inverse Gaussian Distribution

The inverse Gaussian distribution with pdf

$$f_X(x) = \mu(2\pi\beta x^3)^{-\frac{1}{2}} e^{-\frac{(x-\mu)^2}{2\beta x}} \tag{10.3.15}$$

is medium tailed. We have $\gamma = (2\beta)^{-1}$ and $L_X(-\gamma) = e^{\mu\beta^{-1}}$. Also, the df satisfies

$$1-F_X(x) \sim (\frac{2\beta}{\pi})^{\frac{1}{2}} \mu e^{\mu\beta^{-1}} x^{-\frac{3}{2}} e^{-\frac{x}{2\beta}}, \quad x \to \infty. \tag{10.3.16}$$

Thus, if $P'(e^{\mu\beta^{-1}}) < \infty$, the df of the compound distribution satisfies

$$1-F_S(x) \sim (\frac{2\beta}{\pi})^{\frac{1}{2}} \mu e^{\mu\beta^{-1}} P'(e^{\mu\beta^{-1}}) x^{-\frac{3}{2}} e^{-\frac{x}{2\beta}}, \quad x \to \infty \tag{10.3.17}$$

and the stop loss premium (10.2.14) satisfies

$$R_S(x) \sim (\frac{8\beta^3}{\pi})^{\frac{1}{2}} \mu e^{\mu\beta^{-1}} P'(e^{\mu\beta^{-1}}) x^{-\frac{3}{2}} e^{-\frac{x}{2\beta}}, \quad x \to \infty. \tag{10.3.18}$$

Embrechts (1983) has shown that the generalized inverse Gaussian distribution with $\lambda < 0$ (example 4.14.7) is medium tailed (including the inverse Gaussian). As in example (10.3.3), formula (10.3.14) holds if $L_X(-\gamma) < z_0$ where $P(z) < \infty$ for $z < z_0$. The results of the previous section hold if $\theta^{-1} \leq L_X(-\gamma)$. We leave it to the reader to verify that $\theta^{-1} = z_0$ for each of the frequency models in section 10.2.

Embrechts and Veraverbeke (1982) have summarized these results and we may thus classify claim severity distributions as follows:

> **Light Tailed** - (10.2.3) always satisfied
>> Exponential
>> Gamma
>> Generalized Inverse Gaussian $(\lambda > 0)$.
>
> **Medium Tailed** - (10.2.3) sometimes satisfied
>> Inverse Gaussian
>> Generalized Inverse Gaussian $(\lambda < 0)$.
>
> **Heavy Tailed** - (10.2.3) never satisfied (subexponential)
>> Lognormal
>> Pareto
>> Transformed Beta

Since the lognormal has all its moments, it is lighter tailed than the other subexponential distributions.

The results of the past two sections suggest that the right tail behavior of the compound distribution is essentially determined by the heavier of the frequency and severity components. If the claim frequency distribution satisfies (10.2.2) and is thus sufficiently heavy tailed and the claim severity distribution satisfies (10.2.3) and is thus relatively light tailed, then the tail of the compound distribution is determined by the frequency distribution through (10.2.4). It is interesting to note that the Poisson is light-tailed by this classification, and that the tail of the compound negative binomial looks like a gamma tail (see example 10.2.1 and section 4.12). Similarly, the tail of the compound Sichel distribution looks like a generalized inverse Gaussian tail (see exercises). The same comments hold for the compound geometric (exponential tail) and the Poisson-Inverse Gaussian (inverse Gaussian tail, see 10.2.13). In general, for mixed Poisson distributions, the tail of the compound distribution looks like the tail of the mixing distribution (see example 10.2.3). This discussion is also applicable in the discrete case, as is evident from example 10.2.4.

If the claim severity distribution is sufficiently heavy-tailed (subexponential) and if the claim frequency distribution has a moment generating function and is thus sufficiently light, then the right tail of the compound distribution is governed by the severity distribution. Medium tailed distributions such as the inverse Gaussian may or may not determine the tail.

10.4 BIBLIOGRAPHIC NOTES

Much of the material from this chapter has been taken from the papers by Embrechts (1983), Embrechts and Goldie (1982), Embrechts, Goldie, and Veraverbeke (1979), Embrechts, Maejima, and Teugels (1985), Chover, Ney, and Wainger (1973), and Stam (1973). A good review paper is Embrechts and Veraverbeke (1982). A review of asymptotic techniques is given by Bender (1974). Slow variation is discussed in detail by Bingham, Goldie, and Teugels (1987). Other references on asymptotics for discrete distributions are Meir and Moon (1987), Willmot (1989), and Willmot (1990).

EXERCISES

1. **Logarithmic Distribution**

   For the logarithmic distribution with pf

   $$p_n = \frac{q^n}{-n \log(1-q)},$$

   show that (10.2.2) is satisfied, and so, for the compound logarithmic distribution, one has, from (10.2.4),

   $$1 - F_S(x) \sim \frac{x^{-1} e^{-\kappa x}}{-\kappa \log(1-q)}, \quad x \to \infty.$$

2. **Extended Truncated Negative Binomial Distribution**

   For the negative binomial distribution with pf

   $$p_n = \frac{-r \Gamma(n+r)}{n! \Gamma(1+r)[1-(1+\beta)^r]} \left(\frac{\beta}{1+\beta}\right)^n,$$

   show with the help of example 10.2.1 that (10.2.2) is satisfied, i.e.

   $$p_n \sim \frac{-r n^{r-1}}{\Gamma(1+r)[1-(1+\beta)^r]} \left(\frac{\beta}{1+\beta}\right)^n, \quad n \to \infty$$

   and so, for the compound extended truncated negative binomial,

   $$1 - F_S(x) \sim \frac{r x^{r-1} e^{-\kappa x}}{\kappa \Gamma(1+r)[1-(1+\beta)^{-r}][-\beta L_X'(-\kappa)]^r}, \quad x \to \infty.$$

3. **Sichel's Distribution**

   For Sichel's distribution with pf

$$p_n = \frac{\mu^n}{n!} \frac{K_{\lambda+n}[\mu\beta^{-1}(1+2\beta)^{\frac{1}{2}}]}{K_\lambda(\mu\beta^{-1})}(1+2\beta)^{-\frac{\lambda+n}{2}},$$

use the asymptotic formulas for $n!$ and $K_\lambda(x)$ to show that

$$p_n \sim \frac{n^{\lambda-1}}{2\mu^\lambda K_\lambda(\mu\beta^{-1})}\left(\frac{2\beta}{1+2\beta}\right), \quad n\to\infty$$

and hence, for the compound Sichel's distribution,

$$1-F_S(x) \sim \frac{x^{\lambda-1}e^{-\kappa x}}{2\kappa\mu^\lambda K_\lambda(\mu\beta^{-1})[-L_X'(-\kappa)]^\lambda}, \quad x\to\infty.$$

Recover (10.2.12) and (10.2.13) by substituting $\lambda=-\frac{1}{2}$ into the above formulas.

4. The Loggamma Distribution

Hogg and Klugman (1984) construct the loggamma distribution by considering $Y = e^X$ where X has the gamma pdf (4.12.1). Show that the pdf of y is

$$f_Y(y) = \frac{\lambda^\alpha(\log y)^{\alpha-1}}{y^{\lambda+1}\Gamma(\alpha)}, \quad y>1.$$

Show that

$$1-F_Y(y) \sim \frac{\lambda^{\alpha-1}}{\Gamma(\alpha)}y^{-\lambda}(\log y)^{\alpha-1}, \quad y\to\infty$$

and so the loggamma distribution is subexponential by (10.3.4). Thus, show that the df of the aggregate distribution and the stop-loss premium satisfy

$$1-F_S(x) \sim \frac{E(N)\lambda^{\alpha-1}}{\Gamma(\alpha)} x^{-\lambda}(\log x)^{\alpha-1}, \quad x \to \infty,$$

$$R_S(x) \sim \frac{E(N)\lambda^{\alpha-1}}{(\lambda-1)\Gamma(\alpha)} x^{-\lambda+1}(\log x)^{\alpha-1}, \quad x \to \infty$$

where the latter formula holds if the mean of the loggamma distribution is finite (i.e. $\lambda > 1$).

5. Show that, for given mean μ and variance σ^2, the skewness of the gamma distribution is $2(\frac{\sigma}{\mu})$, the inverse Gaussian $3(\frac{\sigma}{\mu})$, and the lognormal $3(\frac{\sigma}{\mu}) + 3(\frac{\sigma}{\mu})^3$, which is consistent with the tail ordering of section 10.3. This suggests that the inverse Gaussian distribution should resemble the lognormal if $\sigma < \mu$.

6. (a) Prove that if $a_n \sim b_n$, $n \to \infty$ where $b_n > 0$, then

$$\sum_{k=n+1}^{\infty} a_n \sim \sum_{k=n+1}^{\infty} b_n, \quad n \to \infty.$$

(b) Show that

$$\sum_{k=n+1}^{\infty} k^{\alpha}\tau^{-k} = \frac{n^{\alpha}\tau^{-n}}{\tau-1} + \frac{1}{\tau-1}\sum_{k=n}^{\infty} \tau^{-k}\{(k+1)^{\alpha}-k^{\alpha}\}.$$

(c) Prove that, if $g_n \sim C_n^{\alpha}\tau^{-n}$, $n \to \infty$ where $C > 0$, $\alpha \in (-\infty,\infty)$, and $\tau > 1$, then

$$\sum_{k=n+1}^{\infty} g_k \sim \frac{C}{\tau-1}n^{\alpha}\tau^{-n}, \quad n \to \infty.$$

(d) Use (c) and example 10.2.4 to establish formulas analogous to (10.2.4) for the tail and (10.2.22) for the stop-loss premium in the discrete case.

7. Suppose, as in example 10.2.4, that $P(z) = K\{F(z)\}$ where $k_n \sim C_1 n^{\alpha_1} \tau_1^{-n}$, $n \to \infty$ where $\tau_1 > 1$, and $f_n \sim C_2 n^{\alpha_2} \tau_2^{-n}$, where $\tau_2 > 1$.

(a) Prove that the radius of convergence of $K(z)$ is τ_1, and that $K(\tau_1) < \infty$ if $\alpha_1 < -1$ but $K(\tau_1) = \infty$ if $\alpha_1 \geq -1$.

(b) Prove that (10.2.18) is applicable if $\tau_2 > \tau_1$ and (10.2.19) is applicable if $\tau_2 < \tau_1$.

(c) Interpret (b) in light of the discussion on tail behaviour in section 10.3.

CHAPTER 11

RUIN THEORY

11.1 INTRODUCTION

The previous chapters have been concerned with obtaining the distribution of aggregate claims for a portfolio. The purpose of this and subsequent chapters is to explore some of the possible applications of these models to insurance situations.

Often in examining the nature of the risk associated with a portfolio of business, one runs into difficulty in quantifying this risk even if one has modelled the distribution of total claims. In addition, it is of interest to assess how the portfolio may be expected to perform over an extended period of time. One approach to answering these and other questions concerns the use of **ruin theory.**

Ruin theory is concerned with the excess of the income (with respect to a portfolio of business) over the outgo, or claims paid. This quantity, referred to as the **insurer's surplus,** may be expected to vary with time. Specifically ruin is said to occur if the insurer's surplus reaches a specified lower bound. One measure of risk is the probability of an event such as this, clearly reflecting the volatility inherent in the business. In addition, this serves as a useful tool in long range planning for the use of an insurer's funds.

The first part of the chapter is concerned with the slightly more mathematically tractable infinite time horizon. In other words, we shall examine the probability of ultimate ruin. The latter part of the chapter will deal with a finite period.

11.2 QUANTITIES OF INTEREST

We begin by assuming that the number of claims process $\{N(t); t{\geq}0\}$, is a Poisson process (section 3.3) with rate λ. In addition, the claim severities will be assumed to be independent and identically distributed non-negative random variables with cdf $F_X(x)$, Laplace transform $L_X(z)$, and finite mean μ. The net premium will be assumed to be payable at a constant rate c over time, where

$$c = (1+\theta)\lambda\mu \tag{11.2.1}$$

and $\theta{>}0$ is the **relative security loading.** The insurance surplus at time t will be denoted by $\{U(t); t{\geq}0\}$. The initial surplus at time 0 will be denoted by $u = U(0)$.

The total claims process $\{S(t); t{\geq}0\}$ is by assumption a compound Poisson process (section 3.7), and thus

$$U(t) = u+ct-S(t), \quad t{\geq}0. \tag{11.2.2}$$

We shall ignore the effect interest earned on the insurance surplus for mathematical simplicity. The event of interest in this section is that $U(t)$ becomes negative for some $t{>}0$. Consequently we define

$$T = \inf\{t \,|\, t{\geq}0, U(t){<}0\} \tag{11.2.3}$$

and define $T = \infty$ if $U(t){\geq}0$ for all t. The random variable T is the time that **ruin** occurs. We define the **probability of ultimate survival** to be

$$\phi(u) = Pr\{T{=}\infty\} \tag{11.2.4}$$

and note the dependency of this function on u. The **probability of ultimate ruin** is the complement $1{-}\phi(u)$.

11.3 THE ADJUSTMENT COEFFICIENT

We begin our study of ruin by introducing a number $\kappa > 0$, called the **adjustment coefficient**, which is the solution to the equation

$$1 + (1+\theta)\kappa\mu = L_X(-\kappa). \qquad (11.3.1)$$

Clearly, $\kappa = 0$ satisfies (11.3.1), but there may exist a positive solution as well (this requires that X have a moment generating function, however, thus excluding distributions such as the Pareto and the lognormal). To see the plausibility of this result, note that $L_X(0) = 1$, $L_X'(z) < 0$, $L_X''(z) > 0$, and $L_X'(0) = -\mu$. Hence, the curves $y = L_X(z)$ and $y = 1 - (1+\theta)\mu z$ may intersect, as shown in figure 11.3.1.

FIGURE 11.3.1

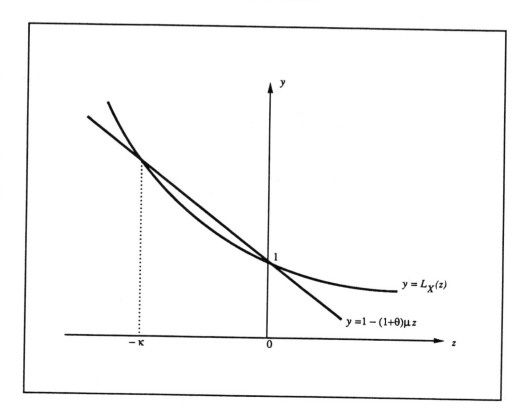

Example 11.3.1. Exponential Claim Amounts

If X has an exponential distribution with parameter β, then $F_X(x) = 1 - e^{-\beta x}$ and $L_X(z) = \beta(\beta+z)^{-1}$, $z > -\beta$. Since $\mu = \beta^{-1}$, (11.3.1) becomes $1 + (1+\theta)\kappa\beta^{-1} = \beta(\beta-\kappa)^{-1}$. This may be solved to yield $\kappa = \beta\theta(1+\theta)^{-1}$.

In general, it will be necessary to solve (11.3.1) numerically for κ. This is normally a straightforward problem which may be handled using the Newton-Raphson method. Thus, define

$$H(z) = 1 + (1+\theta)\mu z - L_X(-z), \tag{11.3.2}$$

and so $\kappa > 0$ is a solution to $H(\kappa) = 0$. Since

$$H'(z) = (1+\theta)\mu + L_X'(-z), \tag{11.3.3}$$

one may compute updated estimates of κ by the formula

$$\kappa_{i+1} = \kappa_i - \frac{H(\kappa_i)}{H'(\kappa_i)} \tag{11.3.4}$$

beginning with an initial estimate κ_0. Since $H(0) = 0$, care must be taken not to converge to the value 0, and so κ_0 should not be too close to 0. If $\mu_2' = E(X^2)$ and $\mu_3' = E(X^3)$, then,

$$L_X(-\kappa) = \int_0^\infty e^{\kappa x} dF_X(x) > \int_0^\infty (1 + \kappa x + \frac{1}{2}\kappa^2 x^2 + \frac{1}{6}\kappa^3 x^3) dF_X(x)$$

$$= 1 + \kappa\mu + \frac{\kappa^2 \mu_2'}{2} + \frac{\kappa^3 \mu_3'}{6}.$$

Thus, from (11.3.1), $1 + (1+\theta)\mu\kappa > 1 + \kappa\mu + \frac{\kappa^2}{2}\mu_2' + \frac{\kappa^3}{6}\mu_3'$. In other words,

$\mu_3'\kappa^2 + 3\mu_2'\kappa - 6\theta\mu < 0$. Since $\mu_3' > 0$, the value of κ is between the two roots of this quadratic. One root is negative and hence is of no use. Hence

$$\kappa < \frac{-3\mu_2' + \{9\mu_2'^2 + 24\mu\mu_3'\theta\}^{\frac{1}{2}}}{2\mu_3'} = \frac{12\mu\theta}{3\mu_2' + \{9\mu_2'^2 + 24\mu\mu_3'\theta\}^{\frac{1}{2}}}, \qquad (11.3.5)$$

where the second equality on the right hand side of (11.3.5) follows from an identity of the form $a - b = (a^2 - b^2)/(a+b)$. Thus, the right hand side of (11.3.5) may be used as a starting value for the Newton-Raphson procedure. If it is inconvenient to calculate μ_3', then a somewhat weaker inequality is obtained by noting that

$$\frac{12\mu\theta}{3\mu_2' + \{9\mu_2'^2 + 24\mu\mu_3'\theta\}^{\frac{1}{2}}} < \frac{12\mu\theta}{3\mu_2' + \{9\mu_2'^2\}^{\frac{1}{2}}} = \frac{2\mu\theta}{\mu_2'}. \qquad (11.3.6)$$

The right hand side of (11.3.6) may also be used as a starting value, although it is poorer than (11.3.5), though simpler to calculate. An example illustrates these ideas.

Example 11.3.2. Gamma Claim Amounts

Suppose the single claim amount distribution has a gamma distribution (section 4.12) with mean $2500 and standard deviation $500. Then, working in units of $1000 for convenience, one finds from (4.11.6) and (4.11.7) that $\alpha = 25$ and $\beta = 10$. The contingency premium is 20% of expected claims, so that $\theta = .2$. From (4.11.4) and (11.3.2), one finds that

$$H(z) = 1 + (1+\theta)\frac{\alpha}{\beta}z - (1 - \frac{z}{\beta})^{-\alpha}$$

and so

$$H'(z) = (1+\theta)\frac{\alpha}{\beta} - \frac{\alpha}{\beta}(1 - \frac{z}{\beta})^{-\alpha-1}.$$

In order to get initial estimates of κ from (11.3.5), one needs the first three moments about the origin. From (4.11.5), with these parameter values, one obtains $\mu = 2.5$, $\mu_2' = 6.5$, and $\mu_3' = 17.55$. Thus an initial estimate of κ is found from (11.3.5) to be $\kappa_0 = .13696$. From (11.3.4), one gets $\kappa_1 = .13561$, and then $\kappa_2 = .13560$. A final iteration of (11.3.4) yields $\kappa_3 = .13560$ and so convergence has occurred. Thus the adjustment coefficient, accurate to 5 decimal places, is $\kappa = .13560$. As a check, one calculates $H(\kappa) = 1.09 \times 10^{-9}$, which is close to 0. Alternatively, one could use (11.3.6) to get a starting value, and this gives $\kappa_0 = .15385$. One more iteration is required to obtain $\kappa = .13560$ than in the previous case. Note that .13560 is less than both initial values, as it must be, but (11.3.5) is much closer to the true value of κ than is (11.3.6).

The adjustment coefficient κ may be used in the derivation of useful approximations for the probability of ruin. A fundamental result is the following.

Theorem 11.3.1. If there exists $\kappa > 0$ satisfying (11.3.1), then

$$1 - \phi(u) \le e^{-\kappa u}, \quad 0 \le u. \tag{11.3.7}$$

Proof

Define $1 - \phi_n(u)$ to be the probability that ruin occurs at the time of or before the n-th claim for any nonnegative integer n. We now prove by induction on n that $1 - \phi_n(u) \le e^{-\kappa u}$. Clearly $1 - \phi_0(u) = 0 \le e^{-\kappa u}$. Next, assume that $1 - \phi_k(u) \le e^{-\kappa u}$, $u > 0$. By conditioning on the time of the first claim (which has an exponential distribution) and the amount, and using the fact that $\{U(t); t \ge 0\}$ has stationary and independent increments, it follows that

$$1 - \phi_{k+1}(u) = \int_0^\infty \lambda e^{-\lambda t} \{1 - F_X(u+ct) + \int_0^{u+ct} [1 - \phi_k(u+ct-x)] dF_X(x)\} dt$$

$$\leq \int_0^\infty \lambda e^{-\lambda t} \{1 - F_X(u+ct) + \int_0^{u+ct} e^{-\kappa(u+ct-x)} dF_X(x)\} dt$$

$$\leq \int_0^\infty \lambda e^{-\lambda t} \{\int_0^\infty e^{-\kappa(u+ct-x)} dF_X(x)\} dt$$

since $1 - F_X(u+ct) = \int_{u+ct}^\infty dF_X(x) \leq \int_{u+ct}^\infty e^{-\kappa(u+ct-x)} dF_X(x)$ because $-\kappa(u+ct-x) > 0$ if $x > u+ct$. Thus,

$$1 - \phi_{k+1}(u) \leq \int_0^\infty \lambda e^{-\lambda t} e^{-\kappa(u+ct)} \{\int_0^\infty e^{\kappa x} dF_X(x)\} dt$$

$$= \lambda e^{-\kappa u} \int_0^\infty e^{-(\lambda+\kappa c)t} L_X(-\kappa) dt$$

$$= \lambda e^{-\kappa u} \int_0^\infty e^{-(\lambda+\kappa c)t} \{1 + (1+\theta)\kappa\mu\} dt$$

$$= \lambda e^{-\kappa u} \{1 + (1+\theta)\kappa\mu\} \int_0^\infty e^{-(\lambda+\kappa c)t} dt$$

$$= e^{-\kappa u} \{\lambda + \kappa[(1+\theta)\lambda\mu]\} \left[\frac{-e^{-(\lambda+\kappa c)t}}{\lambda+\kappa c} \Big|_0^\infty \right]$$

$$= e^{-\kappa u} \{\lambda + \kappa c\} [(\lambda+\kappa c)^{-1}] = e^{-\kappa u}.$$

Thus, by induction, $1 - \phi_n(u) \leq e^{-\kappa u}$ for all n and so $1 - \phi(u) = \lim_{n \to \infty} \{1 - \phi_n(u)\} \leq e^{-\kappa u}$.

This is an important result because it provides an upper bound on the probability of ruin on a portfolio of business. It may be used to provide guidance as to the size of contingency loading needed to keep the probability of ruin manageable. Suppose that it is desired to have the probability of ruin below a specified level α. Then, choose

$$\theta = \frac{u\{L_X(\frac{\log \alpha}{u})-1\}}{-\mu\log \alpha} - 1. \qquad (11.3.8)$$

With this choice of θ, $1 + (1+\theta)\kappa\mu = L_X(-\kappa)$ is satisfied by $\kappa = (-\log \alpha)/u$. Thus, by Theorem 11.3.1, $1-\phi(u)\leq e^{-\kappa u} = e^{\log \alpha} = \alpha$. Alternatively, if market conditions dictate a specified loading θ, then (11.3.1) may be solved for κ and the desired surplus u obtained as

$$u = (-\log \alpha)/\kappa. \qquad (11.3.9)$$

Then $1-\phi(u) \leq e^{-\kappa u} = e^{\log \alpha} = \alpha$ as before.

Freifelder (1976) and others have argued using utility theoretic arguments that, if the loss insured against is a random variable S, then the premium charged should be based on the **exponential utility principle**, namely

$$P(S) = a^{-1}\log E(e^{aS}) \qquad (11.3.10)$$

where $a>0$ is a parameter to be chosen. In the present situation with $S = S_t$ a compound Poisson random variable, (11.3.10) becomes

$$P(S_t) = a^{-1}\{\lambda t[L_X(-a)-1]\}. \qquad (11.3.11)$$

Clearly, premiums are charged at a constant rate c per unit time under (11.3.11). Since

$$a^{-1}[L_X(-a)-1] = a^{-1}\{\int_0^\infty e^{ax}dF_X(x)-1\} > a^{-1}\{\int_0^\infty (1+ax)dF_X(x)-1\} = \mu,$$

it follows that $P(S_t) > \lambda t \mu = E(S_t)$, and so the loading θ is positive. Thus, the premium rate per unit time is $c = P(S_t)/t = \lambda a^{-1}[L_X(-a)-1]$. Since c also equals $(1+\theta)\lambda\mu$, this means that $(1+\theta)\mu = a^{-1}[L_X(-a)-1]$, i.e. that

$$1+(1+\theta)\mu a = L_X(-a). \tag{11.3.12}$$

Comparison of (11.3.12) with (11.3.1) reveals that $a = \kappa$ is the adjustment coefficient. Thus, for a specified ruin probability α and surplus u, one may wish to charge the premium (11.3.11) with $a = (-\log \alpha)/u$. The loading θ is again given by (11.3.8) in this case.

11.4 AN EXPLICIT FORMULA

In this section an explicit formula for $\phi(u)$ will be derived as well as its Laplace transform. We begin by showing that $\phi(u)$ satisfies an integro-differential equation.

Theorem 11.4.1. The survival probability $\phi(u)$ satisfies the integro-differential equation

$$c\phi'(u) = \lambda\phi(u) - \lambda\int_0^u \phi(u-x)dF_X(x), \quad u \geq 0. \tag{11.4.1}$$

Proof

We shall consider what happens in the first h units of time. If no claims occur, the company takes in an additional ch units of premiums. If a claim occurs, then survival beyond time h takes place if the claim is for an amount less than $u+ch$. Since the compound Poisson process $S(t)$ has stationary and independent increments (sections 3.2 and 3.7), it follows from (11.2.2) that $U(t)$ does also, and so $\phi(u)$ is also the conditional survival probability given the history of the process $\{U(t); t \geq 0\}$. Thus

$$\phi(u) = \phi(u+ch)[1-\lambda h] + \lambda h \int_0^{u+ch} \phi(u+ch-x)dF_X(x) + o(h).$$

This may be rewritten as

$$c\,\frac{\phi(u+ch)-\phi(u)}{ch} = \lambda\phi(u+ch)-\lambda \int_0^{u+ch} \phi(u+ch-x)dF_X(x) + \frac{o(h)}{h}.$$

Letting $h \to 0$ yields (11.4.1).

We shall now demonstrate how to obtain $\phi(0)$. First, however, we must prove the following lemma.

Lemma 11.4.1. The Laplace transform

$$L_Y(z) = \frac{1-L_X(z)}{\mu z} \tag{11.4.2}$$

is that of an absolutely continuous random variable with df $F_Y(x)$ and pdf

$$f_Y(x) = \frac{1-F_X(x)}{\mu}, \quad x>0. \tag{11.4.3}$$

Proof

Clearly, $f_Y(x) \geq 0$ for all $x>0$. We also have

$$\int_0^\infty f_Y(x)dx = \int_0^\infty \frac{1-F_X(x)}{\mu}dx.$$

Using integration by parts, we obtain,

$$\int_0^\infty \frac{1-F_X(x)}{\mu}dx = \frac{x[1-F_X(x)]}{\mu}\Big|_0^\infty + \int_0^\infty \frac{xdF_X(x)}{\mu} = 1 + \lim_{x\to\infty}\frac{x[1-F_X(x)]}{\mu}.$$

Now,

$$0 \le \frac{x[1-F_X(x)]}{\mu} = \frac{x\int_x^\infty dF_X(y)}{\mu} \le \int_x^\infty \frac{ydF_X(y)}{\mu}$$

and $\displaystyle\lim_{x\to\infty}\int_x^\infty\frac{ydF_X(y)}{\mu}=0$ because $\mu = \int_0^\infty ydF_X(y) < \infty$. Thus, $\displaystyle\lim_{x\to\infty}\frac{x[1-F_X(x)]}{\mu} = 0$, and so $f_Y(x)$ is a valid pdf. The Laplace transform is given by (11.4.2) as can be seen easily by using (1.3.6), example 1.3.2 with $n = 0$, and (1.3.10).

Equation (11.4.1) will now be used to derive a formula for $\phi(0)$.

Theorem 11.4.2. The survival probability with no initial reserve is given by

$$\phi(0) = \theta(1+\theta)^{-1}, \tag{11.4.4}$$

independently of the claim frequency rate λ or the single claim amount distribution.

Proof

From (11.4.1), one has

$$\phi'(u) = \frac{\lambda}{c}\phi(u) - \frac{\lambda}{c}\int_0^u\phi(u-x)dF_X(x).$$

Integrating this equation with respect to u from 0 to y gives

$$\phi(y)-\phi(0) = \frac{\lambda}{c}\int_0^y \phi(u)du - \frac{\lambda}{c}\int_0^y\int_0^u \phi(u-x)dF_X(x)du. \qquad (11.4.5)$$

Changing the order of integration gives

$$\int_0^y\int_0^u \phi(u-x)dF_X(x)du = \int_0^y \phi(r)\int_0^{y-r} dF_X(x)dr,$$

The inner integral is simply $F_X(y-r)$, and the dummy variable r may be replaced by u, yielding from (11.4.5),

$$\phi(y) - \phi(0) = \frac{\lambda}{c}\int_0^y \phi(u)du - \frac{\lambda}{c}\int_0^y \phi(u)F_X(y-u)du.$$

This may be rewritten as

$$\phi(0) = \phi(y) - \frac{\lambda}{c}\int_0^y \{1-F_X(x)\}dx + \frac{\lambda}{c}\int_0^y \{1-F_X(x)\}dx - \frac{\lambda}{c}\int_0^y \phi(u)\{1-F_X(y-u)\}du,$$

and, making the change of variables $u = y-x$ in the second of these integrals, this becomes

$$\phi(0) = \phi(y) - \frac{\lambda}{c}\int_0^y \{1-F_X(x)\}dx + \frac{\lambda}{c}\int_0^y \{1-\phi(u)\}\{1-F_X(y-u)\}du. \qquad (11.4.6)$$

From Theorem 11.3.1, one has that $1\geq\phi(y)\geq 1-e^{-\kappa y}$ and so $1\geq \lim_{y\to\infty} \phi(y) \geq \lim_{y\to\infty} (1-e^{-\kappa y}) = 1$, and so $\lim_{y\to\infty} \phi(y) = 1$. Similarly, the integral on the right hand side of (11.4.6) satisfies

$$\int_0^y \{1-\phi(u)\}\{1-F_X(y-u)\}du \leq \int_0^y e^{-\kappa u}\{1-F_X(y-u)\}du$$

$$= \int_0^y e^{-\kappa(y-x)}\{1-F_X(x)\}dx = e^{-\kappa y}\int_0^y e^{\kappa x}\{1-F_X(x)\}dx.$$

As $y \to \infty$,

$$\int_0^y e^{\kappa x}\{1-F_X(x)\}dx \to \int_0^\infty e^{\kappa x}\{1-F_X(x)\}dx = \mu L_Y(-\kappa)$$

by lemma 11.4.1. But, from (11.4.2) and (11.3.1), $L_Y(-\kappa) = 1+\theta$. Thus,

$$0 \le \frac{\lambda}{c}\int_0^y \{1-\phi(u)\}\{1-F_X(y-u)\}du \le \frac{\lambda}{c}e^{-\kappa y}\int_0^y e^{\kappa x}\{1-F_X(x)\}dx$$

$$\le \frac{\lambda}{c}e^{-\kappa y}\int_0^\infty e^{\kappa x}\{1-F_X(x)\}dx = \{e^{-\kappa y}\frac{\lambda}{c}\mu(1+\theta)\}$$

and $\lim_{y \to \infty} [e^{-\kappa y}\frac{\lambda}{c}\mu(1+\theta)] = 0$. In other words,

$$\lim_{y \to \infty} \frac{\lambda}{c}\int_0^y \{1-\phi(u)\}\{1-F_X(y-u)\}du = 0.$$

From (11.4.6), letting $y \to \infty$ yields

$$\phi(0) = 1 - \frac{\lambda}{c}\int_0^\infty \{1-F_X(x)\}dx + 0 = 1 - \frac{\lambda\mu}{c} = 1 - \frac{1}{1+\theta} = \frac{\theta}{1+\theta}.$$

Theorem 11.4.2 holds even if there is no adjustment coefficient (see, for example, exercise 4 at the end of the chapter).

We shall solve equation (11.4.1) for $\phi(u)$ using the technique of Laplace transforms (discussed in section 1.3). To do this, define

$$\bar{\phi}(z) = \int_0^\infty e^{-zu}\phi(u)du.\qquad\qquad(11.4.7)$$

The Laplace transform of $\phi(u)$ is given in the following theorem.

Theorem 11.4.4. The Laplace transform of $\phi(u)$ is given by

$$\bar{\phi}(z) = \frac{1}{z}\{1 - \frac{1}{\theta}[L_Y(z) - 1]\}^{-1}.\qquad\qquad(11.4.8)$$

Proof

Taking Laplace transforms of both sides of (11.4.1), we see by (1.3.5) that that of the left hand side is $c[z\bar{\phi}(z)-\phi(0)]$. The Laplace transform of the first term on the right hand side of (11.4.1) is $\lambda\bar{\phi}(z)$. The second term is $-\lambda$ times the convolution of $\phi(u)$ and the density corresponding to $F_X(x)$. Thus, by (1.3.11), it has Laplace transform $-\lambda\bar{\phi}(z)L_X(z)$. Thus, we obtain

$$c[z\bar{\phi}(z)-\phi(0)] = \lambda\bar{\phi}(z)-\lambda\bar{\phi}(z)L_X(z).$$

Using (11.2.1) and solving for $\bar{\phi}(z)$ yields

$$\bar{\phi}(z) = \frac{(1+\theta)\mu\phi(0)}{(1+\theta)\mu z-1+L_X(z)} = \frac{\theta^{-1}(1+\theta)\phi(0)}{z\{1-\theta^{-1}[\dfrac{1-L_X(z)}{\mu z}-1]\}}.$$

Since $\phi(0) = \theta(1+\theta)^{-1}$, (11.4.8) follows easily.

An explicit expression for $\phi(u)$ is easily obtained and is now given.

Theorem 11.4.5. The probability of ultimate survival $\phi(u)$ is the distribution function of a **compound geometric** distribution, i.e.

$$\phi(u) = \sum_{n=0}^{\infty} \frac{\theta}{1+\theta} \left(\frac{1}{1+\theta}\right)^n F_Y^{*n}(u) \qquad (11.4.9)$$

where $F_Y^{*n}(u)$ is the df of the n-fold convolution of $F_Y(u)$, the cdf of the random variable Y with pdf

$$f_Y(x) = \frac{1-F_X(x)}{\mu}, \quad x>0. \qquad (11.4.10)$$

Proof

From (11.4.8), one notes that $\bar{\phi}(z)$ is of the form (1.3.6) with $\bar{h}(z)$ of the form (2.9.7), and with N a geometric variate (section 4.4) with parameter β equal to θ^{-1}, and so the result follows.

If one sets $\theta = 0$ in (11.4.9) one obtains $\phi(u) = 0$ for all $u \geq 0$. This says that ultimate ruin is certain if there is no security loading $(\theta = 0)$ or if $\theta < 0$, therefore.

Equation (11.4.9) is a compound distribution of the same form as, the compound distributions used to model the total claims. Since $F_X(x)$ is a (piecewise) continuous increasing function, the pdf (11.4.10) is a (piecewise) continuous monotonic decreasing function. In particular, if the severity random variable is defined on positive integers, then $f_Y(x)$ is a decreasing step function. The probability of ultimate survival can be computed by first approximating the pdf $f_Y(x)$ by a discrete distribution, $g_Y(x)$, $x = 0, 1, 2,...$ by using, for example, the methods of section 6.15, and then calculating the approximation

$$\phi'(u) = \sum_{n=0}^{\infty} \frac{\theta}{1+\theta} \left(\frac{1}{1+\theta}\right)^n f_Y^{*n}(u)$$

$$\approx \sum_{n=0}^{\infty} (\frac{\theta}{1+\theta})(\frac{1}{1+\theta})^n g_Y^{*n}(x), \quad x = 0, 1, 2,... \qquad (11.4.11)$$

using the recursion (6.6.5) after adjusting the parameters for the probability at zero, $g_Y(0)$, of the approximate "claim size" distribution from table 6.6.1, we have $a = \beta(1+\beta)^{-1} = (1+\theta)^{-1}$ and $b = 0$. The recursive formula for $\phi'(u)$ is then

$$\phi'(u) \approx \frac{1}{1+\theta} \sum_{y=0}^{u} g_Y(y)\phi'(u-y), \quad u=1, 2,... \qquad (11.4.12)$$

Transposing the first term of the right-hand side yields

$$\phi'(u) \approx \frac{1}{1+\theta-g_Y(0)} \sum_{y=1}^{u} g_Y(y)\phi'(u-y), \quad u = 1, 2, 3,... \qquad (11.4.13)$$

The recursive formula (11.4.13) is used beginning with

$$\phi'(0) \approx \sum_{n=0}^{\infty} \frac{\theta}{1+\theta} \{ \frac{g_Y(0)}{1+\theta} \}^n$$

$$= \frac{\theta}{1+\theta-g_Y(0)}. \qquad (11.4.14)$$

Finally $\phi(u)$ is calculated approximately by

$$\phi(u) \approx \sum_{y=0}^{u} \phi'(u), \quad u = 0, 1, 2,... \qquad (11.4.15)$$

This method of direct recursive evaluation of the ultimate survival probabilities, and hence the ultimate ruin probabilities is discussed in detail by Panjer (1988). It should be noted that the only approximation introduced in this method is that of "arithmetizing" the distribution $f_Y(x)$. In general, the methods described in section (6.15) can give any required degree of accuracy by either making the interval size smaller or increasing the number of local moments that are matched.

In the next section methods for obtaining $\phi(u)$ will be discussed.

11.5 SPECIAL CLAIM AMOUNT DISTRIBUTIONS

In the previous section an explicit expression for the probability of ultimate survival $\phi(u)$ was obtained as (11.4.9) as well as its Laplace transform (11.4.8).

When the claim size distribution is exponential (or closely related), simple analytic results for (11.4.9) may be possible. This is illustrated in the following two examples.

Example 11.5.1. Exponential Claim Amounts

Suppose the claim size distribution is exponential (section 4.9) with parameter β. Thus

$$F_X(x) = 1 - e^{-\beta x}, \quad x > 0$$

and

$$L_X(z) = \beta(\beta+z)^{-1}.$$

Thus, from (11.4.8),

$$\bar{\phi}(z) = \frac{1}{z}\left\{1 - \frac{1}{\theta}\left[\frac{1-\beta(\beta+z)^{-1}}{\beta^{-1}z} - 1\right]\right\}^{-1} = \frac{1}{z}\left\{1 - \frac{1}{\theta}\left[\beta(\beta+z)^{-1} - 1\right]\right\}^{-1}$$

$$= \frac{1}{z}\left\{1 + \frac{z}{\theta(\beta+z)}\right\}^{-1} = \frac{1}{z}\left\{1 - \frac{z}{z+\theta(\beta+z)}\right\}$$

$$= \frac{1}{z} - \frac{1}{1+\theta}\ \frac{1}{z+\dfrac{\theta\beta}{1+\theta}}.$$

Using example 1.3.2 with $n = 0$, example 1.3.1, and (1.3.10), we obtain

$$\phi(u) = 1 - \frac{1}{1+\theta} e^{-\frac{\theta\beta}{1+\theta}u}.$$

Alternatively, one could show that $L_Y(z) = \beta(\beta+z)^{-1}$ and use example 2.9.1.

In general, when using partial fractions, it is easiest to write $\bar{\phi}(z) = z^{-1} - \bar{h}(z)$ for some $\bar{h}(.)$, which yields on inversion an expression of the form $\phi(u) = 1 - h(u)$. A second example is given.

Example 11.5.2. Mixed Exponential Claim Amounts

Suppose that the single claim amount distribution is a mixture of two exponentials, with pdf

$$f_X(x) = q\alpha e^{-\alpha x} + (1-q)\beta e^{-\beta x}, \quad x>0.$$

Then $\mu = q\alpha^{-1} + (1-q)\beta^{-1}$ and (11.4.3) is

$$f_{X_1}(x) = p\alpha e^{-\alpha x} + (1-p)\beta e^{-\beta x}, \quad x>0,$$

where

$$p = \frac{q\alpha^{-1}}{q\alpha^{-1} + (1-q)\beta^{-1}}.$$

Thus $f_{X_1}(x)$ is also a (different) mixture of (the same) two exponentials. Now, (11.4.2) is

$$L_{X_1}(z) = p\alpha(\alpha+z)^{-1} + (1-p)\beta(\beta+z)^{-1}$$

and so (11.4.8) becomes

$$\tilde{\phi}(z) = \frac{1}{z}\{1 - \frac{1}{\theta}[p\frac{\alpha}{\alpha+z} + (1-p)\frac{\beta}{\beta+z} - 1]\}^{-1}$$

$$= \frac{1}{z}\{1 + \frac{z}{\theta}[\frac{z+(1-p)\alpha+p\beta}{(\alpha+z)(\beta+z)}]\}^{-1}$$

$$= \frac{1}{z} - \frac{z+\psi}{(1+\theta)z^2 + [\psi+\theta(\alpha+\beta)]z+\alpha\beta\theta}$$

where

$$\psi = \alpha(1-p) + \beta p.$$

This expression may be rewritten as

$$\tilde{\phi}(z) = \frac{1}{z} - \frac{1}{1+\theta}\{\frac{z+\psi}{(z+r_1)(z+r_2)}\}$$

where

$$r_1 = \frac{\psi+\theta(\alpha+\beta) - \{[\psi+\theta(\alpha+\beta)]^2 - 4\alpha\beta\theta(1+\theta)\}^{\frac{1}{2}}}{2(1+\theta)}$$

and

$$r_2 = \frac{\psi+\theta(\alpha+\beta) + \{[\psi+\theta(\alpha+\beta)]^2 - 4\alpha\beta\theta(1+\theta)\}^{\frac{1}{2}}}{2(1+\theta)},$$

as may be seen from the fact that $-r_1$ and $-r_2$ are the roots of the quadratic in the denominator of the term on the right hand side of the expression for $\tilde{\phi}(z)$. Since

$$[\psi+\theta(\alpha+\beta)]^2 - 4\alpha\beta\theta(1+\theta) = \{\alpha(\theta+1-p) - \beta(\theta+p)\}^2 + 4\alpha\beta p(1-p) > 0$$

(check this result), it follows that r_1 and r_2 are real, distinct, and positive. Now,

$$\tilde{\phi}(z) = \frac{1}{z} - \frac{1}{(1+\theta)(r_2-r_1)}\{\frac{\psi-r_1}{z+r_1} + \frac{r_2-\psi}{z+r_2}\}$$

and so inversion of this expression yields

$$\phi(u) = 1 - \frac{1}{(1+\theta)(r_2-r_1)}\{(\psi-r_1)e^{-r_1 u} + (r_2-\psi)e^{-r_2 u}\}.$$

For more general claim amount distributions, the partial fraction technique may not work, and an alternative must be sought to calculate $\phi(u)$.

Theorem 11.5.1. An alternate expression for the probability of ultimate survival is

$$\phi(u) = \frac{\theta e^{u[\mu(1+\theta)]^{-1}}}{1+\theta}\{1 + \sum_{j=1}^{\infty} \frac{[-\mu(1+\theta)]^{-j}}{j!}h_j(u)\} \qquad (11.5.1)$$

where

$$h_j(u) = \int_0^u (u-x)^j e^{-x[\mu(1+\theta)]^{-1}} dF_X^{*j}(x). \qquad (11.5.2)$$

Proof

From (11.4.2), and (11.4.8), the Laplace transform of the probability of ultimate survival is

$$\tilde{\phi}(z) = \frac{1}{z}(\frac{\theta}{1+\theta})\{1 + \sum_{n=1}^{\infty} (\frac{1}{1+\theta})^n [\frac{1-L_X(z)}{\mu z}]^n\}$$

$$= \frac{1}{z}(\frac{\theta}{1+\theta})\{1 + \sum_{n=1}^{\infty}[(1+\theta)\mu z]^{-n}\sum_{j=0}^{n}\binom{n}{j}(-1)^{j}[L_X(z)]^{j}\}$$

$$= \frac{1}{z}(\frac{\theta}{1+\theta})\{1 + \sum_{n=1}^{\infty}[(1+\theta)\mu z]^{-n}(1 + \sum_{j=1}^{n}\binom{n}{j}(-1)^{j}[L_X(z)]^{j})\}$$

$$= \frac{1}{z}(\frac{\theta}{1+\theta})\{\sum_{n=0}^{\infty}[(1+\theta)\mu z]^{-n} + \sum_{n=1}^{\infty}[(1+\theta)\mu z]^{-n}\sum_{j=1}^{n}\binom{n}{j}(-1)^{j}[L_X(z)]^{j}\}$$

$$= \frac{1}{z}(\frac{\theta}{1+\theta})\{\frac{z}{z-[\mu(1+\theta)]^{-1}} + \sum_{j=1}^{\infty}\sum_{n=j}^{\infty}\binom{n}{j}[(1+\theta)\mu z]^{-n}(-1)^{j}[L_X(z)]^{j}\}$$

$$= \frac{\theta}{1+\theta}\{\frac{1}{z-[\mu(1+\theta)]^{-1}} + \sum_{j=1}^{\infty}\frac{[-\mu(1+\theta)]^{-j}}{j!}\sum_{n=j}^{\infty}\frac{[(1+\theta)\mu]^{-n+j}}{(n-j)!}\int_{0}^{\infty}(\frac{n!e^{-zx}}{z^{n+1}})dF_X^{*j}(x)\}$$

where we have used the notation

$$[L_X(z)]^{j} = \int_{0}^{\infty}e^{-zx}dF_X^{*j}(x)$$

for the Laplace transform of the sum of j claim amounts. Define the function

$$(u-x)_{+}^{n} = \begin{array}{ll} (u-x)^{n}, & u \geq x \\ 0, & u < x. \end{array}$$

Then the Laplace transform of $(u-x)_{+}^{n}$ is

$$\int_{0}^{\infty}e^{-zu}(u-x)_{+}^{n}du = \int_{x}^{\infty}e^{-zu}(u-x)^{n}du.$$

Making the change of variables $y = z(u-x)$, this becomes

$$\int_0^\infty e^{-y-zx}(\frac{y}{z})^n \frac{dy}{z} = \frac{e^{-zx}}{z^{n+1}}\int_0^\infty y^n e^{-y} dy = \frac{n!e^{-zx}}{z^{n+1}}.$$

The above expression for $\bar{\phi}(z)$ may then be inverted to give

$$\phi(u) = \frac{\theta}{1+\theta}\{e^{u[\mu(1+\theta)]^{-1}} + \sum_{j=1}^\infty \frac{[-\mu(1+\theta)]^{-j}}{j!} \sum_{n=j}^\infty \frac{[\mu(1+\theta)]^{-n+j}}{(n-j)!} \int_0^\infty (u-x)_+^n dF_X^{*j}(x)\}$$

$$= \frac{\theta}{1+\theta}\{e^{u[\mu(1+\theta)]^{-1}} + \sum_{j=1}^\infty \frac{[-\mu(1+\theta)]^{-j}}{j!} \int_0^u (u-x)^j (\sum_{n=j}^\infty \frac{[(u-x)\{\mu(1+\theta)\}^{-1}]^{n-j}}{(n-j)!}) dF_X^{*j}(x)\}$$

$$= \frac{\theta}{1+\theta}\{e^{u[\mu(1+\theta)]^{-1}} + \sum_{j=1}^\infty \frac{[-\mu(1+\theta)]^{-j}}{j!} \int_0^u (u-x)^j e^{(u-x)[\mu(1+\theta)]^{-1}} dF_X^{*j}(x)\},$$

and the theorem follows.

Theorem 11.5.1 may sometimes be used to derive a computational formula for the probability of ruin. This is the case for the following distributions.

Example 11.5.3. Gamma Claim Amounts

Suppose that

$$f_X(x) = \frac{\beta(\beta x)^{\alpha-1}e^{-\beta x}}{\Gamma(\alpha)}, \quad x>0.$$

Then $\mu = \alpha/\beta$ and $L_X(z) = \{\beta/(\beta+z)\}^{-\alpha}$. Thus

$$f_X^{*j}(x) = \frac{\beta(\beta x)^{j\alpha-1}e^{-\beta x}}{\Gamma(j\alpha)}, \quad x>0$$

and (11.5.2) becomes

$$h_j(u) = \int_0^u (u-x)^j e^{-\beta x/\alpha(1+\theta)} \frac{\beta(\beta x)^{j\alpha-1} e^{-\beta x}}{\Gamma(j\alpha)} dx.$$

Let $y = 1-x/u$ and so $x = u(1-y)$. Then

$$h_j(u) = \frac{\beta^{j\alpha}}{\Gamma(j\alpha)} \int_0^1 (uy)^j [u(1-y)]^{j\alpha-1} e^{-\beta u(1-y)[1+1/\alpha(1+\theta)]^{-1}} u\, dy$$

$$= \frac{\beta^{j\alpha} u^{j(\alpha+1)} e^{-\beta u[1+1/\alpha(1+\theta)]^{-1}}}{\Gamma(j\alpha)} \int_0^1 y^j (1-y)^{j\alpha-1} e^{\beta u[1+1/\alpha(1+\theta)]^{-1} y} dy.$$

In terms of the confluent hypergeometric function (see appendix A), this may be expressed as

$$h_j(u) = \frac{\beta^{j\alpha} u^{j(\alpha+1)} (j!) e^{-\beta u[1+1/\alpha(1+\theta)]^{-1}}}{\Gamma\{j(\alpha+1)+1\}} M\{j+1, j(\alpha+1)+1, \beta u[1+1/\alpha(1+\theta)]^{-1}\}$$

and (11.5.1) becomes

$$\phi(u) = \frac{\theta}{1+\theta} \{e^{\beta u[\alpha(1+\theta)]^{-1}} + e^{-\beta u} \sum_{j=1}^\infty \frac{[-(\beta u)^{\alpha+1}\{\alpha(1+\theta)\}^{-1}]^j}{\Gamma[j(\alpha+1)+1]} M[j+1, j(\alpha+1)+1, \beta u + \beta u\{\alpha(1+\theta)\}^{-1}]\}.$$

A finite number of terms in this expression may be used to evaluate $\phi(u)$. For numerical evaluation, one may write

$$\phi(u) = \frac{\theta}{1+\theta}\{e^{\beta u[\alpha(1+\theta)]^{-1}} + \sum_{j=1}^\infty (-1)^j b_j\}$$

where

$$\log b_j = j\{(\alpha+1)\log(\beta\mu) - \log\alpha - \log(1+\theta)\}$$

$$+ \log M\{j+1, j(\alpha+1)+1, u+u[\alpha(1+\theta)]^{-1}\}$$

$$- \log \Gamma\{j(\alpha+1)+1\} - \beta\mu.$$

Hence, one can compute this expression using the series expansion for $M(a,b,z)$ and then exponentiate (this avoids taking ratios of large numbers) until b_j is sufficiently small.

As a numerical illustration, suppose $\theta = .3$, $\alpha = 6.25$, $\beta = 3.75$, and $u = 4.50$. Then one obtains

j	b_j
1	5.3775365103
2	0.6037032418
3	0.010571542
4	0.0000318997
5	0.0000000208
6	0.0000000000

and so $\phi(4.50) = .73742417$. As a check, we note that $1-\phi(u) \sim .82459530\exp\{-.25430102u\}$, $u \to \infty$ (see example 11.6.1), which yields the approximation $\phi(4.50) \approx .73742464$.

Clearly, the approach is useful as long as the b_j's do not become excessively large, which is the case for βu small and α large.

As a second example, consider the situation with constant claim sizes.

Example 11.5.4. Constant Claim Amounts

If claim sizes are constant and equal to 1, then $\mu = 1$ and (11.5.2) becomes

$$h_j(u) = (u-j)_+^j e^{-j/(1+\theta)}$$

in the notation of Theorem 11.5.1, since the sum of j claims equals j. Hence (11.5.1) becomes

$$\phi(u) = \frac{\theta e^{u/(1+\theta)}}{1+\theta}\{1 + \sum_{j=1}^{[u]} \frac{[(j-u)(1+\theta)^{-1}e^{1/(1+\theta)}]^j}{j!}\}.$$

More generally, for discrete claim amounts one has the following result.

Example 11.5.5. Discrete Claim Amounts

If the claim size distribution is discrete on the positive integers with Laplace transform

$$L_X(z) = \sum_{x=1}^{\infty} f_X(x)e^{-zx},$$

then (11.5.2) becomes

$$h_j(u) = \sum_{k=0}^{[u]}(u-k)^j e^{-k[\mu(1+\theta)]^{-1}}f_X^{*j}(k)$$

where $[x]$ is the greatest integer function and $f_X^{*j}(x)$ the j-fold convolution of $f_X(x)$ with itself. Thus, (11.5.1) becomes

$$\phi(u) = \frac{\theta}{1+\theta}e^{u[\mu(1+\theta)]^{-1}}\{1 + \sum_{j=1}^{\infty}\frac{[-\mu(1+\theta)]^{-j}}{j!}\sum_{k=0}^{[u]}(u-k)^j e^{-k[\mu(1+\theta)]^{-1}}f_X^{*j}(k)\}$$

$$= \frac{\theta}{1+\theta}e^{u[\mu(1+\theta)]^{-1}}\{1 + \sum_{k=0}^{[u]}e^{-k[\mu(1+\theta)]^{-1}}\sum_{j=1}^{\infty}(\frac{k-u}{\mu(1+\theta)})^j\frac{f_X^{*j}(k)}{j!}\}.$$

With $f_X(0) = 0, f_X^{*j}(k) = 0$ if $j>k$ and one obtains

$$\phi(u) = \frac{\theta e^{u[\mu(1+\theta)]^{-1}}}{1+\theta}\{1 + \sum_{k=1}^{[u]}e^{-k[\mu(1+\theta)]^{-1}}\sum_{j=1}^{k}\frac{(\frac{k-u}{\mu(1+\theta)})^j}{j!}f_X^{*j}(k)\}.$$

We remark that Gerber (1988) has derived a similar expansion to (11.5.1).

It is difficult to obtain explicit expressions for $\phi(u)$ in many situations, but for a large family of claim amount distributions which are called phase type, queueing arguments yield tractable results (see Neuts, 1981). One simple such computational algorithm is given.

Example 11.5.6. Mixture of Erlang Claim Amounts

Suppose that the claim size pdf is given by

$$f_X(x) = \sum_{i=1}^{m} q_i \frac{\beta(\beta x)^{i-1} e^{-\beta x}}{(i-1)!}, \quad x > 0$$

where $\{q_1, q_2, \ldots, q_m\}$ is a probability distribution. We remark that when $m = 2$ an explicit formula for $\phi(u)$ is given in exercise 5. Then from Tijms (1986, p. 273), one has

$$\phi(u) = 1 - \sum_{j=1}^{\infty} f_j I(j, \beta u)$$

where $I(n, x)$ is the incomplete gamma function and the probability distribution $\{f_0, f_1, \ldots\}$ may be obtained recursively beginning with $f_0 = \theta/(1+\theta)$ from the formula

$$f_j = \frac{\lambda}{\beta} \sum_{k=(j-m)_+}^{j-1} (f_k \sum_{i=j-k}^{m} q_i); \quad j = 1, 2, 3, \ldots,$$

$(j-m)_+ = \max(0, j-m)$, and λ is the Poisson claim rate.

For more general claim amount distributions, direct inversion of (11.4.8) or evaluation via (11.4.9) is difficult (if not impossible), but we now demonstrate that $1 - \phi(u)$ satisfies a Volterra integral equation, and so $1 - \phi(u)$ may be obtained numerically from an equation of the form (1.3.12).

Theorem 11.5.2. The probability of ultimate ruin $1 - \phi(u)$ satisfies the Volterra type integral equation of the second kind,

$$1 - \phi(u) = \frac{\lambda}{c} \int_u^\infty [1-F_X(y)] dy + \frac{\lambda}{c} \int_0^u [1-F_X(u-y)][1-\phi(y)] dy. \qquad (11.5.3)$$

Proof

From (11.4.8) we have

$$\frac{1}{z} - \tilde{\phi}(z) = \frac{1-\{1-\theta^{-1}[L_{X_1}(z)-1]\}^{-1}}{z}$$

$$= \frac{1-\theta^{-1}[L_{X_1}(z)-1]-1}{z\{1-\theta^{-1}[L_{X_1}(z)-1]\}} = \frac{(1+\theta)^{-1}[\dfrac{1-L_{X_1}(z)}{z}]}{1-(1+\theta)^{-1}L_{X_1}(z)}.$$

Thus,

$$z^{-1}-\tilde{\phi}(z) = (1+\theta)^{-1}[z^{-1}-\tilde{\phi}(z)]L_{X_1}(z)+(1+\theta)^{-1}[\frac{1-L_{X_1}(z)}{z}].$$

The left side of the above equation is the Laplace transform of $1-\phi(u)$. The first term on the right side is the Laplace transform of the convolution of $1-\phi(u)$ and $f_{X_1}(u)$ multiplied by $(1+\theta)^{-1}$. By (1.3.6), example 1.3.2 with $n = 0$ and (11.4.3), $z^{-1}[1-L_{X_1}(z)]$ is the Laplace transform of

$$\int_u^\infty f_{X_1}(x) dx = \int_u^\infty \frac{1-F_X(x)}{\mu} dx$$

multiplied by $(1+\theta)^{-1}$. Thus, inversion yields (11.5.3) with the help of (11.2.1).

Equation (11.5.3) is of the form (1.3.12) with

$$h(x) = 1-\phi(x), \qquad (11.5.4)$$

$$J(x) = \frac{\lambda}{c} \int_x^\infty [1 - F_X(y)] dy, \qquad (11.5.5)$$

and

$$K(x,y) = \frac{\lambda}{c} [1 - F_X(x-y)]. \qquad (11.5.6)$$

Thus, in most situations, $\phi(u)$ cannot be obtained exactly but can be obtained numerically from equation (11.5.3). Techniques for the numerical solution of this type of equation are given in appendix D. Hence, one may obtain ultimate survival probabilities in the same way as one can obtain the pdf of many compound distributions.

11.6 ASYMPTOTIC RESULTS

It was shown in Theorem 11.4.4 that the ultimate survival probability $\phi(u)$ is the cdf of a compound geometric variate. Hence, we may apply the results of sections 10.2 and 10.3 to obtain approximate formulas for $\phi(u)$ for large u. These may be used in place of or in addition to the results of section 11.5.

Consider first the situation where there exists $\kappa > 0$ satisfying (11.3.1). Using (11.4.2), this may be rewritten as

$$1 + \theta = L_Y(-\kappa). \qquad (11.6.1)$$

If κ exists, then by Theorem 11.4.4 and (11.2.8), we have the asymptotic formula

$$1 - \phi(u) \sim -\frac{\theta e^{-\kappa u}}{\kappa L_Y'(-\kappa)}, \quad u \to \infty. \qquad (11.6.2)$$

Differentiating (11.4.2) with respect to z, substituting in $-\kappa$, and using (11.3.1) yields the alternate form

$$1-\phi(u) \sim -\frac{\theta\mu e^{-\kappa u}}{L_X'(-\kappa)+\mu(1+\theta)}, \quad u \to \infty. \tag{11.6.3}$$

Formula (11.6.3) is referred to as **Cramer's asymptotic ruin formula.**

Example 11.6.1. Gamma Claim Amounts

For gamma claim amounts, with

$$L_X(z) = (\frac{\beta}{\beta+z})^\alpha,$$

it is clear from (11.3.1) that $\kappa > 0$ is the positive solution $(\kappa < \beta)$ to

$$H(\kappa) = 1+(1+\theta)\frac{\alpha}{\beta}\kappa - L_X(-\kappa) = 0.$$

Then

$$L_X'(z) = -\frac{\alpha}{\beta}(\frac{\beta}{\beta+z})^{\alpha+1}$$

and (11.6.3) becomes

$$1-\phi(u) \sim \frac{\theta}{(1-\frac{\kappa}{\beta})^{-\alpha-1}-(1+\theta)}e^{-\kappa u}, \quad u \to \infty.$$

In example 11.3.2, with $\theta = .2$, $\alpha = 25$, and $\beta = 10$ it was found that $\kappa = .13560$. In this case, one obtains

$$1-\phi(u) \sim .88447e^{-.13560u}, \quad u \to \infty.$$

If an adjustment coefficient exists then one has the asymptotic formula (11.6.3) and the inequality (11.3.7) for the probability of ruin. It is easily seen that for light tailed claim amount distributions (see section 11.3) such as the gamma or the exponential, one can always find κ satisfying (11.6.1). For the heavy-tailed subexponential distributions such as the lognormal or Pareto, however, (11.6.1) is never satisfied.

Asymptotic formulae are obtainable for the subexponential distributions, however. Embrechts and Veraverbeke (1982) have shown that

$$1-\phi(x) \sim \frac{\int_x^\infty [1-F_X(y)]dy}{\theta\mu}, \quad x \to \infty. \tag{11.6.4}$$

Formula (11.6.4) is the general asymptotic formula for the probability of ruin with subexponential claim amounts. Some examples are now given.

Example 11.6.2. The Transformed Beta Distribution

From example 4.14.6, we have

$$\mu = \lambda_1^{\frac{1}{c}} \frac{\Gamma(\alpha-\frac{1}{c})\Gamma(\beta+\frac{1}{c})}{\Gamma(\alpha)\Gamma(\beta)}, \quad c\alpha-1>0$$

where λ_1 is a claim amount parameter (to be distinguished from the Poisson parameter λ). Also, we have

$$\lim_{x \to \infty} \frac{\int_x^\infty [1-F_X(y)]dy}{x^{-c\alpha+1}} = \lim_{x \to \infty} \frac{-[1-F_X(x)]}{-(c\alpha-1)x^{-c\alpha}} = \frac{\lambda_1^\alpha \Gamma(\alpha+\beta)}{\Gamma(\alpha+1)\Gamma(\beta)}$$

by L'Hopital's rule and example 11.3.1. Hence (11.6.4) yields

$$1-\phi(x) \sim \frac{\lambda_1^{\alpha-\frac{1}{c}}\Gamma(\alpha+\beta)}{\theta\alpha(c\alpha-1)\Gamma(\alpha-\frac{1}{c})\Gamma(\beta+\frac{1}{c})}x^{-c\alpha+1}, \quad x \to \infty. \tag{11.6.5}$$

The corresponding formulae for the **Pareto** $(c = 1, \beta = 1)$, the **Burr** $(\beta = 1)$, the **generalized Pareto** $(c = 1)$, and the **log-logistic** $(\beta = 1, \alpha = 1)$ are the respective special cases of (11.6.5).

Example 11.6.3. The Lognormal Distribution

From formula (4.11.3) with $k = 1$, we obtain the mean $e^{\mu+\frac{\sigma^2}{2}}$. (Note that in this example, μ does not represent the mean.) Using (11.6.4) and example 11.3.2 and a similar argument to that of the previous example yields

$$1-\phi(x) \sim \frac{\sigma^3 e^{-\mu-\frac{\sigma^2}{2}}}{\theta(2\pi)^{\frac{1}{2}}}\frac{x}{(\log x-\mu)^2}e^{-\frac{1}{2}(\frac{\log x-\mu}{\sigma})^2}, \quad x \to \infty. \tag{11.6.6}$$

Asymptotic ultimate ruin probabilities for subexponential distributions are largely determined by the probability of one large claim.

For medium tailed distributions, we note that if $L_X(z)$ exists for all $z \geq -\gamma$ where $\gamma > 0$ and $L_X(-\gamma) < \infty$ (see section 11.3), then from (11.4.2), $L_Y(-\gamma) < \infty$ and $L_Y(z)$ also exists for all $z \geq -\gamma$. Thus there will be a value $\kappa > 0$ satisfying (11.6.1) if $L_Y(-\gamma) \geq 1+\theta$. If $L_Y(-\gamma) < 1+\theta$, no such κ exists and so (11.6.3) does not hold. In this case, however, Embrechts and Veraverbeke (1982) have shown that

$$1-\phi(x) \sim \frac{\theta\gamma\mu}{[1+(1+\theta)\gamma\mu-L_X(-\gamma)]^2}[1-F_X(x)], \quad x \to \infty. \tag{11.6.7}$$

Example 11.6.4. The Inverse Gaussian Distribution

For the medium-tailed inverse Gaussian distribution, (see section 4.13 and example

11.3.3) we have $\gamma = (2\beta)^{-1}$ from (4.13.3). Also, $L_X(-\gamma) = e^{\mu\beta^{-1}}$. Thus, (11.6.3) becomes

$$1-\phi(x) \sim \frac{\theta\mu e^{-\kappa x}}{\mu(1-2\beta\kappa)^{-\frac{1}{2}}[1+(1+\theta)\kappa\mu]-\mu(1+\theta)}, \quad x \to \infty \qquad (11.6.8)$$

if $2\beta(e^{\mu\beta^{-1}}-1) \geq \mu(1+\theta)$. In this case κ is the positive solution of equation (11.3.1), which in this case becomes

$$1+(1+\theta)\kappa\mu = e^{\mu\beta^{-1}[1-(1-2\beta\kappa)^{\frac{1}{2}}]}. \qquad (11.6.9)$$

Note that if $2\beta(e^{\mu\beta^{-1}}-1) = \mu(1+\theta)$, then $\kappa = (2\beta)^{-1}$ and (11.6.8) becomes $\lim_{x \to \infty} e^{\frac{x}{2\beta}}[1-\phi(x)] = 0$. If $2\beta(e^{\mu\beta^{-1}}-1) < \mu(1+\theta)$, we may use (11.6.7) and (11.3.16) to obtain

$$1-\phi(x) \sim \frac{\theta\mu^2 e^{\mu\beta^{-1}}(2\beta)^{\frac{3}{2}}}{(\pi)^{\frac{1}{2}}[(1+\theta)\mu-2\beta(e^{\mu\beta^{-1}}-1)]^2} x^{-\frac{3}{2}} e^{-\frac{x}{2\beta}}, \quad x \to \infty. \qquad (11.6.10)$$

11.7 RUIN OVER A FINITE INTERVAL

We now consider the situation where we are interested in the probability that the insurer's surplus $U(t)$ as defined by (11.2.2) remains non-negative for a finite period rather than permanently. Thus we define

$$\phi(u,t) = Pr\{U(s) \geq 0, 0 < s < t\}. \qquad (11.7.1)$$

Alternatively, in terms of the time to ruin T as defined by (11.2.3), we have

$$\phi(u,t) = Pr\{T > t\}. \tag{11.7.2}$$

As in section 11.2, we assume that the number of claims process $\{N(t); t \geq 0\}$ is a Poisson process (section 3.3) with rate λ and consequently the total claims process $\{S(t); t \geq 0\}$ is a compound Poisson process. Premiums are payable at rate c per unit time where c is defined by (11.2.1).

We now derive the analogous equation to (11.4.1) satisfied by $\phi(u,t)$.

Theorem 11.7.1. The probability of survival to time t beginning with initial reserve u satisfies the partial integro-differential equation

$$\frac{\partial}{\partial t}\phi(u,t) = c\frac{\partial}{\partial u}\phi(u,t) - \lambda\phi(u,t) + \lambda\int_0^u \phi(u-x,t)dF_X(x). \tag{11.7.3}$$

Proof

Consider the first h units of time. If no claim occurs then survival occurs beyond time $t+h$ with probability $\phi(u+ch,t)$ since $\{S(t); t \geq 0\}$ and hence $\{U(t); t \geq 0\}$ has stationary and independent increments. If a claim does occur for an amount x less than $u+ch$ then survival to time $t+h$ occurs with probability $\phi(u+ch-x,t)$. Since the number of claims process is a Poisson process, the probability of non-ruin over the interval $(0,t+h)$ thus satisfies

$$\phi(u,t+h) = (1-\lambda h)\phi(u+ch,t) + \lambda h\int_0^{u+ch}\phi(u+ch-x,t)dF_X(x) + o(h).$$

Rewriting this as

$$\frac{\phi(u,t+h)-\phi(u,t)}{h} = c\frac{\phi(u+ch,t)-\phi(u,t)}{ch} - \lambda\phi(u+ch,t)$$

$$+ \lambda\int_0^{u+ch}\phi(u+ch-x,t)dF_X(x) + \frac{o(h)}{h}$$

and letting $h \to 0$ yields (11.7.3).

The solution to (11.7.3) is quite complicated, and we will find it expedient to derive an explicit expression for the bivariate Laplace transform (section 1.3) of $\phi(u,t)$, namely

$$\bar{\phi}(z_1,z_2) = \int_0^\infty\int_0^\infty e^{-z_1 u - z_2 t}\phi(u,t)du dt. \qquad (11.7.4)$$

This Laplace transform will be used to derive computational formulae for $\phi(u,t)$. We also define the Laplace transform of $\phi(0,t)$ to be

$$\bar{\phi}_0(z) = \int_0^\infty e^{-zt}\phi(0,t)dt. \qquad (11.7.5)$$

We have the following lemma.

Lemma 11.7.1. The Laplace transforms $\bar{\phi}(z_1,z_2)$ and $\bar{\phi}_0(z)$ satisfy the relation

$$\bar{\phi}(z_1,z_2)[z_2+\lambda-cz_1-\lambda L_X(z_1)] = \frac{1}{z_1} - c\bar{\phi}_0(z_2). \qquad (11.7.6)$$

Proof

Define

$$\bar{\phi}_1(z,t) = \int_0^\infty e^{-zu}\phi(u,t)du.$$

Using (1.3.5), (1.3.11), and (1.3.10), we may take the Laplace transform of (11.7.3) with respect to u to obtain

$$\frac{\partial}{\partial t}\bar{\phi}_1(z_1,t) = c[z_1\bar{\phi}_1(z_1,t) - \phi(0,t)] - \lambda\bar{\phi}_1(z_1,t) + \lambda\bar{\phi}_1(z_1,t)L_X(z_1).$$

Taking Laplace transforms of the above equation with respect to t and noting that

$$\bar{\phi}(z_1,z_2) = \int_0^\infty e^{-z_2 t}\,\bar{\phi}_1(z_1,t)dt,$$

we obtain

$$z_2\bar{\phi}(z_1,z_2) - \bar{\phi}_1(z_1,0) = cz_1\bar{\phi}(z_1,z_2) - c\bar{\phi}_0(z_2) - \lambda\bar{\phi}(z_1,z_2) + \lambda\bar{\phi}(z_1,z_2)L_X(z_1).$$

Since, $\phi(u,0) = 1$ for $u \geq 0$, it follows that $\bar{\phi}_1(z_1,0) = z_1^{-1}$. Substituting into the above equation and rearrangement yields (11.7.6).

We are now in a position to obtain an explicit expression for $\bar{\phi}_0(z)$ as defined by (11.7.5).

Theorem 11.7.2. The Laplace transform $\bar{\phi}_0(z)$ is given by

$$\bar{\phi}_0(z) = \frac{1}{cr(z)} \tag{11.7.7}$$

where $r(z)$ is the unique root of the equation

$$z + \lambda - cr(z) = \lambda L_X[r(z)] \tag{11.7.8}$$

for fixed z with $\text{Re}(z) > 0$.

Proof

Consider, for fixed real $z > 0$, the functions

$$y_1(r) = z + \lambda - cr,$$

$$y_2(r) = \lambda L_X(r).$$

Now, $y_1(0) = z + \lambda$ and $y_1'(r) = -c < 0$ by (11.2.1). Also, $y_2(0) = \lambda < y_1(0)$, $y_2'(r) < 0$ for $r > 0$, and $y_2''(r) > 0$ for $r > 0$. Thus the graphs of y_1 and y_2 are given in figure 11.7.1. It is easily seen from the graph that there is exactly one value of r, say $r(z)$, which satisfies $y_1(r) = y_2(r)$. This also follows from the intermediate value theorem since $y_1(r)$ and $y_2(r)$ and hence $h(r) = y_1(r) - y_2(r)$ are continuous for $r > 0$. Since $h(0) = z > 0$ and $h(\frac{z+\lambda}{c}) = -y_2(\frac{z+\lambda}{c}) < 0$, it follows that there is exactly one such r. Thus choosing $z = z_2$ and substituting $z_1 = r(z_2)$ into (11.7.6), it follows from (11.7.8) that the second factor on the left hand side of (11.7.6) is 0, and so the result follows by noting that the right side is also 0.

FIGURE 11.7.1

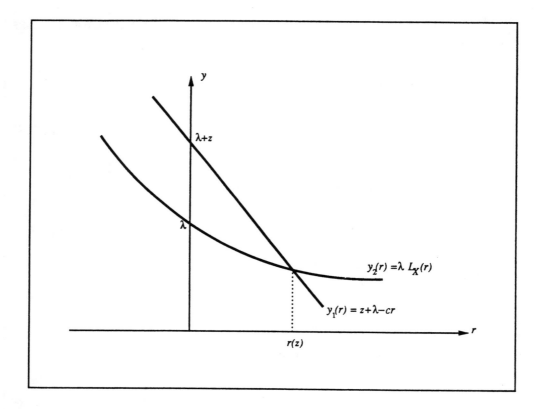

The above analysis assumes that z_1 and z_2 are both real. More generally, for complex z_1 and z_2, Benes (1957) has shown that there is a unique root $r(z)$ of (11.7.8) for Re$(z) > 0$, and so (11.7.7) holds for z with Re$(z) > 0$.

Before finding the bivariate Laplace transform (11.7.4) of the survival probability $\phi(u,t)$, it is desirable first, however, to obtain an explicit formula for $\phi(0,t)$ by inverting the Laplace transform $\bar{\phi}_0(z)$ defined in theorem 11.7.2. We need the following lemma.

Lemma 11.7.2. If $f(z)$ is analytic in and on a contour surrounding the point $\frac{z+\lambda}{c}$, then

$$f[r(z)] = f(\frac{z+\lambda}{c}) + \sum_{n=1}^{\infty} \frac{(-\frac{\lambda}{c})^n}{n!} \frac{d^{n-1}}{dy^{n-1}} \{f'(y)[L_X(y)]^n\} \Bigg|_{y = \frac{z+\lambda}{c}} \qquad (11.7.9)$$

where $r(z)$ is defined by (11.7.8).

Proof

Rewrite (11.7.8) as

$$r(z) = \frac{z+\lambda}{c} - \frac{\lambda}{c} L_X[r(z)].$$

Benes (1957) demonstrates that there exists a contour surrounding $\frac{z+\lambda}{c}$ for which the inequality

$$\left| \frac{\lambda}{c} L_X(z_1) \right| < \left| z_1 - \frac{\lambda+z}{c} \right|$$

is satisfied for all z_1 on the perimeter. Hence one may apply Lagrange's theorem (Whittaker and Watson, 1927) to obtain (11.7.9).

The above lemma may be used to obtain an explicit solution to (11.7.8).

Corollary 11.7.1. The solution $r(z)$ to (11.7.8) is given by

$$r(z) = \frac{z+\lambda}{c} + \sum_{n=1}^{\infty} \frac{(-\frac{\lambda}{c})^n}{n!} \frac{d^{n-1}}{dy^{n-1}} \{[L_X(y)]^n\} \Bigg|_{y=\frac{z+\lambda}{c}} . \qquad (11.7.10)$$

Proof

Substitution of $f(z) = z$ into (11.7.9) yields (11.7.10).

We may also use lemma 11.7.2 to obtain an explicit formula for $\phi(0,t)$.

Theorem 11.7.3. The probability of survival to time t with no initial reserve $\phi(0,t)$ is given by

$$\phi(0,t) = \frac{1}{ct} \int_0^{ct} F(y,t) dy \qquad (11.7.11)$$

where

$$F(y,t) = \sum_{n=0}^{\infty} \frac{(\lambda t)^n e^{-\lambda t}}{n!} F_X^{*n}(y) \qquad (11.7.12)$$

is the df of $S(t)$, the total claims in $(0,t]$.

Proof

By Lemma 11.7.2 with $f(z) = (cz)^{-1}$, we have from (11.7.7)

$$\tilde{\phi}_0(z) = \frac{1}{z+\lambda} - \sum_{n=1}^{\infty} \frac{(-\frac{\lambda}{c})^n}{n!} \frac{d^{n-1}}{dx^{n-1}} \left\{ \frac{[L_X(x)]^n}{cx^2} \right\} \Bigg|_{x=\frac{z+\lambda}{c}}$$

$$= \frac{1}{z+\lambda} - \sum_{n=1}^{\infty} \frac{(-\lambda)^n}{n!} \frac{d^{n-1}}{dz^{n-1}} \left\{ [L_X(\frac{z+\lambda}{c})]^n (z+\lambda)^{-2} \right\}.$$

Now, by applying (1.3.6) twice, followed by (1.3.4), (1.3.2), and (1.3.8) in succession to $f_X^{*n}(y)$, we find that the Laplace transform of

$$h_n(t) = t^{n-1} e^{-\lambda t} \int_0^{ct} F_X^{*n}(y) dy \qquad (11.7.13)$$

is (we leave the details to the reader)

$$\tilde{h}_n(z) = c(-1)^{n-1} \frac{d^{n-1}}{dz^{n-1}} \left\{ [L_X(\frac{z+\lambda}{c})]^n (z+\lambda)^{-2} \right\}. \qquad (11.7.14)$$

Thus,

$$\tilde{\phi}_0(z) = \frac{1}{z+\lambda} + \frac{1}{c} \sum_{n=1}^{\infty} \frac{\lambda^n}{n!} \tilde{h}_n(z).$$

We may invert this latter expression to obtain

$$\phi(0,t) = e^{-\lambda t} + \frac{1}{c} \sum_{n=1}^{\infty} \frac{\lambda^n}{n!} t^{n-1} e^{-\lambda t} \int_0^{ct} F_X^{*n}(y) dy$$

$$= \frac{1}{ct}\int_0^{ct}\left\{e^{-\lambda t} + \sum_{n=1}^{\infty}\frac{(\lambda t)^n e^{-\lambda t}}{n!}F_X^{*n}(y)\right\}dy$$

since all terms are non-negative. Noticing that the integrand is (11.7.12) gives (11.7.11).

To obtain $\phi(0,t)$, one may obtain (11.7.12) using the recursive techniques outlined in chapters 6 and 10 and then obtain (11.7.11) numerically, (numerical integration will normally be required).

To obtain the survival probabilities $\phi(u,t)$ for arbitrary $u>0$, we shall derive the bivariate Laplace transform (11.7.4).

Theorem 11.7.4. The bivariate Laplace transform $\tilde{\phi}(z_1,z_2)$ of $\phi(u,t)$ as defined by (11.7.4) is given by

$$\tilde{\phi}(z_1,z_2) = \frac{\frac{1}{z_1} - c\tilde{\phi}_0(z_k)}{z_2+\lambda-cz_1-\lambda L_X(z_1)} \qquad (11.7.15)$$

where $r(z_2)$ satisfies (11.7.8).

Proof

Substitution of (11.7.7) into (11.7.6) and solving for $\tilde{\phi}(z_1,z_2)$ yields (11.7.15).

We may now invert (11.7.15) to obtain $\phi(u,t)$.

Theorem 11.7.5. The survival probabilities $\phi(u,t)$ are given by

$$\phi(u,t) = F(u+ct,t) - c\int_0^t \phi(0,x)f[u+c(t-x),t-x]dx, \quad u\geq 0 \qquad (11.7.16)$$

where

$$f(x,t) = \frac{\partial}{\partial x} F(x,t), \quad x > 0 \qquad (11.7.17)$$

is the pdf of the total claims in the time interval $(0,t]$.

Proof

Defining $\bar{\phi}_1(z,t)$ as in the proof of lemma 11.7.1, we may take the inverse with respect to z_2 of (11.7.15) to obtain

$$\bar{\phi}_1(z_1,t) = \frac{e^{ctz_1 + \lambda t[L_X(z_1)-1]}}{z_1} - c\int_0^t \phi(0,t-\tau)e^{c\tau z_1 + \lambda \tau[L_X(z_1)-1]} d\tau. \qquad (11.7.18)$$

Multiplication of (11.7.18) by e^{-ctz_1} yields, using (1.3.6),

$$e^{-ctz_1}\int_0^\infty e^{-z_1 x}\phi(x,t)dx = \int_0^\infty e^{-z_1 u}F(u,t)du$$

$$- c\int_0^t \phi(0,t-\tau)e^{-cz_1(t-\tau)}\left\{e^{\lambda\tau[L_X(z_1)-1]} - e^{-\lambda\tau} + e^{-\lambda\tau}\right\}d\tau.$$

If one makes the change of variables $u = x+ct$ in the first integral and notes that the Laplace transform of $f(x,\tau)$ given by (11.7.17) is $e^{\lambda\tau[L_X(z_1)-1]} - e^{-\lambda\tau}$, one obtains

$$\int_{ct}^\infty e^{-z_1 u}\phi(u-ct,t)du = \int_0^\infty e^{-z_1 u}F(u,t)du$$

$$- c\int_0^t e^{-c(t-\tau)z_1}e^{-\lambda\tau}\phi(0,t-\tau)d\tau$$

$$- c\int_0^t \phi(0,t-\tau)\int_0^\infty e^{-\{x+c(t-\tau)\}z_1}f(x,\tau)dx\,d\tau.$$

Now making the change of variables from τ to $u = c(t-\tau)$ in the second last integral and from x to $u = x+c(t-\tau)$ in the last integral, one finds that

$$\int_{ct}^{\infty}e^{-z_1 u}\phi(u-ct,t)du = \int_0^{\infty}e^{-z_1 u}F(u,t)du - \int_0^{ct}e^{-z_1 u}e^{-\lambda t+\lambda\frac{u}{c}}\phi(0,\frac{u}{c})du$$

$$-c\int_0^t\phi(0,t-\tau)\int_{c(t-\tau)}^{\infty}e^{-z_1 u}f\{u-c(t-\tau),\tau\}du\;d\tau.$$

The double integral may be split into two portions, yielding

$$\int_{ct}^{\infty}e^{-z_1 u}\phi(u-ct,t)du = \int_0^{\infty}e^{-z_1 u}F(u,t)du - \int_0^{ct}e^{-z_1 u}e^{-\lambda t+\lambda\frac{u}{c}}\phi(0,\frac{u}{c})du$$

$$-c\int_0^t\int_{c(t-\tau)}^{ct}e^{-z_1 u}\phi(0,t-\tau)f\{u-c(t-\tau),\tau\}du\;d\tau$$

$$-c\int_0^t\int_{ct}^{\infty}e^{-z_1 u}\phi(0,t-\tau)f\{u-c(t-\tau),\tau\}du\;d\tau.$$

If one reverses the order of integration in the last two integrals, one obtains

$$\int_{ct}^{\infty}e^{-z_1 u}\phi(u-ct,t)du = \int_0^{\infty}e^{-z_1 u}F(u,t)du - \int_0^{ct}e^{-z_1 u}e^{-\lambda t+\lambda\frac{u}{c}}\phi(0,\frac{u}{c})du$$

$$-c\int_0^{ct}e^{-z_1 u}\int_{t-\frac{u}{c}}^{t}\phi(0,t-\tau)f\{u-c(t-\tau),\tau\}d\tau\;du$$

$$-c\int_{ct}^{\infty}e^{-z_1 u}\int_0^{t}\phi(0,t-\tau)f\{u-c(t-\tau),\tau\}d\tau\;du.$$

Thus, by the uniqueness of the Laplace transform, one finds that for $u>ct$

$$\phi(u-ct,t) = F(u,t) - c\int_0^t\phi(0,t-\tau)f\{u-c(t-\tau),\tau\}d\tau.$$

By replacing u by $u+ct$, one has for $u>0$

$$\phi(u,t) = F(u+ct,t) - c\int_0^t \phi(0,t-\tau)f\{u+c\tau,\tau\}d\tau$$

which yields (11.7.16) on replacement of τ by $x = t-\tau$.

Once one has obtained $\phi(0,t)$ from the results of Theorem 11.7.3, one can solve for $\phi(u,t)$ from (11.7.16) numerically. Seal (1978) has used this technique extensively.

11.8 BIBLIOGRAPHIC AND OTHER NOTES

Sundt (1984) discusses the adjustment coefficient for the more general renewal claim number process. The proof of Theorem (11.3.1) is taken from Gerber (1979, pp. 119-120). The Laplace transform approach to ruin theory follows that of Seal (1969, p. 120). Gerber (1979, pp. 125-128) interprets the ultimate survival probability $\phi(u)$ as the df of the "maximum aggregate loss" of an insurer. Panjer (1988) takes advantage of this idea in the compound Geometric formulation of ultimate survival. Example 11.5.2 and exercises 4 and 5 are taken from Tijms (1986, pp. 403-404). Theorem 11.5.1 is derived from Shiu (1988). The approximations of Section 11.6 are taken largely from Embrechts and Veraverbeke (1982). Beekman and Bowers (1972) and Tijms (1986, p. 60) suggest approximations to ruin by the use of gamma functions and mixtures of exponentials respectively. Other approximations are discussed by Asmussen (1987, pp. 283-287) and Kremer (1987). Exercise 8 is taken from Gerber, Goovaerts, and Kaas (1987).

The approach to finite ruin follows Seal (1974) and Takács (1962, pp. 55-56). Seal (1978) discusses the numerical solution of (11.7.16) in some detail.

There is a close connection between ruin theory and queueing theory which has proved fruitful to both disciplines. Asmussen (1987, pp. 281-287) identifies this connection and suggests several queueing theoretic diffusion approximations to ruin probabilities.

Exercise 3 is taken from Gerber (1979, p. 113). This reference provides a more advanced treatment of ruin theory. A simpler reference is Bowers et al. (1987). See also Sundt (1984), Beard et al. (1984), Seal (1969), and Seal (1978). Models similar to those in exercises 4, 5 and 6 are considered by Panjer and Doray (1988).

In some instances it is desirable to generalize the assumption of a Poisson process for the number of claims. It is easily seen that all the results in the chapter hold for a compound Poisson claim number process (section 3.7) by simply letting the claim severity random variable X be itself a compound variate with Laplace transform

$$L_X(z) = \sum_{n=1}^{\infty} q_n [L_Y(z)]^n \qquad (11.8.1)$$

for some absolutely continuous non-negative variate Y. If, in addition, one chooses $\{q_n; n = 1,2,3,...\}$ to be members of the $(a,b,1)$ class (section 7.2), then the resulting distribution for $N(t)$ is discussed in detail in chapter 7. Clearly, computation of the pdf for the distribution with Laplace transform (11.8.1) is greatly simplified in this case.

Prabhu (1961) demonstrates that (11.7.16) holds if $\{S(t); t\geq 0\}$ has stationary and independent increments (section 3.2). Many results have been derived assuming that $\{N(t); t\geq 0\}$ is a renewal process. Thorin (1982) considers this model. Embrechts and Veraverbeke (1982) derive asymptotic formulae for ultimate ruin probabilities in this case.

EXERCISES

1. Show, using (11.7.10) or otherwise, that if claim sizes are exponential with mean β^{-1} then the solution to (11.7.8) is

$$r(z) = \frac{1}{2}(\frac{z+\lambda}{c}) - \frac{1}{2}\beta + \frac{1}{2}\{[\beta - (\frac{z+\lambda}{c})]^2 + \frac{4\beta z}{c}\}^{\frac{1}{2}}.$$

2. **The Loggamma Distribution**

    Show, using exercise 11.4, that the asymptotic expression for the probability of infinite ruin for the loggamma distribution is

$$1 - \phi(x) \sim \frac{(\lambda-1)^{\alpha-1}}{\theta\lambda\Gamma(\alpha)} x^{-\lambda+1}(\log x)^{\alpha-1}, \quad x \to \infty.$$

3. **Survival With no Initial Reserve**

   (a) Show that (11.7.11) may be rewritten as

   $$\phi(0,t) = \frac{\theta}{1+\theta} + \frac{1}{ct}\int_{ct}^{\infty}\{1-F(y,t)\}dy.$$

   (b) Show that

   $$1-F(y,t) \le \frac{\lambda\mu_2' t}{(y-\lambda\mu t)^2}.$$

   Hint, note that $E\{S(t)\} = \lambda\mu t$, $Var\{S(t)\} = \lambda\mu_2' t$, and show that

   $$1-F(y,t) = Pr\{S(t)-\lambda\mu t > y-\lambda\mu t\} \le Pr\{|S(t)-\lambda\mu t| > y-\lambda\mu t\}.$$

   Then use Chebyshev's inequality.

   (c) Use (a) and (b) to prove that

   $$\phi(0) = \lim_{t \to \infty} \phi(0,t) = \frac{\theta}{1+\theta}.$$

4. **A Mixture of Two Erlang Distributions**

   Suppose that the single claim amount distribution has pdf

   $$f_X(x) = \{p\beta+(1-p)\beta^2 x\}e^{-\beta x}, \quad x>0$$

   and Laplace transform

$$L_X(z) = p(\frac{\beta}{\beta+z}) + (1-p)(\frac{\beta}{\beta+z})^2, \quad z > -\beta.$$

(a) Find the mean μ and show that the Laplace transform of the distribution of Y given by (11.4.2)

$$L_Y(z) = p_1(\frac{\beta}{\beta+z}) + (1-p_1)(\frac{\beta}{\beta+z})^2, \quad z > -\beta,$$

where $p_1 = (2-p)^{-1}$. Hence find the associated pdf $f_Y(x)$.

(b) Show that the equation satisfied by the adjustment coefficient is

$$(1+\theta)\kappa^2 - \beta[2(1+\theta)-p_1]\kappa + \theta\beta^2 = 0.$$

Prove that the larger of the two roots is

$$\kappa_1 = \beta\{1 + \frac{[4(1+\theta)(1-p_1)+p_1^2]^{\frac{1}{2}}-p_1}{2(1+\theta)}\}.$$

Use this representation for κ_1 to prove that κ_1 cannot be the adjustment coefficient, and hence that the smaller root is the adjustment coefficient, namely

$$\kappa = \beta\{1 - \frac{[4(1+\theta)(1-p_1)+p_1^2]^{\frac{1}{2}}+p_1}{2(1+\theta)}\}.$$

(c) Prove that the Laplace transform of the probability of ultimate survival is given by

$$\tilde{\phi}(z) = \frac{1}{z} - \frac{z+\beta(2-p_1)}{(1+\theta)z^2+\beta[2(1+\theta)-p_1]z+\theta\beta^2}.$$

(d) Show that (c) may be reexpressed as

$$\tilde{\phi}(z) = \frac{1}{z} - \frac{1}{(1+\theta)(\kappa_1-\kappa)}\{\frac{\beta(2-p_1)-\kappa}{z+\kappa} + \frac{\kappa_1-\beta(2-p_1)}{z+\kappa_1}\}.$$

(e) Prove that the probability of ultimate survival is given by

$$\phi(u) = 1 - \frac{1}{(1+\theta)(\kappa_1-\kappa)}\{[\beta(2-p_1)-\kappa]e^{-\kappa u} + [\kappa_1-\beta(2-p_1)]e^{-\kappa_1 u}\}, \quad u>0.$$

5. Mixed Exponential Claim Amounts

In example 11.5.2, show that the adjustment coefficient satisfies the equation

$$(1+\theta)\kappa^2-[\psi+\theta(\alpha+\beta)]\kappa+\alpha\beta\theta = 0.$$

Hence show that the roots of this equation are r_1 and r_2 but r_1 is the adjustment coefficient. (Hint: $L_X(z)$ is defined for $z>\max(-\alpha,-\beta)$ and so $\kappa<\min(\alpha,\beta)$).

6. The Sum of Two Exponentials

Suppose that the single claim amount random variable is the sum of two exponentials with parameters α and β where $\alpha<\beta$. The pdf is thus

$$f_X(x) = \int_0^x \alpha e^{-\alpha y}\beta e^{-\beta(x-y)}dy, \quad x>0.$$

(a) Show that

$$f_X(x) = (\frac{\beta}{\beta-\alpha})\alpha e^{-\alpha x} + (\frac{\alpha}{\alpha-\beta})\beta e^{-\beta x}, \quad x>0.$$

(b) Prove that the distribution of Y given by (11.4.2) is

$$f_Y(x) = p\alpha e^{-\alpha x} + (1-p)\beta e^{-\beta x}$$

where $p = \beta^2/(\beta^2-\alpha^2)>1$.

(c) Hence, show that the probability of ruin is as given in example 11.5.2, where r_1 and r_2 are real, distinct, and positive. Hint: show that

$$\{\psi+\theta(\alpha+\beta)\}^2 - 4\alpha\beta\theta(1+\theta) = \{\alpha(\theta+1-p)-\beta(\theta-p)\}^2 + 4\beta\theta p(\beta-\alpha).$$

7. Continuous Uniform Claim Sizes

Suppose that

$$f_X(x) = \beta^{-1}, \quad 0<x<\beta.$$

Show that

$$f_X^{*j}(x) = \frac{\beta^{-j}}{(j-1)!} \sum_{m=0}^{j} \binom{j}{m}(-1)^m (x-\beta m)_+^{j-1}$$

in the notation of the proof of Theorem 11.5.1. Then show that (11.5.2) becomes

$$h_j(u) = \{\beta^j e^{2u/\beta(1+\theta)} \begin{bmatrix} 2j \\ j \end{bmatrix} \}^{-1} \sum_{m=0}^{j} \frac{(-1)^m}{m!(j-m)!} (u-\beta m)_+^{2j} M\{j+1,2j+1,2(x-\beta m)/\beta(1+\theta)\}.$$

8. The Severity of Ruin

Let $g(u,y)dy$ be the probability that ruin occurs (beginning with initial reserve u), and the deficit (negative reserve) at the time of ruin is between y and $y+dy$.

(a) Prove that

$$\phi(u) = 1 - \int_0^\infty g(u,y)dy$$

(b) Define

$$\bar{g}(s,y) = \int_0^\infty e^{-su} g(u,y)du.$$

Using the fact that

$$\bar{g}(s,y) = \frac{1}{\mu\theta}\{e^{sy}\int_y^\infty e^{-sx}(1-F_X(x))dx\}\{1 - \frac{1}{\theta}[L_Y(s)-1]\}^{-1},$$

where Y is given by (11.4.2), prove that

$$g(u,y) = \frac{1}{\mu\theta}(\phi(u)\{1-F_X(y)\} - \int_0^u \phi(u-x)d_x F_X(x+y)).$$

(c) Use b) to find $g(u,y)$ when the claim size distribution is exponential (example 11.5.1), mixed exponential (example 11.5.2), and discrete (example 11.5.5).

(d) Prove that

$$g(u,y) \sim \frac{\int\limits_0^\infty e^{\kappa x} \{ \frac{1-F_X(x+y)}{\mu} \} dx}{-L_Y'(-\kappa)} e^{-\kappa u}, \quad u \to \infty.$$

APPENDIX A

THE GAMMA AND INCOMPLETE GAMMA FUNCTIONS

Some useful properties of the gamma function are summarized here. More detailed discussions are given in Abramowitz and Stegun (1965).

The **gamma function** is defined as

$$\Gamma(x) = \int_0^\infty t^{x-1} e^{-t} dt, \quad x>0. \tag{A1}$$

It is easily shown that

$$\Gamma(x+1) = x\Gamma(x), \tag{A2}$$

from which it follows that, for r a positive integer,

$$\Gamma(x+r) = \{\prod_{n=0}^{r-1} (x+n)\}\Gamma(x), \tag{A3}$$

and for x a positive integer,

$$\Gamma(x+1) = x! \tag{A4}$$

It can also be shown that

$$\Gamma(\tfrac{1}{2}) = \sqrt{\pi}. \tag{A5}$$

Also, for large x, it follows that

$$\Gamma(x) \sim \sqrt{2\pi} e^{-x} x^{x-\frac{1}{2}}, \quad x \to \infty \tag{A6}$$

where the symbol $\sim$ is taken to mean that the ratio of the two sides tends to unity as $x \to \infty$. When working with factorials, it is sometimes more convenient to use the formula

$$x! \sim \sqrt{2\pi} x^{x+\frac{1}{2}} e^{-x}, \quad x \to \infty. \tag{A7}$$

To compute the gamma function, one would normally use (A3) and choose x such that $1 < x < 2$. Then, for $0 < y < 1$, a good approximation is given by

$$\Gamma(1+y) \approx 1 + \sum_{n=1}^{8} (-1)^n a_n y^n \tag{A8}$$

where

$$
\begin{array}{ll}
a_1 = .577191652 & a_5 = .756704078 \\
a_2 = .988205891 & a_6 = .482199304 \\
a_3 = .897056937 & a_7 = .193527818 \\
a_4 = .918206857 & a_8 = .035868343.
\end{array}
$$

The **incomplete gamma function** is defined by

$$I(\alpha,x) = \frac{1}{\Gamma(\alpha)} \int_0^x y^{\alpha-1} e^{-y} dy, \quad \alpha > 0, \, x > 0. \tag{A9}$$

If α is a positive integer, then

$$I(\alpha,x) = 1 - \sum_{n=0}^{\alpha-1} \frac{x^n e^{-x}}{n!}. \tag{A10}$$

In addition, the gamma function is related to the **standard normal cdf**

$$\Phi(x) = \int_{-\infty}^x \frac{e^{-\frac{y^2}{2}}}{\sqrt{2\pi}} dy \tag{A11}$$

by the formula

$$\Phi(x) = \frac{1}{2}[1 + I(\frac{1}{2}, \frac{x^2}{2})], \quad x > 0. \tag{A12}$$

To compute (A9), note that a finite number of terms may be used in the following expansion

$$I(\alpha,x) = \frac{x^\alpha e^{-x}}{\Gamma(\alpha)} \sum_{n=0}^{\infty} \frac{x^n}{\alpha(\alpha+1)\cdots(\alpha+n)} \tag{A13}$$

obtained by noting that (A9) is closely related to a **confluent hypergeometric function**

$$M(a,b,x) = \frac{\Gamma(b)}{\Gamma(b-a)\Gamma(a)} \int_0^1 e^{xt} t^{a-1} (1-t)^{b-a-1} dt. \tag{A14}$$

A series expansion is given by

$$M(a,b,x) = \sum_{n=0}^{\infty} \frac{\Gamma(a+n)\Gamma(b)}{\Gamma(a)\Gamma(b+n)} \frac{x^n}{n!}. \qquad\qquad\text{(A15)}$$

See Abramowitz and Stegun (1965), chapter 13. The standard normal cdf (A11) may be computed using (A12) and (A13).

APPENDIX B

THE INCOMPLETE BETA FUNCTION

The **incomplete beta function** is defined by

$$B(a,b,x) = \frac{\Gamma(a+b)}{\Gamma(a)\Gamma(b)} \int_0^x y^{a-1}(1-y)^{b-1} dy, \quad 0<x<1. \tag{B1}$$

An alternative expression is obtained by letting $t = y(1-y)^{-1}$ in (B1), yielding

$$B(a,b,x) = \frac{\Gamma(a+b)}{\Gamma(a)\Gamma(b)} \int_0^{\frac{x}{1-x}} \frac{t^{a-1}}{(1+t)^{a+b}} dt, \quad 0<x<1. \tag{B2}$$

It is also easily shown that

$$B(a,b,x) = 1 - B(b,a,1-x). \tag{B3}$$

If b is a positive integer, then

$$B(a,b,x) = \frac{\Gamma(a+b)}{\Gamma(a)\Gamma(b)} \sum_{n=0}^{b-1} \binom{b-1}{n} (-1)^n \frac{x^{a+n}}{a+n}. \tag{B4}$$

If a is a positive integer, then one may use (B3) followed by (B4). Since $B(a,b,x)$ is a hypergeometric function, we may write (Abramowitz and Stegun, 1965)

$$B(a,b,x) = \frac{\Gamma(a+b)}{\Gamma(a)\Gamma(b)} x^a (1-x)^b \left\{ 1 + \sum_{n=0}^{\infty} \frac{(a+b)(a+b+1) \cdots (a+b+n)}{(a+1)(a+2) \cdots (a+1+n)} x^{n+1} \right\} \qquad \text{(B5)}$$

and a finite number of terms from (B5) may be used to calculate $B(a,b,x)$ for arbitrary a and b.

APPENDIX C

THE MODIFIED BESSEL FUNCTION OF THE THIRD KIND

Some useful properties of this function are given here. More details are given in Jorgensen (1982), Sichel (1971), and Abramowitz and Stegun (1965).

The **modified Bessel function of the third kind with index** λ ($\lambda \varepsilon R$) is defined by

$$K_\lambda(x) = \frac{1}{2} \int_0^\infty y^{\lambda-1} e^{-\frac{1}{2}x(y+y^{-1})} dy, \quad x>0. \tag{C1}$$

It can be shown that

$$K_\lambda(x) = K_{-\lambda}(x), \tag{C2}$$

$$K_{\lambda+1}(x) = \frac{2\lambda}{x} K_\lambda(x) + K_{\lambda-1}(x), \tag{C3}$$

$$\frac{\partial}{\partial x} K_\lambda(x) = -\frac{1}{2} [K_{\lambda+1}(x) + K_{\lambda-1}(x)]. \tag{C4}$$

Also, for $n = 0,1,2,...$ we have

$$K_{n+\frac{1}{2}}(x) = (\frac{\pi}{2x})^{\frac{1}{2}} e^{-x} \sum_{k=0}^{n} \frac{(n+k)!}{(n-k)!k!} (2x)^{-k}, \tag{C5}$$

which together with (C2), yields simple formulae for any half-integer value of λ.

Furthermore,

$$K_{\lambda}(x) \sim \sqrt{\pi}(2\lambda)^{\lambda-\frac{1}{2}} e^{-\lambda} x^{-\lambda}, \quad \lambda \to \infty. \tag{C6}$$

APPENDIX D

NUMERICAL SOLUTIONS OF
INTEGRAL EQUATIONS

D.1 INTRODUCTION

Integral equations arise in various places in this book. In chapter 6, the distribution of total claims for continuous severity distributions was shown to be the solution of a **Volterra integral equation of the second kind** of the form

$$g(x) = J(x) + \int_0^x K(x,y)g(y)dy. \tag{D.1.1}$$

In this equation $f(x)$ is a known function, $K(x,y)$ is a known function called the **kernel** and $g(y)$ is the unknown function. Equations of the form also appeared in chapters 7 and 8 in connection with the evaluation of ruin probabilities.

Equation (D.1.1) can be solved in an ad hoc manner numerically by appropriately discretizing the integral in (D.1.1) using the methods previously described in section 6.16. In this chapter, we examine methods developed in the field of numerical analysis for the numerical solution of integral equations. These methods have the advantage that error estimates have been developed and that the methods are shown to be numerically stable in the sense that errors introduced by computer truncation or rounding do not "blow up" and render the numerical results unreliable.

In this chapter we address the solution of equations of the form (D.1.1) rather than the specific equations which arise in various places in this book. In this way we produce a general solution and specific solutions are not necessary each time this kind of equation arises.

Although several approaches can be used to develop numerical solutions to (D.1.1), we prefer to examine only single-step and multi-step methods based on the discretization of the integral in (D.1.1). The results are similar to those developed in section 6.16 but have certain weights attached to each of the terms in the summation which replaces the integral in (D.1.1).

We first examine a single-step method and then proceed to the multi-step method. These techniques were inspired by Stroter (1985) and are based on Baker (1977) who explores a large number of methods.

D.2 A SINGLE-STEP METHOD

For some interval $h>0$, we consider the values of the function $g(x)$ in (D.1.1) at the points $0,h,2h,...$. We now use a quadrature rule of the form

$$\int_0^{kh} \phi(y)dy \approx \sum_{j=0}^{k} w_{k,j}\phi(jh), \quad k = 1,2,... \; . \tag{D.2.1}$$

The approximate integration formula (D.2.1) can be seen to be a linear combination of the values $\phi(0),\phi(h),\dots,\phi(kh)$ with the quantities $w_{k,j}$ serving as "weights".

When (D.2.1) is used to evaluate the integral in (D.1.1), one obtains the formula

$$\hat{g}(kh) = f(kh) + \sum_{j=0}^{k} w_{k,j}K(kh,jh)\hat{g}(jh) \tag{D.2.2}$$

where $\hat{g}(\cdot)$ is an approximation for $g(\cdot)$. Solving for $\hat{g}(kh)$ yields the approximate values

$$\hat{g}(kh) = \frac{f(kh) + \sum_{j=0}^{k-1} w_{k,j}K(kh,jh)\hat{g}(jh)}{1-w_{k,k}K(kh,kh)}. \tag{D.2.3}$$

For a fixed set of weights $\{w_{k,j};\ k = 1,2,...;j = 0,1,...,k-1\}$, equation (D.2.3) can be used to evaluate $\{\hat{g}(kh);\ k = 1,2,...\}$ recursively beginning with the initial value $\hat{g}(0) = f(0+)$. We write $f(0+)$ because $f(x)$ may be defined only for $x > 0$.

The accuracy of the formula (D.2.2) depends upon the smoothness of the functions $K(x,y)$ and $f(x)$, upon the interval size h and upon the quadrature rule used to determine the weights $w_{k,j}$.

When the formula (D.2.3) is used for the $(a,b,0)$ subclass class of distributions (6.12.3), examination of (6.13.1) and (D.1.1) reveals that

$$f(x) = p_1 f_X(x) \qquad\qquad (D.2.4)$$

and that

$$K(x,y) = \{a + b\frac{x-y}{x}\}f_X(x-y). \qquad\qquad (D.2.5)$$

For the Poisson claims frequency distribution, $a = 0$ and consequently $K(x,x) = 0$ eliminating the final term in the summation (D.2.2) and the algebraic quantity in the denominator of (D.2.3).

The values of the weights $w_{k,j}$ are determined by applying simple approximate integration formulas repeatedly. **Simpson's rule** and the **three-eights rule** are discussed in most books dealing with numerical quadrature (c.f. Henrici, 1964 or Burden, Faires and Reynolds, 1981). When these rules are applied once to approximate the integral of a continuous function, they each have an error of approximation of order $0(h^5)$. When k is even, we choose (on the basis of Baker, 1977) a **repeated Simpson's rule** and when k is odd, we choose a **repeated Simpson's rule followed by a single three-eighths rule**. This leads to the system of weights (beginning with a trapezoidal rule) illustrated in Table D.1.

When these rules are used in a repeated manner to evaluate (D.1.1) over some fixed interval of length $R = nh$, the error of approximation wil be of order $0(h^4)$.

It should be noted that when using this technique to solve equations like (6.14.1) or (6.16.5) for the distribution of total claims, only the continuous portion of the distribution is considered. Only approximations to the values of the continuous portion of the density function are produced. In the case of

TABLE D.1

Values of the Coefficients $w_{k,j}$

k | $j =$	0	1	2	3	4	5	6	7	8
1	$\frac{1}{2}h$	$\frac{1}{2}h$							
2	$\frac{1}{3}h$	$\frac{4}{3}h$	$\frac{1}{3}h$						
3	$\frac{3}{8}h$	$\frac{9}{8}h$	$\frac{9}{8}h$	$\frac{3}{8}h$					
4	$\frac{1}{3}h$	$\frac{4}{3}h$	$\frac{2}{3}h$	$\frac{4}{3}h$	$\frac{1}{3}h$				
5	$\frac{1}{3}h$	$\frac{4}{3}h$	$\frac{17}{24}h$	$\frac{9}{8}h$	$\frac{9}{8}h$	$\frac{3}{8}h$			
6	$\frac{1}{3}h$	$\frac{4}{3}h$	$\frac{2}{3}h$	$\frac{4}{3}h$	$\frac{2}{3}h$	$\frac{4}{3}h$	$\frac{1}{3}h$		
7	$\frac{1}{3}h$	$\frac{4}{3}h$	$\frac{2}{3}h$	$\frac{4}{3}h$	$\frac{17}{24}h$	$\frac{9}{8}h$	$\frac{9}{8}h$	$\frac{3}{8}h$	
8	$\frac{1}{3}h$	$\frac{4}{3}h$	$\frac{2}{3}h$	$\frac{4}{3}h$	$\frac{2}{3}h$	$\frac{4}{3}h$	$\frac{2}{3}h$	$\frac{4}{3}h$	$\frac{1}{3}h$

(6.14.1) or (6.16.5), the distribution of total claims has a spike of size p_0 at zero. To obtain the distribution function of total claims,

$$F_S(x) = p_0 + \int_0^x f_S(x)dx, \tag{D.2.7}$$

the same approximate integration rules can be used. Hence, the approximated values are

$$\hat{F}_S(0) = F_S(0) = p_0,$$

(D.2.8)

$$\hat{F}_S(kh) = p_0 + \sum_{j=0}^{k} w_{k,j}\hat{g}(kh), \quad k = 1,2,\dots \ .$$

When the distribution function $F_S(x)$ is approximated, the values of $\hat{F}_S(kh)$ should converge monotonically to one as kh gets large. The deviation of such values from the correct value 1 is the accumulated error arising from all sources and is an indication of the reliability of the intermediate values.

It should be noted that computational errors may arise as the step size h becomes small necessitating a larger and larger number of recursions (D.2.3). With each recursion a numerical truncation error occurs on a computer because of the fixed precision in each arithmetic operation. On the other hand when the step size h becomes large, the error of approximation becomes large. Hence, it is necessary to find a balance between these two types of errors. In practice, this can be done experimentally by examining the error in $\hat{F}_S(kh)$, as kh becomes large for various values of h.

The multi-step method described in the next section attempts to improve on the error propogation by simultaneously increasing the step size h and maintaining the accuracy of the approximation.

D.3 A MULTI-STEP METHOD

Suppose that we wish to find approximate values of the solution $g(x)$ of (D.1.1) for the range $0 \leq x \leq R$. We now let $R = Nph$ where h is the step size, p is a positive integer denoting the number of multi-steps and N is a positive integer. We generalize the single-step method so that in each recursion k, $(k = 0,1,2,\dots,N-1)$ we obtain p approximate values $\{g(kp+1)h), g((kp+2)h),\dots, g((k+1)ph)\}$ by solving a system of linear equations in p unknowns.

Consider the values of $g(x)$ for the interval $kph < x \leq (k+1)ph$. Separating out this interval in (D.1.1) yields (with $x = nh$)

$$g(nh) = f(nh) + \int_0^{kph} K(nh,y)g(y)dy + \int_{kph}^{nh} K(nh,y)g(y)dy. \qquad \text{(D.3.1)}$$

We now use repeated quadrature rules to approximate each interval in (D.3.1) with its own set of weights, so that

$$\int_0^{kph} K(nh,y)g(y)dy = \sum_{j=0}^{kp} w_{n,j} K(nh,jh)g(jh) \qquad \text{(D.3.2)}$$

and

$$\int_{kph}^{nh} K(nh,y)g(y)dy = \sum_{j=kp}^{(k+1)p} u_{n,j} K(nh,jh)g(jh). \qquad \text{(D.3.3)}$$

Substitution of (D.3.2) and (D.3.3) into (D.3.1) yields the system of equations

$$\hat{g}(nh) = f(nh) + \sum_{j=0}^{kp} w_{n,j} K(nh,jh)\hat{g}(jh) + \sum_{j=kp}^{(k+1)p} u_{n,j} K(nh,jh)\hat{g}(jh) \qquad \text{(D.3.4)}$$

for $n = kp+1, \ldots, (k+1)p$ and $k = 0,1,\ldots,N-1$. The system of equations is first solved with $k = 0$ for the approximate values in the third term in the right-hand side of (D.3.4). Next, with $k = 1$, the results of the step with $k = 0$ are used in the second term, and the system of p equations is solved for the next block of approximate values. This process is repeated until all Np desired values are obtained.

The relation of (D.3.4) to the corresponding equation from the single-step method should be noted. If we set $u_{n,j} = 0$ for $j > n$, then (D.3.4) is equivalent to the corresponding equation (D.2.2) from the single-step method. The unique feature of the multi-step method is that the second integral in (D.3.1) is approximated in (D.3.3) by terms that are outside its range of integration.

We now consider the problem of obtaining the weights $w_{n,j}$ and $u_{n,j}$ in (D.3.4). We first consider the weights $u_{n,j}$. To get maximum precision in the second integral we find weights such that the resulting quadrature rules are exact for collocation polynomials. Hence, the values of $u_{n,j}$ must satisfy

$$\sum_{j=kp}^{(k+1)p} u_{n,j}\phi(jh) = \int_{kph}^{nh} P(y)dy \qquad (D.3.5)$$

where $P(y)$ is the interpolating $\phi(y)$ at $y = kph,\ y = (kp+1)h, \ldots, y = (k+1)ph.$

This "block-by-block" approach is reminscent of the method of moment matching for discretization of a severity distribution which was described in section 6.16. In that method $v+1$ points were simultaneously obtained by requiring moments of order v or less to agree. In this approach we require the integral to be exact for polynomials of degree p or less.

The following theorem gives the explicit formula to be used in evaluating the weights $u_{n,j}$ in (D.3.5).

Theorem D.3.1. The weights $u_{n,j}$ in (D.3.5) satisfy the equation

$$u_{kp+r,kp+s} = p^{p+1}h\int_{0}^{r/p} \prod_{i\neq s} \left(\frac{x-i/p}{s-i}\right) dx \qquad (D.3.6)$$

for $1 \leq r,\ s \leq p$ where the product is taken from $i = 0$ to $i = p.$

Proof

The Lagrange formula for collocation of a polynomial $f(y)$ at the points $y_0, y_1, \ldots, y_p$ is

$$f(y) = \sum_{s=0}^{p} f(y_s)\prod_{i\neq s} \left(\frac{y-y_i}{y_s-y_i}\right).$$

Equation (D.3.5) may be rewritten as

$$\sum_{s=0}^{p} u_{kp+r,kp+s}\phi(kph+sh) = \int_{0}^{rh} P(kph+y)dy. \qquad (D.3.7)$$

Letting $f(y) = P(kph+y)$ and $y_s = sh$ for $s = 0,1,\ldots,p,$ and recognizing that

$P(kph+y_s) = \phi(kph+y_s)$ for $s = 0, 1, \ldots, p$ we obtain

$$P(kph+y) = \sum_{s=0}^{p} \phi(kph+sh) \prod_{i \neq s} \left(\frac{y-ih}{(s-i)h} \right).$$

Integration of both sides from $y = 0$ to $y = rh$ yields

$$\int_{0}^{rh} P(kph+y)\,dy = \sum_{s=0}^{p} \phi(kph+sh) \int_{0}^{rh} \prod_{i \neq s} \left(\frac{y-ih}{(s-i)h} \right) dy.$$

Equating coefficients with (D.3.7) gives the result

$$u_{kp+r,kp+s} = \int_{0}^{rh} \prod_{i \neq s} \left(\frac{y-ih}{(s-i)h} \right) dy$$

$$= p^{p+1} h \int_{0}^{r/p} \prod_{i \neq s} \left(\frac{x-i/p}{s-i} \right) dx.$$

It should be noted that the weights are functions of r, s, p and h but not k and that the weights are multiples of h. Consequently, one needs only tabulate values of the coefficents of h in each of the weights. The values of these weights are given in Table D.2 for $p = 2, 4$ and 8. These should be sufficient for the user since larger values of p will necessitate the solution of a large number of equations while may itself cause numerical problems.

The approximation error is now of order $0(h^{p+2})$ within each block since the approximation is based on collocation. The overall approximation by evaluating $g(x)$ in (D.1.1) is then of order $0(h^{p+1})$ as long as the accuracy of the first integral is also of order $0(h^{p+2})$. In order to maintain the accuracy in the first integral of (D.1.1), it is necessary to use integration rules based on the collocation polynomial of order p. The coefficients of such rules can be found by setting $r = p$ in (D.3.6). The values for $p = 2, 4$ and 8 are given in the final row of each section of Table D.2. These integration rules are used for each ''block'' contained in the second summation of (D.3.4). We have thus determined all the necessary weights to maintain an error of order $0(h^{p+1})$.

TABLE D.2

Values of the Weights $u_{kp+r,kp+s}$

p	r	$s =$	0	1	2	3	4
2	1		.416666667	.666666667	-.083333333		
	2		.333333333	1.333333333	.333333333		
4	1		.348611111	.897222222	-.366666667	.147222222	-.026388889
	2		.322222222	1.377777778	.266666667	.044444444	.011111111
	3		.337500000	1.275000000	.900000000	.525000000	.037500000
	4		.311111111	1.422222222	.533333333	1.422222222	.311111111
8	1		.294868000	1.231011354	-1.268902668	1.541930667	-1.386992945
	2		.285511464	1.610088133	-.374726631	1.058977072	-1.023985891
	3		.287522321	1.582633929	.076741071	1.784241071	-1.253571429
	4		.286631393	1.592663139	.017213404	2.310546737	.640564374
	5		.287319500	1.585579255	.052014440	2.193218144	-.027557319
	6		.286428571	1.594285714	.012857143	2.302857143	-.257142857
	7		.288439429	1.575297068	.093954475	2.094787809	.105864198
	8		.279082892	1.661516755	.261869489	2.961834215	1.281128748

p	r	$s =$	5	6	7	8
8	1		.867046407	-.3558239653	.086219687	-.009356537
	2		.658977072	-.274726631	.067231046	-.007345679
	3		.768616071	-.313883929	.075937500	-.008236607
	4		.651287478	-.279082892	.068853616	-.007548501
	5		1.177593144	-.338610560	.078882826	-.008439429
	6		1.902857143	.112857143	.051428571	-.006428572
	7		1.419903549	1.007033179	.430505401	-.015785108
	8		2.961834215	-.261869489	1.661516755	.279082892

The "block-by-block" approach gives maximum local precision for fixed h and p within each block as the values for that block are being computed. It is this increased precision that makes the method more accurate and more stable than the single-step method.

Baker (1977) examines the numerical stability of the procedures described here. The reader is referred to Baker (1977) for detailed analyses of these as well as other numerical procedures.

REFERENCES

Abramowitz, M., and Stegun, I. (1965). *Handbook of Mathematical Functions*. Dover, New York.

Adelson, R. (1966). "Compound Poisson Distributions". *Operations Research Quarterly, 17*, 73-75.

Albrecht, P. (1984). "Laplace Transforms, Mellin Transforms, and Mixed Poisson Process". *Scandinavian Actuarial Journal*, 58-64.

Anscombe, F. (1950). "Sampling Theory of the Negative Binomial and Logarithmic Series Distributions". *Biometrika, 37*, 358-382.

Asmussen, S. (1987). *Applied Probability and Queues*. John Wiley, Chichester.

Atkinson, A., and Yeh, L. (1982). "Inference for Sichel's Compound Poisson Distribution". *Journal of the American Statistical Association, 77*, 153-158.

Baker, C. (1977). *The Numerical Treatment of Integral Equations*. Clarendon Press, Oxford.

Barnett, V. (1982). *Comparative Statistical Inferences*. John Wiley, Chichester.

Beard, R., Pentikäinen, T., and Pesonen, E. (1984). *Risk Theory*, (3rd ed.). Chapman and Hall, London.

Beekman, J., and Bowers, N. (1972). An Approximation to the Finite Time Ruin Function". Scandinavian Actuarial Journal, 55, 41-56, 128-137.

Bender, E. (1974). "Asymptotic Methods of Enumeration". *SIAM Review, 16*, 485-515. Corrigendum (1976), 18, 292.

Benes, V. (1957). "On Queues with Poisson Arrivals". *Annals of Mathematical Statistics, 28*, 670-677.

Bertram, J. (1981). "Numerische Berechnung von Gesamtschadenverteilungen", *Blätter der Deutsche Gesellschaft für Versicherungsmathematik, 15*, 175-194.

Bingham, N., Goldie, C., and Teugels, J. (1987). *Regular Variation*. Cambridge University Press.

Bishop, Y., Fienberg, S., and Holland, P. (1975). *Discrete Multivariate Analysis: Theory and Practice*. MIT Press, Cambridge, MA.

Bowers, N., Gerber, H., Hickman, J., Jones, D., and Nesbitt, C. (1986). *Actuarial Mathematics*, Society of Actuaries, Itasca.

Bühlmann, H. (1970). *Mathematical Methods in Risk Theory*. Springer Verlag, New York.

Bühlmann, H. (1984). "Numerical Evaluation of the Compound Poisson Distribution: Recursion or Fast Fourier Transform?" *Scandinavian Actuarial Journal, 1984*, 116-126.

Burden, R., Faires, J., and Reynolds, A. (1978). *Numerical Analysis*. Prindle, Weber and Schmidt, Boston.

Chover, J., Ney, P., and Wainger, S. (1973). "Functions of Probability Measures". *J. Analyse Math., 26*, 255-302.

Collins, R. (1962). "Actuarial Application of the Monte Carlo Technique". *Transactions of the Society of Actuaries, 14*, 365-384.

Cox, D., and Hinkley, D. (1974). *Theoretical Statistics*, Chapman and Hall, London.

Cox, D., and Lewis, P. (1966). *The Analysis of Series of Events*. Chapman and Hall, London.

Cox, D., and Miller, H. (1965). *The Theory of Stochastic Processes.* Methuen, London.

David, H. (1981). *Order Statistics.* 2nd ed. John Wiley, New York.

De Pril, N. (1986). "On the Exact Computation of the Aggregate Claims Distribution in the Individual Life Model". *Astin Bulletin, 16,* 109-112.

De Pril, N. (1988). "Improved Approximations for the Aggregate Claims Distribution of a Life Insurance Portfolio". *Scandinavian Actuarial Journal,* 1988, 61-68.

Douglas, J. (1980). *Analysis with Standard Contagious Distributions.* International Co-operative Publishing House, Fairland, Maryland.

Embrechts, P. (1983). "A Property of the Generalized Inverse Gaussian Distribution with Some Applications". *Journal of Applied Probability, 20,* 537-544.

Embrechts, P., and Goldie, C. (1982). "On Convolution Tails". *Stochastic Processes and their Applications, 13,* 263-278.

Embrechts, P., Goldie, C., and Veraverbeke, N. (1979). "Subexponentiality and Infinite Divisibility". *Zeitschrift Fur Wahrscheinlichkeitstheorie und Verwandte Gebiete, 49,* 335-347.

Embrechts, P. and Hawkes, J. (1982). "A Limit Theorem for the Tails of Discrete Infinitely Divisible Laws with Applications to Fluctuation Theory". *Journal of the Australian Mathematics Society A, 32,* 412-422.

Embrechts, P., Maejima, M., and Teugels, J. (1985). "Asymptotic Behaviour of Compound Distributions". *Astin Bulletin, 15,* 45-48.

Embrechts, P., and Veraverbeke, N. (1982). "Estimates for the Probability of Ruin with Special Emphasis on the Possibility of Large Claims". *Insurance: Mathematics and Economics, 1,* 55-72.

Engen, S. (1974). "On Species Frequency Models". *Biometrika, 61*, 263-270.

Everitt, B., and Hand, D. (1981). *Finite Mixture Distributions*. Chapman and Hall, London.

Feller, W. (1935). "Uber den zentralen Grenzwertsatz der wahrshcheinlichkeits rechnung, *Math. Zeits., 40*, 521-559.

Feller, W. (1968). *An Introduction to Probability Theory and its Applications*, Vol. 1 (3rd ed.). John Wiley, New York.

Feller, W. (1971). *An Introduction to Probability Theory and its Applications*, Vol. 2 (2nd ed.). John Wiley, New York.

Fisz, M. (1963). *Probability Theory and Mathematical Statistics*. John Wiley, New York.

Folks, J., and Chhikara, R. (1978). "The Inverse Gaussian Distribution and its Statistical Application - A Review". *Journal of the Royal Statistical Society B, 40*, 263-289.

Freifelder, L. (1976). *A Decision Theoretic Approach to Insurance Ratemaking*. S.S. Huebner Foundation, University of Pennsylvania, Philadelphia.

Gerber, H. (1979). *An Introduction to Mathematical Risk Theory*. S.S. Huebner Foundation, University of Pennsylvania, Philadelphia.

Gerber, H. (1982). "On the Numerical Evaluation of the Distribution of Aggregate Claims and its Stop-Loss Premiums". *Insurance: Mathematics and Economics, 1*, 13-18.

Gerber, H. (1984). "Error Bounds for the Compound Poisson Approximation". *Insurance: Mathematics and Economics, 3*, 191-194.

Gerber, H. (1988). "Mathematical Fun with Ruin Theory". *Insurance: Mathematics and Economics, 7*, 15-23.

Gerber, H., Goovaerts, M., and Kaas, R. (1987). "On the Probability and Severity of Ruin". *Astin Bulletin, 17*, 151-163.

Gerber, H. and Jones, D. (1976). "Some Practical Considerations in Connection with the Calculation of Stop-Loss Premiums". *Transactions of the Society of Actuaries, 28*, 215-231.

Gossiaux, A., and Lemaire, J. (1981). "Methodes d'ajustement de distributions de Sinistres. *Bulletin of the Association of Swiss Actuaries, 81*, 87-95.

Griffin, W. (1975). *Transform Techniques for Probability Modeling.* Academic Press, New York.

Haight, F. (1967). *Handbook of the Poisson Distribution.* John Wiley, New York.

Heckman, P. and Meyers, G. (1983). "The Calculation of Aggregate Loss Distributions from Claim Severity and Claim Count Distributions". *Proceedings of the Casualty Actuarial Society, 70*, 22-61.

Henrici, P. (1964). *Elements of Numerical Analysis.* John Wiley, New York.

Hipp, C. (1986). "Improved Approximations for the Aggregate Claims Distribution in the Individual Model". *Astin Bulletin, 16*, 89-100.

Hofmann, M. (1955). "Uber Zusammengesetzte Poisson-Prozesse und ihre Anwendungen in der Unfallversicherung". *Bulletin of the Association of Swiss Actuaries, 55*, 499-575.

Hogg, R., and Craig, A. (1978). *Introduction to Mathematical Statistics*, 4th ed. Macmillan, New York.

Hogg, R., and Klugman, S. (1984). *Loss Distributions.* John Wiley, New York.

Holgate, P. (1970). "The Modality of Some Compound Poisson Distributions". *Biometrika, 57*, 666-667.

Holla, M. (1966). "On a Poisson-Inverse Gaussian Distribution" *Metrika, 11*, 115-121.

Hossack, I., Pollard, J. and Zehnwirth, B. (1983). *Introductory Statistics with Applications in General Insurance*. Cambridge University Press, Cambridge.

Huang, J. (1975). "A Note on Order Statistics from Pareto Distributions". *Scandinavian Actuarial Journal*, 187-190.

Irwin, J. (1975). "The Generalized Waring Distribution. *Journal of the Royal Statistical Society A, 138*, 18-31, 204-227, 374-384.

Johnson, N., and Kotz, S. (1969). *Distributions in Statistics: Discrete Distributions*. John Wiley, New York.

Johnson, N., and Kotz, S. (1970a). *Distributions in Statistics: Continuous Univariate Distributions - 1*. John Wiley, New York.

Johnson, N., and Kotz, S. (1970b). *Distributions in Statistics: Continuous Univariate Distributions - 2*. John Wiley, New York.

Jorgensen, B. (1982). *Statistical Properties of the Generalized Inverse Gaussian Distribution*, Lecture Notes in Statistics 9. Springer Verlag, New York.

Kalbfleisch, J., and Prentice, R. (1980). *The Statistical Analysis of Failure Time Data*. John Wiley, New York.

Karlin, S., and Taylor, H. (1975). *A First Course in Stochastic Processes*, (2nd ed.). Academic Press, New York.

Karlin, S., and Taylor, H. (1981). *A Second Course in Stochastic Processes*. Academic Press, New York.

Kendall, M. and Stuart, A. (1977). *Advanced Theory of Statistics*, Vol. I, Griffin, London.

Knuth, D. (1981). *The Art of Computer Programming, Vol. 2, Seminumerical Algorithms*. Addison-Wesley, Reading.

Kornya, P. (1983). "Distribution of Aggregate Claims in the Individual Risk Theory Model". *Transactions of the Society of Actuaries, 35*, 823-836.

Kremer, E. (1987). "An Improved Approximation of the Ultimate Ruin Probability". *Bulletin of the Swiss Actuarial Association*, 243-245.

Kuon, S., Reich, A. and Reimers, L. (1987). "Panjer vs. Kornya vs. De Pril: A Comparison from a Practical Point of View". *Astin Bulletin, 17*, 183-191.

Kupper, J. (1960, 1962). "Wahrscheinlichkeitstheoretische Modelle in der Schadenversicherung". *Blätter der Deutsche Gesellschaft für Versicherungsmathematik, 5*, 451-503; *6*, 95-130.

Kupper, J. (1965). "Some Aspects of Cumulative Risk". *Astin Bulletin, 3*, 85-103.

Laha, R., and Rohatgi, V. (1979). *Probability Theory*. John Wiley, New York.

Lawless, J. (1982). *Statistical Models and Methods for Lifetime Data*. John Wiley, New York.

Le Cam, L. (1960). "An Approximation Theorem for the Poisson Binomial Distribution". *Pacific Journal of Mathematics, 10*, 1181-1197.

Lehmann, E. (1983). *Theory of Point Estimation*. John Wiley, New York.

Lemaire, J. (1985). *Automobile Insurance*. Kluwer, Boston.

Linhart, H. and Zucchini, W. (1986). *Model Selection*. John Wiley, New York.

Lundberg, O. (1940). *On Random Processes and Their Applications to Sickness and Accident Statistics*. Almqvist and Wiksells, Uppsala.

Marsden, J. (1974). *Elementary Classical Analysis*. W.H. Freeman and Co., San Francisco.

McCullagh, P., and Nelder, J. (1983). *Generalized Linear Models*. Chapman and Hall, London.

McFadden, J. (1965). "The Mixed Poisson Process". *Sankhya A, 27*, 83-92.

Meir, A. and Moon, J. (1987). "Some Asymptotic Results Useful in Enumeration Problems". *Aequationes Mathematicae, 33*, 260-268.

Neuts, M. (1981). *Matrix-Geometric Solutions in Stochastic Models: An Algorithmic Approach*. The Johns Hopkins University Press, Baltimore.

Oberhettinger, F., and Badii, L. (1973). *Tables of Laplace Transforms*. Springer Verlag, Berlin.

Ord, J. (1972). *Families of Frequency Distributions*. Charles Griffin, London.

Panjer, H. (1980). "The Aggregate Claims Distribution and Stop-Loss Reinsurance". *Transactions of the Society of Actuaries, 32*, 523-535.

Panjer, H. (1981). "Recursive Evaluation of a Family of Compound Distributions". *Astin Bulletin, 12*, 22-26.

Panjer, H. (1986). "Direct Calculation of Ruin Probabilities". *The Journal of Risk and Insurance, 53*, 521-529.

Panjer, H., and Doray, L. (1988). "Further Results on the Probability of Ruin With an Absorbing Upper Barrier". *Transactions of the 23rd International Congress of Actuaries*. Helsinki, 257-267.

Panjer, H., and Lutek, B. (1983). "Practical Aspects of Stop-Loss Calculations". *Insurance: Mathematics and Economics, 2*, 159-177.

Panjer, H., and Wang, S. (1992). "On the Stability of Recursive Formulas". *Institute of Insurance and Pension Research Report 92-05*, University of Waterloo.

Panjer, H., and Willmot, G. (1981). "Finite Sum Evaluation of the Negative Binomial-Exponential Model". *Astin Bulletin, 12*, 133-137.

Panjer, H., and Willmot, G. (1982). "Recursions for Compound Distributions". *Astin Bulletin, 13*, 1-11.

Panjer, H., and Willmot (1983). "Compound Poisson Models in Actaurial Risk Theory". *Journal of Econometrics, 23*, 63-76.

Panjer, H., and Willmot, G. (1984a). "Computational Techniques in Reinsurance Models". *Transactions of the 22nd International Congress of Actuaries*, Sydney, 4, 111-120.

Panjer, H., and Willmot, G. (1984b). "Models for the Distribution of Aggregate Claims in Risk Theory". *Transactions of the Society of Actuaries, 36*, 399-446.

Panjer, H., and Willmot, G. (1986). "Computational Aspects of Recursive Evaluation of Compound Distributions". *Insurance: Mathematics and Economics, 5*, 113-116.

Parzen, E. (1962). *Stochastic Processes*. Holden-Day, San Francisco.

Patel, J., Kapadia, C. and Owen, D. (1936). *Handbook of Statistical Distributions*. Marcel Dekker, New York.

Patil, G., and Joshi, S. (1968). *A Dictionary and Bibliography of Discrete Distributions*. Boyd, Edinburgh; Hafner Pub. Co., New York.

Prabhu, N. (1961). "On the Ruin Problem of Collective Risk Theory". *Annals of Mathematical Statistics, 32*, 757-764.

Prentice, R. (1975). "Discrimination among some parametric models". *Biometrika, 62*, 607-614.

Riordan, J. (1958). *An Introduction to Combinatorial Analysis*. John Wiley, New York.

Rosenthal, I. (1947). "Limits of Retention for Ordinary Life Insurance". *Record of the American Institute of Actuaries, 36*, 6-22.

Ross, S. (1983). *Stochastic Processes*. John Wiley, New York.

Ross, S. (1985). *Introduction to Probability Models* (3rd ed.). Academic Press, Orlando.

Sankaran, M. (1970). "The Discrete Poisson-Lindley Distribution". *Biometrics, 26*, 145-149.

Seal, H. (1969). *Stochastic Theory of A Risk Business*. John Wiley, New York.

Seal, H. (1974). "The Numerical Calculation of $U(w,t)$, the Probability of Non-Ruin in an interval $(0,t)$". *Scandinavian Actuarial Journal*, 121-139.

Seal, H. (1978). *Survival Probabilities: The Goal of Risk Theory*. John Wiley, New York.

Seal, H. (1982). "Mixed Poisson - An Ideal Distribution of Claim Numbers?". *Bulletin of the Association of Swiss Actuaries, 82*, 293-295.

Serfling, R. (1980). *Approximation Theorems of Mathematical Statistics*. John Wiley, New York.

Shiu, E. (1988). "Calculation of the Probability of Eventual Ruin by Beekman's Convolution Series". *Insurance: Mathematics and Economics, 7*, 41-47.

Sichel, H. (1971). "On a Family of Discrete Distributions Particularly Suited to Represent Long Tailed Frequency Data". *Proceedings of the Third Symposium on Mathematical Statistics*, N. Laubscher (ed.), Pretoria, CSIR.

Silvey, S. (1975). *Statistical Inference*. Chapman and Hall, London.

Simon, L. (1961). "Fitting negative binomial distributions by the method of maximum likelihood". *Proceedings of the Casualty Actuarial Society, 48*, 45-53.

Stam, A. (1973). "Regular Variation of the Tail of a Subordinated Probability Distribution". *Advances in Applied Probability, 5*, 308-327.

Steutel, F. (1970). *Preservation of Infinite Divisibility Under Mixing and Related Topics.* Math. Centre Tracts 33, Math Centre, Amsterdam.

Ströter, B. (1985). "The Numerical Evaluation of the Aggregate Claim Density Function via Integral Equations". *Blätter der Deutsche Gesellschaft für Versicherungsmathematik, 17*, 1-14.

Sundt, B. (1984). *An Introduction to Non-Life Insurance Mathematics.* Verlag, Karlsruhe.

Sundt, B., and Jewell, W. (1981). "Further Results on Recursive Evaluation of Compound Distributions". *Astin Bulletin, 12*, 27-39.

Takács, L. (1962). *Introduction to the Theory of Queues.* Oxford University Press, New York.

Teugels, J. (1985). "Approximation and Estimation of Some Compound Distributions". *Insurance: Mathematics and Economics, 4*, 143-153.

Teugels, J., and Willmot, G. (1987). "Approximations for Stop-Loss Premiums". *Insurance: Mathematics and Economics, 6*, 195-202.

Thorin, O. (1977). "On the Infinite Divisibility of the Log-Normal Distribution". *Scandinavian Actuarial Journal*, 121-148.

Thorin, O. (1982). "Probabilities of Ruin". *Scandinavian Actuarial Journal, 1982*, 65-102.

Thyrion, P. (1961). "Contribution à l'étude du Bonus pour non Sinistre en Assurance Automobile". *Astin Bulletin, 1*, 142-162.

Tijms, H. (1986). *Stochastic Modelling and Analysis: A Computational Approach.* John Wiley, Chichester.

Tröblinger, A. (1961). "Mathematische Untersuchungen zur Beitragsrückgewähr in der Kraftfahrversicherung". *Blätter der Deutsche Gesellschaft für Versicherungsmathematik, 5,* 327-348.

Vandebroek, M. and De Pril, N. (1988). "Recursions for the Distribution of a Life Portfolio: A Numerical Comparison". *Liber Amicorum Ed. Franckx, Vol. II, Bulletin of the Royal Association of Belgian Actuaries, 82,* 21-35.

Venter, G. (1983). "Transformed Beta and Gamma Distributions and Aggregate Losses". *Proceedings of the Casualty Actuarial Society, 70,* 156-193.

Weber, D. (1970). "A Stochastic Approach to Automobile Compensation". *Proceedings of the Casualty Actuarial Society, 57,* 27-63.

Whittaker, E., and Watson, G. (1927). *A Course of Modern Analysis,* (4th ed.). Cambridge University Press, London.

Widder, D.D. (1946). *The Laplace Transform.* Princeton University Press, Princeton.

Willmot, G. (1986). "Mixed Compound Poisson Distributions". *Astin Bulletin, 16,* 559-579.

Willmot, G. (1987a). "On the Probabilities of the Log-Zero-Poisson Distribution". *Canadian Journal of Statistics, 15,* 293-297.

Willmot, G. (1987b). "The Poisson-Inverse Gaussian as an Alternative to the Negative Binomial". *Scandinavian Actuarial Journal,* 113-127.

Willmot, G. (1988). "Parameter Orthogonality for a Family of Discrete Distributions". *Journal of the American Statistical Association, 83,* 517-521.

Willmot, G. (1989). "Limiting Tail Behaviour of Some Discrete Compound Distributions". *Insurance: Mathematics and Economics, 8,* 175-185.

Willmot, G. (1990). "Asymptotic Tail Behaviour of Poisson Mixtures With Applications". *Advances in Applied Probability, 22*, 147-159.

Willmot, G., and Panjer, H. (1986). "Difference Equation Approaches in Evaluation of Compound Distributions". *Insurance: Mathematics and Economics, 6*, 43-56.

INDEX

THE
RED
ROOM

MARK DAWSON

THE RED ROOM

WELBECK

First published in 2023 by Welbeck Fiction Limited,
an imprint of Welbeck Publishing Group
Offices in: London – 20 Mortimer Street, London W1T 3JW &
Sydney – Level 17, 207 Kent St, Sydney NSW 2000 Australia
www.welbeckpublishing.com

First published in 2023
This edition published by Welbeck Fiction Limited, part of
Welbeck Publishing Group, in 2023

A CIP catalogue record for this book is available from the British Library

Paperback ISBN: 978-1-80279-588-2

Printed and bound by CPI Group (UK) Ltd., Croydon, CR0 4YY

10 9 8 7 6 5 4 3 2 1

To Lucy — for a decade of support that I couldn't do without.

PART I

MONDAY

1

The glass roof of the refectory reverberated with the drumming of the rain as the clouds opened and thunder boomed overhead. Clive Mouton paid for his breakfast and took his tray to the table in the corner he preferred. He removed his green and yellow sash and folded it neatly, leaving it on the seat next to him. He had a bacon bloomer, and the last thing he wanted to do was to spill ketchup onto the sash; also, it marked him out as a guide, and it wasn't unheard of for visitors to ask him questions while he was eating. He was an enthusiastic member of the volunteer team at the cathedral, but he liked to spend the half-hour he took before he started by checking his social media accounts to see the updates from his daughter and grandchildren. He was distracted from his phone today by the storm.

A skein of lightning split across the sky, thunder boomed and the rain kept thudding down, a deluge that raced down the slope of the glass. The gutters had quickly overflowed, and now they spilled the water down the windows in a sudden wash. The southwest of the country had seen an enormous amount of rain since Christmas, with the result that several of the five rivers that converged on Salisbury – including the Avon – had burst their banks. The water meadows were full, and some of the lower-lying villages had flooded.

The refectory served the cathedral and had been built in the space between the nave and the cloisters, replacing the unsightly 1970s prefabricated buildings that had once stood here. Mouton had been head of history at the nearby Chafyn Grove School and had always had a keen interest in his subject. He had studied the cathedral and taught his students about it; volunteering to show tourists around the building was an obvious way for him to fill the spare hours of his retirement. He always finished his tours by taking his guests to the refectory, explaining how it stood on the site of the old plumbery the cathedral's masons would once have used to repair the leadwork on the roof. Mouton would show them how the design had incorporated the ancient buttresses of the cloisters, and then he would point up, through the modern glass and steel roof, to the glorious view of the tower and spire. He was one of the handful of guides who was allowed to conduct tours of the tower itself, and showing visitors the spectacle from the ground just after they had descended the 332 steps from the top was an excellent way to bring the tour to a close.

He looked up now and noted how the pale stone contrasted against the dark grey clouds. The forecast had been for more storms today, and it hadn't been wrong; dawn had broken with the sky an angry purple, and it had quickly grown gloomier and more ominous. The spire stood proud against the fast-moving clouds like the prow of a ship cutting through furious waves.

'Morning, Clive.'

Mouton looked up and saw that the dean had stopped at his table. 'Morning.'

'What a start to the day.'

'It's supposed to rain all week,' Mouton said. 'I was listening to the radio in the car.'

'They're saying it's what's left of Hurricane Louise.'

4

'As if we haven't had enough. You know the Avon's burst its banks? Britford's flooded. I've got friends there. The river's going right through the middle of it.'

'Same with the Ebble. Berwick St John and Bowerchalke look like they might flood. Stoke Farthing, too.'

Mouton nodded. The Met Office was saying that a jet stream strengthened by the warm tropical air pushed northwards by Louise would push low pressure across the country, and that it wasn't likely to move for days.

The dean pointed up at the tower. 'You know who I feel sorry for? Apart from anyone in those villages? David.'

'No. Seriously? He'll still do it today?'

'Just saw him. He's only got another week to go, and then he's done. And he's stubborn as a goat.'

Mouton looked up again at the tower. David Campbell – the cathedral's clerk of works – was a keen amateur photographer and had been undertaking a fundraising project whereby he took a photograph from the same parapet of the cathedral tower every day for a year. An exhibition was planned for when the project was completed. A lot of money had been raised – over fifty thousand pounds – and it had been earmarked for the restoration of the statuary of the West Front of the cathedral. Campbell had been blogging about it, too, posting daily pictures and his reflections as he looked out over the city from the same vantage point. Mouton had been following the blog and knew the dean was right; Campbell's stubbornness was legendary. He had continued with the project through autumn winds that registered at more than a hundred miles an hour on the anemometer atop the spire, and then again through the snows in February; he wouldn't let today's rain stop him and would probably see the storm as a perfect opportunity to take a particularly striking image.

They both looked up to the parapet. 'He's going to get soaked,' Mouton said.

'Rather him than me.'

The dean wished Mouton a good day and took his coffee into the gift shop. Mouton tucked a napkin into his collar. He looked up again as another clap of thunder rumbled overhead. Rainwater swept down the camber of the glass, a ripple that passed through his view of the tower and the spire. Another fork of lightning spread out across the sky as he noticed something up at the juncture where the tower ended and the spire began.

Movement.

A dark blur against the stone.

It took him a moment to realise what it was. A person.

Arms and legs flailing.

Falling down the side of the tower.

He watched for a second and then another.

The body caught against the stone, flipped into a spin and then bounced off a buttress. It spun again, head over heels, limbs flailing, and then disappeared.

Mouton heard the muffled thud of impact as it hit the ground.

He froze, slack-jawed with confusion and not sure what he was supposed to do. The café was quiet for a moment, the silence interrupted by the sound of a dropped tray and then, finally, the first scream.

2

'Come on,' Mackenzie Jones said. 'We need to get in the car or we're going to be late.'

She was trying as hard as she could to keep a sunny temperament despite the challenges that two tired and irritable children were presenting. It had been her weekend to have the two of them and, despite the occasional argument, they had been on their best behaviour and a pleasure to be with. Mack had taken them to enjoy the rides at Paultons Park on Saturday and then to the cinema to see the latest Pixar movie, followed by a visit to the city and lunch at Nando's on Sunday. They had gone to bed much later than would have been the case had they been staying with Mack's estranged husband, Andy, but now – after allowing them to stay up until ten for a midnight feast – she was paying the price. It had been difficult to get them out of bed, and their truculence looked like it was permanent, despite Mack's threats of a trip to the head-master's study should they be late.

'Daddy never shouts at us,' pouted Daisy.

Mack was about to retort that perhaps they should stay with Daddy, then, but bit her tongue. Andy's constant exhortations that she needed to be more patient with them hadn't helped their relationship as it entered its terminal phase, and she couldn't help but imagine his version of the morning routine – beatific smiles and 'pleases' and 'thank yous', whereas all she received were exasperated frowns and grunts – and that was if she was lucky.

Thinking of Andy brought her back to what he had said on Friday night, just after dropping the kids off. He had admitted he was in a relationship with a woman from work and that the two of them were thinking about moving in together. Mack had long since suspected that they had been more than just colleagues and, keeping her voice down for fear of upsetting the children, had asked him how long it had been going on. Andy had confessed that he had been seeing her for six months, their relationship starting when he and Mack had still been together. It would have been the height of hypocrisy for Mack to criticise him for that, given her own dalliance with Atticus Priest, but, as she had lain in bed that night thinking about what he had said, she had found that it made her feel a little better about what had happened. She had convinced herself that the end of the marriage was all her fault, but that wasn't fair. They had both been miserable. Perhaps, if they had been more honest with each other, they might have been able to emerge from the wreckage of their union with a better chance of staying on good terms. That seemed like a lost cause now.

Mack knelt and helped Sebastian as he struggled to tie his laces. 'All right,' she said with a smile. 'Let's get into the car and off we go.'

* * *

Mack navigated the knot of traffic as parents deposited their kids at school, waited until Sebastian and Daisy were safely in the playground, and then repeated the feat as she drove slowly and carefully back towards town. She hadn't had time for her morning coffee and decided to stop and try the café that had opened at Parkwood Gym on the London Road. She left the car outside the gym and, sheltering from the rain beneath Daisy's Peppa Pig umbrella, she hurried inside. She bought a coffee and a pastry to go and was making her way back to the car when she felt the vibration of her phone in her pocket. She climbed back into the driver's seat, rested the coffee on the dashboard, wiped her sugary fingers against her trousers and took out the phone.

It was Robbie Best. 'Good morning.'

'You might want to hold on before you say that, boss.'

She sipped her coffee. 'What's happened?'

'We've got a death. A bad one.'

She put the cup back on the dashboard. 'Go on.'

'It's at the cathedral. The clerk of the works was up in the tower, and he fell off.'

'Jesus.' She paused, allowing that to sink in. *'Jesus.'*

'I'm there now. He fell into the space at the side of the refectory. I'll be honest – he's made a right mess. I think you'd better get down here.'

Best was right: a death *that* macabre had the makings of a story that could get picked up nationally, and was something that she would need to supervise herself.

'Secure the scene,' she said. 'I'm on my way.'

3

'Bandit!' Atticus yelled. *'Bandit!'*

The dog raced away, ignoring Atticus's forlorn attempt to call him to heel. The two of them had gone up to Old Sarum, the ancient settlement that had once been the site of Salisbury itself. It had been defended by way of a motte-and-bailey castle, and the large mound of earthworks remained. It was one of their favourite spots for a walk. Bandit had sprinted off, and Atticus watched as he launched himself down into what was left of the old cathedral. Atticus jumped down into the foundations and jogged over to where the dog was standing over what looked like a rabbit hole.

'What was it, boy? You see a rabbit?'

The dog stood in the classic pose of a German Shorthaired Pointer: one foreleg raised, snout pointing down. Atticus scrubbed the back of his head, clipped the lead to the ring on his collar and gave him a biscuit. He munched it happily and then looked up for another.

'I don't think so,' Atticus said. 'You only get two biscuits when you listen.'

The dog stared up at him plaintively and, his resolve melting, Atticus tossed him a second treat. Bandit caught it in his mouth and wagged his tail happily as he crunched down on it.

10

Atticus led the way out of the foundations and back towards the monument. The rain was still lashing down, but Atticus was wearing his waterproofs, and Bandit didn't care. Atticus didn't care either; it had been a good few weeks and he had been happier than he could remember for months.

His professional reputation had been rehabilitated by two cases that had both received national attention. The first had involved his piercing of the veil surrounding the death of the Mallender family at their house in Grovely Woods. The second, trumping even the first, had seen him solve the mystery of the bodies that had been found in the graveyard of a church in Imber, the village in the middle of Salisbury Plain that had been abandoned to the army. Atticus had been mentioned on the television and radio, and had been interviewed in national newspapers. He had been shrewd in anticipating the publicity and had made sure that he was able to take advantage of it; there had been a flood of enquiries for his assistance and, after quickly filling his own diary, he had cultivated relationships with ex-police officers who were striking out on their own as private investigators in Andover and Devizes. Atticus passed them the cases for which he had no interest in return for healthy finder's fees.

The Imber investigation had had other consequences, too. Atticus's time had also been taken up by working with the police in trying to solve the murder of Richard Miller, the sitting MP for Salisbury. Miller had been released pending his trial for an incident that took place while he was an officer in the army forty years ago. Miller had been in Londonderry and had been implicated in the deaths of two Irish locals. That case had also involved Alfred Burns – the paedophile who had returned to Salisbury and whom Atticus had been pursuing for months – and James York. Miller had admitted that he had stolen from the Irish, but pleaded ignorance as to the murders and said that Burns and York had been responsible. The Crown Prosecution Service had determined that there was insufficient evidence to charge Miller for murder and had limited their prosecution of him to the thefts to which he had confessed.

But the crimes of York and Burns went deeper than that. York had been questioned about the bodies of five teenage girls found at the Methodist chapel at Imber and had admitted that he and Burns had been involved in their deaths. York had confessed that the two of them had been guilty of kidnapping, abusing and then murdering teenagers that Burns had selected from those he worked with as part of a council scheme for disadvantaged youngsters.

Burns – chased out of the country by Atticus's investigation of him – had then blackmailed both York and Miller for the money he needed to maintain his lifestyle. York admitted that he had killed Burns when he realised that the blackmail would never end. York made his confession and then took his own life in his cell. It was discovered later that he had been suffering from terminal cancer.

Miller had been questioned and reported that Burns had been blackmailing him about the Londonderry incident. Atticus had doubted then that the thefts were the extent of his involvement, and his suspicions had been confirmed by Miller's subsequent murder. Atticus had found his body in the back of a car outside his office after a tip-off by someone he knew only as Jack_of_Hearts, his opponent in games of online chess who knew more about Atticus than ought to have been possible.

The affair was complicated, and, while Atticus had made progress in untangling some of it, he knew that Miller and York had lied to him about the extent of their culpability. All three men were dead, but that wasn't good enough for Atticus. His certainty that there were depths to their conspiracy that had yet to be plumbed irritated him beyond measure. He had never been able to leave a puzzle unsolved, and that – together with fear that there were more victims to discover – had seen him working long into the nights to try to uncover new angles that might help him understand how deep things *really* went.

Bandit cocked his head to one side, his tongue lolling out of his mouth.

'What?'

The dog picked up a stick and dropped it at Atticus's feet.

'No time for that. We need to get back to the office.'

Atticus had a busy day ahead of him. He had an appointment to see the senior officer who had been sent down from London to review the stalled investigation into Miller's death, and then a potential new client had arranged to come into the office to discuss the work that she was interested in giving him.

Atticus tried to set off, but the dog pulled against him.

'Come on, mutt.'

Bandit growled at him.

Atticus reached into his pocket and took out another biscuit. 'I'll make it worth your while.'

The dog eyed the biscuit, licked his lips and then relented. Atticus set off to the car before he could change his mind.

4

Mack drove slowly through the High Street Gate and into the Cathedral Close. It was just before nine, and the narrow road beyond the gate was empty, yet to be choked by the tourists who would arrive in their tour buses later. The rain ran along the gutters and pooled around drains that had long since taken all the water they could manage. An inch of water spread across the stone from one side to the other. Mack rolled through the flood to the hut where the attendants checked the credentials of those who wanted to continue deeper into the Close. The guard stayed in the shelter of the hut and indicated that she should lower the window.

'Morning,' she called out. 'DCI Jones.'

She took out the leather wallet that held her warrant card and let it fall open so that the man could see it.

'Bloody awful start to the day,' the man called back.

'You see anything?'

'I was in here, reading the paper. Only found out when the ambulance came, but a fat lot of good that would've done him.'

'You know him?'

The man nodded. 'David Campbell – the clerk of works. Been here for years – almost as long as me. Nice bloke.'

'Thank you. Where should I park?'

14

The man pointed to a row of empty spaces to the right of the hut. 'Anywhere over there.'

Mack backed into the space and killed the engine. The rain hadn't let up at all, but all she had to shelter herself from it was the bright pink umbrella. She certainly couldn't use that, so she grabbed a copy of *The Times* from last week that she had chucked on the back seat and used that as a makeshift shield. She hurried across the grounds towards the cathedral's main door. Mack had been here with Atticus last week to exercise Bandit before they went back to his place. She hadn't seen him over the weekend – she wasn't quite ready to introduce him to her kids – but he had never been far from her thoughts.

Vernon Edwards, one of the uniformed constables who worked at Bourne Hill station, was standing in the doorway at the side of the cathedral that opened on to the cloisters.

He was pale. 'Ma'am.'

'You all right?'

'It's not pleasant. I was close to bringing up my breakfast.'

'Where's Robbie?'

He pointed into the foyer beyond the main entrance to the cathedral. Mack saw that Best was waiting next to the cashier's desk.

'Keep everyone out until we've got a handle on it.'

'Will do.'

She stepped around Edwards and went into the foyer.

Best was speaking to a member of the cathedral staff. He saw Mack and turned as she approached.

'Morning, boss.'

She looked at the man to whom Best had been speaking. 'I'm DCI Mackenzie Jones.'

'Kingsley Lamb,' he said. 'I'm the dean.'

Mack put out her hand and shook Lamb's.

15

'It's a dreadful morning,' Lamb said. 'Absolutely dreadful.'

'The dean has closed the cathedral,' Best said.

Lamb nodded. 'We can't possibly open today.'

'No,' Mack said. 'We'll need to have a good look around, too.'

'Of course. It'll be obvious, though, surely? What happened, I mean?'

'Hard to say until we've been able to examine everything. The man who fell – the clerk of the works?'

'David Campbell.'

'What can you tell me about him?'

'I've been here for ten years, but he's worked here for longer. More than thirty. Incredibly helpful to me when I was settling in. *Incredibly*. He knew everything about the cathedral. If I ever had a problem with the building, he was always the one to go to. Just a really good man. I can't *begin* to tell you how devastating this will be for everyone who works here. He was very popular. And goodness knows how awful this'll be for his family.'

'Thank you. I'd better take a look.' She turned to Best. 'Where do we need to go?'

Best pointed. 'There's a space between the refectory and the tower. He landed in there.'

'Any witnesses?'

'Three. I've got them in the Chapter House.'

'I was in the gift shop when it happened,' the dean said. 'I didn't see anything, but I heard the sound when . . . when . . .'

'Of course,' Mack said. 'Thank you. Do you think you could go to the Chapter House with the others? I'll want to talk to you once I've seen the body.'

'Of course.'

Mack turned to Best and indicated that he should lead on. They went through the gift shop, passed between the racks of trinkets and knick-knacks that the cathedral flogged to tourists with more money than sense, and went into the refectory. The glass ceiling overhead offered a spectacular view of the spire and the storm.

There was a door at the end of the café. They went through it and emerged on the narrow grassy margin that separated the walls of the cathedral from the refectory. The body of a man was sprawled face down across the ground, his head propped up at an unnatural angle against the stone and with his arms and legs spread wide. He was facing away from them. The rain streamed down onto them, living and dead alike, and a steady curtain fell down the wall from where a blocked gutter had overflowed.

Mack abandoned the sodden newspaper and knelt next to the body. She saw that Campbell's right leg had been bent backwards beneath him, both arms were broken and that the hair on the back of his head was matted with blood.

'You weren't kidding,' she said.

'Fyfe is on the way, but . . . well, cause of death is pretty bloody obvious.'

She looked up and blinked through the rain at the tower and the spire, and felt an emptiness in her gut. She had never been great with heights and, as a child, she had found it difficult to stop imagining what it would feel like to fall off something tall.

She stepped back from the body. 'What do we know about him?'

'Sixty-three years old, father of three, lived in Winterslow. Worked here all his professional life – stonemason out of college and then climbed the ladder.' Best paused, thinking about what he had just said. 'Pun not intended. He's raised thousands for the cathedral over the years. This project was on course to make six figures.'

'What project?'

'He was taking photos from the same parapet every day for a year. He called it "A Year in the Life". There was supposed to be an exhibition once he was done. He was raising money for the cathedral. The dean told me about it.'

'I remember. I read about it in the *Salisbury Journal*.'

'There's a blog on the cathedral's website.'

'Which parapet was it?'

'East.'

'Was he up there on his own?'

'Think so.'

'CCTV?'

'Plenty in the cathedral but nothing up there.'

'Is it secured?'

'Yes. Yaxley's up there.'

Mack looked down at the mangled body once more and was grateful that she hadn't had time to finish the pastry. She had seen plenty of dead bodies over the course of her career in the police, but this one was near the top of the list when it came to gruesomeness.

'I'd better go and have a word with the witnesses.'

5

Atticus had been sitting in the waiting area for twenty minutes. Mack had told him that he needed to be on time, that his usual lackadaisical approach to punctuality would be unwise for this particular appointment and that he should be on his best behaviour.

And, for once, he had listened to her.

Detective Chief Superintendent Lee Murphy had been sent by the Metropolitan Police to oversee the investigation into Richard Miller's murder. Murphy worked in counterterrorism and, given that Miller had been an MP, he had been tasked with ruling out terrorism as a motive. Atticus knew that politics had nothing to do with why Miller had been killed, but realised there would be all manner of boxes that needed to be ticked when the victim was this high profile.

DCS Murphy had asked to see Atticus at nine thirty and, with Mack's advice fresh in his mind, he had arrived five minutes early. He was wearing his suit and shirt, freshly laundered at the dry-cleaner's in Waitrose, and drummed into himself the guidance that Mack had given him: be polite, don't show off, don't let Murphy know what you really think of him.

All those things would be difficult, but Atticus was going to do his best.

Atticus had just looked at his watch when the door to the interview room opened. A man stepped out into the corridor, saw Atticus and made his way over to him.

'Mr Priest?'

'That's right.'

'I'm DCS Lee Murphy.'

Murphy put out his hand and Atticus shook it. He was dressed in a navy-blue suit with a white shirt and a blue and white striped tie. He was bald, with a fuzz of hair to each side of his head that had evidently just been trimmed. He wore glasses with rectangular frames, his eyes were small, his nose was large and his top lip curled up just a little, in such a way as to give him an unfortunate and permanent sneer.

'Sorry for keeping you. Appreciate you coming over. Shall we get cracking?'

He gestured to the open door.

Atticus stood. 'How long will you need?'

'Depends on what you have to say. I've spoken to everyone else, but I thought I'd save you until last. Miller's body was found outside your office, after all. You'll definitely have the most interesting perspective on all this, and I don't want to hurry. Please – come inside and we can get started.'

6

Best led the way to the East Walk of the cloisters and then into the Chapter House. John Fulbright, a uniformed constable from the station, had been posted in the vestibule to keep an eye on the witnesses. He nodded to Mack and Best and then held the door open for them. The octagonal building beyond was used to display the cathedral's copy of the Magna Carta; Mack had brought the kids here and had tried – and failed – to interest them in the document that was protected behind thick Perspex. Today, though, her attention was taken by the three people who were sitting and standing inside: one woman, who was dressed in the black uniform of the refectory waiting staff, and two men, one of whom wore chefs' whites, while the other wore the green and yellow sash of a cathedral guide.

'Where's the dean?' she asked Fulbright.

'He said he had to take a call.'

Mack nodded and turned her attention back to the two men and the woman.

'Who got the best look?'

Best pointed to the man with the green sash. 'Him.'

'I've seen him before,' Mack said. 'What's his name?'

Best opened his notebook. 'Clive Mouton.'

The name was familiar, too, and, as Mack looked over at the old man, she realised why: he had been a teacher at the school that she and Andy had been considering when they were looking for somewhere to send the kids.

She made her way across the room to where he was standing. 'Mr Mouton,' she said. 'I'm DCI Mackenzie Jones.' She offered her hand and he took it. 'Do you remember me?'

'Have we met?'

'I came for a visit to the school.'

He smiled. 'Just before I retired. I remember. You had two children? Daisy and . . .'

'Daisy and Sebastian. That's right. You've got an excellent memory.'

'You didn't put them with us, did you?'

'We decided we couldn't really afford it.'

'Shame. Where did you send them?'

'Greentrees.'

'Good school,' he said. 'Are they doing well?'

'Very, thanks.' She indicated behind her in the direction of the refectory. 'DI Best said you saw what happened?'

'I'm not sure I'd go that far.'

'Tell me what you saw.'

'I was having my breakfast. The rain was coming down hard, and it was difficult to see much through it. I caught a glimpse of him falling and heard the noise when he hit the ground.' He paused. 'It's horrible. Poor man.'

'Did you know him?'

'Of course. Everyone did. He *lived* for the cathedral. He told me once that he decided he was going to work here when he was a boy. Do you live in Salisbury?'

'I do.'

'So you know what it's like – you look up and see the spire twenty times a day, the same as everyone else. I remember he told me once how his lifetime ambition was to climb to the top. He did it, too. Look on YouTube – he videoed himself going up to change the anemometer last year.'

'That wouldn't be for me.'

'Me neither. It's bloody high. I'm one of the guides who take people up the tower. That's more than high enough for me.'

'What was he like as a person?'

'Larger than life. I don't know anyone who'd have a bad word to say about him.'

'Could he have been depressed?'

'Why?' Mouton frowned, and then, as he realised what Mack was implying, he shook his head vigorously. 'Oh. You think he might've jumped.' He shook his head again. 'I can't see that at all.'

'We have to look at all the possibilities. An accident is possible, but I think it's unlikely if all he was doing was taking photographs. I've been up to the tower, and the walls up there are quite high, aren't they?'

'The railings come up to here,' he said, holding his hand up to the top of his chest.

'So it would be difficult to fall.'

He nodded. 'I see what you mean. Yes – you're right. He'd have to climb on top of them.'

'Anything to make you think he might have done that?'

'I haven't spoken to him for a while. I'm probably not the person to ask.'

Mack smiled. 'Thank you, Mr Mouton. You've been very helpful.'

Mack asked Best to introduce her to the others and she spoke to them in turn. The woman worked behind the counter and said that she had been looking down at the till when she heard

Campbell hitting the ground. The man was a chef and explained that he had been preparing one of the soups for the lunchtime serving; he had been looking up and saw something fall, but, like it had with Mouton, the rain on the glass roof had made it impossible to make out any detail. He was pale and seemed to have taken what had happened worse than either of the other two; Mack had finished her gentle questions when he held up a hand, swallowed and stumbled for the door. He had only just made it into the cloisters when she heard him retching and then the splatter of vomit on the ground.

Mack went back to where Best was waiting for her.

'I'd better go up and have a look.'

'I'll come up with you,' he said. 'I know the way.'

7

Murphy led the way into the room and indicated that Atticus should take one of the two chairs on the side of the desk. He did, undoing the button of his jacket and sitting down.

Murphy pointed to a jug and two cups that sat on the desk. 'Coffee?'

'Please.'

Atticus looked around as Murphy busied himself with the drinks. He had evidently taken this room as his base. The shelves to the right of the desk had been filled with ring binders arranged alphabetically; the names on the sides referred to people who had been involved in the twin investigations: the murders at Imber and the murder of Miller. Atticus saw ring binders for Alfred Burns and James York and two labelled with Richard Miller's name. Others were labelled with the names of witnesses who had been interviewed during the investigations. Another – to Atticus's surprise and discomfort – bore his name. The desk was neat and tidy, with a notebook next to a closed laptop and a pen laid on top of it. Atticus noticed that everything had been lined up in perfect geometrical symmetry: the laptop, the notebook and the pen were all parallel to one another. It spoke to a punctiliousness that Atticus would bear in mind during the interview.

Murphy handed Atticus one of the two mugs of coffee and took the second around to the other side of the desk. He pulled out his chair and sat down. 'Thank you for coming in, Mr Priest.'

Atticus manufactured an easy smile. 'Happy to help.'

'I'm glad to hear that. Like I said – you're of special interest to this review. You're the only person who's had any contact with the suspect in Mr Miller's death.'

'It seems so.'

Murphy sipped his coffee. 'Do you know how long I've been in Salisbury?'

'A month?'

'Just over. Chief Constable Beckton called my guv'nor three days after Miller's body was found. The two of them decided that they'd give Wiltshire a free run at it for the first week to see what they could turn up and, depending on progress, I'd bring my team down to see if we could lend a hand. You know what they found in the first week?'

'I don't know,' Atticus said.

'Jack shit, Mr Priest. They didn't find anything. Between you, me and the gatepost, I wanted to get down here straight away. You know how it is – the first day or two of any investigation is always the most important. The golden hours. The longer you leave it, the trickier it gets. Evidence is destroyed. Recollections fade. The trail goes cold. That's what's happened here – you had the murder of an MP, they wasted time, the trail went *very* cold very fast, and any advantage we might have had by getting off our arses and acting quickly was lost.'

'I think that's a little unfair.'

'Do you?'

'I do. They got a team on it quickly and did everything that you'd expect.'

'What are you basing that on?'

'Sorry?'

'Your impression that the investigation went as it should – I'm just curious what information you're using to make that assumption. You don't work here any more.'

'No. But I was consulting on the bodies at Imber.'

Murphy stroked his chin. 'That's true, you were. And I have to say – I found that all a little odd. But we'll get into that later.' He reached down, opened one of the drawers in the desk and took out a portable recording device. He laid it on the table and gestured down to it. 'Do you mind?'

'Not at all.'

'Super.' Murphy pressed a button on the side of the device; it gave a bleep to indicate that it was recording. 'This is DCS Murphy with Mr Atticus Priest, previously a DC at Bourne Hill in Salisbury.' He gave the time and the date, and then reached over for the ring binder that bore Atticus's name. He opened it and flipped to a page that had been marked with a yellow Post-it note. 'Now then, Mr Priest – I'm particularly interested in the circumstances of your discovery of the body of Richard Miller. Do you think you could tell me what happened that night?'

'Of course. What would you like to know?'

'How about Jack_of_Hearts. Start there – tell me about him. How did you meet?'

'Jack? I've never met him in person. I play online chess, and he was someone I played against.'

'Random, then?'

'From my point of view – yes.'

'But not his.'

'No. Clearly not.'

'You think he picked you out?'

'I'm sure he did.'

'But you don't know who he is?'

'No.'

'Or where he is?'

'No. And I don't know if he's male or female, either.'

'Noted – but we'll assume he's a man. Tell me about your first interactions with him.'

'He'd leave me comments in the chat box while we played. Nothing out of the ordinary to begin with, but then he started to say things that made it obvious that he knew more about me than he should've.'

'Like what?'

'My name, for one. The game's anonymous, and he shouldn't have been able to find that out. I still don't know how he did it.'

'What else?'

'Things about my personal life.'

Murphy eyed him across the table. 'He knew about you and DCI Jones?'

'Yes.'

'I want to come back to that, too.' Murphy scribbled in his notebook. 'Tell me what happened the night you found Miller's body.'

'Jack messaged me. He said he wanted to meet me in the Cathedral Close. He wasn't there, but he'd left a phone for me in one of the bins.'

'And he called you on it?'

'Yes.'

'What did he sound like?'

'He didn't want me to recognise his voice, so he used software to mask it.'

'Software?'

'An app. There are loads of them. Look on the App Store.'

'What did he say?'

'That he knew Miller was involved with what York and Burns had been doing. He said they were abusing kids. He said he was

28

looking for the names of the customers York and Burns were serving.'

'"Customers"?'

'That's what he said.'

'He said he was involved, too.'

'Yes.'

'What do you think he meant by that?'

'I don't know. He said he was hoping I could help him.'

'But you couldn't?'

'I didn't – I *don't* – know anything about that. Customers? It was the first I'd heard of it. I asked if he had proof that Miller was involved in whatever York and Burns were doing, and he told me not to worry about it. He said it didn't matter. He said Miller had already been taken care of.'

Murphy flicked through the ring binder. 'You said he told you that Miller wouldn't be able to hurt anyone any more.'

'Exactly. He said he was giving him to me. I went back to my office and there was a car on the street outside. I opened the boot and, well . . . I found Miller.'

Murphy looked at the ring binder. 'You said Jack quoted the Bible?'

'Psalm 106, verse three. "Blessed are they who observe justice, who do righteousness at all times." He left me a number of other passages, too. "Vengeance is mine, and recompense, for the time when their foot shall slip; for the day of their calamity is at hand, and their doom comes swiftly."'

Murphy looked down and read. '"Eye for eye, tooth for tooth, hand for hand, foot for foot, burn for burn, wound for wound, stripe for stripe."'

Atticus nodded. 'Exodus twenty-one.'

'I read all the passages he left for you. None of them actually condone revenge.'

'He has a selective understanding of scripture.'

Murphy tapped his pen against the edge of the desk. 'You said that you thought someone might have been watching when you found the body?'

'They were, for sure. My office is on New Street, opposite the multistorey. There was someone down by the junction with Catherine Street.'

'And they waved at you?'

'They raised an arm. I ran down to try to catch them up, but they'd gone.'

'That's a shame.'

Atticus nodded.

'You think it was him?'

'That'd be my guess.'

'And any contact with him since?'

'None.'

'No more chess?'

'There's an open game between us, but he hasn't made a move for weeks.'

'You'll let us know if he does get back in touch, won't you?'

'Of course.'

Murphy scribbled in his notebook again. Atticus tried to see what it was, but it was upside down, and Murphy was obscuring it with his hand.

'Can I help you with anything else?'

Murphy drew a line and looked up. 'Yes,' he said. 'The second thing I wanted to discuss was the nature of your engagement with the police. A consultancy like the one you negotiated is unusual. More than unusual, actually – unprecedented. I've been police for twenty years and I don't think I've ever seen anything like it before.'

Atticus's condition meant that he had never been good at reading people when it came to what they thought of him, but even he could see that Murphy was not approaching the conversation in an even-handed manner. He had an agenda that was dangerous for him and *especially* for Mack. Atticus knew where the discussion was headed and reminded himself to keep a civil tongue. 'What would you like to know about it?'

'Who arranged it?'

'DCI Jones.'

'And the two of you are in a relationship.'

'We are, but I don't see how that's relevant—'

'Seriously? You don't?' The smile stayed on Murphy's face, but his eyes didn't mirror it. 'Why did she think it was a good idea?'

'You'd have to ask her that.'

'I will, but I'm asking *you* now – why do you think she wanted your help?'

'Because I'm very good at what I do.' The tethers that had restrained Atticus's temper were starting to fray. 'You know the murders in Grovely Woods?'

'Yes. You were able to cast some light on them.'

'And the bodies at Imber?'

'That was you, too. I know. No one is doubting you've been able to get results. My question is more about DCI Jones's judgement in bringing you back. You failed a drug test – didn't you?'

'No,' Atticus said. 'I passed a drug test after someone grassed me up.'

Atticus knew who had reported him – Mack's estranged husband, Andy – but there was no point in telling Murphy that.

'Semantics,' Murphy said. 'The urine test showed evidence of cannabis, but you were under the limit. You were asked to take a hair strand test – which you knew you would fail – so you resigned before the board could fire you. The thing I couldn't understand is how you were allowed back in the building without your clearance. So I checked. I called the vetting unit, and it appears that no one thought to tell them what had happened. You still have your clearance.'

'I'm not sure how this is relevant to what happened to Miller.'

'I'm looking at how the investigation was conducted. The DCI's judgement is relevant to that, and she put that in question when she put someone with whom she was in a relationship back on the payroll, especially when that someone – *you*, Mr Priest – has what might charitably be described as a questionable disciplinary record. It's a classic conflict of interest.'

Atticus started to stand. 'Are we finished?'

'No,' Murphy said. 'We're not. You know the next thing that I didn't understand? Surely, I thought to myself, *surely* someone in accounts would've reported that you were being paid.' He opened the ring binder, unfastened the rings and took out a sheaf of paper. He took one from the top and turned it around so that Atticus could see what it was: one of his invoices. 'You set up a new company and invoiced through it. Wiltshire Police pays the company, and I presume it pays you – no one in admin knows any better.'

'Come on,' Atticus said. 'Is that the best you can do? There's nothing wrong with that. It's normal.'

'Yes, it is. But when you add it to the fact that you shouldn't have had clearance, it looks to me that we have a pattern of deceptive behaviour.'

'DCI Jones cleared everything with the chief constable.'

'So I understand. And I'm sure there'll be a conversation about that in due course.'

Atticus rose and slid the chair back under the table. 'We're definitely done.'

'We are,' Murphy said. 'But it's a pause, Mr Priest, not the end of my interest in you. I'm going back to London for a few days, but I'd like to see you again when I'm back.'

8

Mack followed Robbie Best into the cathedral. The door that was used to take visitors up the tower was at the western end of the nave. There was a diorama nearby that showed what the cathedral might have looked like when it was being built, together with silken Regimental Colours that were, according to custom, being allowed to disintegrate into nothingness, at which point the Colour and its pike would be cremated and interred.

Their footsteps echoed against the flagstones as they made their way to the door. Best opened it and gestured that Mack should go through. There was a small vestibule inside, with a bank of lockers along one wall that were used by guests who wanted to leave their bags rather than carrying them all the way up the tower. Best took Mack up a narrow flight of stone steps and then along a passage that traced the wall of the nave, looking down on the dean and a group of volunteers who had gathered below. They continued, climbing another flight of stairs and then passing through the roof space above the nave. She could see the gentle curvature of the walls that held up the tower, as well as the buttresses that had been installed to strengthen the pillars when the spire was added.

A third flight took them into the tower itself. They saw the mechanism of the cathedral's clock and then, on the level above that, the bells. They continued, taking the narrowest stairway yet and emerging in a large square chamber with four doors that led onto the parapets outside. Mack looked up into the spire and saw the wooden scaffolding that had been used by the builders who had erected it nearly a thousand years before.

Another constable – Ryan Yaxley – was standing guard by one of the doors.

'Morning, boss.'

'Morning, Ryan. Which one did he fall from?'

'South door,' Yaxley said. 'This one.'

The doorway was low, and Mack had to duck her head to get through it. The parapet was narrow, and the door had to be closed again to get to the other side. The rain was still falling heavily, and puddles had gathered around the holes in the wall that had been drilled to allow the run-off to drain. The stone flags were soaked, too, sheeted with standing water. Sodden feathers had floated into the corners, and Mack spotted the half-eaten carcass of a pigeon. A tripod had been set up at one end of the parapet.

She pointed down to the dead bird. 'The peregrines did that?'

Best nodded. 'They nest on the other parapet, but they leave dead birds and feathers everywhere.'

Mack went up to the edge and looked down. The top of the tower was more than two hundred feet above the ground. The refectory was directly below them. She could see Campbell's body. An iron railing had been fixed to the wall, high enough to reach the top of her chest. Her first suspicions had been right: it would have been impossible for anyone to fall from the parapet unless they had purposefully climbed the wall.

The rain was still lashing down, and Mack's hair was quickly plastered to her forehead. Thunder boomed and, for a moment, she wondered what would happen if the spire was struck by lightning.

'Let's get back inside.'

They went back through the door and closed it. Mack noticed a case for the tripod and a camera bag on the floor.

'Campbell's?'

'That's what I was told,' Best said. 'He must have put the tripod up first before he got his camera.'

'Probably didn't want to get it wet.'

'So why would he put up his tripod and then jump?'

Best shrugged. 'People do weird things.'

The wind picked up and rattled the doors against their frames. 'It's getting worse,' Yaxley said.

Beneath them, the bells sounded for the hour, and Mack shivered a little in the cold. She put a hand on Best's arm. 'Can I leave you to deal with the follow-up?'

'Of course,' he said. 'What about you?'

'Better go and see the widow.'

9

Atticus concentrated on calming down as he headed back to his office. Murphy was the kind of man for whom he had no respect whatsoever: an overinflated opinion of his own ability contributed to a sneering sense of superiority that would have been hilarious if he didn't have the authority of rank and the potential to make things very difficult for him and – *especially* – for Mack. Atticus knew that he himself could be guilty of arrogance – Mack told him that regularly – but at least he could walk the walk as well as talk the talk. Murphy obviously could not, and having a man like that in a position to tell him what to do had been intolerable. Atticus had just about managed to keep a lid on his temper, but much more of Murphy's sarcasm today and things might have been different.

The rain was still coming down hard as Atticus cut through the Brown Street car park and continued along New Street to his office. He had given some thought to moving to a more impressive address, but, after talking it through with Mack, he'd decided that there was no point in going to the expense. The two rooms that he rented were adequate for what he needed, especially now that he was spending several nights every week with her at the house she was renting in Harnham. She had, however, exhorted him to get a cleaner to keep things neat and tidy and, after finding it more difficult than he had expected to secure the services of someone who was prepared to put up with his mess, he had finally found a woman looking for a handful of hours a week for extra money while her children were at school. Her name was Felicity, and she had already made a significant improvement to the accommodation. She had encouraged Atticus to ensure that there was a clear divide between the smaller room at the rear of the property that he used as his bedroom, and the larger room that overlooked New Street where he worked and met his clients. Atticus had cleared out everything from each room that had no reason to be there, had filled three large bin bags with unwanted junk and had given several pieces of unwanted furniture to the Trussell Trust.

He climbed the exterior staircase at the back of the building to the door that opened into his bedroom. Bandit was waiting for him, his tail wagging so much that it beat out a rhythm against the wall.

'Move,' Atticus said, giving the dog's head a pat and slipping inside.

The bedroom was much more presentable now. Mack had taken him to John Lewis and had picked out new bedding and other soft furnishings that made a difference to how the room looked. Atticus still slept on a mattress on the floor, but, now, at least until he got around to buying a proper bed, it didn't look quite so much like a student squat.

He went to the tiny kitchen that was hidden under the stairs to the flat on the third floor, took out a tin of dog food, opened it and then spooned it into Bandit's bowl. He changed his water and put both bowls in the corner of the bedroom for him to enjoy. Scrubbing the dog behind the ears, he told him to be quiet; Bandit wolfed his food, then curled up on the bed and closed his eyes.

Atticus went through into the office. This room had been transformed, too. He still had the small two-seat sofa in the bay that extended out over the pavement below, but he had exchanged the crate that he had used as a coffee table for a proper one with a glass surface and chrome legs. He had the same large desk with his laptop and two monitors, but had added two new filing cabinets for his case files, and had commissioned a local carpenter to build a bespoke bookshelf upon which he could arrange his extensive collection of textbooks. Tomes on criminology, psychology, forensic science and a host of more ephemeral subjects were on show, with one of Felicity's tasks being to ensure that they were put back in the right place once he was done with them rather than being strewn around the room, as had been the case before.

Atticus opened his diary and checked the entry that he had made when he had set up the appointment for this morning. The woman's name was Nina Parsons, and the email that she had sent had simply asked whether it would be possible to make an appointment. Atticus had searched online to see if he could find anything that would give him an idea about what she wanted to discuss, but 'Nina Parsons' was far from an original name, and there had been dozens of hits. He had replied and asked her to tell him what she wanted to talk to him about, but had been politely rebuffed. The matter was delicate, she said, and she would much rather discuss it face to face. There was intrigue in her secrecy and, finding it impossible to say no, he had agreed to the appointment. If the case was not of interest, he would send it to one of the agencies to whom he had been referring work and pocket the commission.

The bell rang. Atticus left the office, diverted quickly into the bathroom to check that he looked presentable and, happy enough that he did, descended the stairs to the door. He opened it; a woman was standing in the passageway with her back to him, shaking the rain from a large golfing umbrella.

'Nina?'

She turned and smiled. 'Yes, that's right. Atticus Priest?'

'That's me.'

'And we *did* say eleven, didn't we?'

'We did.'

'Thank goodness. I had a blonde moment and thought it might have been twelve.'

Nina was of medium height and build, with short dark hair and dark eyes. She wore no make-up and could, had she been of a mind to put any effort into it, have been strikingly attractive. She was slender, and her fine cheekbones and nose had a pixie-ish quality to them. She put out her hand and Atticus shook it; her fingers were callused and her skin was cold to the touch.

Atticus led the way up the stairs and into the office. Nina followed and, at Atticus's suggestion, handed him her coat and umbrella. He guessed that she was in her mid-thirties, and her clothes – a bulky sweater with a T-shirt and jeans – looked like they might have been pulled together in twenty seconds. Her eyes had an enigmatic quality to them and her mouth suggested cynicism.

She sat down on the sofa. 'Thank you for seeing me.'

'Not at all.'

She looked around the room, taking it in with an appraising eye.

'You're a soldier?' Atticus said.

'I am,' she replied, her eyebrows kinking up in amused surprise. 'I didn't tell you that, though.'

'You've just returned from abroad.'

'Yes.'

'Iraq?'

'Cyprus. I've been back a couple of months and I've been trying to keep my tan up.'

He nodded. 'I haven't done too badly if that's all I've got wrong.'

She eyed him. 'How do you know I'm in the army?'

'You have a military bearing. Your hair is cut short and very neat – that's always a strong indication, especially in a place like

39

Salisbury with so many soldiers. The recent travel is obvious from your tan.'

'That could've been because I've been on holiday.'

'It could, but, when added to everything else . . .' He shrugged. 'Service abroad is indicated by the evidence.'

'It still feels like you're reaching.'

He pointed to the timepiece she wore on her left wrist. 'That's a G10 quartz watch. Standard army-issue with a military strap.'

'It is. But you *can* buy knock-offs.'

'True,' he admitted. 'But it's another useful piece of evidence. It all adds to the picture.'

'Fair enough,' she said. 'Very impressive.'

'Not really,' he replied with false modesty. 'It's just a question of keeping your eyes open.'

'So you can spot the "trifles"?'

That brought Atticus up short. 'Excuse me?'

She stared at him. '"You know my method,"' she intoned. '"It is founded upon the observation of trifles."'

Atticus sat back, unable to prevent the smile of amusement that crept across his face as he realised what she had just said. 'Well played. You know your Holmes.'

'"The Boscombe Valley Mystery,"' she said. 'Not one of my favourites, but still a cut above the usual. I love all the classic authors – Allingham and Christie and Sayers, especially – but Conan Doyle's my favourite. I read everything when I was little – the novels *and* the shorts – and then I read them all again while I was in Dhekelia.'

He chuckled. 'It's my turn to be impressed.'

'Your little demonstration – does it impress people?'

'Usually.'

'And you see yourself as being like him?'

Atticus shook his head, trying to hide his embarrassment at her perspicacity. 'Hardly. Some of his deductions are a little too incredible for me. But do I enjoy reading the stories?' He held up his hands. 'I do. Guilty as charged.'

'You don't need to show off. I'd decided that I wanted you to work on my little problem before today.'

'I'm flattered.'

'I've been reading up about you. The murders at that house in Grovely Woods – you got that man off, didn't you?'

'I did.'

'And then the bodies they dug up at Imber. You solved that.'

'I played a part,' he replied, wanting to say that she was right, yet knowing that boastfulness was a bad look; humility was awkward for him as ever.

'What I have for you isn't nearly as exciting.'

Atticus took his notebook and a pen. 'Tell me about it.'

'It's a little embarrassing. I've been seeing a man. I met him online two months ago. We've seen each other quite a lot since then, and I suppose you could say that we're getting serious. He's nice and we get on well. The thing is, though, I've been married before. My ex-husband was a liar and a cheat, and I promised myself that I'd never put myself in a position where someone could put me through it the way he did ever again. We split up three years ago, and I've been single ever since. It's not that I haven't dated anyone; it's just that I have real trouble trusting anyone. I've never let anyone get close to me, and in the end, they leave.' She shrugged helplessly. 'It's a problem.'

'I can see that it would be.'

'But my new . . . well, my new *boyfriend*, I suppose . . . He's nice. He's kind; he's thoughtful and generous. He's also married – so there's *that* – but he says that he's going to be leaving her. We get on well and I don't want to mess it up because I don't trust him.'

'And you want me to make sure there are no skeletons in the closet?'

She nodded. 'Exactly. I told you it wasn't exciting.'

'My job isn't always exciting. There's a lot of sitting around drinking cold coffee while you wait for someone to maybe turn up. I have no trouble taking the job, but it would be unfair of me if I didn't tell you it would be more expensive than it would have to be. I could refer you to someone who would be able to do an excellent job for you at half the price.'

'Money's not a problem,' she said. 'And I don't want someone else – I want you.'

'I'm not going to turn the work away if you really want me to do it, but I *do* think it's overkill.'

'Like a hammer to crack a nut?'

'Exactly.'

'I *want* a hammer,' she said. 'If I'm going to have a relationship with him, I need to know that there's nothing in his history that might cause problems in the future. I need someone to do that whom I know I can trust. Someone who's good at what they do.' She smiled and gestured to him. 'Hence me being here.'

'Fine,' he replied. 'I'd be happy to do it. What can you tell me about your boyfriend?'

'Do you think I could have a drink before we get into that?'

Atticus put his hand to his forehead. 'My manners – I'm so sorry. Of course. What would you like?'

'Coffee?'

'The kitchen's outside – just a minute.'

Atticus went outside, filled the kettle, plugged it in and flicked the switch to set it to boil. He was happy to take the new work, even as he knew he was going to have to do the most thorough job possible. The woman waiting in his office was not someone he would be able to distract with demonstrations of his intellect.

She had demolished his attempt to impress her, and the only other person who was able to see through his smoke and mirrors in the same way was Mack. Work was work, though, and since he had been honest about what he would cost, and the fact that she could get a report somewhere else for much less, he would charge her the full whack and give her the A1 service.

It was her prerogative to choose him to do the work, just as it was his to charge her enough for him to be able to afford to treat Mack to a romantic weekend in Paris.

10

Mack could have sent one of her junior officers to go and speak to Debbie Campbell. She could think of two officers with training in victim support who would have been able to pass on the news; Francine Patterson, for example, had an especially calming way about her. But Mack was never going to do that. She had long made it her policy not to duck the difficult moments that the job brought her way. Conveying the news of a loved one's death was the most difficult professional conversation it was possible for her to have; she'd never shirked the responsibility so far and didn't mean to start now.

She left Robbie Best to bring the investigation to a close at the cathedral, so that the building could eventually be released back to the dean, and hurried through the rain to collect her car. The dean had provided Campbell's address, and she tapped the post-code into her satnav and waited for it to plot a route. The house was in Coombe Bissett, a small village to the south of Salisbury, and it would take fifteen minutes to get there.

She put the car into gear and pulled out. It had been a busier start to the day than she had anticipated, but at least she had negotiated the weekend without killing the kids, and they were now safely at school and ready for Andy to collect them in the afternoon. He had insisted that he would have the children for most of the time on the basis that he didn't want them to be confused by Atticus's role in her life. Mack hadn't wanted that either, at least not until she had worked out precisely *what* that role was going to be. Atticus was moving a little faster than she would have chosen, and she had recently mooted the suggestion that they go for a long weekend abroad together. She wasn't quite ready for that but hadn't worked out how to tell him without crushing his confidence. For all his brilliance – or perhaps *because* of it – he had difficulty in reading reactions when they concerned him. He was clumsy when manoeuvring through personal relationships, and Mack knew she would have to navigate for him. She needed to find a way to tap the brakes without sending him into a tailspin of doubt.

11

Atticus went into town to get lunch. There was a takeaway in the square that did excellent coffee, so he picked up a bagel and an Americano and took them both back to the office. He opened another tin of dog food for Bandit and refreshed his water, and then placed his meal on his desk and sat down.

While he ate and drank, he looked at the notes he had made during his meeting with Nina. Investigators like him were increasingly being asked to research the contacts that clients made online. Catfishing was an issue, with people pretending to be someone that they weren't to deceive others, and nowhere was that more relevant than in the world of online dating. Atticus had read about people who had been bilked of hundreds of thousands of pounds by fraudsters who had used fake identities to seduce them and then, once they were on the hook, ruthlessly deceived them. It was usually women who were tricked by men, but that was not always the case; he remembered an account of an elderly man who had lost more than a million pounds when the younger woman who had bewitched him had emptied his account. One of the investigators he referred work to in Andover had worked on the case of a man who pretended to be a soldier, tricking his mark into paying for fake medical procedures;

others persuaded their victims to share intimate images and then used the material to blackmail them; yet others deployed more elaborate schemes involving websites that phished for bank account details.

Atticus woke his computer, navigated to Facebook and typed in Nina Parsons' name. The same glut of profiles was returned as before, but this time, with the benefit of knowing what she looked like, he was able to pick the right one. Her account had been established a year ago, with her privacy settings configured so that only friends and family could see her updates and personal information. Atticus sent a friend request to be thorough and then, while he waited for it to be accepted, went to Google and, using the 'site:' qualifier, typed 'Facebook Nina Parsons' and hit search. Facebook users often thought that setting their account to private would prevent their information being observable to others, but that was only true up to a point; all comments were public and indexed by Google.

Atticus used a software tool to scrape all the comments into a spreadsheet and glanced over them; her account appeared to be dormant, with only a handful of comments over the course of the last few months. That wasn't particularly unusual, and he set it aside.

Nina's boyfriend's name was Robin Wintringham. Atticus navigated to the website of the company he used when he was working on background checks and requested a basic DBS report that would reveal details of his criminal record, including any unspent convictions. He paid the fee and added it to his list of expenses; it would take a day for the report to be issued, but, in the meantime, there was more that he could do.

He went back to Facebook, cleared the search bar and searched Wintringham's name. The name was more unusual, and Atticus quickly found his profile. It had been created ten years ago and was full of the kind of content that it would be almost impossible to fake, at least not without significant effort and expertise. He went further, using a tool that he had bought to identify the connections between Wintringham's account and those belonging to the others with whom he interacted most frequently. Atticus was able to trace an outline of his life and then fill in the spaces with the details: he was married, his Facebook status changing from 'In a Relationship' to 'Married' five years previously; his wife, Laura, was a teacher at Godolphin; he had two young children, both girls, the older of whom went to reception at his wife's school and the other who appeared to be looked after by his mother during the week.

Wintringham was injudicious about the quantity of information he left on his public profile. Atticus was able to find out that he worked as a programmer for a large local website developer with an office near Old Sarum; he played hockey every weekend on the Astroturf pitch next to the cricket club on the Wilton Road; he was interested in cycling, and posted his routes on Strava. This last snippet allowed Atticus to locate the street in Laverstock at which all his rides started and stopped. He opened Google Maps, typed in the address and dropped the Street View icon outside the house. It was impossible to be sure, but it looked like Wintringham's house was one of either 27, 29 or 31 Hill Road. He found a photograph on the Instagram account belonging to his wife and swiped back to a photograph of the family in what looked very much like their back garden.

Atticus switched from Street View to the satellite perspective and was able to match several features in the photograph with the house to the left of the terrace: the fence that divided the garden from what appeared to be a communal parking area and, most tellingly, the large conservatory that belonged only to that particular house.

Atticus noted down everything, dictating his findings into a Word document that he would tidy up when he was finished. He would visit the property on foot to conduct a little surveillance, but he was already about as confident as he could be that Wintringham was who he had said he was; there was nothing about him that appeared to be out of the ordinary.

12

The Ebble had flooded at Coombe Bissett, with the A354 outside the Fox and Goose closed after being submerged by half a foot of water. Mack's turning was just before the river and, although there were puddles across the road, she was able to drive slowly to the west until she found Northfields, the house where David Campbell and his family lived. The access from the road was behind a set of wooden gates that bore a sign asking drivers not to block the way. Mack ignored that and buzzed the intercom.

'Hello?'

'Can I speak to Debbie Campbell?'

'Who is this?'

'I'm DCI Jones from Salisbury Police. Am I speaking to Mrs Campbell?'

'Yes. Why? Is something wrong?'

'Do you think I could come in?'

'What's the matter? Is it David? What's happened?'

'Please,' Mack said gently. 'I think it'd be best if I came inside.'

The lock on the gates buzzed and they swung open. The property was larger than Mack was expecting, with an older portion in the middle that was adjoined by two large, modern extensions.

A gravel drive led to a garage next to the property, and there was a large wicker love seat on the far side of the lawn.

The front door to the house was open, with a woman standing outside it. Mack made her way over to her.

'Mrs Campbell?'

'Yes,' she said. 'What is it?'

'Could I come in?'

The woman nodded dumbly, standing aside so that Mack could enter the house. She looked around as she did so, looking for anything that might give her an inkling as to what had happened to David Campbell. The hallway was pleasant, filled with furniture that looked as if it might have been collected over the course of many years, with framed photographs showing the family in happy times. Mack saw a wedding photograph and wondered how long the two of them had been married; she felt the usual discomfort at the news she was going to have to deliver. However long the two of them had been married – thirty or forty years, she guessed from the photo – it had come to an end just a few hours earlier, and Debbie Campbell didn't know it yet.

Debbie had stopped in the hallway. Mack saw that she was confused and unsure what she should do next.

'Could we sit down?'

'Please – this way.'

She led the way into the sitting room and gestured to the sofa.

'Can I get you a drink? Tea or coffee?'

She was procrastinating, finding reasons to stop Mack from delivering the news that she must have known could only have been bad.

'I'm fine,' Mack said. 'You should have a seat, too.'

Debbie sat on the armchair, her knees and feet pressed together and her hands in her lap, her fingers shaking.

'I'm very sorry to have to tell you that your husband is dead. He was on one of the parapets of the cathedral tower this morning, and he fell.'

'Oh my god,' she said, her face crumpling. 'Oh my *god*.'

'I'm so sorry.'

'What am I going to do? I need to tell our children.'

There was a telephone in a cradle on the table. Debbie got up, but her knees buckled, and she had to reach out for the back of the chair to stop herself from falling. Mack stood and helped her to sit back down in the chair.

'I'll introduce you to a family liaison officer. They'll be able to assist with things like that if that would be helpful.'

Debbie dabbed her eyes. 'Thank you.' She paused, looking down at her lap before raising her head. 'What happened? Was he up there taking his photographs?'

'We think so,' Mack said. 'We found his camera and equipment.'

'In this weather?'

'Yes.'

'That project,' she said. 'That *bloody* project. He was obsessed with it. Once he got halfway into the year, there was no way that he would let anything stop him from finishing. He probably saw this weather as an opportunity to get a really good picture.' She closed her eyes, paused to gather herself and then opened them to look at Mack again. 'How did he fall?'

'That's what I'm trying to find out.'

'He was always careful. He would never have done anything that put him at risk. And you must have been up on the parapet?'

'This morning.'

'It was wet?'

'Very.'

'But you still wouldn't be able to fall off.'

'I don't think so.'

52

'Maybe he was up higher? The weather door at the top of the spire? He said that was sticking and needed to be fixed.'

'We don't think so. The weather door is on the other side of the spire. And in this weather? Everything I've found out about him suggests he was a very careful man.'

Debbie nodded, her lips pressed tightly together, then covered her face with her hands in an outburst of grief. Mack waited for a moment to let her compose herself once more. She took the opportunity to glance around the room. It was pleasant, with nicely chosen pieces of furniture and a host of framed photographs that showed the Campbells together in several different locations: hand in hand before the Taj Mahal in India; with two young children at Disney World, Minnie Mouse next to them; on the deck of a cruise liner that looked as if it was passing through the Scandinavian fjords.

Mack turned back to Debbie and took a deep breath. 'I'm sorry to have to ask,' she said delicately, 'but, as I said, the question of *why* he fell is what we need to understand. An accident is one possibility, but, as you've said – and I agree – it does seem unlikely.'

'What are you saying? You think he *jumped?*'

'We have to see that as a possibility.'

'No,' she said with a firm certainty. 'It isn't. It's impossible.'

'Why do you say that?'

'Because I would've *known*. I've been married to David for thirty-three years. Don't you think that I would have realised if he was depressed?'

'I've investigated similar things before. It's always a horrible thing to say, but I'm afraid I've seen cases where the person involved hid the way they were feeling from their loved ones.'

Debbie shook her head. 'No. Not David. We don't have secrets.' Her voice caught, and she paused. '*Didn't*. And he had too much to live for.'

She got up and, steadier this time, crossed the room to the sideboard and picked up one of the framed photographs. She came back and handed it to Mack; it was a picture of the Campbells with a young woman.

'That's Emily, our daughter.' She dabbed at her eyes again. 'She's pregnant. Due next month. We don't have any grandchildren yet – Emily's had trouble conceiving, and David and I had given up hope. They had IVF and nothing happened, and then, when they stopped, it happened. It was a miracle – we both thought so. David was excited – *so* excited. He was supposed to go around to help them decorate the nursery after work today. The suggestion that he would kill himself when he had so much to live for . . .' Her breath came in a shudder, and she had to stop to compose herself again. 'No. You can see why I'd say that now, can't you?'

'He didn't mention any problems?'

'No.'

'Money?'

'We've got plenty.'

'Can you think of anything?'

'He didn't have any concerns. None. The idea that he'd do something like that deliberately . . . it's impossible. Completely impossible. He must have fallen.'

The room fell quiet.

'What happens now?'

'The coroner will have to decide whether to hold an inquest. I think he'll say that the cause of death is unclear and that there should be one. The body will be released for a funeral, and you'll be able to get what's called an interim death certificate that'll help with any administration that needs to be done.'

'What about . . .' Debbie paused. 'What about the practical steps?'

'You'll need to find an undertaker. I can recommend one if you like.'

'It's all right,' she said. 'My friend's husband is an undertaker. I'll ask him.'

Mack took out her card and left it on the table. 'If you need anything in the meantime, please give me a call. I'd be happy to help. I'll arrange for the family liaison officer to be in touch. They'll be able to help you as we investigate what happened.' Mack stood and smoothed down her trousers. 'Once again – I'm very sorry. I'll let myself out.'

13

The rain had gathered strength over the course of the afternoon, and now it lashed the streets with a vengeance. Alice Morris turned the corner, and a gust of wind, racing at her from the opposite direction, turned her umbrella inside out. She sheltered in an empty doorway long enough to fix it and then stepped back out onto the slick pavement and hurried on her way.

The offices of the *Salisbury Journal* were on Rollestone Street in the centre of the city. The buildings around it were a curious mixture: opposite was an old brewery that had been turned into office space, and a Victorian terrace sat alongside. The office occupied by the newspaper was a seventies addition, an ugly brick three-storey block that had been allowed to fall into disrepair by the landlords. There were four large windows on each floor, but the paint on the frames had peeled off, and the wood had started to rot. The ground-floor windows showed off a selection of photographs that hadn't been changed for years, and the branded boards that would once have been used to advertise the day's papers were empty, stacked against the wall with weeds growing up between them. Alice ruefully thought it an eloquent comment on the state of the local newspaper industry.

She huddled beneath her umbrella as she made her way along the street, opening the door to the office and gratefully stepping inside.

'Afternoon,' said Carly, the receptionist who doubled up her work on the front desk by reporting on the council and events at city hall. 'You're drenched.'

'Cats and dogs,' Alice said. 'At least we put a warning on the website.'

Carly chuckled. 'You seen the comments?'

'No? Why?'

'The usual suspects have been arguing.'

'About the *weather*?'

Carly looked at the screen on her desk. 'Lord Salzbrie said it's climate change. Spireman said he's talking out of his arse and that there's no such thing. It all went downhill from there.'

They had tried to moderate the comments for a month but had quickly given it up as a waste of time. The usual suspects just found the Facebook posts that they used to promote the stories and commented there instead. Alice was reconciled to it now and, anyway, it was about the only thing that was lively about the newspaper.

'Have you been at the cathedral?' Carly asked.

'All day.'

'How is it?'

'Horrible.'

'Poor man. What a way to go.'

Alice took off her wet coat and hung it over the bannister. 'Is Eddie in?'

'Upstairs.'

She pushed open the door to the stairs. The death *had* been horrible. She had been given a call by a friend who worked in the PR department at the cathedral and had been the first reporter on the scene. Workplace accidents were not unusual, and Alice had covered many in two years at the *Journal*, but this one – so Gothically lurid – promised to be something else entirely, with the suggestion that the police were considering suicide as a possible cause of death.

It was funny; Eddie Thorpe had been worrying how they were going to fill the newspaper at yesterday's editorial meeting and had reluctantly agreed to run yet another story on the interminable bureaucracy that swirled around the proposed tunnel that would take the A303 away from Stonehenge. It was a lot of nonsense – Eddie dismissed it as 'yet another crock of Salisbury shit' – but it was relevant to the city, and it was all they had. Now, though, they had been given the perfect lead story. The bypass could be relegated to the inside pages, where it belonged, and they could run with Campbell's death. Alice felt a little guilty at her relief, but she'd been a journalist for long enough to know that selling papers – and clicks – was a cut-throat business.

She climbed the stairs to the newsroom and thought, as she usually did, that that was a rather grandiloquent way to describe her place of work. It evoked images of rooms full of noise and life, of reporters on the phone to their sources or arguing with their editors about the merits of their stories. Alice had been a film buff at college and had daydreamed about what it might be like to be a hack, her expectations coloured by *His Girl Friday, All the President's Men* and *The Philadelphia Story*.

The reality was different.

There were three reporters, all of them fresh out of college, with Alice – at just twenty-three – the most senior. Their work was overseen by Eddie and supplemented by an apprentice and a handful of freelancers, including James Ward, the photographer who had been with her to get snaps of what was happening at the cathedral. They shared the space with two desks and three old filing cabinets that Eddie said pre-dated him, and he'd worked in the industry for *years*.

The staff lived in perpetual fear that the owners of the paper would close it down; local news didn't make much money, and newspapers around the country had been swallowed up by conglomerates who then amalgamated them and reduced headcounts to cut costs. Alice had wondered uneasily what she might do if that happened to them and had started to think about going back to college so that she could train for something else. She had friends who were teaching English in far-off climes, and the prospect of decent pay and sunshine was attractive when compared to the dour weather and relative penury that she had here.

Eddie had a tiny office in the corner that looked as if it might once have been a broom cupboard; there was no window and barely enough space for his desk and chair. He was sitting there now, but, upon seeing Alice, he got up and met her halfway.

'Well?' he asked.

'Awful.'

'You've got the front page.'

She sat down on the edge of the desk. 'Feels a bit morbid.'

Eddie shrugged. 'You know what they say.'

'"If it bleeds, it leads." I know. But it doesn't change the fact he's dead and that he died in pretty much the worst way possible. Do you know how long it would have taken him to hit the ground?'

'Please don't say you've googled that.'

'I was bored. Nearly four seconds. *Four seconds.* That's plenty of time for him to think about it.'

Eddie had been a reporter for thirty years. He had worked on Fleet Street when it was still the Street of Ink but had been let go six months earlier when he could no longer square the rampant drinking culture of which he enthusiastically partook with the need to file good copy. He was owed a favour by an old drinking buddy who had moved to the *Journal*'s parent company. He had been given the editor's job after his predecessor quit, citing the exhaustion of covering the stories at Grovely and Imber.

Alice saw Eddie as an example of how not to plot a successful career. He was her opposite: he had started in London and then retreated to Salisbury; she, on the other hand, intended to get the experience she needed here before looking for something more glamorous elsewhere. Alice had been born and raised in Salisbury, but – unlike many of her contemporaries from school whose ambitions did not extend beyond the city limits – she wanted to do great things.

'How much of it have you written?'

'Just notes,' she said. 'I need to put it together.'

'You've got a couple of hours. Photos?'

'James has a couple.'

'I'll take a look. Coffee?'

'Love one.'

'Get cracking, then. I'll put the kettle on.'

14

Mack followed at the back of the group as they left the station and made their way to the Royal George. The pub, on nearby Bedwin Street, was the venue that they invariably decamped to whenever they had something to celebrate. Today was Bob Bradley's birthday.

They reached the pub and filed inside. The television on the wall was tuned to a Premier League match, with a collection of regulars watching it from the bar. Neil Blyford, Bob's best friend at the nick, took their orders for the first round.

Mack intercepted Blyford at the bar.

'I'll get these.'

'Don't be daft, boss.'

'No arguments.'

She took out her purse, thumbed out two twenties and handed them to the barman. She waited for the first pints to be pulled and then took them over to the corner of the room where the others had taken two empty tables. Mack put the glasses on the nearest table and then sat down.

It was a good turnout; Bob had been police for twenty-five years and was a popular fixture at the nick. Robbie Best, Stewart Lynas, Mike Lewis and Francine Patterson had come from CID, with Neil Blyford, James Boyd, Pete Britten and Sam Collison representing uniform. Another five or six were expected to make their way over once they got off shift.

Blyford and the barman brought over the rest of the drinks and distributed them, together with half a dozen packs of crisps and another half-dozen packs of pork scratchings.

'Courtesy of the gaffer,' Blyford said, gesturing to Mack.

The others thanked her.

'Long day,' Mack said, stretching out her back.

'Been at the cathedral?' Collison asked her.

She nodded.

'It's true, then? He fell off the spire?'

'The tower,' Mack corrected him.

'Not that it would've made any difference,' Best said. 'I don't think he could've made any more mess if he'd tried. He bounced off the wall and then . . .' He clapped his hands.

They spoke about the day for five minutes before conversation inevitably moved on to office gossip: Ryan Yaxley was rumoured to have won five thousand on the lottery and was still refusing to pay his way at the bar; the travellers up at the hospital site were being investigated for nicking the lead off the church at Britford; Bob Carver had driven his new Tesla into the back of a car at the college roundabout just two weeks after buying it and was blaming Elon Musk.

Francine got up and went to the bar. She was an impressive young officer. She had been a redcap in the 1st Investigation Company of the Military Police at Bulford before swapping her camouflage for street clothes and joining Salisbury CID. Mack knew from personal experience that it was a challenge to be an ambitious woman in an environment that was still overwhelmingly male, and had taken Francine under her wing. Francine, for her part, had rewarded Mack's early faith with two years of excellent work, and

Mack had recommended that she should be considered for promotion to detective sergeant when the next opportunity arose.

Mack watched as she approached a good-looking man who had just come inside, reaching up to plant a kiss on his lips and then leading him to the table. Mack looked over at Robbie Best and noticed that he had a troubled expression on his face. She knew why: Best had held a candle for Francine ever since she had joined CID and, until recently, had been labouring under the misapprehension that she was single. It wasn't that she had deceived him or led him on, just that she was private and not keen on discussing her life outside of the nick. Her Facebook status had changed from 'Single' to 'In a Relationship' the same day that Best had come into the station with a face like thunder, and Mack had joined the dots from there.

'There's someone I want to introduce,' Francine said. 'This is Charlie.'

Boyd stood up and extended his hand. 'The mysterious boyfriend?'

'Nice to meet you,' Charlie said, shaking Boyd's hand and then nodding to the rest of them.

Francine was obviously nervous about the prospect of introducing Charlie to her colleagues. She knew – and Charlie might not – that they could be a raucous group, especially when they'd had a few to drink. It was early, though. She was wisely making sure that he was properly introduced to them all before too much ale had flowed.

Mack stood up and offered her hand; Charlie took it.

'Drink?' she asked him.

'Thanks. I'll have a lager.' He and Francine took seats beside each other.

Mack went up to the bar and ordered another pint of Amstel. She looked back at the table and noticed Francine holding

Charlie's hand underneath the table. Best was putting on a brave face, but perhaps trying a little *too* hard.

They were talking about the death at the cathedral again when she returned with the pint.

'Charlie was walking through the Close when it happened,' Francine said.

Charlie picked at a crisp from the open packet. 'Didn't see anything. Saw the police and the ambulance, but I only realised what had happened when I got home and heard it on the radio.'

'I was saying it was messy,' Best noted.

'Do you know what happened to him?'

Mack wasn't all that keen on discussing business while a civilian was present, so she shook her head and kept things as vague as she could. 'Can't say for sure.'

'Could he have slipped?'

'Don't know.'

Boyd frowned. 'I've been up there, boss. Took my kids. The parapets on those balconies come up to the top of my chest. How'd he go and slip from there?'

'We don't know that he did,' she said. 'But it's either that or he jumped, and his wife says she has no reason to think he might've been depressed.'

Lynas took a sip of his pint and then put the glass down. 'That doesn't always mean they're not, though, does it? We've all had cases like that – someone tops themselves, and it takes the whole family by surprise. Maybe it's like that here.'

'Maybe,' Mack said. 'Maybe not.'

'Who decides?' Charlie asked.

'It'll be up to the coroner.'

Best, perhaps aware from Mack's succinct replies that she didn't want to discuss the case now, looked over at Charlie and changed the subject. 'What do you do for work?'

'I'm a photographer.'

'Taking photos of what?'

'Whatever takes my fancy. If I could choose, it would be land-scapes, but they don't pay the bills. Corporate work, mostly – photos for catalogues, stuff like that. Not nearly as glamorous as what you do.'

Lynas nearly choked on his pint. '"*Glamorous*?" Jesus, Franny, what shit have you been telling him?' He swallowed another mouthful and put his glass down on the table. 'Mate – what we do couldn't be any farther away from being glamorous if it tried. You think going down the road picking up the bits and pieces of someone who's been in an RTA is glamorous?'

'I don't believe you,' Charlie said amiably. 'Salisbury's been in the papers. The murders at Grovely? And Imber?'

'True,' Bradley said. 'But it's not "glamorous". Not unless you think standing on Salisbury Plain all day and all night in the pissing rain and wind is glamorous.'

'With mud that you find in your boots a week later,' Lynas said.

'With weak tea the only thing standing between you and hypothermia,' added Bradley.

'All right,' Francine said, holding up a hand and chuckling. 'Leave him alone. He was only asking.'

'How long have you two been seeing each other?' Britten asked.

'It was a year on Sunday.'

'Where did you meet?' Boyd asked.

'Online,' Charlie said.

Mack glanced over at Best and saw that he was forcing an amiable smile. She felt sorry for him. His wife had divorced him eighteen months earlier and he hadn't taken it well. Francine was younger than him, and her interest – or the thought that she might be interested in him – had been good for his confidence. Mack wondered whether she should take him out for dinner next week to make sure he was OK. She had known him for years and, at least since Atticus's departure, he was the closest she had to a friend at the nick. He knew about her relationship with Atticus and had been a shoulder to cry on in the aftermath of her separation.

Lewis gestured to the empty glasses on the table. 'Who wants another?'

'*Please* don't tell me you're buying,' Bradley said.

'Don't sound so surprised.'

'You know the last time you took out your wallet?'

'The nineties?' Lynas offered.

Lewis raised his middle finger.

15

Deadlines weren't usually pressing at the *Journal*. With a couple of recent exceptions, breaking news didn't happen in Salisbury, and that meant that they had all week to prepare for the print edition. Copy was written and edited, and pages were set in plenty of time for Eddie Thorpe to give everything the once-over before approving it and sending it off to be printed. Tonight was different. Eddie had called the printer to tell them they would be filing late and had been told that they could wait until eleven-thirty but no longer.

Alice sat down at her desk, opened her laptop and her notebook and began to type.

A distraught family have paid tribute to a popular local man, 63, who tragically fell to his death from the tower of Salisbury Cathedral yesterday morning.

She read it back. 'Distraught' was too formal; she deleted it and tried again.

A heartbroken family have paid tribute to a popular local man, 63, who tragically fell from the tower of Salisbury Cathedral yesterday morning. David Campbell was taking a photograph on the southern parapet when he fell to his death. The preliminary cause of Campbell's death was confirmed as multiple injuries following a fall from height.

She flexed her fingers and typed out a final paragraph.

In a statement, his wife Deborah described Mr Campbell as being a 'great father' and said that 'he had worked at the cathedral all his life.' She has asked for privacy so that the family can come to terms with their loss.

Alice reclined to straighten out her back and read the piece through. It was good, if a little impersonal. She reminded herself that they had an excellent photograph of Campbell from the archive at the cathedral, and that his broad smile would do much to bring his personality across. She had already finished a piece on his life for page three, and that, together with a second photograph of him changing the anemometer at the tip of the spire – so far above the ground that it made her queasy to look at it – would add extra colour.

She scrolled back to the start of the article with the intention of tightening up the flabbier sentences when she saw Carly in the doorway.

'What's up?'

Carly held up a Jiffy bag. 'Parcel for you.'

'What? It's late.'

'Must have been put through the letterbox.'

'By whom?'

She shrugged. 'Sorry – didn't see.'

'When?'

'Don't know. I just noticed it.'

Carly brought it over and handed it to Alice. The bag looked as if it was brand new, and had been sealed at one end with an adhesive strip. She turned it over and looked at the front: her name had been printed onto a label, and the label had been fixed – perfectly dead centre – on the packet. The package wasn't heavy and was perhaps thirty centimetres long and twenty-five centimetres wide.

Carly looked over Alice's shoulder. 'Expecting anything?'

'No,' she said. 'I don't think so.'

She slid her finger into a loose gap at the end of the package and wriggled it until she had torn it all the way open. She turned the packet on its side and tipped the contents onto her desk: it was a glossy black plastic case with a single piece of A4 paper folded in half.

'What is that?' Carly said.

Alice picked the case up and examined it. It had a clear plastic sheath around it and a label had been affixed to the spine. A name and date had been written in black ink on the label.

Campbell, David / 21 June

Alice opened the case.

A videotape was inside.

She got up so quickly that she knocked her chair over. 'Eddie?'

'What?'

'Come here a minute.'

Eddie had his office door half-closed and, when he opened it, a cloud of smoke drifted into the newsroom. He took the cigarette from his mouth and dropped it into a mug of cold coffee that had been left on someone's desk. 'What's up?' He came over to where Alice and Carly were standing.

'Look at this.' She handed over the envelope and the videotape and watched as he examined them.

'A video?'

'Look at the name on the side.'

He turned the case over. 'Weird.'

'Do you think we need to call the police?'

'Why?'

'Because we get this on the day he died?'

Eddie shook his head. 'We don't even know what it is.'

Alice took the piece of paper and unfolded it. Two sentences had been printed in bold type:

It is mine to avenge; I will repay. In due time their foot will slip; their day of disaster is near and their doom rushes upon them.

Carly looked over Alice's shoulder. 'What? What does that mean?'

Alice went to her computer and tapped a key to wake the screen. She went to Google, typed out the first dozen words and searched. The first result was from Biblehub.com and identified the words as from Deuteronomy.

'That's . . .' She stared at the paper, and the sentence drifted away.

'Weird?' Carly offered.

'Very weird.' She put the paper down and picked up the case. 'Do we have something here that'll play this?'

'Not a chance.' Eddie said.

'eBay?' Carly suggested.

Alice laid the case down on the desk and ran her finger over the black plastic. 'I think my dad's got one in the attic. God knows if it'll work. I'll give him a call.'

'Don't forget you need to finish the piece for the front page.'

'Give me ten minutes.'

She sat down and flexed her fingers.

She needed an extra paragraph to fill the space on the front page and had decided that she would include a reference to the photography project that Campbell had been working on all year.

She started to type, but her attention was snagged by the shiny black cassette box next to the keyboard.

PART II

TUESDAY

16

Carl Jeffers parked his car next to the shipping container that was used as his office and pushed the button to open the boot. His dog, Jess, leapt out and proceeded to run in a series of circles, throwing up sprays of muddy water as her legs powered through the puddles that had gathered overnight. It was still raining, just as hard as it had yesterday, and the forecast was the same for the rest of the day and tomorrow. The Avon had burst its banks, and the floodplain between the main river and the carrier was underwater. The level recorded by the gauge at Harnham Bridge was still climbing, and Jeffers had started to wonder whether they might see the businesses on the southern side of Southampton Road flood again. It had happened four years ago, and there had been the threat then that the road itself might flood. Salisbury's traffic was bad at the best of times, but if the main road into the city was forced to close, it was going to be awful. Jeffers drove in that way from his home in Alderbury. The diversion through downtown would mean he'd have to get up an hour earlier, and he wasn't keen on that at all.

He got out of the car, his boots sinking into an inch of mud, and then squelched across to the container. He removed the padlock and opened up, switching on the light and filling the kettle with water that he'd brought from home in a two-litre plastic bottle. He pushed back the sleeve of his waterproof jacket until he could see his watch: it was five-thirty in the morning, and he was expecting a dozen fishermen to come and enjoy the fishery today. He was here a little earlier than normal so that he could walk the banks from one end to the other and make sure that everything was as it should be, and that access was even possible. He picked up his shotgun, put a handful of shells into his pocket, stepped back outside and locked up the office again.

Jeffers was the water bailiff for this stretch of the river. His role was to maintain the river for the fishermen who travelled from all over the country to enjoy it. He arrived early every morning and spent the first hour walking to the trout farm that marked the eastern limit of the angling association's land and then walking the mile and a half back to New Bridge Road, which was the western boundary. He had the shotgun to shoot the cormorants that would, if left unchecked, decimate the fish that the association had released into the river to maintain stocks. The bird wasn't a native species and, because of that, Jeffers was allowed to kill them. It was a different matter with herons, and the heronry in nearby Britford was a problem for which there was no easy solution. He would fire a shot to scare them off when he saw them, but he knew that the clever buggers just waited to return at the end of his shift.

With Jess at his side, Jeffers passed the church, older even than the cathedral that he could see if he turned back to the west, and trudged through the slop of the mud. He stopped to check on the repairs to the wooden platform that he had made last week, satisfied that the planks were strong enough for the fishermen who would set up there so that they could cast out into the deepest part of the river.

He reached the weir that governed the flow of the water at the trout farm, splitting it in half so that the farm had enough for its purposes, and then turned back. He retraced his steps, passing the church and then the first and second bridges that the farmer used to take his cattle to and from the water meadows. He went by the car park for his office and the two fishing lodges. Jess wriggled beneath the fence that guarded the bridge over Manor Ditch, and Jeffers used the stile, continuing along the paved track until the old eel house came into view. The building stretched across the river from one side to the other, a single span on raised stone piers and then a sluice house, built at a right angle so that the whole building was arranged in the shape of an L. The bonded red bricks and dark tile roof stood out against the water and the greenery that surrounded them.

The structure was in a state of disrepair. Some time ago, Jeffers had removed a section of the ivy that had engulfed the walls and had found that one corner was collapsing. The back scouring of the river current had undermined three of the six stone piers upon which the sluice range stood, and the roots of an ash were damaging the foundations. Jeffers had been concerned; the building regulated the flow of the water and, if it had collapsed, the water levels on the city side of the sluice would have plunged and damaged both the upstream and downstream habitats. The Environment Agency was looking into the possibility of making repairs, but every morning that Jeffers approached it, he did so in fear that more of the structure would have been damaged.

The interior of the sluice house contained machinery for operating the sluices, including several large cast-iron gears that were used to raise and lower them. Jeffers looked inside and saw something in the flow.

He thought at first that it was a deer. There were plenty of them here, and it wasn't all that long ago that a fawn had fallen into the river and drowned. The body had been swept down the river by the current until it came to rest against the sluice; Jeffers had had to loop a rope around its neck to haul it out.

He carefully stepped inside the building and saw that it wasn't a deer; he stepped closer still, and his stomach fell as his worst fears were realised.

It was a man.

17

Francine Patterson was woken by the buzzing of her phone on her bedside table. She snaked out a hand, probing the table with fingers still clumsy with sleep, and upended a half-empty glass of water that she had left there last night to help prevent the hangover that she had known would be waiting for her when she awoke.

'*Shit*,' she mumbled.

She found her phone and snoozed the alarm. She blinked the sleep from her eyes until she was able to focus on the time: six-thirty. She usually set two alarms – one at six and the other at half past – and she'd either forgotten to set the first one or had slept through it, and was now going to struggle to get to the nick in time to start the early turn at seven.

There was movement on the other side of the bed and she remembered that Charlie had come home with her after they had gone out with the others for a curry last night.

He groaned.

'You don't need to get up,' she said. 'Go back to sleep.'

'What's the matter?' he mumbled.

'I'm on the early shift, and I'm late. And I've got the hangover from hell.'

She shuffled over to the edge of the bed, slid her feet down to the floor and stood. Her head throbbed, and she felt vomit bubbling up at the back of her throat. She staggered into the bathroom, knelt in front of the toilet and brought up whatever it was that she had had for dinner. She took a moment before she was sick again, a third heave bringing up nothing more than a mouthful of bile. Wiping her mouth with the back of her hand, she flushed the foul-smelling vomit away.

It had gone pretty well last night, she thought, all things considered. The others had taken to Charlie well and, after early nerves that only she would have been able to discern, he had held his own with their banter. She had noticed that Robbie Best had been uncomfortable. That was a shame; Robbie was nice and had been kind to her when she'd swapped uniform for CID. She would've liked to have been able to say something to make him feel better but had no idea where to start without it being embarrassing for them both.

She ran the shower so that the water could warm up and went back into the bedroom to pick up the towel that she had dumped on the floor yesterday. Charlie was still in bed, his face lit by the glow of his phone as he scrolled down the screen.

Francine bent down for the towel. 'How drunk was I?'

'Quite drunk.'

'You were drunk, too – right?'

'I think so.'

'The others?'

'You weren't the worst. Whose birthday was it? Rob?'

'*Bob.*'

'They had to carry him into a taxi.'

'And everyone else?'

'Not as bad as him, but all pissed. Relax. You didn't do anything to disgrace yourself.'

She started to unbutton her pyjama top and then, with a little blush of self-consciousness, paused and went into the bathroom. She remembered Charlie taking off her shirt last night and then, as she closed her eyes and tried to remember everything, was as sure as she could be that they had had sex. She grimaced; it wasn't their first time, but they were early enough in their relationship that she was worried that the experience might not have been up to scratch. She glanced through the crack between the door and the frame and saw that Charlie had put his phone down on the bedside table and lain down again.

Francine undressed and stepped into the shower, letting the water soak through her hair and run down her shoulders and back. She squeezed out a handful of shower gel and scoured herself clean, then took her toothbrush and scrubbed her teeth until the taste of the vomit was replaced by mint. She turned off the shower, then dried herself with a towel before wrapping it around herself and creeping back into the bedroom to find clean clothes that she could wear for work. Charlie was snoring lightly. She crept around the bed so that she could look down at him and allowed herself a smile; he looked happy and comfortable, his chest rising and falling with each breath. She reached down to pull the duvet all the way up so that his shoulders were covered and then went to the wardrobe, taking out the navy-blue wool skirt suit that she had had dry-cleaned last week and a white shirt that she could just about get away with without ironing. Grabbing fresh underwear, she went back into the bathroom to change. It was six forty-five, and she had a short drive to get into the office. She was going to be late, but hopefully not too late for it to be a problem.

* * *

Francine pulled into the car park at the side of the building at Bourne Hill at six minutes past seven. She took her bag and umbrella from the passenger seat, locked the car and made her way into the office. Sergeant James Boyd was waiting for her at her desk. He had been working the night shift, from eleven until seven. The rota had everyone on the team cycling through the three shifts – early, late and night – changing from one to the next every two days before they had two days off.

'What's up?' she said to him.

'How's your head?'

'Sore. How do you know?'

'You don't remember me being there?'

'No . . .'

'We had a complaint. I had to go out and calm things down.'

'What? Really?'

His face broke into a wide grin. 'No, you tit, not really. Although I'm a little concerned you think it's *possible* that you all might have disgraced yourself. Can't wait until Bradley rolls in.'

'He's off today. Lucky bastard.'

'Bet you wish you'd thought of that.'

'Don't rub it in.'

Boyd put on his jacket and picked up the rucksack that he'd left on her desk. 'Time for me to go. I'll walk you down to your car.'

She frowned. 'What? Why?'

'Because we've just had a call from uniform. I'd deal with it, but I'm done for the day.'

'Where?'

'You know the old sluice house on the river down by Churchill Gardens?'

'Think so,' she said. 'Why? What's happened?'

'Bob Carver just called in. There's a body in the water.'

18

Mack was still sleeping when Atticus woke. He swung his legs off the mattress as gently as he could so as not to wake her. She had been out with colleagues from the nick for Bob Bradley's birthday and had texted him late and said that she wanted to see him. He had offered to go over to hers, but she had replied and said that there was no need: she was outside. She was a little the worse for wear and had fallen asleep almost as soon as he had helped her upstairs to the bedroom. He had wakened her so that she could take two aspirin with a pint of water, and then lay down next to her, listening to her breathing as she fell into a deep and dreamless sleep.

After freshening up in the bathroom, he went back into the bedroom to change. He clipped the lead to Bandit's collar and led the way down the stairs and out to the car. He took out his phone and went to his notes, found the address that he had discovered for Robin Wintringham, copied the postcode and pasted it into his map's search bar.

* * *

Atticus drove across town to Laverstock and arrived at Wintringham's address at a quarter to eight. Hill Road was one of the new developments that had sprung up around Salisbury over the course of the last few years, and the houses – neat and tidy, with fresh red bricks and slate-covered porches over their front doors – looked pleasant as the sun broke through the clouds and shone down on them. The Land Registry record that Atticus had purchased confirmed his earlier deduction: Wintringham was the owner of number 27. He drove down the slope that gave the road its name and found a space at the side of the road where he could leave his car and continue his observation on foot.

Atticus recalled the research that he had conducted and, in particular, the layout of Wintringham's property in relation to its neighbours. The house was on the left-hand side of a block of three, with a short drive to the side that led to a residents' parking area. Atticus followed the drive, jumping to peer over a wooden fence that enclosed the back garden. It was a simple space, a rectangle of lawn with a large conservatory extending out from the house. Atticus was able to see into the windows on the first floor and spotted a girl in school uniform looking out before turning her head and mouthing something to someone whom Atticus couldn't see.

'Excuse me?'

Atticus turned to see that a woman had emerged from around the corner of the fence. She was looking at him with obvious suspicion, and he guessed that the girl in the window must have alerted her to him peering over the fence.

'Hello.'

'What are you doing?'

'I'm from Carter and May,' he said, using the name of the first estate agency in town that came to mind. 'We're letting agents for one of the houses over there, and we've had a complaint about noise.'

Her suspicion was allayed and replaced with a prying officiousness. 'At which property?'

'That one,' he said, pointing at the back of number 27.

'Really? The Wintringhams? No – that can't be right.'

'That's definitely the house.'

'I find that hard to believe.'

'Why do you say that?'

'Because they're a very nice young family. Two little girls, both good as gold. They're not the sort of people to create a disturbance. Who made the complaint?'

'I'm afraid I can't tell you that.'

'Well, whoever it was, I'd suggest that they might be making a mountain out of a molehill. This is a good street. Everyone knows everyone else, and nothing's too much trouble.'

'That's good to hear. Sorry to have disturbed you.'

Atticus set off back to the street and had turned left to go and get his car when the door to number 27 opened, and two girls emerged from within. The first was dressed in school uniform and the second in a padded coat that looked as if it would be snug in the brisk weather. They waited by the door until their father, two bags slung on one shoulder and a set of car keys in his hand, stepped out to join them. Atticus recognised Robin Wintringham and gave what he hoped was a sympathetic smile as he stepped to the side to let the girls make their way down to the car parking space where he had just been. Wintringham returned the smile with a wry shake of the head, presuming, perhaps, that Atticus had children and could empathise with the rigours of getting them ready and out of a morning.

Atticus walked to his car. He knew that the woman who had questioned him was probably still in the car park and, although he thought it was unlikely that she would repeat the story that he had given her to Wintringham, for fear of embarrassing him, it wasn't worth waiting to find out.

19

Alice parked outside her parents' home and finished the rest of the strong black coffee in her flask. She had found it difficult to sleep, and now she was paying the price. Her dreams had been unusually vivid: her first had seen her falling from the tower of the cathedral, and then, once that had woken her up, she hadn't been able to stop thinking about the tape that had been delivered to the office. The fact that it had been labelled with the dead man's name was strange and, given the timing, ominous.

She got out of the car, went to the front door and knocked.

Her father opened it. 'Morning, sweetheart.'

He crouched down and picked up the video cassette recorder that he'd placed on the floor earlier.

'Thanks,' she said.

'No idea if it still works,' he said, handing it over.

'Do you have the leads?'

He bent down again and collected a plastic bag, depositing it on top of the recorder. 'Should all be in there. What on earth do you want it for?'

'We were sent a tape last night, but we don't have anything to play it on.'

'Sounds intriguing. Everything all right at work?'

'All good,' she said. 'I'd better get into the office – thanks for this.'

'No problem, love. Want a hand getting it to the car?'

'It's all right – I can manage.'

'See you at the weekend.'

*   *   *

Alice parked the car in Salt Lane car park and carried the VCR the rest of the way to the office. Eddie Thorpe was already in the newsroom.

'Well done,' he said. 'You found one.'

'No idea what I'm supposed to do with it.'

Eddie snorted, muttered something about millennials and took the recorder from her and carried it into the conference room. They had a television on a stand there, and Eddie slid the VCR onto the shelf beneath the screen. Alice looked at the nest of cables and wires in the bag and shrugged her shoulders. Eddie connected the VCR to the television, found a power cord and plugged that in, too, then switched the power on and stood back. The display blinked on. He took the tape from its box and pushed it into the slot. The mechanism whirred as the tape was drawn back into the machine; Alice was suddenly fearful that it would be chewed up and ruined.

'Shouldn't we test it on something else first?'

'It'll be fine.'

He pressed play, and the two of them pulled up chairs and sat down.

The screen was filled with static and then bars of white that rolled from the top to the bottom. An image emerged: a room, lit in luminous red, with a bed shot from above and to the side. A boy was on the bed. He was naked.

Alice felt very uneasy. 'What *is* this?'

Eddie didn't answer. The atmosphere had changed quickly. Their initial curiosity was gone; their scepticism had been replaced with confusion and, in Alice's case, dread. She wondered whether she should reach over and press stop but found that she couldn't. Her hands stayed in her lap, fingers laced together, and her eyes stayed on the screen.

The boy's mouth opened as he said something to whoever else was in the room but out of shot. There was no sound on the recording, but it was obvious from his eyes, wide as saucers, that he was frightened.

'Maybe you were right,' Eddie said. 'We need to think about what we should be doing with this. Maybe we *should* get the police.'

A second person stepped into shot. It was a man, also naked, but he was looking away from the camera so that they couldn't see his face. He said something to the boy, who shook his head. He tried to stand, but it looked as if he was suddenly dizzy. He teetered on the edge of the bed before the man put his hand on his shoulder, and he settled back down. The man sat down next to him and, for the first time, turned and showed his face. He said something to someone off camera; he looked confident and eager, and his arousal was evident. He laughed and turned his attention to the boy.

Alice reached forward quickly and pressed stop.

The man's face was still turned to the camera, frozen and caught amid the bands of static.

Eddie stared. 'Is that who I think it is?'

'It's him. It's *definitely* him. It's David Campbell.'

20

Francine drove into Britford, taking the bridge over the Avon cut and then turning down a rough track that ran between opposing lines of mature elms. There were two old fishing lodges at the end of the track and, to the right, an open area of parking for anglers who had visited the river to fish. A blue shipping container had been left at one side of the space, a door cut into it and a sign fixed to the outside advertising it as the office where fishermen could buy day passes for the fishery. There were four cars parked in the space: a silver Toyota four-by-four, a lime-green Mondeo, a Fiat and a police patrol car. She parked behind the Toyota and opened her door. The car park was unadopted, and the rough surface had been turned into mud by the rain. Francine made her way gingerly around the car to the rear, opened the boot and sat on the edge while she took off her shoes and changed into her waterproof boots.

She stopped to get her bearings: the two lodges were to her left, a deer watched her from the edge of the flooded field to her right, and there was a bridge across the river straight ahead. She had called Bob Carver on the way, and he had told her to go left, taking the track that allowed access to the lodges. She did, noting the lights in the window of the house on the right. There was a narrow concrete bridge that spanned a ditch, and then a gate with a stile to the side.

She crossed the bridge and climbed the stile. The river was to her right, with brambles to the left. The city was close; the spire of the cathedral was visible above the trees. The track had been paved at some point in the past, but it had not been maintained; weeds had punched through the concrete, and chunks of it had been allowed to disintegrate. The river had burst its banks, and long stretches of ground had been submerged. A pair of ducks paddled against the flow, and a bright splash of blue, so vivid as to be almost indigo, signalled a kingfisher as it darted low across the water.

Francine turned the corner and saw a building that she remembered. The playground in Churchill Gardens was on the other side of the water; her parents had taken her there when they were younger. A modern weir had been built across the water and, behind that, it was possible to see the red brick of the old sluice house. She had never had reason to visit it, and it was strange to see the structure from this direction and from close up. The river spread out on this side of the range, the surface whitened with froth as the current pushed out through the sluices.

Francine saw a uniformed officer – Bob Carver – and he raised a hand in greeting as she approached.

'Morning,' she said.

'Morning.'

'What have we got?'

'Dead body found in the water this morning.'

'Where?'

'This way.'

Carver led the way upstream to an opening that offered access to the large cast-iron gears that worked the sluices. Francine saw a man waiting for them, a shotgun leaning against a tree. A dog had been tied to a post, the animal pacing back and forth as far as its lead would allow.

'Who's he?' Francine asked, inclining her chin towards the man.

'The water bailiff. He found the body.'

'Where?'

Carver pointed into the opening. 'In there.'

The inside of the structure was gloomy, and it took Francine a moment for her eyes to adjust. It was loud, too, with the water rushing through the sluices, through the channels and then into the pool on the other side. There were six sluice gates, three of which had been raised for the water to flow through. The river shot through the gates, emerging on the other side in a cascade of spray. Francine looked down and saw that the concrete surface was slick with water. She was careful not to slip as she made her way to the edge so that she could look down into the channel.

The body of a man was floating there, pressed up against the gate by the flow of the water. He was of slight build and dressed in clothes that had seen better days: a leather jacket, ripped jeans, battered boots.

'How did he get in there?'

'I asked the bailiff – he's not sure.'

'Would he fit through the sluices?'

'Maybe.'

'Do we know how long he's been in the water?'

'Jeffers – the bailiff – says he was off yesterday and didn't check inside here the day before that.'

'Up to two days, then?'

Carver nodded. 'Looks like it.'

She looked back down into the throbbing water. 'I'll need to call the coroner.'

Carver nodded. 'We're going to need another couple of lads, too. Fishing him out isn't going to be easy.'

21

Salisbury was a small city, and Alice had worked for the *Journal* long enough to have built up a reasonable contacts book. Her closest police contact was Detective Sergeant Mike Lewis at Bourne Hill, and she had called and said that he needed to come to the *Journal*'s office as soon as he could.

He arrived at the office at eight and rapped on the door until Carly went over to open it.

'Morning,' Alice said.

'It's early,' he grouched. 'What did you want to show me?'

'In the conference room.'

'What is it?'

'I need to show you – this way.'

He frowned, but then saw the expression on her face. 'All right.'

She led the way up the stairs and took him into the room with the VCR and the TV. Eddie was sucking on a cigarette, blowing smoke through the partially open window.

'Eddie,' Lewis said.

'Mike.'

'Alice says you have something for me.'

She pointed to the VCR. 'We were sent a video last night. You need to see it.'

'Go on, then. Let's have a look.'

Alice paused, wondering whether she should warn him that the footage was graphic, then realised that was foolish and just pressed play.

22

The sluice house had been quiet when Francine had arrived, but that didn't last for long. She knew that the death of the man in the water was likely to be classified as unnatural and that they would need to have at least a DS at the scene. She called the station and spoke to Nigel Archer, explaining what had happened and that they were going to need a couple of additional men so that they could get the body out of the water.

Archer arrived at the scene half an hour later with Constables Sam Collison and Philip Newman. He toured the sluice house and surrounding area with Francine and decided that it would be better to report up to the duty detective inspector – it was Robbie Best this morning – for additional support and guidance.

Best sent over a crime scene investigator, and Jeffers unlocked the gate so that he was able to drive his van as close to them as the flood allowed. He took out his camera and started to take photographs. Francine watched him as he went about his business, making sure that he had shots of the body from several angles so as not to miss anything.

Jeffers had found a windlass and had lowered the sluice gates to ensure that the flow of water was a little less fierce. He was resting now with a roll-up cigarette. 'Aren't you going to get him out?'

'We will.'

'When? What are you waiting for?'

'The pathologist.'

'Why'd you need him?'

'We can't rule out foul play. We'll need advice to work out the cause of death, and he'll be able to make sure we get him out in a way that doesn't disturb trace evidence.'

'Foul play? What does that mean – murder?'

'Much too early to say, but . . . yes, of course, it's possible.'

'Murder? Here?' He lit the cigarette and put it to his lips. 'No chance.'

'Why'd you say that?'

'I know the type of blokes who come down here. I just can't see it.'

Francine gestured into the building. 'Do you recognise him?'

'Haven't seen his face yet.'

'His build, though? His clothes?'

Jeffers shook his head. 'I wasn't here yesterday, like I told the other one, but we didn't have no one in the book who was due to come down and fish, so, whoever he is, I'd say there's a good chance he's not a member.'

'Not supposed to have been here, then?'

'That's right. You'd need to be a member – we haven't done day tickets since before COVID. People take advantage, though. You get some who'll come down later when they know I'm not likely to be around. Gypsies, for example. They come down. That might've been what he did.'

'What about at night? Does anyone fish then?'

'Not supposed to, but they do. Good time to go after chub. You use a stinky bait like cheese paste and you'd be surprised what you can get out.'

'What about the day before yesterday?'

'Like I said, I *was* here then. I had half a dozen down, but none of them were dressed like him.' He drew down on his cigarette. 'Never had nothing like this happen in all the years I've been here.'

'How long's that?'

'Thirty years.'

'Who do you work for?'

'London Anglers Association.'

'They own the land?'

He shook his head. 'Lord Radnor owns it. We rent it from the estate – have done since the sixties.'

Francine looked back to the spire of the cathedral and saw the bank of angry dark cloud that was rolling over the city behind it. Her phone buzzed in her pocket and, taking it out, she saw a warning that yet more rain was imminent. She looked at the time on the screen and wished the pathologist would get a move on.

23

Mack reached over for her phone and silenced it, lying back and closing her eyes as she remembered what had happened last night. Bob Bradley's birthday drinks had been predictably messy, and she had made her escape at last orders just as the others were conspiring about where they could go next. There was talk of a lock-in at the Pheasant – or was it the Wig and Quill? – and, knowing that going along with the others would be a certain way to a much worse hangover than the one she was already going to get, Mack had made her excuses and headed over to see Atticus.

She blinked open her bleary eyes and saw the empty water glass on the bedstand. She remembered him insisting that she drink it – all of it – before they went to bed. She had done and, as she lay back and assessed how she felt, she found that her headache wasn't nearly as bad as she might have expected given the number of pints she had put away.

Mack looked the other way and saw that the bed was empty. She reached out a hand and felt the indentation where Atticus had lain; it was cold. She turned back to the bedstand and took her phone, opening her messages to see if he had left anything for her. He hadn't, but she remembered that he had said something about getting an early start. He'd told her he'd been given a new job, that it wouldn't be difficult and that he ought to be able to get it finished in a day if he put his mind to it.

It was seven. She would grab a quick shower, get dressed and then stop off at Boston Tea Party for breakfast on her way to the office. She fancied something greasy and unhealthy.

* * *

Mike Lewis called Mack during her walk to the nick.

'Morning, Mike. What's up?'

'Sorry to disturb you, boss. I'm at the *Journal*. I got a call from Alice Morris. She said she had something I needed to see. She was right. You need to see it, boss. You need to get over here now.'

'Now? *Right* now? I was going to stop and get some breakfast.'

'Sorry, boss. I don't think this can wait.'

24

Francine watched as Professor Allen Fyfe, the Home Office pathologist, made his way along the sodden track to join them.

'You'd think I would've learned by now,' he grumbled, pointing down.

His brogues and the bottoms of his trousers were thick with mud, and he was soaked through despite his umbrella. Francine remembered the same complaints when Fyfe had attended to the bodies that had been discovered at Imber. He was much more comfortable in his inspection rooms at the hospital than out in the field, especially when the weather was unpleasant.

'Thank you for coming, Professor.'

'What've we got?'

'Dead body inside the sluice house. Looks like it's been in the water for a while.'

Fyfe went over to the opening and looked inside. 'Bloody hell. We can't leave him in there getting bumped around like that. We need to get him out.'

'We've just been waiting for you,' Archer said.

Fyfe told them that they should get started. Collison had drawn the short straw and was going to be the one who got into the water to manoeuvre the body while the others pulled him out. Francine watched as he pulled on a pair of waders that Jeffers had fetched for him from the shipping container back near the fishing lodges, hauling them up so that he was covered to halfway up his chest.

'It's going to be bloody cold,' he grumbled as he went to the edge of the channel and sat down.

Jeffers gestured down into the channel. 'Are you sure you wouldn't rather I did it?'

'Better that it's us,' Francine said.

'We'll need you to help pull him out,' Archer said.

'It'll be slippery on the bottom. There'll be mud and silt down there, and the current will be a bastard. Be careful.'

Collison pushed off the edge and lowered himself into the water. It was deeper than it looked, and the glossy surface came up to the top of his chest. The water tried to shove him downstream, and he had to set himself against it. Archer passed him the end of a coil of rope, and Collison carefully looped it around the torso of the dead man. He fed it beneath his arms, secured it around his back and then gently floated the body away from the edge.

Archer and Jeffers took the other end of the rope.

'Ready?' Archer said.

'Ready,' said Jeffers.

'Ready,' said Collison.

'*Pull.*'

It was a joint effort: Collison tried to ensure that the body didn't scrape against the side of the channel, getting his arms around the dead man's waist and boosting him up; Archer and Jeffers and Francine pulled, hand over hand and inch after inch, heaving the dead weight out of the water and then up and over the side. They grabbed him beneath the shoulders and pulled him all the way out, leaving him face down on the concrete floor. Water pooled beneath him and ran back down into the channel again.

'Give me a hand,' Collison said.

Archer reached down and locked his hand around Collison's wrist, grunting with the effort as Collison scrabbled up, his boot finding something to wedge against so that he could boost himself over the edge and out. He remained where he was, on hands and knees, and gathered his breath.

Fyfe stepped forward. 'Let's get him over there,' he said, pointing to a spot where the curve of the riverbank had been flattened out.

The body was limp. Archer took the arms and Jeffers took the legs and, between them, they moved it to the spot that Fyfe had indicated. They lowered the body to the ground and turned it over and, for the first time, Francine was able to look at the man's face. It was angled slightly upward by a small overbite, and his skin was tanned by the weather, with a lattice of tiny veins across his fleshy nose and pitted cheeks. He was unshaven, with water clinging to the unkempt bristles, and his lips were chapped. His hair was thin, a tonsure in the middle of his scalp encircled by dark hair that was run through with grey. His clothes looked as if they would have been dishevelled even before he entered the water; they were torn, and a rip in his shirt revealed an expanse of tattooed skin.

'Recognise him?' Archer asked Jeffers.

'Never seen him before.'

'Not a fisherman?'

'Not a member, put it that way.'

Francine put a hand to her cheek.

Archer noticed. 'Franny? What is it?'

'I know who he is. I've nicked him before.' She closed her eyes and tried to remember the details. 'Rough sleeper, used to doss down in the Maltings, record for petty crime – mostly shoplifting. I picked him up after he took a bunch of clothes from the tailor's on New Street. He flogged them for heroin he got off Tommy Quinn in the Friary. He had a couple of grams he'd hidden in his sock.'

'Name?'

'He's Polish . . .' She scrunched up her face, then put her hands together as she remembered it. 'They called him Lucky Lucjusz.'

'Not *that* lucky,' Collison said as he peeled off the waterproof trousers.

She tried to remember his surname. 'Lucjusz . . . Lucjusz . . . Lucjusz Kajetan.'

Fyfe knelt and started to make a quick examination. 'The deceased is male, late forties to early fifties.'

'How long has he been in there?'

'A body in the water will decompose more slowly than would be the case if it were on land. It's the cold – it delays things. You'll see the usual post-mortem changes – vascular marbling, dark discolouration of skin and soft tissue, bloating, putrefaction. It just takes longer.'

'When, then?' Archer said. 'A day? Two days? The bailiff wasn't at work yesterday and didn't look in here the day before.'

Fyfe nodded. 'A two-day window, then. That's about right.'

Francine was impatient. Fyfe's caution was as predictable, and as annoying, as ever. 'Best guess?'

Fyfe sucked his teeth. 'Anywhere between twelve and eighteen hours.'

'Cause of death?'

'Most likely drowning, but I'll have a look.' He stood up. 'I need to move him. Putrefaction accelerates once a body is taken out of the water. I need to get him into the fridge.'

25

Atticus followed Wintringham, picking him up at the end of the road and then discreetly tailing him as he headed into town. He stopped at Godolphin to drop off his eldest daughter and then continued to Bishopsdown, where he delivered his youngest to an older woman Atticus recognised from Wintringham's social media as his mother. The house was on the same estate as the one that Mack had shared with her ex-husband, and Atticus was irrationally concerned that Andy Jones would see him and confront him for breaking up his marriage.

Atticus had expected Wintringham to drive over to Old Sarum for work, but he didn't; he turned around and headed into the city, leaving his car at the Maltings and hurrying on to Fisherton Street on foot while sheltering beneath a small umbrella. Atticus parked up, put Bandit on the lead and followed, staying a decent distance behind him. Wintringham stopped in Waterstones, where he browsed the shelves for ten minutes. He went outside again, turning left and walking the short distance to St George's Mall, where he diverted to WHSmith. He came out and retraced his steps to Boston Tea Party, the large coffee shop on the high street. Atticus sheltered in the doorway of an empty shop where he could watch without being easily noticed.

Wintringham ordered a coffee and a pastry and then chatted with the barista who served him.

Wintringham came back outside, and Atticus followed him once more as he made his way up Crane Street to the medical practice at the back of the Lush House car park. Atticus waited behind a car and watched as Wintringham went into the surgery, spoke to the receptionist and then disappeared.

Having waited for a minute and then started back to his car. There was nothing about Wintringham that gave him any cause for concern. He was just as Nina had described him: a father of two children with what appeared to be a normal, mundane life. There wasn't much else for him to do. He would go back to the office and write up his report, add the relevant links to the social media profiles that he had used, and then, when he had received the DBS check and the entry on the Land Registry for the Wintringhams' house, he would bundle it all together with his invoice and send it over to Nina.

It was boring work, but it paid well, and Atticus wasn't in the habit of turning down easy money.

26

Francine drove back across the city to the nick. Fyfe had arranged for the body to be taken to the hospital, where he would go through the motions of confirming what they already suspected: Lucjusz Kajetan had fallen into the water and drowned. He said that he would test the blood for the presence of alcohol and drugs; Francine remembered Kajetan and was confident that he would have been under the influence of one or the other – or both – when he died. It all seemed grimly predictable: another unfortunate who had fallen on hard times and was dead because of it.

Francine was cold and damp, and in need of a hot drink. Robbie Best was in the kitchen, filling the kettle at the tap. She paused, worrying that it might be awkward, but he defused any possible awkwardness with a friendly smile as he held up a teabag. 'Want a brew?'

'Please. It's bitter out there.'

Best flicked the switch on the side of the kettle. 'How was it?'

'Unpleasant.'

'You get the body out?'

She nodded. 'Remember Lucjusz Kajetan?'

'Name's familiar. Where do I know him from?'

'Rough sleeper. I nicked him for possession. It's a sad story – came over from Poland twenty years ago and set up as a builder, got in too deep with the bank and lost it all. He ended up on the street with a drug habit, which is where he was when I pulled him. He got a suspended sentence and disappeared. I heard on the grapevine that he'd gone to Andover, but maybe not.'

'What was he doing in the river?'

'I think he might have been sleeping in the sluice house and fell in. It's dark and slippery, and if he was pissed or high, like he probably was . . . I don't think it'd be too hard to go over the edge and drown.'

'What does Fyfe think?'

'He's going to take a look at the body and let me know.'

The kettle boiled. Best took out two mugs from the cupboard, dropped a teabag into each and was about to pour the water when they heard footsteps approaching from outside.

Mack stopped in the doorway. 'Meeting in the conference room in fifteen minutes,' she said. 'Grab everyone who's here, Robbie. No exceptions.'

'What is it, boss?'

'David Campbell,' she said. 'It *definitely* wasn't an accident on the tower yesterday.'

27

The memory of what she had watched at the *Journal* – and what it might mean – was fresh in Mack's mind as she went through into the same space that they had only recently used as the Major Incident Room for the Imber enquiry. There was a long table with enough chairs to seat twenty. Mack had brought the package with the video and, once the evidentiary requirements had been taken care of, had asked the IT department to digitise the footage so that it could be more easily distributed and viewed. They would also ensure that it was stored safely, in the event that it became important evidence in any subsequent investigation into the events leading up to the death of David Campbell. There was a screen on the wall, and Mack took out her laptop and connected it, thumbing the remote to the correct input so that she was able to share her screen.

She went to one end of the table, pulled out the chair and sat down. She tried to get her thoughts in order as she waited for the others to arrive. She was buzzing with the adrenaline of a new challenge, a death that had been tragic until this morning, when it had suddenly become much more than that: now it was mysterious and most likely sinister.

Debbie Campbell had been convinced that her husband had not taken his own life, and now, considering what she had seen on the video, Mack was inclined to believe her.

Suicide was possible, but, if it was, then blackmail was involved. Murder was in play, too.

Robbie Best marshalled those officers who were working the day shift and sent them into the conference room. Nigel Archer took the seat to Mack's right, and Francine Patterson took the seat next to him. Archer had only just been promoted from detective constable, his career already characterised by huge ambition and the willingness to put in the hours that others might not have been prepared to invest. Francine's hair was damp, and Mack had noticed mud on her trousers; she had been told that a body had been found in the river and that Francine had been the first detective on the scene.

DC Stewart Lynas sat down at the opposite end of the table. He was ambitious, too, but, unlike Archer and Francine, Mack wasn't sure that he had the ability to back it up. He was the son of wealthy parents who had not stinted on his education, sending him to a succession of expensive private schools. These had given him an overinflated sense of self-worth and a habit of looking down on others but had been unable to improve a sluggish intellect.

She tapped her knuckles against the table. 'All right, quieten down. We've had a development on the death of David Campbell at the cathedral. We *had* been working on the assumption that he had either fallen by way of an accident or that he'd jumped. An accident always felt like a bit of a long shot, and there's been a development this morning that makes it even less likely.'

She looked around the table at the faces of her officers. They were all rapt, Campbell's death was already grotesque, but the suggestion that it might have been something other than a dreadful accident gave it an edge that had been missing before. The suggestion of a darker motivation raised the stakes.

Mack turned to her laptop and moused over to the folder that she had been given by the evidence handler. The envelope that had contained the tape had been photographed and then transferred to a sterile container and filed. Mack double-clicked the folder and then clicked again on the sub-folder that was labelled with the details of the envelope. She picked a photograph taken from above and gestured to it on the screen.

'At some point yesterday,' Mack continued, 'this package was delivered to the offices of the *Journal* on Rollestone Street.'

She dragged the image of the package to the other side of the screen and opened two additional top-down photographs of the video cassette: one showing the label and the other showing the back. She opened another folder and clicked on the images that showed the case, with Campbell's name written on the slip of paper that had been pushed down against the spine.

'The tape was in the case,' she said.

Best pointed to the image that showed the spine. 'David Campbell?' he said.

'That's right. He's on the tape. You need to see this first.'

Mack clicked again and opened a photograph of the piece of paper.

'"It is mine to avenge,"' Best read out. '"I will repay. In due time their foot will slip; their day of disaster is near and their doom rushes upon them." What is that? From the Bible?'

'Deuteronomy chapter thirty-two, verse thirty-five.'

'Didn't Jack leave Bible verses with Atticus after he left Miller's body?' Francine said.

Mack nodded. 'He did.'

She clicked back, jumped across to the folder that had the digitised version of the video and double-clicked it. The file opened and auto played, showing the room with the bed, everything lit in red. No one spoke as the boy appeared in the shot and then the man. He turned so that his face was exposed to the camera.

'Shit,' Best said.

Mack pointed to the screen. 'I haven't had it absolutely confirmed yet, but I'm about as confident that we can be that that is Campbell, albeit maybe twenty or twenty-five years ago. We'll have to ask his wife, but that can wait for now.'

'And the boy?'

'Young,' Mack said. 'Hard to say how young, but I wouldn't be surprised if he was under sixteen.'

'Definitely under sixteen,' Lynas said.

Mack moved the cursor to the top right of the video and closed it.

Archer laid his palms flat on the table. 'And this went to the *Journal?*'

She nodded.

'Why?'

'We don't know, but it'd be a very big coincidence that Campbell happens to fall to his death on the day that this video comes to light. An accident was always unlikely. He knew the cathedral well, and they've made it safe up there. He slipped?' She shook her head. 'No.'

'Blackmail?'

'That'd be my guess. Maybe Campbell was sent this by someone who was trying to make money. Either he didn't have the money, or he was worried that the tape would come out anyway.'

'Or he paid it, and they still put it out.'

'Possible.'

Lynas clucked his tongue. 'What about the verse?'

'I don't know,' Mack said. 'But Franny is right. It does remind me of Jack.'

'Could it be him?'

'We never made it public that he was into the Bible,' Mack said. 'I mean, it *might* just be one of those things, but I don't know . . .'

Lewis leaned back. 'So it's murder?'

Mack spread her hands. 'There's no evidence that there was anyone else up there with him.'

'No CCTV?'

Best shook his head. 'Checked. None once you get through the door at the back of the nave and start to climb the tower.'

'What about the cameras they *do* have?' Archer said.

'We've reviewed them, didn't see anything that would suggest that someone else was up there.'

'That's not to say that we can rule it out,' Mack said. 'I think it's less likely than suicide, but we need to eliminate it.' She paused. 'We don't have any choice but to open an enquiry. I want it to be discreet at the moment. Campbell's wife lost her husband yesterday, and the last thing I want is for her to have to worry about this until it's absolutely necessary.' She gestured to Francine. 'Can you very carefully get a crop of the video that shows just his face – nothing else if you can help it – and take it over to her and get her to confirm that it's him?'

'And if she asks where we got it from?'

'We can't shield her from it completely. Maybe just try to be vague. Tell her we've seen a video of him from a long while ago that he might have found embarrassing. Tell her that she doesn't have to see it, but that we need her to confirm that it's him.'

Francine nodded. 'It's possible she knows something about it and didn't want to say.'

'Maybe. See how she reacts. And ask her if she had any reason to think that he might've been blackmailed. Had he moved money out of a joint account or asked if she had any he could use – anything like that.'

Archer pointed to the screen. 'What about the package?'

'That's got to be our focus,' Mack said. 'We need to find out who delivered it.' She pointed at Lynas. 'Go and check all the cameras on Rollestone Street. See if there's anything that shows someone dropping a package off. They don't think it was there before lunch, and they found it around ten. Eight hours. That's your search window.'

Lynas said that he would get to it right away. Mack didn't doubt that he would find the task menial and beneath him, but she had decided that he was going to have to get used to doing the running around before she gave him the more interesting and consequential jobs.

'What about the boy?' Archer said. 'Who is he?'

Lynas scratched his cheek. 'We're saying that's twenty years ago? He'd be mid to late thirties now.'

Mack shrugged. 'Look for mispers around the time. You can dig out the files from Imber – we already spent hours on it. No point doing the work twice.'

'And if nothing shows up?'

'Public appeal?' Archer suggested.

'Not yet,' Mack said. 'Not without making things a million times worse for Mrs Campbell.'

He nodded his agreement. 'Hold off until we don't have any other choice.'

'Agreed.' Mack nodded to Best. 'Can you sort forensics? We need to get everything looked at – the package, the video, the box, the paper. We'll need disqualifying prints from everyone at the *Journal*, so get that done and then see if there's anything else. Maybe we get lucky and there's a hit.'

'Will do.'

Mack stood. 'Good. I don't want to make a song and dance about this yet, so let's not talk about it out of school.'

Best drummed his fingers on the table. 'Look, I don't want to sound the alarm unnecessarily, but do you think this could be connected to Imber?'

'Go on.'

'We had missing girls there. I don't know – seems like that video was shot at around the same time they were killed. Maybe they had it away with boys, too.'

'We can't rule anything out. See if you can find a match with the boy in the video and the girls we dug up in the graveyard. Anything. Think laterally. Go on – get to it. Dismissed.'

The team dispersed. Mack stayed where she was for a moment, thinking about what Best had said about Imber. The thought had crossed her mind, too, and she wondered whether she should mention what they had discovered to Atticus.

28

Atticus had been surprised to receive the text message from Mack asking if he was available for lunch. He had spent a quiet morning writing up his notes following his background check on Robin Wintringham. He had prepared a short two-page report that laid out what he had found – or, precisely, what he *hadn't* found – and had just about finished it when his phone buzzed with Mack's invitation. He had given the dog a quick walk so that he could relieve himself and then had walked to the market square. Mack had suggested that they meet at Henderson's and was waiting for him at a table inside.

'This is a pleasant surprise,' he said as he sat down. 'Is everything all right?'

'I thought it would be nice to see you,' she said.

'Really?'

'I don't need a reason for that, do I?'

'Of course not.'

Mack wouldn't admit that there *was* a reason, but Atticus could see that she was agitated: the glasses on the table held cutlery and paper napkins, and Mack had taken out one of the napkins and torn it into squares. She was fidgeting, too, and a tightness in her neck suggested stress. Atticus's instinct was to point out what he had noticed, but, for once, he managed to hold his tongue.

'What are you having?' she asked him.

'A sandwich,' he said, rising before she could. 'I'll get them. What do you want?'

'You choose.'

He went to the counter and ordered two sandwiches – the cheese and tomato that she liked and a pastrami for him – together with drinks. He paid for them and went back to the table.

Mack had taken out a second napkin and was in the process of shredding that one, too.

Atticus couldn't hold his tongue any longer. 'What is it? Something's up.'

She sighed, pushed the pieces of the napkin into a pile, and nodded. 'I could do with your opinion.'

'Work?'

She nodded. 'You know I've been looking into the man who fell from the tower of the cathedral?'

'What about him?'

'I don't think it was an accident.'

His eyes widened. 'Really?'

'This doesn't go any further – right?'

'Of course not.'

'Atticus – I'm serious.'

'It's strictly between us.'

She leaned forward a little. 'A package was sent to the *Journal* yesterday. We only found out about it this morning. It was a video of Campbell from about twenty years ago. He was doing things with a boy that he really oughtn't have been doing.'

'Have you seen it?'

She nodded.

'Cheese and tomato and pastrami?'

The girl from the counter had their sandwiches and two cans of Diet Coke.

'Thanks,' Atticus said, smiling as she set the food and drink down on the table.

Mack waited until she had gone back behind the counter.

'This video shows up on the day that he falls off the tower and dies?' She spread her hands over the table. 'I mean – come *on*. You can see why I don't think it was an accident now, right?'

'Blackmail?'

'That'd be my guess.'

'He's blackmailed, and *then* he jumps off the tower.' Atticus's mind started to race with questions and angles that would have to be investigated; he held up his hand, as much to tell himself to slow down as anything. 'Right – give me the details. When did they get the package?'

'Yesterday afternoon or evening.'

'Can they be more specific than that?'

'No. That's the best they can do.'

'How was it delivered?'

'We think by hand. It wasn't posted.'

'So it was delivered yesterday afternoon or evening, and Campbell died in the morning. Why would they do that?'

'Maybe he didn't pay?'

'Or maybe he did. Maybe someone wants to ruin his reputation. His death wasn't enough.'

'Suicide, then?'

He paused again, prodding a finger against his untouched sandwich.

'Atticus?'

'Someone pushed him?'

'Why?'

'There's an argument. It gets physical.'

'Why would there be an argument on the cathedral tower? It's hardly convenient.'

'I agree, but humour me. Would anyone have known he was there?'

'He was taking photos for a project. He's been up the tower at the same time every day all year. He blogs about it.'

'*That's* interesting.' Atticus paused. 'We need motive, means and opportunity – predictability gives us opportunity.'

'But means and motive? I don't know.' Mack toyed with the napkin again. 'Let's say it's blackmail, and he *didn't* jump. Why murder him? It couldn't be that he didn't pay. Maybe you'd kill him, but like that?'

'The lack of discretion? Yes – strange. But how about this – maybe whoever pushed him *wants* the attention. They want this to make the news. It's why the video was sent after he was dead. It's about publicity.'

'*Not* blackmail, then?'

'It's the most likely motive, but it wouldn't have to be that. Maybe someone wants to kill him *and* ruin his reputation.'

'Murder him twice,' she suggested.

'That's a nice way to put it.'

'There was something else, too,' Mack said. 'There was a piece of paper in with the tape. It had a Bible verse printed on it. "It is mine to avenge; I will repay—"'

He finished for her. '"In due time their foot will slip; their day of disaster is near and their doom rushes upon them." Deuteronomy thirty-two, verse thirty . . . thirty . . .'

'Five,' Mack said. 'Thirty-five.'

'And that was in the package?'

Mack sighed. 'Yes.'

'Right. *OK.*' He clapped his hands together. '*Now* I get it – you think this is Jack?'

'He referred you to a Bible verse when Miller was left.'

'And gave me a Bible with all his favourite verses highlighted.'

115

'Was that one of them?'

'No, but the Bible's not short on revenge. Especially not the Old Testament. He'd have *lots* to choose from.'

'So – what do you think? Could it be him?'

'I don't know. You never made the fact he left verses for me public, did you?'

'No. Did you tell anyone?'

He shook his head. 'I can see why you think I might be interested.'

She pushed her food away and looked at him. 'Are you?'

'Of course.'

'Why?'

'Because . . .' He started, noticed that Mack was looking at him quizzically, and stopped.

'This all goes back to Burns. You went after him like a dog with a bone, then Imber, and you haven't really stopped.'

'Because I knew Burns was guilty. And because there's more to what he and Miller and York did than we've found out so far.'

She was watching him carefully as he spoke, and he found it unnerving.

'OK.'

Atticus reached across the table and took her hand. 'What is it?'

There was concern in her face as she squeezed his hand. 'You'll always be honest with me, won't you?'

'Of course,' he said. 'What is it, Mack?'

'I'm always here if you want to talk.'

He shook his head. 'Where's all this coming from?'

She squeezed his hand again and let go. 'All right. I just wanted to make sure you knew that.'

'I do.'

'Good. And thank you. I'm grateful for your help.'

'Could you call the cathedral for me? I'll go up to the tower and have a look. Tell them I'm coming and to let me up.'

'There's nothing there. We've been over it from top to bottom.'

'So there's no harm in me having a check, is there?'

Atticus could see from Mack's body language that she was reluctant. He knew that her decision to involve him would be rescinded if she found out that he had butted heads with Murphy yesterday; she had been too drunk to ask him about the interview last night, and he hadn't volunteered his account of it. He would have to tell her about it eventually – especially given that Murphy looked like he had her in his sights, too – but it could wait until tonight.

'I don't know,' she said.

'Just a quick look. Up and down in half an hour.'

She sighed.

'You wouldn't have spoken to me about it if you didn't want my help.'

'I wanted to *talk* to you about it. That's a *long* way from wanting you to get involved.'

'It's up to you. But a second opinion might help you get a little closer to what happened.'

'I suppose I could say that you're consulting again.'

He thought of what Murphy had said and ignored it. 'Just like before.'

'But please – don't embarrass me.'

Atticus picked up his sandwich, opened the wrapping and took a bite.

'I'll be good.'

29

Atticus went back to the office, took Bandit into the courtyard for five minutes so that he could relieve himself, and then walked the short distance to the cathedral. Mack had called ahead, and one of the guides who led the tours up to the tower was waiting for him in the cloisters.

'Mr Priest?'

'That's right.'

'I'm Clive Mouton. You want to go up the tower?'

'Please.'

'Anywhere in particular?'

'I'd like to see the parapet Mr Campbell was on when he fell.'

'I thought the investigation was finished?'

'I'm just checking a couple of things before we close the file.'

Atticus didn't know whether Mouton had been told that he wasn't a policeman, but, if he didn't know, Atticus wasn't minded to correct him. It would be a useful misconception and would make securing his cooperation a little easier.

Mack had explained that Mouton was one of the witnesses who had seen Campbell falling from the tower, Atticus didn't expect that he would be able to extricate anything from him that he hadn't already provided to the investigation, but it would be helpful to be able to have his perspective.

'This way,' Mouton said, going through the door and into the nave of the cathedral. They crossed over to the doorway in the corner of the building that was used for the tours. 'Have you been up the tower before?'

'I haven't. Would Mr Campbell have come this way?'

'Definitely.'

'Any other ways up?'

'A couple,' Mouton said, 'but those doors are kept locked.'

'Where?'

'There's a door in the north transept and another in the sacristy.'

'Would you be able to show me later?'

'If it'd help.'

Atticus was looking for CCTV cameras and had spotted half a dozen between the entrance and the doorway through which they were about to pass. Mack had said that they had checked the recordings and hadn't seen anything that would suggest that anyone other than Campbell had climbed the tower yesterday morning.

'It was suicide, wasn't it?' Mouton said. 'Seems most likely.'

'Did you know him?'

'We all did. He was a popular man. He'd been here a long time.'

Mouton took a key from his pocket and unlocked the door. Atticus followed him into the waiting area with the lockers on the left-hand side and the passage on the right that would continue up into the rest of the building.

'No cameras in here?'

'No,' Mouton said. 'There's no need. The public can't come up unless they're with a guide, and the door is locked.'

Atticus followed Mouton up the stairs, across the passage that ran along the wall of the nave and then up two flights of stairs until they reached the clock. They climbed again, paused for a moment while the bells chimed the quarter hour, and then climbed the final set of stairs that brought them to the top of the tower and the four doors that led out onto the parapets.

Atticus tried to orient himself. 'Which door?'

Mouton pointed to the door on the right. 'That one.' He walked over and turned the handle. The door was unlocked, and he opened it, stepping aside to let Atticus pass. Atticus stepped through and onto the narrow parapet on the other side. He looked over the edge of the balcony to the roof of the refectory below. He could see that what Mack had said was likely correct; it would be very difficult for anyone to fall over the barrier accidentally. It would have had to have been an intentional act on Campbell's part. He thought about the other possibility – that he was pushed – and found that prospect less likely now.

'How big was Campbell?'

Mouton frowned. 'Sorry?'

'Was he a large man?'

'Yes. A couple of inches taller than me.'

'How old?'

'Early sixties.'

'Fit? Unfit?'

'Very fit. You know he was in the army? The discipline never left him. He was in good shape. Ran a marathon every year to raise money for the cathedral and worked out two or three times a week. Why?'

'Just wondering about whether he might have climbed up onto the railing and then slipped. More likely if he was frail.'

'Frail is the *last* word I'd use to describe him.'

Atticus looked at the balustrade. The fact that Campbell was still fit and strong made foul play less likely. It would have taken effort to get him up and over the barrier, especially if he was struggling.

Was it possible? Yes.

Likely? No.

Atticus stood with his hands on the metal bar and looked out over the city. The rain started to fall again, but he ignored it, closing his eyes and concentrating on the explanations for what might have happened here the day before.

Three options.

An accident? That seemed unlikely. There was no reason for Campbell to have put himself in a position where he might fall. Everything Atticus had been told about him suggested that he was careful.

Foul play? Also unlikely. Atticus had been unable to find any evidence to suggest that there was someone on the tower with Campbell yesterday morning, and, even if he wasn't alone, it was difficult to see how it would have been possible to get him into a position where he could be tipped over the edge.

Suicide, then. More likely. Campbell was being blackmailed and, fearing the ruination of his reputation, he had come up to a place that he loved and taken his own life. But the blackmailer had released the footage anyway. Atticus tried to find the weaknesses in the argument but could see only one: that Campbell's wife had detected nothing to suggest that her husband was considering taking his own life. Atticus agreed with what Mack had suggested; there was no guarantee that she would have realised his intentions, especially when the thing that Campbell wanted to avoid – his shame – would have been guaranteed if he had been honest.

But, saying all that, Atticus still felt the nag of doubt.

He needed to see the tape.

30

Mouton took Atticus to the doors that he had mentioned in the north transept and sacristy. The transept was first. Atticus tried the handle.

'It'll be locked,' Mouton said.

It was.

Atticus knelt and, ignoring the looks of confusion from the worshippers and tourists who were ambling around the building, leaned in close to examine the wood around the keyhole for any suggestion that the lock might have been picked.

'What is it?' Mouton asked him.

Atticus ignored him. The wood was old and had been scratched and scraped over the course of its life, but there was nothing that looked new.

They went to the sacristy, and Atticus confirmed that that door, too, was secured. There were cameras covering both doors, and, as he looked up and down the nave, he doubted whether anyone who might have wanted to do Campbell harm would have been able to use either door to climb the tower without being seen.

Atticus thanked Mouton for his help and exited the nave, walking through the cloisters and then going outside. The rain was falling more heavily now, but Atticus had an idea and was distracted from the fact that he was getting wet by his desire to test it.

He skirted the cathedral until he reached the Trinity Chapel at the easternmost side of the building. He remembered from walking the dog that the walls here were covered with a lattice of scaffolding across the whole flank. The exterior of the Lady Chapel and its vast stained-glass window were accessed by way of six levels of boarded platforms, each level reached by a ladder. The nave was also being maintained, and another nine platforms reached up from the roof of the chapel to the points of the three decorative pillars that stood at the eastern end of the main building. There was no obvious means of access to the tower that sat over the junction of the nave and the north and south transepts, but that was not reason enough for Atticus to abandon the suspicion that nagged at him as he looked up at the building.

What if there was a way into the tower from the outside?

The bottom of the scaffolding had been protected behind a series of interlocking portable fences that had been erected all the way along the length of the wall. Atticus followed the fence until he came to a gate; he looked around and, seeing no one who might oppose him, tried the gate and found that it was unlocked. He pushed it all the way back and passed through the opening, turning left and then right until he saw the ladder that led up to the first platform ten feet above him. He climbed it, reaching the wooden boards and then taking a second and third ladder until he was thirty feet above the ground. He was up close to the stained-glass window that celebrated prisoners of conscience, the view into the cathedral obscured by the coloured glass to the extent that the people inside were no more than indistinct shadows.

Atticus climbed the next ladder, then the next and, finally, the ladder that took him up to the platform that allowed access

to the apex of the roof. He was high up here; the boards continued around the top of the cathedral and, hidden from the ground
on the southern side of the building, he saw two stonemasons
who were working on the weathered marble piers. They both saw
Atticus as soon as he climbed up to the platform, and the man who
was closest stood up and picked his way around the boards.

'What are you doing?' the man said angrily.

Atticus held up his hands. 'It's OK.'

'You can't be up here.'

'It's fine.'

'No, it's not. Who are you? You need to get down right away.'

'I'm with the police.'

'Oh.' The man stopped. 'Because of David?'

'That's right. We're looking into what happened.'

'You still shouldn't be up here, mate, especially not by yourself.'

He smiled. 'I'm not by myself now, am I? The two of you
are here.'

'Come on. That's not—'

Atticus interrupted him. 'Could you answer a couple of questions for me?'

'You need to—'

Atticus cut across him again. 'What's your name?'

'Tristan.'

'The dean knows I'm up here, Tristan, but feel free to go and
have a word with him if that'd make you feel better.'

He fidgeted uncomfortably. 'What was your name?'

'Atticus Priest.'

'And you're police?'

'That's right.'

'And what do you want?'

'Just a couple of questions.'

'Go on, then.'

'Are you up here every day?'

'Yes.'

'What time do you start?'

'Usually around nine.'

'Yesterday?'

He shook his head. 'Didn't come up – not after what happened.'

Atticus hadn't expected to find out anything useful, but that wasn't why he had asked his questions; he needed a delay while he looked for what he was really interested in.

'I remember reading about a workshop in the attic, above the nave – is it still there?'

'Yes. Why?'

'Have you ever been inside?'

'No. It's not being used at the moment.'

'Where is it?'

Tristan pointed across the leadwork roof to a hatch that Atticus hadn't noticed.

'Could you show me?'

Atticus followed the stonemason around the platform until he reached the outward bulge that marked the start of the choir transept. The hatch was made of wood that was banded with iron straps; it had received a battering from the weather over the years. It had a handle and looked as if it was secured by way of a mortice.

Atticus gestured to it. 'Locked?'

'Never tried it.'

Atticus stepped around him, reached for the cold iron knob and turned it.

The hatch opened.

The space inside was dark and Atticus was unable to see anything once the gloom swallowed up the daylight.

'Where does it go?'

'It's above the nave, but, like I said, I've never been in.'

'But it might run to the tower?'

'I mean, it *might*, but—'

Atticus took out his phone, activated the flashlight and shone it inside. He could see a little farther now, but still not enough to satisfy his curiosity. The tower was still at least a hundred feet away; the only way to see whether it was possible to access it through the roof was to go in and check.

Atticus took a step over the threshold, and the mason grabbed his arm.

'You can't go in,' he said. 'Not without someone from the works department.'

'So either come in with me or go and get someone.'

The man turned back to his mate and called out that he was going to have to borrow his phone. Atticus took his opportunity, he shook the man's hand off, and, shining the torch down to light the way, he stepped inside.

31

Atticus held his phone out in front of him in the hope that the torch might light the way enough for him to see where he was going. He remembered reading an article about a secret workshop in the roof that was used by the stonemasons and glaziers who had been involved in restoration work across the life of the building. The attic space was full of the beams that supported the roof. Long cross braces stretched from one side of the space to the other, with more modern – yet still ancient – metal trusses locking everything into place. The wood was old – hundreds of years old – and Atticus breathed in its aroma. The attic was furnished with one vast table that would have been used by masons and glaziers working on larger items that couldn't easily be brought up from the ground.

Atticus counted his steps to the other end of the workshop and reached fifty; he guessed that he still had the same distance again before he reached the start of the tower.

The room ended in a triangular wall formed by the angle of the roof. Atticus shone his torch up and saw that there was a door in the wall, and that it was open. He shone his light down on the floor and carefully stepped over the sill and into the next room beyond.

'Hey,' he heard from behind him. 'Stop! You can't just go in there.'

It was the mason; Atticus ignored him and carried on.

The second room was an attic that didn't look as if it had ever been used. A wooden gangway led down the middle of the space, with the false ceiling of the nave bulging upwards. Holes had been drilled into the slaked lime so that water could drain, in the event that there was ever a fire. Atticus followed the gangway as it took him above the presbytery. He tried not to focus on how high above the floor of the cathedral he was and hoped that access to this space was not restricted on account of it being unsafe. He didn't know, but couldn't stop walking; he felt that he was close to making a discovery that could be important in determining what had happened to Campbell. His single-mindedness – Mack would call it impetuosity – might land him in trouble, but the game would be worth the candle if he could give her an explanation as to what might have happened on the tower yesterday morning.

He came to the end of the roof space and tried to picture the plan of the cathedral. It was laid out in the shape of a cross, with the tower atop the junction where the nave and the north and south transepts met. He guessed that he had travelled beyond the choir transepts and that he must now be near to the tower.

He shone his torch ahead and saw another door in the wall. It was made of wood and looked as old as the beams behind him. The door had an iron handle; Atticus covered his hand with the sleeve of his jacket and tried it. The handle turned, and the door opened. Atticus knelt and shone his torch on the door, checking the wooden frame for signs of damage and finding none. He focused on the lock itself; it was antique, although newer than the door. He got in closer and recognised a double-acting tumbler design.

His knowledge of locksmithing was extensive, and he knew that this lock would have dated from around the mid-1700s. He concentrated his light on the decorative plate that protected the keyhole and saw a scrape, a straight line that started at the hole and extended an inch below it. Atticus held the torch as close to the door as he could and then leaned in even closer; it was impossible to say for sure, but the scratch looked recent. He covered his fingers with his sleeve and very carefully touched the iron handle, gently pulling the door back so that he could look at the bolt. It was undamaged. He would need to have the door removed so that he could look at the mechanism; he made a note to himself to mention it to Mack when he spoke to her.

He went through the doorway and emerged onto a landing before a set of stairs that he remembered from his visit to the tower earlier.

Satisfied, he turned and retraced his steps, passing through the second and then the first door and returning to the hatch that opened onto the roof. The masons were still there, but a third man – someone Atticus hadn't seen before – had joined them.

The newcomer approached him. 'What do you think you're doing?'

'Who are *you*?'

'The deputy clerk of works. Who are you?'

'I'm with the police.'

'I just *called* the police. They said there's no one supposed to be here.'

'I'm a consultant,' he said patiently. 'Speak to DCI Jones.'

'Don't worry, mate – I intend to.'

'She'll explain everything.' Atticus turned and pointed into the dark attic. 'There's a door at the end of the gangway in the second room, just before the staircase in the tower. Please don't go inside, and *definitely* don't let anyone touch it. I'm going to arrange for a crime scene investigator to come out and see if there are any fingerprints on the handle. Do you understand?'

'Fingerprints? What do you mean?'

'When's the last time that you went in there to have a look?'

'Beyond the workshop? Never. It's not safe.'

'And was the door locked or unlocked?'

'We never go in there,' the clerk repeated. 'We don't use that door. I have no idea whether it's locked.'

'Please listen carefully,' Atticus said. 'Don't go inside now. Absolutely do not touch *anything*. There could be evidence there that'll help us to understand what happened to your boss.'

'What do you mean? Evidence of *what*?'

'I need you to meet the CSI and show him where he needs to go. All right?'

The man looked baffled, his earlier indignation with Atticus for trespassing inside the building now replaced by confusion.

'Is that all right?' Atticus repeated.

'Yes. I'll show them.'

'Good man.' Atticus smiled. 'Is there anything else?'

All three men looked completely bemused.

'No? Good.'

Atticus went over to the ladder and started to descend before any of them could raise any further objections. He knew that he had gone a little further than he ought, and that Mack was going to be angry, but, on the other hand, he had made a breakthrough. He still wasn't sure how anyone would have been able to force someone as large as Campbell over the side of the parapet, but he had demonstrated that it was possible that someone *could* have joined him in the tower without having to use the internal doors that were covered by cameras. There might have been a perfectly good reason for the scratch on the lock, but there was a chance that the damage had been done while someone was trying to pick it.

Atticus reached the ground, went through the gate in the fence and looked up at the cathedral. He took out his phone and called Mack.

It went to voicemail.

'It's me,' he said. 'I need to speak to you.'

32

Alice had been busy all morning, pushed on by the adrenaline of working on a story that she knew was going to be big. Eddie had told her they were going to include a piece about the video with Campbell. He had recorded it on his phone before the police arrived and said he wanted her to write up something they could illustrate with a still. He was going to write a piece from the point of view of the newspaper, explaining how the tape had come to be in their possession. He was particularly interested in the scripture that had accompanied the tape and wanted to include a photograph of it that he'd taken before the police had removed everything to the station.

Alice had been surprised that he would be that ballsy, but reminded herself that he had ink beneath his fingernails and that life on a provincial paper after time spent breaking stories on the *Sun* and the *Mirror* had to be depressing. He had never spoken about it, but she suspected he had been bruised by the end of his career in London and that he saw his job at the *Journal* as a backwater where he would see out the last few years before his retirement. He was an old newshound at heart, and this was his chance to publish something important again.

'Shit!'

The shout came from Eddie's office. Alice looked up from her desk and saw that he was standing, the handset of his phone held out in front of him.

'Shit, shit, *shit!*'

For a moment, Alice thought he was going to crash the phone against his desk. He didn't. He replaced it, and then, a moment later, he came out into the newsroom.

'Sorry,' he said. 'Lost my rag for a moment.'

'What was it?'

'I was speaking to Andy Clarke,' he said.

'Who?'

'My boss. He's taken an interest in Campbell.'

'What did he say?'

'He said he'd heard we'd been sent a video of Campbell and that, if we wanted to run anything on it, we had to clear it with head office first. I said I wanted to cover it, maybe find a still we could use to illustrate it, and he said no. It was the lawyers, he said. They'd had a think and said that there was no way we could do it. We can't mention the scripture, either.'

'What? Why?'

Eddie waved a hand in irritation. 'Reporting restrictions. Don't want to impede the investigation. Blah, blah, blah. It's all bollocks. What about freedom of expression? I said. What about the right to impart and receive information? He told me to get back into my box.'

'How does he even *know* about the video?'

'*We* didn't tell him,' he said bitterly, 'and the only other people who know are Old Bill. Someone must've put pressure on them to make sure we don't print anything they want kept quiet.' He reached into his pocket for his packet of cigarettes. 'Anyway, you might as well leave the video for now. I'll push him on it again tomorrow.'

Alice had plenty of other work to be getting on with and would have carried on all the way through her lunch break, but Eddie insisted she go for a sandwich to clear her mind before they all knuckled down for what would probably end up being a very long day. He was going out for a walk, he said, and she should, too. She didn't protest; she had dry-cleaning to pick up from Waitrose and could grab a bite to eat while she was there. Alice hadn't had the best night's sleep, and a couple of shots of caffeine and a sandwich would help her negotiate the rest of the day. She told Eddie where she was going, grabbed her coat and set off.

It was still raining, and she borrowed an umbrella from Carly at reception before stepping outside and hurrying to the car park on Salt Lane. She drove onto the ring road but saw, to her annoyance, that there was a long queue of traffic waiting to get around the roundabout at St Marks.

Alice turned on the radio but couldn't focus on it. Her thoughts drifted. It was obvious now that Campbell's death wasn't accidental, and that it was much more likely that he had killed himself after being blackmailed by whoever had delivered the tape to the office. DCI Jones had questioned them all at length about whether they had any idea who that person might have been; she'd asked whether there had been any other communication, and whether they had any cameras that might have recorded any footage that could help. Eddie had answered in the negative to all three questions, and Jones and Lewis had departed with the proviso that they would need them all to come down to the station and provide statements to that end.

Alice reached the obstruction on the road – a broken-down bus – and pulled out to go around it. It took only another few minutes to reach Waitrose, and she parked up and hurried inside. She collected her dry-cleaning and then stopped by the café for an egg and cress sandwich and a coffee to go. She put the umbrella up again, shared a rueful expression with an old man who didn't have one, and set off back to the car.

She had reversed into a space between two others, and the angle meant that she didn't see that something had been left next to the driver's side door until she was almost alongside. She knelt: it was a waterproof satchel of the sort used by bicycle couriers. She stood up again and looked around her for any sign of the person who might have left it there. The car park wasn't busy, and the only people that she could see looked to be going about their business: shoppers either going into or leaving the stores; a man in a Waitrose uniform pushing a long line of trolleys.

Alice picked up the satchel, opened the door to the car and put her dry-cleaning and lunch onto the passenger seat. She lowered herself inside, placed the satchel on her lap and opened it.

She felt a twist of anxiety as she reached into it and withdrew a Jiffy bag. It was the same as the one that had been delivered to the office yesterday: brand new, her name printed on a label and the label fixed in the middle of the packet.

She knew she should put it down and call the police, but couldn't.

She slipped her finger into a gap at the end and carefully peeled back the adhesive strip. Turning the packet up, she shook it so that the cassette box inside slid into her lap. She reached a hand into the envelope and drew out a piece of paper, folded once down the middle. She unfolded it and read.

If you do wrong, be afraid, for he does not bear the sword in vain. For he is the servant of God, an avenger who carries out God's wrath on the wrongdoer.

She turned the cassette box onto its side and read the label.

Kajetan, Lucjusz / 15 May

33

Atticus left the lawns of the cathedral and made his way to North Walk, the road that marked the southern perimeter of the cathedral and its grounds within the Close. He continued to the junction with Bishop's Walk and then walked west, looking for any security cameras that might offer footage that would help him to prove the validity of the theory that he was considering. He came to Sarum College, passed through the ornate iron gate with the lantern atop it, and looked up at the side of the building. There was a camera fixed to the wall just beneath the eaves of the roof, and, as he squinted up at it, Atticus saw a green light that suggested that it was powered and operating. The college was connected to the cathedral and offered courses on theology and ecclesiastical history, among other things.

Atticus went inside, buffeted by a warmth that was the opposite of the cold and wet outside.

The reception was empty, but there was a small bell on the desk that gave a melodic tinkle as Atticus pressed his hand against it. He went over to a rack of leaflets advertising the courses that were planned, picking out one – Reading Scripture Together – that promised to illuminate the Book of Jonah. Atticus had just opened it out to read when he heard footsteps and turned to see a woman.

'Can I help you?'

'I hope so. I'm with the police. I'm looking into what happened to the man who fell from the tower yesterday.'

Her smile faded. 'Dreadful. Completely dreadful.'

'It was,' he said, slotting the leaflet back into the rack. 'You have a camera on the wall outside.'

'Yes.'

'Do you know whether it's recording at the moment?'

'It is. We had lead taken from the roof a month ago. The police said we needed to improve our security, so the camera was put up after that.'

'Do you think I could have a look?'

'Can I ask why you're interested in it?'

'It's to do with what happened on the tower.'

She looked shocked. 'You think it might have recorded it?'

'Probably not,' he said, smiling reassuringly at her. 'He was on the other side of the tower when he fell. I'm just being thorough. I doubt I'll be long.'

* * *

The woman took Atticus into a room with a computer sitting between stacks of books on a small desk. She switched on the machine, waited for it to boot up and then, after consulting with a colleague on the phone, managed to navigate to the portal that showed the footage from the camera outside.

'I'm afraid I've never used it before. I'm not sure how much help I can give you.'

'It's fine,' Atticus said. 'I can manage from here.'

'I'll just be outside. Let me know if you need anything.'

Atticus waited for her to go and then reached back and pushed the door so that it was nearly closed. He turned back to the screen, considered the interface and then navigated to the calendar that showed the last two weeks' footage. That, at least, was a good start; not every camera would retain that many days' worth of content. The feed from the camera was uploaded to the cloud, and Atticus double-clicked on the icon to access the footage.

He scrolled back to the evening before Campbell's death and pressed play. There was a reasonable distance between the camera and the cathedral, and, although the paths were lit, it was impossible to make out any detail from the figures who occasionally passed along them. Atticus increased the playback speed by three times, and then focused his attention on the area around the scaffolding. He saw a man walking just inside the boundary of the cathedral grounds and then what looked like a man and a woman taking a seat on one of the benches that were arranged inside the wall. The two of them stayed on the bench for twenty minutes before they stood and retraced their steps. The clock in the corner of the screen showed eleven p.m., and Atticus knew that the gates to the Close were shut at around that time.

Eleven became twelve and then two, and there was no sign of any activity. The minutes went by in chunks, and Atticus started to worry that his theory would be disproved.

The clock showed two-fifteen when he was rewarded: the figure of a person, their features invisible in the dark, passing through the gap in the wall and then leaving the path to make a direct approach to the scaffolding. They headed for the gate that Atticus had used earlier, and he watched, agog, as the figure knelt where the padlock that fastened the gate would have been placed.

It didn't take long, the gate opened, and the figure rose and stepped inside, hidden by the fencing for a moment before Atticus caught them again on the first ladder. It was even more difficult to see anything now that the figure's dark clothes were up against the stone, hidden by the night and sheltered by the scaffold and the boards, but he could see movement as the figure progressed up the second ladder and then the third.

Atticus leaned forward, his nose just a few inches away from the screen, and watched as the figure climbed all the way up to the uppermost platform and then headed in the direction of the hatch in the roof that Atticus had used a few hours earlier.

Atticus scrubbed back in the footage and played it again, straining his eyes for anything that might give him an idea as to the identity of the figure scaling the ladder. It was in vain; it was too dark and the figure was too far away from the camera to reveal anything other than the fact that they were wearing black. Atticus knew that the fence was around six and a half feet tall and, judging by how high up the fence the figure reached, he estimated that they were between five feet eight and five feet ten. It was either a woman who was a little taller than average or a man who was right around the median for his sex.

He let the footage play, keeping an eye on the time in the top left of the screen so that he could reference it to the moment that Campbell fell to his death. The angle of the camera didn't show the tower, and, even if it had, the parapet from which Campbell had fallen was on the other side; Atticus wouldn't be able to see him fall, but he hoped that he might see something else that would give him a clue as to what had happened. He focused his attention on the top of the roof, especially the area of the door that led into the passage that he had used earlier.

Night became dawn, and then the gates to the Close opened. Cars started to crawl down to the Cathedral School. A van parked, and the driver emerged to set a ladder against the wall of one of the buildings. A DPD driver looked for the address of his delivery. People made their way across the lawn.

Atticus blinked, trying to maintain his focus as the clock in the corner of the screen showed seven and then eight. At ten past eight, a clutch of people came into view and gathered in front of the cathedral, perhaps talking about the news that someone had fallen to their death. A police constable wandered from one side of the shot to the other.

Midday came and went.

Dusk fell, and then it started to grow dark.

The woman from reception shuffled up behind him. 'Anything useful?'

Atticus paused the playback. 'Maybe. I just need to concentrate for a moment.'

'Sorry, love. I'll leave you to it.'

Atticus pressed play again and kept his eye on the screen as the clock showed seven and then eight p.m.

At twenty past eight, he saw what he had been waiting for: it was dark again, but he noticed movement on the ladder and, after three minutes had passed, a figure emerged through the gate in the scaffolding. They stayed off the main path and left the cathedral grounds at Bishop's Walk, turning left and continuing north, then turning right on North Walk and disappearing out of sight in the direction of St Ann's Gate.

Atticus scrubbed all the way back to the arrival of the figure in the early hours of the morning. There was a button at the bottom of the screen that allowed him to select a clip from the footage and then attach it to an email; he sent it to himself, and then, in an abundance of caution, he played the footage again and recorded the screen with his phone. He did the same for the fifteen-minute period that showed the figure's departure.

He was checking the recording on his phone when it rang with an incoming call.

It was Mack.

He pressed answer. 'I've been trying to—'

She cut across him. 'Where are you?'

'At the cathedral. I think I've found—'

Her voice was tight with tension. 'I need you to come in.'

'Why? What's happened?'

'There's been a second package.'

He felt a buzz of excitement. 'When?'

'This afternoon. It was left next to the reporter's car when she went to Waitrose for lunch. I'm going to the office now. Can you come?'

'Are you sure? You didn't want me to—'

'Just get over there,' she said. 'We'll deal with it later.'

He stood up. 'I'm on my way.'

34

The *Journal*'s office on Rollestone Street was close to the nick. Mike Lewis led the way, with Mack and Francine Patterson along-side him; they were approaching the office when they saw Atticus hurrying towards them from the other direction.

They met him at the door.

'Tell me everything,' Atticus said without preamble.

'I've told you everything I know,' Mack said. 'They've had a second package. Came this afternoon.'

'How?'

'Didn't say.'

'Another video?'

'They said it looks the same as the first.'

'And a verse from the Bible?'

She nodded.

Lewis was quiet. Mack glanced over at him and saw that he was glowering in Atticus's direction. She knew that she wouldn't be able to continue justifying Atticus being included on an ad hoc basis, and that, if she wanted him to work on the case – if she thought the circumstances warranted it – she would have to revive the consultancy arrangement that they had used before. The others would gossip about his involvement and what that might mean, but putting things on a professional footing was something that she would need to do sooner rather than later.

Atticus turned to the door. Mack laid a hand on his arm. 'Information only gets released to the press – or to anyone – when Beckton says. All right?'

She couldn't tell whether Atticus realised that she had chided him on account of Lewis, but he nodded his agreement. 'I know.'

'Keep it in mind,' Lewis muttered. 'You've got form for messing things up.'

* * *

They tried the door to the office, only to find that it was locked. Atticus rapped his knuckles against the glass pane and then waited until he saw movement from inside. The door was unlocked and opened by Eddie Thorpe.

'Come in.'

They did, and Eddie shut the door after them.

'Thanks for coming, Mack.' He turned to Lewis. 'Mike, Francine.' He turned to Atticus. 'And you are?'

'Atticus Priest,' Mack said. 'Atticus – this is Eddie Thorpe. The editor.'

Eddie squinted at Atticus. 'Of course. You were on the Grovely case.'

'He's working for us as a consultant,' Mack said. 'I'd be grateful if you'd answer his questions just the same as you'd answer mine.'

'Of course.'

'Where's the package?' Atticus said impatiently.

'You'd better come up.'

They went up to a conference room on the second floor. Alice Morris was sat at the table, and a television on a trolley had been set up at one end. An old VHS recorder sat beneath the TV. Mack saw an opened Jiffy bag on the table in front of the woman.

'You didn't open it . . .' Atticus said.

'Excuse me?'

'The package. You didn't—'

Alice cut over him. 'I'm sorry, who are you?'

'Mr Priest is working with the police,' Eddie said. 'This is Alice – she works at the paper.'

'And you're the one who got the package?'

'Yes.'

'And you touched it?'

'Obviously, but I was very care—'

'I *wish* you hadn't.'

'As I said, I was very careful.'

'Wearing gloves?'

'No. But I was—'

'Have you watched it?'

'Some of it.'

Mack gestured with her hand that Atticus should throttle back. 'It would have been better if you'd waited,' she said. 'There could be forensic evidence on it that will help us to find out who sent it.'

'I *did* tell her,' Lewis said, looking over at Mack in fear, perhaps, that she might blame him. 'I asked her to call us straight away.'

'Hang on.' Eddie shook his head. 'This has to be cooperative. We're involved here – the newspaper is involved, and Alice is involved *personally* – and I'm not going to let things head off in another direction without us.'

'The investigation has to come first,' Mack said.

'Of course it does, but we want to be able to run the story. I've been doing this for long enough to know that the nationals are going to be all over this like flies on shit when it gets out, and we all know that it *is* going to get out. I'm not going to sit around and let them scoop us. I can tell you now – that's *not* going to happen.'

Mack raised her hands to mollify him. 'It won't. You have my word. We have to be careful how and when we release information, but this is your story to break. OK?'

Eddie looked at Alice and then back at Mack. 'OK.'

'I'm sorry,' Alice said. 'This has been difficult for us to negotiate.'

'How's that?' Mack said.

'We've been told that we have to be careful what we publish.'

'By whom? Someone at the police?'

'No,' she said. 'The owners of the paper.'

'It's just internal politics,' Eddie said. 'We don't need to bother them with that.'

Atticus was clearly itching to gather up as much information as he could. 'There was a Bible verse?'

Alice nodded and pointed to the piece of paper on the desk.

Mack looked down and read aloud: "*If you do wrong, be afraid, for he does not bear the sword in vain. For he is the servant of God, an avenger who carries out God's wrath on the wrongdoer.*"

'It's from Romans,' Alice said.

Atticus waved a hand dismissively. 'Chapter thirteen, verse four.'

Francine came around the table so that she could examine the cassette box.

'How was it delivered?' Atticus asked.

'I went to Waitrose at lunchtime,' Alice said. 'It was in a waterproof bag next to my car when I came back.'

'Do you still have the bag?'

She nodded. 'It's downstairs.'

'Did you see who left it?'

'No.'

'No one who looked suspicious?'

'No.'

'You didn't notice anyone following you?'

'No,' she said. 'No one.'

Atticus turned to Mack. 'You'll need to check CCTV in the car park.'

'We will.'

Francine gasped.

Mack turned. She had her hand over her mouth.

Eddie looked at her with suspicion. 'What?'

Francine shook her head. 'Nothing.'

'I don't believe you. What is it?' He pointed down at the name on the box. 'Kajetan – do you know who that is?'

Francine bit her lip and looked over at Mack for help.

'We'll need to discuss this back at the nick, Eddie,' Mack said. 'We'll share everything that we're able to share.'

'Really? I can't help feeling that we're being pushed to the side.'

'This is a police matter,' she said, a little more sternly. 'I've promised that we will let you have what we can, and we will. But you need to keep in mind that a man has died in suspicious circumstances, and finding out what happened to him must be the priority. OK?'

She waited, and, eventually, Eddie gave a grudging nod of assent.

'Good.' Mack pointed to the tape player. 'We'd better have a look.'

Eddie walked around the table and pressed play on the recorder. The screen was filled with a blizzard of static. They waited until the interference dissolved away and the footage that had been recorded became visible. Mack watched carefully: the bed; the naked bricks of the wall behind it; the blood-red glow that came from lights that were below the shot, a red that was so deep as to be almost purple, brightest at the foot of the wall and faintest at the top.

Atticus spoke without taking his eyes off the screen. 'Is this like the first video?'

'You haven't seen it?' Eddie asked him.

'Not yet. Is it?'

'Looks like the same place,' Lewis said.

A man, naked apart from his underwear, came into the shot and sat down on the bed. He looked to be in his mid-forties and was solidly built. He had tattoos down both arms and another on his chest.

'Stop it there,' Mack said.

Eddie pressed pause, and the image froze, save for the thin bands of static that rolled from the top to the bottom of the screen.

The man was looking straight into the lens.

Mack thought she recognised him.

* * *

They left the office and set off back to the station. Mack could see that Francine was bursting with whatever it was that had provoked her when they had watched the video; they turned the corner on to Bedwin Street and then stopped outside the almshouse.

Atticus was fizzing with excitement. 'You know him,' he said to Francine. 'Don't you?'

'It's Lucky Lucjusz.'

'Who?' Atticus said.

'I've seen him before, too,' Mack remarked. 'Where?'

'I nicked him,' Francine replied. 'But that's not it.' She spoke slowly and deliberately, trying to keep a lid on her obvious excitement. 'He's dead, boss. We pulled him out of the river this morning.'

35

They continued back to the station, sharing the cover of two umbrellas. Atticus walked alongside Mack and was distracted, trying to sort out the developments that had quickly cast the death of David Campbell in an entirely new light. He had initially agreed with her: his death had looked very much like suicide. The discovery that he had made by way of the security-camera footage cast doubt on all of that, and now this – a second possible victim, with a second tape – made things look very different indeed.

Atticus was left with the sensation that there were depths to what had happened that they hadn't even *begun* to plumb.

He could see that Mack shared his animation, but there was a trepidation on her face that he knew was inspired by the fear that they were about to be plunged into their third major murder enquiry in the last two years. Francine looked to share the anticipation, although not the misgivings; she was new enough in her CID career to be insulated from the practical considerations with which Mack would need to grapple. Lewis was excited, too, but he knew it was tempered by an irritation that Atticus was involved in the investigation that he was making no effort to hide.

They stopped at the doors to the station. 'Go and get the others,' Mack said to Lewis. 'Meeting in the conference room in ten minutes.'

Lewis said that he would take care of it and went ahead.

'Can you give me a minute with Atticus, Franny?'

'Of course, boss. See you upstairs.'

She followed Lewis into the building.

Mack and Atticus stayed outside, the rain thrumming against the umbrella that Atticus held over both of them.

'Shit,' Mack said. She looked out over the Greencroft and the playground, where a mother was pushing a child in a pram, and then turned to him. 'Would I be right in thinking you'd like to be involved again?'

'Very much so.'

'Same as before? Your company invoices, not you?'

'I'd do it for free.'

'No, it has to be professional.'

Atticus knew that he ought to tell Mack about his interview with Murphy. He knew that Murphy would be very much against the idea of his involvement in the investigation, but, given that he had said he was going back to London, Atticus was prepared to operate on the basis of out of sight, out of mind. He didn't know what Mack would say if she learned of Murphy's reservations, but there had to be the possibility – the likelihood, even – that she would change her mind. Atticus knew that it was selfish, but this case was so intriguing that he was prepared to hold his tongue. The thought that Murphy was investigating Mack, too, gave him the most pause; he concluded, again, that it wouldn't matter if he waited a day or two before telling her.

'Come on, then.'

'I'm in?'

'You're in.'

Atticus folded the umbrella and shook it off. 'Thanks.'

'Just *try* not to show off.'

'Can't promise,' he said and, as she frowned, he tried to reassure her with a wink that just deepened her scowl.

36

Atticus followed Mack through the CID room and into the same conference suite that they had used for the Major Incident Room in the Imber investigation. It still hadn't been cleared of everything from that case: the map of Salisbury Plain that they had stuck to the wall had not been taken down, and there were files of witness statements and other evidence stacked in the bookshelves. Atticus took a seat and waited for Lewis to corral the others who would be working on the enquiry: Robbie Best and Nigel Archer came inside first, both perplexed as they looked at Atticus; Francine Patterson sat next to him; Stewart Lynas followed her, double-taking as he noticed Atticus and then exchanging a look of incredulity with Archer that he made no effort to hide. Lewis came next and then Mack.

She shut the door and went to the head of the table.

'Right,' she said. 'First things first – for reasons that will soon become obvious, the Campbell case is going to be more complicated than we thought. There are aspects of it that are starting to look as if they might be very troubling, and I've asked Atticus to consult with us again in the same way that he did for the murders at Imber. Everything is the same as it was then – please treat him as a member of the team.'

'Really, boss?' Lynas said. 'No disrespect, Atticus, but—'

'It's funny,' Atticus cut over him. 'Whenever someone says that, it usually means the complete opposite.'

'I'm fine with him being here,' Best said. 'I'm sure he'll play nicely.'

'*Really*, gaffer?' Lynas pressed. 'It's a distraction.'

'He'll be reporting directly to me,' Mack replied. 'For reasons that, as I said, will become obvious in a moment, I think we should be open to the offer of help. Right?'

Atticus looked around the table: Lynas didn't hold his eye, and Archer looked to be stifling his objection.

'Good,' Mack said, keen to put potential disagreements to the side so that they could move on. 'We've had a development in the case – *several* developments, actually. You've probably heard that we had a body in the river at Britford this morning. Francine went out and took charge of getting him out. Franny?'

She cleared her throat. 'I recognised him – Lucjusz Kajetan. Polish immigrant, used to run a building business until it went under. His life went off the rails after that, and I ended up nicking him for possession. Last I heard, he was sleeping rough in the car park underneath Sainsbury's. We had Fyfe out to have a look, and his initial assessment was that he drowned. No obvious signs of trauma on the body. It seemed likely that he was sleeping rough in the sluice house, got pissed or high, or both, slipped, fell in and drowned.' She looked over at Mack. 'But we don't think that now.'

'No,' Mack said. 'We don't. A second video was sent to the *Journal* today. It's the same set-up as the first – a man in the same location as before with what looks like a teenager. Francine recognised Kajetan. On that basis, it's impossible that either his death or Campbell's was accidental. We've had two bodies in two days, with videos of the dead men in very compromising situations sent to the paper both times.'

'Blackmail, then?' Lynas said. 'Blackmail and suicide?'

'Maybe,' Best said.

Atticus shook his head. 'No.'

Lynas turned to him. 'What?'

'Two murders.'

Lynas exhaled and, when he spoke again, his usual supercili-ousness was coloured with disdain. 'That's ridiculous. How can you say that? You can't be sure.'

'Of course I can.'

'Why not blackmail?' Best asked. 'That's what we're looking at for Campbell.'

'No,' Atticus said firmly. 'Campbell may or may not have been blackmailed, but he was *definitely* murdered. And Kajetan.'

Lynas appealed to Mack. 'Come on, boss. Not this again.'

Mack was looking at him uncomfortably. 'Atticus?'

Atticus had forgotten how disagreeable he found Lynas; the man's public-school arrogance blinded him to deficiencies that were obvious to everyone else. Robbie Best had said once that Lynas was 'a legend in his own lunchtime', and Atticus agreed. He remembered what he had promised Mack and tried to keep the scorn from his voice.

'I'm sorry, Mack. There are a couple of things I haven't had a chance to tell you yet – I was going to call, but then you told me about the video.'

She frowned. 'Tell me now.'

He held his palms together and worked out how to explain what he was thinking in as efficient a way as possible. 'Let's assume Campbell was being blackmailed. Can I accept him jumping off the tower in shame? Yes. Definitely. But Kajetan's different. He was homeless, so blackmail doesn't make sense.'

'It still *could* be,' Lynas protested.

'Whatever,' Atticus said. 'But committing suicide by drown-ing? *That* would be unusual.'

'Rubbish,' Lynas said.

'What? You think he drowned himself?'

'Why not?'

'Because it would be very uncommon.'

'It happens.' Lynas looked at the others as if appealing for support. 'You remember the woman who died in the river at the back of the Maltings? That wasn't an accident, was it? She drowned herself.'

'I didn't say it *couldn't* be suicide,' Atticus countered. 'I just said it would be *uncommon*. Do you know the percentage of suicides by drowning last year?'

Lynas folded his arms and leaned back in his chair. 'I have no idea.'

'I do – less than three per cent. What about death by falling?'

Lynas shrugged. 'I'm sure you'll tell us.'

'*One* per cent. So, if we are looking at two suicides, it'll be two of the most unlikely methods in terms of relative prevalence. Possible? Yes. Likely? No. Not likely at all. We have to proceed on the basis that these could be murders. It would be nice if they weren't, but, even then, we've still got evidence that the two of them were filmed having sex with partners who look very likely to be under the age of consent. And whether it's murder or blackmail and suicide doesn't make a huge difference in practical terms to how we're going to have to deal with this – it's salacious either way, and the press is going to be all over it.'

'The *Journal*, for certain,' Lewis said. 'Both tapes were sent to them. Both had Bible verses about revenge that'll make it even *more* salacious, especially when they connect it with Jack from before.'

'Is the *Journal* onside?' Lynas asked.

'They've said that they'll cooperate with us,' Lewis answered, 'but it'd be naïve to think that we're going to be able to keep a lid on it for long.'

Mack nodded her agreement. 'This is going to have cut-through. It's definitely prurient enough. The media will be interested. Beckton is going to want this cleared up before the nationals and the TV get wind of it.'

'Absolutely,' Lynas said with conviction. 'That's why it's irresponsible to talk these up as murders when there's no evidence to suggest it.'

'I agree with Stewart,' Lewis said. 'They look like suicides to me.'

Atticus couldn't stop the impatient roll of his eyes.

Lewis noticed. 'You haven't changed a bit.'

'Neither have you,' Atticus said. 'You're as slow and predictable as ever.'

'Piss *off*.' Lewis turned to Mack in exasperation.

Atticus looked at her, too, mouthed an apology and then cut across her attempt at mollification. 'It's murder – I guarantee it.'

'You keep saying that, but you have *nothing* to back it up.'

'Fine,' he said. 'There's the similarity with Jack, for a start.'

'He didn't leave videos,' Lewis said.

'No, he didn't. But he did speak to me about the Bible, and that's never been made public.'

'Tenuous.'

'Yes, on its own, but not when you add it to everything else. I went to the cathedral today and went up to the tower for a look around. I couldn't find anything that made me think Campbell's death wasn't what you think – that he jumped. It's obviously not an accident – it's too hard to fall from the parapet without meaning it. That leaves us with two possibilities: Campbell killed himself, or someone else threw him over the side. But Campbell was big, and he was in good shape.'

'So pushing him over the edge wouldn't have been easy,' Best said.

'Absolutely. That's why I thought murder was unlikely, especially when there was no obvious way for anyone to get up on the tower without being seen.'

'We checked the cameras,' Best said. 'They don't show anything.'

'And I checked the only other doors that would let someone get up to the tower. Both were locked.'

Best gestured for him to continue. 'Why do I get the feeling there's a "but" coming?'

'There is. I went outside and walked around the grounds. The east side of the cathedral has scaffolding all the way to the top. I had a look and saw how easy it would have been to climb up.'

Mack closed her eyes. 'Please don't say what I think you're about to say . . .'

37

Atticus spread his arms helplessly. 'I had to look, and it was as easy as I thought it would be. There's a gate in the fence at the bottom, and then it's just a question of climbing the ladders up to the roof.'

Mack put her head in her hands.

Atticus continued before she could speak, hoping that *what* he had discovered would quickly cancel out any qualms she might have had about *how* he discovered it.

'I found a hatch that opens into an old stonemasons' work-shop above the Lady Chapel. I went inside and followed it, went through a door into an attic space and then ended up at another door. They were all unlocked, although I don't think they should have been. I can't say for sure because it was pitch black, but it looked to me like there was a scratch on the last one that might have been from someone picking the lock.'

'That doesn't prove anything at all,' Lynas said.

'It does. The one thing that always mitigated against there being someone else involved was that we didn't see anybody apart from Campbell going up to the tower. But finding out that you can get up there from the outside changes everything. It *would* be possible for someone to get up to the tower without being seen.'

'Are there any CCTV cameras in the tower?' Lynas asked.

'Not once you're on the stairs,' Mack replied.

Lewis shook his head. 'So this is still speculation. All you've shown is that it *might* be possible. That doesn't mean that anyone actually *did* go up that way.'

'Yes, you're right.' Atticus tried hard to ensure that his patient reply didn't sound exaggerated and sarcastic. 'So I went back outside again and found a security camera on Sarum College that's pointing at the east side of the cathedral. I was there this afternoon – I reviewed everything from the evening before Campbell died. Robbie – could you pass me the remote for the TV, please?'

Best took the remote control and slid it across the table. Atticus turned on the screen, took out his phone and found the two clips from the camera that he had emailed to himself. He cast his phone to the television and tapped to begin playback. They saw the shape of the cathedral in the gloom of the night.

'What are we looking at?' Lewis grumbled. 'There's nothing.'

'Wait.'

Francine pointed at the screen. 'Look there – by the fence.'

'Keep watching.'

Atticus found that he was holding his breath as the figure went through the gate in the barriers and climbed the ladders to the roof. Atticus let the footage continue until whoever it was had disappeared out of shot.

He stopped the playback.

Mack pointed to the screen. 'The time on the screen – is it right?'

'I think so.'

'Six hours before Campbell fell.' Atticus nodded. 'Give or take.'

'What are we supposed to do with that?' Lewis said. 'It could be anyone. It's not even clear whether it's a man or a woman.'

Mack ignored his grumble. 'Do we see them come down again?'

'Yes,' Atticus said. 'Much later.'

'Can we see it?'

Atticus opened the second clip and played it until the figure descended the ladders.

Mack pointed to the time on the screen. 'They were up there for *hours*.'

'They stayed out of sight until it was dark again. Most likely they hid in the attic space.'

The figure on the screen stepped out through the gate in the fence and crossed to Bishop's Walk.

'I can't make out anything useful,' Mack said. 'Any other cameras?'

'Not at the college. I didn't have time to check between there and Exeter Street, though.'

'The school's down there,' Francine said. 'They could have a camera.'

'There's the dentist, too,' Mack said.

'And an architect?' Lewis offered.

'Maybe one of them has a video doorbell.'

'Let's check *all* the cameras in the Close,' Mack said. 'All of them. We're due some luck. We might be able to wrap this up before there's any more chaos.'

Atticus chewed his lip.

Mack saw him. 'What?'

'I'm not optimistic. Think about how this has been planned.' He pointed at the figure on the screen. 'Whoever that is, they're careful. Clever, too. They knew that they would've been filmed if they'd followed Campbell when he went up the tower, so they found another way. And I think they knew there's a camera at the college. They knew they couldn't avoid it altogether if they wanted to use the ladders, so they worked around it. Look at how precise they've been. Look at the route they chose to get back to North Walk. The quickest way would've been to follow the path diagonally up, but they didn't do that. They took the long way to make sure there was distance between them and the camera. And then, even when they got closer, they were looking down the whole time. It's hard to be sure, but it looks like they've covered their face, too. *Look.* They scouted this all out. This has been planned. They know the places they need to avoid, and I'll bet you whatever you like that they knew exactly where the cameras are on the way back to Exeter Street, too. I don't think those will show us anything.'

'So how did they know about the other way up to the tower?' Lewis asked.

'Could it be someone who works at the cathedral?' suggested Francine.

Atticus gave a nod. 'That would be a good place to start. There's something else to check, too – I remember reading something about the cathedral offering a tour of the secret rooms in the attic just after COVID. They had a budget shortfall and were looking for ways to make it up. It might be worth seeing if they have a record of everyone who's been up there.'

Best noted it down. 'I'll check.'

'What about Kajetan?' Atticus said. 'Much as I'm loath to take anything Fyfe says without a very large dose of scepticism, what did he suggest about the cause of death?'

Francine gave a shrug. 'Not much. No sign of anything that would suggest it was suspicious.'

'He didn't know what we know now, though,' Mack said. 'When's the post-mortem?'

'Tomorrow morning.'

Atticus turned to Mack. 'I'd like to go.'

'We'll both go.'

Mack brought the meeting to a close. Atticus could see from the way that she was glaring at him that she was irritated about something – he guessed it was the fact that he had blindsided her with what he had found at the cathedral – but there had been nothing else for it, and he hoped that she would forgive and forget, just as she usually did.

'Mack,' he said, 'can I have a word?'

'I've got to go and see Beckton. What is it?'

'I need to see Campbell's video.'

'Franny,' Mack called out, stopping Patterson at the door, 'could you show Atticus the first tape?'

'Of course, boss,' she said. She turned to him. 'I've got it on my computer. This way.'

Atticus turned back to Mack, but she had left the room and all he saw was her back as she made her way down the corridor to Beckton's office. He winced; he supposed that she *had* told him that she didn't want him freelancing and that she didn't want surprises, and she probably thought that he had already let her down. He knew he had to try harder, but it was difficult when he had the scent of the chase.

38

The enquiry team knew that they were going to be working longer days as the investigation gathered momentum. Francine had come on shift at seven that morning and would normally have clocked off at five, but it was half past eight when Mack told her and the others that it was time to knock off for the night. She would have been happy to stay, but Mack was not the kind of boss who required staff to stick around when there was no good reason for it.

They had made a good start in establishing the structure of the team that would be responsible for the investigation, and Francine had been given the responsibility for setting up the database that they would use to collate and cross-reference the information and evidence that would be collected. It was known as the Home Office Large Major Enquiry System, and was very much a case of a product's name being crowbarred to fit the acronym that had been chosen for it. HOLMES 2 was a cloud-based system that allowed all the officers on the team to both input and interrogate data at the same time. Francine's role as disclosure officer would require her to assess the incoming data, determining whether the information met the disclosure test so that it could be provided to the defence in any subsequent trial that came out of the investigation.

Francine snagged her jacket from the back of her chair. Atticus was sitting in it and watching the video of David Campbell. She had given him access after the meeting, but that was an hour ago, and he was still going over it.

'Find anything?'

He didn't take his eyes off the screen. 'Nothing useful.'

'Do you think it's him?'

Atticus paused the recording. 'Who? Jack?'

She nodded.

'Yes,' Atticus said. 'I think it's possible.'

'Why, though? What do Campbell and Kajetan have to do with Miller?'

'That's what I'm trying to work out.'

'Jack said that Miller was involved with Burns and York – right?'

Atticus pushed away from the desk and swivelled the chair so that he could look up at her. 'That's right.'

'And he said that the three of them were abusing kids.'

'He said they were being paid to do it,' Atticus added. 'And that he was involved.'

'How? As one of the kids?'

'Maybe. Or maybe he was a customer. Or maybe he was working with the three of them. It's impossible to say.'

'So this is Jack getting revenge?'

Atticus looked at the screen and breathed out. 'That's where I'd put my money.'

Francine put on her jacket. 'Switch off when you're done.'

He turned back to the screen. 'Will do.'

Francine left him and paused at Mack's open door. 'See you in the morning, boss.'

Mack looked up. 'Will do. Get a good night's sleep. We're going to be busy tomorrow.'

39

Francine went down to the car park and drove back to St Ann Street, pleased to see that there was a space for her to park on the road outside her house. She had a little two-bedroom place that was just a hundred yards from the Close by way of St Ann's Gate. She had bought it a year ago, using the inheritance she had been left when her father passed away. The estate agent who had showed her around had described it as 'compact', and it certainly was that; there was a study, sitting room and kitchen on the ground floor and two small bedrooms and a bathroom above. It was quaint, though, and although owning a property that was hundreds of years old presented ongoing challenges – her mother warned her it would be like maintaining the Forth Bridge – Francine was happy to accept that rather than living in one of the boxes that were being constructed at great pace as the city slowly spilled out at the sides. She had a view of the spire from her front door, too, and she stopped to look at it as she reached for her door key. The red light at the top glowed out, and the floodlights lit the stone in amber. The thought of Campbell falling to his death made her shiver a little.

She opened the door and went inside, taking off her boots and hanging her jacket on the bannister. She went into the kitchen and opened the fridge to see what she had for dinner and was dithering over the remains of Sunday night's lasagne or a microwave chicken chasseur when there was a knock on the door.

She went back down the hall and opened it: Charlie was outside with a bunch of flowers.

'Oh,' Francine said.

'Sorry . . . are you busy?'

'No, of course not. Did you say you were coming over? Did I forget?'

'I thought I'd surprise you.' He held up the flowers. 'I thought these might help you feel better.'

'The hangover?' She waved that aside. 'I'm fine now – but thanks, they're lovely.' She stepped aside. 'Want to come in?'

He did, taking off his shoes and coat and then giving her a kiss.

'I was just going to cook dinner,' she said. 'Have you eaten?'

'Not yet. I'm starving.'

She took out the tray of lasagne. 'There's enough here for the two of us.'

He looked over her shoulder. 'You've got salad leaves, carrots, tomatoes . . . I could make a salad to go with it.'

Francine put on Radio 4 just as *The World Tonight* began, the presenter trailing ahead to what they would be discussing. The chancellor had delivered a mini budget that afternoon, and there had been a development in a doping scandal involving racehorses that Francine had been following.

Charlie took the packet of tomatoes from the fridge and tipped them out onto a chopping board. 'How was your day?'

'Long.'

He started to halve the tomatoes. 'Anything interesting?'

She nodded. 'Body in the river.'

He stopped. 'Where?'

'You know the sluice house on the Avon?'

'Other side of the river at Churchill Gardens? Other side from the playground?'

She nodded.

'What happened to him?'

'Looks like he drowned, but we won't know for sure until they do the post-mortem tomorrow.'

'You had to deal with it?'

'I was the first detective there.'

They listened to the discussion on the radio as the chancellor's plans for dealing with inflation were skewered by an expert on fiscal policy and then derided by an opposition MP.

'Got any mustard?' Charlie asked. 'I'll make a dressing.'

'In the cupboard,' she said, pointing.

The discussion on the economy ended, and the presenter handed over to the newsreader for a summary of the day's news.

Francine opened the oven and slid the lasagne inside.

'*A man who fell to his death from the tower of Salisbury Cathedral has been named as David Campbell.*'

'Turn it up,' Francine said.

'*Mr Campbell, who was sixty-three, was the clerk of works at the cathedral. He was pronounced dead at the scene.*'

'That's what we were talking about last night,' Charlie remarked.

Francine put her finger to her lips as the announcer continued.

'*While the police have indicated that they believe Mr Campbell's death to have been an accident, the Health and Safety Executive will be conducting an enquiry to ensure that the proper procedure was followed.*'

The announcer moved on to the next item.

Charlie whistled. 'You're going to be famous.'

'Hardly.'

'Why are they reporting it?'

'Duh,' she said. 'He fell off the tower. It's macabre.'

'I guess.' He shivered. 'What a way to go. Wouldn't have been how I'd do it.'

'Do what?'

'Top myself.'

'We're not so sure that's what it was now.'

'Him topping himself?'

She went over and turned the radio down.

'What, then? An accident?'

'It would've been hard to fall unless you did something really stupid, and, by all accounts, he was careful.'

'Suicide, then.'

She shrugged.

Charlie laid the knife on the chopping board. '*Murder*? Seriously?'

'Atticus thinks so.'

'Atticus? Who's that?'

'I haven't told you about him?'

'I think I'd remember a name like that.'

'He used to be in CID until he got fired or resigned for using drugs – depends on who you ask. Mack's brought him in as a consultant.'

'Is that usual?'

'Not at all. He's seeing Mack, too. Makes it more complicated.'

'She hired her *boyfriend*?'

Francine nodded. 'With form for doing drugs. I know.'

'Why would she do something like that?'

'Because he's seriously clever. Weird, too, and hard to deal with, but you can't argue with the fact he gets results. He found things out at Grovely and Imber that no one else did. And he found things at the cathedral that we'd missed.'

'And he thinks Campbell was murdered?'

'He thinks someone climbed the tower just before Campbell fell. We thought he was alone, but it looks like we might've been wrong about that.' She paused, her cheeks flushing. 'Shit. I didn't tell you that, all right?'

Charlie used the back of the knife to push the tomatoes into the bowl with the rest of the salad. He gave a knowing wink. 'Tell me what?'

Francine hadn't had a serious boyfriend since she had joined the force, and she could see that she was going to have to be careful with what she told Charlie. She trusted him, but that didn't mean that he might say something that he shouldn't. He might not mean to do harm, but it would put her in a difficult position.

Charlie spooned mustard into a bowl and slowly whisked in olive oil. 'Poor bastard, either way – whatever happened to him.'

Francine thought back to the clamour that had accompanied the discovery of the bodies at Imber, and coming home to watch footage from helicopters that had been flown over the church-yard during the excavation. She was tempted to tell Charlie about the video that had been sent to the *Journal*, but she knew that that information hadn't been released to the public yet and that it would be unprofessional to discuss it with him.

But . . . *still*.

Charlie finished the salad and edged around her, his hands on her hips, as he made his way to the fridge. He opened it and, with a happy clap of his hands, took out the bottle of Chablis that she had put inside to chill the day before yesterday. He found two glasses in the cupboard and a corkscrew in the drawer. He uncorked the bottle, poured out two large glasses and gave one to Francine.

'Cheers,' he said, leaning around and planting a kiss on her lips. 'Sounds like you need this.'

40

Mack had gone into her office after updating Beckton with what had happened. Atticus watched her over the top of the screen on Francine's desk. She was busying herself with the administration that accompanied any large enquiry and was so lost in the minutiae that she didn't notice when he went over and knocked on the door.

'Yes?'

'Can I have a word?'

He started to close the door so that they could have some privacy, but she told him to leave it open. He looked at her quizzically before noticing her knowing gaze out to where the others were working at their desks and understood: a shut door might suggest intimacy, and she wasn't ready for the others to reach that conclusion.

'Sorry,' he said quietly.

She spoke more loudly. 'What's up?'

'Are you staying late?'

'Beckton wants me to send him the details by email. It'll take me an hour, maybe two.'

Atticus kept his voice low. 'After that?'

Stewart Lynas stopped at the open door. 'Night, boss.'

'Night. See you tomorrow.'

Atticus waited for him to go. 'Want me to cook?'

Mack got up from behind the desk and went to the door. She looked around him and, seeing that the office was empty, reached across and laid her hand on Atticus's arm. 'Go back to mine and let yourself in. You know where the keys are.'

'Shall I wait so we can walk back together?'

'Better if we don't. Better, for now, if we keep this – *us* – to ourselves.'

He wanted to protest, but he saw how awkward this was making her feel. 'I'll see you later, then.'

She very quickly ran her fingers down his arm and then went back to her desk.

*　*　*

Atticus walked to Mack's rented house in Harnham. It was a small two-bedroom property that she could just about afford. Mack and her husband still had the mortgage on the family home in Bishopsdown, and taking on another property had, she had confided, put their joint finances under strain. Atticus had been tempted to suggest that it would all be sorted out once they divorced but had managed to hold his tongue; even he realised that that would have sounded hopelessly self-interested. Mack didn't speak about her relationship with Andy, and although Atticus wanted her to tell him what she was thinking about it – and what she was thinking about *them* – he knew that particular conversation could only happen at her instigation.

Mack kept the key in a lockbox that was fixed to the wall, and the combination was the birthday of her daughter. Atticus felt awkward as he turned the dial and opened the box; he still hadn't been introduced to her children. He had suggested they all go to the park last weekend, but Mack had quickly dismissed the idea.

She had seen his hurt feelings and had been tender in explaining that the time wasn't right and that it would just confuse them.

There wasn't much food in the fridge. Atticus took out a tray of chicken breasts that were just within date and then collected an onion, the last two cloves of garlic, a piece of ginger, a can of chopped tomatoes, a bag of rice and jars of turmeric, cumin and dried chillies. He took out a wok, tipped in the last dregs from a bottle of cooking oil and heated it up. Chopping the onion and garlic, he tossed them into the wok, and, once those were hot, added the chicken, the spices and the chillies. He tipped in the tomatoes and lowered the heat so that the curry would simmer rather than boil.

He ran the tap to wash up the things that he had used and thought about Mack telling him to leave work without her. He knew why: she was still nervous about advertising the fact that the two of them were seeing each other. Atticus was less concerned about what the others thought – it was the opposite: he *wanted* them to know – but it was different for her. She worked with them every day, and, if they knew that she and Atticus were romantically involved, it could lead to them doubting her judgement. He had complained to her about a similar situation during the Imber investigation and, knowing how difficult he found it to put himself in someone else's shoes, she had explained: she had already gone out on a limb to bring him on to the team, and the last thing that she'd needed then, as now, was for someone to suggest that her motives were coloured by her feelings.

Atticus found it impossible to navigate topics like this, but wondered whether it would have been the same if the roles had been reversed. Mack had often suggested that a career in the police was more difficult for a woman; was this the kind of thing that she meant?

He cleaned the utensils and the plates that he had used, stood them in the rack and wiped his hands. His condition made it difficult to be as sensitive to Mack's concerns as he knew she would have liked and, although he had told himself that he would try to be better, he knew that it was going to be a challenge. He was lucky, then, that Mack was sympathetic; Atticus couldn't imagine many partners sharing her patience.

41

Atticus heard Mack's key in the lock and looked at his watch: it had taken her nearly two hours to finish in the office. She came into the kitchen-diner and sat down at the little table.

She took off her shoes. 'What a day.'

'Are you OK?'

'Robbie wanted to talk to me, and then Beckton called me back. I couldn't get away.'

'I've eaten,' Atticus said. 'There's a plate for you in the oven. I'll get it for you.'

'Thank you.'

Atticus went to the oven, put on a glove and took out the bowl with the rest of the curry. He took it over to the table, along with a knife and fork, and set it down in front of her, then sat down on the chair across from hers.

'What did Robbie want?'

'He was concerned about you.' She held up a hand to stop his protest. 'Don't be defensive. It wasn't like that. He wasn't negative.'

'He can leave that to Lynas and Lewis.'

'He actually *likes* you. He just wanted to tell me that he has reservations after what you said at the meeting.'

'After I said *what?*'

'Going off and doing your own thing again. At the cathedral . . . I mean, come on. He has a point. You know that's not the way we work.'

'I got carried away.'

'You *always* get carried away. Robbie knows how good you are. That's why he's concerned. He's worried you'll find out something really important and it'll be inadmissible because of *how* you got it. If it's not done right . . .' She let the sentence drift and sighed. 'If it's not done right, it could be damaging. He's not sure if it's worth the risk.'

Atticus looked at her, saw that she was annoyed, and, for a moment, he worried that she might have decided to take him off the case.

'You're right. *He's* right.'

'It's not as if you're just a consultant we've brought in to help. You've worked with most of them before. You have a history. And they all know about us.'

That brought Atticus up short. 'Really? But you said—'

'At least I *think* they do,' she interrupted. She sighed, wearily this time. 'I know you miss details like that when it comes to you because of . . .' She fenced for the right word that wouldn't insult him.

'Because of my condition.'

'Yes, because of that. None of them will bring it up with me, but they're talking. And because of that – and because Beckton might not agree with my decision to bring you on again – you have to be especially careful not to piss them off. Beckton won't need an excuse to get rid of you, but he'll criticise me for my decision, too, and, with everything that's going on with Andy and the kids – and with us – it's not something I can afford. Understand?'

'Yes. I need to stop and think.'

'You promise? No more impetuousness?'

'Promise. I'll run everything by you.'

'Good.'

Atticus knew that she was tired, and that it wasn't just the fatigue that came with a long day. She was in charge of the investigation, and he could see that the weight of it was bearing down on her. Most detectives, even of senior rank, would never have to deal with the media attention that would be aroused by a case that became a *cause célèbre*. Mack had had the misfortune to have been given two big investigations to deal with in the last two years, and now he was quite sure that she was about to receive a third.

'There's something else,' he said.

She looked dejected. 'What is it now?'

'Don't worry – it's not the investigation. It's Murphy.'

'I forgot you went to see him. Sorry. I got distracted.'

'Don't worry about it. It's fine.'

'What did he say?'

'He's not my biggest fan. And he wasn't happy with me consulting during Imber.'

'I cleared it with Beckton,' she protested.

'I know you did. But I doubt you told him about my clearance not being revoked when it should've been. And he thinks the billing arrangement was set up to be deceptive.'

'He doesn't care that you helped us to clear up the murders?'

'Like I said – he's not a fan.'

'You didn't . . .' She stopped.

He grinned. 'Tell him what I thought of him?'

'*Please*, Atticus . . .'

'But he's *so* mundane.'

'You have to play the game. Someone like him . . . It's easy – you just flatter his ego and you'll have him eating out of your hand. The other way, though? A man like him won't take well to someone who makes him feel inferior, and you have a particular knack of giving people the idea that they don't impress you.'

'And that's because they usually don't.'

'Fine. I know. But you need to learn to keep that to yourself.'

He got up and went around her chair so that he was behind her and started to massage her shoulders. 'He's going to ask why you brought me back for Imber.'

'So he won't be a fan of you working on this.' He felt her muscles tense and took his hands away.

'No,' Atticus said, 'but he's in London for the rest of the week. There's no reason why he'd know.'

'Until he comes back,' she pointed out.

'We can cross that bridge when we come to it.'

She sighed and rested back in the chair.

He kneaded her shoulders again. 'We might have worked it all out by then.'

'I wish I could believe that. What you were saying in the meeting – do you really think it's murder?'

'I do,' he said.

'And Jack?'

'Francine was asking me about that,' he said. 'I think it's possible. The verses from the Bible . . . it'd be weird if it was someone else. You're sure that was never made public?'

'Not by us,' she said.

'In private?'

'I can only speak for myself, and I haven't spoken to anyone outside the investigation about it.'

'Someone from the team?'

She sighed. 'I don't think so, but can I say for certain?' She spread her hands helplessly. 'Of course not.'

'The post-mortem might help,' he said. 'We need to look and see if there are any similarities with Miller.'

'Be careful with what you say. Fyfe's already said he thinks Kajetan was an accident, and he won't take kindly to you coming in and asking questions.'

'He just doesn't like his mistakes being pointed out to him.'

She lowered her shoulders so he could really dig his fingers in. He could feel the knots in her muscles. 'Did you hear what I said about making people feel inferior?'

'I did. I know. And I'll be nice.'

She turned her head and looked back up at him. 'Do you want to stay?'

'Can't. I need to see to the dog.'

'You could bring him over, you know.'

'You said the lease said no pets.'

'It does, but is anyone really going to find out?'

'Look at you – breaking all the rules.'

'Are you sure you don't want to stay?'

'Tomorrow,' he said. 'I want to spend a little time going over my notes when I get back tonight, and you *need* to eat. Go on – before it gets cold.'

'OK.'

He lowered his head and kissed her. 'I'll see you in the morning at the hospital.'

'You will. I know you don't like Fyfe, but please try to be civil with him.'

'It's not that I don't like him. It's more that I have absolutely no respect for him.'

'*Atticus.*'

PART III

WEDNESDAY

42

Atticus was up at six, early enough to go for a longer walk with Bandit so that the dog was tired out for the rest of the day. He followed the longer of their usual loops: through the cathedral grounds, up into Harnham and around the cricket pitch, then following the river to the Old Mill pub and taking the town path through the water meadows and back into the city and home. He took out his phone and filleted his inbox as he walked, deleting everything until he looked down with satisfaction and saw that there were no messages left. His smugness was only temporary, though; moments after he shoved it back into his pocket, his phone buzzed and beeped with an incoming message.

He took the phone out again, opened his mail client and saw it was from Nina Parsons. She wanted to come back into the office to discuss the report on her boyfriend that Atticus had prepared. She said, with apologies, that she was leaving the country on military business tomorrow and that she wouldn't be able to relax while she was away without having had the chance to clarify a couple of points.

Atticus opened his calendar: he had the PM for Kajetan first thing and had blocked out the rest of the day to dig into the case for Mack, but he would be able to find thirty minutes for Nina without too much bother. He hadn't had the chance to provide her with his invoice yet, either, and this would be a good opportunity to do that.

He tapped to reply to the message and said that he was available at midday if she could come to the office again. He sent it and, a moment later, she replied: that was fine, she said. She thanked him for fitting her in and closed with a breezy 'see you later' and an informal 'Nx'.

Bandit scampered over the bridge that led into Queen Elizabeth Gardens and chased a duck until he was up to his chest in the water. Atticus called him back and, after trotting out of the river and shaking himself dry, the dog ambled up and waited as Atticus fitted the lead to his collar.

'Time to get back. It's going to be a busy day.'

43

Max Mason had been following the same morning routine for years. He was woken by his butler, Ross, at five minutes past seven, with a breezy 'Good morning, sir,' as he crossed the bedroom and opened the curtains. Ross brought a tray over to the bed with his breakfast – eggs Benedict and a cafetière of strong black coffee – and copies of the *Sun*, the *Mail* and *The Times*, together with a printout of his diary for the day ahead. Mason allowed himself a moment for his eyes to adjust to the sunlight and then shuffled up the bed, allowing Ross to put two cushions behind his back so that he could sit more comfortably.

'How are you this morning, sir?'

'Not bad,' he said.

'You wanted me to remind you about the Wednesday Morning Club.'

'Yes, that's right. Thank you. Are they all coming?'

'No one has said otherwise.'

'Good. Thank you.'

Ross dipped his head and made his way out of the bedroom. Clarendon was a large house, and, given the fact that Mason was approaching eighty, it wouldn't have been possible to live here without help. There were two cleaners, a chauffeur, a handyman and two gardeners, with Ross as the glue that held them all together. All of them worked for Mason on a full-time basis, and it gave him a sense of pride to think that he was supporting them and their families. He had been born in the area and had never been tempted to leave it for somewhere that might have been seen as more glamorous; he had a *pied-à-terre* in London and a house in Florida, but he spent most of his time here. Even now, though, and after all these years, the fact that he had people working for him was still apt to bring him up short. It was quite something when he considered where he had come from.

He finished his eggs and got out of bed, making his way slowly to his en suite bathroom. He relieved himself and then went to the window and looked out over the grounds. The manor house was in Redlynch, south of Salisbury, and Mason had bought it at the end of the eighties when his fame had provided him with more money than he really knew what to do with. The estate had cost him three million, and he had spent the same again on renovating it and its outbuildings, plus a further two to buy additional land from a farmer who owned the neighbouring fields. It had been a huge outlay, yet it had still proven to be a shrewd investment. Mason's banker had arranged for the property to be valued, and the report had come back suggesting that, if he were ever to sell, offers would need to include seven zeroes.

Mason's rise from humble beginnings had been stratospheric, and the story was one that he never tired of telling. The poverty of his youth and the snubs that might have set him back had given him a chip on his shoulder, and the house and its grounds, and everything else that he had accumulated, were the ultimate denunciation of those who had doubted him.

He had been born in Broad Chalke to Roman Catholic parents, the youngest of eight. His father had worked on a farm, and all the family could afford was a tiny two-bedroom house in the village. He had been an abject failure at school and had left as soon as he could and taken a job as a labourer. He worked on the Southampton docks and then found a job as a concert promoter and DJ. He found that his brashness was perfectly suited to show business, and his swift rise through radio and then television seemed preordained.

Success had piled upon success, and now Mason enjoyed a position as television royalty, one of the best-loved celebrities in the country. It would have been easy to look out at the lawn and the lake and the hundred acres beyond that and feel that he didn't deserve it, but that kind of doubt was alien to him. There had been some good fortune along the way, but Mason had worked hard to get where he was and, as far as he was concerned, he deserved every last scrap of it. You could make luck with hard work, and that's what Mason had done.

He went into his dressing room and opened the wardrobe with his suits. He had more than twenty, each made to his precise measurements by his tailor on Savile Row. They were his trademark: he had them in all the colours of the rainbow, from electric blue to bright yellow to lime green. He never allowed himself to be seen in public when he wasn't looking his absolute best, and people had come to associate him with the striking colours that he matched with similarly garish shirts and ties. He ran his finger along the rail; each suit was freshly dry-cleaned and cloaked in a protective plastic sheath. He stopped at a three-piece that was ketchup red and took it down, tore off the plastic and laid it across the back of the chair that sat in front of his make-up table. He selected a shirt of the same hue and then added suede shoes, also in red. His guests this morning all had an idea of what to expect of him, and Mason had never been one to let anyone down.

44

Atticus dropped the dog back at the flat and drove over to the hospital. It was eight o'clock, and the car park was beginning to fill with staff and people visiting patients. Fyfe's office was behind the mortuary, reached by way of a series of functional corridors that led to the basement of the hospital. Atticus reached the door to the two post-mortem suites and held down the doorbell. The lock buzzed, and he pushed the door open and went through. Mack and Fyfe were in the reception area.

'Morning,' Atticus said.

Fyfe turned. 'Morning.'

'Morning,' Mack said. 'I was telling Professor Fyfe that you were going to come over. He was just telling me that he was able to move up the PM to yesterday evening.'

'I was hoping to be here for it,' Atticus remarked.

'I'll run you through the results,' Fyfe said, as defensive as always. 'Very straightforward. Could probably have done it by email, to be honest.'

'Nothing like seeing the evidence in person,' Atticus replied with a smile. 'Shall we get started?'

Fyfe found each of them a disposable gown and handed out pairs of nitrile gloves and hairnets. They put them on and followed

Fyfe into the examination room where the post-mortem had been carried out. Kajetan's body was laid out on the examination table. He was naked, the dark ink on his arms contrasting starkly with his pasty-white flesh and the gleaming steel beneath him.

Fyfe went up to the table and stood at the head of the body. 'It's straightforward, as I said. Kajetan wasn't subjected to prolonged attempts at resuscitation, and there hasn't been significant decomposition. I pressed down on his chest and saw exudation through the mouth and nose of pink froth. The manifestation of the subject's last attempts to breathe on a mixture of residual air and water, plus oedema fluid in the lungs are a very clear sign of drowning.'

'But not conclusive,' Atticus said. 'You see it in drug overdoses and congestive heart failure.'

'True,' Fyfe said, making it obvious that he was humouring him. 'But add it to the fact that he was found in water? I think we can say with a *very* high degree of confidence that he drowned.'

'Anything else?'

'Mud in his nostrils and mouth and in his scalp. Washer-woman's hands, too.' He pointed down at Kajetan's pale and wrinkled hands. 'You see that when there's been dermal absorption of liquid.'

'You'll be pleased to know that I can't disagree with any of that. He was certainly drowned.' Atticus approached the body. 'How long do you think he was in the water?'

'Hard to be sure,' Fyfe said. 'Somewhere between one and two days.'

Mack came up to the table, too. 'That ties in with what the water bailiff said.'

Atticus decided not to ask whether Fyfe had been made aware of that when he visited the river. He suspected he would find that in Francine's report, and that Fyfe – lazy as always – had tied in his findings to match what she had said.

187

Fyfe gestured down at Kajetan's chest. 'I could open him up to have a look at the lungs, but I don't think it's warranted when cause of death is as obvious as this.'

Atticus pointed. 'What about that? He's bruised around the neck and shoulders.'

'He is,' Fyfe said. 'Likely caused after death. My operating hypothesis is that it was caused by him being jostled against the concrete in the channels by the current.'

'Really? Are you sure?'

Atticus knew that Fyfe found him confounding. He had contradicted the man's findings when they had found the bone on Salisbury Plain, and that had just been the most recent of their disagreements. Atticus had never been impressed with Fyfe's abilities and, as always, he was struggling now with keeping his opinions to himself.

Remembering his promise to Mack, he smiled as benignly as he could. 'I'm not trying to be impertinent – just trying to encourage a vigorous examination of the facts. You're confident he drowned first?'

'Yes – on the balance of probabilities.' Fyfe said it with less certainty this time.

'So you should welcome an open exchange of views. I'm sure you'll still be right at the end of it – and your conclusion will be bolstered by the process.'

Fyfe turned to Mack and spread his arms in a silent plea for help.

Atticus noticed the smile that was playing on the corner of her lips. 'It can't hurt, can it? Go on, Atticus.'

Atticus nodded his thanks. 'So – we can agree that he drowned. But *how*? It's either natural causes or foul play. Can we agree on that?'

'Of course.'

'So it all comes down to the bruising. You surmise that he was alive when he went into the water and that the bruising was caused by him being bumped around.'

'That's the most likely outcome,' Fyfe began. 'Indeed, you might—'

'It's the *least* likely,' Atticus said over him. He turned to Mack. 'What do we know about bruises?' He didn't allow her a chance to answer. 'A bruise is a collection of blood, visible to the naked eye as an area of discolouration, which has extravasated into the surrounding tissues after vascular disruption, usually after trauma.'

'That doesn't help you in the slightest,' Fyfe said.

'Yes, it does. Blood seen in the tissue after death can be misinterpreted. What we have here is very significant bruising. Look at it.' He pointed at several key spots. 'I read a study last year that examined whether blunt force trauma delivered *after* death could cause the extravasation of blood and tissue damage that was indistinguishable from bruising produced *before* death. The study showed that producing post-mortem bruises, like these, requires considerable force. Even when they used a mallet, the resulting bruise was always smaller than would have been the case before death.'

Mack looked down at the bruising. 'What are you saying?'

'I'm saying that bruises as extensive as this could not easily have been produced by jostling a dead body against the sluice house.'

'Fine,' Fyfe said. '*Fine*. I'll play along. Let's say he had a heart attack. He falls into the water, still alive, and he's bruised before he drowns.'

'Possible,' Atticus conceded. 'But more unlikely than the alternative.'

'Being?' Mack said. 'That he was murdered?'

'That he was attacked in the sluice house, leading to the bruising, and then drowned.'

Fyfe snorted. 'You're speculating.'

'Maybe. But maybe not.' He turned to Mack. 'I think you should tell him about the videotape.'

Fyfe frowned in confusion.

'A tape was sent to the *Journal* yesterday,' Mack said. 'Like the one for Campbell. Given the context, we have to assume that this is either suicide or murder.'

'You didn't tell me that,' Fyfe protested.

'Sorry,' Mack said. 'It's a fast-moving enquiry.'

'Well, yes,' he blustered. 'Obviously, it changes everything. I can't see how this was suicide. I mean, it's possible, but—'

'Very unlikely,' Atticus said. 'What about David Campbell?'

'I looked at him two days ago. I'm sending the report over today.'

'The potted version?'

His face puckered a little. 'He was a mess. Falling from as high up as that? Not pleasant.'

'Cause of death?'

'Impact. Obviously.'

'Any sign of struggle?'

'Not easy to see with all the other injuries, but no – no obvious signs.'

'What about toxicology?'

'I've taken blood and urine. They'll be tested next week.'

'Same for Kajetan?'

'Yes. I know what we'll find for him – alcohol or drugs. Probably both.'

'Can you expedite the tests?'

'Why? What are we looking for?'

'Kajetan probably *was* out of it, I agree, but there's no suggestion that would be the case for Campbell. It was early in the morning, and he wasn't a drinker. He was also fit and healthy. It would've been difficult to get him over the edge of the parapet.'

'Meaning what?' Fyfe said. 'You think he was pushed?'

'Let's say he was. He would've put up a fight, wouldn't he? Unless . . .'

Mack finished the sentence. 'Unless he was drugged.'

'Maybe,' Atticus said. 'I'd like to check.'

45

Alice had forced herself to get out of bed without snoozing her alarm and had gone to the gym so that she might start the day properly. She hadn't worked out for over a week, and it had started to bother her; she found it embarrassingly easy to find a reason to ignore her early-morning routine, but always felt bad when the day ended and she hadn't done any exercise. She had been one of the first into the building that morning and had done forty minutes of cardio, followed by a few gentle laps of the pool.

She reversed the car onto the drive, taking it back until the proximity warning bleeped and then applying the brake and switching off the engine. She took a moment to sit quietly, closing her eyes as she realised just how tired she was. It had been a hard week so far. David Campbell's plunge from the cathedral tower was two days ago, and there had been a lot of follow-up work to do even after the story had run. Subsequent events had changed the complexion of the story radically, and she had been hurrying to catch up ever since.

She breathed in and out, grabbed the plastic bag of groceries from the passenger seat and reached for the door. She had stopped at the Marks & Spencer outlet at the petrol station to pick up some muesli and fresh fruit, and the thought of breakfast made her hungry. She would make herself a bowl, listen to the *Today* programme on Radio 4 and then get into the office.

She crossed the short path across her front lawn to the door and let herself in. There was a pile of post on the doormat, but she needed to eat, so she stepped over it and went into the kitchen. She had bought the house six months earlier. It was her first property, and she had been thrilled to move out from her parents' and into a place of her own. The costs of the transaction had been steep, and the mortgage was at the limit of what she could afford. She had had no choice but to be frugal with furnishing the place, and her father had hired a van and driven her down to the IKEA in Southampton, where he had helped her buy the things that she needed right away. There was the Grönlid sofa and Ypperlig coffee table in the living room; the Hemnes sideboard and Malm ottoman bed in the bedroom. The rooms still looked bare, but Alice couldn't afford everything she wanted straight away. But she had a list and would work her way through it, item by item, as funds allowed.

Alice put the bag on the counter and took out the muesli and fruit, poured the cereal into a bowl, chopped the strawberries and grapes, added milk and then ambled back into the hall. She looked down at the post: there was an envelope that looked as if it might contain a bill, two packets from Amazon that probably contained the books on the cathedral that she had ordered and, hidden beneath them, the corner of a yellow Jiffy bag.

She set her bowl aside, then knelt and reached for it, her hand freezing before she touched it. In the kitchen, she took out a freezer bag and put her hand inside it. It wouldn't be as good as a glove, but it would do for now. She went back to the front door and very carefully picked up the package, gripping it between thumb and forefinger at its edge. She took it into the kitchen, set it down on the counter and then stared at it: there was a label on the side that faced up, and her name had been printed on it, just as had been the case with the package that had been delivered to the office. It was the same size as the previous Jiffy bags, and the shape of it suggested that something similar was inside.

Lewis had told her to call him at once should anything like this happen, but, as she reached for her phone, she stopped.

Wouldn't the police just take it away?

Would she even be told what was inside?

She felt awkward, as if ignoring the instructions that she had been given was going to get her into trouble, but mastered her unease for the sake of what she might find, and what *that* might mean for what was looking like the story of a lifetime – and what *that* might mean for her career. She would say that she had opened it without realising what it was.

She took a knife from the knife block, slid the tip inside the seal, then drew it back with just enough force to cut through the paper but not enough to cause unnecessary damage. She lifted the parcel and tipped it up, careful not to touch the contents as they slid out and onto the counter. It was the same as before: a black plastic box of the sort used to store videotapes. She turned the case and saw that it, like the others, had a label that had been pushed into the plastic sleeve that lay against the spine.

Hartnett, Dominic / 31 August

There was a sheet of folded paper, too. She opened it out.

Whoever kills an animal must take restitution, but whoever kills a human being is to be put to death.

Alice exhaled, looked back at the cassette box and the note and forgot all about her breakfast. She took out her phone and scrolled through the contacts. She found the entry for Lewis, called the number and waited for it to connect.

46

Atticus had asked Francine Patterson to search the Police National Database for everything that could be found about Lucjusz Kajetan, and when he got back from the hospital and woke his computer, he found that there was an email waiting for him. He opened the report attached to it and scanned it. The database held records of Kajetan's cautions and convictions, and Atticus saw that there were a *lot* of them: most were for possession of controlled substances, along with one for assault. There was a witness statement that Kajetan had made when he had been interviewed by Francine after his most recent arrest for possession. He told her that he was born in Warsaw in 1973 and that he had arrived in London at the turn of the century. He had lived in London for five years, working for a Polish builder, and then, after marrying a local woman, he had moved down to Salisbury and set up his own business. Things had been good until the financial crash; the banks called in their loans and, with no one starting any new projects, the business was choked of the funds it needed. After limping on for a year, it died. Kajetan's house was repossessed, his marriage failed, and, with nothing left, he ended up on the street.

Atticus gave a low whistle, and Bandit, who had been sleeping in the other room, lifted himself off the mattress and trotted over.

'Another walk?'

The dog bounded with excitement as Atticus put on the harness, clipped the lead to it and led the way down the stairs.

* * *

Atticus and Bandit walked through the city, along the high street and then on to Fisherton Street, eventually turning right and following the signs to the office where the Shopmobility team hired out their wheelchairs and scooters. The office was on the ground floor of the two-level car park at the Maltings, beneath Sainsbury's. Atticus continued around the corner until he reached the area used by the local homeless as a place to shelter and sleep. The council had been trying to move them on for months, and Atticus remembered the consternation when they had installed metal fencing to prevent access to the areas that they favoured. There had been a campaign in the *Journal* about it, he recalled, and the fencing had been removed.

There were three men and two women there as Atticus approached, surrounded by the detritus of the terminally poor: empty cans of cheap lager, empty bottles of supermarket own-brand cider and fragments of glass from crushed vials that crunched underfoot. They had spread out a series of mismatched duvets to soften the concrete, and there were orange carrier bags from the nearby Sainsbury's, some stuffed with empty food wrappers and more empty cans. They had a cooker that ran off a bottle of Calor Gas, and one of them had found, and moved in, an armchair that was now accommodating a sleepy-looking Labrador. Bandit wagged his tail enthusiastically at the prospect of an introduction to the dog, but the Labrador stayed where he was and closed his eyes.

Atticus had been down here regularly when he had been a detective. There were usually six or seven rough sleepers, and, although the precise membership of the group varied from time to time due to some moving on and others passing away, Atticus had been able to form useful relationships with several of them over the years. He approached now and saw a man he recognised.

'Ricky,' he said.

The man looked up at him. 'Haven't seen you for a while.'

'Months.'

'Still police?'

'Not any more. I'm working on my own now.'

'Doing what?'

'Private detective.'

'For real? Like on the telly?'

Atticus smiled with self-deprecation. 'Don't you read the papers? I'm famous.'

'Bollocks you are.'

'How are you?'

'Same as always.'

'I thought you were waiting for a room at Alabare?'

'I had one for a week,' he said.

'And?'

'They kicked me out.' He shrugged. 'Caught me shooting up, and that was that. There's no way I'm ever going to stop. Don't *want* to stop. Anyway, it doesn't matter – I've got everything I need.'

Ricky had been a soldier, like so many of the other men and women who ended up down here. Their military careers came to an end and, without preparation or training for their transition to Civvy Street, they fell between the cracks and were forgotten.

'I'm looking for information on someone who used to sleep down here. Do you think you could help me?'

'Depends,' he said.

'On what?'

Ricky put his hand out.

Atticus took out his wallet, opened it and removed the little wad of notes that he kept inside. He peeled off a ten and gave it to the man. 'Same again if you can help me.'

'Fair enough – what do you want?'

'Do you know Lucjusz Kajetan? The police nicked him here for possession three or four months ago. He had a nickname. They called him—'

'Lucky,' the man interrupted, then gave a hacking laugh. 'Lucky Lucjusz. He thought that was hilarious.'

'Did you know him?'

'Same as I know any of the others around here. People come, people go. You'll get blokes turn up and sleep down here for a few nights, then they'll get a bed somewhere until they get kicked out and end up here again.'

'What can you tell me about him?'

'Not much to say. He's Polish, used to be a builder, I think, until his business went under and his life went to shit.'

'Did he ever give you any reason to think that he had enemies?'

Ricky shrugged. 'Don't think so. He's a good bloke. Hard not to like him.'

'*I* don't like him,' said the man to Ricky's right. His name was Jezza, and Atticus remembered him as being an airman who had, if memory served, seen action in Afghanistan. He was rolling a joint.

'Why not?'

'Has a temper on him. You wouldn't want to be around him when he was in the wrong sort of mood.'

'Shut up,' Ricky said. 'He's all right.'

The Labrador reached out with a paw and scratched itself on the snout.

'When was the last time you saw him?'

Ricky paused for a moment, his face puckering as he gave thought to the question. 'Last week, I think. The police come around here and move us on every now and again. Like you said, Lucky got nicked not all that long ago, and I think it freaked him out. He said he'd found somewhere else to kip where he wouldn't get trouble.'

'Did he say where?'

'Not to me,' Ricky said. 'You get somewhere good, somewhere you might get a bit of peace and quiet, you don't always tell anyone else. You keep it to yourself.'

'*I* know,' Jezza said, putting out his hand. 'He told me. But you're going to have to pay me if you want me to tell you, though. Nothing comes for free.'

'Nice try,' Atticus said. 'I know where it was – the old eel house on the river.'

Jezza finished rolling his joint and lit it. 'S'right.' He didn't seem remotely concerned that his ploy for Atticus's money had failed. 'He told me last week.'

Ricky was confused. 'Why are you here asking about him if you already know where he is? Has he done something wrong again?'

Atticus watched their faces for a reaction. 'He's dead. He was found in the water yesterday.'

Both men reacted as Atticus would have expected: with surprise, if not necessarily shock. It wasn't unusual for the men and women who ended up down here to find themselves in medical difficulty, and death would be a more regular occurrence here than would have been the case in the world outside.

'What happened?' Ricky asked.

'The police aren't sure. Might have been an accident – he gets drunk; he slips; he falls in and drowns.'

Jezza was looking at him shrewdly. 'But that's not what you think. You were asking whether he had any enemies.'

'That's the other possibility. Ricky said he didn't. What do you think?'

Jezza cocked an eyebrow, smiled suggestively and put out his hand again.

Atticus took another ten-pound note and held it out.

Jezza reached for it, and Atticus pulled it back. 'You first.'

The man stared at Atticus, then smiled, baring a mouthful of blackened teeth. 'Fine. There was a bloke down here, back end of last week. He was like you, asking around about Lucky. Had a picture of him from before – didn't recognise him until he said that he was Polish, and then it could only really be him. He told me he was a lawyer and that he was looking for him because one of his relatives had died and left him some money in a will.'

'And you told him where he was?'

He nodded. 'He gave me fifty notes.'

'When was this?'

'I said—'

'You need to be precise,' Atticus interrupted. '*Exactly* when?'

'I have no idea, mate. One day is the same as any other. I don't even know what day it is today.'

'Tell me what happened.'

'I already said – a bloke came down here asking where he could find Lucky, and I said I thought he was down on the river.' He took a draw on his joint.

'Don't do that now,' Atticus said. He reached out and batted the joint from his fingers.

'Hey!'

Atticus took out two more ten-pound notes and added them to the first, holding them up so that Jezza could see what he stood to make by cooperating. 'What did he look like?'

Jezza picked up the joint and screwed up his face as he tried to remember. 'Younger than me. Thirties. Dark hair. About your height.'

'What was he wearing?'

'Jeans, I think. And a leather jacket.'

'Was there anything about him that was unusual?'

'Not that I can think of.'

'Anything at all.'

He sucked his teeth. 'I didn't think he was a lawyer. He didn't have that kind of air about him, if you know what I mean. He had an *edge*. I said I'd help him if he'd make it worth my while, and the way he reacted made me think that he wasn't someone that I'd want to piss off. I mean, he paid up – generous, too – but I got the feeling that he might have a nasty side.'

Atticus knew that there was no point in pushing things too much further. He gave him the notes and a business card that he took from his pocket. 'There's another hundred in it for you if you can think of anything else that helps me to find him.'

'What about me?' Ricky protested.

'You too.' He took out a second card and handed it over, plus the additional ten he'd promised him. 'Here's my number. Call me if you think of anything useful.'

47

Max Mason waited in the library as his guests arrived. He could hear the crunch of the wheels of their cars as they rolled to a stop on the gravelled turning circle in front of the house, and then Ross's voice as he welcomed them and showed them through into the drawing room. Mason's chef – a Frenchman named Claude whom he had poached from the kitchen of Michel Roux – had prepared pastries to be served with coffee, and Ross had brought out a humidor with a selection of cigars from Mason's extensive collection. Mason listened to the buzz of conversation as his guests greeted one another and waited for their host's arrival.

The Wednesday Morning Club had been a fixture in Mason's diary for the last forty years. He cultivated social contacts the way a gardener might attend to his garden; he added new members who he thought might add colour to his collection and pruned those for whom he had no further use. A few of the men – and they were always men – whom he had invited had turned out to be disappointments, but, by and large, Mason had extracted value from the weekly gatherings.

On the one hand, it did his ego no harm at all to have the great and the good of local society under his roof and enjoying his hospitality; he remembered where he had come from and remembered the snubs that his father had received when he had tried to advance himself. On the other hand – and more importantly – the connections that he had made during those countless mornings together had stood him in good stead.

The men who came to him had nothing to do with the glitz and glamour of Mason's life in London, but they were all important in the local community. The complement changed over time, but it had included businessmen, doctors, lawyers, judges, army officers and men from the police. Mason was a spider, weaving a web that stretched out from Salisbury to all corners of Wiltshire and beyond. His guests willingly flung themselves into its strands, all of them attracted by the glow of his celebrity.

There was a knock.

'Yes?'

Ross opened the door. 'Everyone is here, sir.'

'Thank you.'

Mason straightened his jacket, fastening the last button but one, and then crossed the hallway to the reception hall and then the drawing room. His guests were waiting for him: Allan Ellsworth, the owner of a local estate agency, was pouring coffee while talking to Craig Loome, a landlord who owned a swathe of the industrial park near to the airfield; Connor Gallagher, a retired judge who still enjoyed extensive connections at the High Court in London, was sat in an armchair opposite Chief Superintendent Alexander Beckton; Richard Claire and William Mackintosh, both involved in finance in London, were chatting by the big mullioned window.

Mason clapped his hands. 'Good morning, gentlemen. How are we all doing?'

The others turned to him; they were sycophantic toadies to a man, but, rather than be irritated by the transparency of their obsequiousness, Mason found it amusing. It was almost flattering; the son of a farmhand, a former labourer and stevedore who didn't have a pot to piss in while he was growing up was able to hold court and attract the great and the good of Wiltshire society to his door. It was another sign of how far he had come.

He went to the humidor, opened the lid and took out an Arturo Fuente Opus X, a big seven-inch stogie that cost fifty pounds. He went to where Beckton and Gallagher were sitting and held out the ebony box; Gallagher passed, but Beckton obliged, taking out another of the Arturos.

'How are you both?' Mason said as he took a cutter and snipped off the end of his cigar and then Beckton's.

'Very good, Max,' Gallagher said.

'I saw the show at the Palladium,' Beckton remarked.

'*The Royal Variety*?' Mason waved a hand dismissively. 'Things aren't what they used to be. Do you know the first year I did it?' Beckton shook his head. 'Seventy-five. Nearly fifty years ago. The bill in those days . . . my god, it put last weekend to shame. Michael Crawford swung over the stage with a rope tied to one ankle. They had to insure him – a hundred and fifty grand. Harry Secombe and Vera Lynn were there. Charles Aznavour sang. There was a Zulu troop there – KwaZulu, I think, if memory serves – and I remember the controversy about whether they could dance with their tits out like they did in their West End show. Do you know what Buckingham Palace said?'

They both shook their heads.

'"The Queen has seen topless ladies before."'

They laughed.

'Telly Savalas was there – do you know the security wouldn't let him in on account of the fact that he looked suspicious? God knows how they didn't recognise him – how do you not recognise Kojak?'

Mason noticed the way that Gallagher and Beckton both leaned in towards him, big smiles fixed to their faces as he regaled them with stories from his career. He had long since realised that he had that effect on people and had always taken advantage of it; the stories he could tell told of a different time, of gossip and intrigue, when celebrity meant something, rather than the ephemeral fluff that passed for glamour these days. He could make them feel part of something exclusive, give them a glimpse into the world that would otherwise have been closed off to them. His career had been long enough for him to *embody* show business, and it was catnip to those with boring, dull, provincial lives.

He took out his lighter and offered to light Beckton's cigar. 'How are things with you?'

'Still dealing with what happened at Imber.'

'What happened with the Met?' Gallagher asked.

'They sent a man from the counter-terrorism team,' Beckton said. 'It took a lot of effort to persuade him that it had nothing to do with that.'

'This is Richard Miller?' Mason said. Beckton nodded.

Mason had heard about Miller's death from Beckton on the occasion of his last visit. He had explained that Miller's body had been found in the back of a car and that the suggestion was that he had been involved in a murder connected to the deserted village at Imber. Mason had prompted him for more information, but Beckton had been a terrible bore and told him that it was under investigation and he had to be careful what he said.

No harm in trying again. 'Have you found out how he was involved?'

Beckton drew down on his cigar and then blew the smoke up towards the ceiling. 'It's still not clear. Miller confessed to a robbery in Londonderry when he was in the army. We charged him and bailed him, and then he was found dead in the back of a car on New Street.'

'Found by the private detective.'

Beckton nodded. 'Priest.'

'Do you know why he was left there?' Gallagher asked.

'We still don't know. Someone – the murderer, most likely – called Priest and told him that Miller was involved with the two men who we think were responsible for the Imber killings. This person – whoever he is – thought Miller would get away with it, so he decided to take matters into his own hands.'

'How extraordinary,' Gallagher said.

Beckton blew out another mouthful of smoke. 'That's one way of describing it. We still don't have any idea who he is.'

'But you're investigating?'

'We are,' Beckton said. 'With help from the Met. They've accepted it's not terrorism, but Miller was an MP, and they have to be seen to be treating it seriously. It's made things much more difficult for us, of course. That's the thing with the Met – they come down to a place like this and think that we don't know what we're doing. You know my dad was an officer?'

'I don't think you've ever mentioned that,' Mason said.

Beckton nodded. 'Down here, too – Salisbury. He got to detective inspector before he retired. Did a case with the Met back in the seventies. It was the same then, too. He said they treated them like country bumpkins. You know what they called them?'

Mason shook his head.

'Swedes – like turnips. It hasn't changed.'

Mason told Beckton to enjoy the cigar and left to circulate around the room. He had been to Imber, and the thought of the bodies in the graveyard sent shivers up and down his spine. He had followed the investigation through the reports in the newspapers at first, swiping through the pages from front to back with the morbid curiosity of a rubbernecker at a car crash. The reporters had run out of fresh material as the investigation foundered, and

Mason had taken advantage of Beckton's friendship in an attempt to get the inside line. Beckton had been coming to the house for several years, but, in truth, Mason had always found him rather dull. Beckton was a senior officer, though, and now Mason was prepared to hold his nose in the hope that he might be able to learn something that would otherwise have been beyond him.

He noticed that Beckton had been eyeing the crystal decanter on the table with the Glenfiddich. He indicated it with a flick of his fingers. 'Fancy a Scotch?'

Beckton feigned reluctance. 'Surely it's too early?'

'Never. That's the Grande Couronne – twenty-six years old. I picked it up in an auction in London for . . . well' – he grinned – 'it wasn't cheap.' Mason raised a hand, and Ross was alongside almost before he could lower it. 'Pour the chief superintendent a glass. I'll take one, too.'

'Right away, sir.'

Mason watched as Ross went to the table and selected two tulip-shaped glasses with tapered necks, perfect for allowing the concentrated aroma to hit the nose through a narrow rim.

'So,' he said to Beckton as Ross unstopped the decanter and poured, 'bring me up to date about Imber. I'm dying to know what's happened since you were last here.'

48

Atticus went back to the office, made Bandit comfortable in the second room and spent ten minutes reviewing the file that he had prepared for Nina Parsons. He got up from his desk at a little before midday and went to the bay window, where he could look down on the street below. He saw Nina making her way along the pavement and then passing beneath him, where she would turn right into the passageway that led to his door.

The bell rang, and he went down to let her in.

'Mr Priest,' she said.

'It's Atticus.'

'Atticus,' she said, smiling, 'thanks for seeing me on short notice.'

'Not a problem. You said you were going away?'

'Estonia.'

'You're Royal Welsh?'

'First Battalion. How'd you know?'

'I had a case before I left the police – an infantryman from Tidworth crashed his car outside the barracks after a night out. He was Royal Welsh – just rotated back from Eastern Europe.'

'Well, that's me.'

'The weather won't be quite as nice as Cyprus.'

208

'No, it won't. You'll have more of a challenge next time.'

'How do you mean?'

'You'll have to find something else to impress me with other than what my tan might tell you.'

She wasn't criticising him, but rather, judging from the sparkle in her eye, was very gently ribbing him for his earlier attempt to impress.

'You're never going to let me live that down, are you?'

'Probably not.'

Atticus wasn't sure, but he was left with the impression that she was flirting with him. 'Well,' he said, 'unless you have some other work you'd like me to do, I'm not sure that our paths will cross again. I've finished looking into Mr Wintringham for you.' He held up a copy of the report that he had printed out.

'Do you have time to go through it with me?'

'Of course.'

'Tell you what – why don't I have a quick flick through it while you make me a coffee?'

Atticus clapped his hands together. 'I'm *so* sorry. That's the second time I've been a terrible host. How do you take it again?'

'White, no sugar.'

'White, no sugar. I'll just be a moment. Here.'

He handed her the report so that she could take it, then got up and made his way to the kitchen outside. He filled the kettle and flicked the switch to set it to boil, then prepared the mugs with coffee granules and milk. He found that he was impressed once again with Nina's assurance; she had had no problem calling him out on his attempts to show off, and her easy banter was the same today as it had been before. It was unusual, especially in a client; coming to see an investigator was out of the ordinary and disconcerting, and the prospect of discussing intimate personal matters would have made most people cringe. It was much like going to the doctor with an embarrassing condition. Nina did not show any of the usual symptoms of nerves, though, and Atticus found himself wondering whether her poise might be thanks to her career as an officer. Those in the military often had that same self-possession; perhaps she held a more senior rank than he had assumed. It made him curious, and he decided to check once he had a moment.

His phone chirped with an incoming text just as the kettle boiled. He took it out of his pocket, saw that it was from Mack – *Call me!* – and resolved to get back to her as soon as he was finished here; it wouldn't be long. He poured the hot water into the mugs and took them back into the office. Nina had got up from the sofa in the bay window and was standing next to the desk when he returned, looking at one of the large whiteboards that he had fixed to the wall. He had used the board to note down his thoughts on the continuing investigation into Alfred Burns, only recently wiping it away. He had returned to the office last night and had doodled a series of inchoate thoughts on the deaths of Campbell and Kajetan, trying – and failing – to find anything to connect them beyond the peccadillos that had been exposed by the videos that had been received at the *Journal*.

The scribbles would have made no sense to anyone else, and Nina showed no interest in them. Atticus handed her one of the mugs, and she took it over to the bay window and sat down once more.

'Thank you,' she said, then proffered the printed report. 'You didn't find much.'

'There's not much *to* find. He's a fairly normal man. I didn't find anything that says he's anything other than what he told you he was. Married, two kids, mortgage on his house with Barclays, drives a sensible car, shops at Waterstones and has coffee at Boston Tea Party.'

'You followed him?'

He nodded. 'I went to his house, spoke to one of the neighbours, who said that the family was very nice, and then followed him into the city.'

'What about online?'

'That's pages five and six,' Atticus said, gesturing to the report, 'but the précis is the same: standard Facebook profile of long standing, reasonably active, posts a little too much about his family to be safe; has a Twitter account but doesn't use it; posts pictures of local landscapes taken from a drone on his Instagram. None of it is even remotely controversial.'

She flicked through the pages, scanning the screen-caps that Atticus had taken from his various profiles. 'It's funny,' she said. 'I'm relieved he's what he said he is, but I can't help feeling foolish that I've had you go to all this trouble when I should just have trusted him.'

'It was no trouble at all,' Atticus said. 'And I don't blame you. You had a bad experience – it's not unreasonable to try to do everything you can to make sure it doesn't happen again.'

'Yes – you're right.' She stood, opened her bag and slid the report inside. 'Can you email a copy to me as well, please?'

'Of course.'

'And a copy of your bill? I'll pay before I fly out.'

Atticus took her outstretched hand. 'Why are you going to Estonia?'

'There's a battlegroup out there – we're training them in how to use NATO gear. Can't really say much more than that.'

'Of course.'

She paused at the door. 'I meant to ask you – did you get out to Imber during the investigation?'

'I did,' he said. 'Several times.'

'What did you make of it?'

'It's one of the strangest places I think I've ever been. You must have been?'

'When I was training, but that was years ago. You're right about it being weird, though. It's the buildings that they just left, as if they were always going to come back . . . I found it a bit spooky. And the bodies were found in the graveyard?'

'They were.'

She shook her head. 'Awful what they did. Awful.'

Atticus opened the door for her. 'Let me know if there's anything else I can do for you.'

'I will,' she said. 'And thanks for taking care of this so promptly. I appreciate it.'

* * *

Atticus watched Nina walk back up New Street, took his phone from his pocket, woke the screen and saw that Mack had sent another two messages after the first. The first asked him to call her back, the second asked again, and the third – in all caps – practically *demanded* it.

He called her. 'What is—'

She didn't let him finish. 'Where are you?'

'At the office. I had a meeting with a client.'

'You need to come in.'

He noticed the edge to her voice and guessed immediately what it was. 'There's been another video?'

'At Alice Morris's house this morning. She's bringing it into the nick.'

'Wait for me,' he said, reaching for his jacket. 'I'll be there in fifteen minutes.'

49

Atticus hurried to Bourne Hill, negotiated the woman at the desk and rushed up to the CID room. The desks were empty, and he could see and hear the activity in the enquiry room.

He went inside. The team were taking the seats around the table. Mack saw him and turned. 'Good. We're all here.'

Atticus pointed at the open envelope on the desk.

'Another?'

'Another.'

'Who opened it?'

'They did. The *Journal*.'

'What? Didn't we tell them not to?'

'We did,' Lewis said. 'It was Alice. She said she wasn't thinking.'

'Did she touch it?'

'Just the envelope,' Lewis said. 'Not the tape or the case or the note.'

Atticus muttered a curse and turned to Mack. 'Where's the tape now?'

'It's being digitised.'

'When will it be ready?'

She went over to the computer on the desk and tapped the keyboard. 'Now.'

Mack cast the laptop's screen onto the larger screen on the wall and double-clicked on the most recently added file. The video player opened with the same background that had become familiar from the two previous videos: the bed, the bare brick wall behind it lit from below by red uplighters on the floor. The footage ran for thirty seconds without anyone appearing in it, but then a man crossed into the shot from the left and sat down on the edge of the bed. He was bare-chested and, sharing a conversation with someone off camera, he gave a laugh that carved lines around his mouth and nose.

'Stop the tape,' Best said.

Mack did, freezing the frame with the man looking straight into the camera with a grin on his face.

Atticus recognised him. 'You know who that is?'

Best pointed down to the label on the case. 'Dominic Hartnett.'

'Yes – and?'

'Shit.' Mack's jaw fell open as she realised. 'The MP for Devizes.'

Atticus jabbed his finger at the screen. 'He's younger, but it's him.'

Best took out his phone and, after a moment, turned it around so that the others could see the display. He had found Hartnett's website: the MP was standing with his hands behind his back and a smile on his face. His hair was grey now – it was dark brown in the video – and his skin was wrinkled with age, but there was very little doubt that the two images were of the same man.

Atticus's thoughts ran around his head in crazy circles, and he had to close his eyes in order to try to corral them. 'What day is it today?'

'Wednesday.'

'There was a vote in Parliament yesterday evening.'

'How do you know that?' Best said.

'It was on the radio. I had it on in the background last night. Things – random things – stick in my mind.' He took out his phone, opened a browser and navigated to the website that listed how individual MPs had voted in the chamber. 'He wasn't there.'

'So?' Lynas said.

'So it was a three-line whip. He *had* to be there, and he wasn't.'

Best held up his phone. 'I've got the number for his constituency office.'

'Call it,' Mack said.

Best placed the call and, after waiting for it to connect, introduced himself and asked if it was possible to speak to the MP. Atticus couldn't hear the response, but, as the conversation continued, Best shook his head and turned his face away. He thanked the other person for their help, asked them to stay on the line and then muted his microphone and put the phone on the table.

'He's dead.'

50

Atticus sat bolt upright. 'How?'

'You were right – he wasn't there for the vote last night. They couldn't get in touch with him, so they went to the place in Fulham he has for when he's in Parliament. He was in bed. Dead.'

'*How?*'

'They think he had a heart attack.'

'He didn't have a heart attack,' Atticus muttered.

'They said it didn't look suspicious.'

Atticus ignored that. 'I need to go and see for myself.'

'No,' Mack said. 'You can't. That'll be for the Met.'

'They'll mess it up.'

Mack stared at him and shook her head.

'What about the post-mortem?' he said. 'Someone from here needs to go.'

Mack held up a hand to try to calm him. 'First things first – we need to make sure Murphy knows. That's two dead Wiltshire MPs in less than two months. And Hartnett's apartment is on their patch. I know it's frustrating, but we don't have any choice.'

Atticus threw up his hands. 'But Murphy is *hopeless*.'

Mack held his eye until he remembered to take a breath. 'This is what we're going to do. I'm going to go and speak to Beckton. I don't know what he'll want to do about it, but that'll be for him and Murphy to decide. I'd suggest you speak to the tech department and make sure that the other two videos have been put somewhere convenient so that we can all look at them. OK?'

'What? Why?'

'I want to make sure we can get to them as easily and conveniently as possible.'

Atticus realised what Mack was suggesting: she anticipated, as did he, that Murphy would return with reinforcements and take control of the investigation from top to bottom. Atticus would definitely be barred from offering his assistance; it might lead to the freezing out of the officers from Salisbury, too. Mack was hinting at a way that he could remain involved: if he were to have a copy of those videos, then he could continue to investigate them even if he was no longer on the team.

'Good idea,' he said. 'I'll do that. What about the message?'

Mack held up an evidence bag with a piece of A4 paper inside.

Atticus read: '"Whoever kills an animal must take restitution, but whoever kills a human being is to be put to death."'

'Leviticus,' Francine said. 'Chapter twenty-four.'

'It's him,' Atticus said. 'It has to be.'

'Jack?'

'It must be. There's too much pointing in that direction to ignore it: the scripture, the kids in the videos.'

'Let's say it is him,' Lynas began. 'Why is he including the scripture with the tapes? Because he's religious?'

'Maybe,' Atticus said.

Mack eyed him. 'But you don't think so?'

'I don't know. He could be – it's possible. But if he is, he's butchering the meaning. None of the verses actually *condone* revenge. At best, they say it's not our place to intervene and God will sort everything out.'

'No one is suggesting he's rational,' Best said. 'Maybe he has his own spin on them.'

Atticus shook his head. '*I* think he's rational.'

'So?'

'I think he's including them because he knows that when they get out – and we all know they *will* get out, eventually – it's going to make the story even bigger than it would already have been. Think about what the hacks from the nationals will say when they get wind of it? It'll be like catnip for them.'

Lynas frowned. 'You think he *wants* publicity?'

'It wouldn't be unusual. I can think of a dozen killers who craved notoriety. David Berkowitz, Richard Ramirez, Dennis Rader – what did they all have in common?'

'Apart from the fact that they were psychopaths?' Best asked.

'Apart from that. They sent letters to the cops and the newspapers because the thing they wanted most of all was a public image.'

'You don't think he's like *them*, though?' Best said. 'I mean – those are all serial killers.'

'He's killed multiple times,' Atticus said. 'So there's that. But, no, I don't think he's like them. His victims aren't random. There's an agenda. He's choosing them. It's something to do with the videos.'

Atticus sat back, put his hands on his head and laced his fingers. The room was quiet as they digested the implication of what had just been discussed.

Best tapped his knuckles on the table. 'What do you want the rest of us to do, boss?'

'Work on the leads we've been following.'

Lynas raised a hand. 'I've got something on that.'

'The cameras near the *Journal*?'

He nodded. 'I went up and down Rollestone Street, looking for cameras. There's a surgery on the other side of the road from the office. They have a camera above the door that looks out on to the street.' He paused and shrugged. 'I went through the footage carefully. Nothing.'

Atticus frowned. 'There must be *something*.'

'There isn't. The staff from the paper go in and out, but it was raining all day – *really* heavy, remember? – and there was hardly anyone around. The only people who went in through the front door were the editor, the reporter, the receptionist and another bloke they told me was the photographer. That's it. If you don't believe me, you can go and check it out yourself.'

'Then how was the tape delivered?'

Lynas spread his arms. 'I don't know – with the post?'

'No,' Lewis said. 'I checked with the receptionist and she's sure it wasn't.'

'Do we trust that she's right?' Atticus said. 'It looked disorganised there when I went in.'

'It is disorganised,' Lewis said, 'but she was sure. The post comes in the morning and she says it wasn't there then. It could've been a courier . . .'

'But then they would've been on the camera,' Lynas finished, 'and they weren't.'

'We need to get to the bottom of that,' Mack said.

The talk of cameras spurred a thought. 'What about the cameras around the cathedral?' Atticus asked. 'Anything after he went by the college?'

'No,' Best answered. 'The only one that was working was up high above the door to the school. We've got him going by, but his face was covered. You were right. He knew how to get through without letting us get a good look at him.'

'I'm not surprised,' Atticus said.

Best held up a finger. 'There's one other thing. I checked with the cathedral to see if they had a record of everyone who went up on the tour of the attic. They only did it twice – six people each time. I checked them all, and none of them ring any alarm bells. One family – mum and dad and three kids. Four of the others were women from the Women's Institute. The other three didn't look likely, but I checked them out to be sure, and they all have alibis.'

Atticus slumped back in his chair. He had hoped that they might be destined for a little luck, but it seemed not.

Mack brought the meeting to a close, making sure that everyone was assigned a task and dismissing them with the injunction that they clear their diaries: there was going to be a lot of overtime until they were able to find out who was behind the deaths.

51

Mack went to Beckton's office but found he wasn't there. She went to his secretary and asked her to ensure he called her as soon as he returned, explaining that it was important they speak before the end of the day. The secretary said she would see to it; Mack thanked her and went back to the CID room.

The door to the enquiry room was closed. She looked through the opaque window to the side and saw a blurred figure in the glass.

She knocked on the door, waited a moment, and then opened it.

Atticus was standing with the boxes of documents that had been generated during the enquiry set out on the floor by his feet. The table was covered with papers, and Atticus was standing over them, taking a picture of each before replacing it with the next and repeating the process.

'Shut the door,' he said without looking up.

She did. 'What are you doing?'

'What does it look like I'm doing? I'm copying as much of this as I can. Pass me Miller's statement – it's in the box over there.'

She opened the lid and took out the statement. 'I'm not sure this is a great idea.'

'You suggested it.'

'I meant the videos – not all this.'

'I've already emailed myself the videos,' Atticus said, checking the images on his phone. 'It's not enough. I need these, too. I need all of it, really. The statement, please. Give it to me.'

Mack went around the table and looked over his shoulder. She saw he had just finished photographing the last page of James York's statement. She dropped Miller's on top of it.

'You think there's a connection between Imber and now?'

'I think it's likely.'

'What, though?'

'York and Burns abused and murdered teenagers. We know that. Miller was involved, too, beyond what he admitted to, anyway. Jack told me that.'

'And we believe him?'

'Why wouldn't we?'

'Go on.'

'All three videos involve kids.'

'True. But we've got nothing beyond that.'

'What did Jack say to me?'

'That Miller wasn't just guilty of the murders in Londonderry.' He gestured for her to continue. 'What else?'

'That the three of them were being paid to rape the girls.'

'What did he tell me – the exact words?'

'I can't remember, Atticus. I'd have to—'

He spoke over her. '"I don't know the names of the customers." That's what he said. "The *customers*." What if Campbell, Kajetan and Hartnett were involved in it, too? Maybe it was a business – what if you could buy the kids? What if they were being prostituted?'

'But why would they have been filmed?'

'Look where the camera is – up high, hidden in the corner. I'll bet you anything you like that the three of them didn't know it was there.'

'So they could be blackmailed.'

'We know Alf Burns was into blackmail. Or maybe it was so the tapes could be used for protection. Or leverage.'

'OK,' she said. 'OK. Let's assume, for the sake of argument, that I buy that. Who's topping them? Who's sending the tapes? You *really* think it's Jack?'

He stared at her as if she had just asked a stupid question. 'It's him.'

'Next question, then. How's he got the tapes?'

'Don't know.'

'And why's he sending them to the paper?'

Atticus was about to answer, but, before he could speak, there was a knock at the door.

'Hold on,' Mack said. She put Miller's statement back into the box. 'And that one,' she hissed to Atticus, pointing at York's statement. She waited until he had put it away before raising her voice again. 'Come in.'

Murphy opened the door. 'DCI Jones,' he said. 'Mr Priest. What are you doing?'

'Discussing the enquiry,' Mack said.

Murphy turned to Atticus. 'With him?'

'That's right.'

'Why?'

Mack paused.

'It's true, then – you brought him back again.'

'Atticus works for us as a consultant. I cleared everything with the chief superintendent.'

'I just spoke to him about that,' Murphy said. 'And other things. But never mind – it can wait.' He came inside and drummed his fingers on the top of the nearest cardboard box. 'I've just got back from London. And DCS Beckton's been speaking to my boss. There's not really any point beating around the bush – we'll be taking over.'

'How much?'

'All of it. You've had two MPs murdered in the space of six weeks. You're out of your depth.'

Atticus stiffened. 'And you're not?'

Murphy glowered. 'Thank you, Mr Priest. We won't need you any more.'

'You don't know what you're doing. You're going to make a mess.'

Murphy pointed at the door. 'Out.'

'No.' Atticus shook his head. 'I'm not going anywhere.'

'Yes, you are. But not too far, please. I've still got some questions I want to ask you.'

'I answered your questions.'

'Not satisfactorily. I'll be in touch.'

Mack could see that Atticus was close to losing his temper. She reached a hand out and rested it on his elbow, but he brushed it off.

'Mack doesn't need your help,' Atticus told him. 'And handing the investigation over will slow things down and cause confusion. This is *local*. Can't you see that? The dead men all have connections to Salisbury. There's no reason for you to be involved other than politics.'

'I'm afraid politics is an excellent reason for us to be involved.'

Mack tried again. 'Atticus.'

'No, Mack. You know as well as I do that this is wrong.'

Murphy folded his arms. 'Go on, then. Indulge me. What do you think happened?'

'You've seen the tapes? The three dead men all featured in them. At first I thought it was blackmail and then suicide, but it isn't that. They were *murdered*. It's Jack – he's getting revenge. They were killed and then the tapes were sent to the newspaper to discredit them. Killing them isn't enough. Throwing Campbell off the tower of the cathedral isn't enough. The motive here is *intensely* personal. Jack wants them dead *and* he wants their reputations ruined.'

'Speculation. We won't get anywhere with random guesses.'

'You think I'm going to stop looking into this?'

'Yes – I do.'

'I won't.'

Murphy's brows lowered. 'Yes, you *will*. Interfering with an investigation is a crime. I'd like you to leave the building now, please. I don't know the details of your *arrangement* with DCI Jones, but I'm sure we can take care of any formalities. That can all be dealt with later. I need to speak to her privately now about how we can work together from now on. And you need to leave.'

Mack listened to the way Murphy sneered 'arrangement' and knew that he knew about them. Atticus must have realised, too, but was seemingly too angry to respond.

Mack tugged him aside. 'Atticus – come with me.'

'Don't be long,' Murphy said to her. 'There's a press conference tomorrow morning, and I need to talk to you about it.'

52

Francine was exhausted when she got home, and there were no spaces outside the house where she could park. She drove along St Ann Street until she found somewhere she could leave the car and, ignoring the fact that her permit wasn't valid this far down the road, she pulled up to the kerb and walked back to the house. It was only when she opened the door that she remembered that Charlie had offered to cook dinner for her. The light in the kitchen was on, and she could hear the radio, tuned to the channel that played the nineties indie tunes that he preferred. The music was loud and, as she slipped off her boots and hung up her jacket, she recognised the Manic Street Preachers.

'Hello?' she called out.

The volume on the radio was turned down, and Charlie stepped into the doorway. He was wearing her apron and, as she smiled at the incongruity of it, he gestured to the slogan printed on to the front.

'"Wine goes in, wisdom comes out,"' he read. 'Recent events would suggest otherwise.'

'Very funny.'

'We could put it to the test tonight?' He reached for the counter and held up a bottle of red. 'I had a bottle of this last year. It's bloody nice.'

Francine followed him into the kitchen and saw that he had already gone to an effort to make the evening special: he had laid the table with cutlery for three courses and had lit a candle that flickered above the two settings.

'Look at all this,' she said.

He pulled out her seat and, with a theatrical sweep of his arm, indicated that she should sit down. He went to the counter and brought out the first course: mussels with chorizo, beans and cavolo nero.

'So,' he said, sitting down and pouring out two glasses of the wine. 'How was your day?'

'Difficult.' She took a bite of the mussels. They were delicious, and she said so.

'Thank you,' he said. 'So, what happened?'

'You know the death at the cathedral?'

'The bloke who fell off the tower?'

She nodded. 'It wasn't an accident. We're sure about that now.'

'You said that someone went up the tower with him.'

'It's not just that.'

She knew that she should keep her mouth shut, but she had been thinking about it all day, and she knew it would help her to relax if she could tell someone else about it, too.

'A video was sent to the *Journal* on the day he died. An old videotape – VHS.'

'Why would that have made him jump?'

'It's a sex tape.'

'With him in it?'

'When he was younger.'

'Oh.'

'That's not all. The boy in it was borderline legal – hard to say, one way or the other. Teenage.'

'Seriously?'

She nodded.

'So why push him off the tower?'

'Maybe he wouldn't pay. Maybe the blackmailer wanted him dead and his reputation ruined. We don't know.'

Charlie rose and cleared the plates away and then replaced them with the main course: baked sea bass with lemon caper dressing. Francine finished her glass and refilled it, Charlie held his out and she topped that up, too.

She swallowed a mouthful. 'That's not all. You mustn't tell anyone *any* of this.'

'I won't.'

'I'm *serious*. I'll be in the shit if anyone finds out.'

'Not a word,' he said. 'Promise.'

She exhaled; talking *was* helping, as was a decent meal. 'There have been two more videos and two more deaths.' She dug into the sea bass. This, too, was excellent, and she felt herself relaxing, even though the subject matter was anything but.

'Shit, Franny.'

'I know. Remember the body in the river yesterday?'

He nodded. 'The guy who drowned.'

'His name was Lucjusz Kajetan. Another video was sent to the *Journal*. The same as before – another sex tape. Teenage girl this time.'

'So he didn't drown?'

'He definitely drowned,' she said. 'But maybe it wasn't an accident. And then we got another tape today. Dominic Hartnett.'

'Who's that?'

'Another MP.'

Charlie's mouth fell open, and he set down his fork.

'I *know*,' she said, 'it's nuts. He died last night in London. They're saying it was a heart attack, but a video was delivered, so it obviously wasn't.'

'Do you have any idea who might have done it?'

'No. None.'

'How do you go about investigating something like that?'

'We look at the victims and see if there's anything in their pasts that might give us an idea about who might have wanted to kill them. Or we try to find out where the videos came from. It looks like they were shot in the same room.' She caught herself; she had already gone too far. 'I can't say anything else about that.'

He took away the empty plates, opened the fridge and, with a melodramatic 'Ta-da!', brought out the dessert: a white chocolate and cardamon tart.

'You didn't buy this from a shop?'

'How dare you,' he said in mock offence. 'Iceland doesn't do these.'

They finished the bottle of wine and took their time over the tart. It looked good and tasted even better.

Francine cut off a slice with her fork, put it in her mouth and savoured it as it dissolved on her tongue. 'You can see why it's messy now?'

'I can.'

'Promise to keep it to yourself?'

He laid his fork down and looked her in the eyes. 'Of course.'

'Because I probably shouldn't have told you.'

Charlie stood, went to the cupboard where Francine kept her alcohol and took out a bottle of whisky. He found the glasses and poured out two generous measures. He brought the glasses back to the table, gave one to her and held the other up for a toast. She touched her glass to his and took a sip; the whisky burned her throat as it slid down into her stomach.

'Thank you for doing this,' she said. 'It's been a tough day. Just what I needed.'

'My pleasure.'

Francine got up and took the plates to the counter. It was a running joke in her family that she was the messiest cook imaginable, with a reputation for leaving her work surfaces strewn with dirty pots and pans and utensils, and smeared with whatever ingredients she was working with; Charlie, by contrast, had cleaned up as he worked, and there was no sign that he had prepared a meal for them both at all.

'I was going to do the washing up,' she said, 'but you've done that, too.'

He shrugged. 'I can't stand leaving a mess.'

She went to the table, sank what was left of her whisky and reached down for his hand. 'There must be another way I can thank you,' she said.

PART IV
THURSDAY

53

Atticus had intended to go to Mack's overnight but found that he wasn't in the mood. He worked until three, studying the papers he had copied in the hope of finding something that might now be cast in a different light, and then – disappointed with his lack of progress – retreated to bed, where he managed a couple of hours of unsatisfactory sleep. He woke just before dawn, decided that he might as well get up and get started again.

He made himself a cup of strong black coffee and took the mug to his desk. After connecting his phone to his computer, he set about copying across the photographs that he had taken of the documents that were being used in the investigation. He hadn't had the luxury of time when going through the boxes, and, apart from the fact that the photographs had been hastily taken and were often badly framed, he knew that there would be plenty that he had missed, either because he was rushing or because he didn't know that they would be relevant. He would need Mack's help with that.

He navigated to the folder where he had stored the digital copies of the videotapes that had been delivered to the *Journal*. He had been unable to quieten his mind, his thoughts continually returning to the three dead men. It was possible that one might have killed himself in shame or through fear of being exposed, but not two and certainly not all three. They had been murdered, and he was sure it was Jack. There had to be something that would give him a clue as to what had happened and, with little else to go on, Atticus knew that his best chance of making a breakthrough lay in the footage.

Atticus double-clicked on Campbell's video and watched it. It was unpleasant, but he forced himself to watch every frame in the hope that something might give him an angle he could pursue. He got to the end of the footage and let it run. There was a minute of static that filled the screen before it disappeared, to be replaced by black. He reached for his mouse but then decided not to stop the playback. The entire tape had been digitised and, with nothing else presenting itself, he settled back in the chair and kept his eyes on the screen in the event that there might be something else that had been missed. The black continued, interrupted intermittently by flashes of static and horizontal bars that rolled from the top of the screen to the bottom. Atticus kept watching, occasionally nudging the mouse to bring up the counter so that he could gauge how long he had left.

Ten minutes went past.

Twenty minutes.

The city awoke. Atticus heard traffic passing on the street outside the window but ignored it, his attention fixed on the monitor.

An hour passed, and then an hour and a half.

He could have fast-forwarded through it all, but that would be a shortcut that might not be worth taking. It was a long shot that he would find anything, but he had little else to go on, and he didn't want to miss something because of his impatience.

Three hours passed before he got to the end.

Nothing.

Atticus double-clicked to close the player and got up.

Bandit was sitting behind him, patiently waiting for his walk.

'Come on,' Atticus said. 'We both need some fresh air.'

54

Mack made her way into the meeting space that had been chosen for the morning's press conference. It had been hastily arranged, but, despite the short notice, the room was full of journalists from the press and TV. The leaking of the news of Dominic Hartnett's death – and its possible connection with the murder of Richard Miller – had meant that the media caravan had decamped to Salisbury for the third time in two years.

Mack had delivered the briefings on the previous occasions and, although she was relieved that the responsibility had been passed to Murphy this time, she still felt a burn of irritation that the Met had muscled on to their patch and taken charge of an investigation that should have remained with local officers. She shared Atticus's annoyance in that regard, but, whereas he was unable to keep his anger to himself, she would bite her tongue and let Murphy get on with things. It had been difficult enough to advance in her career as far and as fast as she had, and she didn't want to torpedo her prospects by giving Murphy or Beckton any reason to be aggrieved with her.

The two men came into the room together. Mack had seen Mary Winkworth, the constabulary's media liaison, in the room that the two officers had used for preparation and knew that they would have been primed with answers for the most obvious questions that would be received. There wasn't very much that they would be able to discuss, and Mack had wondered about the good sense of having the conference at all, but it had been decided that something had to be said, even if it would be obvious under even the gentlest questioning that they had nothing substantial to go on by way of a lead.

A table had been set up with two seats behind it. Beckton took the seat to the left and Murphy the seat to the right.

'Hello, everyone,' Beckton began. 'Thank you for joining us today. I'm Chief Superintendent Beckton from Wiltshire Police and I'm here with my colleague Detective Chief Superintendent Lee Murphy from the Metropolitan Police. What I intend to do today is read out a short statement of the facts as we know them so far. We will then be available for some brief questions.'

He took a sip of water from the glass on the table, cleared his throat and then continued.

'Just after midnight on Tuesday, officers from the Metropolitan Police were called to a flat in the Fulham area of London. The body of a fifty-five-year-old man was found at the scene. A Home Office post-mortem was carried out this morning and police are now treating the incident as suspicious. Formal identification has been carried out by the family of the deceased, and I can confirm that it is Dominic Hartnett, the member of Parliament for Devizes. You will be aware that the member of Parliament for Salisbury, Richard Miller, was murdered six weeks ago. Although we have yet to demonstrate a link between the two deaths, we are proceeding on the basis that they might be connected. I'd like to hand over to DCS Murphy now – he's a member of the Metropolitan Police's anti-terror task force and is responsible for the investigation of these two deaths.'

Murphy thanked Beckton and leaned forward so that he could speak into the microphone.

'Thank you, Chief Superintendent.' He cleared his throat and Mack saw, with satisfaction, that he was nervous. 'I've been in Salisbury working on the investigation into Mr Miller's death for the last few weeks. The death of Mr Hartnett is suspicious, and I want to assure everyone that it will receive the closest possible scrutiny. We are examining the last few weeks of both men's lives in the event that we might be able to find a connection. Obviously, Mr Hartnett's death is very recent and our enquiries have only started in the last few hours. Mr Miller's death – his murder – was some time ago and, as you would expect, things are a little more advanced on that front.'

There was a shout from one of the journalists. 'So who did it?'

'We don't know that at this time,' Murphy said. 'As I say, Mr Hartnett was only found during Tuesday night and the initial suggestion was that he had passed away from natural causes. That may not be the case, hence we are now treating his death as suspicious.'

'Why? What made you change your mind?'

'I'm not able to discuss that at the moment,' Murphy fenced.

'Don't you think the public should be told?'

'Not at the risk of jeopardising an ongoing investigation. We'll provide additional information when the time is right to do so.'

'Who did it?' asked another reporter.

'We don't know,' Murphy said.

'You must have *some* idea,' the same journalist called back. 'Or a lead, or *something*.'

'As I say,' Murphy repeated patiently, 'it's very early in the investigation. We have several lines of enquiry that we are looking to pursue, but you'll understand when I say that we're unable to go into any detail on them now. However, there is one appeal that I would like to make. We would like to speak to the person who has been in contact with a local man, Mr Atticus Priest. This person, who uses the name "Jack" when speaking to him, had information regarding the death of Mr Miller, and we believe he might also have information on the deaths of Mr Hartnett and two local men – David Campbell and Lucjusz Kajetan. We would ask him to make contact with police.' Murphy gave a nod. 'Thank you. We're happy to take a few more questions.'

A forest of hands shot up. Murphy pointed to a woman at the front of the room.

'You mentioned the two local men who died this week.' She looked at her notes. 'Campbell and Kajetan. What can you tell us about them?'

'We're not in a position to speculate upon that,' Murphy said.

'What about James York and Alfred Burns? The police investigation into their deaths suggested that they were involved with Miller. What's going on here, Mr Murphy? It doesn't feel as if we've been given anything like the full picture.'

'I've told you everything I'm able to say at the moment.'

'That might be so, but it's not going to fill local people with much confidence, is it? I've lost count of the number of murders that have happened in the city during the last two years – this is the third time I've been back here in that time. It's *Salisbury*, not the Bronx.'

Beckton leaned into the microphone. 'It's true that there have been a series of deaths here. There are no two ways about it – we've been unlucky. But I can say with confidence that the murders in Grovely Woods have nothing to do with the deaths that we are investigating now.'

'And the murders at Imber?'

'We can't comment on that at the moment,' Murphy said.

A reporter whom Mack recognised from before put up his hand. 'What about the videos?'

The surprise was evident on Murphy's face. 'Sorry?'

'Have you read the paper this morning?'

'No,' Murphy said. 'Sorry. Who are you?'

'Ian Bird from the *Sun*. We received a video last night that we understand was also sent to the Salisbury *Journal*. A man who looks very much like Mr Campbell is shown having sex with a teenage boy. Could you comment on that?'

Murphy took a moment to gather himself.

'DCS Murphy?' Bird pressed. 'You must've seen the video?'

'I can't comment on anything beyond what has been said already.'

'We ran a still from it in the paper this morning. I can let you have a copy afterwards if you'd like.'

The offer raised laughter from the other reporters.

Both officers were obviously uncomfortable and, with a look over at Winkworth, they pushed back their chairs and stood.

Winkworth came to stand in front of the table, covering the officers as they made their retreat. 'Thank you for coming,' she said. 'You all have my number. Please do call if there's anything else that you need.'

Mack got up and made for the exit with the others.

'DCI Jones, hang on a minute.'

Mack turned and saw that Bird was hurrying to reach her. Mack had found him charming and completely untrustworthy during their previous interactions, his cheerfulness a mask that he used to disguise the fact that he was an ambitious snake who had been working her in the hope that her guard might slip and he might learn something useful.

'*That* was a waste of time,' he said.

'Not much to say at the moment.'

'What about the video?'

'Can't comment on that.'

'Look. I've got it here.'

His phone was in his hand. He tapped the screen and showed it to her before she could get away. She looked down: it was a still of the room that had become familiar from the three videos. Campbell was on the bed, looking right into the camera.

'We only ran the still,' Bird said, 'but the video is disgusting.'

'How did you get it?'

'Can't say.'

'You need to speak to DCS Murphy about that.'

'We will,' Bird said. 'My editor tried to speak to him earlier. Can you give me *any* idea what's going on?'

She shook her head. 'Nothing more than what you just heard.'

'There's other footage, isn't there?'

'Why would you say that?'

'There was a message with the video. It said that if we ran this, we'd get more.'

Mack didn't want to have to lie, but she couldn't very well confirm that he was right. She smiled in a way that she hoped included a little innocent nonchalance and shrugged. 'I can't talk about the case. You really will have to speak to DCS Murphy.' The queue shuffled forward enough for Mack to spy a way out and, with a cheerful farewell, she passed through the door and used her key card to swipe open the door that led to CID.

55

Mack went back to the nick and was shanghaied by Beckton's secretary as soon as she stepped through the door.

'Boss wants to see you upstairs.'

Mack wasn't surprised in the slightest and took a moment in the bathroom to compose herself before taking the lift. Beckton was a proud man, and he wouldn't have enjoyed being caught on the hop like that. Mack didn't know Murphy at all, but it had been obvious that he had also found the experience of being surprised in front of the press to be an excruciating one. The two of them would be looking for someone to blame and, as Mack's father had often been fond of saying, 'shit runs downhill.'

She braced herself and knocked on the door.

'Come.'

She went inside. Beckton was sitting behind his desk, and Murphy was pacing.

'How did he know about the tapes?' Murphy said.

Mack closed the door behind her. 'He says the one with Campbell was sent to them.'

'You spoke to him?'

'He grabbed me on the way out.'

'Do you know him?'

'Not really. He covered the Imber enquiry.'

'And?'

'And he says it came with a message promising more if they ran it. His editor has been trying to speak to us.'

'No one spoke to *me*,' Murphy said.

'Or me,' Beckton said.

The door opened and Beckton's secretary appeared with a copy of the *Sun* in her hand. Beckton thanked her, took the newspaper and opened it to pages two and three. He laid it out on the desk so that they could all see it. The top half of the left-hand page was taken up with a still image that she recognised from the first video: Campbell's grinning face was frozen, his eyes sparkling as he looked into the camera, the red light behind him lending him even more of a demonic aspect.

Murphy threw his hands up. 'How can they just run that?'

'I know,' Beckton said. 'They've crossed a line. The CPS can deal with it.'

Murphy stabbed a finger against the photograph. 'How did they get it?' He turned to Mack. '*How?*'

'I have no idea.'

'*Speculate.*'

'Like I said . . . it was sent to them last—'

'I know it was sent, but by whom?'

'I think it's obvious.'

'Yes,' Murphy said, staring at her. 'I agree. Your boyfriend.'

Beckton looked from Murphy to Mack and back again. 'What?'

Murphy stared at her. 'Tell him.'

Mack took a breath. 'Fine,' she said. 'I'm in a relationship with Atticus. I'm sure DCS Murphy will say it's an abuse of my position, and perhaps it is, but I'd suggest that it might be better to save that discussion for another day rather than have it distract us now.'

Beckton held her eye and then nodded. 'I agree. But, just for the record, and just so it's clear, you've never given me a reason to doubt your professionalism.'

'Thank you, sir.'

He looked to Murphy. 'And you might want to think carefully before you impugn the reputation of one of my senior officers.'

Mack thought for a moment that Murphy was going to insist that they discuss her behaviour there and then, but – perhaps because of Beckton's vote of confidence, or perhaps because he recognised that she was right, and they couldn't afford the diversion – he muttered something under his breath and shook his head.

'Well?' Beckton said. 'Could it have been him? He strikes me as the sort of man who'll throw his toys out of the pram if he doesn't get his own way.'

Mack knew Atticus well enough to know that his hand was rarely stayed by whatever he had been told to do or not do, and, although she doubted he would do anything to damage the investigation, he could go off-piste if he disagreed with a decision and thought that he knew best. Could he have been frustrated with the pace or direction of the investigation and decided to take things into his own hands? She really hoped not.

'No,' she said. 'He wouldn't do that.'

'Who, then?'

'The *Journal*?' Beckton suggested.

Mack shook her head. 'Doesn't make sense. They're desperate to break the story themselves. Why would they let themselves be scooped?'

'No,' Mack said. 'It's not Atticus and it's not anyone on my team, and it's not the *Journal*. It's him. *Jack*. He's upped the ante. Things aren't going as fast as he wants, so he's changed his tactics.'

'Maybe,' Murphy said.

'Probably,' Mack corrected him.

'And we think this is him?' Beckton said. 'Jack, I mean?'

'Atticus does,' Mack replied.

Beckton turned to her. 'Call the *Sun* and tell them we need to see what they've been sent.'

'Yes, sir.'

Murphy turned back to Beckton, putting his back to Mack and ignoring her as if she weren't there. 'We'll have to decide when we can make it public.'

Mack went out into the corridor and set off for the CID room. She would call the newspaper, but, before that, she needed to speak to Atticus.

56

Atticus found it difficult to keep his attention on the screen. His eyelids had grown heavy from lack of sleep and, as he blinked them to try to stay awake, the footage on the Kajetan tape ran to the end and stopped.

He froze.

He blinked.

He didn't know if he had imagined it, but he thought he had seen something just before the tape ran out. Reaching for his mouse, he scrubbed back for ten seconds and pressed play. He stared hard at the screen; there was nothing of interest, just more of the unending black that had taunted him for the last three hours. The counter ticked up to the end, and then, just a moment before it came to a stop, something new *was* there: a woman standing on a balcony and, behind her, a row of houses.

His eyes were tired. He rubbed them.

Atticus scrubbed back again and clicked play, waited until he got to the footage and then hit pause. The clip was short and contained little other than the woman smiling at the camera and a bird flying over the tops of the houses. He selected the start and end of the clip and copied it, then uploaded it to YouTube, not because he intended to publish it but because it made it easier to use the

FFmpeg tool to break it down into a collection of still images that would be clearer to examine than the video itself.

The length of the clip was just under a second, and the tool turned the video into thirty-two still images. The shot jerked a little to the left and right, suggesting that the camera had been handheld when the footage was taken. Atticus examined the still images one by one in an attempt to find anything useful that might have appeared in only one of them, but, despite the small variations in the field of vision, there was nothing useful.

He selected the image with the greatest clarity, printed it out and laid it on his desk. He took his magnifying glass from its sleeve and subjected the printout to a minute examination. The image had been taken from the third or fourth storey of a building and showed the street outside and the buildings opposite. He saw a row of apartment buildings with black balconies and one with an extruding bay window that had been painted white. The buildings were of varying heights and designs, with unusual tiled roofs that did not look like the sort that would have been used in the UK.

Somewhere in Europe?

He could see a much larger and more modern building behind the terrace, and, beyond that, a blue sky criss-crossed with aircraft contrails. The foreground of the image included a white car, a sign from an estate agent, an unusual cast-iron lamp that was attached to one of the buildings, the number of one of the properties – 62 – and a pavement that had been laid with some sort of dark grey stone slabs. The street appeared to be narrow, without trees or free-standing street lamps.

Atticus copied the most noticeable features of the image – the polished wooden door, the extruding white bay window, the balconies – and ran them through a reverse-image look-up. The results provided nothing useful.

He enlarged the licence plate of the car. The letters and numerals were not discernible, but he was able to see that they were dark red in colour. Atticus opened a browser and navigated to a website dedicated to licence and registration plates found all around the world. He selected Europe, then went through the countries until he found a match; Belgium was the only country that he could find that used that particular colouring. It wasn't conclusive, but it was a start.

He went out to the kitchen and boiled the kettle.

While he waited, he went back to his screen and focused on the estate agent's sign. It was attached to the wall at ground level and, when he enlarged it, he was able to make out part of a business name, a phone number and a word in French – VENDU – that added to his suspicions that the picture was taken in Belgium. He opened another browser and searched the phone number, bringing up a website for Calao Consulting, a real estate agency based in Brussels. The name and logo matched what he could see on the sign.

Belgium.

Brussels.

He was getting somewhere.

He heard the kettle click off and went back to the kitchen, then made a cup of strong black coffee and took it to his desk. Bandit was waiting for him, his tail wagging and his lead in his mouth. Atticus scrubbed him on the back of the head, took a slurp of coffee and sat back down.

He visited the agency's website and saw that the business had only a single office in the Forest district of the city. That was helpful; he doubted that they would work on properties that were outside of their patch. He looked at the properties on their website now and plotted them on a map, showing the districts of Uccle, Forest, Anderlecht and Sint-Jans Molenbeek. He opened Street View and wandered through those areas, finding that they often included dark metal balconies and buildings that had been constructed with similar materials.

His quick scout did confirm that the streets in Brussels were unusual for often having a distinct style of street lamp that varied from district to district. The variation was *so* distinct that an open-air museum had been established to celebrate the various styles. He visited the museum's website and spent half an hour reviewing the contents. He saw the ornate nineteenth-century lanterns that were prevalent in the older parts of town, the bronze gas lamps that could be found in Schaerbeek, and the orange 1970s orbs that had been installed on the outskirts.

He returned to Street View and examined the areas that were served by the agency. He looked for the street lamps and saw that in neighbourhoods like Forest, with broad streets and newer buildings, they were not fixed to the sides of the properties and were more modern in design. It was only in the more densely built areas in the middle of the city that they were found on the buildings; these areas had similar designs, too.

Atticus narrowed down his search to the area around Barrière de Saint-Gilles. It was easy from that point, and it only took him another ten minutes to locate the particular lamp, the dark glossy door and the house that was marked with 62.

He rotated the camera and looked back at the building from which the video must have been taken: 75 Albaniëstraat.

It was a four-storey building with two large windows on each floor, a narrow sliver that was jammed in between a similarly narrow building to its right and a larger neighbour to its left. The bricks had been painted magnolia and its door and window frames were made from varnished wood.

Atticus dragged the mouse to angle the camera and looked up at the two windows on the top floor. The video had been shot there – he was certain of it – and now all he needed to know was by whom.

57

Max Mason gazed into the camera and delivered the same closing lines that had made him famous: 'Thank you very much, ladies and germs. *I've* been Max Mason; *you've* been amazing. I'll see you again next time for more . . .'

The audience roared out: '*Couples Clash!*'

Mason bowed. 'Good night!'

He waved and held his smile until his cheeks ached. He waited until the floor manager counted down from three and announced that they were out.

The audience continued to applaud.

Mason clapped them, turning through a half circle so that they were all included. 'Thank you,' he called up to them. 'Thank you. You were easily the best audience we had today.'

Laughter rolled down from the gallery, the audience humouring a joke that he had used on countless occasions in the past. They had recorded two episodes of the show this morning and the audience had been the same for both.

Mason made his way to the side of the studio. His assistant, Clara, was waiting with a bottle of water.

'How'd I do?' he asked her.

'You were brilliant. They loved it.'

He cranked off the top of the bottle and took a swig. 'I would've loved for them to have won the jackpot.'

'I can't believe they didn't get it.'

'I know. How long is an Olympic swimming pool – who doesn't know that?'

'What did they say? Twenty-five metres?'

'Twenty-five metres,' he confirmed. 'Come on. Ridiculous. That cost them thirty grand. Thirty! They were kicking themselves – I almost felt bad for them.' He set off towards the backstage area, and Clara followed. 'I *definitely* felt bad for us – would've been great telly.'

Bob Nicholls, the floor manager, was waiting by the door. 'Good job, Max. Two good ones in the can.'

Mason gave a heavy theatrical sigh. 'And back tomorrow for another two.'

'You love it.'

He winked. 'I love what they pay me.'

The studio had been constructed within what had once been an old warehouse on the banks of the Thames. Max's production company had purchased it forty years ago when it had been ready to fall into the river, and he had gambled by sinking every last penny in his name into the renovation. It had been the shrewdest thing that he had ever done. *Couples Clash* had shown signs of promise, but it was only when he'd moved the recording here that its success had really taken off. Mason had gone from having nothing to his name but a speculative project in an unseemly part of the city to having a beautiful new studio and a contract that had paid him more every time it had been renewed. And, what was more, the area around the studio had been gentrified in the same way as all the other run-down ex-industrial quarters in London, with the result that the property, bought for a song, was now worth thirty million.

The studio itself was a large open space with four rows of raked seating that surrounded the contestants' chairs and the lectern from which Mason presided over affairs. Each audience was composed of three hundred members of the public who had been given a seat by way of a raffle. The contestants were picked from the audience in a process that was reputed to be random, but which was anything but. They had quotas to meet, and each episode was sure to include the necessary demographic qualities to ensure that all the relevant boxes were ticked. That was something that had changed during Mason's career, and he wasn't sure it was for the best.

The backstage area was a warren of corridors that led to the production suite, storage areas and changing rooms.

Mason gestured for Clara to keep up. 'What have you got for me?'

She walked briskly to match his pace. 'They want you on *This Morning* to discuss the retrospective.'

'When?'

'Next Wednesday.'

'Am I free?'

'You are.'

'Book it in. Next?'

'The People's Choice Awards are next week. A little bird tells me you're going to get a gong.'

'For what?'

'Quiz show.'

'Who's getting the Bruce Forsyth Award?'

'Ant and Dec.'

'Tell them I can't make it.' They turned the corner and arrived at the door to his dressing room. 'Anything else?'

'Corporate gig for Vodafone.'

'Fee?'

'Hundred thousand.'

'Do it. Next.'

'The BBC asked if you'd do a vox pop for a show they're doing with Jonathan Ross.'

'Can't stand him, not interested. Next.'

She put her phone away. 'That's it.'

'Good. Thank you. What do I have on for the rest of the day?'

She took the phone out again. 'Lunch with Mic at the Ritz and dinner with George at Nobu.'

'Good,' he said. 'I'd forgotten about that.'

'I've left a suit and a clean shirt on the hook inside. The car's coming to get you in an hour.'

Mason went into the dressing room and closed the door behind him. He had a rule that he was not to be disturbed when the door was closed. This was his sanctuary, a space where he could relax after however many hours he had just spent pandering to the public. The false jollity, the catchphrases, the legendary rapport with the audience that was supposed to be natural, but which was, in fact, just one more pretence from a career that had been built on a stack of them; the whole thing was exhausting. He took off his jacket and the shirt that had grown damp with sweat after he had stood underneath the stage lights all morning. He removed the rest of his clothes and showered, drying himself off with a monogrammed towel and then pulling on the robe with the same mark – the intertwined Ms – on the breast pocket.

His backstage requirements were modest: a pot of fresh tea and the day's newspapers. He had flicked through the broadsheets before recording started this morning, leaving him with the trashy red-tops. The teapot had been refilled with a fresh brew; Mason poured himself a cup and took it, and the papers, to the sofa on the other side of the room.

Clara went through the papers before giving them to Mason every morning and marked anything that she thought might be relevant with sticky tabs: yellow tabs were stories that mentioned him, while red tabs were those that mentioned people on the list that Mason provided to Clara, usually rivals whom Mason enjoyed seeing in difficulty. There had been nothing of note in the broadsheets and only a handful in the tabloids.

He checked the yellows first: a sniffy review of his autobiography; a short article trailing the anniversary of *Couples Clash* that was due to run over the weekend; a recipe for pulled pork that he had provided to one of the supplements; an account of his sponsored cycle ride around the country that had raised six million for charities. There were more red tabs than yellow today, and he finished his tea while enjoying the travails of celebrities and other public figures who had attracted his ire over the course of his career.

He picked up the *Sun* and was flipping through to the single red tab when he glanced at the photograph that accompanied a story on pages two and three. He was about to turn the page when something in the photograph caught his attention. It looked like a still from a video, with a room that was lit with deep red light. There was a bed in the centre of the shot with a topless man sitting on it.

Mason felt a queasiness that came out of nowhere. He read the headline:

SEX TAPE SENSATION OF CATHEDRAL DEATH MAN

Mason stared back down at the still image. It didn't look as if it had been taken recently.

There was a knock on the door.

Mason quickly closed the newspaper and tossed it on top of the others. 'What is it?'

It was Clara. 'Just checking you're getting ready. The car will be outside in ten minutes.'

'I'll be ready,' he said.

Mason stared across at the paper and felt the pinprick of pressure in his temples that always heralded one of his headaches. He closed his eyes until the pressure eased and then got up. He couldn't deal with that now. He needed to have lunch with his agent and then meet his son for dinner. He hadn't seen George for weeks, and the last thing he wanted was to spoil the evening by worrying about something that was probably, he hoped, a fuss about nothing.

But, even as he told himself that, Mason knew that the image was a problem and that it was not going to be something that he would easily forget.

58

Atticus wiped down Bandit's muddy paws, filled his bowl with biscuits and changed his water, and then went back to his desk. He navigated back to the folder where he had placed the three videos and double-clicked on the file with the footage that he had been examining.

His phone rang. He picked it up, expecting to see that Mack was calling, but didn't recognise the number. It was probably a marketing call, so he killed it and put the phone down.

He pressed play.

The phone rang again.

Atticus grabbed it. 'I'm not interested.'

'That's no way to speak to an old friend.' He froze.

The voice was disguised, like before, but Atticus knew: it was Jack.

He put the call on the phone's speaker. 'You've been quiet.'

'I've been busy.'

'I'm sure you have.'

'See the press conference?'

Atticus took a digital recorder from the cubbyhole underneath the surface of the desk. 'I did.'

'They want me to get in contact with them.' Jack chuckled. 'Why would I want to do a thing like that?'

Atticus hit the button on the device to record and put it down next to the phone. 'It was you, then? Campbell and Lucjusz and Hartnett? You killed them?'

'They got what they deserved. They're dead *and* everyone knows what they did. I know you might not agree, but *I* think that's justice.'

'Are we going to find anyone else?'

'I told you, didn't I? The last time we spoke.'

Atticus pushed the recorder a little closer to the phone. 'I can remember exactly what you said. I asked if it was just York and Burns, and you said that there were others.'

'And I'll get to them all eventually.'

'Wouldn't it be easier to just tell the police?'

There was anger in Jack's reply. 'They can't be trusted. They didn't help then and they won't help now. Nothing has changed. I thought we agreed on that.'

'They'll find you in the end. You'll make a mistake and they'll find you.'

'Probably. But I'm *good*.'

'Are you?'

'You have no idea who I am, do you?'

'I don't.'

'I have the deepest respect for you, Atticus, and if *you* can't find me, well . . . I'm not likely to lose sleep over the police, am I?' He paused, then chuckled again. 'Listen to me. So rude. I hope you don't think I'm insulting your girlfriend.'

The reference to Mack and their relationship was deliberate: *I know all about you.* It was a tactic that he had used on their previous call, too.

Atticus ignored it. 'Tell me about the videos.'

'What do you want to know?'

'Where did you find them?'

'Do you remember Derek Burns?'

'Alf's brother. He disappeared.'

'He knew that they'd come after him, so he ran and took them as insurance. But he was an amateur. He wasn't hard to find.'

'"*Wasn't*"? Past tense?'

'He knew what Alf had done, and he did nothing about it. That made him culpable.'

'You killed him?'

There was no answer. Atticus went to the window and looked out on to the street. There was no sign of anyone there.

'How many tapes do you have?'

'More.'

'Where are they?'

Jack tutted. 'No, no, no – *that's* not going to happen. I need them. How long do you think it'll be before the police talk about what's on the tapes? About the red room?'

'I don't know.'

'Soon. They're stuck, and they'll have to appeal for help. They'll describe the room and hope that someone will come forward and say that they were there, that they know where it is. Can you imagine how anyone who's ever been there will feel? They'll *panic*.' He chuckled. 'They'll lose their shit. It'll be in their heads all day and all night. They won't be able to sleep. They won't be able to kiss their wives or hug their kids without thinking it might be the last time. I don't have a tape for everyone who's ever been inside, but *they* won't know that.'

A line of cars had formed up outside, with cars trying to exit the multistorey car park and others jammed up against the two sets of lights that stood between them and Brown Street.

'You're the only one smart enough to stop me,' Jack continued, 'but I don't think you will.'

'Is that right?'

'You hated Burns. Why do you think I got in touch with you in the first place? You knew there was a risk that he'd wriggle free, and he did. That's what I mean – the police can't be trusted even when they do mean well. Don't tell me that the thought hasn't crossed your mind that this way – *my* way – is better. I give them what they deserve. I punish them for the things that they did.'

'There's a line between justice and vengeance.'

'*Boring*, Atticus. You don't believe that, and neither do I. Their guilt isn't in question. It's right there on the screen. And you know what makes it worse? They would've forgotten about the children they hurt as soon as they'd finished with them. They used them and tossed them aside like it'd never happened. Not a second's thought. They wouldn't have lost sleep then, would they? Now they will.'

The queue started to move.

'What do you want?'

'Just to speak to you. What I do can be lonely.'

'You still haven't told me *why* you're doing it.'

'Isn't it obvious?'

Atticus was looking up at the multistorey car park when he thought he saw a shadow moving across the roof. He grabbed his phone and ran for the door, startling Bandit into thinking that he was about to get a bonus walk. With an apologetic 'Stay, boy,' to Bandit, he let himself out, pulling the door shut behind him. He took the stairs two at a time, fumbled with the lock and, once he had got the door open, barrelled out into the passage and then the street.

There were two flights of stairs that offered access to the five floors of the multistorey; Atticus thought that the figure he had seen had headed towards Exeter Street, so he went right, dodging between two cars and then skipping back as a motorcyclist had to skid to a halt to avoid hitting him. There was a cacophony of horns behind him as Atticus shouldered the door open and started to climb; he took the stairs two at a time and then, when his thighs started to burn, just one. He was gasping for breath when he reached the top floor, shoved the kick bar to open the door and staggered out into the cold early-morning air. A car was pulling out of a space on the other side of the roof; Atticus ran for it but saw that it was driven by an old lady who gaped fearfully at him as she went down the ramp. There were a dozen other cars, but none were occupied, and there was no one else save him on the roof.

He went to the spot where he thought he had seen the figure. It was directly opposite his window and, as he looked down, he saw that Bandit had clambered onto the sofa and was looking out, perhaps wondering where his master had disappeared to in such a hurry. Atticus looked left and right and saw nothing; he looked down and spotted a pair of footprints that had been left on the damp concrete and the smouldering end of a cigarette.

He remembered that he was still clutching his phone. He looked at the screen and saw that the call had ended. He was still looking at it when an incoming text was announced with a buzz and a chime.

NOT YET. WAIT UNTIL I'VE FINISHED.

59

Mason would have liked to have gone straight back to Wiltshire, but he had a long-standing lunch appointment with his agent that he couldn't postpone. Mic had booked them a table at the Ritz, knowing that it was one of Mason's favourite places to eat, and was waiting for him as the endlessly deferential maître d' accompanied him to the back of the room.

She stood, beaming at him as he approached. 'Max, so good to see you. How are you?'

'Good,' he said, thanking the maître d' as he pulled out a chair for him.

The man put his hands together in an expression that managed to look particularly obsequious. 'Your usual?'

Mason was thirsty and the thought of something alcoholic was tempting after the discovery that he had just made. 'Yes, please.'

Mason tried to pay attention as Mic ran through the news that she was obviously excited to deliver. She was gleeful, announcing a slew of potential new endorsements that would amount to several million pounds over the lifetime of the deals; Mason was perfunctory in his enthusiasm, his mind fixed on what he had read in the newspaper. He couldn't stop his thoughts drifting back to the picture and what it might mean.

'What is it, Max?'

He looked up. 'What?'

'You don't seem pleased.'

Mason managed to force a smile. 'I'm sorry. I *am* pleased – *delighted*. I've got a couple of things on my mind, that's all.'

'Anything I can help you with?'

'It's just something at home. It's all under control.'

The waiter arrived at the table with their drinks: Mic had a glass of Krug, while Mason took a tall glass with the drink he always ordered when he came here: a Bull Shot, combining vodka, sherry and vegetable juice with herbs, sauces and spices.

Mic raised her glass. 'Cheers, then.'

'Cheers,' Mason said. 'And, really, thank you – I can see you've been working hard on all this, and I'm grateful.'

He tried to be more present for the rest of the meal but was relieved when the plates were cleared away and he was able to make his excuses and leave. He called his chauffeur, Steve, and told him that he was ready to be picked up and, after thanking Mic again, he left cash on the table to cover the bill and made his way outside to where his Bentley Flying Spur was waiting.

Steve got out and opened the door. 'Back home, sir?'

'Yes,' he said, then added, 'just give me five minutes. I need to make a quick call.'

He walked in the direction of Green Park and found a quiet alley off Piccadilly where he would be able to make the call without being bothered by anyone who might recognise him. He found the number and tapped the screen to dial it, putting the phone to his ear as he walked a little deeper into the alley.

Harry Summers picked up at once. '*Max*, this is a surprise.'

'Is it?'

'Yes – why would you say that? We don't have anything in the diary for you, do we?'

'I need to see you.'

'OK. Where are you?'

'London.'

'I'm afraid I'm at the house in Wiltshire—'

'I'm coming back this afternoon,' Mason said, cutting across him. 'I'll be there around five. Make sure you're in. This can't wait.'

60

Mack had been at the nick all day, working with Murphy to ensure that his team had everything they needed as they formally took over the investigation into the death of Miller; they also took responsibility for the deaths of Campbell, Kajetan and Hartnett. Mack had already formed an opinion of Murphy as someone with an unfortunate mix of bombast and incompetence, and the time they spent together only reinforced that. He swanned around the CID room, dispensing instructions with an air of easy superiority, oblivious to the fact that most of the things he wanted doing had either already been done or were in hand. He made no effort to smooth over the friction that had been caused by him taking control; Mack had watched her team with pride as they got on with their work without complaint. They would convene in the pub after work to put the world to rights, and none of the London interlopers would be invited. Mack decided that she would take the initiative and arrange the drinks herself.

She was composing a WhatsApp message to the others when her phone rang with an incoming call. She checked the screen, saw that it was Atticus and went into the bathroom so she could take it in private.

'What's up?'

'I need to see you.'

'What is it?'

'Not on the phone.'

'I'm really busy, Atticus.'

There was a manic edge to his voice that suggested he was having – or about to have – an episode. Mack could have asked him to explain why he needed to see her, but she knew him well enough to know that that would make him impatient, and that he would become more and more insistent until she gave in.

'I *need* to see you. He called me.'

'What? Who?'

'*Jack.*'

'When?'

'Just now.'

'Shit.'

'There's something else, too. Maybe more important. But you need to come here.'

'OK, OK. I'm coming.'

'Come *now*, Mack – I'm serious. I've made a breakthrough.'

61

Mack went through the passageway to the courtyard at the back of the building and climbed the metal steps so that she could knock on the door that led into Atticus's bedroom. She was rewarded with a bark from Bandit before the dog moved the curtain out of the way and pressed his damp nose against the glass; Atticus followed soon after, cursing as he tripped over something in his way.

He opened the door. 'What took you so long?'

'I came as soon as I could,' she said.

He stepped aside and gestured that she should come in. 'I've got something to show you in the office.'

Atticus went through with Mack following and Bandit trotting alongside. Mack's heart sank as she saw that Atticus had made a dreadful mess: there were papers strewn across the desk and the floor, splayed-open ring binders on the table, and the whiteboards had been wiped clean and then filled again with notes that made no sense, decipherable only to a mind like Atticus's. He was standing by the desk, his hands opening and closing, his eyes blinking a little more often than normal, and his jaw clenching and unclenching. She had seen him like this before; he was on the precipice of an episode.

'Have you taken your pills?'

'Not today.'

'You know you need—'

'Forgot. Too busy. And I needed everything sharp and focused. The pills slow me down.'

'They also stop you from ending up in hospital. Where are they? In the bathroom?'

'Never mind them. I need to show you this.'

'I'm not looking at *anything* until you take them.'

She opened the door and started to cross the landing to the bathroom.

'*Fine,*' Atticus said after her. 'In the cabinet above the sink.'

Mack found the plastic bottle of Prozac that bore a label with his details. She had googled to learn how the pills might be helping him and learned that some doctors believed it gave those on the spectrum a better chance of controlling their impulsiveness. She opened the bottle, tipped out two pills and carried them, together with a glass that she filled with water at the sink, back into the office.

'Take them now, or I'm going back to the nick.'

He muttered under his breath but put the pills in his mouth. Mack stood, her arms crossed, and waited until he drank from the glass and then, giving her an ironic shrug, opened his mouth so that she could confirm that he had swallowed the pills.

'Happy?'

'Go on, then – start with Jack.'

'He called me. Disguised his voice again, like last time. He said he killed the three of them, that there are more and that he isn't going to stop. I recorded the call. I'll play it to you.'

He dug a recorder out from underneath a pile of papers, switched it on and played back the call. Mack listened intently. It was the first time that she had heard Jack's voice and, even though it was distorted, she felt an immediacy that she hadn't felt when Atticus had recounted their first call.

Atticus went to the window and pointed across the street to the car park. 'He was there. He was watching me.'

'Did you see him?'

'He was gone by the time I got there, but he was definitely there. He texted me. Look.'

He handed her his phone and showed her the message.

'I found this, too.'

Atticus held out a small plastic freezer bag. Mack looked at it and saw the dog-end of a cigarette.

'How do you know that was his?'

'It was still lit when I got there. It'll be worth testing for forensics.'

She took the bag. 'I'll get that done.' She pointed to the recorder. 'I'll need to take that, too. Murphy will want to listen to it.'

'Fine,' Atticus said.

She looked at him curiously. He would normally have grumbled about that but had agreed as if it was of trifling importance. She could see that whatever it was he had discovered was exciting him much more than the conversation with Jack.

'Go on, then,' she said. 'What else is there?'

62

Atticus went to his laptop, tapped the keyboard and woke the screen. It displayed an image of a woman standing on a balcony with a terrace of tall houses behind her.

'What is that?'

Atticus didn't answer. He clicked his mouse and the image moved, the woman smiling at whoever was behind the camera for less than a second before the frame froze once more.

Atticus pointed. 'That was recorded at the end of Kajetan's tape.'

'What?'

'It was there *before* what we saw was recorded over it. I investigated how tapes work. You can get machines that wipe them – they erase the original recording before the next recording re-magnetises the tape with new, stronger information. Either the machine didn't work all the way to the end, or they got sloppy, but this clip was left.'

Mack stared at the woman looking out at them from the screen. 'And you think whoever that is might be involved in all this?'

'Impossible to say. Maybe whoever filmed Campbell bought a job lot of second-hand tapes, wiped them and then used them. Or maybe this was a one-off, and this is a personal tape that was wiped and reused.'

'We'd prefer the latter.'

'We would.'

'So we need to know where that' – she tapped her finger against the screen – 'was filmed.'

Atticus grinned. 'Brussels. Seventy-five Albaniëstraat in Barrière de Saint-Gilles.'

He took a piece of paper and put it down on the desk next to the keyboard. It was a screengrab from Google Street View. Mack looked from the image on the screen to the screengrab and saw that, although the images had been taken at different times, it was definitely the same building.

'I bet you can't wait to tell me how you worked that out.'

'Maybe later,' he said, so excited by his discovery that he was prepared to postpone a demonstration of his brilliance. 'Once I figured out where the building is, I just needed to know who might have owned it at the time that video was filmed. I contacted the Belgian Federal Ministry of Finance and asked for a search of the land register and got lucky. The most likely owner was always going to be a Belgian, and we would've had to fly over there on the off chance that he or she might have been able to remember who visited the property twenty years ago when the video was taken. But it *wasn't* owned by a Belgian. It was owned by an Englishman.'

'Go on,' Mack prompted.

He took out a second piece of paper and laid it down on top of the first. It was a printout of an official document that bore the logo of the Belgian government and the headline KADASTER. The contents were in French, but it looked like a record of the owners of the property listed as 75 Albaniëstraat.

Atticus had ringed one of the names in red ink.

'General Sir Harry Summers,' he said. 'Originally commissioned into the Intelligence Corps and then transferred to the

Parachute Regiment. Multiple tours in Northern Ireland and then the Balkans.'

'And in Brussels because of NATO?'

'Exactly. Commander of the Allied Rapid Reaction Corps during the Kosovo War. Came home after six years and was promoted to full general and appointed to commander-in-chief, Land Command. He retired a decade ago and set up a very successful private intelligence business. Corporate clients, a hundred staff, multi-million-pound contracts. Companies House says they had a turnover of a hundred million last year.'

Mack looked at the still from the video and laid a finger on the woman smiling into the lens.

'And she is?'

Atticus took a third sheet of paper and handed it to Mack. It was a printout of a website from Tatler's, a restaurant in the New Forest that Mack had visited before. The photograph was from the website's 'About' section and showed the chef-proprietor, Samantha Summers. It reported that she had started the restaurant but had passed away several years ago. The woman in Brussels was younger than the woman in the picture – maybe twenty years younger – but it was obvious that it was her.

Mack put the paper down on the desk and exhaled. 'Shit. Why do I get the feeling this is going to get worse before it gets better? Why would footage shot in a property belonging to Summers end up on a dead man's sex tape?'

'It could be a coincidence.'

'But you don't believe in coincidences.'

'No. I don't.'

She could see from the gleam in his eyes that he was excited by the discoveries that he had made, and that she was going to have to rein him in for fear of him doing something outrageous. During the last case on which they'd worked together, the mystery of the bodies at Imber had taken a turn with the revelation that Miller had been involved, and that had required a delicate touch that, for all his brilliance, Atticus just did not possess.

This had the potential to be even more sensitive. 'You don't do *anything* with this,' she said.

'I know. I'm not stupid.'

'Where does he live?'

'Big place out near Sixpenny Handley. West Woodyates Manor.'

Mack exhaled. 'I need to go and speak to Murphy.'

'Really? Are you sure that's a good idea?'

'He's in charge of the investigation. I don't have a choice.'

'I disagree.'

'Atticus . . .'

'Just go and have a look. You don't have to do anything else. Tell Murphy you were checking it out and leave it up to him to arrange an interview.'

'Just like that?'

'Come on,' he said. 'Where's the harm? You're just being thorough. The last thing you'd want to do is to waste his time with something that you haven't checked out first.'

'And I suppose that's something you'd be up for helping me with?'

'I have nothing on this afternoon. Bandit could do with a walk, and the countryside is lovely down there.' He shrugged. 'I don't know – sounds like it might be something I could help you with.'

She stared at him. 'Please tell me you're not going to put me in a difficult position?'

'I won't,' he said. 'Trust me – for once?'

63

Harry Summers lived in a house at the centre of a near-thousand-acre estate two miles north-east of Sixpenny Handley and eleven miles south of Salisbury. Mason's driver took him straight there, turning off the road and passing through the open gates with the sign on the left-hand pillar that announced West Woodyates Manor. The area was picturesque and the entire estate set within an Area of Outstanding Natural Beauty. There was open farmland all around and then the oak forests of Cranborne Chase, the big house set in the hollow of the landscape. Mason didn't pay any of it the slightest bit of attention; he had read and reread the story in the *Sun*, looking at the picture of the red-lit room with the bare stone walls and knowing, with a certainty that filled him with dread, that he had been there.

Steve parked the car and stepped out and around so that he could open the door. Mason got out just as Summers opened the door to the house and made his way down the flight of stone steps to the gravelled turning area.

'Max,' he said, shovelling on the charm, 'how are you?'

'I'll be better once I've had a chance to ask you some questions.'

'Come inside.'

Mason told Steve to wait in the car and followed Summers to the front door and then into the house. He looked around as they passed through the entrance hall and saw the pictures of Summers that had been hung on the wood-panelled walls. There were photographs of him with local and national dignitaries, all of them speaking to the fact that he was a man of influence. His military background bestowed upon him an air of unflappable sangfroid, and his career – brimming with tales of derring-do with which he never tired of regaling his company – had given him authority among the many retired senior officers who had made Salisbury and its neighbouring villages their home. The jaw-dropping success of the business that he had set up following his retirement had given him gravitas in London, too, meaning that his reputation was assured in both town and country.

'Cup of coffee?' Summers said.

'No.'

'Something stronger?'

'*No.* This isn't a social call.'

'I didn't think it was. It's about the report in the newspaper today?'

'What else? What's going on, Harry?'

'Nothing you need to be concerned about. I can help put your mind at ease.'

Mason's stomach sank. He realised that he had been holding on to the hope that the whole thing was an unfortunate misunderstanding, that the image he had seen in the paper did not show the room he remembered from twenty years ago, but Summers' suggestion that there was nothing to worry about had the opposite effect.

'It's right, then? The picture *was* what I thought it was? The red room?'

'Yes.'

'How did it get into the paper?'

Summers sat down on one of the leather sofas and indicated that Mason should do the same. 'You know about the man who died at the cathedral?'

Mason lowered himself onto a nearby Chesterfield. 'Of course – they thought he killed himself. Jumped off the tower.'

'David Campbell. He was a customer from twenty years ago.'

'So why was he on film?'

'There used to be another man in the business with me and my partners. We found out recently that he was using a hidden camera to record our customers. We think he had a mind to blackmail them, although he never did – at least not as far as we know.'

'Who is he?'

'You don't need to be concerned about him—'

'I disagree.'

'Because he's dead, Max.'

'You *killed* him?'

'There's no need to go into what happened, but let's just say I don't tolerate betrayal, and I take the privacy of my customers seriously. *Extremely* seriously.'

'How many customers did he film?'

'No more than a handful.'

'And not me?'

'No, Max. Not you.'

'How can you be certain?'

'Because the videos we found were all made in the autumn of 1999. You didn't start going out to Imber until after that.'

'Late 2000.'

'There you are, then. Months later. You have nothing to worry about.'

'Is that why you stopped using the house in Imber?'

'Because of that?' Summers shook his head. 'No, that was a business decision – things are much easier to scale online.'

Mason remembered: the house at Imber had been closed down not all that long after his final visit. The operation had changed, with personal participation curtailed in favour of streams distributed on the dark web and, these days, paid for by way of cryptocurrency. The aesthetic – the red room – had been kept.

'Anything else, Max?'

'You haven't explained how the newspaper has the video. You said he was dead.'

'We're looking into that with all the urgency you'd expect.'

'You're holding something back. Remember who you're talking to, Harry. I'm not just anyone.'

He nodded. 'No, you're quite right – you're not. The situation with my colleague was very unpleasant, as you can imagine. We dealt with the problem, but we couldn't find all the recordings we think he made. There was a brother involved, and he's gone missing. We think he might have the tapes, and now *he's* trying to make money off them.'

'You're guessing?'

'Educated guessing, and I'm afraid it's the best I can do at the moment. One thing I can say with absolute certainty, though, is that you were never filmed. We were able to speak to him before he died, and he was clear about that.'

'You believed him?'

'We were persuasive, and he had no reason to lie. There's nothing – and I really do mean *nothing* – that would implicate you. You have my word on that, Max.'

'I'd like to say that makes me a little more confident, but I can't. I trusted you. It was all about discretion. That was the selling point, *especially* for someone like me. You've let me down.'

Summers spread his hands. 'I understand why you would say that. I'd feel the same.'

Summers kept agreeing with him, and that made it more difficult to remain angry.

'What about the police? You said you had connections there.'

Summers nodded. 'I do. It has to be managed with discretion, but we have sources who'll let us know of anything that might be helpful.'

Mason thought of Beckton. 'I have a connection. Senior.'

Summers shook his head. 'Keep it to yourself. It's in hand. Why bring any attention on to yourself by asking questions? There's no point. Leave it to us.' He stood. 'Now – are you *sure* I can't get you a drink?'

Mason stood, too. 'I need to be getting back. I'm filming again tomorrow.'

'We're planning another performance soon. Two very pretty girls who'd be right up your street. I'll tell you what – why don't I see about you having access to the stream for free? I feel bad that you've been worrying. Let me start to make it up to you.'

That was tempting.

'Sort this mess out first,' Mason said. 'Then we'll see.'

64

Atticus had reviewed the manor house on Google before making the twenty-minute drive south. It was grand and had been bought by the general after his corporate intelligence company had made profits in what had turned out to be just the first in a series of stellar years. Atticus had downloaded the particulars from the website of the high-end estate agents who had been engaged to sell it and had noted from the Land Registry details that the asking price – more than £18.5 million – had been exceeded by thirty per cent. The *Evening Standard*'s society page suggested that Summers had been caught up in a three-way auction with a well-known singer and a *nouveau riche* dilettante who had recently received the fruits of a multi-million-pound inheritance and wanted the estate as a place to run a shooting business. Summers had bid aggressively to close the deal.

Atticus pulled over at the side of the road within sight of the track that the map suggested led to the property.

He turned to Mack. 'How much are you comfortable with?'

'I'm not comfortable with any of it.'

'You don't have to be here. I can take Bandit on my own.'

'And what happens when someone sees you?'

'I was walking the dog and he went after a deer. I'm very sorry to have trespassed, but I would've lost him if I didn't go after him.'

'What's the point?' Mack muttered. 'We need to speak to him, not look around his gardens.'

'So let's do that.'

'And Murphy?'

'You're a DCI,' Atticus reminded her. 'Do you need to ask his permission before you do anything?'

'No,' she began. 'No, but—'

He cut across her. 'Tell him this was just speculative, that it's almost certainly nothing and you didn't want to waste his time.'

Atticus had known that Mack would be tempted. She wouldn't have agreed to come out here with him without at least considering the idea that they might go a little further than they had agreed and try to speak to Summers. He knew her well enough to know that she would have been fuming at her replacement as the head of the investigation; he had seen that she had no respect for Murphy, and had no doubt that the fact that he was male and from outside the area would have exacerbated her irritation. Atticus had tempted her with the prospect of a breakthrough that she would be able to wave in the faces of those who doubted her; Murphy and Beckton wouldn't be able to complain that she had gone off the reservation if she could show them that her initiative had brought them closer to understanding what had happened to the three murdered men.

Atticus might have given thought to the propriety of taking advantage of how well he knew Mack, but that wasn't something that came naturally to him; and, besides, it wasn't as if he was suggesting something that wasn't important. The fact that he would get to come along and speak to Summers himself had been in his thoughts, too. Murphy would never have allowed it, and he wouldn't be able to get a gauge on the man without sitting opposite him where he could watch his body language for useful tells.

Mack sucked on her teeth. 'I suppose we could see if he's in.'

Atticus nodded. 'Where's the harm in that?'

'Who does the talking?'

'You do,' he said.

'Sure?'

He put a finger to his lips. 'Not a word.'

65

Mack led the way to the pillars that accommodated the gates for the property. The gates were open, but, rather than walk down the track unannounced, she pressed the intercom.

They waited a moment before the speaker crackled into life. 'Hello?'

'Hello,' Mack replied. 'Is that Harry Summers?'

'No. Who is this?'

'Detective Chief Inspector Mackenzie Jones from Salisbury CID. Is Mr Summers at home?'

'What do you want?'

'We're making some enquiries and Mr Summers' name came up. We'd like to speak to him, and it'll be much easier if we do it here rather than asking him to come to the station. Is he around?'

There was a pause, and Atticus thought he could hear hushed conversation. He and Mack shared a glance, but, before he could say anything to her, the intercom crackled with static once more.

'He's got twenty minutes before he needs to go out. Will that be enough?'

'Plenty,' she said.

'Follow the drive and park in front of the house.'

They went back to the car. Atticus turned off the main road, passed between the pillars and through the gate. The estate was reached by way of a single-track road that was hemmed in between a converted farm building and a row of new houses. A car approached them. It was a big Bentley Flying Spur, and it took up all the width available. There was a passing space behind them, and Atticus reversed back into it. The driver of the Bentley didn't acknowledge them as he passed.

'Who's that?' Mack said, craning her neck to watch the Bentley.

Atticus glanced up at the rear-view mirror. The car turned the corner and passed out of sight. 'No idea. But there's obviously a lot of money here.'

The track continued between hedges that divided otherwise open farmland for three-quarters of a mile. The halfway point saw a Dutch barn and a parking area where tractors and equipment were stored, and then, as they continued, Atticus saw the beginning of the estate proper; the farmland turned into lawns and then manicured gardens. The manor house was to the left, bracketed by a long barn to the north-east and formal gardens, with topiary and striped grass, to the south.

They reached the parking area at the rear of the house and Atticus rolled the car to a halt next to a brand-new Land Rover Discovery. The two of them looked from the car to the house and then to the immaculate grounds.

'A *lot* of money.'

They got out of the car and started towards the house. The front door opened before they were halfway there, and a man dressed in red tweed trousers and a salmon-coloured shirt came out to meet them.

'Detective Chief Inspector Jones?'

'That's right.'

Summers put out his hand and Mack shook it. 'Harry Summers. Good to meet you.' He turned to Atticus. 'And you are?'

'Atticus Priest.'

Summers shook his hand, too. 'Police?'

'I'm a private investigator.'

'He's a consultant,' Mack explained. 'He has some experience with the case that we're investigating and I thought it would be helpful to have him here.'

Summers released Atticus's hand and gave him another broad smile. 'Absolutely. Please, come inside – I only have twenty minutes, but you're both very welcome.'

Summers led the way through the house. The entrance hall had doors to what looked like the drawing room, a grand flight of stairs to the first floor and an arch that led down into a library. The walls were panelled in oak and hung with pictures of men and women who looked as if they might have been connected to the house in years gone by; small plaques beneath them identified previous owners and family members. Other framed photographs showed Summers with politicians and the occasional celebrity that Atticus, who had little time for such people, half recognised.

'Can I get you both a coffee?'

'Yes,' Mack said. 'Thank you. That would be nice.'

They continued into a vast dining hall with a table that would have been big enough to seat twenty and then into the kitchen. Atticus couldn't help but be impressed with the property. He knew how much Summers had spent on it, and it served as a reminder of how successful he had been since he had retired from the military. His experience had evidently been put to lucrative use in his new business.

'Thank you for agreeing to see us, Sir Harry,' Mack said.

'Please – it's Harry. I'm not one for formality. Take a seat.'

Summers filled a kettle and stood it on one of the hotplates of the large Aga that warmed the kitchen. Atticus looked around the room and saw more examples of Summers' wealth. The pictures on the wall were of his family, while those arranged on the large dresser that stood against the wall showed him in uniform during his years of service. Atticus wandered over so that he could look at them more closely.

'You had a very interesting career,' he said.

Summers nodded. 'Certainly can't complain.'

Atticus saw photographs of him in ceremonial garb with the Queen; in conversation with the host of the *Today* show on Radio 4; crossing the line at the end of the London Marathon; in a mud-smeared uniform as he stood with a rifle before a tank. Atticus picked up a photograph of Summers as a younger man standing with a group of officers in what he guessed was a parade ground at Sandhurst. Summers was watching him, and Atticus thought he detected discomfort.

'How can I help you?' Summers said.

Mack was looking at Atticus too, her frown suggesting that he should stop interfering with the general's things. He took the hint and put the photograph back on the shelf.

'It won't take long,' Mack said. 'Just a few questions. I'm grateful you've found time for us.'

Atticus clenched his jaw. Her deference was irritating; he knew why she was treating Summers carefully – he was an important man who could have caused them enormous trouble if his feathers were ruffled – but Atticus was impatient and wanted to get stuck into the questions. Mack's equanimity also cast light on the fact that it was something that *he* lacked, and that annoyed him, too.

Summers took the kettle from the Aga, poured hot water into the cafetière and then stood it on the tray with three mugs and a plate of biscuits. He brought it over to the table, set it down and took a seat next to Mack.

'Fire away.'

'This is going to sound a little unusual,' Mack began. 'I'd like to show you a picture if that's all right?'

Summers pushed down on the plunger of the cafetière. 'Of course.'

Mack opened her bag and took out the still image of the woman on the balcony of the house in Brussels. She put it on the table. Summers poured the coffee, replaced the cafetière and put on a pair of glasses so that he could examine the photograph.

Atticus watched his face carefully.

'Where did you get this?'

'Do you recognise it?'

'Yes, of course,' he said. 'That's Samantha.'

'Your wife?' Atticus said, taking over.

'Ex-wife.'

'Where was it taken?'

'Brussels. Must be twenty years ago.'

'What were you doing there?'

'I was based there. I was the UK representative to NATO.'

'And where in the city was it taken?'

'Our house in Barrière de Saint-Gilles. Up on the balcony.' He tapped his index finger against his lips. 'I don't remember this as a photograph, though. I'm pretty sure we were messing around with a camcorder.'

'You're right,' Atticus said. 'That's a still from a video.'

Summers looked at the image and shook his head. 'How on earth did you get it?'

'We can't tell you that,' Mack said.

'What? No, Detective Chief Inspector, that won't do.'

She put her hands together. 'Very sorry, sir, but I can't go into that at the moment.'

Summers shook his head with exasperation. 'How extraordinary. How is it relevant?'

Atticus ignored the question and asked another of his own. 'Can you tell us where you've been over the last week?'

'Why?'

'Please – just answer the question.'

'No, I'm sorry. Why are you asking me that? Am I being investigated for something?'

'No,' Mack said. 'Not at the moment.'

'Meaning that you *might* investigate me in the future?' Summers folded his arms in a classic pose of defence. 'You said this was a simple matter. Do I need to speak to my lawyer?'

Atticus could see that the conversation was sliding out of control. He looked at Mack and saw that she could see it, too.

'We're not investigating you, sir,' she said, 'but if you feel you need a lawyer, then you—'

Summers snapped across her. 'I don't need a lawyer because I've done nothing wrong. My goodness – this is a strange thing to drop on someone like this. If you must know, I've been at my flat in London. I was in the office yesterday and the day before, and I went out to the theatre with my girlfriend. My PA will be able to confirm that.'

'Thank you, sir,' Mack said. 'That's very—'

Atticus couldn't stay silent any longer. 'The videotape of your wife in Brussels – do you still have it?'

'Of course not,' he said. 'Who keeps *videotapes*? I imagine it was thrown out years ago.'

'Are you sure?'

'I'm not *sure*,' Summers replied. 'But it's the kind of thing Samantha would've done. And it would've been years ago, as I said.'

'We need to be sure about what happened to that tape.'

'Yet you won't tell me why!'

Summers was losing his temper, his earlier urbanity pierced by the indignation of a senior officer unused to being put on the spot like this by two civilians. Atticus would have loved to push him a little closer to the edge, to prod and poke him until he forgot where he was and said something he might regret, but Mack put up a hand to forestall him.

'Thank you, Sir Harry. We have enough to be getting on with.'

The moment had passed, and Summers' courtliness returned, albeit with a hint of hauteur about it. 'I'm sorry – shouldn't be so impatient, but it's frustrating when you can't tell me what it's about.' He handed back the image of his ex-wife. 'It's a worry that you can't tell me how you came by this.'

'I understand. I'll be very happy to tell you more when I'm able.' Mack got to her feet, and Summers and Atticus followed suit.

Summers put out his hand and Mack shook it. 'Thank you, Detective Chief Inspector.'

'*Do* ask your ex-wife, though,' Atticus said.

Summers withdrew his hand and stared bleakly at Atticus. 'She's dead.'

'Oh,' Atticus said. 'I didn't know.'

'Cancer. Five years ago.'

'We're very sorry to hear that,' Mack said.

'Yes,' Atticus said. 'Very sorry. But do let us know if you think of anything that might be helpful.'

Summers held Atticus's eye. 'I will.'

66

Bandit was excited to see them as they made their way back to the car. They got inside, turned around and drove away from the house.

'Did you *really* have to do that?' Mack said.

'Do what?'

'Wind him up.'

'Putting someone under a little pressure is the only way to test whether they're telling the truth.'

'Fine. And? Was he?'

'What do you think?'

She sighed in exasperation. 'That's why I brought *you* along.'

'You first.'

'I don't think he told us everything.'

Atticus tapped both hands against the wheel. 'He *definitely* didn't. Did you see how he changed? Friendly and affable when we arrived.'

'But nervous.'

'Yes,' he said. 'He did a good job hiding it, but there were signs. His posture was stiff, his arms were folded and the whole coffee thing? Who offers coffee when they've just said they've only got twenty minutes? It was an excuse to turn away from us, to give his hands something to do to stop him from fidgeting.'

'None of that's unusual. You know what it's like when you interview someone – they always think that they must've done something wrong. It's human nature.'

'It is,' Atticus said. 'And that might have been the reason for it. But did you notice how he changed once we showed him the picture of his wife?'

'He was vague.'

'Very vague.'

'You think he's lying?'

'He repeated questions before he answered them – he was giving himself time to think. He spoke in fragments of sentences – that's the same. The bluster at the end? Manufactured. He was trying to hide his reaction by distracting us with something else.'

'He pressed his finger to his lips, too – did you see that? He was literally telling himself not to answer.'

'Very good,' Atticus said. 'You've been paying attention.'

'Jesus,' she said, rolling her eyes. 'Could you be any more patronising?'

'Sorry. Didn't mean it like that.'

'You're hopeless,' she said. 'But never mind.'

They reached the end of the drive. Atticus waited for a car to go past and then followed the road to the north.

Mack drummed her fingers against the dash. 'Could he be involved?'

'In the murders?' Atticus drew in a breath and then exhaled. 'We can't say that. All we *can* say is that a tape that he used to record his wife twenty years ago *was* used again to record David Campbell. That's suspicious, at the very least.'

'Fine – let's play it out. Say the same tape was used twice. How did that happen? Maybe his ex-wife threw it out. Maybe she gave it to a charity shop and they sold it to whoever used it again.'

Atticus gazed out into the gathering darkness at the side of the road.

'Atticus?'

'Possible,' he said.

'But unlikely?'

'I think so.'

'I need to speak to Murphy and Beckton. I can't sit on it any longer. I wouldn't put it past him to call the nick and make a complaint.'

'I'll drop you off.'

'What are you going to do?'

'Bandit's never going to talk to me again if I don't give him the walk I promised.'

She looked across at him.

'What?'

'Nothing,' she said. 'Do you want to come over later? I wouldn't mind talking it over with you.'

'When?'

'Ten? I'll be back by then.'

'Ten it is,' he said.

67

Atticus dropped Mack at the station and then drove back to the office. He let Bandit out of the back seat, took his lead and knelt to hook it to the dog's collar.

'Who's been a patient boy?' Atticus said as the dog pushed its muzzle into his neck, licking his cheek and ear.

He walked to the cathedral, unclipped the lead and watched as Bandit sprang away. His gaze was drawn up to the spire and then down to the tower; the floodlights from below splashed it in white light that was visible from miles around.

Bandit raced towards him at full speed, dodging to the side at the last moment and then haring away again.

Atticus looked absent-mindedly at the floodlights until he realised what he was doing and blinked the brightness away. He didn't believe what Summers had told them, or at least didn't think that he had been frank with them. He couldn't say for sure how Summers might be involved in what had been happening, but he knew that if he was, then the longer they waited, the greater the opportunity Summers would have to come up with a credible story and dispose of anything that might speak to his involvement.

Bandit rushed by him at full pelt just as Atticus's phone rang. He took it out, expecting to see that Mack was calling, but, instead, it was a number he didn't recognise.

He answered it. 'Hello?'

'Mr Priest?'

'Yes,' he said. 'Who is this?'

'Harry Summers.'

Atticus switched the phone to his right hand and started towards the nearest vacant bench. 'I didn't give you my number.'

'It's on your website.'

'So it is.' Atticus sat down. 'How can I help you?'

'I've had a think about that video you were interested in.'

'Yes?'

'I wonder – I know this is going to be inconvenient but would you be able to come back out to the house to see me?'

'Couldn't you come into the station? DCI Jones is the one you need to speak to.'

'Can't, not really. I'm going away tomorrow for a week, and I'd much rather get this off my chest now.'

'I'm sure she'd see you tonight. I could call her if—'

Summers spoke over him. 'I don't want to be seen going into the police station. And I'd rather this wasn't *official* – do you know what I mean? I'd rather it was you. Of course, you can speak to her yourself when we're finished, and I'll be happy to cooperate if she thinks that'd be useful. I'm hoping that won't be necessary, though. I think – I *hope* – I can put your mind at ease.'

Atticus bit down on his lip. It was an unusual offer, and one that made him suspicious. Summers had become unfriendly during the questioning, especially towards him, and it was difficult to understand why he would invite Atticus back to his house.

'When?'

'Now? Are you free?'

Atticus watched as Bandit gambolled happily across the grass. He hurtled at Atticus again, swerving around the bench and then slowing right down, his belly low to the ground as he sprang away once more.

'Mr Priest?'

'OK,' he said. He looked at his watch. 'I've got a couple of things to do first. I'll be with you in an hour.'

'Thank you. I appreciate it.'

Atticus ended the call and then tried Mack's number. It went straight to voicemail. Atticus ended the call and drummed his fingers against his knee. Mack had explained that she would be seeing Murphy and Beckton, and she was probably still with them now. How long would she be? An hour? Two? He knew that he ought to wait until he had spoken to her, but that would require patience that he didn't have. Summers' offer was intriguing, and he wanted to understand why he had made it. There was a reason he wanted to speak to him and not Mack, and Atticus couldn't work out what it might be; an unresolved question like that was agony for him, and he needed to have it answered.

He called Mack again and, this time, waited to leave a message. 'It's me,' he said. 'I just had a call from Summers. He wants to talk to me. I know I should wait for you, but he says he's going away tomorrow and he doesn't want it to look "official". Anyway, I just wanted you to know that I'm going to go out there and I probably won't be back until after ten. I'll come straight to you when I'm done.'

Atticus called Bandit back to him, gave him a biscuit and reattached his lead, and went back to the office.

68

Atticus fed Bandit, changed his water and then tried to call Mack again, with the same result. He took his spare digital voice recorder and slipped it into his pocket and went down to get his car. He sat down and fastened his belt and rested his hands on the wheel, reluctant to start the engine. He knew why: he was suspicious of Summers's motive but, at the same time, unable to resist his invitation. It was as if a lure had been dropped into the water and, even though he knew that taking it would be a bad idea, there was nothing he could do to stop himself. He reminded himself that, beyond the video, there was nothing to suggest that Summers was involved in any of the crimes that they were investigating. That might have been true, but, as Atticus turned the key and started the engine, it didn't ameliorate the sickening feeling in the pit of his stomach that he was wandering into a situation without really appreciating what it might mean.

* * *

Atticus followed the same route that he had taken with Mack earlier, arriving at the house at half past eight. He gazed at the house, which was now bathed in the silvered glow of the moon.

Light escaped between the curtains of the windows on the ground floor. Atticus parked the car next to the Land Rover Discovery they had noticed earlier, opened the door, stepped out onto the gravel and started over to the door. It opened before he was halfway there, and Summers stepped out.

'It's cold,' he called over. 'Come in.'

Atticus hurried across the gravel as Summers stood aside. 'Evening.'

'Thank you for coming,' Summers said. 'Please – let me have your coat.'

Atticus shrugged off his jacket, and Summers took it, hanging it on a hatstand that was next to the grandfather clock that Atticus had noticed earlier.

'We'll go through to the drawing room,' Summers said. 'This way.'

The library was straight ahead, but Summers turned right and showed Atticus into a vaulted room that was dominated by a stone fireplace, the stone blackened by soot that must have gathered over time. Wooden beams supported the ceiling and the polished floor was softened by large rugs. There was a huge bay with leaded windows and a chandelier glittered overhead. Speakers in the ceiling played Vivaldi at low volume.

Summers indicated that Atticus should take one of the armchairs and went over to a table next to the window.

'Can I pour you a drink?'

'I'm fine,' Atticus said.

'No, that won't do. I've got a *really* good twenty-five-year-old bottle of Ardbeg that I was going to open tonight. Let's have a glass.'

It wasn't a suggestion; Summers had decided, and that was that. He took two heavy glasses, opened the bottle and poured out two generous measures. He brought the glasses over, gave one to Atticus and kept the other one for himself. He found a remote control on the table, muted the speakers and raised his glass.

'Cheers.'

Atticus touched glasses. 'Thank you.'

'So,' Summers said, sitting and crossing one leg over the other. 'You were interested in the videotape.'

'We are – have you had a chance to think about it?'

'I have, and I remember what happened to it. My wife took it to a charity shop in town.'

'When was this?'

'We divorced ten years ago – must've been around then.'

'Ten years.'

'Yes – what about it?'

'You have a good memory.'

He looked at Atticus and smiled. 'I suppose so.'

'To remember something like that? It's a bit random, isn't it? And you couldn't remember it earlier.'

'I just needed to put my mind to it,' Summers said. 'It's come back to me now. We had a collection of videos. I used to be a video buff. I had an old JVC camcorder, used to bring it out all the time, usually to do with the children, of course. Sports day, Nativity plays, learning to ride a bike, my daughter's first gymkhana – you name it. We had a wardrobe in one of the bedrooms with a box full of tapes. Samantha took the box and gave them to a charity shop in town.'

'Why did she do that? Family memories. She'd just get rid of them?'

'I transferred them to DVD,' Summers said. 'There was no point in keeping the tapes after that. They were just taking up space.'

'So why not just throw them out?'

'I suppose she thought the charity might be able to get something for them.'

'For used VHS tapes? Really?'

'She never liked to just bin something if she thought it might have value.'

Atticus sipped his drink and looked at Summers over the top of his glass. It was a decent enough story, with – fortunately for Summers – no way for Atticus to disprove it. It smelled very much like the sort of explanation that he might have cooked up after he had been questioned earlier.

'You asked me to come all the way here to tell me that? Wouldn't it have been easier to tell me or DCI Jones on the phone?'

'I wanted to give you the opportunity to ask me anything else you might want answering, and it's easier to do that face to face.'

Atticus had the impression that Summers had brought him out here so that he could better assess his reaction to the story that he had just provided, plus any others that he was preparing to tell. He was surer now than he had been that Summers was being economical with the truth; he was lying, or – at the very least – holding something back. He decided that it was worth turning up the temperature a little to see how he reacted.

'I hope you don't mind me saying that it all seems a little unlikely.'

Atticus watched for a change in Summers' demeanour and was rewarded with several tiny defensive movements: a stiffness in his posture, a dab of his finger to the side of his face and then, as he noticed that Atticus was observing him, a classic cross of the arms.

'I don't think it's unlikely at all. We had some videos, we didn't need them any more, we got rid of them. End of story. You haven't even told me why it's so important.'

'That'll be something you can discuss with DCI Jones.'

'I will.'

Summers stood and went to the table where he had left the bottle of Ardbeg. He finished his drink and poured another, then turned back to Atticus.

Atticus smiled pleasantly. 'I don't know, Harry. I can't help thinking you're hiding something.'

Summers didn't offer Atticus a refill. 'Why would I want to do that?'

Atticus kept his eyes on him. 'I don't know. Why would you?'

The easy smile on Summers' lips disappeared, and his brows lowered into a scowl. 'Can I give you a word of advice, Mr Priest?'

'Please do.'

'You should be careful about the way that you present yourself to other people.'

'Should I?'

'You really should. You have an unfortunate tendency to rub people up the wrong way.'

'Sorry you feel that way.'

'But it's not just me, is it? I have a business that works with law enforcement, among other things.'

'I know. I've looked into it – the business, your background.'

'And I've looked into *you*. I know about your career. Your dismissal.'

'My *resignation*.'

'Semantics. You resigned before they could fire you. I know all about it. I have a friend in Wiltshire constabulary who was able to let me have a look at your annual appraisals. They were dreadful. I mean . . . *really* dreadful. I'm surprised you lasted as long as you did. You're clearly intelligent, but you don't play well with others.'

'Am I supposed to be impressed?'

'With what?'

'That you were able to get my appraisals.'

'Not at all.'

'What is it, then? You're trying to intimidate me?'

He laughed. 'Don't be so *paranoid*. I just want you to know that I've got my eye on you. I don't enjoy having my character called into question. It's important to me – my integrity and my reputation – and anyone impugning either can expect a response.'

Atticus stood. The convivial atmosphere had always been tenuous, but the façade had fallen away completely now, and Summers' icy threats were evident even to him. It was time to leave. 'Duly noted. Thank you for your time this evening. I'll make sure that DCI Jones is up to speed the next time you see her.'

'I doubt there'll be a next time,' Summers said. 'I can't imagine what else she might want to ask me.'

Atticus made to leave the drawing room and collect his jacket from the hatstand in the hall, but, as he approached the open door, he saw that a man was waiting just the other side. He was bigger than Atticus, with an obvious solidity that spoke of hard muscle. His forehead had an atavistic slant that ended with heavy eyebrows and, beneath small and pitiless eyes, his nose was squashed flat to his face.

Atticus was about as sure as he could be that he had seen him before. It had been dark that night in Alfred Burns' flat, and his recollection had been scrambled a little by the blow to the head that had knocked him out, but he would have laid a sizeable bet that the man in front of him now was the man who had attacked him.

'Mr Doyle,' Summers said, 'would you show Mr Priest to the door, please?'

The big man nodded but didn't immediately step out of the way. He blocked Atticus for just long enough for him to be sure that his presence there was not an accident but a threat; if Atticus continued to make a nuisance of himself, or if Summers concluded that he was being harassed, then the next interaction would be with his pet gorilla instead of him. Doyle glared at him, then took a step back so that Atticus could make his way out and into the hall. He took his jacket from the hatstand and went to the door.

Summers followed. 'Thanks for coming, Mr Priest. Pass on my best wishes to DCI Jones. I doubt she has any other questions to ask me, but, if she does' – he spread his arms – 'then, of course, I'd be happy to answer them.'

The smile was back on Summers' face now, but he made no effort to disguise the fact that it was a pretence. Doyle opened the door and Atticus stepped outside. The door slammed shut behind him before he had taken even a handful of paces towards his car.

69

Atticus made his way down the drive, turned on to the A354 and started back in the direction of Salisbury. He couldn't stop thinking about the conversation with Summers; he was sure that the general was lying to him, and that he'd invited him to the house to assess and then threaten him. Atticus was also sure that he had already come off second best in an encounter with Doyle and had no wish to arrange a repeat performance, but he was not about to be daunted by threats.

He reached the turning for the nature reserve at Martin Down, saw a lay-by and, without really thinking about it, pressed down on the brake and pulled over. He gripped the wheel tightly and ground his teeth. He had been given a problem to solve and was surer than ever that Summers had information that would help him to do that; he wouldn't be intimidated into turning away.

He checked his mirrors, then swung the car around and drove south again, turning off the road at the junction for the manor house and then turning left, following a short drive that gave access to the rear of one of the cottages that came with the estate. There was a space at the end where it was possible to park two cars; the space was empty and Atticus reversed into it. Save the fact that he was going to need to trek north-west for a mile to get back to the house, it was a good place to leave the car.

He opened the glovebox and took out one pair each of the nitrile gloves and overshoes that he kept there, putting both into his pocket. Better to have something and not need it than to need it and not have it. He wasn't intending to break in – probably – but he knew himself well enough to know that it was a possibility if he found something that looked like it might be interesting. He reached inside the glovebox again and took out his penlight and the leather sleeve that held his collection of lock picks. He put those in his pocket, too.

The moon hung overhead, a glowing gem amid the dark of a sky that was, for the first time in days, without cloud. Atticus would have much preferred the conditions of the last week so that visibility was not quite as good, but there was nothing to be done about that now. He would just have to make his approach a little more carefully.

He joined the drive and started walking. He followed it for the first half a mile before clambering over a gate and continuing through the fields, and then the oaks that enclosed the house. He reached the start of the formal gardens and found a spot among the topiary that allowed him to watch without being seen from the house. The lights were still on and, as he watched, the glow from one of the bedrooms on the first floor dimmed as someone walked in front of the window. Atticus kept his focus on that window; the person returned, their shadow thrown out into the middle of the square of light that was cast on the grass, and closed the curtains.

He tried to recall the map of the estate that he had studied before coming here with Mack. The house and gardens were ahead of him, with a long range of brick stables behind them and to the north-east. There was another lawned area to the rear of the house and then the first of a series of cottages that would once have been tithed to the men and women who worked on the land. There was a chapel behind those buildings and then nearly a thousand acres beyond that.

Atticus wanted to look around the grounds and the other buildings. That might involve breaking in and risked severe consequences were he to be caught. He doubted that he would be able to resist it but knew that he'd have to wait until he was confident that Summers was asleep.

He looked at his watch and wondered when the general would turn in. He lowered himself to the ground and settled in to wait.

PART V

FRIDAY

70

Atticus crept closer, taking a wide path to avoid exposing himself directly to the house. He took advantage of another line of neatly kept trees, moving along it until he reached the stone wall that encircled the formal gardens. The drive that he had used to get to the parking area at the back of the house was to his right; he went left, staying down low and working his way around the western side of the building. There was a large barn there. The door was unlocked and Atticus peered inside. It looked as if it was used to store the machinery that kept the grounds in order: he saw a sit-on mower, a roller, then strimmers and blowers and brush cutters and other pieces of agricultural machinery that he didn't recognise. None of it warranted a second look and there was nothing else of interest inside. He backed out, carefully pulled the door closed and went around the side so that he could look at the rear of the house.

He heard footsteps across gravel and stepped back so that he could hide behind the barn. It sounded like the movement was coming from the direction of the door that he had used to get inside earlier. He followed the long edge of the barn and then picked his way between the shrubs and the trunks of the smaller trees that he found on the other side until he was able to peek through the vegetation.

Summers and Doyle were walking to the north, following a path that skirted the lawn in the direction of two cottages and, beyond those, the old chapel. Atticus watched and waited, wondering whether this was the opportunity to look around the house. He remembered that the door was on a latch and wondered whether it might have been left unsecured; even if it *was* locked, it would still have been easy enough to get inside. He agonised over it for a moment before deciding that it was too risky: he didn't know how long Summers and Doyle would be away, and didn't want to have to rush. He was curious, too, to see what the two men were doing outside at such a late hour.

He waited until they were out of sight and then followed, making his way across the gravel as quietly as he could before he reached the path they had taken. Stopping there for a moment, he listened for any sign that Summers or Doyle might be coming back. After hearing nothing and, waiting another beat to be sure, he continued to follow them. The path went north beneath the shelter of another two large oak trees and then continued between a pair of lawns to a junction where it intersected with a path running east to west. Summers and Doyle turned right, following an avenue of trees, then turned left and carried on until they reached the chapel. Summers paused at the door, reaching into his pocket for a set of keys, then opened it. The two men went inside.

Atticus looked around for somewhere that he could wait without being seen when they came back out. There was another path bracketed by hedges, but he would have had to cross an open area of lawn to get there, and the risk of exposure was too great. He decided his best option was to go left at the intersection of the two paths rather than right, and to find a spot between the trunks of the trees where he would be able to watch.

He had a good vantage point from here, where he was able to look across the lawn to the chapel. It was a gable-ended stone building topped by a pitched roof with a stone ridge. An arch was set around the timber door, with a small window above that showed the red glow from a light inside.

Atticus waited in the trees for ten minutes, looking for anything that might give him a clue as to what Summers and Doyle were doing. He thought that he could hear conversation but couldn't be sure.

The timber door opened again, and the two men emerged.

'He's a troublemaker,' Summers said. 'I'm not sure we're in a position to take the chance that this goes away, especially not now.'

'What do you want me to do?'

Summers rubbed his scalp. 'We've got to move the stuff.'

'I'll take care of it. Where shall I take it?'

'Put it in the van for now and find storage in the morning. There's a place up at South Newton.'

'Black Hole Storage.'

'That's it. Get a unit and dump the gear. We'll leave it there until this mess goes away.'

'What about him?'

'Who – Priest?'

'I could sort him out tonight, boss. I know where he lives.'

'I know you do, but we can't. What if he told someone he was coming out here? What if he told his girlfriend? It wouldn't take a genius to work out that I'm involved. No. He gets a reprieve for now, but we need to keep an eye on him.'

'And after that?'

'I don't care. Do what you want to him. I've been up all day dealing with this shit, and I'm done in – move the stuff and tell me when it's been done tomorrow.'

'What about the girl?'

'Just take care of it.'

'I'll go and get the van and get started.'

Doyle left Summers and headed east; Atticus guessed he was going to the farm that he remembered from the satellite map. Summers set off back to the house. The path would take him very close to Atticus's hiding spot, and he had no option but to hope that the gloom between the trunks of the trees would be enough to shield him. Summers approached and then stopped, close enough that Atticus would almost have been able to reach out and touch him.

Atticus waited, watching Summers as he began walking again and made his way back to the house, and then, once the coast was clear, he turned back to the chapel. He reached into his pocket, pulled out the nitrile gloves and overshoes and put them on.

The timber door looked as if it was decades old, pitted with knots and whorls that felt rough through the synthetic rubber as he laid his palm against the wood. The door had been fitted with a substantial hasp, which was then secured with a padlock. Atticus reached into his pocket for the leather pouch and took out a long, straight pick. He slid it into the padlock and, once he felt a little resistance – indicating it had been inserted fully – he twisted it to the right. It took him twenty seconds to pop the lock; he removed it from the hasp and then slowly and carefully pushed the door open.

The interior was about as different from what he had expected as it was possible to be. There was a flagstone floor, an ancient timber with dogtooth ornamentation above the door, a wind-braced roof and a single window on the eastern end of the building that still retained fragments of stained glass.

It wasn't the architecture that gave Atticus pause for thought, though; rather, it was the modern equipment that was arrayed around the space. There were two professional video cameras, each mounted on a pedestal; there were microphones and fold-back speakers; two video monitors for visual feedback and a mixing desk for sound. A bed had been placed in the middle of the room, the cameras arranged so that they could cover it from two separate angles. Uplighters had been placed at the bases of the walls. Atticus went to the socket that provided them with power and, heedless of the risk that the illumination might be visible from the house, flicked the switch to turn them on. He had known what to expect and was not disappointed; the lights were fitted with coloured bulbs that filled the room – the *studio*, he corrected himself as he acknowledged the sickening feeling in his stomach – with a deep blood-red glow.

He switched the lights off and took out his flashlight. Beyond the equipment, there was nothing else of note. The bed was covered with a duvet and, when he lifted it and looked beneath, he saw that the sheets had been recently changed. He looked under the bed and saw a wooden crate; he dragged it out, opened the lid and looked inside: there were handcuffs and a selection of sex toys. He bit down on his lip; he knew what had happened here from the videos that he had seen this week. Those were old, though, from twenty or twenty-five years before, and the thought of how many films must have been shot here – or in places that looked just like this – was enough to make the blood rise in his cheeks. Summers had owned this property for only five years, meaning they had developed their aesthetic somewhere else and then imported it. It was as if the red lighting was the brand for their filth; the thought of it made Atticus sick.

He heard an engine from outside and, remembering Doyle, he hurried to the door.

71

Harry Summers walked back to the house. It was after midnight and he was angry. He had always been a man who liked to be in command of events and, recently, it felt as if things had run away from him. Control had been important in the military and then as he made the switch to business, and to lose it – as he most certainly had – was difficult. Max Mason insisting that Summers see him on short notice had been bad enough, and having to put up with his self-important bluster and bombast had been a test. But the visit by DCI Jones and her tame private investigator had been something else; he had suffered their impertinent questions and Priest's knowing looks and asides while maintaining his pretence as the perfect host, confused and concerned about what he was being told.

He had decided to bring Priest back to the house again so that he could gauge how much he knew – and how much danger Summers was in – without the detective chief inspector around. He had concluded the answers were 'too much' and 'enough'.

Summers had been aware of Priest ever since he had been involved in the police investigation against Alf Burns. That had been inconvenient and, the more Summers had come to think about it, Priest's relentless hounding of Burns had been the inflection point for everything that happened next. Burns' legal difficulties had led to financial difficulties, and they had led, in turn, to his foolish attempts to blackmail Summers, Miller and York. Burns had been killed because of that, and Summers had hoped that that might have been the end of the matter.

It wasn't.

He had been wrong.

It had just been the *start*.

Priest's investigation had revealed some of their old operation at Imber. Summers had moved it out to West Woodyates years ago, within months of buying the house. Imber had served a purpose in the early days, but they had outgrown it. It had always felt amateurish, and the fact that they couldn't control it meant that it was riskier than Summers would have liked. His new place had allowed them to install a purpose-built studio and, as technology moved on, to take it entirely online. It was discreet and professional and safe.

But the police investigation in Imber had been effective enough to mean that their past put them at risk, and it had eventually meant there was no choice but to find a fall guy. York had terminal cancer and was the obvious choice; a razor blade slipped to him by a corrupt lawyer was all they needed. Miller would have needed to take his medicine, too, but it should have been limited to what happened in Londonderry. He had been out to the house to talk it through on the night he died; Summers still hadn't been able to get to the bottom of what had happened to him, but the fact that his body had been deposited outside Priest's office suggested that he – and the police – knew more than Summers did, and that rankled.

Doyle had suggested that he pay Priest a visit. The two of them had met before, at Alf Burns' flat, and it had been a pity that Doyle had only knocked him out. He could have topped him then, and that might have avoided all the present difficulties. Summers was a good judge of character and, although he could see that Jones was dangerously sharp in her own right, it was Priest who gave him cause for the most concern. Summers had told Doyle to stand down, but he wondered now whether that had been a mistake. Murdering Priest now would be a brazen move, and one that could easily have him implicated as a suspect, but perhaps it would be better than letting him continue to tug and pull at the loose threads that Summers had been unable to snip. If he kept doing it – probing and prodding and making a nuisance of himself – there was no way of knowing what he might turn up.

And now old customers were being murdered, and Burns' old blackmail tapes were being sent to the press. Summers had no influence over events, and that bothered him more than anything else.

72

Atticus looked out through the door. The noise of the engine wasn't coming from the house, but – as he had guessed – from the direction of the farm. He slid outside and edged around the chapel until he could look behind it. There was a paddock between the building and the farm, and a van was approaching, the headlamps bouncing up and down as the wheels negotiated the uneven surface. Atticus shut the chapel door but knew that he wouldn't have time to lock it again; he left it as it was, looked back to the house to be sure that Summers wasn't in view, then crossed back over into cover again. He found the same spot in the trees as before and waited as the van edged through a gap in the fence and reversed until the cargo doors were next to the chapel door.

Doyle got out of the cab and paused, evidently confused at finding the door unlocked. Atticus held his breath and froze as Doyle turned and looked out over the lawns. He knew that he was well hidden, but there was a moment when Atticus was afraid that Doyle had seen him; he tensed, ready to run if Doyle were to make a move in his direction.

He didn't.

Instead, he turned back to the door, pushed it all the way open, then went inside. He emerged a moment later with one of the large cameras cradled in his arms. Atticus watched as Doyle opened the doors at the rear of the van, carefully lowered the camera inside and then went to get the tripod.

Atticus waited for Doyle to put the mixer and then a second camera into the van, and then left the undergrowth, moving quickly with his head down until he was alongside the vehicle. He took out his penknife, unfolded a serrated blade and made a quick and forceful strike into the side wall. He pushed the blade deeper into the tyre and yanked it to the side. Air rushed out through the split in the rubber; it was loud at first – Atticus was sure that Doyle would hear it – but then quieter, a low hiss that was less obvious.

Atticus heard Doyle's footsteps and saw the van's suspension dip as he put something heavier inside. He walked back inside. Atticus knew that Doyle would notice the tyre eventually and that now was the time to beat a retreat. He reached the path and followed it back to the house, looking up and seeing that two of the windows on the first floor were now lit.

He hid in the gloom beneath the boughs of one of the old oaks and put in his earbuds. He took out his phone and, shielding the light of the screen with a cupped hand, he called Mack. He felt a buzz of nervousness as the call rang. She was going to be angry with him.

She picked up. 'Where are you? You said you'd come over and—'

He cut across her. 'Did you get my voicemail?'

'No. Why?' She paused. 'And why are you whispering?'

'There's something you need to see.'

'It's past midnight. What is it? Where are you?'

'At Summers' house.'

She didn't respond.

'It's not what you think,' Atticus said. 'He called me and he asked me to come. I sent you a voicemail, but . . . well, you didn't get it.'

'What did he say?'

'He lied through his teeth and then threatened me, but it doesn't matter. I've found a room that looks just like the one in the videos. The red room.'

'You "found" it? *Please* don't tell me you've broken the law.' She paused. 'What am I talking about? Of *course* you broke the law.'

'I didn't. Summers invited me here, and I had a look around the grounds afterwards. I suppose, technically, it might be described as trespassing . . .'

'"Technically"? You're there without permission. That's the *definition* of trespassing.'

'And it's a civil matter, not criminal. Anyway.' He took a beat. '*Anyway* – it was worth it. Summers and a man who works for him went inside the chapel, and I looked inside, through the door. He's got a little film studio and it's been made to look like the one in the videos.'

'What good does this do us? What do you want me to do? Come over and ask him nicely if he'd show me?'

'No, Mack. You've got grounds to suspect there's evidence relating to an indictable offence on the premises.'

'You don't need to teach me what PACE says,' she said, referring to the Police and Criminal Evidence Act.

'It's definitely connected to the three deaths and Summers knows we're on to him. They're moving everything out. You need to get here before it all disappears.'

'How? I've got no grounds to be there, save what you've told me, and you only know that because you're there when you shouldn't be.'

Atticus stopped. He thought he heard something. He frowned, closed his eyes and concentrated on listening as carefully as he could.

Had he?

There was nothing now, nothing obvious, save the call of a night bird from somewhere in the dark overhead.

But that wasn't it.

It was the sound of breaking glass.

'Atticus.'

Atticus looked back up at the house and saw that another light had come on downstairs.

'Atticus, are you still there?'

'Something's happening.'

He stepped out from behind the tree and then ran across the grass to the main house. He reached the wall and edged around it until he was outside the door that he had used earlier. That door was still closed and there was no sign of broken glass. He continued, reaching the corner of the house and another door that he recalled as opening into the storeroom next to the ground-floor office. There was a pane of glass in this door and it had been smashed; the door, when he touched it, swung open.

'*Atticus?*'

He heard a loud cry from somewhere in the house.

73

Atticus pushed the door back with his fingertips and stepped into the dark space beyond. His recollection of the plan of the property was right; the space was used as some kind of store, with shelving on the walls and a low unit pushed up beneath the single covered window. There was an open door to his right; he stepped through it into the office and then froze at the sound of an angry shout from somewhere upstairs.

He only had to pass through the office and the boot room to get to the hall, and from there it was just a short distance to the stairs that would take him up to the first floor. The master bedroom was above the kitchen, with the bay window perhaps ten metres away from where he was standing now.

He heard voices.

Two men: one of them angry, the other afraid.

Atticus crept forward, passing between the desks in the office and gently opening the door to the boot room. An exterior door was to his left. There was a sink in the corner and, beneath it, a cupboard. He opened it and found a plastic box that stored a variety of tools that could be used for household maintenance. He took it out and picked up a screwdriver with a heavy plastic handle, wondering whether it would serve as something he could use to defend himself. He put it down, reached into the box again and took out a hammer.

Atticus stepped into the hall. There was a second flight of stairs directly to his right that ascended to the landing on the first floor.

The voices were clearer now. He could make out what was being said.

'Put it down,' Summers said.

'You don't remember me, do you?'

'How would I? I've never met you before.'

'Yes, you have. But I was younger then.'

Atticus started up the stairs. They were made of dark hardwood, with ornate balustrades and a curved handrail. The treads were old and loose, and they creaked as he put his weight on them. Atticus froze, but the voices continued. He resumed climbing.

'What do you mean?' Summers said from the floor above.

'Tell me you remember me.'

'I don't.'

Atticus reached the landing. It was grand, with high ceilings and large windows that were covered by thick curtains. The floor was covered by a plush carpet that meant he could approach the master bedroom without making a sound. Eleven doors opened onto the corridor that ran along the middle of the house, some of them grand and imposing.

The voices were coming from the master bedroom.

'It's too late for that.'

'For what?'

'For playing the innocent.'

'Put that *down*.'

Summers muttered something, and there was the sound of a scuffle, then a thud as something heavy fell to the floor. There was a shriek – from Summers, Atticus thought, but he wasn't sure – and then another thud.

He reached the doorway. His heart hammered in his chest, and he could feel sweat on his palms beneath the gloves and in the small of his back. Atticus waited for a beat and then turned and looked into the bedroom.

A figure, dressed in black and with a knife in his hand, turned to face him.

74

The man was dressed in black from head to toe. He was of average appearance: his hair was dark and of a medium length, worn in a practical cut; his blue eyes were a pale, almost greyish shade; his features were neither overly sharp nor overly soft, lending him an ordinary appearance. He would have been entirely unexceptional, were it not for the knife in his hand.

'Atticus,' he said, 'why did you have to come back? You should've kept driving.'

'How do you know my . . .' He stopped, the pieces of the puzzle locking into place. 'What do I call you? Jack?'

'That'll do.'

Atticus looked at the knife and saw that the blade was stained red. Summers was spreadeagled across the floor, his arms and legs splayed wide. A slowly expanding pool of blood leeched out from beneath his torso.

'Put it down.'

Jack shook his head. 'Can't do that. I'll take it with me. But I don't want to hurt you.'

Atticus raised the hammer with one hand and held up the other, as if that might be enough to ward him off. 'What have you done?'

'He got what he deserved. You saw what they were doing. Miller, Burns and York? You've seen the videos. You *can't* disagree with me. Summers was involved from the start. He had the money and a place to film when they couldn't use Imber.' He stepped away from Summers. 'He's as guilty as sin, and he got what he deserved.'

'You need to stop. They'll catch you in the end.'

'No, they won't. They haven't got a clue.'

'*I've* found you. They will, too. Give up.'

'When I'm done. But not now – there's more to do. There are others.'

'Customers?'

'Men who paid to rape kids. I've got a list of them, and I'm going to work through it from top to bottom.' He took a step towards the door. 'Get out of my way.'

Atticus heard a car rolling across the gravel drive and saw headlights raking the room through the uncovered window.

'I told you,' Atticus said. 'You can't run.'

Footsteps approached the house across the gravel, and then there was a heavy knock on the door. 'Police – is anyone inside?'

Jack raised the knife and turned his wrist so that the tip of the blade was pointing at Atticus's chest. He jabbed it at him, forcing him to step back, then darted through the open door and turned left, hurrying along the corridor to the landing. He took the stairs two at a time, the treads creaking in protest.

'*Police!*' came the shout from below.

Atticus was frozen. Jack had a knife and Atticus had no desire to be stabbed. On the other hand, he knew that Jack was cunning and cautious, and there was a good chance that he would disappear forever if he was allowed to leave now.

Atticus had no choice; he *had* to know who he was.

He followed, sprinting along the corridor and onto the landing, then descending the stairs as fast as he could. The police sounded as if they were outside the door to the entrance hall. Jack had come in through the office store and would be able to use that to get outside again. And, thanks to the angle of the house, he would be invisible to the officers who were trying to get inside.

'Mr Summers?' the voice called out. 'Atticus? *Open the door.*'

Atticus reached the foot of the stairs, ran into the library and leapt up the three steps to the entrance hall. He stopped, removed the gloves and overshoes, undid the latch and opened the door. Bob Carver was on the threshold.

'The owner of the house has been stabbed,' Atticus said.

'Where is he?'

'Upstairs.'

The blue and red lights of a patrol car pulsed against the walls of the house and cast enough light for Atticus to glimpse a figure running north, between the trees that bracketed the path that ended with the chapel.

Atticus stepped around Carver and ran.

75

Atticus put his head down and sprinted, passing the two cottages and following the path towards the chapel. He slipped on a patch of wet grass, his legs sliding out from underneath him so that he crashed down on to his side. He got up again and ran, reaching the path and pressing on as fast as he could.

He heard an exclamation from ahead and then a dull thud. He came around the corner and saw Doyle and Jack on the ground next to the van. Doyle was struggling to get astride Jack and, as he managed it, he used his knee to press down on Jack's left arm. Jack's top was pulled up and Atticus saw a scar, a couple of inches long, on the lower-right side of his belly. Doyle punched down at Jack's head: once, twice and then a third time. Each blow was hard, with all of Doyle's weight behind it, and blood splashed on Jack's face.

'Hey!' Atticus yelled.

Doyle turned at the sound, his face twisted with fury. He turned back to Jack and drew back his fist to deliver another blow, but didn't notice Jack scrabbling with his free hand, his fingers probing for the knife that must have fallen from his grasp. He found the tip of the blade, then the handle. Doyle saw, but too late; Jack swung his arm up and around, burying the knife into Doyle's torso, the point slicing in between his ribs. Doyle gasped.

Jack pulled the knife out and then plunged it in for a second and then a third time.

Doyle stiffened, his arms falling limply to his sides.

Jack lay back and gasped for breath. His face was smeared with blood.

Doyle groaned and slumped to the side. He slid off Jack's body, bounced off the van and then hit the path.

The knife had fallen from Jack's hand again and lay on the path next to him. Atticus used the toe of his boot to push it away and knelt next to him.

'It's over.'

'Why are you . . . doing this?' He coughed, and blood bubbled out of the corner of his mouth. 'You want . . . you want . . . same thing as me. Burns, York . . . Miller . . . the others . . .' He swallowed the blood, his words slurring. 'Just the same . . .'

'Not like this.'

Atticus heard footsteps from behind him and glanced around as another uniformed officer – Pete Britten – raced up to them. He slowed and stopped and muttered a curse.

'What's happened?'

'This is Jack,' Atticus said, then pointed at Doyle. 'He works for Summers. Jack stabbed him.'

Britten took his cuffs from his belt, opened the bracelets and secured Jack's wrists.

Atticus sat down next to Jack.

Britten spoke into his radio. 'Bravo November four-five to control. I need an ambulance to West Woodyates Manor.'

Atticus closed his eyes.

'Ambulance is already on its way, four-five.'

'I need another one. I need the on-call DI, I need CSI, I need the Major Incident Team . . . I need the whole bloody circus.'

76

Atticus got up and went over to check Doyle. He put his fingers to his neck and felt for a pulse.

Britten looked over. 'And?'

'Dead.'

They both heard footsteps and turned to see another uniformed officer approaching.

'Sarge,' Britten called out, 'over here.'

It was James Boyd. He changed direction and swore as he saw the two bloodied men.

Britten explained what had happened. Jack looked as if he was unconscious now. Boyd radioed control to see where the ambulance was and was told that it would be with them in ten minutes. The two officers made sure that Jack was breathing before Boyd stood and turned to Atticus.

'Anything I need to know?'

'Look in the chapel.'

'Why?'

'You'll see.'

He did as Atticus suggested. 'Empty. What am I looking for?'

Atticus went inside, went over to the plug and switched on the lights.

The room was bathed in red.

'Shit,' Boyd said.

'The dead man's name is Doyle. He worked for Summers. He was moving the kit from here into the van.'

'Why?'

'There was a little too much heat here for them.'

'Let me just try to get this straight,' Boyd said. 'Are you saying that Summers and the bloke outside – Doyle . . . Are you saying that they're responsible for making the videos?'

'They were involved.'

'And what are you doing here?'

'Summers asked me to come over to see him tonight. I was outside when all this kicked off.'

Boyd reached out and put a hand on Atticus's shoulder. 'Better go up to the house. Mack's on her way. You'll have to explain it to her.'

* * *

Atticus left the chapel and walked back to the house. An ambulance and two other patrol cars were parked there, and he could hear the howl of more ambulance sirens and patrol cars in the distance. Atticus saw a man being stretchered out of the door and loaded into the back of the ambulance. He drew nearer and saw that it was Summers.

Bob Carver was standing at the door.

'How is he?' Atticus asked.

'Alive.'

'Is he going to make it?'

'They don't know.'

Atticus stepped back, waiting for the paramedics to shut the doors and for Carver's attention to be distracted as they got into the cab and started the engine. The door to the house was closed, and rather than have Carver notice him opening it again and going inside, he made his way around the house and used the door that Jack had forced. Atticus went upstairs, emerging on the top landing and orienting himself with his memory of the plan of the property.

The door to Summers' bedroom was open; it was the only room that was lit, with a warm glow falling out across the carpet. Atticus took it all in quickly: the duvet on top of the bed was disturbed; a glass of water on the bedstand had been overturned; the bloodstain on the floor had grown a little larger.

He left the room and checked the others. The bedrooms had been made up, but none of them were being used. A door at the end of the corridor was closed and, when Atticus tried the handle, he found – to his irritation – that it was locked. He was going to try to pick it when he heard a car outside. He went back to the master bedroom, glanced out of the window and saw another patrol car and, beyond that, the lights of several additional vehicles approaching along the long drive.

They drew nearer and he saw that Mack's car was bringing up the rear.

Time to leave.

77

Atticus went back outside and stepped around the corner of the house as Mack pulled up in the parking area. He went with Carver to join her.

'What's going on?' she said. 'I passed an ambulance on the way in – what happened?'

'The owner of the house has been stabbed,' Carver said.

She looked to Atticus. 'Summers?'

Atticus nodded.

'Dead or alive?'

'Alive,' Carver said. 'But it looks bad.'

'What happened?'

'It was Jack,' Atticus said. 'He broke in and attacked him.'

'You saw him?'

'I was in the room with him. He ran when the first patrol car arrived. We got him, though.'

'Where?'

Atticus pointed. 'By the chapel. He was jumped by one of the men who work for Summers. There was a struggle between the two of them – Jack knifed Summers' man, but he's taken a beating. Britten and Boyd are with him.'

A second ambulance arrived and slowly made its way through the gardens in the direction of the chapel.

'What does Jack have against Summers?'

'The videos. Summers was involved with Miller and the others. Jack killed Miller, he killed the customers – Campbell, Kajetan, Hartnett – and he tried to kill Summers. He admitted it.'

'You've spoken?'

'Yes, but not for long. You'll need him to repeat that in an interview.'

'And if he won't?'

'He'll talk to me.'

'That's not going to happen, though, is it? You're not police.'

Robbie Best pulled up in his car, got out and listened carefully while Mack updated him. Atticus paced, anxious to return to the chapel. He needed to be doing something. The police would search the house and the grounds and, although Atticus was desperate to be involved, he knew that Mack wouldn't – *couldn't* – allow it.

Mack finished with Best and turned to Atticus.

'Show us where he is,' she said.

Atticus led the way, following the strobing blue lights of the ambulance to the chapel. One of the paramedics was crouched over Doyle; he looked for a pulse, shook his head, and covered the body with a sheet. The other medic was with Jack. He had been propped up against the side of the van, his cuffed wrists in his lap, while the woman checked him over.

Mack stopped dead. 'Shit.'

'What is it?'

'*Shit.* That's Francine's boyfriend.'

Atticus frowned. 'What do you mean it's her boyfriend?'

'I can't remember his name. I met him in the pub this week.' She turned to Best. 'You were there – Bob Bradley's birthday. That's him, isn't it, or am I going mad?'

Best stared. 'You're not going mad. It's definitely him.'

'What's his name?'

'Charlie.'

They watched as Jack – or Charlie, or *whoever* he was – was helped up.

Mack put her head in her hands. 'Someone's going to need to tell Franny.'

'Can't be a coincidence,' Best said.

'Of course it's not,' Atticus said. 'He's used Francine to get a line into the investigation. *Jesus.* How much has she told him?'

Mack frowned at him. 'Maybe she hasn't told him anything. She knows this is sensitive.'

'And you've never shared anything out of school?'

She glared at him, then turned to Best. 'Follow the ambulance to the hospital.'

'Will do.'

Mack gestured to Atticus with her finger. 'Walk back to the house with me.'

She set off, and he followed.

'You've done it again,' she muttered.

'Done what?'

'Messed up! I told you not to let me down, and you said – you promised – that you wouldn't.'

'I told you,' he reminded her starchily. 'Summers called me. He asked me to come. I tried to let you know, but you didn't pick up.'

'I was with Beckton and Murphy.'

'Did you listen to my message?'

'Yes, but you still should've waited. You know I would have told you it needed to be done properly. By a police officer who's prepared to respect the rules.'

'I thought he might have called me because he was panicking about what you might know, so he brought me over so that he could get a sense of it without it being official. And I thought *if* he was panicking, it would potentially be too good an opportunity to wait until tomorrow when he might not have been.'

She cut across him. 'You really should listen to yourself sometimes. The shit that comes out of your mouth. You can try to dress it up however you like. We had a plan and you ignored it.'

'I know, and I've said I'm sorry.' He knew that Mack was going to tear a strip off him, but he was growing frustrated that she wasn't paying attention to the progress that had been made. 'Look – you can beat me up about it for as long as you like once this is over and done with, but, for now, you need to focus on what we've found out. It's *done*. It's *over*. You can put this whole thing to bed tonight. We wanted to find out what's been going on, and now we have. Jack has been murdering the men who made the videos and the men who were in them. Summers was involved in making them.'

'You could have caught either of them in the act, and it wouldn't make a blind bit of difference if the evidence is inadmissible because of how you got it. Let's assume he doesn't die and we have enough to build a case against him—'

'We do,' he said.

'Let's *assume* that we do.' She pointed back up the garden to the house. 'Look at this place. It cost eighteen million when he bought it. Eighteen million! He has enough money to afford the kind of lawyer who'll make *us* look corrupt when we get him to trial. There are rules that we have to follow about evidence. I know you find them tedious, but there we are – they exist, they're there for a reason, and we *can't* ignore them.'

'I haven't done anything wrong. He asked me to come, and I came. That's it.'

'Fine. When did this all happen?'

'Just after midnight.'

'Why were you still here, then?'

Atticus was quiet for a moment. 'I see what you mean. Yes. We'll have to think of a reason to explain that.'

She put her head in her hands.

'I'll say I forgot something, came back to get it, went to the door, saw that it had been forced.'

'And called me.'

'Yes,' he said, hoping that she might be prepared to play along. 'I heard a scream and went inside to see if I could help. I saw a man with a knife. He ran. I chased him. Look, Mack – we can argue later, but, right now, you need to search the property.'

'How are we going to do that? We can't ask Summers for permission.'

'Say that there's a risk that evidence would be destroyed if we had to wait to get a warrant?'

Mack thought about it, then shook her head. 'No. We've already taken enough risks in getting to where we are now. We'll make an expedited application for a warrant. We need to be sure that we do this by the book.' She stared at him meaningfully. 'No more shortcuts.'

The ambulance drove by them, following the path back to the house.

Atticus turned back to Mack. 'How much have you told Francine?'

'About what?'

'About Summers? About what I found on the tape?'

She shook her head. 'I haven't seen her today.'

'So how did Jack know that Summers was involved?'

'I don't know. Maybe—'

'Don't say coincidence,' he cut over her. 'He's out here the *same* day that we find out about Summers.'

'It's possible.'

'No, it's not. He's got close to Francine to keep an eye on the investigation. You need to find out exactly what she's told him.'

'Could he have been watching you?'

'And then followed me here?' Atticus closed his eyes and tried to recall whether there might have been a car on the road with him out to the estate on either of his two visits yesterday. 'I don't know.'

'We'll ask him,' she said. 'He'll need to be checked out, but once we have the green light, we'll get him in the interview room and see what he's got to say.'

They both noticed another car as it came around the house and slowed as the driver looked for a spot to park.

Atticus squinted at it but was blinded from seeing who was inside by the glare of the headlamps. 'Who's that?'

'Looks like Murphy,' she said. 'He'll want to take over here.'

'What about Francine?' Atticus said.

'I'll go and see her now. Want to come?'

'OK.'

She pointed to her car. 'Get in before Murphy sees you.'

78

Mack drove to Francine Patterson's place on St Ann Street. She parked in an empty space and then led the way back down the hill to the house. There was a light on in the downstairs window.

She put out a hand and took Atticus by the elbow. 'I'll do it. This is going to be very difficult for her, and I don't want her to feel like it's her fault.'

'Can I come in and listen?'

'Be gentle.'

Mack knocked on the door. Francine opened it and blinked out at both of them. Her face was pale and her eyes were damp.

'Is it true?'

'How do you know?'

'Robbie called me. It *is* true, then? About Charlie?'

'Yes,' Mack said. 'I had a look as they loaded him into the ambulance. It's definitely him. Can we come in?'

A hand fluttered up to her throat. 'Sorry. Of course.'

She stepped back to allow Mack and then Atticus to come inside. They went into the kitchen.

'I feel like I've been punched in the face,' Francine said.

'Sit down. Atticus – make us all a brew.'

Francine distractedly told him that the teabags were in the cupboard above the sink. He found them, filled the kettle and flicked the switch to set it to boil.

Mack quickly recounted what had happened at Summers' house, that Charlie looked to have broken his arm and that he had been taken to hospital.

Francine put a hand to her mouth. 'Are you sure he did what you say he did?'

'I was there,' Atticus said. 'He was in the house with a knife.'

'My god.'

Mack reached out and grabbed her wrist. 'It's fine. It's not your fault.'

'I still feel like a complete fool.'

The kettle boiled. Atticus put teabags into three mugs and poured in the hot water. He put the mugs on the table and opened the fridge for the milk.

'It's off,' Francine said. 'Charlie was going to pick up a bottle on his way over.'

'I'll have it black,' Mack said.

There were only two chairs at the table, so Atticus stood with his back against the wall. 'How did you meet him?'

'Online. I've got a profile on Bumble. He sent me a message.' She waved a hand vaguely. 'It was all totally normal.'

'He's very smart,' Atticus said.

'Is Charlie even his real name?'

'We don't know yet,' Mack said. 'We'll find out when we speak to him.'

'When?'

'Depends what the doctors say – later this morning or this afternoon.'

'Can I be there?'

'Probably best if you aren't.'

Atticus looked around. 'Where's your phone?'

'Why?'

'Can I see the messages he sent?'

Francine looked down and bit her lip; Mack thought she might be about to cry. 'This is going to be so embarrassing,' she said.

'It's important. We—'

Mack looked up at Atticus and gave a gentle shake of her head. 'We can wait until later for that.'

Francine breathed in and out and, when she looked up again, there was steel in her eyes. 'What can I do to help, boss?'

'Are you sure? I don't mind if you take a little time to get yourself together.'

'I'd rather get straight back into it, if it's all the same. Doing something useful will take my mind off it.'

'OK – that's good. We need to get a search warrant for Summers' house. Liaise with Robbie – you'll need to go and wake a judge up.'

She nodded.

Mack gripped her hand. 'And it's *not* your fault. No one blames you. There was no way of knowing.'

'I know,' she said, although the tremor in her voice suggested that she hadn't yet been able to persuade herself that that was true.

'We'll get to the bottom of it. Call Robbie, go and get the warrant, and we'll take it from there.'

79

The search team assembled at the property at nine. Mack got out of her car and finished what was left of the coffee that she had brought with her from the office. She had managed to grab an hour or two of sleep on the sofa in the break room, but she knew that she was going to be working for hours in a row as the investigation picked up speed, and that she was going to need caffeine to stay upright.

Murphy and his team arrived, parking next to her and exiting to join the others who were milling around. There were a dozen of them, a mixture of plainclothes – from Salisbury and London – and uniform. Atticus had wanted to be here, too, but Mack had vetoed it. Murphy had made his feelings about him very obvious, and it made no sense to antagonise him. Mack felt vulnerable, too; she knew that her feelings for Atticus – and her confidence in his ability to make breakthroughs that were beyond everyone else – could sometimes blind her to his methods. There were occasions when the ends justified the means, but it felt as if parading him in front of Murphy now would be asking for trouble. He had been predictably outraged, but she had won him over with a promise that she would share anything useful that they discovered with him.

Still, she had arrived at the house with a sense of trepidation, half expecting to find Atticus waiting for her. Thankfully – and for once – he had been good to his word.

Robbie and Francine had applied to a judge to obtain the warrant that they would need to search Summers' property. Robbie had made the application with Francine, taking contemporaneous notes to provide the audit trail in the event that the warrant was disputed at trial. They had visited the judge at home and reported that she was easily persuaded by their evidence and that the process had been over in less than fifteen minutes.

'Ladies and gents,' Murphy said now, clapping his hands together to bring them to order. 'We've had a development. DCI Jones will bring you up to speed, and then we're going to be busy.'

Mack briefed them all so that they understood the background to the search and why a warrant was necessary. She explained first that she had questioned Harry Summers following the discovery that images of his ex-wife had been found at the end of one of the videos that had been sent to the *Journal*. She said that he had then been attacked here yesterday evening, leaving out the information that Atticus had been the one to interrupt the assault and likely saved his life. She had briefed Murphy at the nick earlier, and he was now aware that Atticus was responsible for the discovery. He had also made it plain that he was going to want to discuss Atticus's continuing involvement in the case – 'despite his clear instructions' – with Beckton.

They were each assigned a part of the house to search, and set off.

Mack was paired with Francine, and the two of them headed off through the gardens to the buildings at the rear. There were two barns that it was necessary to clear, and it looked as if both had been converted: the first was being used as accommodation, while the second seemed to have been adapted to provide office space for Summers' business.

'What was Summers like when you spoke to him?' Francine asked her as they started to look through the first cottage.

'Polite.'

'How did he explain his ex-wife being on that tape?'

'He didn't. He couldn't explain it.'

'And you believed him?'

'I didn't think he was telling us everything.'

'What did Atticus think?'

'The same.'

They cleared the first cottage and moved into the second. The interior of the building had been divided into two separate sections: the first provided two large conference rooms, a kitchenette and staff break-out areas; the second was reserved for an extra-large office. There was a huge desk with two external monitors that looked as if they would have cost the same as reasonable family cars, and the walls were bedecked with sporting memorabilia, including signed shirts, a pair of football boots in a Perspex case, and a football, complete with the signatures of the 1966 England World Cup winning team, displayed on a pedestal. Other framed photographs showed Summers with the great and the good from the worlds of entertainment, sports and politics.

'Look at all this stuff,' Francine said, pointing up to a pair of boxing gloves in a clear case, a plaque beneath them noting that they had been used by Mike Tyson in his defeat of Frank Bruno. 'It must've cost a bomb.'

'He's not short of money.'

Mack tapped the keyboard to wake the two screens, but the computer to which they were attached was locked.

'Boss,' Francine said, 'look at this.'

She was on the other side of the office, bent over a circular coffee table that held an open lever-arch file. Mack crossed over to look at it and saw that it contained a thick stack of papers.

The page at which it had been left open was a printout of a spreadsheet that looked as if it recorded a list of payments. The payments started in 2020 and the recipient of at least half of them was listed as KBank.

'KBank,' Mack muttered.

'Kasikornbank,' Francine said with a nod of confirmation. 'It's Thai, isn't it?'

'The bank that Alfred Burns used in Bangkok. That's where Miller and York said they were making payments after he blackmailed them, isn't it? What are we saying? Burns was blackmailing Summers, too?'

Mack took out her phone and snapped a picture of the spreadsheet so that she could show it to Atticus. She was sure now, that he was right in his suggestion that Summers was involved with Miller, York and Burns and that his ignorance about the videotape was feigned. The sense that they were closing in on a breakthrough that would throw the whole case open was now too tantalisingly close to ignore.

'Come on,' she said, pointing to the door. 'Let's see what they found in the chapel.'

As they reached the door, Mack heard a muffled noise from somewhere beneath the floor.

'Did you hear that?'

Francine had stopped, too. 'I think so. What was it?'

'It sounded like a voice.'

They both stood still and listened.

It was clear this time: a muffled shout, coming from somewhere beneath their feet.

Mack looked around. 'There's got to be a cellar.'

They each looked around the room, searching for a trapdoor or any other means of access that would allow them to get down to a basement. There was no obvious opening. Mack went back to the desk and heaved it to the side, hoping to see something beneath it, finding nothing, save freshly scuffed floorboards. She went to the sofa, pushing that away from the wall and finding nothing.

The noise came again.

'Shit,' Francine said. 'There's someone down there.'

There was a cupboard on the other side of the room that was secured with a padlock. Mack found a heavy metal paperweight on the desk and took it over, raising it up and bringing it down as hard as she could so that the edge caught the shackle. The metal was dented but didn't break. She hit it again and again, and then, with the fourth blow, the shackle came away from the body and she could open the door.

Mack had been wrong: it wasn't a cupboard.

It was a set of stairs that led down into darkness.

She took out her phone and switched on the flashlight. The beam wasn't strong enough to cast light all the way to the bottom, but Mack thought she could make out another door.

'Stay here,' she said. 'I'm going to have a look.'

She started down the stairs, taking them one tread at a time and listening carefully for anything that might suggest danger.

There came another muffled cry; it *was* a person. Mack was sure about that now.

She reached the foot of the stairs and turned to face another wooden door. This one was locked, but the key had been left in it. Mack turned it and, with the phone held up so that the light shone inside, pushed the door open. The room beyond was cramped, not much more than a cubby hole, and the flashlight could reach all four walls. Mack shone the light down and saw a girl. Her hands and feet had been secured with plastic ties, and a cloth had been stuffed into her mouth and then held in place with tape.

Mack's heart raced.

'Franny!' she yelled. 'There's a kid down here.'

The girl said something, but her words were rendered unintelligible by the cloth. Her eyes were wide with fear.

Mack knelt beside her. 'It's all right. My name's Mack. I'm with the police. Let me get this off you.'

She gently peeled away the edge of the tape and pulled it back, trying not to yank the strands of blonde hair that had been caught in the adhesive. She removed it all, dropped it to the side, and removed the cloth from the girl's mouth.

'Everything's going to be fine,' Mack said. 'You're safe now.'

80

Mack remembered seeing a pair of scissors on the desk upstairs and told Francine to bring them down. Mack used them to cut through the ties and then put her arm around the girl's waist and helped her to stand. She took her to the stairs and helped her to climb up to the ground floor.

Francine was waiting, and bit down on her lip as the two of them emerged. Mack could see the girl more clearly now: she couldn't have been much more than fifteen or sixteen and was dressed in a dirty T-shirt and tracksuit bottoms. Her feet were bare, and her wrists and ankles were chafed from where she had struggled against the plastic ties. She blinked her eyes against the light; Mack realised that she might have been kept down there, in the pitch dark, for hours.

'Franny,' Mack said, 'can you get her a drink of water?'

Mack took the girl to the sofa and indicated that she should sit down. She sat, too, turning her body so that they were almost facing each other. She reached out and took both of the girl's hands in hers.

'What's your name, love?'

Her voice was hoarse. 'Maria.'

'What's your surname?'

'Zankovetska.'

'Where are you from?'

'Ukraine.'

'All right. That's good. Do you speak English?'

'I learn it.'

'I'm Detective Chief Inspector Jones, although you can call me Mack. My friend over there is Francine. She's a policewoman, too. A detective – like me. Like I said – you're safe now.'

She shook her head, her eyes wide. 'I'm not. What about them?'

'"Them"? Who do you mean?'

'The men. The men who . . .' She swallowed, unable to finish the sentence.

'You're *safe*,' Mack said. 'There are a lot of police officers here apart from us. They're outside now. A dozen – more than a dozen. And we know what happened.'

The girl squeezed Mack's hands tight. 'The *men*. They . . .' She choked up again.

'Do you mean Mr Summers?'

She shook her head. 'Don't know names.'

'The men who kept you down there have been sorted out. I *promise*. You're safe, Maria. You don't need to worry about them, not any more. We won't let *anything* else happen to you.'

Francine brought over a plastic beaker of water and gave it to the girl. She gulped it down quickly, as if worried it would be taken away.

'Maria,' Mack said, 'I'm just going to leave you with Francine for a moment. Is that OK?'

The girl shook her head and tightened her grip on Mack's hand.

'Francine,' Mack said, 'come over and say hello.'

Francine knelt in front of the girl and rested a hand on her knee. She smiled. 'You can call me Franny. I'll stay with you, I promise.'

'And I'll be back in a moment,' Mack said. 'I just need to tell the other officers that you're here.'

81

Mack left Francine in the cottage and hurried back to the rally point at the front of the house. Murphy was waiting there, along with a detective constable from his team and Robbie Best. All three of them turned as Mack crunched through the gravel and made her way over to them.

Best had a clear plastic evidence bag in one gloved hand. 'Look at this, boss.' He held the bag up so that Mack could see what was inside: a leather-bound book.

'What is it? Address book?'

'Don't know. It was in an office upstairs.' He unsealed the bag and carefully removed the book. Mack put on a fresh pair of gloves and took it. 'Turn to C.'

Mack did as she was told. The page contained eight names, all ordered alphabetically.

The name at the top was David Campbell.

'Now go to H.'

Mack flicked forwards, found the page behind the tab for H, and found another six names.

At the top, once more, was a name that she recognised immediately: Dominic Hartnett.

She didn't need to be told what to do next, and flipped forward another three tabs until she reached K. There were only three names listed, but Lucjusz Kajetan was the second of them.

Murphy was watching her. 'Any idea what that might mean?'

Mack tried to order her thoughts. The investigation had multiplied over the course of the last day, and it was difficult to keep track of the angles that were shooting off in all directions. She needed to write down her thoughts before they ran away with her; she needed to speak to Atticus even more.

'DCI Jones?'

'I think this is a customer ledger. I think Summers has been running some sort of dirty video business, or whatever passes for that online.'

'From the studio in the chapel?'

'Yes, and probably for years – at least twenty. I think he used to run it with Burns, York and Miller.'

'And the man who attacked Summers last night?'

'It's Jack,' she said. 'I think he was one of the children they abused, most likely at Imber. He killed Miller and three customers and then went after Summers when he learned he was involved.'

'And how did *you* work that out?'

'Sir?'

'How did you know to come out here and speak to him? Priest was involved again, wasn't he?'

'He was, sir, but, with respect, I think that's going to have to wait.'

'No, Detective Chief Inspector, I don't agree with that at all. I gave him explicit instructions to—'

'Please,' Mack cut across him, '*please*, for once, just *shut up*.'

'*Excuse* me?'

'Shut up and *listen*. We found a young girl in the cellar of one of the cottages. She was tied up, and the door was locked.'

Murphy's mouth fell open. 'Shit. Where? Which cottage?'

Mack pointed. 'There. It's not really a cellar – not big enough. More of a crawlspace. I've no idea how long she's been down there.'

'Is she OK?'

'No, she's not. She's traumatised. I don't even want to think about what she's been through. Francine Patterson is with her now, but we need someone from the child abuse investigation team down here pronto. We'll need a translator, too – she's a Ukrainian refugee, and I don't know how well she speaks English.'

'I'll sort it out,' Best said.

'She'll need to be checked out at the hospital, too.'

'Has she said anything?' Murphy asked.

'She's scared. I haven't been able to get much out of her yet.'

Murphy muttered another curse. 'What a mess. You really think this goes back to Imber?'

'I do. We know Burns was blackmailing Miller and York, and we know they killed him for it. I found bank statements in the cottage suggesting that Burns was blackmailing Summers, too. All four of them must have been working on the business together until they fell out.'

'We need to speak to Jack,' Murphy said.

'Have you heard from the hospital?'

'They've given him the all-clear on the concussion.'

'When can we question him?'

'After lunch.'

'And Summers?'

'They operated on him. He lost a lot of blood. They've intubated him. It's fifty-fifty.'

Mack knew they needed to speak to him, but she couldn't stop thinking of the girl in the cellar. She wouldn't have been remotely upset if he never recovered.

The officers dispersed to carry on with the search. Mack wandered over to the trees that fringed the parking area and took out her phone. She saw she had three missed calls from Atticus and knew that he would be beside himself with agitation and anxiety.

She tapped his number and he answered on the first ring.

'What's going on?'

She updated him on what had been found.

'What about Summers?'

'Not in a good way.'

'And Jack?'

'He's been cleared for interview. It'll be later.'

'I want to be there.'

'Murphy won't go for that.'

'Persuade him.'

'How?'

'I'm a witness,' he said.

'And he'll see that you're interviewed about that, but I can't see any chance that he'll let you be involved.'

'I *need* to be there, Mack. No one else has the experience with him that I do.'

'I'll speak to Murphy,' she said, 'but don't hold your breath.'

82

Even by recent standards, it had been a busy morning. Mack had stayed at Summers' house until lunchtime. An officer from the child protection unit had arrived to help with Maria Zankovetska, but she had refused to leave the cottage unless Francine went with her. Mack was happy to approve that and watched as the girl was checked out by the paramedics before going with Franny to the hospital for a more thorough examination. They would need to take a statement from her, but it could wait. In the meantime, they had established that her parents had both been killed by shelling in Kramatorsk and that her older brother was in the military. Mack worried it wouldn't be easy to find a relative who could be responsible for her and that they would have to rely upon Social Services.

Robbie Best had investigated the man Jack had stabbed to death outside the chapel. He had a wallet in his pocket and the name on his driving licence and credit cards was Paul Doyle. They had run a PNC check and had been rewarded with a litany of previous convictions: public order and violence offences, including assault and criminal damage. Best reported that Doyle had been a soldier and that he had been jailed for eighteen months after a court martial in Osnabrück found him guilty of mistreating Iraqi prisoners at an aid depot near Basra. Doyle had been dishonourably discharged upon his release and employed by Summers shortly thereafter. A check of his DNA matched a sample taken in Derek Burns' flat in Andover; Atticus had been attacked there and, although the incident had never been recorded because Atticus shouldn't have been in the flat at all, Mack knew they had found the man who had been responsible.

Mack went through the office to the custody suite where suspects were held until they were ready to be questioned and then to the interview room at the end of the corridor. Murphy was sitting at the table with papers and photographs spread out in front of him.

She cleared her throat, and he looked up. 'DCI Jones.'

'Afternoon, sir.'

'So – Jack.'

'It's probably Atticus you need to be talking to,' she said. 'He's the one who has been in contact with him.'

'I'm not having him anywhere near this investigation. We still need to talk about what he was doing at the house last night.' He waved a hand as if swatting away an irritation. 'I understand Jack has been in a relationship with one of your officers.'

'Yes, sir – DC Patterson. She knows him as Charlie.'

'I can understand why Jack might want a relationship like that – it's an excellent way to get an idea of what we're thinking.'

'Francine says she didn't tell him anything.'

'Come on, it's human nature. She would have said *something*.'

'Maybe,' she allowed. 'But I will not see this as an error on her part.'

'What about Priest? Why's Jack interested in him?'

'Jack – *Charlie* – knew Atticus was the one pushing to investigate Alfred Burns, and he obviously had a reason to want him brought to justice. He told Atticus that he was involved with what Burns, Miller and York were doing. We didn't know what that meant then – being "involved" – but we can make an educated guess now.'

Murphy took notes. 'Charlie called Priest after you'd arrested and released Miller and told Priest that there were others involved in what was going on – more than just Miller, Burns and York.'

'Yes. And he said that he was involved. He must be one of the kids. You'll have to ask him.'

Murphy scribbled a line. Mack looked at him and wondered whether he was equipped for a conversation with Charlie. She knew that Atticus's own interactions with him had been cursory, but he had reported that the man seemed unusually smart.

'I want you to come in with me,' Murphy said. 'It's my interview, but we'll benefit from having your knowledge of him.'

83

Mack sat quietly with her hands in her lap as Charlie was brought into the interview room. His face was a mess: one eye had been closed shut, and there were cuts and bruises everywhere. He moved gingerly and winced as he lowered himself into the chair. There were two cameras in the room: one focused on all three of them from above and to the side, while the second focused only on Charlie. Murphy had a ring binder with him and he set it down on the table, opening it and taking out several pieces of paper: a map and crime scene photographs Mack recognised from Summers' house.

'OK,' Murphy said. 'Let's get started. This interview is being both audio and visually recorded and may be given in evidence if your case is brought to trial. At the conclusion of this interview, you'll be supplied with a form explaining what will happen to the recordings and how you may gain access to them. We're in interview room 2 at Bourne Hill Police Station in Salisbury. The time now is one in the afternoon, and the date is 17 February. I am Chief Superintendent Lee Murphy of the Metropolitan Police, and I'm with Detective Chief Inspector Mackenzie Jones of Wiltshire Police. I know that we don't have your full name yet – it would be helpful to have it.'

'Thomas Chandler.'

'Not Charlie?'

'No.'

'Or Jack?'

'No. It's Tom. Call me Tom.'

'I must caution you that you don't have to say anything, but that it may harm your defence if you don't mention when questioned something which you later rely on in court. Anything you do say may be given in evidence. The first part of the caution is simple: you have the right to remain silent or refuse to answer any of my questions. The second part says that if you exercise your right to silence or, alternatively, if you change any of your answers in a later court trial and you then specifically rely on those changed answers in your defence, the court may be less willing to believe you. The interview is being audio and visually recorded, as I said, so the content of our discussion will be played in court at any subsequent trial if it gets to that. Do you understand?'

'Absolutely.'

'And I understand that you've decided you don't need a solicitor.'

'I don't.'

'I just need to be *very* clear about that.'

'Don't want one.'

'Thank you.'

Murphy flicked through his notebook while Mack watched Tom. He was eerily calm.

'OK, Tom. Shall we start with what happened at West Woodyates Manor earlier this morning?'

'There's much more to talk about than that.'

'Is there?'

'We'll need hours if we're going to get through it all. What about what happened to Richard Miller?'

'You'll talk about that?'

'Happily. And the three men from this week. I'll give you everything, but – no offence – I need someone else to be here when I do.'

'Who?'

'Atticus Priest. Is he here? In the station?'

'He's not. Mr Priest isn't a police officer.'

'I know that. But I'll need him to be here if you want me to talk. Go and get him, please.'

'I can't do that. He's not a police officer. It's impossible.'

Mack leaned forward, knowing exactly what Tom was about to say and impressed, in advance, with his astuteness.

'I have mental health issues, Mr Murphy, plus I've been hit on the head. I'm worried that I won't understand what you're asking me. I want Atticus to be here as my appropriate adult.'

Murphy didn't reply at once. Mack could see the tension in his body – he clenched his jaw and his fists were bunched in his lap – and he looked down at the papers on the table before glancing up into the camera, his face darkening with a scowl.

'Fine.' He looked at his watch. 'I'm going to stop the interview here, and we can pick it up again later. It's ten past one.'

84

Atticus took Bandit for a walk down by the river in Churchill Gardens. The water had risen with the amount of rain that had fallen over the last few weeks, and now it had spilled over the banks, flooding the path and encroaching on the children's play area. A swan, baffled by its change in circumstances, paddled in the lake that had been used for football the last time Atticus had brought the dog here.

He had needed to get out of the office. Mack had told him that the interview with Jack – or Charlie, or whatever he was really called – was due to commence at one, and he knew that he would obsess about it if he didn't give himself a distraction. As he'd stood staring out his window earlier, Bandit had padded over to him and nudged his leg with his muzzle. Atticus would have liked to credit the dog with the anticipation to have known that he would need to get out, but he knew that Bandit just wanted to go and cock his leg. It didn't matter. Fresh air was an excellent idea, and Atticus didn't need persuading.

He picked up the stick that Bandit had collected and tossed it into the water, watching as the dog threw up clouds of spray as he pursued it. The exercise was good, but not enough of a distraction for Atticus to be able to forget the interview. He knew that

Mack had a good grasp of the case and had spent an hour earlier making sure she had everything that she needed with regard to Atticus's interactions with Jack, but it could only ever be a substitute for him being present for the interview.

Bandit returned with the stick clenched between his teeth. Atticus leaned down to take it, but the dog hopped back and, before Atticus could retreat, shook himself dry.

Bandit dropped the stick and waited patiently for Atticus to pick it up.

'You've got to be kidding. After that?'

The dog looked up at him with pleading eyes.

Atticus picked up the stick and heaved it away again, sending it end over end until it landed with a splash in the middle of the lake. Bandit paused at the edge of the water, decided the stick was too precious to ignore, and then bounded after it again.

Atticus took out his phone to check the time just as it buzzed with an incoming call.

He didn't even check to see who it was. 'Mack?'

'Where are you?'

He barely heard her. 'How did it go? It can't have finished already?'

'Where are you? Please say you're in Salisbury.'

'Churchill Gardens.'

'Get to the nick.'

'Why?'

'Because your friend said he'd tell us everything, but only on one condition – you need to be in the room, too.'

Atticus couldn't stop chuckling.

'I know,' Mack said. 'Hilarious. Murphy finds it *particularly* funny.'

'He's playing with us.'

'I know he is,' she said. 'But can you get here – please?'

359

'Wouldn't miss it for the world.' He put his fingers to his lips and whistled. 'I'll be there as soon as I can.'

Bandit trotted back to him. He had swapped his stick for an even larger one, dragging it through the water and then up the slope. Atticus clipped the lead to the dog's collar and gently worked the stick out of his mouth.

'Sorry, boy. They need me after all.'

85

Mack was waiting for him in reception when Atticus arrived.

'Is Jack here?'

'His name isn't Jack. It's Thomas Chandler.'

'And he's ready to confess?'

'Only if you're in the room as his appropriate adult. He's saying he's worried he might be concussed.'

'Oh, that's delicious. I bet Murphy *loved* that.'

'He's not thrilled.'

'I should've been here from the start.'

She took his arm. 'Don't be a dick.' She looked at him. 'OK? Can you do that?'

'I want answers as much as you do,' he said. 'We just need to let him talk – that's it.'

'Good.'

'I'll rub Murphy's nose in it afterwards.'

'Atticus.'

'Kidding,' he said, although he wasn't. 'Where is he? Interview room?'

She nodded.

'Better get up there, then.'

*   *   *

Mack took Atticus to the interview suite. Murphy was waiting in the corridor and indicated that they should follow him into one of the rooms. It was empty.

'I just want to put it on record that this is absolutely *ridiculous*. I've been a policeman for twenty years, and this is the first time that I've had to deal with a shitshow like this.'

'You can say what you like about him,' Atticus said, 'but he's smart. He knew he'd be caught eventually, and he's prepared for it. This will be part of his plan.'

Murphy folded his arms. 'I don't care. If he thinks he's going to be able to give me the runaround, then . . .' He paused, breathing in and then out again. 'Then he's going to get a nasty surprise. I'm not going to pander to him.'

'You *should*,' Atticus said. 'Humour him. He wants to confess.'

'But only to you.'

'He thinks we have a connection. It'll be worth going along with him if it means we can clear everything up. It might stick in the craw to play his game, but remember what's at stake.'

Murphy bit down on his lip. Atticus could read him easily enough: he was balancing his distaste for him on one hand and the possibility that he might be able to help on the other. Murphy reminded Atticus of other young officers he had come across during his interactions with the Met. You only got to his rank if you had the right upbringing, or you were driven by ambition. Murphy was a working-class grafter who had outpaced his contemporaries with ruthlessness and hard work. He might not like Atticus, but if he thought he offered him an advantage in solving the case, then he would take it.

'There are going to be some ground rules if we're going to do this,' he said.

'Fire away.'

'One – you're there as his appropriate adult. You're *not* interviewing him.'

'Understood.'

'Two – anything he says stays confidential. You don't tell *anyone* outside of this building.'

'I don't have any friends,' Atticus said. 'No one to tell.'

Murphy's brows lowered. 'Three – this is not a joke, just a laugh, or some sort of *riddle* that you've set yourself to solve. Four men have been murdered, and Chandler says he'll admit to killing all of them.'

Atticus held his eye. 'I know it's not a joke. Five girls were murdered, too, and I never felt we got to the bottom of that, including whether there are more. I think there *are* more, and I'd like to find them. You don't have to worry about me – I want the answers as much as you do.'

'Good.'

Mack looked at him. 'Is there anything you want to say now?'

'About Jack? Don't underestimate him. He's clever. He's already manipulated you by making you bring me here. And he's played me for months. We should break at regular intervals so that we can compare notes. I might see something you've missed.'

'We'll break every thirty minutes,' Murphy said.

'And you're welcome.'

'What?'

'You're welcome – I was enjoying a walk with the dog. I've changed my plans to help you out.'

Murphy stared at him. 'Thank you *very* much,' he said. He straightened out his jacket and cleared his throat. 'Right – shall we try again?'

86

Atticus followed Murphy down the corridor and into the interview room. Chandler – it was difficult for Atticus to think of him as anything other than Jack – smiled at him as he took the empty seat next to him.

'Thank you for coming.'

'No problem.'

'I'm pleased you could. I want you to hear this.'

Murphy resumed his seat on the other side of the table and ran through the preliminaries for the second time.

'We've been joined by Mr Atticus Priest,' he said once he had repeated the caution. 'Mr Chandler has indicated that he would like Mr Priest to be here as his appropriate adult.' He turned to Atticus. 'Mr Priest – you are not here to act simply as an observer. Your role here is to advise Mr Chandler, facilitate communication and ensure that the interview is conducted fairly.'

It was the rote wording for when an appropriate adult was requested by a suspect, but Atticus could only just hide his satisfaction that Murphy was forced to recite it.

Murphy turned to a fresh page in his notebook and picked up his pen. 'You're still sure you don't want a lawyer, Tom?'

'I told you – I don't need one.'

'And you know you're being investigated for very serious crimes?'

'I do. And I already explained why I don't want one – I want to confess.'

'To what?'

'That I killed four men this week.'

'Four?'

He nodded. 'Summers and the other three.'

'Mr Summers isn't dead.'

Chandler showed the first flicker of emotion. 'Shame.' He paused as his irritation became resignation. 'Doesn't matter. I'll make sure you've got everything you need to prosecute him for what he's done. Not even the CPS will be able to mess it up.' He looked over at Atticus. 'Not like they did with Alf Burns – right?'

Atticus nodded but held his tongue.

Murphy drummed his fingers on the table. 'Shall we start?'

'Who should I tell you about first?'

'Let's start with Mr Miller.'

'Can I go back a little before that? The context will be useful.'

'Of course.'

Chandler turned so that he was addressing Atticus. 'It's relevant to you, actually. I know we've chatted, on and off, but I've never really given you all the story. I started paying attention to you when you first investigated Burns. You knew that he was guilty of a lot more than he was being charged with. And you were frustrated when he went to Thailand. That's why I messaged you – *lots* in common.' He paused, arranging his thoughts, and then started again. 'Burns and York and Miller were working together. You know that, and you know York killed Burns when Burns blackmailed them. You know *some* of what the three of them were doing, but not all of it. I tried to tell you when we spoke, but I don't think you were really listening. I was disappointed about that. I thought you would've worked it all out.'

'Why don't you tell us now,' Murphy suggested.

'Miller and I had a long chat,' Chandler said, still looking at Atticus. 'Before I cut his throat. Burns and York met him when they were in the army, and they got into business together. They started in Northern Ireland with robberies and moved into prostitution. They made money and carried it on when they got back home. He said it was normal to start with – they were pimps, basically, found women who wanted extra cash and set them up in properties they owned where they could entertain clients. But they got requests for illegal stuff – kids – and saw there was more to be made. Miller said he and York didn't want to do it at first, but Burns showed how they could make a packet and told them about a way they could do it without being found out.'

'How was that?'

'Burns was working at Grosvenor House youth club in the city. He'd find vulnerable kids, groom them and then he'd bring them out to the old Manor House at Imber. He'd worked out there for the MOD after leaving the army. He had the keys for all the properties and knew it'd be quiet. There was never anyone there aside from when the army were doing exercises, and those were always posted in advance. They set up in this big old room and then brought the customers out there. They did videos, too. Made to order. They did that exclusively when they moved out of Imber. Less risk, I suppose.'

'And that's when you got involved? You were one of the children?'

'Yes,' he said. 'They took me there more times than I can remember – I tried to black it out. I was perfect for them. I was fourteen and I'd had a shitty childhood. My dad died when I was a baby, and I was just a pain in the arse for my mum. I was with her until I was three; then they put me in care when she got wasted one too many times; then I was back with her again when she cleaned up and promised it'd all be different.' He chuckled bitterly. 'It was never different, though. She'd make a promise and then break it, over and over again. I had a friend from school and she took me to Grosvenor House. She said it'd be a laugh. She said one of the helpers there would give the kids booze and fags.'

'Burns?' Murphy asked.

Chandler nodded. 'I was easy pickings. He had a bottle of vodka in his office and he'd pour me drinks. He had weed, too, and he'd roll joints, and we'd smoke them together out the back. He made me think I was his friend, and then, once he was sure I could be trusted, he offered me money if I'd do things for him.' He swallowed and was silent for a moment. 'They took me out there a lot. Alf used to pay me a tenner every time. He told me I could never tell anyone, and I said I wouldn't. He must've believed me because, well . . . I'm still here, aren't I? The ones they killed must've given them trouble.'

Atticus was rapt. 'These are the girls we dug up?'

'Yes.'

'Did you know any of them?'

'There was one girl, one time – the customer paid extra for the two of us. We got talking afterwards, when they drove us back.'

'Do you know her name?'

He shook his head. 'Can't remember. She said she was going to tell the police what they were doing. I never saw her again after that. A man who said he was her dad turned up at the club and asked if anyone knew where she was. I didn't make the connection at the time, but it's obvious what happened – they saw she was trouble and got rid of her. Killed her and dumped her like the others.'

'Do you think there were more?'

'Than the ones you found?' He chuckled bitterly. 'I was involved with them more than twenty years ago, and they never stopped. You saw what Summers had set up in the chapel. What do *you* think? You could dig the whole bloody village up and you still wouldn't find them all.'

'What happened to you?' Murphy said.

'The council sent me to a family in Warminster who actually cared about me. I never went back after that. I tried to forget about it, but I never could. I can't form relationships. Can't trust anyone. I get nightmares, every night, always the same. They ruined my life.'

'What about the men this week?' Murphy asked. 'Campbell and the others. They were all customers?'

Chandler nodded.

'How did you find out about them?'

'You know Alf ran out of money and that he blackmailed Miller and York for cash. Miller told me that Alf had a hidden camera in Imber, and he filmed everyone who went there. Alf told them unless they paid him, he wouldn't have any choice but to go to the punters and squeeze it out of *them*. So they killed him and went looking for the tapes he said he had. Miller told me they broke into his place in Andover.'

'They did,' Atticus said, thinking about the night that Summers' goon had knocked him out.

'But they didn't find the tapes. Derek Burns had them.'

'Derek was Alf's brother,' Atticus explained for Murphy's benefit.

'They went after him,' Chandler continued, 'but he got the drop on them and ran. He wasn't as clever as Alf, though, and it didn't take me long to find him. He told me where he'd hidden the tapes, and I picked them up. You've seen what they're like – all labelled, nice and neat, plus Alf had a ledger, too, with details of the customers. It was easy to match one to the other. I had a plan – Burns and York and Miller first, then I'd work through the list. I killed them and sent their tapes to the papers so that everyone knows what they did.'

'Why?' Murphy asked.

'Why?' He looked surprised at his question. 'Why'd I send them to the papers? Seriously? Have you watched them? It's the only way men like them are ever going to be held to account.'

87

Chandler spoke with an expansiveness that suggested that he was intent on making good on his promise to confess. Murphy would guide him to a topic and then had nothing more to do than occasionally nudge him back on track. Chandler would answer the question and then expand upon it, offering the additional information with an ease that was enough to convince Atticus that he was being truthful.

'Let's move on to Miller,' Murphy said. 'What happened?'

'I waited outside his house after he was released,' he said. 'I got him into the back of his car and drove him away.'

'He didn't struggle?'

'I came up behind him and hit him with a hammer. Knocked him out. I drove him out to Downton. There's a road up by the leisure centre – you can get right into the countryside. There's never anyone there, not at that time of night. We had a talk. He told me everything.'

'And then?'

'I cut his throat, drove him back into town and left him outside Atticus's office.'

Atticus looked over at Mack. It was obvious from her raised eyebrows that she shared his opinion that Chandler was telling the truth. He was giving them everything they would need to bring charges against him and for those charges to lead to a conviction.

'What about Campbell?' Murphy said. 'Why him?'

'I know why,' Atticus said. 'He was one of the men who abused you.'

Chandler nodded with a smile. 'How'd you work that out?'

'You have an appendectomy scar,' Atticus said, pointing down to Chandler's belly. 'I noticed it when you were struggling with Summers' man. The boy on the tape with Campbell has the same scar.'

Chandler nodded. 'That was a good spot. I looked through the videos to see if I could find myself, and I did – in the video with him. He went right to the top on my list. I didn't want to take the chance that I'd get caught if I went after someone else before him. He was easy to find. His name was on the video, and he's got a decent online footprint – that blog he's been doing, the photos he was taking at the cathedral – I just had to google him, and there he was. I watched him for a week and scouted for the best place to do it. I went up the tower on one of the tours to get a look around.' He looked to Atticus. 'There are several ways to get to the stairs – you knew that?'

'I did.'

'They've got cameras that'll show anyone going through the door they use to get the tourists up, but that's it – once you're on the stairs, there's nothing. They did this special tour last month where they'd take people to look in the attics that the masons and glaziers used. I could see that it was perfect – there's a way through the attic above the nave onto the tower stairs.'

'When did you take the tour?' Murphy asked him.

'A week or two before.'

'Because we can check.'

'Then check. Why would I lie about something like that?'

'What next?' Atticus pressed.

'Campbell had been taking photos at the same time every day for months. I knew he'd be up there. I climbed up the scaffolding early in the morning, used the attic to get to the tower and waited for him.'

'What happened?'

'I drugged him.'

'Why?' Murphy said.

'Takes the fight right out of you. I wanted to have a chat with him before I threw him over the side.'

'With what?' Atticus asked.

'Ketamine.'

'How'd you get hold of that?' Murphy asked.

'It's not that hard to find. You go down to the Priory and ask around.'

'The Priory?' Murphy said.

'Not the best part of the city,' Atticus explained.

Chandler made a fist and thumped it against his thigh. 'I injected him in the leg, just enough to make him woozy – not enough to knock him out completely. I wanted him to know who I was and why I was there. And I wanted him to know that I was going to ruin his good name *after* I'd killed him.'

'Did he remember you?'

'He said that he didn't. But he admitted he'd been at Imber. I got him over the side and waited in the attic until the evening – it wasn't hard to get away without anyone seeing me.'

'Why do it there?' Murphy said.

'You mean why be so dramatic?'

Murphy nodded.

'He *wants* to be dramatic,' Atticus answered for him. 'He wanted everyone to know.'

Chandler tapped his nose and then pointed at Atticus. '*Exactly*. I doubted I'd get through all the tapes, even if I was lucky. You would've caught me eventually. And, besides that, what about the men who'd been at Imber who Alf *didn't* record? Or all the ones who bought their videos afterwards? There must be dozens of customers I don't know about, but that doesn't mean I can't make them *think* I know. I can scare the shit out of them, scare them that they'll be next. The only way to do that was to make as much noise as possible. Think about it – you open a newspaper and you see a photograph of *that* room. It's distinctive. You'd remember you were there or that you watched something shot there. It's not the sort of thing you'd forget. I knew that if I could make it lurid enough, it'd get attention. And then, if I sent the tapes . . . every newspaper and TV station is going to run a story like that. It'll be all over social media. Facebook, Twitter, TikTok – and it all happened that way, just like I knew it would. You'd see that room on the TV and you'd shit yourself. Every time you hugged your kids, you'd think it might be the last time. Every time you kissed your wife, you'd be terrified that you'd be next.'

Atticus nodded. 'Is that why you included the Bible verses with the tapes? To be lurid?'

'That's exactly why.'

Mack scribbled notes on the pad in front of her. Murphy took a moment to compose his thoughts.

Chandler shuffled in his seat. 'Shall I move on to Kajetan?'

'Please,' Murphy said.

'Harder to find. I asked around, and one of his homeless friends told me he was living in the sluice house on the river. I found him there, but it didn't go as smoothly as Campbell. I tried to inject him, but he saw me coming. There was a scuffle. He was pissed, and I was able to get him into the water. I held him down until he drowned.'

'And Hartnett?'

Chandler took a sip from his water. 'More challenging, obviously, because he was an MP. I followed him after he left Parliament, broke into his flat and killed him there.'

'Ketamine?'

He nodded. 'I messed up with him – used too much. He overdosed.'

'What about Summers?'

'Miller told me about him when we had our chat. I don't know exactly when he got involved, but it was early on. As far as I can make out, they had a close call at Imber and decided that they needed to move. He'd just sold his company and bought the big house. He suggested they could use the chapel. They made it look like Imber and started again, but, this time, everything was online. They'd film scenes and distribute them to everyone who paid whatever it was they were asking. More professional all around – dark web servers so they couldn't be tracked and cryptocurrency for payment.'

'That's strange,' Atticus said.

Chandler cocked an eyebrow. 'What is?'

'The timing. I only made the connection between Summers and the tapes yesterday. And you went out there yesterday evening.'

He shrugged.

'You don't think it's unusual?' Atticus said.

'I think it's one of those things.'

'Francine didn't know anything about it,' Atticus said. 'She couldn't have told you.'

'Miller did – he told me.'

'Really?'

'Yes, Atticus. *Really*. I'm telling you everything. Look – I'm *confessing*. Why would I lie about something like that?'

Atticus watched Chandler as he spoke and, for the first time that afternoon, he didn't believe him.

88

Atticus tried to take the stick from Bandit's mouth so that he could throw it again, but the dog was having none of it.

'Give,' Atticus said.

Bandit tightened his jaws around the stick and growled playfully, jerking his head from side to side as he tried to loosen Atticus's grip.

'*Give.*'

The dog bit down harder until the wood splintered, and then let go, tail wagging frantically as he waited for Atticus to throw it again.

'Ready.' He drew back his arm. 'Go!'

The stick looped end over end and landed in the water, with Bandit racing after it at full speed.

'He looks happy,' Mack said.

'He'd be up for doing this all day if he could. He never gets tired.'

She slipped her hand into his as they followed the path around the park. The interview with Chandler had lasted for seven hours, and when it finally finished, Atticus saw it was nearly eight o'clock. They had the right to hold him for twenty-four hours before they needed to charge him, apply for an extension, or let him go.

Murphy had sought – and received – an extension for a further forty-eight hours, but they all knew they wouldn't need it.

Chandler had been returned to the custody sergeant and taken to a cell where he would be held until the CPS had decided whether there was enough evidence to charge him. It would be automatic; Chandler had provided a full confession and been credible throughout, and there was no question as to his capacity. The suggestion of a concussion was an obvious excuse to have Atticus present to witness the denouement to the investigation. The police doctor had confirmed that he was fit to be interviewed, and there was nothing to show any kind of impairment. Chandler had given consent for his fingerprints and DNA to be taken and had not complained when he was told that he would be held until a charging decision had been made.

Chandler had stopped in the doorway as he was being taken out of the interview room, turning back to look at Atticus. He said that he hoped Atticus would be at the trial. Atticus had said that he would, and Chandler had nodded in satisfaction and smiled as he was led away.

It had been gloomy when Atticus had returned to the office, and Bandit had leapt on him as soon as he opened the door. Atticus had struggled to fit the excited dog into his harness, clipped on the lead, and met Mack in the park.

'What do you think?' she said.

'I'm still trying to work it all out.'

'Murphy seemed pleased.'

'Of course he is. He gets to go back to London and claim the credit for solving the case.' They walked on, watching as Bandit splashed off in pursuit of a startled duck. Atticus turned to her. 'Did you believe him?'

'I think he told us the truth, or he's a world-class liar. What do you think?'

'Most of it is true. Fyfe should be able to find ketamine when he does the bloodwork for Campbell. It'll last thirty days in urine. Four months in hair. He might even find bruising from where the needle went in, assuming he's able to do his job properly.'

'That might be unfair,' she said. 'His body was a mess.'

'Maybe,' Atticus conceded, 'but it'll still be in his blood. It'll be the same for Hartnett, and there shouldn't be any problem in finding where the needle went in with him. No one else can say they know about that – the ketamine. It'll be powerful evidence to back the confession.'

She stopped, his hand still in hers. 'So what's bothering you?'

Atticus exhaled. 'He was at Summers' house just *hours* after us. I didn't tell anyone about that. You say you didn't tell anyone—'

'I didn't.'

'Not Francine?'

'No one, Atticus. I didn't tell anyone.'

'So either he's been following me, or it's a coincidence. I don't think I was followed, and you know my view on coincidences. It's lazy thinking. It's what we say when we can't see the levers and pulleys that connect everything. So no – it's not that.'

'What is it, then?'

'I don't know.'

Bandit returned with the stick in his mouth.

Mack let go of Atticus's hand and knelt in front of the dog. 'Drop.'

Bandit stared at her, his tail wagging with frantic enthusiasm. Mack took hold of the stick and braced herself as Bandit tried to wrench it free.

'*Drop*,' Atticus said.

Bandit opened his mouth to release the stick and sat expectantly as Mack straightened, drew her arm back and then threw it as far as she could. The dog spun around and sprinted after it, spray flying as he leapt into the water again.

'What about the cigarette I found on the roof of the car park? Has it been tested yet?'

'I sent it to the lab,' she said. 'But you know what it's like – they're not always the fastest.'

'Can you expedite it?'

'Why?'

'I just want it confirmed that it was him.'

Mack turned to stand in front of Atticus, put her hands on his shoulders and reached up to kiss him.

'Can I say something?'

He nodded.

'You've been preoccupied with this for months. It's normal to have doubts, but they might be misplaced. Chandler gave us a credible explanation for what happened – I know you'll keep picking away at it, but it could be just as simple as he said.'

'Maybe.'

They walked on.

She took his hand again. 'Do you want to come back to mine?'

'I would, but . . .'

'But you want to work on the case?'

'I want to check a couple of things.' He glanced over at her. 'Sorry. I could come over afterwards?'

'Come over when you like,' she said, squeezing his hand again. 'Just promise me you won't obsess over this. It's not good for you.'

'I know. I'll try.'

89

Max Mason looked out of the Bentley as his chauffeur flicked the indicator and turned on to the long private drive through the forest that would finally bring him home. The drive rose gently between an avenue of lime and cherry trees, passed the ponds and then reached the circular driveway at the southern end of the house.

Mason felt the same flutter of pride that he always felt when he returned home. This was his favourite view of all: the huge Jacobean manor, lights shining out from the windows to welcome him home, a shimmering jewel that nestled in the green forests and fields that protected it, and its owner, from the intrusions of the world beyond. The house had been built in the 1600s and was unusual in that it was constructed in the shape of a Y that was believed to represent the three arms of the Trinity. Mason had always found that amusing; he had always considered religion to be a huge joke, and some of the things that he had done inside the house would have scandalised the owners who had lived here before him.

Steve rolled up to the front of the house and brought the Bentley to a stop. The evening was cold and wet, and Mason waited inside the car as Ross hurried out of the house with an umbrella. He opened the door and held the umbrella up so that Mason could shelter beneath it.

'Evening, sir. Good drive?'

'Traffic on the 303,' he grumbled. 'Crash near Andover.'

Steve went to the rear of the car, took out Mason's small suitcase and followed Mason and Ross to the house.

'Do you need me tomorrow, sir?'

'No. I'm going to be here over the weekend.'

Ross stepped aside so that Mason could make his way into the entrance hall. Mason took off his coat and the indigo-coloured suit jacket that he had been wearing at filming today. Ross took both, hanging up the coat in the cupboard beneath the stairs and keeping the jacket so that he could have it dry-cleaned.

'Shall I ask Claude to prepare a light dinner for you?'

'I'm tired. I'm going to bed.'

Mason went up to the first-floor landing and walked through to his bedroom. A fresh set of pyjamas had been laid out for him, but he decided to take a quick shower to warm up before changing into them. He undressed, stood in front of the gilt mirror and examined his reflection. He had put his body through all manner of surgical interventions through the years: blepharoplasty on his eyelids, a rhytidectomy to tighten the skin on his forehead, dermal fillers to add fullness to his cheeks and lips. He had Botox injections every three months, and as he prodded his forehead, he could see that he might have to increase the frequency. His body was harder to maintain. His skin was withered and wrinkled, and the flesh beneath his arms hung loose. His hands were gnarled, the skin thin and translucent. That didn't matter so much as his face, though. He could cover everything else up beneath his bright suits.

He stood under the warm water and scrubbed shampoo through his hair. His mind wandered. He had watched the news on his phone while Steve had driven him home. There had been a second murder in Salisbury, and the *Journal* had been sent a video that, once again, featured the red-lit room that looked so similar to the one that he remembered from twenty years ago.

He thought of how Summers had been adamant that there was no tape with him on it, but how could he be sure? What else could Summers have said? Mason had fretted at it all day and had reached the vaguely reassuring conclusion that, if there *was* evidence that he had been there, then it would have been released first given his fame. Whoever was responsible for the murders was looking for as much publicity as possible; a video showing Mason's involvement would have made for a huge story, and the fact that there had been nothing about him was encouraging.

Encouraging, but not a reason for complacency. He would ask Ross about looking into additional security until the police had caught whoever was behind the murders.

He changed into his pyjamas, tracing his finger over the monogram of his initials on the breast. He was tired and he needed to get to sleep. A full-time security guard at the house. Another camera. Floodlights in the gardens. He would mention it to Ross at breakfast tomorrow.

PART VI

SATURDAY

PART VI

90

Mason woke with a start.

He sat up and blinked until his eyes had adjusted to the darkness, the gloom lightened only by the faint silver moonlight that shone through curtains he had forgotten to close. His breathing was rapid, and he closed his eyes until he was able to slow it down. He opened his eyes again and tried to work out what had woken him. The house was quiet, with just the ticking of the grandfather clock in the hall and a regular dripping from the tap in his en suite; he had asked Ross to see that it was fixed and was annoyed that it hadn't been done.

There it was again: the creaking of a floorboard.

'Ross?' he called out.

Mason swung his legs out of bed and padded across the thick rug to the hook where his dressing gown was hung. He put it on, slid his feet into his slippers and went to the door. He opened it and stepped out into the corridor. The curtains were drawn, and it was too dark to see anything.

'Ross?'

He took a step, and the infrared motion detector lit up, bathing the corridor with a flash of soft blue light. He stopped, and the light flicked off.

He heard the creak again.

'Ross? Is that you?'

The blue light flicked on again and, this time, it wasn't because of him.

91

Atticus worked until five and then tried to sleep. He managed a couple of hours before he woke, and, as he opened his eyes, his mind was still buzzing with the same doubts and questions that he had been unable to shut out when he had lain down. He got out of bed, washed his face with cold water and dressed. Bandit opened a single eye as he stepped around the bed and then buried his head beneath the duvet and went back to sleep. Atticus envied him his peace of mind.

He went into the other room, cleared the pages of notes from his desk and dumped them on the sofa. He had tried to work in a more organised fashion, but it hadn't worked. The case was finished now, and, thinking of what his cleaner would say when she visited, he tried to put the room back into the professional state that she had left it in.

He picked up a textbook on evidence and put it back on the shelf, then binned the two cans of Diet Coke and the paper bag that had held the cheese straws that had sufficed as his dinner. He used his hands to corral the crumbs of the cheese straws onto one of the sheets of paper, then binned that and the others.

He was left with the report that he had written for Nina Parsons on Robin Wintringham. He had forgotten all about that;

and had emailed her the report with his invoice, but, at least as far as he could remember, she hadn't acknowledged receipt or paid. He tossed the report into the bin and tapped the keyboard to wake his computer. He navigated to his email and saw, with a sinking feeling, that his failure to attend to his inbox in a prompt manner had seen more than a hundred unanswered messages pile up.

He confirmed that Nina hadn't replied and then checked to see if the email had bounced; it hadn't.

He dialled her number, but the call went straight to voicemail so he rang off rather than leaving a message.

He opened the first email that she had sent him. There was nothing remotely unusual about it: it had been sent from a nondescript Gmail account – ninaparsons2918 – with a signature strip at the bottom that had a link to her Facebook and Instagram.

Atticus drummed his fingers on the desk and chewed his lip. Something was wrong. He took his mouse, maximised the email from Nina and clicked on the icon with three dots at the top of the screen, selecting the option to show the original format of the message. The screen broke down the email into its constituent parts – message ID, creation date, sending account and receiving account, SPF and DKIM data – and then, in a large window below, a plain-text version of the full header. Atticus opened the search box and typed in 'received', looking for the numeric IP address that would give him the geographical location from which the email had been sent.

He found it: 84.66.44.160.

He opened an IP look-up tool, pasted in the IP address and waited for the results: the email had been sent from Boston Tea Party, the large café in the middle of the city.

That struck him as odd. Nina *might* have composed and sent the email while she was out and about, but surely it was more likely to have been something that she would have done at home.

Emailing a private investigator about a sensitive matter was not something that one would do on a whim over coffee and cake.

And, in his experience, people tended to use public Wi-Fi when they wanted to prevent someone from finding their real address.

Why would Nina have done something like that?

He pushed his chair away from his desk, stood up and grabbed his jacket. Bandit looked up in hope that he was about to get a walk.

'When I get back,' Atticus said, scratching the dog behind the ears. 'There's someone I have to see first.'

92

Atticus got into his car and drove to the address in Laverstock that belonged to Robin Wintringham. He recalled the details of the file and knew that the conversation that he was going to have to have might be difficult. That wasn't what was making him uneasy; he knew it was necessary. Rather, it was what he suspected he might discover.

His phone rang: it was Mack. He answered it. 'Hi.'

'Hello, stranger,' she said. 'Are you OK?'

'I'm fine. Why?'

'You were going to come over last night.'

He winced. He'd forgotten. 'I fell asleep at my desk. By the time I woke up, it was too late. Sorry.'

'It's all right,' she said, then paused. 'Are you sure you're OK?'

'Absolutely.'

'Where are you?'

'Taking the dog out for a walk.'

The lie came easily enough. He wanted to tell her his fears and what they might mean, but it would have to wait. He knew she would be busy with Chandler, and the theory he couldn't get out of his head was based on nothing more than guesses and conjecture. Mack would tell him to stop, and he wasn't about to do that. He had to follow his thoughts to their conclusion for good or ill.

'I just thought you'd want to know that the CPS has agreed that there's enough evidence to charge Chandler. We'll have him in front of the magistrates this afternoon.'

'He still says he's going to plead guilty?'

'Yes.'

'What time's the hearing?'

'Two. Why? Want to come?'

'Do you think that'd be OK?'

'Probably. Murphy's in a good mood. He's been crowing about solving this all morning.'

'I'll see you there, then.'

'One other thing,' she said. 'We heard from the hospital this morning about Summers. He took a turn for the worse last night.'

'How bad?'

'Bad as in they don't think he's going to make it.'

'Shit. I wanted to speak to him.'

'Doesn't look as if that's going to happen.'

'What about the DNA test on the cigarette?'

'Nothing yet,' she said. 'I'll chase the lab.'

Atticus arrived at the address. He glanced over at the house as he went by, then turned around and found a space to park.

'Where are you?'

'Figsbury Ring,' Atticus said. 'Bandit's excited. I'd better go.'

'I'll speak to you later,' she said, and rang off.

93

Atticus climbed the hill to the house, walked up to the door and pressed the doorbell. He heard the ring from somewhere inside, and then saw the shape of a person coming to the door through the frosted-glass panel.

The door was opened by Laura Wintringham. 'Hello?'

'Hello. Sorry to disturb you.'

'Can I help you?'

'Could I have a word with your husband?'

'He's with the kids – I'm sorry, who are you?'

'I'm a private investigator.'

She frowned in confusion and then concern. 'Why do you want to speak to my husband?'

'It's probably best if I speak to him about that. I'm sorry to be so vague. It's nothing to be concerned about.'

Robin Wintringham appeared in the hallway behind his wife. He had a child's rucksack in his hand. 'Who is it?'

'Says he's a private investigator, and he wants to talk to you.'

'I'm sorry – *what?*'

'It won't take long, Mr Wintringham.'

'Go on, then.'

'Might be better if we speak in private.'

'Say whatever you've come to say – the kids are just eating their breakfast and then I've got to get them to their clubs. You'll have to be quick.'

Atticus had done his best to be discreet; Wintringham was about to be put in a difficult position that he could have been spared if he had only taken the hint.

'This is a little delicate, but . . . never mind. Do you know a woman called Nina Parsons?'

He frowned. 'Who? No, I don't think so.'

'She's about thirty years old, about the same height as your wife, slender, dark brown hair and brown eyes.'

'I don't know anyone like that.'

Laura folded her arms. 'Why are you asking?' She turned to her husband. 'Robin – why is he asking?'

'A woman with that name hired me because she said that your husband was in a relationship with her. She wanted me to carry out what we'd call a background check. She wanted me to confirm that everything he'd told her was true.'

Atticus watched Wintringham for a reaction. An accusation like that would elicit confusion in the innocent as a first response; on the other hand, someone with something to hide might react with indignation or an overcompensation that would signal that there was truth to what had been said. Wintringham's mouth fell open, and his brow creased with a perplexed frown before – perhaps remembering that his wife was standing next to him – the angry denunciation followed.

'That's bullshit.'

His wife was watching for his reaction, too, and Atticus guessed that there had been something in their relationship in the past that gave her grounds to think that a transgression was possible.

Wintringham noticed the stiffening of her posture and made a quarter-turn so that he was facing her. 'It's bullshit. *Complete* bullshit.'

'For what it's worth,' Atticus said, 'I believe you. I've been concerned that my client was lying to me, and now I'm sure of it.'

'*Thank* you,' Wintringham said with a mixture of sarcasm and relief.

His wife wasn't quite ready to let it go, though. 'That doesn't make any sense. Why would someone ask you to investigate something that wasn't true?'

'That's something I need to work out. I'm sorry for bothering you.'

He turned and walked down the middle of the road back to his car, keen to put some distance between himself and the domestic spat that he had just caused. He thought of what had happened over the last week and of what had happened at Harry Summers' house, and how Chandler had been there just hours after Atticus and Mack.

Mack's suggestion was wrong: he *hadn't* been followed.

It was something else.

He was still in the road when a car approached and had to stop abruptly. The driver pressed the horn. Atticus was hardly aware of it. A realisation struck him like a hammer. He put his hands to his head and, with an incredulity that grew as he made one connection and then another and then the next, he started to trot and then run back to the car.

He needed to get back to the office.

94

Atticus double-parked, sprinted to the door, fumbled his key into the lock and opened it, taking the stairs two at a time. He was out of breath when he reached the door to the office and stopped himself just in time from opening up and going inside. He went to the bathroom, ran the cold tap and rolled up his sleeves. He held his right wrist under the flow and concentrated on how it felt, closing his eyes and willing his pulse to slacken. Atticus switched wrists, opened his eyes and stared at his reflection in the dirty mirror. His eyes were wide and there was a sheen of sweat on his skin. He cupped his hands, filled them with water and then dunked his face. He did it again, wiped himself dry and took another moment until his breathing was under control.

He couldn't be agitated.

He needed to be himself.

To be normal.

Atticus took another deep breath and, finally calm, he went to the door and opened it. Bandit bounded out and leapt up at him, planting his front legs against his hips so that his head was in range for a scratch. Atticus obliged him and looked around; the office felt different – less trustworthy – and it made him feel uncomfortable.

'OK, boy. Let's get you some lunch.'

Atticus went into the hallway again, opened a can of wet food and scooped it into the dog's empty bowl. He took it back, set it down and looked around again.

He knew he was right, but he didn't know where to start.

He took out his phone, connected it to the Bluetooth speaker, opened Nick Cave's *Push the Sky Away* and pressed play. 'Jubilee Street' started playing, and Atticus turned it up enough so that it would – he hoped – mask the sound of what he had to do.

He reached up for the spotlights that were fitted to a track on the ceiling, unscrewed the first, examined it in minute detail, then set it aside and unscrewed the second. There were four on the first track and another four on the second. He removed them all, one by one, and found nothing. He screwed them back into the holders, stood with his hands on his hips and looked around the room.

They've made a fool of me.

The song picked up pace, matching Atticus's heartbeat. He stared left and right and then moved the sofa in the bay window out of the way. He knelt and examined the router and cable that connected it to the socket. There was nothing out of place.

Where is it?

He pushed the sofa back into place and went to the large set of drawers that he used to store his papers. The speaker was on top of it, flanked by two large wooden lamps.

It's here. I know it's here.

Atticus slid his fingers between the back of the drawers and the wall and pulled, moving it out enough to get to the dual socket. The lamps and the speaker were connected to a power strip, leaving the second socket free.

But it wasn't.

A USB plug had been pushed into it. It looked just like a standard Apple product: white, with a port at the bottom into which a charging cable could be inserted. It looked normal and innocuous and might have escaped detection, save for the fact that Atticus knew that he was looking for something like this, and he knew the device had not been there last week.

The song raced to its crescendo.

Atticus stared at the plug for a long minute, wondering what he should do. He reached down for it and then pulled his hand back again; decided that he would speak to Mack and then changed his mind. He knew his options, and that one of them – regardless of however long he thought about it – would always be the course that he chose.

He set his phone down on the desk in front of him and switched off the music, found a piece of paper and a pen and noted down the things that he wanted to say. He ran through them, point by point, until he was confident that he could deliver the message convincingly.

He drew in a breath, exhaled, and started to speak.

95

Atticus walked across town to the magistrates' court. A jumble of thoughts cluttered his mind, and he tried listening to music as a distraction; it didn't work. He took the earbuds out, put them back into their case and dropped them into his pocket. He thought about what he had discovered: the client who had disappeared into thin air and the device that looked like a plug but almost certainly wasn't.

He thought about the gamble that he had taken and wondered if it had any chance of paying off.

Turning the corner on Wilton Road and he saw that the press had arrived at the court before him. Newspaper and TV journalists jostled for the best position, armed with microphones, cameras and notebooks. The atmosphere was charged with excitement. Atticus saw Mack speaking to a reporter beneath the stencilled letters on the wall that read SALISBURY LAW COURTS. She noticed him, held up a hand to indicate that he should wait, finished the conversation and came over to him.

'Everything OK?' he asked.

'It's bedlam,' she said, indicating the crowd.

'Feels like we've been here before,' he replied. He gestured to the reporter. 'What did he want?'

'The usual – what could I tell him about Chandler, did I think he did it, why didn't we catch him more quickly than we did?'

Mack led the way through the main door. They queued to go through security, emptying their pockets into plastic trays and then passing through the scanner.

'Should all be straightforward,' Mack said. 'He says he'll plead guilty. The case will be allocated to the Crown Court and that'll be that. In and out.'

Atticus looked up at the screen on the wall and saw that *Crown v Chandler* was being heard in court number two. He slid between two reporters and followed Mack to the door that led into the area of the court that was reserved for the prosecution.

'Anything else about Summers?' he asked her.

'Nothing more than I told you this morning,' she said. 'They don't think he's got long. He's been in a coma ever since they brought him in. They gave him a transfusion but the damage was already done. His heart wouldn't have been able to pump the blood he had left. His organs would've shut down and he's probably got brain damage. That's what they said.'

'No one's told Chandler?'

'Not as far as I know.' She nodded to the corridor beyond the door. 'You'd better stay here. Let's not push it.'

Atticus would have protested, but, before he could speak, he was interrupted by Murphy. He pushed the door open, saw Mack and Atticus and gave a nod that was somewhere between satisfaction and irritation.

'Good,' he said. 'You're here.'

'What's up?' Mack asked him.

'Chandler's being difficult again.' Murphy pointed a finger at Atticus. 'He wants to have a word with you before he goes up and pleads. I've no idea why – he wouldn't say. I'd have no trouble sending a couple of brawny lads down there to drag him up, but it'll probably be a lot less of a headache if you just go and see what he wants.'

96

The cells were in the building's basement. Murphy led Atticus down the stairs and along a corridor with four cells, two to the right and two to the left. There were no doors, just wide spaces blocked by bars painted a bright shade of blue. Blue-rimmed white squares had been painted on the floor with markings that identified them as 'search areas'. There were cameras on the walls and a panic strip had been fitted at waist height. The building in Salisbury was more modern than many that Atticus had visited and, as a result, the cells were in better condition. That didn't mean that they were pristine; the walls of all of them had been marked with graffiti by the prisoners who had been held here.

'Where is he?'

'Last on the right,' Murphy said. 'There's five minutes before they take him up. I'll be at the end of the corridor.'

Atticus walked along the corridor. The cell had a bench that had been fitted to two walls in the shape of an L. There was a window just beneath the ceiling, through which an oblong of dim light fell across the vinyl floor. Chandler was sitting on the bench. His back was against the wall, his knees were drawn up and his chin rested on them. He had always looked confident before, but, now, at the start of a chute that would deposit him in the bowels of the legal justice system for the rest of his life, he looked vulnerable and alone.

Atticus cleared his throat.

Chandler looked up. 'You came.'

'You wanted to see me?'

'I thought this might be the last chance we get to speak before the trial.'

'Probably,' Atticus said. 'How are you?'

He shrugged. 'Just wrapping my head around it. I knew it'd come, eventually – getting caught – but that doesn't make it any easier to deal with.'

'You got a lawyer?'

'Scrape the barrel for a brief on Legal Aid? No thanks.'

'You know what they say about a man who is his own lawyer?'

'He has a fool for a client. It's fine – I don't need one.'

'You're pleading guilty?'

Chandler got up and nodded. 'I'm not interested in fighting. You were right – it's over. I've done as much as I could. I'd like to have done more, but it is what it is.'

He came over to the bars and Atticus took a corresponding step back.

'I'm glad you're here,' Chandler said. 'It's good to have a proper talk. I'm sorry about all the deception from before.'

The vulnerability disappeared as he spoke, and now Chandler's voice had the confidence that was at odds with what might have been expected from him, given his circumstances. He had been insouciant about his legal situation when they had interviewed him yesterday, and the indifference had continued despite his imminent first appearance before the bench. Atticus had noted it before, and it was even more obvious now; Chandler had expected to be caught and had approached the prospect without concern.

'Can I ask you a couple of questions?' Atticus asked.

'If I can ask you one after.'

'OK.'

'Go on,' Chandler said. 'What do you want to know?'

Atticus paused, focusing on the graffiti that had been scratched into the wall. 'I'm curious about the videos.'

'What about them?'

'The first one – Campbell. How did you get that to the *Journal*?'

'I dropped it off.'

'When?'

'I don't know exactly.'

'Campbell was killed in the morning.'

'You know he was.'

'But you stayed in the attic until the evening.'

'And?'

'There's a camera outside the office. No one put anything through the letterbox from lunchtime onwards. But you were in the attic until the evening.'

'Yes.'

'How did you do it?'

'I went over there as soon as I got out of the cathedral.'

'But you didn't – the camera doesn't see you.'

'I don't know what you want me to say.'

Atticus paid attention to his body language. Chandler hardly blinked, a sign that he was struggling with a heavy cognitive load and needed to give careful thought to everything he was saying. He was staring at Atticus, as if to reassure himself that his explanation had had the desired effect.

'OK,' Atticus said. 'The night when you attacked Summers – how did you get out there?'

He frowned. 'Why is that important?'

'It's twelve miles from Salisbury.'

'I know. What's your point?'

'Did you drive?'

Chandler didn't answer.

'That's rhetorical. I know you didn't – I've been out there, Thomas. I've been up and down the roads and, when I found nothing, I walked every single track I could find. There's nothing there. No car, no motorbike, not even a bicycle. Nothing.'

'I walked.'

'Really? Twelve miles.'

'Prove I didn't.'

Atticus took a moment. Chandler was becoming uncomfortable, and he wondered whether he might work the carapace loose a little if he kept prodding. His assurance – so uncanny in his interviews – looked as if it might be failing.

'Is that it?' Chandler asked.

'What about the video that was sent to the *Sun*. Was that you?'

'Yes.'

'Why send it?'

'Because the story wasn't spreading quickly enough. I decided that using the *Journal* was a mistake.'

'Why didn't you go straight to the *Sun* from the start?'

He closed his eyes and breathed out. 'I didn't think I'd need to. The *Journal* did a good job with Imber, and I knew the story would get picked up if they wrote it first. I didn't really think much beyond that.'

Atticus kept watching and noticed the way he closed his eyes and how the timing of his sentences was slightly off; he was trying to give the impression that he was frustrated, but it was unconvincing.

'How did you send it?'

'Email.'

'But you'd sent the tape to the *Journal*.'

'Not before I digitised it. I needed to keep a copy for myself.'

His eyes darted left to right, and Atticus was left with the impression that, for the first time, he wasn't sure what to say. He was confident that Chandler had told the truth in his confession, but now he wondered what he had left out.

'Is that it?' Chandler said.

'I still don't understand why you felt you had to do this all yourself,' Atticus said. 'You knew you'd be caught. And you knew what the cost would be when you were caught. Your life – you've thrown it away.'

Chandler laughed bitterly. 'What life? They took it from me.'

'You could have sent the tapes to the police. You could've sent them to me.'

'That would never have led to anything. Men like Summers and Miller and Hartnett have resources. They have money, or influence, or both. They get to act with impunity. What happened to them is *justice*. They got what they deserved.'

'Justice or vengeance?'

'Are we doing this again? Spare me the semantics.'

'I'd rather make a case and then let a judge and jury decide.'

'Your faith in the system is quaint.'

'I know it's not perfect.'

'That's an understatement. It failed you before.'

'With Burns? Yes. You're right – it did. But it doesn't mean that I've given up on it.'

Chandler chuckled. 'Hypocrite. You broke into Burns' flat. And what about trespassing on Summers' property? You've never followed the rules and you've always been frustrated with those who do – that's why you left the police.'

'I left the police because—'

'Because you did drugs?' Chandler shook his head. 'No, you didn't. You'd given up on your career by then. You'd seen enough, so you gave them an excuse to get rid of you.'

Atticus was unnerved. It was unusual for him to find someone he considered his equal. He was the one who was able to get into the heads of others, yet, resting against the bars of his cell with an enigmatic smile playing on his lips, here was Chandler, getting into *his* head.

'Think about the men who were running their dirty little scheme,' Chandler said. 'Maybe Burns *would've* been caught and jailed, but he was a nobody – he cheated justice for years, and *he* didn't have *their* resources.' He waved a hand dismissively. 'York would never have been caught were it not for what happened with his daughter. But Miller? A decorated soldier and serving MP? *No.*' He rapped his knuckles against the bar. 'He would've been given a slap on the wrist. And Summers? A *general*? No. *Never.*' He hit the bars again. 'Men like them never answer for their crimes. You know it as well as I do. And you know there are others. All those customers I'll never be able to punish. This week will have put the fear of god into them, but once they see I've been caught and put away, they'll relax. And men like that, with those perversions. Do you think they'll just stop?' Chandler shook his head. 'No. They won't stop. Other kids will suffer. I don't blame you for what you did, but me being in here will let those men – and there are *dozens* of them – it'll let them get right back to what they were doing as if nothing happened.'

'So give me the videos. Tell me where they are and let me figure it out.'

'How are you going to do that?'

'DCI Jones will go after them.'

'She's one officer. One *woman* – not that I mean to sound chauvinistic, but we both know her face doesn't fit. It's an old boys' club, and she'll always be on the outside looking in. Look at Murphy – he's not even from Wiltshire and they parachute him in to save the day. How long do you think it'd take for someone above her who's either implicated or bought to shut her down?'

'"Implicated"?'

'You don't think the police are involved? Paid to turn a blind eye?'

'Can you prove that?'

'No, they're too careful. But I know.'

'There are other ways you could go after them,' Atticus pressed. 'The tapes could still be used. Give them to a reporter. It'd be a scandal. And the police would *have* to investigate then.'

'I don't share your optimism. My way was best. You won't be able to persuade me otherwise.'

Murphy cleared his throat at the end of the corridor. 'Time's up.'

'You said I could ask you a question,' Chandler said.

'Go on.'

'Why were you so interested in Burns?'

'Because I knew he was guilty and I didn't like the idea of him being out on the streets.'

'No. It was more than that. You were obsessed. I mean, it was why I was drawn to you in the first place, but then I started wondering why.'

Atticus shuffled. 'I wasn't any more interested in him than with any other case.'

The roles had been reversed: before, Atticus had watched Chandler for evidence of mistruth; now Chandler was looking at him.

Chandler shook his head. 'No. *No.* I don't believe you.'

'There's nothing I can do about that.'

Chandler stared at him. 'Did you know him from before?'

Atticus felt a moment of nausea. 'No.'

'Did you go to Grosvenor House?'

Atticus shook his head. 'No.'

'Are you sure?'

'Completely sure. I didn't go to Grosvenor House.'

Atticus was distracted and didn't notice Chandler sliding his arm through the gap in the bars. He reached out and grabbed Atticus by the wrist.

'Who was it then? Your dad? An uncle? A friend of the family.'

Atticus tried to free himself, but Chandler held on with a firm grip.

Murphy hurried over. 'Hey!'

'A little fiddling late at night. What did they say? It'll be a secret – just them and you?'

Atticus tried to shake his arm loose, but Chandler held on.

'I told you before – you and I are alike. More alike than you're prepared to admit.'

He let go.

Atticus stepped back.

'Are you OK?' Murphy said.

Atticus felt blood in his cheeks and the hammering of his heart.

'Atticus?'

'I'm fine.'

Chandler held on to the bars. 'You can't kid a kidder. Come and see me after the trial. You can tell me all about it.'

'I don't think so.'

Atticus turned on his heel and hurried back to the stairs.

97

Atticus went to the bathroom and took a moment to compose himself again. He ran the cold tap, cupped his hands and filled them, lowering his head so that he could dunk his face in the water. It ran between his fingers, so he did it again, clenching his fists and using his knuckles to rub his eyes. The nausea had passed, but his heart was pumping hard, and he took deep breaths – in and *hold* and out, in and *hold* and out – until it stopped racing.

He had been very close to losing it. It would have been bad enough if it were just Chandler, but Murphy had been there, too. What if Murphy said something to Mack? Atticus would have to think of a response, something that he could say – something glib and throwaway, something she would expect of him – so that he was able to change the subject.

He looked up into the mirror and stared into his own eyes. He had panicked. *Panicked*. Chandler had caught him by surprise, and he had only just been able to maintain his equanimity. Atticus already knew that Chandler was perceptive, but his acuity – his instincts – looked as if they might be the match of his own. Atticus found that he was relieved he was in the basement cell and not on the street. It was unheard of for him to be daunted by someone else, yet Chandler had managed it with just one facile observation.

And that moment of intuition had brought a torrent of memories back. It had been all he could manage to staunch the flow. He had managed it – just – but now he found himself with doubt to contend with, too.

Atticus closed his eyes again. He took another deep breath, held it and exhaled.

There was an irritated knock on the door.

'Wait!'

Atticus yanked a paper towel from the dispenser and patted his face dry. He balled up the towel, dropped it in the bin and – with a final look at his reflection – he unlocked the door and went outside.

Murphy was waiting with his arms crossed.

'You took your time. What were you *doing* in there?'

'I felt a bit sick.'

'You don't look great.'

'I think I'm coming down with something.'

It was the closest that the two of them had come to a normal conversation, and it was obvious Murphy felt awkward. 'I'll see you inside.'

Atticus stepped aside, then turned back before Murphy had closed the door. 'Can I ask you a question?'

'I need a piss – be quick.'

'Does Chandler smoke?' He looked puzzled. 'What?'

'He didn't ask for a cigarette break during the interview when I was there. What about afterwards?'

'No,' Murphy said. 'Not as far as I know. Why?'

'It's nothing,' Atticus said.

He turned away.

'Priest? Why's that relevant?'

Atticus didn't answer and made his way down the corridor before Murphy could ask him anything else.

98

The courtroom was full. Atticus came inside and stepped carefully along the row to the seat that Mack had reserved for him. He sat down.

'How was he?' she asked.

'No change. Full of himself.'

'And still pleading guilty?'

'He says he is.'

'So what did he want with you?'

'I told you – he thinks we have a common cause. A connection.'

'You know you don't have to humour him.'

'It's worth the aggravation if it means locking him up is easier.'

'Not if he gets under your skin.'

'That'll be the last time. They can send guards down with rubber truncheons if he kicks up a fuss again. I'm finished with him.'

Atticus looked dead ahead. He saw Murphy, another officer from his team and Robbie Best. The small public gallery was taken up by members of the press, their notepads ready. The usher, a large bald man whom Atticus recalled from the Mallender proceedings, looked more anxious than he remembered. The atmosphere was tense and expectant.

He knew that Mack was looking at him, but he didn't want to catch her eye. He needed to repair the façade that Chandler had nearly knocked down.

She reached for his hand. 'Are you sure you're OK?'

'I'm fine.'

'You look like you've seen a ghost.'

He could feel a bead of sweat rolling down from his scalp, and the small of his back was damp. 'I'm *fine*.'

The usher caught the eye of another member of staff and cleared his throat. 'All rise.'

'Here we go,' Mack murmured.

The proceedings were before three magistrates, two of whom were familiar to Atticus and one – the chief magistrate – who was not. They came into the court, nodded to the others in the room and sat. The legal advisor to the justices stood and spoke to them; they listened and, when he sat back down, they frowned with a solemnity that spoke to the unusual gravity of the afternoon's work. The solicitor from the Crown Prosecution Service was sitting to Atticus's left, but the desk to the right – usually accommodating the solicitor for the defence – was empty.

The chair looked to the usher. 'Bring the defendant up, please.'

Mack squeezed Atticus's hand.

Chandler emerged from the doors at the side of the court and was led into the dock. There were two guards with him; one of the men removed his handcuffs and took up position with his colleague directly behind Chandler. They looked alert and on edge; Atticus couldn't see any prospect of Chandler being able to escape. He looked around the room until he found Atticus; he gave a nod and a smile. Atticus might have disturbed his sangfroid before, but the façade had been put back in place. Atticus looked away and ignored him.

The legal advisor glanced at his papers and then at Chandler. 'You don't want legal representation, Mr Chandler?'

'That's right.'

'And you *do* understand the charges against you are serious?'

'I do – and I still don't need a lawyer. Can we get on with it, please?'

'What's your name?'

'Thomas Chandler.'

'You are charged with murder. How do you plead?'

'Guilty.'

'To all of the charges that have been laid against you?'

'Yes,' he said. 'To all of them. I killed them all.'

The advisor conferred with the justices. The chief justice nodded his understanding and leaned in close to his microphone. 'Thank you, Mr Chandler. As you know, sentencing for charges *this* serious can only be dealt with at the Crown Court. Your case will be sent up to Winchester Crown Court and the matter will be dealt with there as quickly as possible. We can adjourn now.' He turned to the security guards. 'Take the defendant down again.'

Mack leaned back and sighed. 'Done. Thank God for that.'

Atticus was glad that she was still holding his hand. It stopped it from shaking.

* * *

Mack and Atticus shuffled out of the courtroom into the lobby outside.

'There are drinks tonight,' she said.

'First I've heard about it,' he said.

'Just a chance to let off steam. Everyone's been on edge. You should come.'

413

Atticus shook his head. 'I'm knackered. I haven't been sleeping well – you know what I'm like when I get my teeth into something.'

'Sure?'

'I'm fine. I'll go home and get an early night.'

'Want me to come over?'

'When you're pissed, like last time?' He smiled at her. 'No thanks. Go home. I'll see you tomorrow.'

99

Atticus waited in the queue to get outside. The lobby was busy as the courtroom emptied, the flow not helped by the journalists who were clustered around on the pavement outside the entrance. Outside broadcasts were being prepared, with reporters recording pieces to camera explaining what had just taken place inside. Passing cars slowed down as the drivers gawped at the scene and, as Atticus slipped through the door, a delivery van braked just in time to stop it from ploughing into the back of a Volvo that was at the end of a queue waiting to get onto the roundabout.

Atticus saw a man he recognised. It was Ian Bird, the reporter from the *Sun* who had broken the story about the Campbell video. Atticus remembered him from the Imber investigation, too; he was a typical hack, single-minded and ruthless and with a questionable interpretation of ethics.

Atticus was about to go over to him when he saw Eddie Thorpe heading in the same direction. He waited and watched as the two men shook hands. Thorpe said something to him, Bird replied and, after shaking hands again, Thorpe moved away.

Atticus squeezed through the crowd to intercept Bird.

'Mr Bird? Could I have a moment?'

Bird turned to meet him with a smile. 'I remember you.'

'We spoke during the Imber enquiry.'

'Atticus, isn't it? Like in the book.'

'That's right – Atticus Priest.'

'What can I do for you?'

'It's about the case. I need to know who sent the video to you.'

He frowned. 'I assume it was Chandler. I can't be sure, but who else would it have been?'

'I don't think it was.'

'Why?'

'You know I've been involved with this investigation?'

'Yes,' he said. 'The word I heard used was "peripheral".'

'Who told you that? Murphy?'

'Maybe.'

'He would say that.'

Bird grinned at him. 'Looks like he's hurt your feelings.'

Atticus was tempted to tell Bird what Murphy was like, but he realised there was no profit in it. 'Let's just say it's in the DCS's best interests to minimise my involvement and maximise his.'

Bird chuckled. 'Fine. Indulge me, then – why don't you think it was Chandler who sent it?'

'I spoke to him before they brought him up for the hearing, and I asked him. He said that it was, but I think he was lying.'

'Why would he lie about something like that?'

'I don't know. That's why I'm asking. How was it sent?'

'Email. We sent it to the nerds at the office. They poked around, but they couldn't get anything useful. They said it was sent through a VPN – the IP address would've been masked.' Bird took a beat. 'Who do you think sent it if it wasn't him? Who else has even seen it?'

'The police and the *Journal*.'

'Can't be the paper. Why would they scoop themselves?'

'I don't know. Maybe someone got paid.'

'Not by us.'

'What about the police?'

'No. We didn't pay, and we'd *never* pay a police officer.'

'Of course not,' Atticus said.

Bird gave a shrug. 'It's true. Maybe a few years ago, but not now. It's not worth the hassle.'

'What about Eddie Thorpe? You were just talking to him.'

'Eddie? I used to work with him. We were just catching up.'

'You didn't pay him?'

'You're like a dog with a bone,' Bird said. 'No. It wasn't him, and we did not.' He reached into his pocket and took out a business card. 'You'll let me know if you ever have anything useful? I scratch your back, you scratch mine?'

Atticus took the card. 'You'll be the first person I call.'

100

Atticus went back to the office, sat down at his desk and turned so that he could look at the plug; he stared at it for what felt like an age and knew that his gambit was both uncertain and reckless. He knew he was right about what he had found but had no guarantee that the bait he had laid would be taken. Atticus also knew that if it was taken, then he would be on his own to deal with the consequences.

It was too early to head out to West Woodyates, so he took the dog for a walk in the hope it might help him clear his mind. He started towards the cathedral and then, realising that seeing the spire would have him questioning what had happened on the tower again, he changed course and went to Churchill Gardens instead. Bandit raced across the sodden turf, collected a branch and then tried to persuade Atticus to wrestle it out of his mouth. He did, eventually, and tossed it as far away as he could manage. The dog sprinted after it, his tail held high.

A discarded page from this week's *Journal* had blown out of a bin and into the river.

Atticus stared at it as it went by.

'You all right, mate?'

It was an old man on a mobility scooter. Atticus was blocking the path.

'Sorry. Million miles away.'

Atticus stepped aside so that the man could continue on his way. The newspaper was out of sight now, but he couldn't stop thinking about the idea it had triggered.

He called the dog back to him, attached his lead and set off back to the office.

He dried Bandit's paws, changed his water and biscuits, and went over to his desk. He woke his computer and navigated to the *Journal*'s website. Things were already getting back to normal, with the headlines that usually filled the front page: 'Mini smashes into Pret window in Salisbury after handbrake left off'; 'Man left with broken arm after challenging would-be burglars in driveway'; 'Ferrari 488 clocked at 103mph on the A303'.

Atticus wasn't interested in any of those; he clicked to the day of Campbell's death and then went through the headlines and articles, hoping to find something that might lend credence to the idea that was too tantalising to dismiss.

101

Atticus drove out to West Woodyates and parked his car in the same lay-by as before. The rain had picked up on the drive south and, now, at just after eight in the evening, it was a deluge that hammered against the road and thrummed against the roof of the car; the wipers struggled to keep the windscreen clear.

He switched off the engine and reached back to the rear seat for his waterproofs. He put on the jacket and cursed that he had left the trousers in the office; it didn't matter, he would just have to get wet. He reached back again for his binoculars, taking them out of their case and hanging them around his neck. It was dark, and the rain made it difficult to see too far ahead, but it would be better to have them than not.

Atticus opened the glovebox and took out his torch and lock picks. He had a second phone in the glovebox, too, one with a disposable SIM that he kept in the eventuality that he might need to make a call that wouldn't be traced back to him. He took the phone and put it into his pocket with the picks and the torch.

Atticus took a moment to compose himself.

He felt lonely and exposed, but he was caught up in the mania of the hunt and knew himself well enough to know that

420

it would be impossible for him to walk away without knowing if he was right.

He took a breath, then another, then opened the door and stepped outside. The wind lashed at him, and the rain quickly soaked through his trousers. He ignored both, closing the door behind him and looking for a gap in the hedge so that he could approach the house away from the track and without being seen.

PART VII

SUNDAY

102

Atticus raised the binoculars to his eyes and scanned the house again. The windows were all dark, and the door that had been damaged when Chandler had forced his way inside had been protected with sheets of plywood. The place looked empty.

He took a moment to choose the best approach and, after checking that there was no one who might see him, he hurried to the French doors that gave access to the garden from the drawing room. The doors were enormous – nearly three metres tall – with leaded windows. The curtains were drawn, so Atticus couldn't see inside, but, like the rest of the house, there was no suggestion that anyone was there. Atticus knelt and examined the lock: it was an old mortise with a brass doorknob above the keyhole. He put on his gloves and quickly picked it. He turned the handle, opened the door and, after pausing for a moment to listen, slipped between the curtains and into the drawing room.

Everything was dark. He could remember the layout of the house from his previous visit and, using his torch to light the way, he passed through the entrance hall and the library and then the dining hall. He took the stairs to the first floor and went to the master bedroom. The bloodstain on the carpet was still there, and the dishevelled bed had not been made. The curtains had been closed. Atticus opened them an inch and then went over to the bedside table and switched on the lamp. He went back outside to the corridor and switched on the lights there, too. He looked around for another minute, turned on a third light – this one in the family bathroom – and then went back down the stairs.

His phone buzzed with a message as he was halfway down. He stopped and saw it was from Mack.

Summers died tonight. Thought you should know.

He stared at the message, imagining for a moment how she would react if he had told her how apt it was that she had sent that message now, given where he was.

He typed a reply.

Anything from the lab?

The phone indicated she was typing.

Nothing. Sorry. I'll chase tomorrow.

There was a pause, then another message.

Come over?

Atticus stared at the screen. She had likely just returned home after the celebratory drinks. She was probably the worse for drink and would – probably – collapse into bed. He replied he was tired, he needed to sleep and that he would see her later. He switched the phone off and dropped it back into his pocket.

He went to the drawing room, switched off the torch and let himself out, closing the doors behind him and using his picks to secure the lock. He waited by the wall, allowing his eyes to adjust to the darkness, and then ran back into the shelter of the trees. He settled back into place and, shivering in his sodden clothes, he watched.

103

It was four in the morning, and Atticus had been sheltering in the cover of the trees for hours. The rain was coming down harder than ever, and, although the stout boughs overhead offered some protection, their leaves were gone, and Atticus had quickly been soaked through. He shivered, trying hard to ignore the impulse to go home and have a shower. Or, he thought, he could go and have a shower at Mack's. Either option would be a vast improvement on staying out here on what was increasingly looking like a waste of time.

He had started to doubt himself. Perhaps his ruse had been transparent? The voicemail to Mack that he had pretended to leave had tested his acting ability to its limits: he had spoken of his outrage that Summers was being discharged and his frustration that the evidence they had found in the chapel had been deemed inadmissible due to his flouting of the law. He had reported back the news that he *said* he had received: Summers was returning home tonight, and the fear was that he would be leaving the country before a more successful case could be made against him.

It wasn't true, of course, but he knew that it would be tempting.

But now he wondered: had he gone too far?

He looked up at the lights in the upstairs windows and doubted that strategy, too. They would've been switched off by now. Surely anyone watching would have realised that they had been left on to foster the impression that someone was home.

Lightning crackled across the sky, and thunder boomed a moment later. Atticus looked at his watch and started to entertain the thought of leaving. The prospect of warmth – a warm shower and a warm bed – was attractive. It was only his stubborn refusal to accept that he was wrong that had kept him here, but the wasted hours that had passed had eroded that.

The storm grew stronger and the crash of the rain hammering down ever harder almost – but not quite – obscured the noise of footsteps on gravel.

Atticus held his breath and froze.

He reached for the binoculars but left them where they were; he could see the person on the way to the door with his naked eyes. Visibility was limited by the rain, but he could still discern that the figure was dressed in black with a black backpack and a black cap pulled all the way down over the face so that the brim offered cover from the rain.

Atticus reached up slowly and wiped the water from his eyes with the back of his hand. He blinked, trying – and failing – to make out anything else that might be useful.

He had given thought to what he would do if he was fortunate enough to find himself in this position and, despite the urge to step out and stop whoever it was, he decided that it made better sense to stick to his plan. He wanted more than just a confrontation; he wanted answers to all his questions.

The person went to the damaged door, ignored it and continued to the main door that led into the entrance hall. They stopped at an uncovered window, cupped a hand against the glass and peered into the darkened room inside. They moved on, edging around the building until they reached the door. Atticus was still holding his breath; the figure, facing away from him, tried the handle with a gloved hand. It was locked. They moved on, continuing around the house until they reached the French doors that Atticus had used. He had to change position a little to be able to watch, and, as he lowered himself behind a rhododendron bush, Atticus heard breaking glass.

Lightning crackled overhead; the flash showed the newly opened door and a glimpse of the figure passing inside. A torch was switched on. Atticus could see the glow of the beam against the thin curtains, the light moving into the entrance hall and leaking out through the single uncovered window next to the cloakroom.

Atticus crept forward, looking for a better place to hide where he could be closer to the open door. He risked stepping out of cover and, keeping low, he went to another collection of well-kept shrubs. There was less cover here and he knew there was a chance that he would be seen when the person emerged outside again. On the other hand, he was close enough now that he ought to be able to get a better look at them.

Atticus looked at his watch: the person had been inside for five minutes. It must have been obvious: the house was empty.

Why were they taking so long?

Thunder rolled over the countryside again.

The door was pushed open and the person stepped outside.

Veins of lightning lit up the sky.

The person turned and looked up.

The flash was brief but enough.

Atticus got a good look at her face.

He had been right.

It was Nina Parsons.

104

Nina put up her hood, rested her torch on the ground and closed the door. She paused for a moment, looking – and listening – for anything that might suggest that she was not alone. Atticus held his breath. She turned her head so that she was looking right at the bushes behind which he was hiding, then glanced away again; she picked up the torch and walked away.

Atticus waited for thirty seconds, ensuring that there was enough distance between them that he would be able to hide his pursuit. Nina went north, past the chapel and into the fields behind it, then continued in that direction until she reached the tree line that separated the first field from the even larger field behind it. The ground was treacherous from the days of steady rain; it was muddy in most places, occasionally deepening to a quagmire that had to be skirted for fear of getting stuck in the middle. Atticus stayed well back, grateful that Nina was herself staying close to the boundaries of the fields. It would have been difficult to remain hidden if she had gone directly across the field; even with the rain, a glimpse back would have meant that his pursuit would have been obvious. But here, close to the boundary, there was enough vegetation to break up the line of his silhouette.

Nina passed through the trees and continued to follow the southern boundary of the next field. The going was tough and the route challenging; it took Nina twenty minutes to reach a large tract of trees, another twenty to circumvent it and another fifteen to cross a final field to the road that ran north to south. This final field was the most open yet and Atticus had no choice but to wait by the hedge that divided the previous field from this one, which gave Nina the chance to stretch out her lead a little more. He dared not wait too long, though, and, fearing that she might well have left a vehicle in the road, he hurried after her.

He saw the lights of a car glowing through the hedge when he still had a quarter of the distance to cover. He picked up speed, ignoring his sodden feet and his wet, mud-splattered legs, trying to plot a course across the field that combined the soundest footing and shortest distance. He slipped and fell, slapping into the mud face first, but, desperate with the fear that the car would leave and he would lose his chance to test his hypothesis, he plunged his hands into the slop all the way up to his wrists, shoved himself upright, found his footing again and staggered on.

He reached the hedge and found a spot that was low enough for him to look over. There was a one-lane track road beyond, and a passing space opposite with a metal five-bar gate behind it. A car – an old Volvo Estate – was pulling away.

Atticus wiped the rain from his eyes and stared at the back of the car.

The number plate was muddied, too, but he thought he could make it out.

YKN 207X.

The car picked up speed, turned into the gentle right-hand bend and disappeared. He saw the glow of the tail lights for a moment longer until they, too, passed out of sight.

He took out his phone, opened his notes and found the details of the officers at the nick that he had noted down before he left. He found the number of the PNC Bureau and called it. The operator picked up on the second ring.

'This is Sergeant Neil Blyford,' Atticus said. 'Oscar November nine-two-three-four from Bourne Hill in Salisbury. Could you PNC a vehicle for me, please?'

'Go ahead, nine-two-three-four.'

'Yankee Kilo November two-zero-seven X-Ray. Code two.'

'Reason for request?'

'Erratic driving. I'm going to pull it over.'

Code two indicated a moving vehicle that had not yet been stopped. Atticus knew that the operator had asked for his reason for making his request so that the right box could be ticked. He didn't expect any follow-up questions and none came.

'Reading back, nine-two-three-four: Yankee Kilo November two-zero-seven X-Ray. That right?'

'That's it.'

'One minute, please.'

Atticus walked along the raised verge until he found the gap in the hedge that Nina had used to get on to the road.

'Nine-two-three-four, I have your details for you. The car is registered to an Elizabeth Chandler.'

'Address?'

'Betts Farmhouse, Betts Lane, Britford.'

'Thank you.'

Atticus ended the call and opened his map. It was twelve miles to Britford from here, but the pursuit across the fields had left him two miles away from the spot where he had left his car. He ought to be able to get to it in thirty minutes if he walked briskly, and then it would be another thirty to drive to Britford.

He turned to the south and started walking.

105

It was early in the morning and the roads were empty. Atticus followed the A354 back towards Salisbury, continuing through Coombe Bissett until he could see the red warning light at the tip of the cathedral's spire shining out over the fields. The road was long and straight for the mile before it reached the city, and Atticus had to fight back the urge to speed up. He was tense with nervous energy and the anticipation of what the next hour might bring, and there was no point in risking an accident or the attention of the police when there was still so much to learn.

He turned off towards the hospital, continued on to the A338 and then took the left turn and drove into the tiny village of Britford. He stopped and checked his map: Betts Lane was an unadopted dirt track that ran down to the Avon. He located the opening of the track – just off the village green – switched off the engine and got out of the car.

Atticus grabbed his phone and continued on foot, checking the map as he negotiated the deep puddles of water that stretched across the surface of the road. The track continued into the countryside before it split at a junction: the branch to the right ended at a trout fishery and the branch to the left headed north to the farm at which the Volvo was registered. The track terminated at those two points; the Avon cut around them as it looped from east to south, forming a border with no obvious way to get across the water to Alderbury on the opposite bank.

There were two mailboxes attached to a post that had been driven into the ground at the junction. One of them was labelled TROUT FARM and the other CHANDLER. Atticus opened the second one, reached a hand inside and withdrew a collection of letters. He shone the light of his torch down on the envelopes and flipped through them: most of them were marketing circulars, but there was one that looked official. It was a letter from British Gas. He read it: the letter confirmed that the account held in the name of Elizabeth Chandler had been closed by reason of the account holder's death and that there was nothing left to pay.

He put the letter in his pocket, replaced the circulars in the mailbox and switched off the torch. He put it in his pocket and continued along the right-hand track. It cut through fields that were used to graze cattle and sheep, dotted with poles carrying telephone lines and fibre to the farm buildings. A chalk stream ran to the right, and the water bubbled and burbled as it poured over and around stones and branches that disturbed the flow. Atticus heard the scream of a fox and saw a flash of movement as the animal burst out from the hedgerow behind him and scurried away; a cow lowed; somewhere overhead an owl screeched.

It took him five minutes to reach the farm. He stopped and, shielding his phone behind the trunk of an old tree, checked the map. The farm was arranged on either side of the track. There was a series of seven large outbuildings to the left and the farmhouse itself on the right. The farm was bracketed by fields with the Avon at its eastern boundary, a hundred yards away.

The map made it worryingly clear: Atticus was alone, more than a mile away from the nearest property.

It didn't matter.

He wasn't about to turn back now.

106

Atticus edged around the side of the first barn and saw that a space had been formed between the buildings. The track continued to the river with the farmhouse to the left. The space itself was empty, save for a mud-spattered Volvo Estate.

He crept over to it and used it to shelter from anyone who might be approaching from the nearby buildings. He could hear a ticking from the exhaust; the hot gas had made the metal expand and, now that it was cooling again, it was contracting.

Atticus didn't need to check the numberplate to know that the car was the one that Nina had used to leave West Woodyates.

He slipped around to the side and tried the door. It was unlocked. The backpack that Nina had been wearing at the house had been left on the passenger seat. Atticus reached in, undid the clasps, opened it and looked inside. There was a large knife with a serrated blade and, beneath that, a small plastic container. He opened the lid and looked inside: there were three syringes – their points sheathed in plastic nipples – and a glass bottle with a silicone sleeve. He took out his phone and, hiding behind the car, switched on his flashlight. The label on the bottle identified the contents as Anesketin, and, below that, 'Solution for injection for dogs, cats and horses'.

Atticus heard a sound – a door squeaking on rusty hinges – somewhere to his right, most likely from the farmhouse. He switched off the light and stayed behind the Volvo. He heard footsteps and saw the beam of a torch, the yellow light shining through the windows of the vehicle. Atticus shuffled around the vehicle so that he could glimpse around it. Nina had crossed into the yard and was walking towards the brick shed that was between the two largest barns. Atticus watched as she turned a key in the lock and opened the door.

He took out the burner phone, powered it up and dialled 999.

'Hello, 999. Which service do you need?'

'Police,' he whispered.

'I'll connect you now.' The call was transferred.

'Police,' the handler said. 'What's your emergency?'

He kept his voice low. 'I'm being burgled.'

'OK – just confirming, you say you're being burgled now?'

'*Right* now. A man just forced his way into my house.'

'What's your address?'

'Betts Farm, Betts Lane, Britford.'

'I've dispatched a car now. Are you in immediate danger?'

Atticus killed the call and powered the phone down. He closed his eyes and, sweating despite the frigid weather, left his hiding spot and walked towards the brick shed.

107

The building appeared to be some sort of storage shed. Atticus edged up to the corner and peeped around it: the door was open and light from inside was spilling out, glistening in the puddles that had gathered in the yard. Atticus turned around the corner of the shed and stepped over to the open door. He looked inside. The shed had been equipped with racks of metal shelving along the two long walls. Each rack had three shelves, and the shelves were filled with videotapes. There was a table in the middle of the shed with a pile of empty Jiffy bags on it.

Nina stood at the table with her back to him. She was sealing a cassette into a Jiffy bag.

'Nina.'

She turned, saw him and swore.

'Take it easy.'

She chuckled bitterly. 'You clever, *clever* bastard. You tricked me.'

'I was hoping I might be wrong.'

She finished sealing the bag and set it down on the table, then turned fully to face him. 'You found it, then?'

'Yesterday. You left it the second time you came to the office – right? When you asked me to make you a coffee? The first visit was to scope it all out, find somewhere to leave it, and the second visit was to fit it.'

'I was going to come back and take it away, but I had to wait – I told you I was going abroad.'

'You did, and I checked that out. I don't know why I called you Nina – it's Zoë, isn't it? Lieutenant Zoë Chandler. You're seconded to the Royal Welsh from the Royal Army Veterinary Corps, just rotated back from Estonia, won't be sent out again for another six months.'

'Didn't think you'd go to the trouble of checking.'

'They said they didn't have a Nina Parsons. I sent them a still from the security camera in the alley beneath my office and they found you from that.'

'How did you work it out? What gave it away?'

'Your brother's attack on Summers. If you'd waited a month, I doubt it would've caught my attention. But you went after him the *same day* I worked out that he had something to do with the tape. And the thing is, I didn't tell anyone apart from DCI Jones, and I know she kept it to herself. I couldn't understand how you got to him so soon. I'd almost persuaded myself it was just one of those things. *Almost.* There was something that stuck in the back of my mind about you, and then, when you ghosted me . . . well, I checked. I spoke to Wintringham. I told him what you'd said, and he nearly had a heart attack.'

She chuckled. 'Must have been uncomfortable.'

'It was in front of his wife, so yes . . . it was. I knew you'd used me then; I just had to find out how you'd done it. I went back to the office and found the bug and . . .' He shrugged. 'I thought it was worth a try to see if I could get you to break cover.'

She clapped her hands in sardonic applause. 'I'm *actually* impressed this time. I shouldn't have made fun of you. That was clever – using it against me. I fell for it. Summers was the worst of them. I thought tonight was the only chance I'd have to get to him.'

'If it's any consolation, it doesn't matter. He's dead.'

'Really?'

'He died tonight.'

She gave a brief nod. 'Whatever. I hope he suffered.'

Atticus looked around the room for any sign of a weapon that Zoë could use against him. There was a tape dispenser with a serrated edge on the table, but, save that, there wasn't anything obvious.

'Who knows about your little trap?' she asked him. 'Your girlfriend?'

'She doesn't know I'm here. No one does.'

'That's risky.'

'I wanted us to talk. There're a few things I'd like to understand.'

'About me and Thomas?'

'That'd be a good place to start. He's older than you?'

She nodded. 'A year.'

'He told us he didn't have any relations.'

She shrugged. 'You didn't think he'd be honest about everything, did you?'

'Is that what you decided – if either of you got caught, that person would confess to everything to protect the other?'

'Something like that. What did he tell you?'

'That he had a tough childhood. That he was in care.'

'*That's* true. We both were. Dad was a thug and Mum was a prostitute. She died – overdose – and we were taken away when it was obvious that he didn't give a shit about us. They sent us to a family in Salisbury.'

'And how was that?'

'Better. They cared for us. Gave us a chance to make a fresh start. Excellent school, nice holidays on the coast. Didn't last,

441

though. My stepmum and stepdad split up and Mum had to work two jobs just to keep food on the table. She sent us to Grosvenor House in the evenings so we had something to do, and that's when we met Burns. And you know what happened after that.'

He gestured to the tapes. 'Are you on any of them?'

'With Kajetan and Hartnett and a handful of others.'

'And your brother was on the tape with Campbell.'

She nodded. 'Why'd you think we started with those three?'

'Who killed them?'

'What did Thomas say?'

'He said he did.'

She nodded. 'There you go, then.'

'But you were involved, too. I saw the ketamine in your bag. Is that from work?'

She nodded. 'We were a team. I did the planning and he went after them.'

'I'm sorry about your stepmum,' Atticus said. 'When did she die?'

'How do you know that?'

Atticus reached into his pocket and took out the letter.

He held it up.

'Last year,' she said. 'I've been slow to shut the accounts down.'

'And this was her place?'

'Yes,' she said. 'How did you find it? You didn't follow me tonight.'

'I saw you leave in the car and checked the number plate. It's still registered to her at this address.'

'Shit,' she said. 'DVLA. I forgot.'

'You and your brother were abused at the same time?'

She shook her head. 'He was first – I was a year after. We didn't know it had happened to us both until we saw Alf Burns in the papers. Thomas told me first and then I told him.'

'And you did nothing until your mum died?'

'Didn't want her to know. She would have been distraught. It would've been pointless and cruel.'

Atticus noticed she looked over his shoulder and to the left, back in the house's direction.

'Is that your dad?'

She clenched her fists.

'Eddie?' Atticus called out. 'Come inside – you'll get soaked.'

He took a quarter-turn so that he could look back as Eddie Thorpe stepped into view.

He had a large kitchen knife in his right hand.

108

Atticus's mouth was bone dry, but he did his best to ignore it. 'I'm right, then – you're Zoë's stepdad?'

'Well done.'

Atticus looked to Zoë. 'And Chandler is your stepmother's name.'

She nodded. 'Thomas and I took it when they divorced.'

Thorpe stepped closer, the knife held in a steady grip. 'How'd you find us?'

'He tricked me,' Zoë said. 'He found the bug and set a trap. We walked right into it, and he followed us here.'

Atticus looked back to Thorpe, trying to ignore the knife. 'Were you driving tonight?'

He didn't answer.

'And you drove Thomas that night, too? Actually, you don't need to answer – I know you did. I spoke to him earlier, and he tried to persuade me that he walked. He obviously didn't do that.'

Thorpe glanced over at Zoë. 'I *told* you we should never have involved him, and *now* look where we are.'

'It's happened,' Zoë said. 'No point worrying about it now.'

'Come on, Eddie,' Atticus said. 'Don't blame them. You made mistakes, too. Look at how you delivered the Campbell

444

tape. There's a camera over the road from the *Journal*. Carly said someone must've dropped it off by hand, but, when we checked it, no one went into the office in the only times it could've been left. No one apart from you, her and Alice, and it obviously wasn't either of them.'

Thorpe held up the knife. 'You talk a good game for someone neck deep in shit.'

Atticus was frightened, but he found that talking – and his usual showboating – helped. 'Who decided that going to the *Sun* was a good idea?'

Thorpe glared at him.

'Well, it wasn't. You worked at the *Sun* – I checked your LinkedIn profile. Did you know Ian Bird endorsed you?'

Thorpe didn't answer.

'You sent it so he'd think it was from Jack.'

'Things were going too slowly,' Thorpe muttered. 'I wanted to run the still from the video, but my boss said I couldn't. He was so *timid*. I tried and tried, but it was like banging my head against the wall – "we can't prejudice the police enquiry", "we need to run it by the police first", "we don't want to do anything that puts them under pressure". It was bullshit.'

'But the *Sun* would print it?'

'Yes, they'd see how important it was and they'd have the balls to run it. We needed to make it as big a story as we could as fast as we could so we could put the fear of god into those bastards that they might be next.'

'I spoke to Alice,' Atticus said. 'She told me you were pushing for the picture to be run. You take that, add the fact that it had to be one of the three of you who left the video at the office, and it all points to you. And there was another thing, too. Getting up to the tower through the attic would have taken some planning. I knew the cathedral was offering tours, so I had the police check out who was on them. There was no one interesting, but then I wondered if it might have been the kind of local interest piece that the *Journal* would've run. And it was. You wrote it. David Campbell took you up there himself.'

Thorpe brandished the knife. 'I didn't know it'd be him who showed me. It was all I could manage not to do him there and then.'

'But you didn't. You've been cleverer than that.'

'Why did you come out here if you knew all that?'

'I had to be sure I was right. Curiosity is one of my many weaknesses.'

Thorpe turned to his stepdaughter. 'Can you go and put the kettle on?'

'No, Dad.'

'Please – I don't want you to have to watch this.'

'We're not going to hurt him.'

'What choice do we have?' Thorpe stabbed the knife in Atticus's direction. 'Haven't you been listening? He knows *everything*.'

She breathed out. 'So maybe it's over. We knew they'd figure it out eventually.'

'*No*, Zoë,' he snapped. 'You've got the rest of your life ahead of you. I'm not having you spend it in prison like Thomas. Not after what you've been through.'

Eddie took a step towards Atticus.

'*Dad*.'

Atticus held up a hand. 'One more thing you need to think about. You smoke, don't you? Your fingers are stained with nicotine and the office stank of it.'

'So?'

'You were careless when you called me from the car park. You dropped a cigarette. The police are testing it for DNA. You ever done anything that'd mean your DNA is on file?' Thorpe clenched his teeth and Atticus knew that he had. 'What are you going to do when there's a match?'

It was a gamble. Atticus hadn't had the results from the lab yet and, if he was wrong about it being Eddie who made the call, there was a chance that Thorpe would call his bluff. The tapes on the racks behind Zoë were all the evidence that Atticus needed to know that they weren't finished with the work that they had started. Thorpe might decide that Atticus's murder would be balanced out by the additional justice that they would be able to mete out.

Atticus heard a siren from outside. Thorpe and Zoë heard it, too.

'I called the police fifteen minutes ago,' Atticus said. Thorpe clenched his jaw. 'I didn't have a choice – this is the only way. We agree on everything apart from what justice means. Murdering those men makes you as bad as them.' He nodded at the shelves. 'I'll make sure they're punished, but it'll be done the right way. There'll be an enquiry; they'll be prosecuted; they'll be sent to prison.'

Zoë grabbed Thorpe's arm. 'Dad,' she urged, 'let's go. It's done.' She held up the Jiffy bag that she had just sealed. 'We've just got this one left.'

He nodded, and the two of them went into the yard and headed left, following the track east towards the river. Atticus watched them as they were absorbed by the rain and the dark and wondered if he had done the right thing.

The siren was louder now and, as he turned in the direction that he had arrived from, he could see red and blue pulsing through the branches of the trees that lined the track. He left the door to the shed open and the light on, making sure that it was impossible that the officers who were on their way to the farm could miss it. They would investigate and see the tapes inside.

447

The enquiry was a *cause célèbre*, and it was unthinkable that they wouldn't understand the significance of their find. They would see that the owner of the property had been the wife of Eddie Thorpe, and from there, it would be easy to join the dots.

Atticus made his way between the shed and the barn and clambered over the post-and-rail fence that formed the boundary of the paddock that he had seen on his way to the farm. He crouched down behind the hedge as the patrol car bumped and splashed through the potholes, waiting until it was out of sight behind the outbuildings before picking a way through the mud and heading back to the spot where he had left his car.

EPILOGUE

Francine Patterson woke up with the absolute certainty that she was about to be sick. She slid out of bed, stumbled to the bathroom and sank to her knees, holding her hair out of her face as she vomited into the toilet. She got unsteadily back to her feet, flushed, rinsed her mouth at the sink, turned to go back into the bedroom and stopped in the doorway. Someone else was in her bed. He was face down, but the glow from the street lamp outside the window fell through a crack in the curtains and washed over his face. It was Robbie Best. The sheets had fallen to reveal a Celtic band tattooed around his bicep, and he was snoring loudly.

Francine bit her lip as she recalled the night's festivities. They had started in the Royal George and then crossed town for a lock-in at the Huntsman. They had gone somewhere after that, too, she thought, although she couldn't put her finger on the details for the life of her. She remembered Robbie walking her back and inviting him to come inside.

It had been a raucous night. They had all been wired tight during the investigation, and all that pressure and stress had been released now that it had come to an end. Francine had kept herself busy to help stop her thinking about Chandler and how he had involved her in his scheme. She had spent time with the girl they had found beneath the cottage in Summers' property, gently extracting her story from her. Maria had explained over the course of several gentle sessions that she had fled to Poland after the invasion started and had been offered a room in a house in Salisbury by a man she later identified as Doyle. She had been taken to Summers' house and told that, unless she took part in the films that they produced there, she would be hurt. Her compliance had been won with fear and then drugs, and the doctor had found evidence of barbiturates in her blood. Social Services were involved now, and she had been found a safe place to live while efforts were made with the Ukrainian embassy in London to find her brother.

Francine crept back around the bed and lowered herself onto the mattress, keen not to wake Robbie. She didn't know what she would say to him and, although there would be no way of avoiding it, she would rather do it when her head wasn't pounding quite so much.

She looked over at the bedside clock, saw that it was just after four, and closed her eyes again. She tried to work out how she felt about what had happened. Robbie was senior to her – a DI to a DC – and ten years older, too. But she knew he had always fancied her and, if she was honest, she had found him attractive, too. She knew she had had too much to drink last night, but the alcohol had only made it easier to do something that she would have liked to have done anyway. Her friend Jules had texted her last night with the ribald advice that, 'the best way to get over someone is to get under someone'. Robbie had been flirting with her all night, was a consenting adult able to make his own choices, and, as some of the memories emerged from the fog that the drink had left behind, Francine remembered they had both had fun.

Where was the harm in that?

She held her breath as Robbie stopped snoring. He turned over, grunted, and reached out an arm and draped it over her. She snuggled into him, enjoying his warmth, and allowed herself to fall into sleep once again.

*   *   *

Atticus went back to the office, collected the dog and walked across the city to Mack's place in Harnham. It was an hour before dawn and the streets were quiet. Atticus tried not to think about what had happened that night, but it was impossible. He didn't know how long it would take the police to work out what had happened at the farm and start to look for Thorpe. It wouldn't be long. There would be plenty of forensic evidence to confirm that both stepfather and daughter – and, presumably, stepson – had been at the property. Atticus doubted that they would need his help, but, if they did, he would be able to provide judicious and anonymous hints to nudge them in the right direction.

It was coming up to five when they arrived at the house. Atticus opened the lockbox, took out the key and unlocked the door. Bandit would normally have barrelled straight up the stairs in search of Mack, but, perhaps aware that it was early, he went into the front room and curled up on the sofa. Atticus took the blanket that Mack used to keep warm when she was watching television and covered the dog with it.

He climbed the stairs, undressed in the bathroom and left his clothes on the floor. They were damp and dirty, but he was bone-tired, and they could wait until later. He went through into the bedroom and sat down on the edge of the bed.

Mack stirred. 'Hello,' she mumbled, her voice thick with sleep.

'Do you remember what you asked me when we had lunch in the square?'

'Mmm.'

'About why I haven't been able to let this go? About Burns and what happened at Imber?'

She started to reply, then drew in a breath, rolled over and exhaled. Atticus waited a moment, listening as her breathing slowed and became more rhythmic, the soft sound of the air passing through her slightly parted lips.

'Don't worry,' he whispered. 'We can talk about it another time.'

He lay down beside her and closed his eyes. He heard a car driving by as he waited for sleep to come.

* * *

Mack awoke to the buzzing of her phone's alarm. She had left it on the bedstand next to her glass of water, and, as she blearily reached out for it, she nudged the glass and sent it tumbling onto the floor. She cursed under her breath, sat up and carefully slid her feet down on to the now-soaked carpet. Atticus was on the other side of the bed, the sound of his breathing a quiet murmur that was audible over the engine of a car as it ran along the street outside the house. She looked at the clock: it was seven.

She felt a weight at the end of the bed and, when she looked down, saw that Bandit was curled up between their feet. He opened a single eye and glanced up at her, then closed it and, with a sigh of contentment, went back to sleep. Mack remembered: Atticus had come around earlier that morning and must have brought the dog with him. She had been asleep and had probably still been drunk after the drinks to celebrate the end of the enquiry had become raucous. She had a headache now and needed to wash down a couple of Nurofen with a pint of cold water.

Mack got up and went into the bathroom, switched on the light above the mirror and stared at her reflection. She felt as if she had aged over the course of the last year, but it wasn't evident in her face. Her skin was still good, and, save the odd wrinkle here and there, she was confident that she could pass for a woman a good few years younger than she really was. She thought of Atticus and was reminded of the age difference between them. She had been his boss, and she had always wondered how much of that had led to his initial attraction to her. She had joked about it with him, hoping to prompt him into explaining why he wanted to be with her, but he'd always been obtuse when it came to identifying personal feelings and emotions or those of the people close to him. Mack had come to accept the fact that he wanted to be with her and that she, despite the damage that it had done to her family, wanted to be with him.

She showered, dried herself off and put on her dressing gown.

Atticus had left his clothes in a pile on the floor. She picked them up and noticed that they were filthy: his trousers, in particular, were damp and caked in dried mud.

She bundled the clothes up, dumped them into her washing bin and took it and her phone downstairs. She opened the washing machine and checked the pockets of the trousers before putting them in. His wallet was there, together with two items that she hadn't expected: a mobile phone that she didn't recognise and a leather roll-up pouch that, when she undid the clasp and opened it, revealed a set of lock picks. She put the phone on the counter and ran her finger over the picks. The phone was curious enough, but she wasn't worried about it; some might see a second phone as proof of a cheating partner, but Atticus was a bad liar, and Mack knew that she would have seen infidelity in him without needing evidence.

It was the picks that she wasn't sure about.

She rolled the pouch up again and weighed it in her hand. She didn't think he kept it with him all the time; it was bulky, and she would have noticed.

So why was it in his pocket last night?

She put it on the counter next to the phone, tipped washing powder and fabric softener into the machine's tray and started the program. She knew that there were things that he didn't tell her about, and that was fine. There were things in *her* life that she kept to *herself*, and she knew that that was usual in any relationship. The difficulty she had was when Atticus ignored her clear instructions about matters that could have an impact on her professionally. She knew that he had only a passing relationship with the rules of procedure that governed the police and had seen more than once how he was prepared to break the law when he thought it would bring him closer to answering a question that had been vexing him. She had tried to knock sense into his head, warning him that he would eventually find himself in trouble that he couldn't talk his way out of, and that, when that happened, he might end up dragging her down with him.

She tapped a finger on the pouch and then turned her back to it and went into the kitchen, where she took the kettle and filled it at the sink. She wondered whether she should take the picks upstairs and confront him about it but decided to leave it where it was and give him a chance to volunteer an explanation.

Her own phone rang as the kettle boiled. It was Mike Lewis.

'Morning, boss.'

'Morning, Mike. What's up?'

'We had something weird last night, and I thought you ought to know before you got into the nick.'

She took a mug from the cupboard and reached for the coffee. 'Go on.'

'Two things, really. Dave and Phil responded to a 999 about a burglary in the early hours. It was in Britford, this empty farmhouse at the end of the track. Thing is, when they got there, it looked like a crank call.'

'Right. So?'

'They had a look around. One of the barns was open, and a light had been left on. They went inside and found videos. *Lots* of them.'

Mack's stomach fell. 'Like . . .'

'Like the same as the ones we've been looking at.'

Mack leaned back against the counter. 'Shit.'

'That's not all of it. We had a walk-in at the nick in Andover an hour ago. You remember Eddie Thorpe.'

'Eddie Thorpe from the *Journal*?'

'Yes. He turns up and says that he wants to speak to an officer and, when he does, he says that Thomas Chandler is his stepson and that the two of them were working together.'

'*What*?'

'I know. He says the place in Britford belonged to his ex-wife before she died, and they'd been using it. Thorpe said he decided to hand himself in after we got Chandler.'

'And he did it the same night we find the videos?'

'I know. It's weird. Maybe he called about the burglary himself?'

She looked at the burner phone and the lock picks and thought about Atticus's filthy clothes and shook her head.

'Boss?'

'We'll find out when we speak to him. Where's Murphy?'

'Went to London yesterday. Should I let him know?'

'Tell Beckton. He can do it.'

'What about you, boss?'

'Call Andover and tell them to bring Thorpe back to Bourne Hill. I'll get dressed and get over there. Give me thirty minutes.'

* * *

Alice had been in the office since six. The murders had shaken the city, and the revelation that Thomas Chandler had been charged had acted as a balm to frayed nerves. It had also generated a huge amount of interest, and, with connections to the local police and criminal justice community that national reporters couldn't match, she had found herself in high demand. She had been interviewed for half a dozen different newspapers, and her profile had been included on websites with traffic that made the *Journal*'s look puny by comparison. It was the fulfilment of her childhood ambitions, but there had been no time to sit down and savour any of it. She had been working twelve hours a day all week, and now, with the case closed and the media circus moving on to the next sensation, she had her work to consider. Eddie had cleared ten pages of the new edition for the story, and Alice had agreed to take on most of the writing herself.

She went into the kitchen, filled the kettle, and set it to boil.

'I'll have one if you're brewing up.'

She turned: it was James Ward, the freelance photographer they used when they needed something for the paper. 'You're early.'

'I took a million snaps last week, and I need to go through them. Thought I might as well come and get started. Have you seen your email?'

'Not yet. Why?'

'There's one from Andy at Storyville. He sounds pleased – says we've had the best week of revenue for years.'

Storyville was the publishing company that owned the *Journal*. They all knew that they had been one of the worst-performing papers on the roster and had been living in fear that they would be merged with another local and then downsized.

'And remember that Eddie's been asking for the cash for me to go full time? Andy says he's going to OK it.'

'That's great.'

'It's good timing,' Ward said. 'Suzy's pregnant again.'

'Congratulations.'

Ward opened the cupboard, took out two mugs and a jar of instant coffee. He unscrewed the lid and spooned two scoops into each mug. 'What are you doing?'

'Finishing the profile on Chandler.'

'Can't be easy.'

'Why?'

'Because he's so *average*.'

'*So* average. And you know what's weird? The banality of it all. You wouldn't look twice at him if he went by on the street, but he killed four people, and he would've kept killing if he hadn't been caught.'

Alice heard footsteps coming up the staircase from the ground floor and, as she poured water into the first mug, Carly burst through the door. Her eyes were wide, and the blood had drained from her face.

Ward turned to her. 'Are you all right?'

Carly held up her hands as she tried to regain her breath. 'You will not believe this. I went out to my car this morning, and this was on the bonnet.'

She held up a package.

Alice put on a pair of disposable gloves that she had bought from Boots and took the package from Carly. She took the end of the flap and peeled it back, careful to make sure that nothing was ripped, then tipped the package up so that the cassette box inside could slide out on to the desk. She picked up the box and turned it over so that they could see the label that had been slipped down the spine.

Mason, Max / 3 February

Ward swore.

Alice stared at the box with an open mouth.

'Max *Mason*?' Carly said.

'That's what it says.'

'No way. I mean – *no* way. Not him. It can't be.'

'Jesus,' Ward said. 'What are you going to do with that?'

Alice put the box on the desk. 'Where's Eddie? I need to speak to him.'

Atticus Priest will return.

ACKNOWLEDGEMENTS

Thank you to my advance readers and special thanks to my police advisors for making sure I didn't make too much of a meal of the procedure; all mistakes, of course, are mine.

WANT MORE
MARK DAWSON?

Building a relationship with my readers is the very best thing about writing. Join my Reader Club for:

1. The correspondence that passed between the police and Atticus in the lead-up to his resignation from the Force; and

2. A free copy of 'Tarantula', a short story from my multi-million-selling John Milton series.

You can get your content **for free**, by signing up at my website.

Just visit www.markjdawson.com/atticuspriest

ABOUT THE AUTHOR

MARK DAWSON is the bestselling author of the
Beatrix Rose, Isabella Rose and John Milton series
and has sold over four million books. He lives in
Wiltshire with his family and can be reached
at www.markjdawson.com

www.facebook.com/markdawsonauthor
www.twitter.com/pbackwriter
www.instagram.com.markjdawson